Practical Dojo Projects

Frank W. Zammetti

Apress®

Practical Dojo Projects

ISBN-13 (pbk): 978-1-4302-1066-5

ISBN-13 (electronic): 978-1-4302-1065-8

Printed and bound in the United States of America 9 8 7 6 5 4 3 2 1

Lead Editor: Steve Anglin
Technical Reviewer: Herman van Rosmalen

Senior Project Manager: Sofia Marchant
Copy Editor: Sharon Wilkey
Associate Production Director: Kari Brooks-Copony
Senior Production Editor: Laura Cheu
Compositor: Dina Quan
Proofreader: Liz Welch
Indexer: Carol Burbo and Ron Strauss
Artist: Kinetic Publishing Services, LLC
Cover Designer: Kurt Krames
Manufacturing Director: Tom Debolski

Distributed to the book trade worldwide by Springer-Verlag New York, Inc., 233 Spring Street, 6th Floor, New York, NY 10013. Phone 1-800-SPRINGER, fax 201-348-4505, e-mail orders-ny@springer-sbm.com, or visit http://www.springeronline.com.

For information on translations, please contact Apress directly at 2855 Telegraph Avenue, Suite 600, Berkeley, CA 94705. Phone 510-549-5930, fax 510-549-5939, e-mail info@apress.com, or visit http://www.apress.com.

Apress and friends of ED books may be purchased in bulk for academic, corporate, or promotional use. eBook versions and licenses are also available for most titles. For more information, reference our Special Bulk Sales–eBook Licensing web page at http://www.apress.com/info/bulksales.

The source code for this book is available to readers at http://www.apress.com.

I've written four books now, including this one, and I've thanked a lot of people. From the usual suspects such as my wife, children, parents, and friends, to the unusual: fictional characters, various food, alien species, and even myself! At one point I said I had dedicated a book to everyone who matters, but it was my mother-in-law who pointed out I hadn't dedicated anything to her and thus hadn't dedicated a book to everyone who matters.

That got me to thinking. I've actually left out a few important people along the way, so let me try to cover all the bases this time around:

Albert Einstein, Babe Ruth, George Washington, Francis Ford Coppola, Jean-Luc Picard, Rick Wakeman, John Adams, Galileo Galilei, Lenny Bruce, Les Paul, Leonard Nimoy, Mickey Mantle, Steve Wozniak, Karl Schwarzschild, Lee Majors, Bruce Campbell, Robert Kennedy, Wicket the Ewok, Rodney Dangerfield, Ric Flair, Lee and Bill Adama, Scott Baio, Christian Troy, Wally Schirra, Wilton Parmenter, Rod Serling, Nikolai Volkoff, the two old men on The Muppet Show, *and of course Davros and The Doctor.*

Oh yes . . . and my mother-in-law.
Now stop bugging me! ☺

Contents at a Glance

About the Author . . . xiii
About the Technical Reviewer . . . xv
About the Illustrator . . . xvii
Acknowledgments . . . xix
Introduction . . . xxi

PART 1 ■■■ Setting the Table

■ **CHAPTER 1** Introduction to Dojo . . . 3
■ **CHAPTER 2** Dojo Core . . . 41
■ **CHAPTER 3** Dijit . . . 115
■ **CHAPTER 4** DojoX . . . 157

PART 2 ■■■ The Projects

■ **CHAPTER 5** That Human Touch: Contact Manager and Client-Side Persistence . . . 215
■ **CHAPTER 6** A Place for Your Stuff: Dojo Code Cabinet . . . 265
■ **CHAPTER 7** Idiot Blob: The Game! . . . 329
■ **CHAPTER 8** When the Yellow Pages Just Isn't Cool Enough: Local Business Search . . . 379

■ **INDEX** . . . 441

Contents

About the Author xiii
About the Technical Reviewer. xv
About the Illustrator xvii
Acknowledgments. xix
Introduction. xxi

PART 1 ■■■ Setting the Table

CHAPTER 1 Introduction to Dojo 3

JavaScript: A Study in Evolution 3
- Birth of a Language 3
- Reasons for JavaScript's Early Rise 5
- Something Is Rotten in the State of JavaScript 5
- The Unarguable Problems with JavaScript 6
- As Ballmer Said: "Developers! Developers! Developers!..." 7
- Standardization: The Beginning of Sanity 9
- The Times They Are a Changin': The Experienced Come to Bear. 10
- What's Old Is New Again: JavaScript in the Present 11
- The White Knight Arrives: JavaScript Libraries. 12

The Cream of the Crop: Introducing Dojo!. 13
- Let's Take It from the Top: A Brief History of Dojo. 13

The Philosophy of Dojo. 15

The Holy Trinity: The Three Components of Dojo. 16
- Core 17
- Dijit. 20
- DojoX 25

Dojo in Action: What Else? Hello World (Sort Of) 30
- Getting Dojo onto the Page. 32
- Importing Style Sheets 33
- Configuring Dojo 34
- Importing Other Parts of Dojo 35
- Finally: Dijits! 35

Getting Help and Information. 36
Summary. 39

CHAPTER 2 Dojo Core 41

Core vs. Base 41
The Dojo "Include" Mechanism 42
"Trimming the Fat": Creating a Custom Dojo Build. 43
Come Fly with Me: Core in Detail 45
- dojo 46
- dojo.back. 90
- dojo.behavior 92
- dojo.cldr. 94
- dojo.colors. 96
- dojo.currency 96
- dojo.data 98
- dojo.date 98
- dojo.fx 101
- dojo.i18n 104
- dojo.io 105
- dojo.number 107
- dojo.regexp. 110
- dojo.string. 111

Summary. 114

CHAPTER 3 Dijit 115

Dijit at a Glance 115
- Getting Started with Dijit. 116
- Declarative vs. Programmatic Dijits 116

Common Dijit Methods and Attributes. 118
Dijits Directly Under the Dijit Namespace 119
- ColorPalette. 120
- Dialog. 121
- Editor 122
- InlineEditBox. 123
- Menu, MenuItem, and MenuSeparator 125
- ProgressBar 126
- TitlePane 127
- Toolbar. 128
- Tooltip 130
- Tree 131

The dijit.form Package 132
Button 132
CheckBox 133
ComboBox. 135
ComboButton 136
CurrencyTextBox, DateTextBox, NumberTextBox, and TimeTextBox 137
DropDownButton 140
HorizontalSlider and VerticalSlider 141
NumberSpinner 142
RadioButton 143
TextBox 144
Textarea. 145
ToggleButton 146
ValidationTextBox 147
The dijit.layout Package 148
AccordionContainer and AccordionPane 148
ContentPane 150
LayoutContainer. 151
StackContainer and StackController. 152
TabContainer 154
Summary. 156

CHAPTER 4 DojoX 157

dojox.charting 158
Line Chart 159
Area Chart. 160
Fancy-Pants Line Chart (StackedLines Chart) 161
Bar Chart. 161
dojox.collections 162
ArrayList 162
Dictionary 166
Stack 169
dojox.fx 171
addClass() and removeClass() 171
crossFade() 173
highlight() 175
sizeTo() 177
slideBy(). 178

dojox.gfx ... 179
- Surface ... 182
- Line ... 182
- Polyline ... 183
- Rect ... 183
- Circle ... 183
- Ellipse ... 184
- Text ... 184
- applyTransform() ... 184

dojox.grid ... 185
dojox.math ... 188
- degreesToRadians() and radiansToDegrees() ... 190
- distance() ... 190
- factoral() ... 191
- gaussian() ... 191
- midpoint() ... 191
- range() ... 192
- sd(), or Standard Deviation ... 192

dojox.string ... 192
- Builder ... 194
- sprintf() ... 195

dojox.timing ... 195
- Timer ... 195
- Sequence ... 197

dojox.uuid ... 199
dojox.validate ... 202
- isEmailAddress() ... 204
- isInRange() ... 205
- isIpAddress() ... 205
- isNumberFormat() ... 205
- isValidCreditCardNumber() ... 205
- isValidIsbn() ... 206
- isValidLuhn() ... 206

dojox.widget ... 206
- Fisheye List ... 206
- TimeSpinner ... 206
- Toaster ... 208

Summary ... 211

PART 2 The Projects

CHAPTER 5 That Human Touch: Contact Manager and Client-Side Persistence 215

Requirements and Goals 215
How We Will Pull It Off 216
- Dojo and Cookies 217
- The Dojo Storage System 218
- Gears 220

Dissecting the Solution 223
- Writing styles.css 226
- Writing dojoStyles.css 229
- Writing index.htm 230
- Writing goodbye.htm 240
- Writing EventHandlers.js 240
- Writing Contact.js 245
- Writing ContactManager.js 250
- Writing DataManager.js 256

Suggested Exercises 262
Summary 263

CHAPTER 6 A Place for Your Stuff: Dojo Code Cabinet 265

Requirements and Goals 265
How We Will Pull It Off 266
- The dojo.data Namespace 266
- Gears Database Component 268

Dissecting the Solution 270
- Writing index.htm 271
- Writing styles.css 293
- Writing CodeCabinet.js 295

Suggested Exercises 327
Summary 328

CHAPTER 7 Idiot Blob: The Game! 329

Requirements and Goals 329
How We Will Pull It Off 331
- Revenge of the Demented Video Game Designer 332

Dissecting the Solution . . . 333
Writing index.htm . . . 335
Writing styles.css . . . 342
Writing LevelMaps.js . . . 346
Writing GraphicsSubsystem.js . . . 348
Writing GameClass.js . . . 365
Suggested Exercises . . . 376
Summary . . . 377

CHAPTER 8 When the Yellow Pages Just Isn't Cool Enough: Local Business Search . . . 379

Application Requirements and Goals . . . 380
The Yahoo APIs and the Dynamic <script> Tag Trick . . . 381
JSON-P and Dojo . . . 384
Yahoo Web Services Registration . . . 385
Yahoo Local Search Service . . . 386
Yahoo Maps Map Image Service . . . 389
Dissecting the Solution . . . 391
Writing index.htm . . . 392
Writing styles.css . . . 408
Writing App.js . . . 411
Suggested Exercises . . . 439
Summary . . . 440

INDEX . . . 441

About the Author

FRANK W. ZAMMETTI is a Sun worshipper who never really got over the cancellation of *The Greatest American Hero* in the '80s. He is an avid indoorsman who spends his time contemplating all the possible ways he may one day depart this mortal coil involving tomatoes, giant foam fingers, and/or caterpillars. In addition, Frank is a developer of software applications for a large, global bank. He is a father, husband, and walker of the family dog. He lives, works, but mostly plays in the northeastern United States (although clearly not all of his mind inhabits that same location). Frank has now written four books, including this one, covering a wide range of topics from JavaScript, DOM Scripting, and Ajax to DWR (an Ajax library) to Ajax with Java technologies, and of course Dojo, which includes Ajax functionality. He continues to work on various world-changing technological advancements on the side that will likely be released as finished products by real companies some time next week, as is usually the case with every good idea he's ever had. He is a contributor to a number of open source projects (even some that probably would prefer he wasn't!) and is leader/founder of a couple, too.

Frank also rarely takes anything seriously, in case you hadn't figured that out by now!

About the Technical Reviewer

HERMAN VAN ROSMALEN works as a developer/software architect for De Nederlandsche Bank N.V., the central bank of the Netherlands. He has more than 20 years of experience in developing software applications in a variety of programming languages. Herman has been involved in building mainframe, PC, and client/server applications. Since 2000, however, he has been involved mainly in building all sorts of Java EE web-based applications. After working with Struts for years (pre-1.0), he got interested in Ajax and joined the Java Web Parts open source project in 2005. Herman also served as technical editor for the Apress titles *Practical Ajax Projects with Java Technology*; *Practical JavaScript, DOM Scripting, and Ajax Projects*; and *Practical DWR 2 Projects*. Herman lives in a small town, Pijnacker, in the Netherlands with his wife Liesbeth and their children, Barbara, Leonie, and Ramon. You can reach him via e-mail at `herros@gmail.com`.

About the Illustrator

ANTHONY VOLPE is the name of the dude who did the illustrations for this book. He has worked on several video games for various platforms with author Frank Zammetti, including Invasion: Trivia!, IO Lander, K&G Arcade, Spinshot, and Ajax Warrior. Anthony lives in Collegeville, Pennsylvania, and works as a graphic designer and front-end web developer. His hobbies include recording music, writing fiction, making video games, and going to karaoke bars to make a spectacle of himself. To check out all the madness, go here: `www.planetvolpe.com`. You'll find that Anthony is a supremely multitalented guy and also a little . . . off-kilter . . . but in a very good way!

Acknowledgments

This is actually one of the few places in this book where I'm (err, mostly) serious, not my usual tongue-in-cheek self.

I quickly came to realize, upon writing the acknowledgments for my first book a few years ago, that a project of this nature doesn't get done without a lot of help from a lot of folks. Sure, the author is effectively the engine driving things, but an engine without wheels, or a steering wheel, or headlights, or a real good stereo system doesn't make a car on its own, and such is the case with writing a book.

So, I'd like to take this opportunity to thank all those who helped get this one out the door: Steve Anglin, editor, for getting this thing going in the first place. Sofia Marchant, project manager, who kept me on schedule throughout. Sharon Wilkey, copy editor, who made my gibberish (somewhat) coherent. Laura Cheu, production editor, for making it all look good. Herman van Rosmalen, technical reviewer extraordinaire, for making me pay attention to IE7. Anthony Volpe, illustrator, for saving me from having to draw stick figures colored with crayons. And also Joohn Choe, Jimi Browne, and Dominic Shakeshaft for making my experience with Apress what I've come to expect it to be: a very pleasant experience all around.

I'd also like to thank all the fine programmers contributing to the Dojo project itself. Not only did your efforts enable me to write this book (and by extension to make some extra money!), but you've also helped me get things done at my regular day job that would have otherwise taken months of effort to do myself. I think I can safely speak for everyone using Dojo when I say thank you very much; your efforts are most definitely appreciated.

Last but most definitely not least, I'd like to thank *you*, dear reader, for purchasing this book. It's cliché for sports figures to say they couldn't do it without the fans, but there's truth in it, just as there's truth in an author saying I couldn't do it without the readers. You are very much appreciated by this author!

Oh yeah, I almost forgot: thank you to the Higgs boson. *None* of us could've done *any* of it without you! See you later!

Introduction

I've been developing software for a *long* time, by anyone's count: over 25 years, about 15 or so of that "professionally" (meaning 15 years or so I've been getting paid to pretend I know what I'm doing). I've been doing web development specifically for something like 10 or so of those years. I can say, with all honesty, that I was ahead of the curve a number of times. I was writing what we all now call RIAs back around 1998 (two of the apps I wrote in that time frame are still in production, amazingly). I was one of those people who invented Ajax way back then, but didn't think it was anything special and didn't come up with a cute name for it, and hence I am not the one rich and famous for coining an acronym!

None of this is especially important, and I'm not even trying to impress you by saying any of it. I'm just setting the foundation for being able to honestly say this: I've seen a lot. I've done a lot of client-side development. I've seen the evolution from doing absolutely everything yourself, dealing with all the complexities and cross-browser issues, to where we are today, where you basically don't write anything from scratch anymore, you find a good library (or combination of libraries) and proceed from there. This is the same evolution that every other programming language and/or platform has taken; it's just the natural way of things. People over time figure out what works, encapsulate it in some generic, reusable code (a library), and everyone is the better for their efforts.

I've used a large number of libraries over the years too. Some have been very good; some have been very bad; some, of course, were somewhere in the middle. One of the biggest today also happens to be one of the best ever: Dojo.

However, Dojo in a way suffers from its own goodness: it's a bit difficult to wrap your brain around. It's capable of doing so much that understanding what it can do, and understanding how to use it, can be a challenge.

That's why I've written this book. You see, I've used Dojo in a highly complex application on the job, and I've seen the power it offers, but I've also faced the challenge I'm talking about here. My hope is that this book saves you some of the effort I went through and gets you to the point of using Dojo to its full (and considerable) potential quickly.

I also wrote this book because I believe many developers want and really need a "practical" way to learn something like Dojo. We've all seen the articles on the Net that purport to teach you something but do so by showing you simplistic, contrived, limited examples. This sometimes works, but often you hear people saying, "I wish I had a real application so I could see what this article is talking about in a larger context." Many developers like to have code they can rip apart and comprehend on their own, and that's what I'm trying to offer with this book.

I think you're going to like Dojo a lot. In fact, I *know* you will because it will make some very complex things amazingly simple. It will save you a ton of time and effort and enable you to impress your boss in short order! It is without question one of the most forward-looking libraries out there today. There are always very cool new features being explored in Dojo, stuff that you often wouldn't even think is possible in a browser. It's just plain fun to play with sometimes!

Now, if you like and have even half as much fun with this book as you do with Dojo, then we're in good shape . . . but that's my job, isn't it?

Overview of This Book

This book is divided into two parts. The first is more "introductory" in nature:

- Chapter 1 is an introduction to Dojo. We'll start by looking at client-side development more generically, talk about JavaScript's evolution a bit, and finally the evolution of libraries. We'll look at Dojo's philosophy, its overall structure, and some of what it offers.
- Chapter 2 is where we'll delve into the first major component of Dojo: Core. We'll see many of the functions it has to offer, and see examples of each. (Yes, these are small, contrived examples, contrary to what I've said elsewhere, but that's what's needed in this section.)
- Chapter 3 is a detailed look at Dijit, which is where the Dojo GUI widgets are housed.
- Chapter 4 takes a look at DojoX, where the eXperimental components in Dojo live (and, in my opinion, where some of the very coolest parts of Dojo can be found).

In Part 2 we'll jump into the four applications:

- Chapter 5 is where we'll build a contact management application that uses the Dojo storage system to store contacts client-side. We'll get a look at our first dijit too, as well as an introduction to Google's Gears project.
- Chapter 6 presents the code cabinet, an application where you can store code snippets, categorize them, and search for them. We'll get into Dijit a great deal more and see Dojo's data abstraction layer.
- Chapter 7 gives you a break from the more serious applications and shows you how to create a game using Dojo. You'll see Dojo's extensive graphics capabilities in action here.
- Chapter 8 is where you'll find a mashup that uses some publicly available web services to look for businesses around a given area, and show a map of that business. You'll be able to store favorites client-side with this application. You'll see much more of Dijit, the storage system, and lots of Core functionality.

There's lots to cover, but by the end I believe you'll have a good feel for Dojo and will be able to leap ahead in your own projects with it.

Obtaining This Book's Source Code

I remember the days when programming books came with a CD containing all the source code presented in the book. These days, with the advent of the Internet, publishers can frankly save some money, and ultimately generate more profit, by using the Internet to provide that source code, and that's precisely the case with this book.

To obtain the source code for this book, hop on over to `www.apress.com` and click the Source Code/Download link. Find this book in the list and you'll be able to pull down a (fairly large) archive with all the code.

Please note that this book is written with the assumption that you have done this, and have the code ready to look at. Unfortunately, when writing a book you sometimes have to make compromises in the interest of keeping the page count down (and also of not having 50 pages of code in a row, which no one would want to read!). This compromise often means that some of the code isn't printed in the book, and such is the case here. I have a personal philosophy that you should be able to read a programming book in the bathroom, gross as that may seem! Therefore, I've tried very hard to show as much code as possible, and to always show the truly pertinent parts when I couldn't show something in its entirety. Still, it is assumed that you have the code, can (or already have) played with the applications when you begin each chapter, and can refer to the full code as needed. This will all enhance your ability to understand things as you progress through the chapters.

Besides that, the applications are fun to play with, so if for no other reason than that, download the source bundle and have it available before you go too much further.

Obtaining Updates for This Book

No expense has been spared to ensure the accuracy and correctness of everything in this book. We've sacrificed goats to the gods, paid off politicians, tossed salt over our shoulders, and otherwise worked very hard to do our best.

All of that likely won't matter, though, because we're human, and mistakes unfortunately happen.

Because of this, a current errata list is available on the home page for this book on the Apress web site. You can, and I thank you in advance if you do, submit errata for anything you find. Hopefully you won't need to, but few books of this nature get through unscathed. Everyone on the team that made this book happen has done their best to make this one of those few books, but you never know.

I personally apologize unreservedly in advance. I know that I'll rue the day mistakes are found. (*Rue the day*? Who talks like that?) If you find any, I'll buy you a car. I don't have a car; it's my dad's. But then again, didn't anyone ever tell you to make sure your optics are clean?

Contacting the Author

Like most authors, I despise people and like to interact with them as little as possible. I'm a hermit who lives beyond the Dune Sea, content to make Sand People run trembling in fear from my ability to throw weird sounds wherever I choose.

But, if you'd like to contact me anyway (perhaps you have some droids you believe may be mine?), you can contact me at `fzammetti@omnytex.com`.

(That was of course sarcastic. I don't despise people. Well, some of them, but that's for another book. Feel free to contact me about anything you want. Sending money would be better, but I'll take a "hello, how you doin'" too!)

PART 1

Setting the Table

There are two ways to write error-free programs; only the third one works.

—Alan J. Perlis

Computer programming is tremendous fun. Like music, it is a skill that derives from an unknown blend of innate talent and constant practice. Like drawing, it can be shaped to a variety of ends—commercial, artistic, and pure entertainment. Programmers have a well-deserved reputation for working long hours but are rarely credited with being driven by creative fevers. Programmers talk about software development on weekends, vacations, and over meals not because they lack imagination, but because their imagination reveals worlds that others cannot see.

—Bruce Eckel and Larry O'Brien

No matter how slick the demo is in rehearsal, when you do it in front of a live audience the probability of a flawless presentation is inversely proportional to the number of people watching, raised to the power of the amount of money involved.

—Mark Gibbs

Most software today is very much like an Egyptian pyramid with millions of bricks piled on top of each other, with no structural integrity, but just done by brute force and thousands of slaves.

—Alan Kay

I would be delighted to offer any advice I can on understanding women. When I have some, I'll let you know.

—Captain Jean-Luc Picard

There comes a time when you look into the mirror and realize that what you see is all that you will ever be. Then you accept it, or you kill yourself. Or you stop looking into mirrors.

—Londo Mollari

CHAPTER 1

Introduction to Dojo

The evolution of client-side development has been a remarkable journey spread out over a very short period of time. From the early days, which were only ten years or so ago, to the present, we have seen a huge change in the way things are done, the expectations placed upon those doing the work, and the results they generate. No longer is it acceptable for someone lacking a real programming background to churn out code for a web page in his or her spare time. No, there's a certain degree of professionalism now asked of us developers, and it's our job to figure out how to deliver the required results in what is usually a very compressed time frame.

Fortunately, because of this evolution, delivering powerful, good-looking, professional-quality web-based applications is far easier than ever before. You are no longer on your own, required to write every last bit of code, or at least to find snippets here and there and cobble it all together into some sort of coherent whole. No, those days are, for the most part, long gone, and it's thanks to things like Dojo that I can say that.

Before we get to Dojo, though, and all the wonderfulness it brings us, let's look back for a little bit of a history lesson, because only then can you fully appreciate what Dojo brings to the table.

JavaScript: A Study in Evolution

In honor of Charles Darwin, let's now take a brief tour of JavaScript and how it's evolved over time. This is in no way meant to be a detailed history lesson, but I think it'll give you a good overview of the past decade or so of client-side web development involving JavaScript.

Birth of a Language

The year was 1995, and the Web was still very much in its infancy. It's fair to say that the vast majority of computer users couldn't tell you what a web site was at that point, and most developers couldn't build one without doing a lot of research and on-the-job learning. Microsoft was really just beginning to realize that the Internet was going to matter. And Google was still just a made-up term from an old *The Little Rascals* episode.[1]

---

1. The word *google* was first used in the 1927 Little Rascals silent film *Dog Heaven*, to refer to having a drink of water. See `http://experts.about.com/e/g/go/Google.htm`. Although this reference does not state it was the first use of the word, numerous other sources on the Web indicate it was. I wouldn't bet all my money on this if I ever made it to the finals of *Jeopardy*, but it should be good enough for polite party conversation!

Netscape ruled the roost at that point, with its Navigator browser as the primary method for most people to get on the Web. A new feature at the time, Java applets, was making people stand up and take notice. However, one of the things they were noticing was that Java wasn't as accessible to many developers as some (specifically, Sun Microsystems, the creator of Java) had hoped. Netscape needed something simpler and more accessible to the masses of developers it hoped to win over.

Enter Brendan Eich, formerly of MicroUnity Systems Engineering, a new hire at Netscape. Brendan was given the task of leading development of a new, simple, lightweight language for non-Java developers to use. Many of the growing legions of web developers, who often didn't have a full programming background, found Java's object-oriented nature, compilation requirements, and package and deployment requirements a little too much to tackle. Brendan quickly realized that to make a language accessible to these developers, he would need to make certain decisions, certain trade-offs. Among them, he decided that this new language should be loosely typed and very dynamic by virtue of it being interpreted.

The language he created was initially called LiveWire, but its name was pretty quickly changed to LiveScript, owing to its dynamic nature. However, as is all too often the case, some marketing drones got hold of it and decided to call it JavaScript, to ride the coattails of Java. This change was actually implemented before the end of the Navigator 2.0 beta cycle.[2] So, for all intents and purposes, JavaScript was known as JavaScript from the beginning. At least the marketing folks were smart enough to get Sun involved. On December 4, 1995, both Netscape and Sun jointly announced JavaScript, terming it "complementary" to both Hypertext Markup Language (HTML) and Java (one of the initial reasons for its creation was to help web designers manipulate Java applets easier, so this actually made some sense). The shame of all this is that for years to come, JavaScript and Java would be continually confused on mailing lists, message forums, and in general by developers and the web-surfing public alike!

It didn't take long for JavaScript to become something of a phenomenon, although tellingly on its own, rather than in the context of controlling applets. Web designers were just beginning to take the formerly static Web and make it more dynamic, more reactive to the user, and more multimedia. People were starting to try to create interactive and sophisticated (relatively speaking) user interfaces, and JavaScript was seen as a way to do that. Seemingly simple things like swapping images on mouse events, which before then would have required a bulky browser plug-in of some sort, became commonplace. In fact, this single application of JavaScript, flipping images in response to user mouse events, was probably the most popular usage of JavaScript for a long time. Manipulating forms, and, most usually, validating them, was a close second in terms of early JavaScript usage. Document Object Model (DOM) manipulation took a little bit longer to catch on for the most part, mostly because the early DOM level 0, as it came to be known, was relatively simplistic, with form, link, and anchor manipulation as the primary goals.

2. As a historical aside, you might be interested to know that version 2.0 of Netscape Navigator introduced not one but two noteworthy features. Aside from JavaScript, frames were also introduced. Of course, one of these has gained popularity, while the other tends to be shunned by the web developer community at large, but that's a story for another book!

Reasons for JavaScript's Early Rise

What made JavaScript so popular so fast? Probably most important was the very low barrier to entry. All you had to do was open any text editor, type in some code, save it, load that file in a browser, and it worked! You didn't need to go through a compilation cycle or package and deploy it, none of that complex "programming" stuff. And no complicated integrated development environment (IDE) was involved. It was really just as easy as saving a quick note to yourself.

Tying in with the theme of a low barrier to entry was JavaScript's apparent simplicity. You didn't have to worry about data types, because it was (and still is) a loosely typed language. It wasn't object-oriented, so you didn't have to think about class hierarchies and the like. In fact, you didn't even have to deal with functions if you didn't want to (and wanted your script to execute immediately upon page loading). There was no multithreading to worry about or generic collections classes to learn. In fact, the intrinsic JavaScript objects were very limited, and thus quickly picked up by anyone with even just an inkling of programming ability. It was precisely this seeming simplicity that led to a great many of the early problems.

Something Is Rotten in the State of JavaScript

Unfortunately, JavaScript's infancy wasn't all roses by any stretch, as you can see in Figure 1-1. A number of highly publicized security flaws hurt its early reputation considerably. A flood of books aimed squarely at nonprogrammers had the effect of getting a lot of people involved in writing code who probably shouldn't have been (at least, not as publicly as for a web site).

Figure 1-1. *JavaScript: The ugly ducking of the programming world?*

Probably the biggest problem, however, was the frankly elitist attitude of many "real" programmers. They saw JavaScript's lack of development tools (IDEs, debuggers, and so on), its inability to be developed outside a browser (in some sort of test environment), and apparent simplicity as indications that it was a *script-kiddie* language, something that would be used only by amateurs, beginners, and hacks. For a long time, JavaScript was very much the ugly duckling of the programming world. It was the Christina Crawford[3] of the programming world, forever being berated by her metaphorical mother, the "real" programmers of the world.

■Note *Script-kiddie* is a term from the hacker underground that refers to a hacker who has no real ability and instead relies on programs and existing scripts to perform his exploits. The term is now used in a more generic sense to describe someone who relies on the ingenuity of others to get things done—for example, coders who can Google real well and copy the code they find rather than writing it themselves. Make no mistake, copying existing code is generally a good thing, but someone who isn't ultimately capable of writing the code if they had to is a script-kiddie.

The Unarguable Problems with JavaScript

Although it's true that JavaScript wasn't given a fair shake early on by programmers, some of their criticisms were, without question, true. JavaScript was far from perfect in its first few iterations, a fact I doubt that Netscape or Brendan Eich would dispute! As you'll see, some of it was a simple consequence of being a new technology that needed a few revisions to get it right (the same problem Microsoft is so often accused of having), and some of it was, well, something else.

So, what were the issues that plagued early JavaScript? Several of them tend to stand out above the rest: browser incompatibilities, memory usage, and performance.

Browsers for a long time implemented JavaScript in a myriad of different ways. Very simple things such as methods of the `String` object would frequently not work the same way in one browser vs. another. (Anyone who remembers trying to do simple `substring()` calls on a string around the 1996 time frame will know all too well about this!) Today, the differences in JavaScript implementations are generally few and far between and tend to be rather easy to work around. That's certainly not to say you won't occasionally be burned by differences, but typically you'll find that JavaScript itself is probably 99 percent or better compatible between all the major browsers. It's usually differences in the DOM, which there are still plenty of, that can bite you from time to time.

---

3. Christina Crawford was the daughter of Joan Crawford, and her story is told in the classic movie *Mommy Dearest* (`www.imdb.com/title/tt0082766`). Even if you don't remember the movie, you almost certainly remember the phrase "No more wire hangers!" uttered by Joan to Christina in what was probably the most memorable scene in the movie.

Memory usage with early implementations also left a lot to be desired. JavaScript, being an automatic garbage-collected language, leaves all the memory allocation/deallocation in the hands of the browser and the JavaScript interpreter. It used to be common to find objects gumming up the works long after they should have been destroyed. This is rightly considered an outright bug in the JavaScript engine, but thankfully these types of things rarely occur anymore. To be sure, you can have memory leaks in JavaScript, but they are a result of more-sophisticated techniques being employed; it's rarely the engine itself misbehaving.

Performance was a big problem for a very long time, and even today continues to be an issue. In the early days, it was rare to see an arcade-type game written in JavaScript because the performance of the JavaScript engines was just nowhere near good enough for that. Today, games like that can be found with little problem. Performance problems definitely still exist, and worse still they aren't always consistent. String concatenation is known to be much slower in Microsoft Internet Explorer today than in Mozilla Firefox, and it's probably not even as fast as it could be in Firefox. Still, overall, performance is hugely improved over what it once was.

As Ballmer Said: "Developers! Developers! Developers!..."

All that being said, though, there was one true reason JavaScript wasn't embraced by everyone from the get-go, and that's developers themselves!

Early JavaScript developers discovered that they could do all sorts of whiz-bang tricks—from fading the background color of a page when it loaded to having a colorful trail follow the cursor around the page. You could see various types of scrolling text all over the place, as well as different page-transition effects, such as wipes and the like. Although some of these effects may look rather cool, they serve virtually no purpose other than as eye candy for the user. Now, don't get me wrong here, eye candy is great! There's nothing I like more than checking out a new screen saver or a new utility that adds effects to my Windows shell. It's fun! But I always find myself removing those things later, not only because they hurt system performance, but also because they quickly become annoying and distracting.

Here's a quick test: if you are using Microsoft Windows, take a look at the Performance options for your PC (accessed by right-clicking My Computer, selecting Properties, clicking the Advanced tab, and clicking the Settings button under the Performance group). Did you turn off the expanding and collapsing of windows when minimized and maximized? Did you turn off shadows under the cursor? Did you disable the growing and shrinking of taskbar buttons when applications close? Many of us make it a habit to turn off this stuff, not only because it makes our systems snappier (or at least gives that perception), but also because some of it just gets in the way. Seeing my windows fly down to the taskbar when I minimize them is pretty pointless. Now, you may argue that it depends on the implementation. On a Macintosh, the effects that come into play when windows are minimized and maximized are better and not as annoying—at least most people seem think that, and to a certain extent I agree. But you still have to ask yourself whether the effect is helping you get work done. Is it making you more productive? I dare say the answer is no for virtually anyone. So although there may be degrees of annoyance and obtrusiveness, certain things are still generally annoying, obtrusive, and pointless. Unfortunately, this is what the term *Dynamic HTML (DHTML)* means to many people, and while I wish it weren't so, it isn't at all an undeserved connotation to carry. Some people even go so far as to say DHTML is the Devil's buzzword!

Early JavaScript developers were huge purveyors of such muck, and it got old pretty fast. I don't think it is going too far to say that some people began to question whether the Web was worth it, based entirely on the perception that it was a playground and not something for serious business.[4] A web site that annoys visitors with visual spam is not one they will likely use again. And if you're trying to make a living with that site and your company's revenues depend on it, that's going to lead to bad news real fast!

This obviously was not a failing of the technology. Just because we have nuclear weapons doesn't mean we should be flinging them all over the place! I suppose equating nuclear war to an annoying flashing thing on a web page is a bit of hyperbole, but the parallel is that just because a technology exists and enables you to do something doesn't necessarily mean you should go off and do it.

ARE EFFECTS JUST THE DEANNA TROI OF THE ENTERPRISE BRIDGE CREW? (READ: JUST FOR LOOKS)

Let's tackle one question that often comes to mind first: why do we need effects at all? Isn't it just a bunch of superfluous eye candy that doesn't serve much purpose other than to make people go "ooh" and "aah"? Well, first off, if you've ever designed an application for someone else, you know that presentation is an important part of the mix. The more people like how your application looks, the more they'll like how it works, whether it works well or not. It's a relative measure. That's the lesser reason, although one that should not be quickly dismissed.

The much more important reason has do with how we perceive things. Look around you right now. Pick up any object you want and move it somewhere else. Did the object just pop out from the starting point and appear at the new location? No, of course not! It moved smoothly and deliberately from one place to another. Guess what? This is how the world works! And furthermore, this is how our brains are wired to expect things to work. When things don't work that way, it's jarring, confusing, and frustrating.

People use movement as a visual cue as to what's going on. This is why modern operating systems are beginning to add all sorts of whiz-bang features, such as windows collapsing and expanding. They aren't just eye candy. They do, in fact, serve a purpose: they help our brains maintain their focus where it should be and on what interests us.

In a web application, the same is true. If you can slide something out of view and something else into view, it tends to be more pleasant for the users, and more important, helps them be more productive by not making them lose focus for even a small measure of time.

And seriously, how exactly does the ship's shrink manage to always be around on the bridge? Is she necessary personnel for running the Enterprise? I know, I know, she finally passed the bridge crew test and was promoted to commander in the episode "Thine Own Self," but still, she was always floating around the bridge long before then. I suppose she was on the lookout for space madness or something, who knows.

4. I remember a television commercial of a bunch of web developers showing their newly created site to their boss. The boss says there needs to be more flash, like a flaming logo. The developers look at him a little funny and proceed to put a flaming logo on the page. It was pretty obvious to anyone watching the commercial that the flaming logo served no useful purpose, and in fact, had the opposite effect as was intended in that it made the site look amateurish. It's so easy to abuse eye candy that it's not even funny!

So, when you hear *DHTML*, don't automatically recoil in fear, as some do. This term still accurately describes what we're doing today from a purely technical definition. However, you should, at the same time, recognize that the term does have a well-earned negative connotation, brought on by the evils of early JavaScript developers,[5] not the technology they were using. And at the end of the day, that was the underlying source of the problems people saw back then (and still today, although thankfully to a lesser extent).

Part of the evolution of the JavaScript developer was in starting to recognize when the super-cool, neat-o, whiz-bang eye candy should be put aside. Developers began to realize that what they were doing was actually counterproductive, because it was distracting and annoying in many cases. Instead, a wave of responsibility has been spreading over the past few years. Some will say this is the single most important part of JavaScript's overall evolution toward acceptance.

You can still find just as many nifty-keen effects out there today as in the past, perhaps even more so. But they tend to truly enhance the experience for the user. For example, with the yellow fade effect (originated by 37signals, `www.37signals.com`), changes on a page are highlighted briefly upon page reload and then quickly fade to their usual state. Spotting changes after a page reload is often difficult, and this technique helps focus users on those changes. It enhances users' ability to work effectively. This is the type of responsible eye candy that is in vogue today, and to virtually everyone, it is better than what came before.

■ **Note** To see an example of the positive usage of the yellow fade effect, take a peek at the contact form for Clearleft at `http://clearleft.com/contact`. Just click the Submit button without entering anything and see what happens. You can also see the effect all over the place in the 37signals Basecamp product, at `www.basecamphq.com/` (you'll need to sign up for a free account to play around). You can get a good sense of where and why this seemingly minor (and relatively simple technically) technique has gained a great deal of attention. Other 37signals products use this technique, too, so by all means explore; it's always good to learn from those near the top! And if you would like to go straight to the source, check Matthew Linderman's blog entry at `www.37signals.com/svn/archives/000558.php`.

Standardization: The Beginning of Sanity

In early 1996, shortly after its creation, JavaScript was submitted to the European Computer Manufacturers Association (ECMA) for standardization. ECMA (`www.ecma-international.org`) produced the specification called ECMAScript, which covered the core JavaScript syntax, and a subset of DOM level 0. ECMAScript still exists today, and most browsers implement that specification in one form or another. However, it is rare to hear people talk about ECMAScript in place of JavaScript. The name has simply stuck in the collective consciousness for too long to be replaced, but do be clear about it: they are describing the same thing, at least as far as the thought process of most developers goes!

---

5. I'm not only the hair club president, but I'm also a client. I have some old web sites in my archives (thankfully, none are still live) with some really horrendous things on them! I certainly was not immune to the DHTML whiz-bang disease. I had my share of flaming logos, believe me. I like to think I've learned from my mistakes (and so would my boss).

The reason this standardization is so important is because it finally gave the browser vendors a common target to shoot for, something they hadn't had before. It was no longer about Microsoft having its vision of what JavaScript should be, and Netscape of course *knowing* what it should be, having created it and all. Now it was about hitting a well-defined target, and only *then* building on top of it (think enhanced feature sets that one browser might provide that another might not). At least if the underlying language implementation was based on a common specification, we developers would no longer have to hit a moving target (well, to be fair, not quite as active a moving target anyway). Without standardization, it's likely that JavaScript would never have become what it is today, wouldn't be used as much as it is today. Either that or we'd have settled on one browser over another just to make our lives as developers easier, and that's no more a desirable outcome than no JavaScript at all.

The Times They Are a Changin': The Experienced Come to Bear

After the initial wave of relatively inexperienced developers using JavaScript, and many times doing so poorly, the next iteration began to emerge. Certain common mistakes were recognized and began to be rectified.

Perhaps most important of all, the more-experienced programmers who had initially shunned JavaScript began to see its power and brought their talents to bear on it. Those with true computer science backgrounds began to take a look and point out the mistakes and ways to fix them. With that input came something akin to the Renaissance. Ideas began to flow, and improvements started to be made. It wasn't the final destination, but an important port of call along the way.

Although a lot of the early problems with JavaScript undoubtedly did come from less-experienced programmers getting into the mix, certainly that didn't account for everything. Overnight, thousands of otherwise good, experienced programmers got stupid all at once!

As I mentioned earlier, working on JavaScript was almost too easy in a sense: throw some code in a file, fire up a browser, and off you go! In most other languages, you have a compile cycle, which tends to ferret out a lot of problems. Then you often have static code-analysis tools, which find even more things to fix. You may even have a code formatter to enforce the appropriate coding standards. None of this is (typically) present when working with JavaScript. I put *typically* in parentheses because modern development tools now exist to give you all of these features, save for the compile part at least.

Maybe "the bubble" had something to do with it, too. I'm referring to that period when everyone thought they had the surefire way to make a buck off the Web, and when the public was just starting to get online and figure out how cool a place the Web was. There were 80-hour work weeks, powered by Jolt Cola, jelly donuts, and the incessant chant of some flower shirt–wearing, Segway-riding (okay, Segway wasn't out then, but work with me here!) recent college grad with an MBA, who promised us that all those stock options would be worth more than we could count. Maybe that caused everyone to just slap the code together so it at least appeared to work, in a pointless attempt to implement the business plan, and is really what caused all the trouble.

Yeah, you're right, probably not. Ahem.

The good habits that developers had learned over time, such as code formatting, commenting, and logical code structure, had to essentially be relearned in the context of JavaScript. And, of course, those who hadn't done much programming before had to learn it all anew. But learn they did, and from that point, JavaScript started to become something "professional" developers didn't thumb their noses at as a reflex act. It could start to become a first-class citizen, now that developers had the knowledge of how to do it right.

Of course, the last step was yet to come.

What's Old Is New Again: JavaScript in the Present

We've arrived at the present time, meaning the past three to four years. JavaScript has really come into its own.

The whole Ajax movement has certainly been the biggest catalyst for getting JavaScript on a more solid footing, but even a bit before then, things were starting to come around. The desire to build fancier, more-reactive, user-friendly, and ultimately fat-client-like web applications drove the need and desire to do more on the client. Performance considerations certainly played a role, too, but I suspect a lot smaller one than many people tend to think.

The bottom line is that JavaScript has moved pretty quickly into the realm of first-class citizen, the realm of "professional" development, as Figure 1-2 demonstrates. Perhaps the best evidence of this is that you can now find terms such as *JavaScript Engineer, JavaScript Lead,* and *Senior JavaScript Developer* used to describe job offerings on most job search sites. And people now say them with a straight face during an interview!

Figure 1-2. *No longer the object of scorn, JavaScript now gets the respect it deserves.*

So, aside from Ajax, what are the reasons for this relatively current trend toward respectability that JavaScript seems to have earned? Let's have a look.

Browser compatibility isn't so much of an issue anymore, at least when it comes to JavaScript itself (DOM differences are still prevalent, though). Object-oriented design has found its way into JavaScript, leading to much better overall code structure. Graceful degradation is commonplace nowadays, so web sites continue to work even when JavaScript isn't available. Even internationalization and accessibility for those with disabilities is often factored into the design of the code. In fact, this is all a way of saying that JavaScript developers have learned enough that they can be far more responsible with what they design than they ever could before. JavaScript is no longer something for script-kiddies to mess with but now provides a respectable vocation for a developer to be in!

The White Knight Arrives: JavaScript Libraries

JavaScript libraries have grown leaps and bounds over just the past few years, and this is perhaps one of the biggest reasons JavaScript has gone from pariah to accepted tool in the toolbox of good web developers. It used to be that you could spend a few hours scouring the Web looking for a particular piece of code, and you would eventually find it. Often, you might have to, ahem, "appropriate" it from some web site. Many times, you could find it on one of a handful of "script sites" that were there expressly to supply developers with JavaScript snippets for their own use. If you were fortunate enough to find a true library rather than some stand-alone snippets of code, you couldn't count on its quality or support down the road.

Using libraries is a Good Thing™, as Ogar from Figure 1-3 can attest (and which Tor is finding out the hard way).

Larger libraries that provide all sorts of bells and whistles, as exist in the big-brother world of Java, C++, PHP, and other languages, are a more recent development in the world of JavaScript. In many ways, we are now in a golden age, and you can find almost more options than you would want! While some libraries out there focus on one area or another (graphical user interface, or GUI; widgets; Ajax; effects; and so on), other libraries try to be the proverbial jack-of-all-trades, covering a wide variety of areas such as client-side storage, widgets, Ajax, collections, basic JavaScript enhancements, and security.

Figure 1-3. *Be like Ogar, not Tor: use those libraries; don't always reinvent the wheel!*

The one thing all these libraries have in common is that their quality is light-years beyond what came before, and they all will make your life considerably easier! Not only are they more solid, but they are better supported than ever before with real organizations, both commercial and otherwise, backing them up.

There's usually no sense in reinventing the wheel, so libraries are indeed a good thing. If you are implementing an application using Ajax techniques, unless you need absolute control over every detail, I can't think of a good reason not to use a library for it. If you know that your UI design requires some more-advanced widgets that the browser doesn't natively provide, these libraries can be invaluable.

There are oodles of libraries out there today, all with their own pluses and minuses. Most of the bigger names out there—jQuery, the Yahoo! UI Library (YUI), Direct Web Remoting

(DWR), Prototype, script.aculo.us, MooTools, and Rico, just to name a few—are all top-notch, and you can hardly go wrong picking one or the other. However, they all have a somewhat narrow focus, for the most part. jQuery is about accessing parts of the DOM as efficiently as possible. YUI is about widgets. DWR is about Ajax. Script.aculo.us is about effects, as is Rico. Prototype and MooTools are both a bit more general-purpose in nature, which is closer in philosophy to the library we're here to discuss, that of course being Dojo.

Without further ado, let's meet the star of the show, the Dojo Toolkit!

The Cream of the Crop: Introducing Dojo!

Dojo, or more precisely, the Dojo Toolkit (but from here on out it'll be just *Dojo* for short) is an open source JavaScript library. No surprise there! Dojo is licensed under either the Academic Free License (AFL) or the BSD license. The AFL is the more liberal of the two and is favored by the Dojo Foundation, which is the parent foundation under which Dojo lives. However, the Free Software Foundation (FSF) has created some ambiguity between the AFL and the two licenses that the FSF is famous for concocting: the GNU General Public License (GPL) and Lesser General Public License (LGPL). So, the fine folks at Dojo give you the choice to use the BSD license or the AFL, the BSD license being compatible with both the GPL and LGPL licenses, as the FSF says.

Dojo seeks to be your "one-stop shop" for all your JavaScript needs. Many libraries out there focus on just one or two areas, which means that you as a developer will usually have to combine two or more libraries to get everything you need done. With Dojo, that's not the case. Dojo covers all the bases, from core JavaScript enhancements to UI widgets, from browser-independent drawing functions to offline storage capabilities.

The kicker to it all, though, is that Dojo does this well! I bet you've seen libraries that purport to do it all, and in fact they do pretty much cover all the bases, yet they fail in one important regard: they're not very good! They tend to have lots of bugs, incomplete functionality, and no support for any of it. Dojo turns that idea upside-down and not only gives you virtually everything you'd need to create rich modern web applications, but enables you to get everything from the same source, and that's definitely a plus.

There's an underlying philosophy to Dojo, and a big part of it is what I just talked about. But before I get any further into that, let's step back and take a quick look at how Dojo came to be in the first place.

Let's Take It from the Top: A Brief History of Dojo

The year was 2004. The air was musky. Oh wait, sorry, I thought I was writing a novel for a moment. Anyway, the year was 2004, early 2004 to be precise. A gentleman by the name of Alex Russell was working for a company named Informatica doing DHTML development. Alex was the creator of a library called netWindows that allowed for creation of a windowed interface (much like the Windows operating system, which was unfortunate as you'll see!). He began looking to hire someone to help him in that work, and so some prominent members of the DHTML programming community on the Web were contacted. This need led to a more generalized discussion among the DHTML community about the future of DHTML, and web development overall.

Ultimately, the job (one of them as it turns out) went to Dylan Schiemann (the other job went to David Schontzler, who worked at Informatica for the summer). As the job progressed,

Alex and Dylan, along with some others, started to have discussions about developing what would be a "standard" library for JavaScript, much like the standard libraries that exist for most other languages, such as C for instance.

A new mailing list (ng-html, which later became the dojo-developer list) was created, initially with folks including Aaron Boodman, Dylan Schiemann, Tom Trenka, Simon Willison, Joyce Park, Mark Anderson, and Leonard Lin on it. Discussions on licensing, intellectual property (IP) rights, coding standards, and such began in earnest. After not too long a time, the really difficult job began.

That job, of course, being what the heck to name the whole thing!

A while earlier, Alex had received a cease-and-desist letter from Microsoft over his use of the word *windows* in his netWindows project. Seriously! I mean, I like to think I'm a pretty creative guy, but even I couldn't make up something that wacky! Which reminds me, I need to go trademark the terms *sock, sky, person,* and *water*. But I digress. The folks on the mailing list tossed around a bunch of ideas with one of the stated goals (I'd be willing to guess one of the top one or two goals!) to make it something that wouldn't get them sued. Leonard Lin proposed the name *Dojo*, and the rest was history.

The first early code was committed by Alex and Dylan, with the support of Informatica. Soon after, two companies, JotSpot and Renkoo, got behind the project and provided early support. By this point, good momentum was starting to build on the mailing list, with everyone starting to contribute bits and pieces they had lying around, and a JavaScript library was born!

The Dojo Foundation was founded in 2005 to house the copyrights for the Dojo code. The foundation is a 501(c)(6) organization, which is a type of tax-exempt nonprofit organization under the United States Internal Revenue Service code. Alex serves as the president of the foundation, and Dylan is the Secretary/Treasurer.

None of this is terribly important to us code monkeys, I know! But it's interesting to know the history nonetheless, and with those details embedded in our brains, we can move on to more-interesting things, starting with the underlying philosophy behind Dojo.

CODE MONKEY? WHAT DID YOU JUST CALL ME?!?

Some people consider the term *code monkey* to be derogatory, but I never have. To me, a code monkey is someone who programs for a living and enjoys writing code. I suppose by that definition you wouldn't even have to earn a living from programming, so long as you love hacking bits. Either way, it's all about the code!

By the way, just because someone is a code monkey doesn't mean they can't do architecture, and vice versa. If you like all of the facets of building software, if you like being up 'til all hours of the night trying to figure out why your custom-built double-linked list is corrupting elements when you modify them, if you like playing with that new open source library for no other reason than you're curious, if you like the feeling you get from seeing a working application come spewing out the back end of a development cycle (even if it's some otherwise dull business application), then you're a code monkey, plain and simple, and you should never take offense to being called that name.

Of course, some people do mean it in a derogatory way, and you'll know who they are, in which case you should be a good little code monkey and throw feces at them. (Frank Zammetti and Apress cannot be held liable if you actually follow this advice!)

Oh yes, and no discussion of the term code monkey would be complete with referencing the fantastic parody song "Code Monkey" by one Jonathan Coulton. His web site is here: `www.jonathancoulton.com`. Sadly, at the time I wrote this, it appeared to be having problems. Hopefully they are just temporary, but in any case, if you like Weird Al–style funny songs and want to hear a good one about us code monkeys, of which I am proudly one, try that site, and failing that, spend a few minutes with Google trying to find it. (I don't even think the Recording Industry Association of America, or RIAA, the American organization famous for suing grandmothers, children, and even dead people for illegally downloading pirated music, will have a problem with it, but you never can tell, so I'm not suggesting any file-sharing networks you might try!)

The Philosophy of Dojo

Dojo's development has been driven by a core philosophy instilled in the project by those founding members mentioned earlier, and nurtured since by additional contributors who have taken part in making Dojo what it is today. The underlying philosophy is an important aspect of any open source project for us, consumers of the project, to understand. Why is that?

Well, to begin with, understanding the philosophy can give you a feeling of comfort with the project. When you use open source, you are essentially counting on two things: support of those who wrote the code, and the code itself. Being open source means you can get in there and maintain the code as necessary, which is great if the original authors go away. Still, especially if you work in a corporate environment where you may well be betting the future of your company on an open source project, you really want to have some "warm fuzzies" with regard to the prospect of the original authors sticking around to help you when you run into trouble.

More than that, you want to have some understanding of what they're thinking, what they plan to do, and how they plan to do it. An all-volunteer open source project has no real obligation to provide any of that, yet most do because they recognize a certain degree of civil responsibility, so to speak. They recognize that just dumping code into the wild, no matter how good or well-intentioned the motives are, isn't all there is to it. Those involved in most projects feel they have some degree of responsibility to support those who choose to use their code. I'm not talking about coming to their houses and helping them use the code, nor am I talking about reacting to every last issue or feature suggestion everyone makes. It's volunteer work after all. But there's a certain "something" there, for most people, a certain degree of responsibility that they feel obligated to meet.

The Dojo team clearly has that sense of responsibility because they've gone so far as to clearly spell out the philosophy that drives them. Because I've seen it written in a couple of places in a couple of different ways, I'll paraphrase the tenets of the philosophy, try to synthesize it into my own words:

- People should *want* to use your code. I've seen this stated as "minimize the barrier to entry." This covers quite a bit of ground, from how the code is packaged, how it's licensed, how it's designed, how easy it is to get started with, how well it's documented, and so on. The point is, the Dojo team tries to reduce the number of reasons anyone would have for *not* choosing Dojo. You could probably sum it up concisely by simply saying this: produce the best possible code in the best possible way, given the talents of those involved. That's a great motivation and a great guiding principle for any community-driven project.

- Performance is a secondary concern to ease of use. Let me head off a negative thought at the pass here: this in no way, shape, or form implies that Dojo isn't high performance, nor does it imply that the Dojo team doesn't care about performance and strive for it. Quite the opposite, in fact! What it means is that their primary concern is ensuring that the consumers of the library have as easy a time consuming it as possible (and sometimes at the expense of it being more difficult and complex for the library developers themselves). When that goal has been satisfactorily met, only *then* is it time to kick performance up a notch. You may well have heard the saying about never prematurely optimizing code and all the evils that can lead to. This is a variation on that theme.

- Write code that is as simple as possible, but no simpler. Conversely, write code that is only as complex as it needs to be. Don't try to do more than necessary. This is all a way of saying that if the environment the code is running in (read: the browser) can do something, there's no need to do a bunch of heavy lifting to duplicate that functionality in JavaScript. Fill in the gaps between JavaScript and the browser, but don't introduce more pieces than are truly necessary.

- Try to be a "full-stack" library. Dojo tries to be everything to everyone, and tries to do so with a high level of quality, and by and large it succeeds. While other libraries may pick an area or two and focus on them, Dojo tries to do it all so you don't have to worry about the potential difficulties of meshing two or more libraries together to meet all your needs. Much like Java/Java Platform, Enterprise Edition (Java EE) or .NET tries to cover all the bases, so too does Dojo for the JavaScript/web-client world.

- Collaboration is the way. Dojo has, from the outset, been all about talented individuals with similar goals coming together to make something better then they likely could have on their own. This is true of any good community-driven project, and Dojo is certainly no exception.

The Dojo team has also clearly indicated in their own documentation that although these are the goals the project strives for, they may not all be met, or met as fully as the team would like, all the time. The point is, as developers who may look to use Dojo, we know what guides them, we know their underlying thought process, and that's extremely valuable. We can also clearly see that the members of the team, all of whom one presumes buys into these guiding principles, share that sense of civic responsibility and are trying to do right by everyone, to put it in simplest terms. This has to give you a good feeling, a feeling of confidence, in your choice to use Dojo. Indeed, any community-driven/open source project that doesn't seem to share these same goals is likely one you'd be better off avoiding!

The Holy Trinity: The Three Components of Dojo

A long time ago, finding what you needed in Dojo was quite a challenge. There didn't seem to be as much rhyme or reason to the overall structure as you might like. In the end, Dojo users spent a lot of time hunting things down.

That, I'm happy to say, is no longer the case! The Dojo team has now organized the project into three high-level conceptual components, each with a specific focus. Figure 1-4 shows the breakdown.

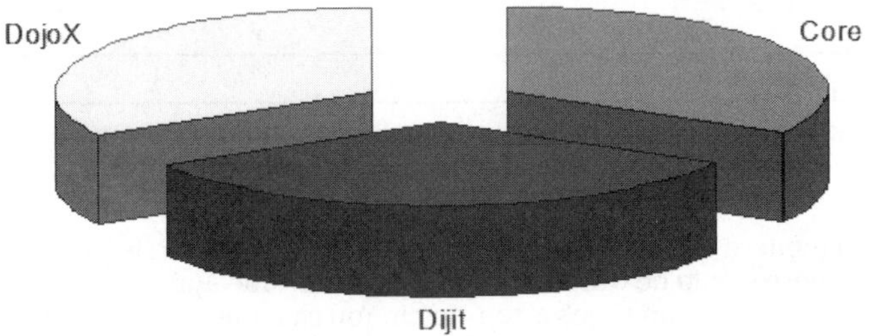

Figure 1-4. *Dojo's three conceptual components. (Note: These are not necessarily scaled to reflect their real sizes in terms of their percentage of the overall Dojo pie.)*

The Holy Trinity, as I like to call it, consists of Core, Dijit, and DojoX. Let's look at each part in turn, at a high level, to see what they're all about.

Core

Like the solid foundation home builders strive to build on, Core provides everything else in Dojo a great foundation to build on. More than that, though, Core offers you, as a JavaScript developer, a whole host of functionality to build your own applications on top of.

As you'll see shortly, using Dojo begins with importing `dojo.js`. What this does for you, in a small amount of space (23KB of code at the time of this writing) is automatically give you a ton of functionality. Beyond that, you'll use the Dojo `include()` mechanism (again, you'll see this in action very shortly), which enables you to "pull in" other parts of Dojo. As far as Core goes, this gives you the ability to bring in more "base" functionality, which is possible because Dojo is designed with a modular approach. Don't worry, this will all make sense very soon. The point for now is simply that Core is, in a sense, split in half: those things you get automatically all the time when using Dojo, and those things that are still part of Core but which you have to explicitly "bring in" to your page.

There's a *ton* of stuff in Core, and you frankly won't even see all of it in this book. There's simply too much to cover, unless the entire book were about Core. Still, I'll do my best to cover and then use in the projects those things you're likely to use most, and as much other stuff as I can. In the meantime, let's run down what's in Core, at a very high level. As you dissect the projects later in the book, you'll see a lot of this in more detail. Table 1-1 and Table 1-2 provide this high-level look. Table 1-1 lists the stuff you can access immediately just by virtue of including `dojo.js` on your page, and Table 1-2 shows the "extra" stuff that's part of Core but that you have to `include()` in your page explicitly.

Table 1-1. *"Automatic" Dojo Core Functionality*

Core Functionality Group	Description
Browser detection	Dojo can tell you whether your application is running in Internet Explorer, Firefox, Opera, Konquerer, and even whether the client is a web browser!
JSON encoding/decoding	Dojo provides functions to turn any object into JavaScript Object Notation (JSON) string, a standard way to represent JavaScript objects, and to turn a JSON string into a JavaScript object.

Continued

Table 1-1. *Continued*

Core Functionality Group	Description
Package loading	The Dojo `include()` mechanism enables modular components to be loaded in a way similar to how packages are handled in languages such as Java and C#.
Powerful Ajax support	No modern JavaScript library that purports to be general-purpose would be worth its salt if it didn't include Ajax functionality, and Dojo's is top-notch. You can quickly and easily make remote calls for content from your client code, all without having to worry about all the potentially sticky issues that can sometimes come into play.
Unified events	Dojo provides a way to hook events to objects of virtually any kind in a consistent manner, allowing for aspect-oriented programming (AOP) techniques in JavaScript. I'm not just talking about the typical UI events you deal with all the time, such as mouse click events, but *events* in a much broader sense. For instance, when one function calls another, that's an event you can hook into.
Animation/effects	Dojo provides all the nifty-keen UI animation effects that are all the rage in the Web 2.0 world. Your UI will be flying, fading, pulsing, sliding, expanding, and shrinking in no time with Dojo!
Asynchronous programming support	I think quoting the Dojo application programming interface (API) documentation here is not only the best bet in terms of accuracy, but frankly it made me chuckle, and I think you will too: *"JavaScript has no threads, and even if it did, threads are hard. Deferreds are a way of abstracting nonblocking events, such as the final response to an* `XMLHttpRequest`. *Deferreds create a promise to return a response at some point in the future and an easy way to register your interest in receiving that response."* Or, to paraphrase: Dojo provides publish-and-subscribe functionality to JavaScript.
High-performance Cascading Style Sheets (CSS) revision 3 query engine	The ability to look up objects in the DOM of a page is the bread and butter of modern JavaScript programmers, and having a way (or multiple ways even better!) to look up objects quickly and efficiently is of paramount performance. Dojo has you covered!
Language utilities	Dojo supports all kinds of "enhancements" to JavaScript itself, things like collections, array utilities, string manipulation functions, and so on.
CSS style and positioning utilities	The ability to manipulate elements on a page, specifically their style and position attributes, is again a fundamental thing to have to do, and Dojo has all sorts of goodies to help here. This in many ways goes hand in hand with the query engine mentioned previously because usually you'll look up an element, and then manipulate it, and Dojo can make it all a lot easier.

Core Functionality Group	Description
Object-oriented programming (OOP) support	When people first learn that they can do object-oriented development in JavaScript, it's something of an epiphany. Then, especially if they're more familiar with OOP in more-traditional languages such as Java, they quickly begin to realize the limitations. Inheritance, for instance, isn't quite the same as in Java, and there are some things you simply can't do in JavaScript (overloading methods, for instance, isn't possible, at least not in the accepted way). Dojo seeks to overcome most of these limitations by implementing OOP capabilities outside the language in a sense, giving you back all those neat tricks you're used to using elsewhere.
Memory leak protection	Dojo provides some extra event handler hooks that enable you to do some extra cleanup work when your page environment is being destroyed, with the intent, of course, of avoiding memory leaks that can happen in JavaScript sometimes.
Firebug integration	Dojo includes built-in debugging support in the form of integration with the very popular Firebug extension to Firefox. More than that, as you'll see in the next section, it provides a way to get at least some of what Firebug gives you in browsers that don't have Firebug, such as Internet Explorer, without you having to think about it.

Table 1-2. *Functionality in Dojo Core That You Have to Manually Add to the Mix*

Core Functionality Group	Description
Unified data access	Provides functions to read and write data independent of the underlying mechanism
Universal debugging tools	Provides Firebug Lite, which is a much slimmed-down port (really just console logging) of the Firebug plug-in for Firefox to Internet Explorer
Drag and drop	Gives you the ability to implement drag-and-drop functions with little effort
i18n support	Internationalization of text strings on the client
Localizations	More internationalization support
Date formatting	Functions for formatting dates in various ways
Number formatting	Functions for formatting numbers in various ways
String utilities	Additional string functions including `trim()`, `pad()`, and `substitute()`
Advanced Ajax transport layers	Provides ways to execute Ajax requests without using the typical `XMLHttpRequest` object, such as IFrames and JSON with Padding (JSON-P)

Continued

Table 1-2. *Continued*

Core Functionality Group	Description
Cookie handling	Provides functions for reading, writing, and otherwise manipulating cookies
Extended animations	Provides animations and effects built on top of the baseline animations and effects you get automatically
Remote procedure calling	Provides functions for executing remote procedure calls, including JSON-P based services
Back button handling	Provides functions for working with browser history
Baseline CSS styling	Provides functionality for setting uniform font and element sizes

As you can see, there's more variety in Dojo Core than there are alien species represented in the cantina scene of *Star Wars*! It's just the beginning, though, as the Dojo developers have gone on to create two great sequels to Core: Dijit and DojoX. (Unlike George Lucas, who managed only one great sequel with *The Empire Strikes Back*, plus one decent one with *Return of the Jedi*. Of course, the less said about the three prequels the better, although I kind of like *Revenge of the Sith*—the final fight scene was pretty intense—even though it still burns me how quickly and easily Anakin turned; it just didn't make sense.)

Oops, slight tangent there, sorry about that. Let's move on to Dijit, shall we?

Dijit

Perhaps the number one thing that first draws people to Dojo is the widgets, and for good reason: they are overall a very good batch of highly functional and good-looking UI components. What's more, they tend to be quite easy to work with, to get into your application.

What used to be a fairly disorganized collection of widgets is now a lot clearer because they are all grouped together in one place, namely Dijit. (Get it? Dojo widget = Dijit.)

What makes Dojo widgets attractive? A few key points, which most people latch on to pretty quickly, are summarized here:

- Theme support. All of the dijits are *skinnable*, meaning you can rather easily change the look and feel of them just by writing some CSS. Dojo also comes with two built-in themes: Tundra and Soria. Tundra especially is rather nice looking and is designed to blend in well with existing color palettes. Although it may not be a perfect match to your existing application, chances are it will blend decently and not look like an eyesore out of the box.

- Dijits provide a common programming interface. Because all dijits are created from a common set of templates, and because they all extend some baseline classes, they share a basic API. This means that a function that exists for one will often exist for another, at least as far as the basic types of behaviors and features you'd expect any UI widget to have (naturally, each widget will have its own specific features and requirements). This not only means you'll have an easy time picking up widgets, but it also means...

- Creating your own dijit isn't terribly difficult, and it'll automatically, by virtue of having the same basic structure as the rest, work well with Dojo-based applications. Dijit isn't just a collection of ready-to-use UI widgets, although that's the part that you notice first. It's also a complete, powerful, and fully extensible widget architecture that you can build on top of with confidence.
- Dijits are fully accessible by providing keyboard navigation and high-contrast modes built in. Dijits are also built with screen readers in mind, further expanding their accessibility to those with disabilities.
- Dojo exposes a markup-based way of working with dijits, and this leads to graceful degradation by enabling you to have fallback markup present easily.
- Dijits inherently support internationalization and localization, with more than a dozen languages supported right now and more on the way.

I know, I know: that's all well and good; you're excited, but what does Dijit actually *look* like? Well, in the following figures I'll show you examples of Dijit in action, beginning with Figure 1-5, which is the mail reader application you can find on the Dojo web site.

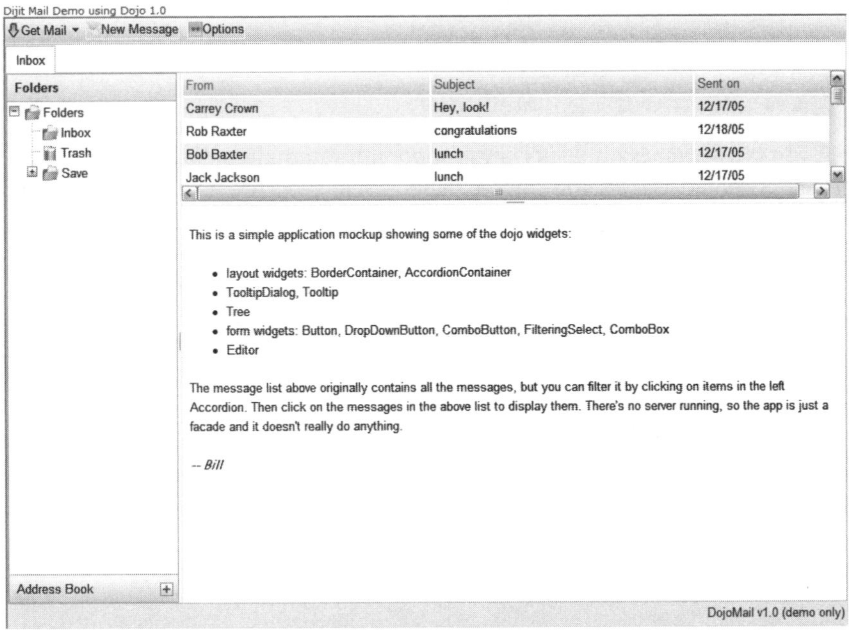

Figure 1-5. *The Dijit mail reader application*

In Figure 1-6, you can see an example of many of the form dijits that are available for building more-complex, powerful, and frankly prettier forms than is possible with basic HTML form elements.

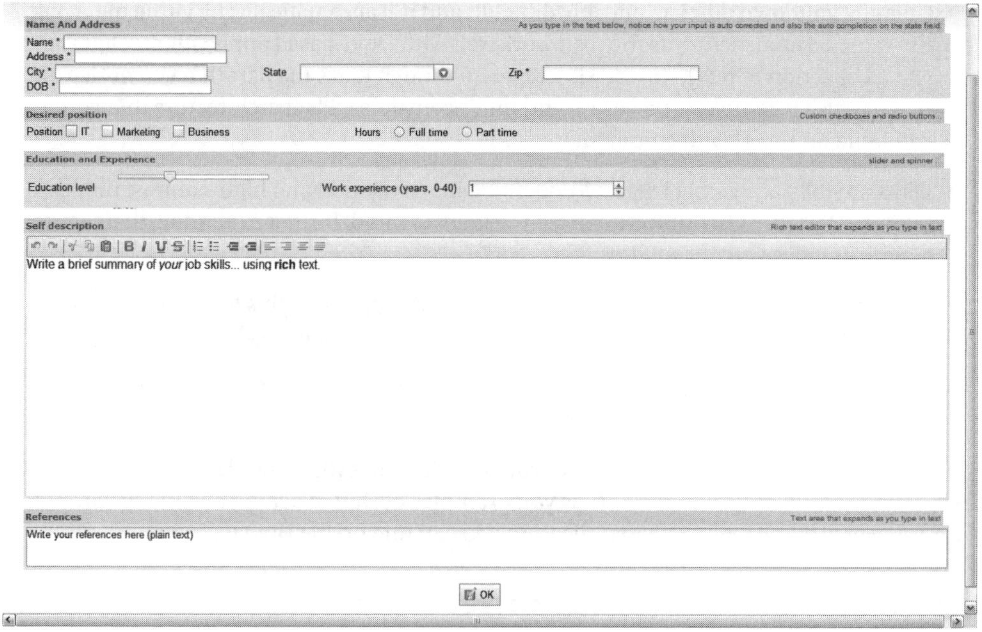

Figure 1-6. *The Dijit form elements in all their glory*

In Figure 1-7, you can see an example of Dijit's support for internationalization, usually, and quite cleverly, abbreviated as *i18n*. You can see that I've selected a new locale from the list, which changes how the form field values are displayed.

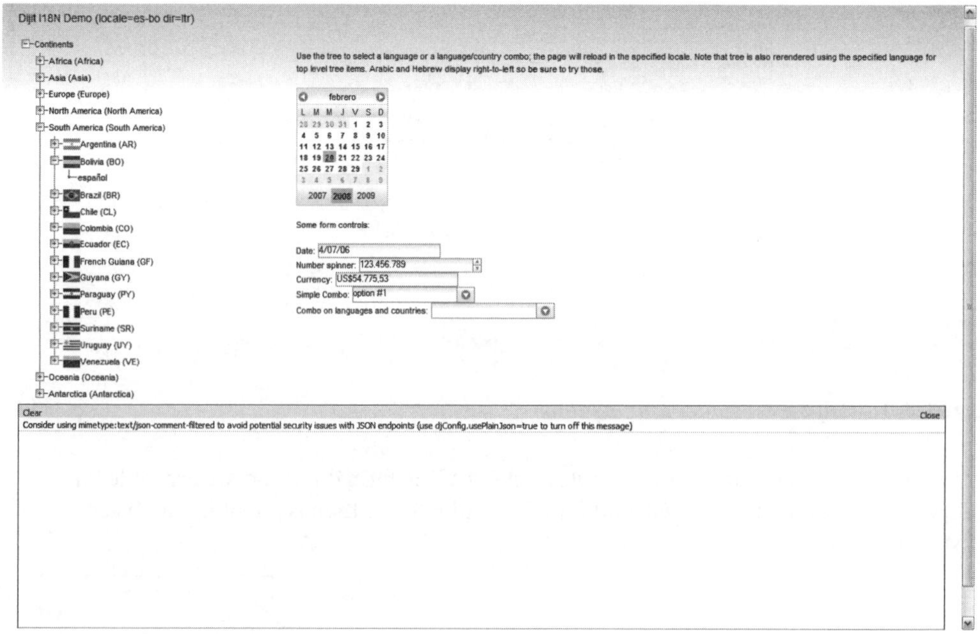

Figure 1-7. *An example of i18n support in Dijit*

Figure 1-8 shows some of the various toolbars Dijit provides. You can also see a tool tip pop-up that is quite a bit more than the usual tool tip: it includes form elements embedded in it.

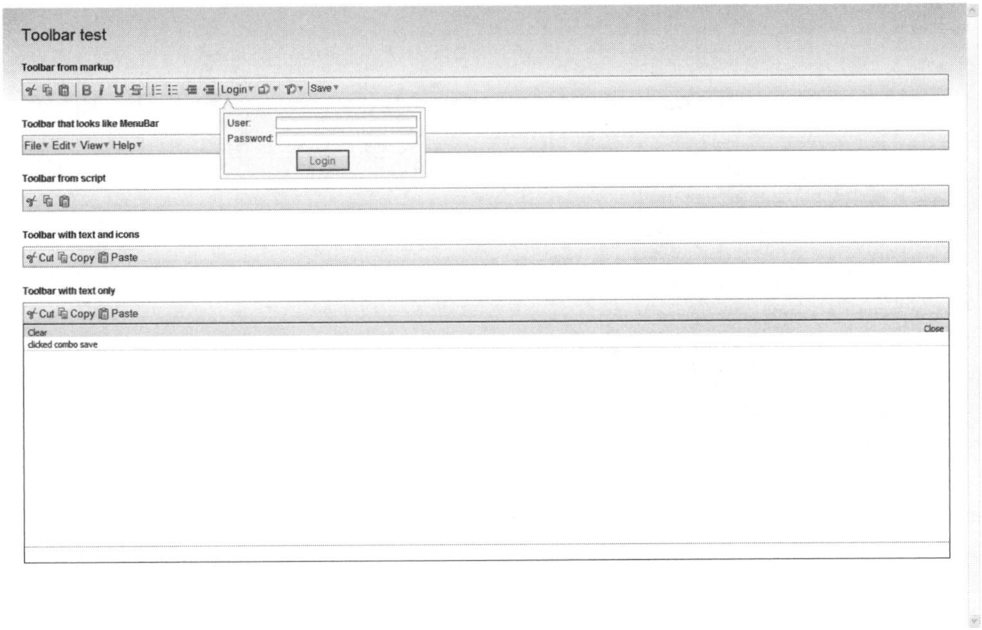

Figure 1-8. *Toolbars in Dijit*

The next few figures are all taken from the Theme Tester application, which comes with the Dojo download bundle. For example, in Figure 1-9, you can see this application with a modal dialog box popped open. This figure is showing the default Tundra theme in action. Unfortunately, this not being a computer screen, you can't get the full effect from the black-and-white pages of a book. Not to worry, though: The examples in this book will use the Tundra scheme quite a bit, so you'll have a chance to see it in all its color and graphical glory as you play with the projects.

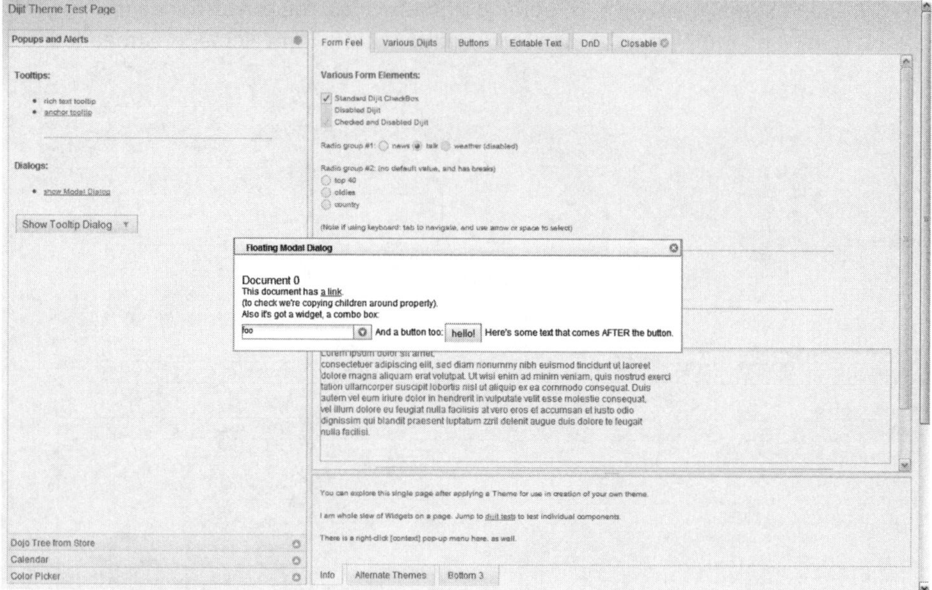

Figure 1-9. *The Theme Tester application, with modal dialog opened up*

Figure 1-10 is another view of this application, but this time you can see a whole slew of dijits! You can also see that I've switched to the Soria theme, and the difference is quite apparent. Note the tabs along the top and bottom. Also note how the right side is an accordion widget, and this time I'm showing a calendar in it.

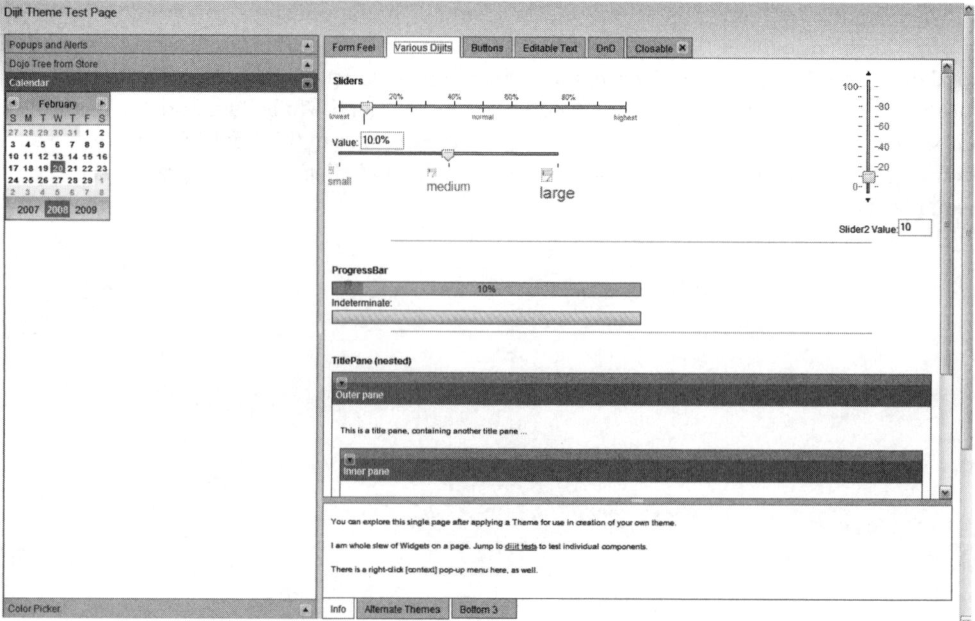

Figure 1-10. *Theme Tester, part 2*

Figure 1-11 provides our final look at the Theme Tester application, this time showing a few more dijits, buttons mostly, plus a color picker on the left. This is again the Soria theme.

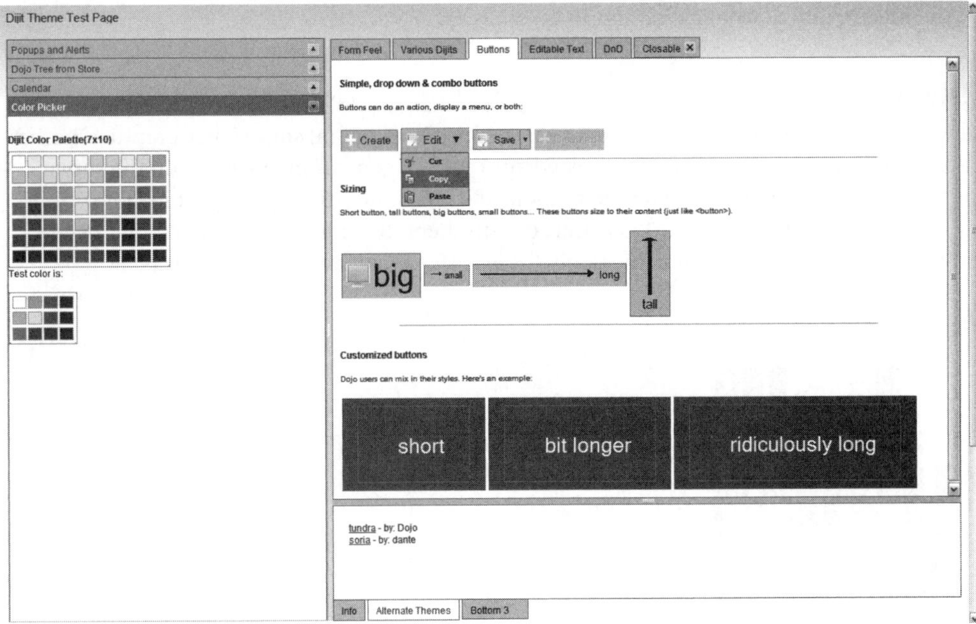

Figure 1-11. *Theme Tester, part 3*

As you can plainly see, Dijit has a lot to offer! There are a whole bunch of other widgets that you haven't seen here, and many of those won't be used in this book. I'll try to use as many as possible, but I'll most definitely miss some because there are so many. I encourage you to download Dojo and have a look through it. You'll find numerous example and test HTML files that show all Dijit has to offer.

Now, we have only one stop remaining, and that's DojoX, where we'll walk on the wild side and look at the future of Dojo.

DojoX

The final component of the Dojo project is DojoX (*component* being my way of stating the organizational structure, not a reference to a component in the software design or the GUI component sense of the word). In short, DojoX is a playground for new features in Dojo. It's similar to the Incubator at Apache, where new projects are developed before being moved into the main project itself. (In the case of the Incubator, they may become projects themselves rather than additions to existing projects; DojoX stuff is obviously all going to land in Dojo.)

This makes it sound like the code in DojoX is highly experimental, and indeed in some cases that's true. However, that's not a completely accurate picture. Much of the code found there has been around for quite a while and is rather stable and completely usable; it's just not "final" yet and hasn't graduated into Dojo completely. You should in no way hesitate using DojoX stuff in my estimation because with few exceptions, it's likely to be quite good.

So, what kind of "stuff" is there in DojoX? Let's have a look, shall we? Once again, I need to point out that there's too much to cover every last bit, but I'll hit the big ones that you'll likely find most interesting. You should definitely spend some time exploring outside this book to get the full breadth of what DojoX has to offer.

Charting

Generating charts on a web site is usually an exercise in either (a) some fancy graphics-based client-side code or (b) the more time-tested approach of generating the chart on the server and returning a dynamically-rendered graphic of it. With the charting support in DojoX, you can do what you see in Figure 1-12 entirely on the client dynamically. You won't even need static graphic resources to build this up; it's drawn 100 percent on the fly, so to speak.

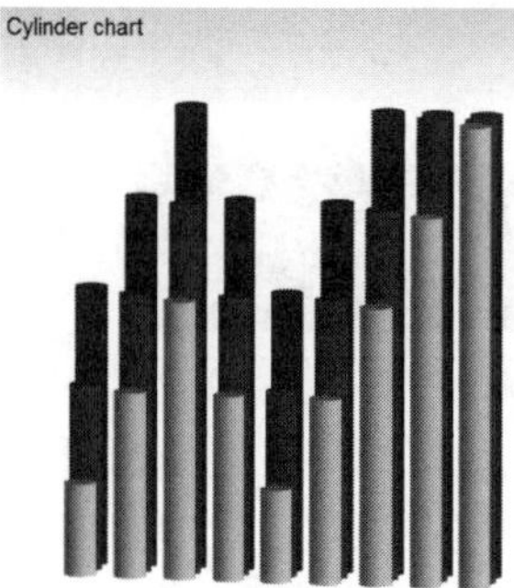

Figure 1-12. *A cylindrical bar chart rendered entirely client-side by DojoX charting support*

And because I'm a big fan of pie, as my ample midsection would likely clue you in on, here's an example in Figure 1-13 of a pie chart, courtesy of DojoX.

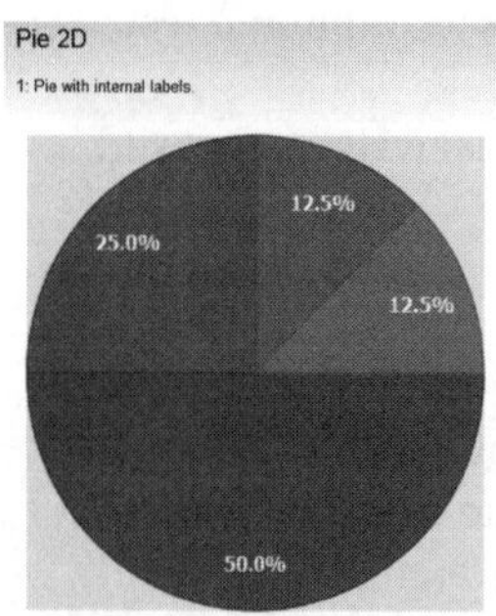

Figure 1-13. *A pie chart (as Homer Simpson would say, "mmmmmm, pie...agh-agh-agh-aga")*

The benefit of not having graphics to download and of not having server processing time involved to generate these charts is a great benefit in many situations. The charting support in DojoX can generate numerous types of charts, including line, pie, bar, area, and so on, with all sorts of options, so it likely has everything you need for any occasion. Better still, the charts are updatable on the fly, which means, mixed in with some Ajax, you can have a bar chart showing stock values in real time as one example. And of course, because Dojo gives you all the pieces you need to build such a thing, you have just a single library to learn and work with.

Drawing

Typically, showing graphics in a browser means downloading static images that are, at best, generated dynamically on the server (but they're still static in the browser). There are animated GIFs too, which are dynamic in the sense that they are animated and move, but still static in the sense that the file retrieved from the server doesn't actually change at all. You can get into things like Adobe Flash and Microsoft Silverlight if you need to draw graphics from primitive components such as line and circles, but doing that from pure HTML and JavaScript is a hopeless cause.

Or is it?

As it happens, DojoX has just the ticket! The `dojo.gfx` package provides a vector-based drawing API that is cross-browser and 100 percent client-side. If you're familiar with Scalable Vector Graphics (SVG), you have a good idea of what `dojo.gfx` is all about.

Want to see it in action? Your wish is my command; see Figure 1-14.

Figure 1-14. *Oooh, how pretty! Better still, it's drawn in real time on the client!*

What's more, there's even a `dojo.gfx3d` package to let you create three-dimensional graphics! Obviously, I can't show you on the printed page, but with the Dojo download comes a boatload of examples of both packages, and a number of them actually perform animation by using this drawing API. (The animation occurs from rapidly redrawing the image.)

This type of capability is something that simply wasn't possible a short time ago, and really, Dojo is beginning to bring it to the masses for the first time.

DojoX Offline

DojoX Offline is, for all intents and purposes, a more robust API wrapped around Google Gears, which is now simply called Gears. (Gears, which you'll see more of in Chapter 5, is a browser extension that provides capabilities typically needed for running a web app without a network.) In short, DojoX Offline enables you to ensure that the resources (images, HTML files, and so on) that make up your application are available even when the network, or server, is down. This enables you to run your application in an "offline" mode.

This API provides many capabilities that Gears by itself doesn't—encryption, for instance. You may well want to ensure that the resources that are saved client-side for use when the application is offline are encrypted if they are sensitive in nature. DojoX Offline provides this capability on top of Gears, which is a really nice addition.

DojoX Widgets

As if Dijit by itself wasn't enough to fill all your GUI widgets desires, there are even more widgets in DojoX!

One example is the DojoX Grid, shown in Figure 1-15. This is a very good grid implementation that rivals any others out there. What's more, this particular widget integrates with other parts of Dojo, such as `dojo.data` (which is a package for, what else, data access, enabling you to share data between widgets).

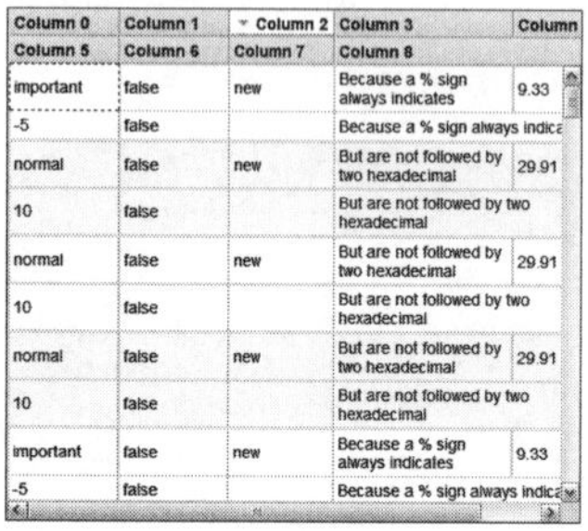

Figure 1-15. *The DojoX Grid widget*

The Grid widget is much more powerful than it seems at first blush because it can essentially host other dijits. For instance, in Figure 1-16, you can see a rich Text Editor dijit in the field I've selected, enabling me to edit the value of that field in place.

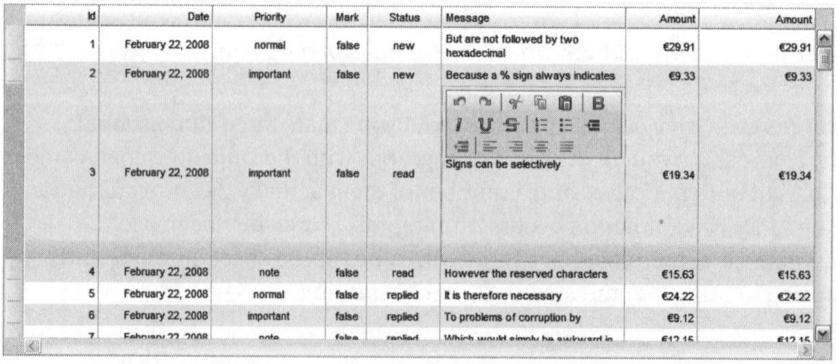

Figure 1-16. *The DojoX Grid hosting other dijits*

The Date fields show a pop-up calendar, and many of the other fields show a drop-down selection dijit when clicked.

But the grid isn't the only widget in DojoX. No, there are plenty more. For instance, the ColorPicker is shown in Figure 1-17.

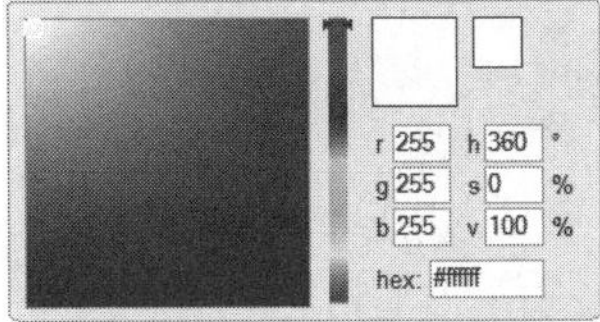

Figure 1-17. *The DojoX ColorPicker widget*

Then there's the ImageGallery widget, as seen in Figure 1-18, which enables you to show a bunch of images in a graphically pleasing way.

Figure 1-18. *The DojoX ImageGallery widget*

Another good one is the (now) standard Lightbox, which you can see in Figure 1-19. It can contain text, graphics, and quite a bit more.

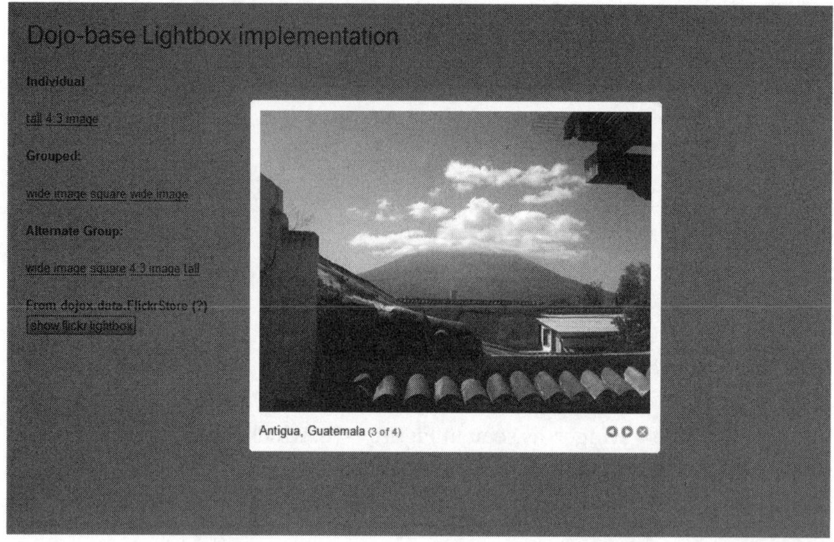

Figure 1-19. *Dojo's take on the typical lightbox pop-up*

Another one worth mentioning, indeed the best of the bunch for many, is the Fisheye List widget. I won't show that here because I want to keep you in suspense until Chapter 5 when you see it in action for the first time. Rest assured, though, it's a very impressive widget!

The Rest of the Bunch

As I mentioned before, DojoX has quite a bit more. Some of the other things you can find include the following:

- Implementations of many well-known cryptographic algorithms, including Blowfish and MD5
- A set of validation functions for validating things like form input in a variety of common ways such as phone numbers, e-mail addresses, and so on
- A package of XML functionality including, for example, a DOM parser
- Advanced math functions
- A batch of collection classes such as ArrayLists and Dictionaries

You'll see a fair bit of this stuff throughout the projects in this book. Indeed, I'll strive to use as much of it as possible so you can see it in action.

Dojo in Action: What Else? Hello World (Sort Of)

At this point, you've had a decent overview of what Dojo is, how it came to be, its philosophy, and of course what it has to offer. What you've yet to see is an example of it in action. Well, I'm about to remedy that right now!

Listing 1-1 provides your very first (presumably) exposure to Dojo. Take a look at it, and then we'll proceed to rip it apart so you can understand exactly what's going on.

Listing 1-1. *Fisher Price's My First Dojo App!*

```
<html>

 <head>

  <title>My First Dojo App</title>

  <link rel="StyleSheet" type="text/css"
   href="js/dojo/dojo/resources/dojo.css">
  <link rel="StyleSheet" type="text/css"
   href="js/dojo/dijit/themes/tundra/tundra.css">

  <script type="text/javascript">
   var djConfig = {
    baseScriptUri : "js/dojo/",
    parseOnLoad : true,
    extraLocale: ['en-us', 'zh-cn']
   };
  </script>
  <script type="text/javascript" src="js/dojo/dojo/dojo.js"></script>
  <script language="JavaScript" type="text/javascript">
   dojo.require("dojo.parser");
   dojo.require("dijit.form.Button");
   dojo.require("dijit._Calendar");
  </script>

 </head>

 <body class="tundra">

  <div style="position:relative;top:10px;left:10px;width:80%;">
   <button dojoType="dijit.form.Button" id="myButton">
    Press me, NOW!
    <script type="dojo/method" event="onClick">
     alert('You pressed the button');
    </script>
   </button>
   <br><br>
   <table border="0"><tr>
    <td valign="top">
     <input id="calEnglish" dojoType="dijit._Calendar" lang="en-us" />
    </td>
    <td width="25"> </td>
    <td valign="top"
```

```
            <input id="calChinese" dojoType="dijit._Calendar" lang="zh-cn" />
          </td>
        </table>
      </div>

    </body>

</html>
```

As you can see, there's not a whole lot of code involved. Before we tear it apart, though, let's have a quick look at the "application," such as it is! I admit it's not going to rival Adobe Photoshop in terms of complexity, but I think it's a good introduction to Dojo. You can be the judge by looking at Figure 1-20.

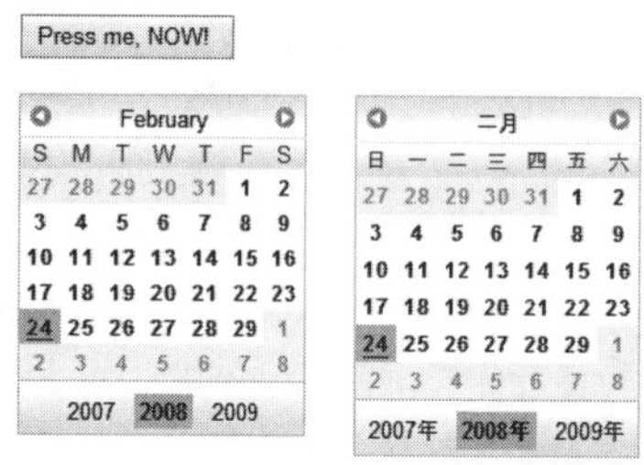

Figure 1-20. *Look, ma, my very first Dojo application!*

Clicking the button results in a simple `alert()` pop-up. As you can see, the two calendars use different locales, showing how Dojo can simply provide internationalization of its dijits.

So, what's the code all about, you ask? Let's get to that now!

Getting Dojo onto the Page

The way Dojo is brought onto a page, an HTML document here, is simple. First, you access the Dojo web site and download Dojo. Then you decompress the archives you download. This results in the directory structure shown in Figure 1-21.

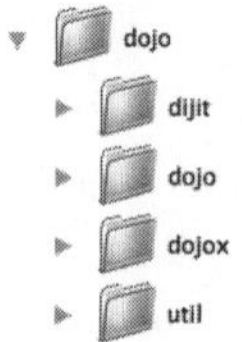

Figure 1-21. *The directory structure of Dojo, as it is when you downlad it*

Next, you add the following to your HTML document:

```
<script type="text/javascript" src="js/dojo/dojo/dojo.js"></script>
```

That's the absolute simplest permutation of using Dojo. This will get you all the stuff in Core that isn't optional. The path itself is as you see it because the `dojo` directory is located in the `js` directory, which is in the root of this mini-application. Under the `dojo` directory is *another* directory named `dojo`, which could have just as easily been named *core*, because that's really what it is, all the Dojo Core code.

There is also another approach that saves you from having to download and host anything on your own web server: the Content Distribution Network. CDN is essentially a simple way of saying that someone has hosted shared content on servers that are designed to handle high levels of traffic from clients all around the world. The Dojo team has partnered with AOL to provide Dojo via CDN, which means you can use Dojo without having to have any of its code present on your own server. This saves you bandwidth and makes setting up your application easier because there are less resources you need to get deployed on your own servers; you just need to point your code at the appropriate URLs and you're off to the races. If you wanted to use this approach, you could use the following line in place of the previous one:

```
<script type="text/javascript"
  src="http://o.aolcdn.com/dojo/1.0.2/dojo/dojo.xd.js "></script>
```

This is indeed handy, and efficient in terms of your own server infrastructure and the traffic it'll have to handle. Even still, I've chosen to not use this approach throughout this book for no other reason than when you write a book, you naturally try to make all the code in it as likely to work as possible. I didn't want to have one more potential point of failure—for example, what if the network is down, or AOL's servers are unavailable, or something like that? Better to have all the Dojo code local so I can be assured (as assured as possible anyway!) that things Just Work as expected.

Importing Style Sheets

Moving on, as you can see from the code in Listing 1-1, there's more to it than just `dojo.js` being imported. Another important piece, which typically matters when you're using Dijit (although it can come into play elsewhere) is to import the appropriate style sheets. This is accomplished thusly (Thusly? Who talks like that?):

```
<link rel="StyleSheet" type="text/css"
  href="js/dojo/dojo/resources/dojo.css">
<link rel="StyleSheet" type="text/css"
  href="js/dojo/dijit/themes/tundra/tundra.css">
```

The first style sheet, `dojo.css`, is a baseline style sheet that Dojo needs to do many things. In this example app, if this style sheet is not present, you'll find that fonts aren't sized quite as they should be. Omitting the style sheet is not a drastic thing here; arguably you could call it optional in this case, but in general you will likely want to import this style sheet and not have to worry about what its absence might do.

The next import is far more critical. Recall earlier that I talked about dijits being fully skinnable and supporting various themes? Well, here's one part of the formula for selecting a theme. Here, I'm using the Tundra theme, which, to my eyes, is somewhat Apple Mac-ish in appearance.

The other part of the formula, which you can see in the `<body>` tag, is to set the class on the body of the document to the theme you wish to use, like so:

```
<body class="tundra">
```

That's all you need to do! From that point on, all dijits you use will use that same theme automatically. Sweeeeeeet, as Eric Cartman[6] would say!

Configuring Dojo

The next step in using Dojo, which is optional although very typical, is configuring Dojo. This is done via the `djConfig` object. This is a JavaScript object that you define *before* the `dojo.js` file is imported. The object contains options you can set, but here we're using only three of them:

```
var djConfig = {
  baseScriptUri : "js/dojo/",
  parseOnLoad : true,
  extraLocale: ['en-us', 'zh-cn']
};
```

The first option, `baseScriptUri`, defines a relative path to the base directory where Dojo is located. All other resources that Dojo loads automatically will use this value when URIs are dynamically written by the Dojo code.

The `parseOnLoad` option tells Dojo to parse the entire document when loaded for Dijit definitions (we'll get to that shortly!), to create those dijits automatically. Alternatively, you can set up an `onLoad` handler to tell Dojo specifically which page elements to parse for dijits, or you can create all your dijits programmatically. This approach, however, is by far the simplest approach.

Finally, `extraLocale` tells Dojo to load additional localizations, other than your own, so that translations can be performed. Here, we're telling Dojo that we want to support English and Chinese. Interestingly, if your system locale is English or Chinese, that language does not need to be specified here. For example, on my PC, which is English-based, I can remove the `en-us` value and things still work as expected. As the name of the option implies, only *extra* locales need to be loaded. But there's no harm in specifying a locale that is the default, so this works just fine, and it also means that if someone happens to run this on a Chinese system, they'll see the English version of the calendar as well.

---

6. I doubt that many readers don't know who Eric Cartman is. He's almost on the level of Captain Kirk in terms of being in the public psyche worldwide. But, on the off chance that you lead a sheltered life: Eric Cartman is the fat kid on the Comedy Central television show *South Park*. He's neurotic, self-centered, spoiled, and extremely funny. If you want to wet yourself laughing (and really, who doesn't want that?), I highly suggest digging up a copy of "Cartman Gets an Anal Probe," which was the pilot episode. I'm sure you'll have no problem finding it on The Internets, and I have every confidence you'll love it.

Importing Other Parts of Dojo

As I mentioned earlier, importing dojo.js gets you all the non-optional Dojo Core stuff—and if that's all you need, you're all set. But what if you want to use some of the optional stuff in Core, or you want to use some dijits or something from DojoX? In those situations, you need to get into one of the neatest things about Dojo in my opinion, and that's the include mechanism. This mechanism is on display in this snippet of code:

```
<script language="JavaScript" type="text/javascript">
  dojo.require("dojo.parser");
  dojo.require("dijit.form.Button");
  dojo.require("dijit._Calendar");
</script>
```

With this code, we're telling dojo that we want to use three optional components: the parser, the Button dijit, and the Calendar dijit.

The parser component is what creates dijits for us. (I promise, we're getting to that very thing next!) The dijits are, I think, self-explanatory. The nice thing to note here is that you aren't specifying all the resources that might be required, that is, graphics, extra style sheets, or even other JavaScript files. Dojo takes care of those dependencies for you! You just specify the high-level part you want to include, write the appropriate dojo.require() statement, and you're off to the races!

Just as a way of teasing something you'll read about in later chapters, you also have the capability of creating a custom build of Dojo, which essentially allows you to get away without even using dojo.require(). Basically, everything gets rolled into dojo.js and then that's all you need to deal with. But, using dojo.require() means that you can keep Dojo modular and then dynamically add pieces as you need them. This *will*, however, increase the number of requests needed to build your page, so there are some performance considerations, which is where custom builds come into play. As I said, though, you'll look at that in more detail in later chapters. For now, dojo.require() is the way to go, and the way you'll see most often throughout this book.

Finally: Dijits!

Okay, okay, I've put you off long enough—let's see how those dijits are created! You've already seen the code, of course, but just to focus you in on the appropriate snippet:

```
<div style="position:relative;top:10px;left:10px;width:80%;">
  <button dojoType="dijit.form.Button" id="myButton">
    Press me, NOW!
    <script type="dojo/method" event="onClick">
      alert('You pressed the button');
    </script>
  </button>
  <br><br>
  <table border="0"><tr>
    <td valign="top">
      <input id="calEnglish" dojoType="dijit._Calendar" lang="en-us" />
    </td>
```

```
    <td width="25"> </td>
    <td valign="top"
      <input id="calChinese" dojoType="dijit._Calendar" lang="zh-cn" />
    </td>
  </table>
</div>
```

Whoa, wait a minute, that's just plain old HTML; where's the code? In this case, there is none! Remember that `parseOnLoad` option in `djConfig`? Well, this is what Dojo will be looking for when that option is set to `true`, as it is here.

The parser component, which we imported via `dojo.require()` earlier, scans the page looking for elements with an expando attribute of `dojoType`. This tells Dojo that the element is to be transformed from plain old HTML markup to Dijit, including all the markup and JavaScript that entails. You don't have to write a lick of code yourself to get these dijits on the page. You simply have to tell Dojo to parse the page for dijit definitions and create said definition as done here. Would could be easier? And best of all, from an author's perspective, there's really nothing here for me to explain! Even the `lang` attribute on the `<input>` tags for the calendars is standard HTML, although it's not used too often. Here, it tells Dojo what locality to use to translate the string in the dijit. That's neat, right?

■ **Note** An expando attribute, which might be a term you haven't heard, is when you add an attribute that didn't exist before to an object. This term is usually used in the context of HTML tags (which are ultimately objects in the DOM, remember) when you have an attribute on the tag that isn't strictly allowed given the definition of that tag. Remember that browsers simply ignore things they don't understand, so doing this doesn't break anything (although it *does* make your HTML invalid and it will thus fail strict validation, which some people complain about when it comes to the `dojoType` attribute). Expando attributes are also frequently added to the `document` object, and can in fact be added to virtually any object in the DOM.

You'll be seeing a lot more examples of this markup-based approach to dijit creation as you progress through this book. I think you'll agree that this is a fantastic way to create GUI widgets—although it's not the only way, as you'll also see later.

Getting Help and Information

For all the benefits Dojo has to offer (and as you'll see throughout this book, Dojo has plenty), many times you'll need to get a little help with it. Aside from help, you'll clearly want documentation and examples.

Then again, this book should give you everything you need, so really, you may never need to look elsewhere.

Ahem.

I kid, I kid. In all seriousness, one of the biggest benefits of Dojo is that it has a thriving, helpful community to back it up, and by that I don't just mean the development team, although they certainly count. Tons of fellow users will come to your aid at a moment's notice. Documentation is constantly evolving and getting better for you to refer to. There are message forums and mailing lists and all that good stuff that we've all come to expect and love about open source projects.

You just have to know where to look!

Fortunately, Dojo has a great web site. In fact, have a look for yourself, in Figure 1-22.

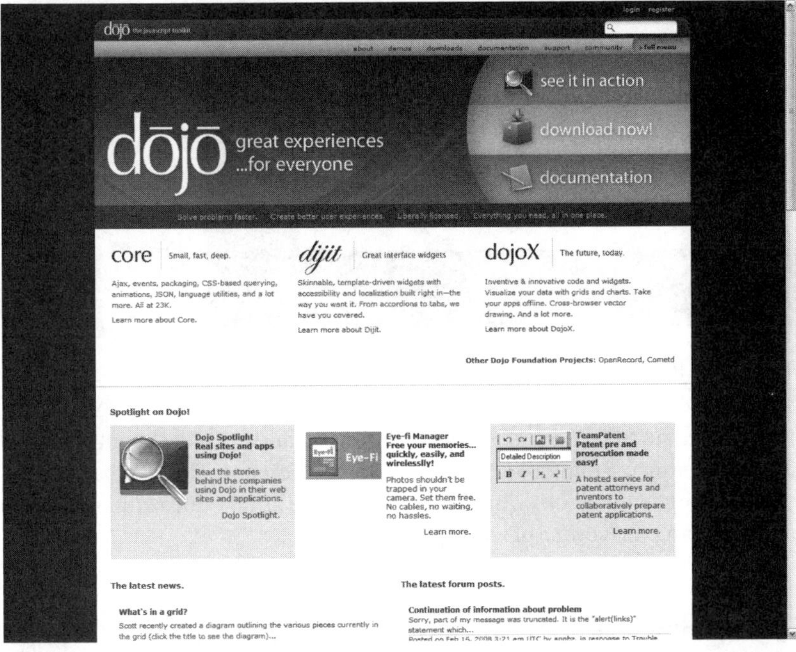

Figure 1-22. *The Dojo web site—'nough said!*

From this site (`www.dojotoolkit.org`) you can reach the message forums, through which most support and discussion takes place. You can also find mailing list archives and subscription information. There is even information on frequently visited Internet Relay Chat (IRC) channels. All of this is available from the Community link on the menu bar up top.

Naturally enough, you can also download pages and issue trackers and even a time line for planned upcoming releases. Not every open source project does this, but it's a really nice thing to do for the community.

One other thing I feel is worth pointing out is the online API documentation, which is generated directly from the Dojo source code and the comments within it. This reference material is one area of the web site you should definitely become acquainted with in a hurry. To access it, visit the Documentation link under the menu bar. Figure 1-23 shows an example of this documentation.

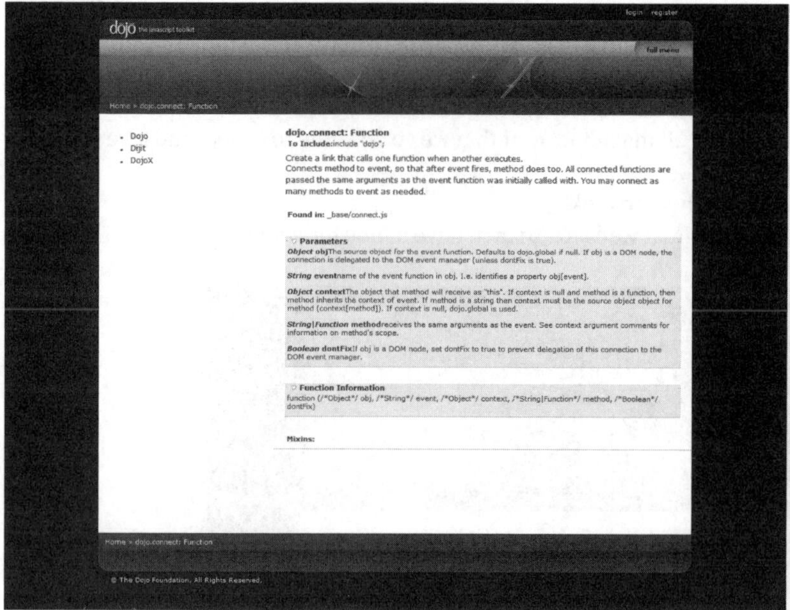

Figure 1-23. *The Dojo online API documentation*

Note that this isn't simple static text: it's all nicely hyperlinked and even uses some cool Dojo effects and widgets, making it a dynamic, interactive bit of reference. This can be very, very helpful when you're trying to figure out what something in the library does (and believe me, I visited it frequently during the course of writing this book!).

THE GOOD...AND THE POSSIBLY NOT SO GOOD

For all the good things about Dojo, and of that there's plenty, one thing that has historically lagged a bit, in my opinion anyway, is documentation and examples. My experience with Dojo started early on, with the very early beta releases. Back then, you had to spend most of your time simply looking at the code to understand how things worked, or how to use this function or that. It was rather difficult, and the fact that Dojo was changing rapidly (which is of course something you accept when using early release code) didn't help matters.

The situation has improved leaps and bounds, especially with the recent 1.0 release (as of the writing of this text). The APIs, outside DojoX anyway, have all stabilized, and documentation has been seriously beefed up. I can also say with complete confidence that the Dojo team is aware that this area needs some work even still and they are diligently putting in effort in this regard.

All of this being said, I feel it's still fair to issue the same caution I've issued in the past about Dojo: if you plan to use it, do yourself a favor and also plan some extra time to find information you need, to research, and to figure things out. The Dojo community is top-notch in terms of extending a helping hand, and that'll likely be your primary resource, not any documentation or examples that you may find on the Web. I've never failed to get an answer to a question I had in short order, and it's always been from polite and helpful people, both Dojo developers and plain old users like me.

Still, if you go to the Dojo web site expecting to find documentation of every last thing, or examples of everything, I believe you will be disappointed. Looking through the source code is often still your best bet. But that's part of the reason I'm writing this book, after all! Hopefully, I will save you a lot of that research time and will answer a lot of the questions you may have, all in one place. You'll certainly have a lot of well-documented example code to look at in these pages; that much I can promise! If I didn't think Dojo was worth all this effort, I wouldn't have written this book, nor would I ever counsel someone to use Dojo.

The fact is, you get out of it a lot more than the effort you put into it, and that's ultimately what you'd want from a good library or toolkit, so don't be put off if you can't immediately find the exact bit of information you need when working with Dojo. Crack open the actual Dojo code, join the community (the forums most especially), ask questions, and I guarantee that you'll get the information you need and Dojo will prove to be an invaluable tool for you. And by the way, I know the Dojo team will thank you very much if you contribute some documentation, so don't be shy! If you've ever wanted to get involved in an open source project, documentation is always an easy inroad into a community.

Summary

In this chapter, we discussed the history and evolution of JavaScript and how it has been applied to client-side development. We looked at the causes of its early, somewhat negative impression and how it came from those humble beginnings to something any good web developer today has to know to some extent. We then took a quick look at Dojo, got a high-level feel for what it's all about, its history, its philosophy, and its structure. We moved on from there to see a basic example of it in action and saw the basics of how to add it to an application. Finally, we saw how to get further help and information about Dojo.

In the next chapter, we'll begin to peel back the layers of the onion and get into detail about what Dojo has to offer, starting with the Core component. Hold on to your hats; you're in for a wild ride from here on out!

CHAPTER 2

Dojo Core

The Core component of the Dojo Toolkit is the foundation on top of which everything else is built, and on top of which you can build your own applications. Core contains all of the basics—string manipulations, collection classes, debugging functions, and so on.

In this chapter, we'll take an in-depth look at what Core has to offer. We'll see plenty of examples of it in action so that as we move into the projects a few chapters down the road, they will all make sense quickly and easily.

We'll also take a look at Dojo's custom build capabilities, which enable us to create our own tailored version of Dojo with just the parts we want in it. We'll examine the include mechanism Dojo provides in detail (as much detail as something so relatively simple, from our perspective at least, deserves!) and we'll look at the configuration options available to control Dojo more precisely to our needs.

Core vs. Base

We're here to talk about Dojo Core, but there's another concept very closely related to this lurking just below the surface that we need to discuss at the same time, and that's Base. Conceptually, you can think of Base as a layer below Core. If you go to the Dojo web site, you'll see that it talks about the three parts I discussed in Chapter 1: Core, Dijit, and DojoX. If you click the link to delve into the Core details a bit, though, you'll see that Core in a sense has a split personality—half of it called Base, and the other half of it, paradoxically, called Core!

Base is the part you can more or less think of as you do the kernel of an operating system. It's contained within a single JavaScript file, the aptly-named `dojo.js`, and it's very tiny on its own. Some of the tasks Base handles are bootstrapping (loading and starting) the toolkit. Base includes a number of basic functions and language extension-type functions, and also includes simple Ajax functions. It has within it a mechanism for simulating client-side object-oriented techniques such as class-based inheritance, something JavaScript itself doesn't by itself provide. It also includes the packaging mechanism that you'll look at next, which keeps Dojo from polluting the global namespace with its own junk.

Core sits on top of Base, or maybe alongside it is really the more apt mental picture. It extends Base in numerous ways and provides many of the neat functions you'll see here and beyond. Dijit and DojoX sit clearly on top of the foundation of Base and Core combined. There's also a Util grouping, architecturally speaking, which includes utilities that are, by and large, used during Dojo builds, testing, and so on.

The key differentiation point between Base and Core is that what's contained within Base is always available to your code 100 percent of the time. Simply by importing the `dojo.js` file, which you always have to do, you have access to everything in Base. Then there are optional components that you explicitly have to import onto a page, and this is the other half of Core.

It's a little bit confusing certainly, and I'm not sure the Dojo web site does as good a job as it could in explaining it, but hopefully I have!

For those who enjoy a pretty picture, take a gander at Figure 2-1, which seeks to explain this architecture graphically. Any resemblance to any famous cartoon mouse, living or dead, is strictly coincidental!

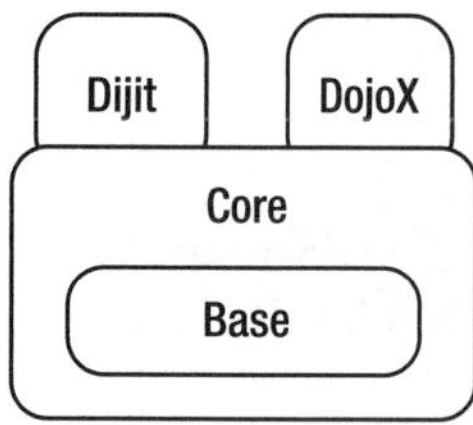

Figure 2-1. *The overall architecture of Dojo, at a high level*

The bottom line is pretty much this: the Core component of Dojo is composed of some capabilities that are required for you to use Dojo at all, and that stuff is called Base. There are also optional parts of Core, sort of sitting "around" the stuff in Base, or on top of it if you prefer.

From this point on, I'll generally be talking about Core as it is represented on the Dojo web site, meaning the combination of what's in Base and what's in the rest of Core. I'll simply refer to Core and not make the differentiation, unless it's really necessary. In general, it's not necessary to differentiate when using Dojo; there's simply Core, and that's that.

The Dojo "Include" Mechanism

One of the really neat features that Dojo provides is the include mechanism, or `dojo.require()` function. In short, this enables you to include parts of Dojo outside the Base code that comes in `dojo.js` (including the optional stuff in Core). This is conceptually just like the `import` statements in Java or the `using` statement in C# that allow you to "include" references to external code in your own programs. In fact, most high-level languages have a similar concept, and with Dojo, JavaScript is no longer an exception!

You will always do a standard JavaScript import of the `dojo.js` file, like so:

```
<script type="text/javascript" src="dojo/dojo/dojo.js"></script>
```

This gets *all* of Dojo Base on your page, ready for you to use. When you need to do a little more, though, that's where the require mechanism comes into play.

The modules that you add to your page with this mechanism correspond, roughly at least, to `.js` files under the Dojo root directory. You'll also find later when you look at Dijit and DojoX in detail that there are subdirectories (`dijit` and `dojox`) under the Dojo root, and you will use this mechanism there as well.

As is typical these days in most languages, modules (or *packages*, as they are often called) are specified by constructing a path to the component or module you wish to import by use of the typical dot notation. For instance, in Java, you can import a HashMap class via the following:

```
import java.util.HashMap;
```

In Dojo, you do much the same. For example, if you want to use the AdapterRegistry class, something you'll look at shortly, you would do this:

```
dojo.require("dojo.AdapterRegistry");
```

The Java import statement and the dojo.require() function are conceptually equivalent in this way. This syntax is a little shorter to type than the usual <script> tags. (Compare the preceding <script> tag to the dojo.require() statement—it's not night and day, but dojo.require() is clearly shorter, and perhaps more important, doesn't include any hard-coded path information.) The other big benefit is that there's no chance of importing a script twice, as there is with a simple <script> tag. Dojo ensures that the code gets imported only once.

The dojo.require() function also includes wildcard support, enabling you to pull off amazing feats like this:

```
dojo.require("dojo.lfx.html.*");
```

This does precisely what you'd expect: all classes within the dojo.lfx.html package are added to your page, ready for your code to use. It should be noted that packages here can also be referred to as *namespaces*, because that's what they represent, JavaScript namespaces.

You will see numerous examples of dojo.require() from here on out, but in general I won't say much more about it unless there's something unusual to point out. Otherwise, what's been described here should give you the understanding you need to parse the imports pretty easily in the code to come.

"Trimming the Fat": Creating a Custom Dojo Build

Dojo allows you to do something that for a long time was fairly unique to Dojo. As they say, imitation is the sincerest form of flattery, and this capability is implemented in other libraries now. Still, Dojo's take on it is still somewhat unique. I'm talking here about the ability to build a custom version of Dojo.

The dojo.js file that you always import in your page includes a bunch of stuff, but how can you know for sure what's in it? As it turns out, the dojo/dojo directory includes a build.txt file that you can read to see what's included. For example, for the version of Dojo that was used for this book, build.txt tells me this:

```
dojo.js:
./jslib/dojoGuardStart.jsfrag
./../../dojo/_base/_loader/bootstrap.js
./../../dojo/_base/_loader/loader.js
./../../dojo/_base/_loader/hostenv_browser.js
./jslib/dojoGuardEnd.jsfrag
./../../release/dojo-release-1.0.2/dojo/_base/lang.js
```

```
./../../release/dojo-release-1.0.2/dojo/_base/declare.js
./../../release/dojo-release-1.0.2/dojo/_base/connect.js
./../../release/dojo-release-1.0.2/dojo/_base/Deferred.js
./../../release/dojo-release-1.0.2/dojo/_base/json.js
./../../release/dojo-release-1.0.2/dojo/_base/array.js
./../../release/dojo-release-1.0.2/dojo/_base/Color.js
./../../release/dojo-release-1.0.2/dojo/_base.js
./../../release/dojo-release-1.0.2/dojo/_base/window.js
./../../release/dojo-release-1.0.2/dojo/_base/event.js
./../../release/dojo-release-1.0.2/dojo/_base/html.js
./../../release/dojo-release-1.0.2/dojo/_base/NodeList.js
./../../release/dojo-release-1.0.2/dojo/_base/query.js
./../../release/dojo-release-1.0.2/dojo/_base/xhr.js
./../../release/dojo-release-1.0.2/dojo/_base/fx.js
```

Now, in and of itself, that's pretty useful information. What's more useful, though, is that if I go to http://download.dojotoolkit.org/release-1.0.2, which is on the Dojo web site and is a repository for all the 1.0.2 releases, I can grab dojo-release-1.0.2-src.zip (or dojo-release-1.0.2-src.tar.gz if you prefer that archive format), which in either case is the Dojo 1.0.2 source tree. The reason this is useful is that contained within it is, obviously, the full source for Dojo, but more important, the ability to build your own version of Dojo with just what you want!

To do this, you will need to have Java version 1.4.2 or later installed on your system. To actually do a custom build, all you do is navigate to <dojo_source_directory>/util/buildscripts and execute build.bat (or build.sh for you *nix guys out there). Passing no options gives you some help and shows you the available options. (You may want to step away now, grab that archive, unzip it, and do this so you can see the help text yourself.)

In short, the command to do a build is basically like this:

```
java -jar ../shrinksafe/custom_rhino.jar build.js profile=base action=release
```

This tells Dojo what JavaScript interpreter to use (Rhino in this case), what build script to use to run the build (build.js), what profile to use (base), and what action to perform (build a release).

Now, you typically wouldn't touch the build script; it should pretty well suit your needs all the time. The profile, however, is a different story. The profile describes what you want your custom build to look like. As an example, assume we had a file named test.profile.js in the <dojo_source_directory>/util/buildscripts directory:

```
dependencies ={
  layers : [{
    name : "customDOJO.js",
    dependencies : [
      "dijit.Button",
      "dojox.encoding.crypto.Blowfish"
    ]
  }],
  prefixes: [
    [ "dijit", "../dijit" ],
```

```
    [ "dojox", "../dojox" ]
  ]
};
```

Dojo custom builds work off the concept of a *layer*, which is a fancy way of saying a bunch of JavaScript smashed together into a single .js file. Inside each layer you specify dependencies, which are all the modules you will be calling upon. The Dojo build system is smart enough to figure out dependencies of these modules for you, so you don't have to traipse through the Dojo source to figure out what dependencies you have. Sweet! Also note that all the Dojo Base stuff is included by default, but code in Core (generally, those namespaces you need to use dojo.require() to gain access to) are not.

The prefixes section lists the modules that need to be included. Here, because we're building in the Button dijit, and the Blowfish encryption from DojoX, we'll need to include those.

After this is done, all it takes is a command line to produce customDOJO.js:

```
java -jar ../shrinksafe/custom_rhino.jar build.js profile=test action=release
```

What you get is not just customDOJO.js, but also a complete tree of Dojo "stuff" that you can drop into your web app. This is just like what you get when you download the standard Dojo distribution, except this has not only what you want it to have, but also the "extra" modules that aren't necessarily part of customDOJO.js but that are available for you to use if you decide you need to via require() statements.

A couple of notes are important to understand here. First, Dojo uses ShrinkSafe, a JavaScript compressor, on the layer files, to make them as small and efficient as possible (efficient in terms of network transit time). Second, part of the build process is interning of certain external resources. For instance, with dijits, you have an HTML template for each dijit. *Interning* that template, that is, turning it into a string and including it in the JavaScript file, makes it more efficient because that's one less resource that has to be fetched during loading.

Lots of options are available during a build: changing the version number, changing the name of the release, telling the build how to optimize the layer files, setting log verbosity settings, and more. But, what I've described here are the basics that you'd need to know to do a custom build.

Come Fly with Me: Core in Detail

As you explore this section, you'll discover that there are essentially three things we'll be looking at within each namespace. The first are *constructors*, or *classes* as I'll frequently call them, and they are exactly what their name implies: functions that are called to instantiate a given object. The second are *functions*, which really are methods of a given class, and they are the main thing we'll be concerned with because that's where the majority of the features you'll be interested in live. Last are *properties*, just data fields you can access to get at certain information Dojo has to offer.

Also note that I've flattened the namespaces out here a bit. For instance, dojo.cldr.monetary is actually a namespace, monetary, under another namespace, cldr, which is itself under the dojo namespace. I've done this simply to be able to present everything as one consolidated list. Of course in JavaScript, dojo.cldr.monetary.getData() is a perfectly valid function call. You can think of the entire thing as simply the name of a function (which of course it is) that just happens to have periods in the name. Under the covers, though, what we're really dealing with are functions within functions within functions (and so on).

Yet another note: Unless stated otherwise, each constructor, function, or property is available to you by virtue of importing `dojo.js` only. As you'll recall, these represent the "nonoptional" pieces of Dojo Core. Other items that are optional will state which `dojo.require()` call is, err, *required*, to get at that functionality.

One final note before we rock and roll: Although I tried to include virtually every member that appears in the Dojo API documentation, I left out all hidden members, and I also dropped a few members that were more or less used internally (for example, `toJsonIndentStr` is the character used when using the `toJson()` function, and telling you it's just a tab escape string is kind of pointless—aside from telling you about it here just to tell you it's pointless, that is!). In the same vein, you may find a few items listed here for which I couldn't find any documentation and couldn't reasonably figure out the purpose. Such is the difficulty with Dojo and documentation that you sometimes come across. I don't believe there are any major omissions, and I've been able to get at least some description for nearly everything, so in many ways this is a step up from the API documentation itself.

Anyway, with all that out of the way, let's get to it, dig in and see what Dojo Core has to offer. There's definitely plenty of meat on them bones!

dojo

It all starts with the `dojo` object! Everything that follows is a namespace underneath this one, which means Dojo will nicely coexist with most any other JavaScript library out there.

Constructors

The following is the list of constructors available directly under the `dojo` namespace.

dojo.AdapterRegistry()

```
dojo.require("dojo.AdapterRegistry");
```

An `AdapterRegistry` object enables you to set up processing rules for a given data type such that the adapter will examine an argument, determine what type it is, and call the appropriate function that you previously registered with it. For instance:

```
var ar = new dojo.AdapterRegistry();
ar.register("stringRule", dojo.isString, function(inString) {
  return inString.toLowerCase();
});
ar.register("arrayRule", dojo.isArray, function(inArray) {
  return inArray.toString();
});
alert(ar.match("HeLlO"));
alert(ar.match(["John", "Connor"]));
ar.unregister("arrayRule");
```

Here, we're instantiating a new AdapterRegistry and then registering two rules with it: one for processing strings and the other for processing arrays. Using the dojo.isString() and dojo.isArray() functions (passed as arguments to the register() function) lets us determine whether the rule should fire. Then we call the match() method of the AdapterRegistry object twice and show the results via an alert() pop-up. The AdapterRegistry then finds the matching registered rule, if any, and calls the specified function. This results in the first pop-up, shown in Figure 2-2.

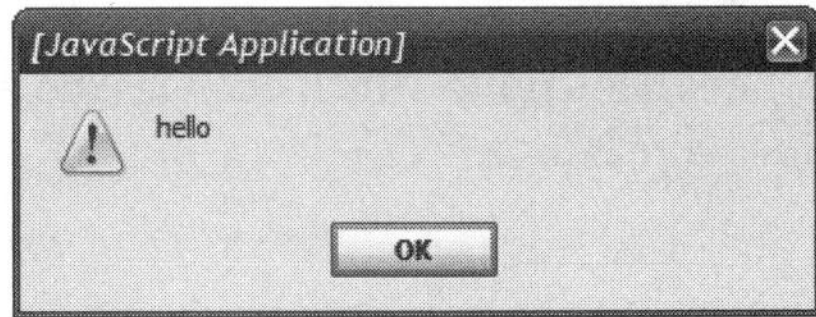

Figure 2-2. *ch2_AdapterRegistry.htm first result*

The second alert() pop-up that follows is shown in Figure 2-3.

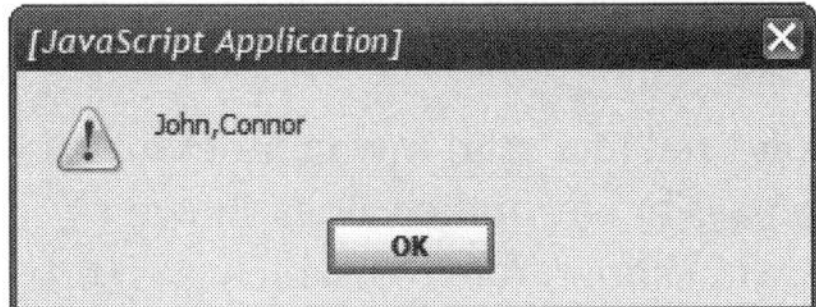

Figure 2-3. *ch2_AdapterRegistry.htm second result*

Last, we can unregister rules by using the unregister() method of the AdapterRegistry object.

The benefit of using this class is the ability to handle various incoming data types without having to explicitly know what that type is at runtime. This is an especially important capability given the dynamic, loosely typed nature of JavaScript.

dojo.Color()

This nifty little object enables you to pass in various forms of colors and get various forms out of it, without having to worry about the details of how to do such conversions. With it, you can do things like this:

```
var c = new dojo.Color("red");
alert("toCss = " + c.toCss() + "\n" +
  "toHex = " + c.toHex() + "\n" +
  "toRgb = " + c.toRgb() + "\n" +
  "toRgba = " + c.toRgba());
c.setColor([0,255,0]);
alert(c.toHex());
```

The first alert() that appears can be seen in Figure 2-4.

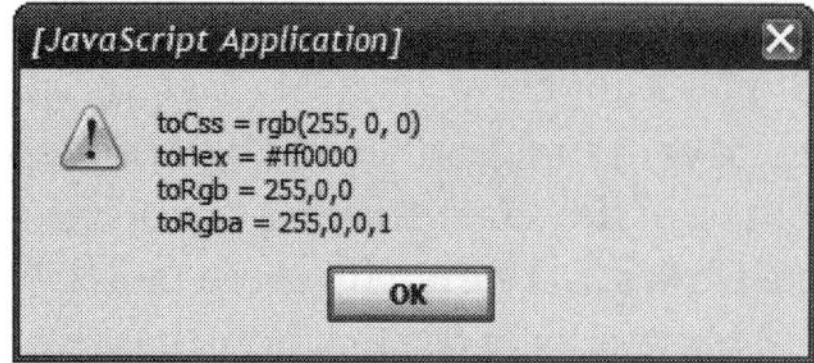

Figure 2-4. *ch2_Color.htm first result*

The second `alert()` occurs after the call to `setColor()` has been done, which changes the color the `Color` object represents. This `alert()` is shown in Figure 2-5.

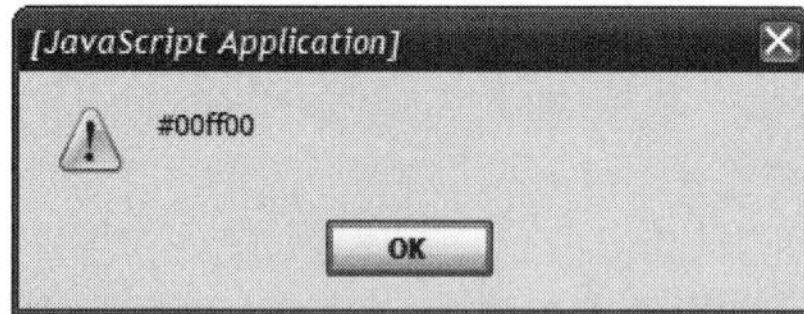

Figure 2-5. *ch2_Color.htm second result*

Note that all the function call results represent the color red in a valid way in other forms. Not only can you pass in a string such as `red`, but you can pass in any of the values shown by the alerts to get the other forms. For instance, the fifth `alert()` shows `#00ff00`, which is green, corresponding to the array of values `0,255,0`. You can also see how the `setColor()` method can be called to change the color that the `Color` object currently holds.

dojo.loaded()

This function is called when the initial Dojo environment is loaded, and when all loading of Dojo packages is complete. This is internally what you're "hooking into," so to speak, when you use `dojo.addOnLoad()`, which is described shortly. When running within a browser, all dijits created declaratively will be instantiated by the end of this method (and before any you connect to this are called). There's no need to demonstrate anything here because `dojo.addOnLoad()` is really what you should use (or `dojo.connect()` alternatively, also described later), and there is a demonstration of that to come.

Functions

You'll now look at the functions exposed through the `dojo` namespace. These are, by and large, what you'll be using, and they constitute the real core of Dojo because everything else depends on these functions to varying degrees.

dojo.addClass() and dojo.removeClass()

The `dojo.addClass()` function enables you to add a style class to a given DOM node. For example:

IBM

Richard Watts
Senior Development Manager
Rational

550 King Street
Littleton, MA 01460 6245

Tel 978 899 3633
Fax 845 463 5576

```
<html>
  <head>
    <link rel="StyleSheet" type="text/css"
      href="js/dojo/dojo/resources/dojo.css">
    <style>.myClass { color : #ff0000; }</style>
    <script type="text/javascript">
      var djConfig = {
        baseScriptUri : "js/dojo/"
      };
    </script>
    <script type="text/javascript" src="js/dojo/dojo/dojo.js"></script>
  </head>
  <body onLoad="dojo.addClass('myDiv', 'myClass');">
    <div id="myDiv">Testing, 1...2...3!</div>
  </body>
</html>
```

The result of loading this document is that the text in the `<body>` is turned red when the page loads.

There is also `dojo.removeClass()`, which of course does the exact opposite. If we were to call that after the `dojo.addClass()` call here, the text would again be the default color, black usually, because the style setting it to red would no longer be applied.

dojo.addOnLoad()

Typically, when you want something to fire when the page loads, you use the `onLoad` event. The problem with this is that the browser waits for all resources to be loaded, meaning all images, all CSS, all JavaScript files, and so on, before that event fires. It also builds the entire DOM and puts everything on the screen before it fires the `onLoad` event and executes your code. Sometimes this is exactly what you want (even need) to happen, but sometimes you need to do some work before that time, if for no other reason than to make your application appear faster to load than it is.

Dojo provides a mechanism to do this. Calling `dojo.addOnLoad()` and passing it a function reference results in Dojo calling that function as soon as the DOM has loaded, and after all dijits declared in markup are instantiated. Although the dijit markup and CSS are guaranteed to have been loaded, other resources on the page may not be.

To use `dojo.addOnLoad()`, you simply do this:

```
dojo.addOnLoad(function() {
  alert("DOM loaded");
});
```

Alternatively, you can use this syntax if you prefer:

```
function onLoadHandler() {
  alert("DOM loaded");
}
dojo.addOnLoad(onLoadHandler);
```

dojo.addOnUnload()

Similar to `dojo.addOnLoad()` is `dojo.addOnUnload()`, which does the same thing but at page unload time. Syntactically it is identical to `dojo.addOnLoad()`.

dojo.blendColors()

This function enables you to blend two `dojo.Color` objects together by using a given weight (indicating which color has dominance over the other). This is easy to demonstrate with a weight of 0.5 (0–1 being the valid range of weights), as follows:

```
alert(dojo.blendColors(new dojo.Color([100, 100, 100]),
  new dojo.Color([200, 200, 200]), .5));
```

The resultant pop-up is shown in Figure 2-6. In the case of a weight of 0.5, where all the color component values are 100 for one color and 200 for the other, blending essentially means averaging them, so 150 in this case. Play with the weight factor to see different results if you have any doubt about how this works.

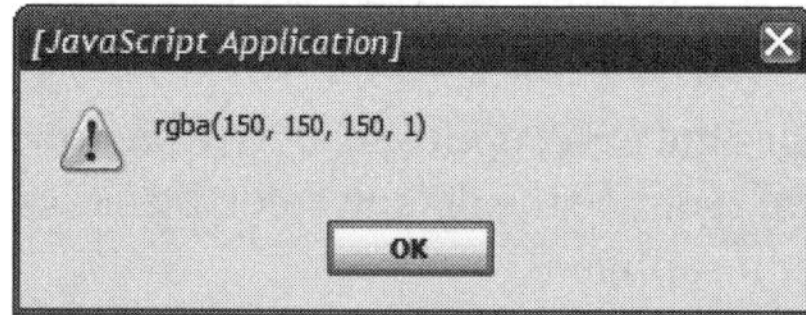

Figure 2-6. *ch2_blendColors.htm result*

dojo.body()

This function simply returns the body element of the current document to you. Keep in mind that Dojo likes to provide functionality that mimics what you can do easily with standard JavaScript and DOM manipulation so that you can always be working with the Dojo API and have to learn only that. This is a nice philosophy for a lot of people who would prefer not to have to know how to get a reference to the body element themselves, for instance, and would prefer to just look to Dojo to handle the details. This also allows Dojo to add value around such relatively simple things should the need arise. For example, the `dojo.body()` function could conceivably return a reference to a DOM in memory rather than the actual DOM of the page so that Dojo can have control over when the screen gets updated instead of the browser.

dojo.byId()

You've no doubt heard of `document.getElementById()`, right? Are you sick of typing it? I know I am! Other libraries, such as Prototype, offer the `$()` function, which is roughly equivalent (I say *roughly* only because `$()` provides extra functionality that `document.getElementById()` does not).

Dojo's version accepts a string that is the ID of a DOM node, or a DOM node itself (the latter representing a no-operation condition (in other words, you'll get the node you passed in back; dojo.byId() doesn't really do anything in that case). Optionally, you can also pass a reference to a document element, enabling you to search other documents. By default, the value of dojo.doc, which is an alias for the current document (that is, window.document) is used.

I haven't shown an example here because this function is used in many other examples throughout this chapter, so it would be a little redundant (more so than writing this sentence was in the first place!).

dojo.clone()

The dojo.clone() function enables you to clone an object, which—most interesting, I think—can be a DOM node. So, this function enables you to do things like this:

```
<html>
  <head>
    <link rel="StyleSheet" type="text/css"
      href="js/dojo/dojo/resources/dojo.css">
    <script type="text/javascript">
      var djConfig = {
        baseScriptUri : "js/dojo/"
      };
    </script>
    <script type="text/javascript" src="js/dojo/dojo/dojo.js"></script>
    <script>
      function doOnLoad() {
        var originalNode = dojo.byId("originalNode");
        var clonedNode = dojo.clone(originalNode);
        clonedNode.innerHTML = "I am the cloned node";
        dojo.body().appendChild(clonedNode);
      }
    </script>
  </head>
  <body onLoad="doOnLoad();">
    <div id="originalNode">I am the original node</div>
    <br>
  </body>
</html>
```

This results in the browser display shown in Figure 2-7. Cloning an object is clearly a pretty handy thing to be able to do. Keep in mind that dojo.clone() doesn't apply just to DOM nodes; it applies to virtually any object you throw at it.

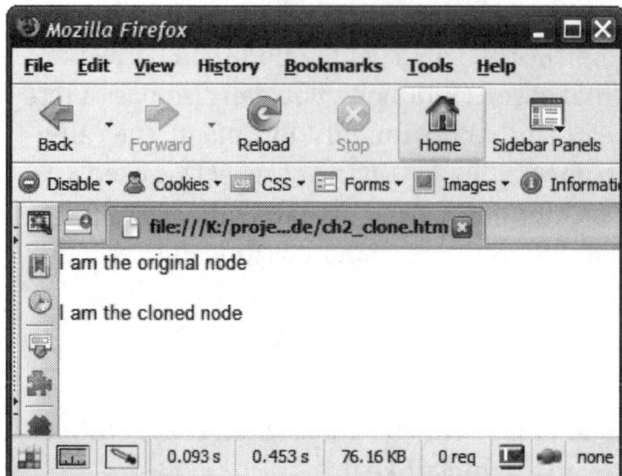

Figure 2-7. *ch2_clone.htm result*

dojo.colorFromArray()

This function enables you to convert an array of RGB(A) values to a `dojo.Color` object. You can either get a new object from it or update an existing one. For instance:

```
var c1 = new dojo.Color([100, 100, 100]);
var c2 = dojo.colorFromArray([150, 150, 150]);
var c3 = dojo.clone(c1);
dojo.colorFromArray([200, 200, 200], c3);
alert("c1 = " + c1 + "\nc2 = " + c2 + "\nc3 = " + c3);
```

Executing this produces the pop-up seen in Figure 2-8.

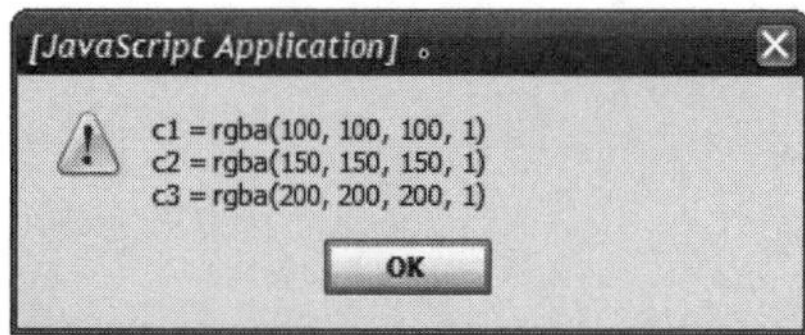

Figure 2-8. *ch2_colorFromArray.htm result*

dojo.colorFromHex()

Similar in concept to `dojo.colorFromArray()` is `dojo.colorFromHex()`, which takes a hex string prefixed with a # character (12-bit RGB shorthand format) and converts it to a `dojo.Color` object. So, for example, you can do this:

```
var c1 = new dojo.Color([255, 0, 0]);
var c2 = dojo.colorFromHex("#00ff00");
var c3 = dojo.clone(c1);
dojo.colorFromHex("#0000ff", c3);
alert("c1 = " + c1 + "\nc2 = " + c2 + "\nc3 = " + c3);
```

That gets you the pop-up shown in Figure 2-9.

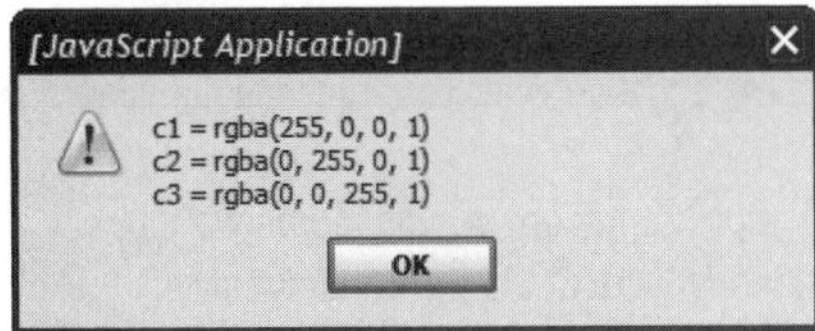

Figure 2-9. *ch2_colorHex.htm result*

dojo.colorFromRgb()

This function works much like `dojo.colorFromHex()`, except that it is capable of handling the four current Color Module formats specified by CSS3: Red/Green/Blue (RGB), Red/Green/Blue/Alpha (RGBA), Hue/Saturation/Lightness (HSL), and Hue/Saturation/Lightness/Alpha (HSLA). It can also handle the optional percentage values that can be specified with the RGBA format.

I'll skip demonstrating this function because it is, by and large, similar to `dojo.colorFromHex()` and `dojo.colorFromArray()` in terms of syntax and arguments accepted.

dojo.colorFromString()

The `dojo.colorFromString()` function rounds out the `dojo.colorFrom*()` functions, and it's in many ways a jack-of-all-trades. It can accept values in any form that `dojo.colorFromArray()` accepts, hex strings in the form `#rrggbb`, or `rgb()`/`rgba()` strings such as `rgb(10,20,30)` or `rgba(10,20,30,40)`.

Once again, I'll skip the demonstration because you've already more or less seen this in action. It's just like the previous couple of functions; it just does more!

dojo.connect()

The `dojo.connect()` function is the entry into the Dojo aspect-oriented programming (AOP) world. This function enables you to do something seemingly simple but incredibly powerful: it allows you to set up a call to a given function whenever another is called. If that doesn't sound like a big deal, give it a second to sink in and take a peek at the following sidebar.

A BRIEF ASIDE ON ASPECT-ORIENTED PROGRAMMING

Aspect-oriented programming (AOP), sometimes called aspect-oriented software development (AOSD), is the technique whereby you identify so-called *cross-cutting concerns* and externalize them from the code in question.

A commonly used example is that of logging. Frequently, you want to output a log statement every time a given function is called. Typically, you would include some sort of log statement directly in the function. This works well enough, but the problem you quickly see is that you have logging code strewn all over the code because in all likelihood you want to do this in many functions.

AOP enables you to do the equivalent of telling your runtime environment, "Hey, do me a favor, buddy; output a log statement every time function A is called," without you having to specifically include the code to do so in the function. This is also an example of separation of concerns because what your function actually does is separated from the logging concern.

How this AOP approach is accomplished depends on the AOP implementation you use. Some work by modifying your code at compile time; others do so at runtime. Some truly work at the environment level, meaning your code is not modified and the function calls are instead intercepted somehow. The implementation isn't terribly important; the underlying concept is.

So, to give you a concrete example of the types of magic you can achieve, have a look at this bit of code:

```
function MyClass() {
  this.sayHello = function(inName) {
    alert("Hello, " + inName);
  }
}
function interceptor(inName) {
  alert("Just said hello to " + inName);
}
var myObject = new MyClass();
dojo.connect(myObject, "sayHello", null, interceptor);
myObject.sayHello("Hayden");
```

The result is two consecutive `alert()` pop-ups, shown in Figure 2-10. I hope you'll notice that there's something a little amiss with these.

Figure 2-10. *ch2_connect.htm result*

The thing that's a bit amiss is that the `interceptor()` function didn't intercept anything; it was called *after* the original call. Now that's still plenty cool, but it isn't quite what I explained previously. Unfortunately, the ability to intercept methods (as well as the ability to have *around advice,* AOP parlance for calling some function or functions both before and after an event) has been removed from Dojo. At this point, there is no concrete plan to bring it back. This is disappointing certainly, but it shouldn't take away from the utility of this function. The ability to call a series of methods based on a triggering event without having to explicitly code all the calls is still extremely useful. (The event can be a DOM event, by the way, such as `onClick`, not just method calls as in this example.)

Also note that there is a `dojo.disconnect()` function that removes a given connected function. This is something you'll want to keep in mind because you can cause memory leaks if you connect things and then don't disconnect them later under some circumstances. Simply put, always use `dojo.disconnect()` when you no longer need the functions to be triggered, and all should remain right with the world!

dojo.publish(), dojo.subscribe(), dojo.unsubscribe(), and dojo.connectPublisher()

Here is a group of four functions that I've chosen to describe all as one group because they are intimately linked. These all deal with the concept of publish/subscribe, which is just a computer science term meaning that one object sends a message while one (or more) other objects gets the message and reacts to it, without the sender having explicitly called any of the listeners.

Using this group of functions is remarkably simple, as you can see for yourself:

```
var s = "";
function MyClass() {
  this.myFunction1 = function() {
    s += "myFunction1 called\n";
  }
  this.myFunction2 = function() {
    s += "myFunction2 called\n";
    dojo.publish("myMessage", [ "Hello!" ]);
  }
}
function callback(inMsg) {
  s += "Message received: " + inMsg + "\n";
}
var o = new MyClass();
o.myFunction1();
s + "----------\n";
var hndl = dojo.subscribe("myMessage", null, callback);
o.myFunction2();
s + "----------\n";
dojo.unsubscribe(hndl);
o.myFunction2();
s + "----------\n";
var hndl = dojo.subscribe("myMessage", null, callback);
dojo.connectPublisher("myMessage", o, "myFunction1");
o.myFunction1();
alert(s);
```

The resultant pop-up is shown in Figure 2-11.

Figure 2-11. *ch2_connectPublisher.htm result*

The first line of the `alert()` is a result of calling `myFunction1()` on the instance of `MyClass` named `o`. This is just a straight method call—no publish/subscribe going on just yet. After that is executed, we subscribe to the `myMessage` event, and we are saying that `callback()` will be called whenever that message is published. Next, we call `o.myFunction2()`, generating the second line of the `alert()`, and which then does a `dojo.publish()` to publish a `myMessage` event. We also pass a message via the array, the second argument to the call. This results in `callback()` being called, and the array passed into it, and that's where the third line in the `alert()` comes from. Next, we use `dojo.unsubscribe()` to stop listening for that `myMessage` event. Note that the call to `dojo.subscribe()` returns a handle that you then pass to `dojo.unsubscribe()` to stop listening for that message. But remember, you can listen for the same message more than once, so there still may be something that happens if that message is published again. Following that `dojo.unsubscribe()`, we again call `o.myFunction2()`, and the fourth line of the `alert()` occurs, just to prove there's nothing happening as a result of the `dojo.publish()` call within it. Finally, we make a call to `dojo.connectPublisher()`, which basically says that every time `o.myFunction1()` is called, we want to publish a `myMessage` event. This is nice because you'll note that `o.myFunction1()` does not explicitly publish `myMessage`, but it will act as if it did as a result of the `dojo.connectPublisher()` call. So, when we again call `o.myFunction1()`, we get line 5 of the `alert()`, and then line 6 as a result of `myMessage` being published and `callback()` being called a result.

■ Note All this publish/subscribe stuff may seem a bit pointless if this is your first exposure to it. Why not just call these methods directly and not bother with all this? The point to it all is that it keeps your code decoupled. For instance, `MyClass` does not have to know about `callback()`—and even better with `connectPublisher()`, it doesn't even have to explicitly know to publish a given message. All of this behavior can be "wired up" externally, keeping low coupling between your code. So long as your code still publishes and subscribes to the correct messages, things should continue to work as you planned regardless of implementation. It's a really good design paradigm to get comfortable with and use.

---

dojo.cookie()

```
dojo.require("dojo.cookie");
```

Dojo makes dealing with cookies very, very easy, and the `dojo.cookie()` function is the singular way to do so. This nifty little function works like so: it can accept three parameters. The first is the name of the cookie. The second, which is optional, is the value of the cookie. The third, which is also optional, is an object with various options for the cookie.

In other words, say you want to set a cookie that expires in five days. All you have to do is this:

```
dojo.cookie("myCookie", "This is my cookie", { expires : 5 });
```

To read that cookie back, you simply do this:

```
dojo.cookie("myCookie");
```

It couldn't be simpler! The other options you can specify in that third argument object are `domain`, which sets the cookie for the specified domain (by default the domain of the page is used), `path`, which is the path the cookie should be set for (by default the path of the page is used), and `secure` (`true` or `false`), which will set the cookie only under a secure connection. Note that for the `expires` option you can also send a date, after which the cookie will expire; or zero, which means the cookie will expire when the browser closes; or a negative number or past date, which will delete the cookie.

dojo.coords()

This function returns to you an object that contains a number of attributes, namely `l` (left), `t` (top), `w` (width), `h` (height), `x` (essentially left again), and `y` (essentially top again). This describes the size and position of a given element on the page. It technically gives you information about the margin box model of the element.

For example, given the following <div>:

```
<div style="width:200px;height:100px;position:absolute;left:20px;top:30px;"
  id="myDiv">
  I am myDiv
</div>
```

. . . and then the following code:

```
function doCoords() {
  alert(dojo.toJson(dojo.coords("myDiv")));
}
```

. . . results in the `alert()` pop-up seen in Figure 2-12.

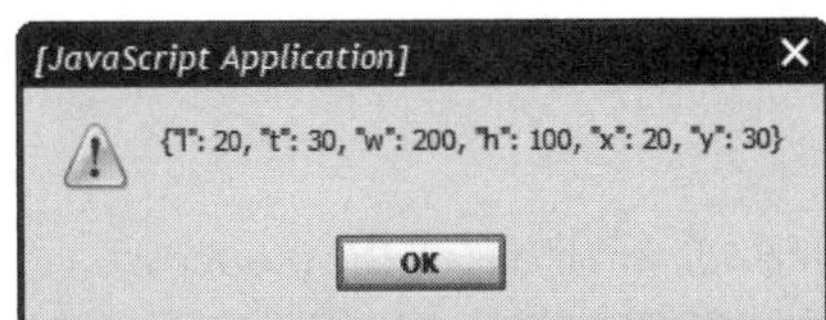

Figure 2-12. *ch2_coords.htm result*

dojo.declare()

The `dojo.declare()` function is what I'd call wickedly cool in that it gives you a powerful mechanism to do some cool object-oriented development in JavaScript.

Let's say you want to create a new class and you want it to be a subclass of two others. We're talking C++-like multiple inheritance here! Let's further say that you want to add some additional properties and methods, as is typical in such cases. You could pull this off with plain JavaScript if you tried hard enough, but I suspect you'd prefer to do the following instead:

```
function MyClass1() {
  var firstName = "Mick";
  this.getFirstName = function() {
    return firstName;
  }
}
function MyClass2() {
  var lastName = "Foley";
  this.getLastName = function() {
    return lastName;
  }
}
dojo.declare("com.omnytex.AnotherClass", [ MyClass1, MyClass2],
  { middleName : "William",
    getMiddleName : function() {
      return this.middleName;
     }
   }
 );
 var o = new com.omnytex.AnotherClass();
 alert(o.getFirstName() + " " + o.getMiddleName() + " " +
   o.getLastName());
```

Running this code nets you the pop-up in Figure 2-13.

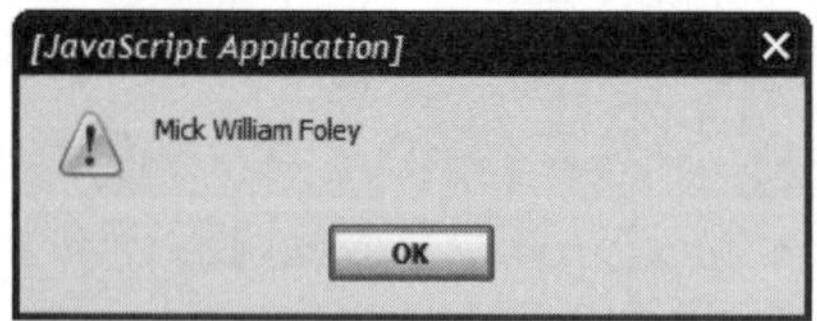

Figure 2-13. *ch2_declare.htm result*

Yes indeed, the class `com.omnytex.AnotherClass` is created, and it has all the properties and methods of `MyClass1` and `MyClass2`, as well as some new ones, namely `middleName` and `getMiddleName()`. The `dojo.declare()` method accepts as its first argument the name of the class to create. The second argument is `null` if you don't wish to inherit anything, or the name of an existing function, or an array of existing functions as seen here. The last argument, which is optional, is an object that specifies the unique properties and methods this class will have in a nice, neat, compact object notation. Nifty indeed!

dojo.eval()

This is another example of Dojo wrapping something relatively simple so you can stay within the Dojo API. This is a wrapper around the usual `eval()` function in JavaScript. Use this instead of using `eval()` directly. I assume here that you know all about `eval()`, in which case you know all about `dojo.eval()` too, so let's move on, shall we?

dojo.every()

This is an interesting little utility function that enables you to take a list of values in array form and determine whether every element in that array meets some criteria as defined by a function you provide. JavaScript 1.6 provides this all by its self, so Dojo's version will be used only when JavaScript 1.6 isn't being used.

Here's a simple example to determine whether all numbers in an array are greater than 10:

```
function checkFunc(inVal) {
  return (inVal > 10);
}
alert(dojo.every([23, 15, 71, 19, 99], checkFunc) + ", " +
  dojo.every([23, 15, 71, 19, 9], checkFunc));
```

This nets us the amazingly thrilling pop-up in Figure 2-14. Seriously, though, it's a pretty useful little function, and because you can do arbitrarily complex things in the check function, and you can pass any type of value in the array, I'm sure you can see the potential uses for this dancing around in your head already.

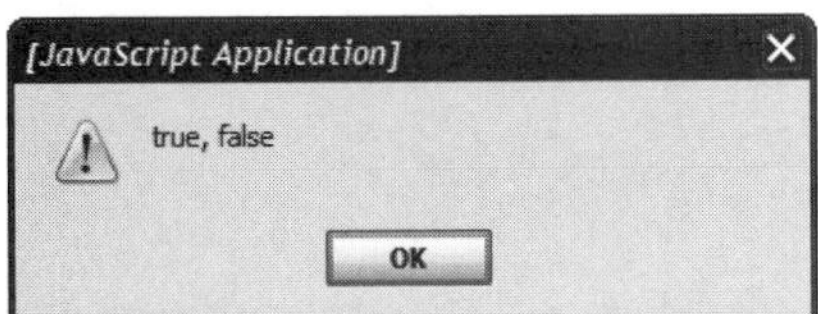

Figure 2-14. *ch2_every.htm result*

dojo.exists()

This is a nice function that can tell you whether an object supports a given method. For example:

```
var myObj = {
  myProp : 123,
  myFunc : { }
};
alert(dojo.exists("myObj.myFunc") + ", " +
  dojo.exists("myFunc", myObj) + ", " +
  dojo.exists("myObj.myFunc2") + ", " +
  dojo.exists("myProp", myObj));
```

The pop-up shown in Figure 2-15 is the outcome.

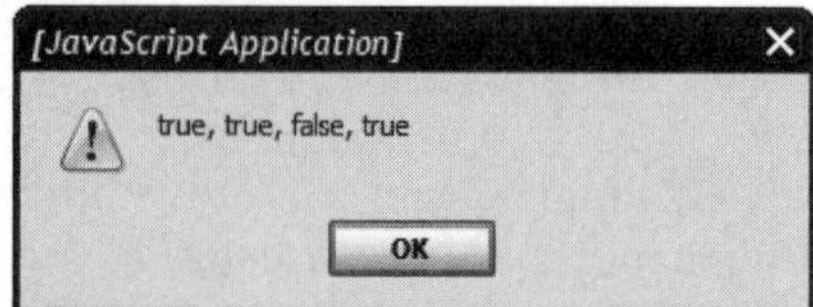

Figure 2-15. *ch2_exists.htm result*

Although the Dojo documentation doesn't say so, you can see here that you can test for properties as well as methods. In other words, any member of a given object can be checked for.

You will also note that you can specify the check in two ways. One is simply a complete path to the member you want to check for (`myObj.myFunc`, for example). The other way is to specify a scope. In the case of `dojo.exists("myFunc", myObj)`, this makes `myObj` the scope of the check. This is nice because you can set a variable equal to the scope and make multiple calls to `dojo.exists()` without having to specify the complete path for every call.

dojo.extend()

This is a really neat function that allows you to add all the properties and methods of a given object or objects to another's prototype, thereby making them available to all subsequent instances of the constructor.

In more-concrete terms, it enables you to do things like the following:

```
function MyClass1() {
  var firstName = "Mick";
  this.getFirstName = function() {
    return firstName;
  }
}
function MyClass2() {
  var lastName = "Foley";
  this.getLastName = function() {
    return lastName;
  }
}
function MyClass3() {
  this.sayName = function() {
    alert("I am " + this.getFirstName() + " " + this.getLastName());
  }
}
dojo.extend(MyClass3, new MyClass1(), new MyClass2());
var mc3 = new MyClass3();
mc3.sayName();
```

Running this code gives you the pop-up shown in Figure 2-16. As you can see, the instance of MyClass3 includes the methods and properties from MyClass1 and MyClass2. As you can also see, the dojo.extend() method enables you to pass multiple objects to inherit from at one time, or just one if you like, or even inline object definitions.

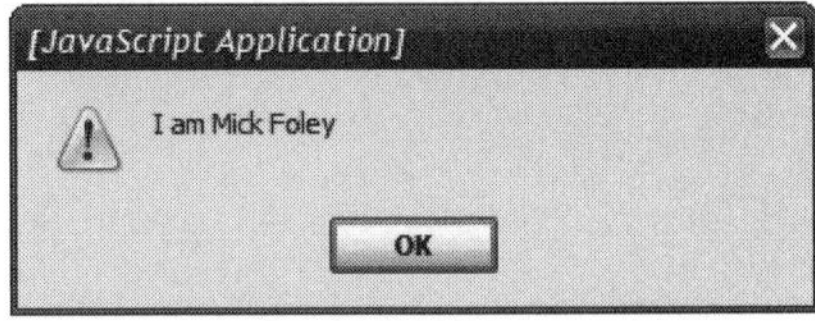

Figure 2-16. *ch2_extend.htm result*

dojo.fadeIn() and dojo.fadeOut()

I'm covering both of these functions together because they're identical except in the direction they do something, namely fade a given DOM element. Let's me first show you the example code for this and then I'll explain it a bit:

```
dojo.fadeOut({node : "myDiv", duration : 2000, onEnd : function() {
  dojo.fadeIn({node : "myDiv", duration : 2000}).play();
}}).play();
```

Because this is an animation, it wouldn't make a whole lot of sense to put a static image here, so you'll just have to take my word for it (or try it, because the example is included in the source download for this book) when I tell you this will fade some text out, and then fade it back in over a period of about 4 seconds. First, we kick off the fade-out by calling dojo.fadeOut(). As you can see, this function accepts an object with some properties in it, namely node, which is the ID of the DOM node to fade, and duration, which is in milliseconds, stating how long the effect will take. Also included is onEnd, which is a function to execute when the animation completes. In this case, it's simply a call to dojo.fadeIn() to get our text back to being visible. You get back a Dojo Animation object from these calls, so calling the play() method on them is required to make things go.

dojo.filter()

This is another of those nifty little utility functions that you'll probably find yourself using frequently now that you know about it. This function enables you to take a list of values in array form and filter it, returning an array with only those items matching the filter in it. This too is something built natively in JavaScript in version 1.6 and thus the native version is delegated to by Dojo when appropriate and available.

Here's a simple example that will return only those values greater than 10:

```
function checkFunc(inItem, inIndex, inArray) {
  return (inItem > 10);
}
alert(dojo.filter([2, 5, 71, 19, 99], checkFunc));
```

What gets spewed forth onto the screen is Figure 2-17.

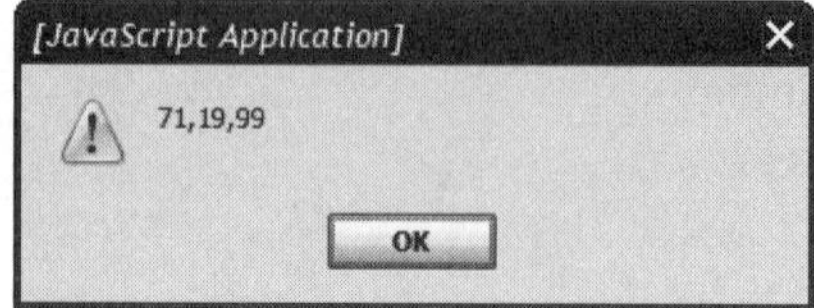

Figure 2-17. *ch2_filter.htm result*

dojo.forEach()

In the same vein as `dojo.every()` and `dojo.filter()` comes `dojo.forEach()`! This function iterates over an array and executes the specified callback method. The callback does not return a value as the other two do. Instead, this function is meant for when you want to do something for every element of the array. As in previous cases, Dojo was ahead of its time a little: JavaScript 1.6 includes this natively as well!

Here's a simple example that will `alert()` each element of the array:

```
dojo.forEach(["Star Wars", "Stargate"], function(inVal) {
  alert(inVal);
});
```

This function is not terribly exciting in action, but nonetheless, Figure 2-18 shows the two pop-ups you'll see when this code is run.

Figure 2-18. *ch2_forEach.htm result*

dojo.formToObject(), dojo.formToQuery(), and dojo.formToJson()

For the sake of brevity, I am describing these three functions together because they all do essentially the same thing, just varying in their output. As their names imply, they take an HTML form and convert it to some format, be it an object, a query string, or JSON, respectively.

So, given a form like so:

```
<form name="myForm">
  <input type="text" name="firstName" value="Steve">
  <input type="text" name="lastName" value="Austin">
</form>
```

. . . and given the following bit of code:

```
alert("formToJson(): \n" +dojo.formToJson("myForm", true) + "\n\n" +
```

```
  "formToObject(): \n" +dojo.formToObject("myForm") + "\n\n" +
  "formToQuery(): \n" +dojo.formToQuery("myForm")
);
```

. . . you get Figure 2-19.

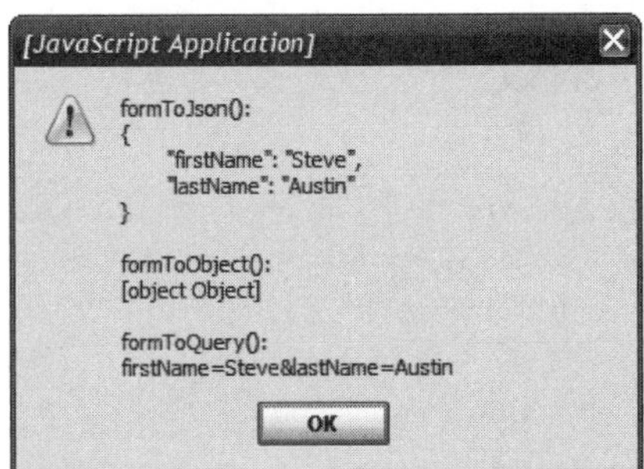

Figure 2-19. *ch2_formToJsonQueryObject.htm result*

The `dojo.formToJson()` function differs just slightly from the other two in that you can pass an optional second argument that tells Dojo to print the JSON in a "pretty" way. Now personally, I find it to be *less* pretty, but that comes down to the classic debate on whether to put braces opening a block of code on the end of a line or on a line by themselves. I prefer the former, many people prefer the latter, and the latter is more like what passing `true` for this argument does. So, whatever floats your boat, Dojo provides!

dojo.getComputedStyle()

This function will return to you a *computed style* object, which is a fancy way of saying it's like the style object you can get at by using `dojo.byId("nodeID").style`—only it's the current rendered state of the node, not necessarily as it was declared. For example, assuming you have this `<div>` defined:

```
<div id="myDiv">I am myDiv</div>
```

. . . then this code:

```
var o = dojo.byId("myDiv");
alert(dojo.getComputedStyle(o).borderWidth);
```

. . . yields the `alert()` in Figure 2-20.

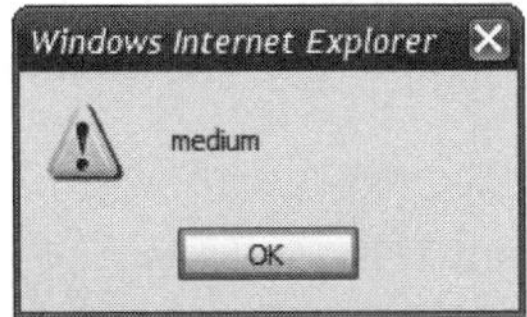

Figure 2-20. *ch2_getComputedStyle.htm result*

Now, the interesting thing to note is that this is an IE pop-up. If you run this code in Firefox, you'll get a blank `alert()` message. The results of `dojo.getComputedStyle()` can vary from browser to browser, and from platform to platform.

dojo.getObject()

This handy function lets you quickly traverse an object hierarchy to get at exactly the object you need. In addition, it allows you to add expandos to an object.

As an example, check this out:

```
function com() { }
com.omnytex = function() { };
com.omnytex.method1 = function() { return "method1 called"; }
alert(dojo.getObject("com.omnytex.method1")() + ", " +
  dojo.getObject("com.omnytex.method2", true) + ", " +
  dojo.getObject("com.omnytex.method2", false));
```

This code begins by creating a function named `com` and then adding a new function named `omnytex` to it. Next, it adds a method to `com.omnytex` named `method1`, which returns a string. This is all done just so we can test `dojo.getObject()`, as seen in the `alert()` function. The first call to `dojo.getObject()` gets us a reference to `method1`, which we then execute, and it returns the string for us. The next call to `dojo.getObject()` uses the optional second parameter, which by default is `false`, but here is `true`. What this does is add `method2` to `com.omnytex` automatically. It's an empty function at this point, but it's there, as you can see in the dialog box in Figure 2-21.

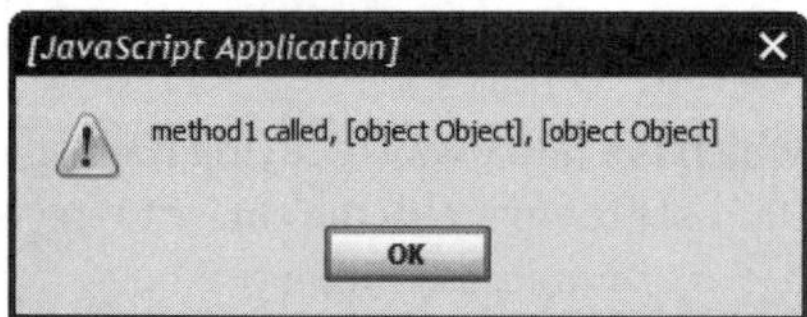

Figure 2-21. *ch2_getObject.htm result*

Just to prove that point, I added the third call to `dojo.getObject()`, specifically telling it *not* to create the requested object if it doesn't exist. Yet, as you can see in the figure, in both of the last two calls it returns us an object, proving it is in fact there.

dojo.hasClass()

This is a simple but useful function that returns `true` if a given DOM node has a given style class applied, `false` if not. So, if you have this markup on a page:

```
<div class="myClass" id="myDiv">myDiv</div>
```

. . . and assuming you have `MyClass` defined in your style sheet, then doing this:

```
alert(dojo.hasClass('myDiv', 'myClass'));
```

. . . will spit out the `alert()` dialog box shown in Figure 2-22.

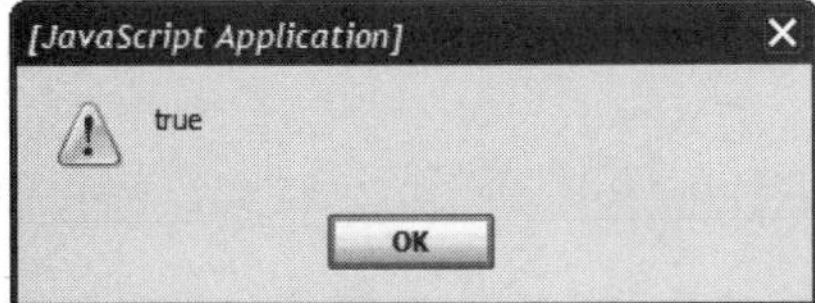

Figure 2-22. *ch2_hasClass.htm result*

dojo.indexOf()

This function mimics `indexOf()` in the standard `Array` object, but with a little more functionality. Here's a quick example:

```
var a = [ "Shatner", "Nimoy", "Kelley", "Spiner", "Nimoy" ];
alert(dojo.indexOf(a, "Nimoy") + ", " + dojo.indexOf(a, "Stewart") +
  ", " + dojo.indexOf(a, "Nimoy", 0, true));
```

And for the stunning outcome, look no further than Figure 2-23!

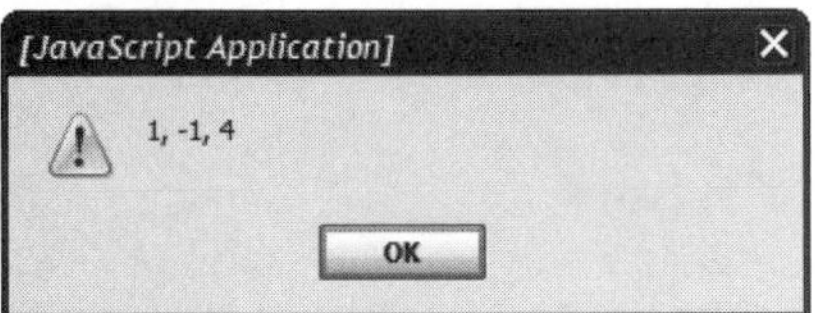

Figure 2-23. *ch2_indexOf.htm result*

The first call to `dojo.indexOf()` results in 1 because that's the index of the first occurrence of *Nimoy* in the array. The second call results in –1 because *Stewart* does not appear in the array. Finally, the third call yields 4 because that's the index of the last occurrence of *Nimoy*. The first argument is obviously the array to search, while the second argument is the element to search for. The third argument, which is optional, is where to begin the search. I specified it only here, in the third call, and it's 0, which is the default and equates to the start of the array. The fourth argument, also optional, defaults to `false`, but when `true` tells the function to search for the last occurrence of the given element.

dojo.isArray()

I'm going to go out on a limb here and bet you can figure out precisely what this function does without having to be told. If you imagine that the following code:

```
var s = new String("I am a string");
var a = new Array();
var i = 5;
alert(dojo.isArray(s) + "\n" + dojo.isArray(a) + "\n" + dojo.isArray(i));
```

. . . results in the pop-up seen in Figure 2-24:

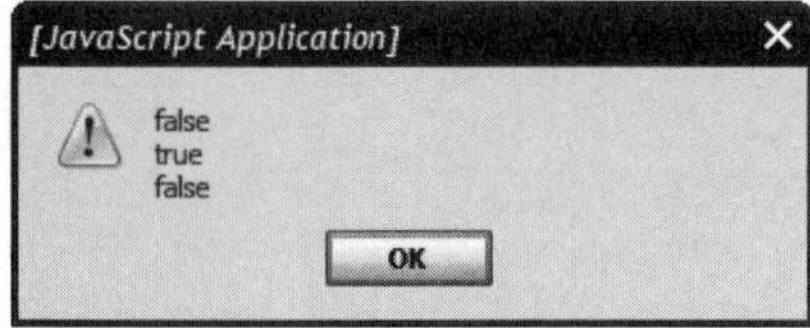

Figure 2-24. *ch2_isArray.htm result*

. . . then you must also have deduced that `isArray()` tells you whether its argument is an array. And if you think that's neat, check out the next one.

dojo.isArrayLike()

The `dojo.isArrayLike()` function is just like `dojo.isArray()`, but what it checks for is that its argument isn't a string or a number, and that is has a length property. So, for example, assuming you have the following markup on the page:

```
<body onLoad="doOnLoad();"><div id="myDiv">I am myDiv</div></body>
```

. . . then the code in `doOnLoad()`, like so:

```
function doOnLoad() {
  alert(dojo.isArray(document.body.childNodes) + ", " +
    dojo.isArrayLike(document.body.childNodes));
}
```

. . . gives you the oh-so-amazing pop-up shown in Figure 2-25.

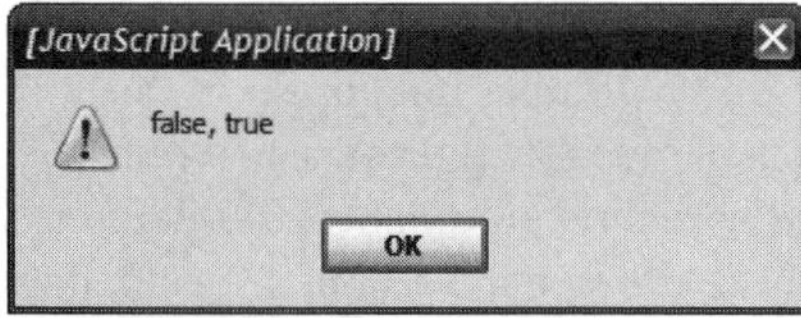

Figure 2-25. *ch2_isArrayLike.htm result*

dojo.isDescendant()

If you need a way to determine whether a given DOM node is a child of another, `dojo.isDescendant()` is just the ticket. With it, you can, for example, examine this markup:

```
<span id="div1"></span>
<span id="div2"><span id="div3"></span></span>
```

. . . with this code:

```
alert(dojo.isDescendant(dojo.byId("div3"), dojo.byId("div1")) + "\n" +
  dojo.isDescendant("div3", "div2"));
```

. . . and the result will be Figure 2-26.

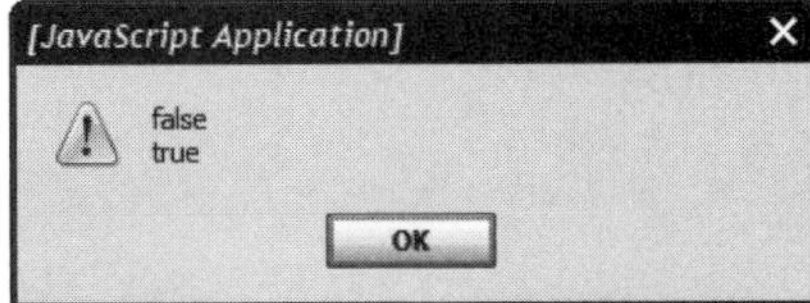

Figure 2-26. *ch2_isDescendant.htm result*

The first argument is a reference, or the ID of the node to examine. The second argument is the possible parent node, or ID of said node. If the first node descends from, or is a child of, the second, then this function returns `true`; otherwise, it returns `false`.

dojo.isFunction()

This is another *identity* function, meaning it tells you whether a given argument is a type of something, and in this case it tells you whether the argument is a function. This enables you to do things like this:

```
var f1 = function() { };
var f2 = new Function();
function func() {
}
var f3 = func;
var f4 = "test";
var f5 = 1;
alert(dojo.isFunction(f1) + "\n" + dojo.isFunction(f2) + "\n" +
  dojo.isFunction(f3) + "\n" + dojo.isFunction(f4) + "\n" +
  dojo.isFunction(f5));
```

When executed, you get the `alert()` in Figure 2-27.

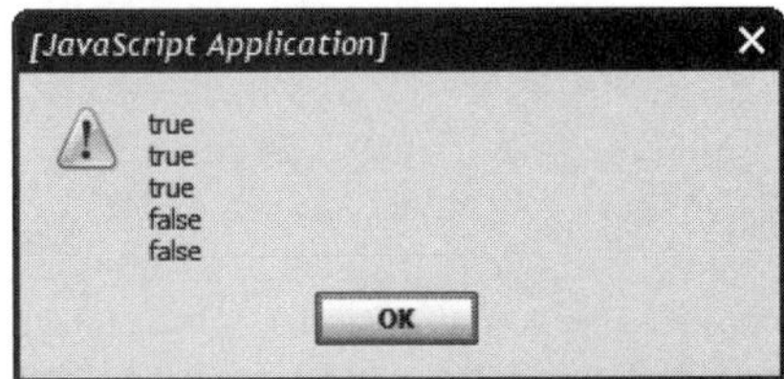

Figure 2-27. *ch2_isFunction.htm result*

dojo.isObject()

The `dojo.isObject()` function returns `true` if the argument passed to it is an object, `false` otherwise. It enables you to do all the nifty-keen checks in this code snippet:

```
var s1 = "string";
var s2 = new String("string object");
var i = 1;
var o = new Object();
```

```
var a = new Array();
alert(dojo.isObject(s1) + "\n" + dojo.isObject(s2) + "\n" +
  dojo.isObject(i) + "\n" + dojo.isObject(o) + "\n" +
  dojo.isObject(a));
```

The outcome is shown in Figure 2-28.

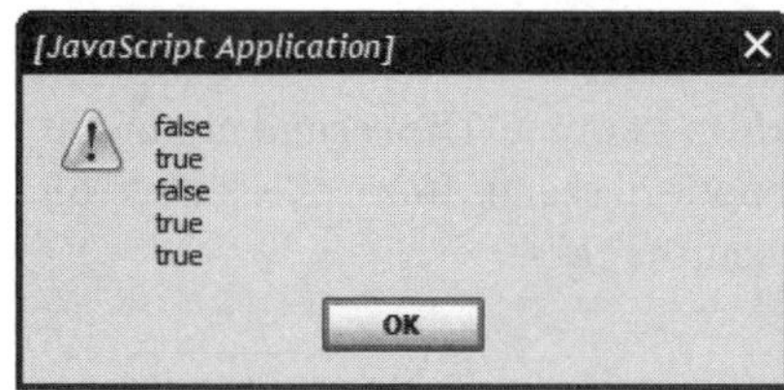

Figure 2-28. *ch2_isObject.htm result*

The only surprise may be that the variables `s1` and `s2` are not both `true`. Remember that there is a difference between string literals and strings constructed using `new String()`. Also remember that arrays are objects in JavaScript, hence the `true` returned for the variable a.

dojo.isString()

The last identity-type function is `dojo.isString()`. It's I think pretty self-explanatory, but for the sake of completeness, here's an example:

```
var s1 = new String("I am a string");
var s2 = "I too am a string";
var s3 = 100;
alert(dojo.isString(s1) + ", " + dojo.isString(s2) + ", " +
  dojo.isString(s3));
```

This tells you whether each of the variables is a string, as you can plainly see by looking at Figure 2-29.

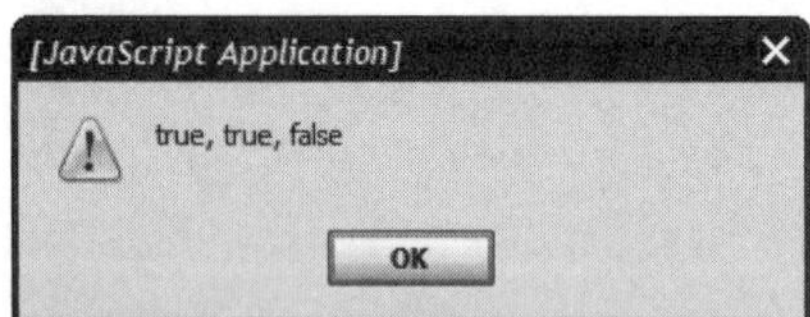

Figure 2-29. *ch2_isString.htm result*

dojo.lastIndexOf()

This function mimics `lastIndexOf()` in the standard `Array` object, but with a little more functionality. Here's a quick example:

```
var a = [ "Boxleitner", "Jurasik", "Katsulas", "Jurasik", "Biggs" ];
alert(dojo.indexOf(a, "Jurasik") + ", " + dojo.indexOf(a, "Furlan"));
```

And for the stunning outcome, look no further than Figure 2-30!

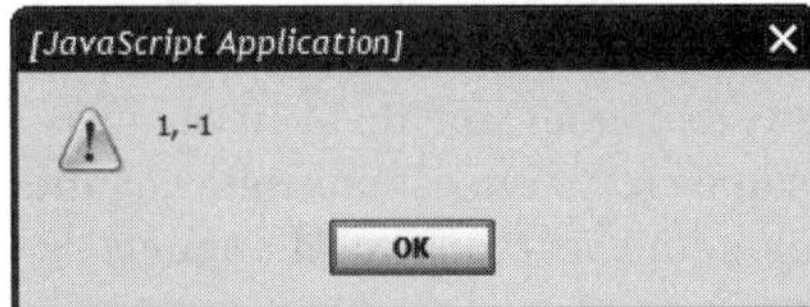

Figure 2-30. *ch2_lastIndexOf.htm result*

The first call to `dojo.indexOf()` results in 1 because that's the index of the first occurrence of *Jurasik* in the array. The second call results in –1 because *Furlan* does not appear in the array (no offense to Delenn![1]). The first argument is obviously the array to search, while the second argument is the element to search for. The third argument, which is optional, is where to begin the search.

dojo.map()

This is another of the functions Dojo provides for dealing with arrays. With this one, you pass it an array as the first argument, and then a function (or reference to a function) as the second. For each element in the array, the function will be called and passed the next item in the array. The function can do something with the item if it wishes, return it, and `dojo.map()` will return the array, with any changes the function has made.

To put this in concrete terms, check out the following bit of code:

```
var a = [ 2, 4, 6, 8, 10 ];
a = dojo.map(a, function(item) {
  return item * 2;
});
alert(a);
```

What you'll see on your monitor is what you see in Figure 2-31.

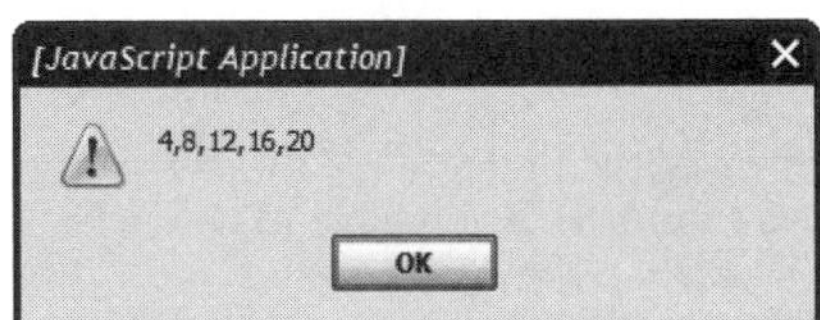

Figure 2-31. *ch2_map.htm result*

1. In case you don't recognize the reference, Delenn in a character from the television show *Babylon 5*. In my opinion, *Babylon 5* is the best sci-fi television series of all time, bar none. Some people agree with me very strongly; others disagree just as strongly. If you've seen the show, you have your own opinion already. If you haven't seen it, I highly recommend doing so, if for no other reason than to understand many of my references! For info, the Internet Movie Database (IMDb) shall provide: `www.imdb.com/title/tt0105946/`.

dojo.mixin()

The `dojo.mixin()` function always reminds me of that ice cream store, Cold Stone Creamery.[2] You see, aside from pumping you full of calories and saturated fat (mmmm, saturated fat!), this place lets you have *mix-ins*, which are all sorts of candy and other stuff that you can mix into the ice cream of your choice. You can come up with some crazy concoctions this way, and Dojo gives you the digital equivalent of that here (err, without the heart disease at a young age!).

Seeing is believing, so here you go:

```
function Class1() {
  this.firstName = "Robert";
}
function Class2() {
  this.lastName = "Redford";
}
var o = dojo.mixin(new Class1(), new Class2());
alert(dojo.toJson(o));
```

Simply put, all the properties of the second argument, an instance of `Class2` here, are added to the first argument, an instance of `Class1`, and the new object is returned. (Note that neither of the arguments—the objects, I mean—are affected by this. The returned object is a whole new animal.)

What, you don't believe me? Well, have a look at Figure 2-32 for proof.

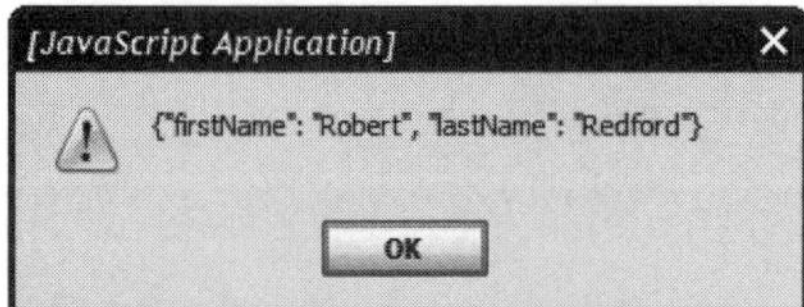

Figure 2-32. *ch2_mixin.htm result*

dojo.objectToQuery()

If you need to construct a query string from an array of name/value pairs, this is just the function you want. It takes care of URL encoding for you too, so there's little you have to worry about other than providing the data.

Here it is in action, both the code and Figure 2-33 showing what the function spits out for you:

---

2. For more information—most important, where one of these stores is near you because, believe me, you haven't had ice cream until you've had some Cold Stone—go here: `www.coldstonecreamery.com`. But, I am in no way, shape, or form responsible for your gym bill or doctor bill after you down tubs of this stuff!

```
alert(dojo.objectToQuery( {
  chipmunk1 : "Alvin Chipmunk",
  chipmunk2 : "Simon Chipmunk",
  chipmunk3 : "Theodore Chipmunk"
} ));
```

By the way, I have absolutely zero clue what the last names of the chipmunks actually are, and I'm frankly too lazy (and too scared how it might impact my macho persona) to look it up. In any case, I simply wanted to demonstrate how spaces get encoded properly to a value of %20; that's the important bit.

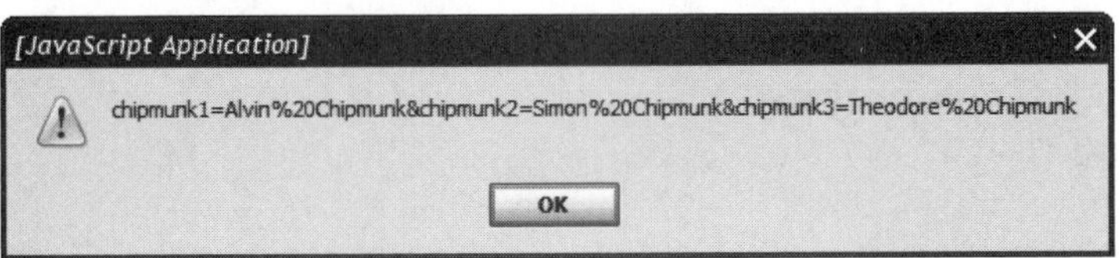

Figure 2-33. *ch2_objectToQuery.htm result*

dojo.place()

The `dojo.place()` function enables you to move DOM nodes around, if they already exist, or place new ones where you want.

Let's say we have three `<div>`s on our page, two of them together and another off on its own. Let's say we want take that loner `<div>` and stick it in-between the other two. The markup might look something like this:

```
<div id="node1">Node1</div>
<div id="node3">Node3</div>
<br><br>
<div id="node2">Node2</div>
```

Then, to move `node2` in-between `node1` and `node3`, we could do this:

```
dojo.place("node2", "node1", "after");
```

The display on the screen after that would be as follows:

```
Node1
Node2
Node3
```

The first argument is the node to move, the second is a node to position relative to, and the third is the position relative to the second argument. This third argument can also be a number that specifies the location in the second node's `childNodes` collection to insert the first node into. Other valid text values for this third argument include `before`, `after`, `first`, and `last` (`first` and `last` indicate that the node should be the first or the last, respectively, in the `childNodes` collection).

dojo.platformRequire()

The `dojo.platformRequire()` function is a brethren of the `dojo.require()` function that enables you to optionally include modules depending on what environment or platform the code is running in.

The `dojo.platformRequire()` function takes as an argument a "map" of arrays, where each element in the map is a value known to Dojo corresponding to a specific platform, plus two additional ones: `common`, which are modules that will always be loaded regardless of platform, and `default`, which will be loaded if none of the platform-specific lists are used.

By way of example, you could do this:

```
dojo.platformRequire({
  browser : [ "dojox.Button" ],
  common: [ "dojo.behavior", "dojo.currency" ],
  default: [ "dojo.AdapterRegistry" ],
});
```

This would load the DojoX button widget only when the code is running within a web browser. It would always load both `dojo.behavior` and `dojo.currency`, and would additionally load `dojo.AdapterRegistry` when not running in a browser.

dojo.query()

If you need to look up DOM nodes on your page by using CSS node selector support, and you need to do it efficiently, this function will be right up your alley. This function is similar to the `$$()` function in Prototype or `$()` in jQuery, if you happen to be familiar with either of those. It enables you to search the entire DOM tree, or just a subsection of it that you specify.

The `dojo.query()` function supports a large set of CSS3 selectors:

- Simple class selectors, such as `.myStyleClass`
- Selection by node type, such as `span` or `div`
- Descendant selectors
- Child element selectors (>)
- Style ID selectors, such as `#someID`
- Universal selector (*)
- Immediate predecessor sibling selector (~)
- Preceded-by-sibling selector (+)
- Attribute queries, including the following:
  - `[xxx]`: Check for existence of a selector
  - `[xxx='yyy']`: Find attribute with a given value
  - `[xxx~='yyy']`: Find attribute with matching value from list

    - [xxx^='yyy']: Find attribute with a value starting with a specified value
    - [xxx$='yyy']: Find attribute with a value ending with a specified value
    - [xxx*='yyy'] Find attribute with value matching substring
- Positional selection for first and last child (:first-child, :last-child)
- Empty content selector (:empty)
- Positional style calculations (:nth-child(n), :nth-child(2n+1))
- Positional selectors (:nth-child(even), :nth-child(odd))
- Negation pseudo-selectors (:not(...))

Moreover, you can combine these selectors in many varied and complex ways to get at just the elements you need.

As a simple example, take the following markup:

```
<body onLoad="testIt();">
  <div id="div1" class="myStyle"> </div>
  <div id="div2"> </div>
  <div id="parentDiv">
    <div id="div3" class="myStyle"> </div>
  </div>
</body>
```

Say we want to find all elements with a style class of myStyle. We can do this:

```
alert(dojo.query(".myStyle") + "\n" + dojo.query(".myStyle", "parentDiv"));
```

The result is the pop-up shown in Figure 2-34.

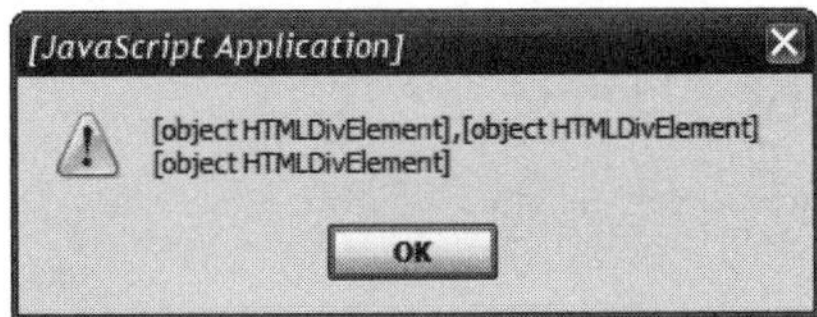

Figure 2-34. *ch2_query.htm result*

Here, I show the ability to scope the search to a specified sub-branch of the page's DOM tree, as shown with the second line of the alert().

dojo.queryToObject()

The dojo.queryToObject() function is the bizarro universe's evil twin of the dojo.objectToQuery() function. This one takes a string in the form of a query string and converts it to an object. With it, you can do things like this:

```
var s = dojo.objectToQuery({
  chipmunk1 : "Alvin Chipmunk",
  chipmunk2 : "Simon Chipmunk",
  chipmunk3 : "Theodore Chipmunk"
});
alert(dojo.toJson(dojo.queryToObject(s)));
```

Here I've used `dojo.objectToQuery()` to build the query string from an anonymous object. Then I take the resultant string and convert it to an object by using `dojo.queryToObject()`, and finally use our friendly neighborhood `dojo.toJson()` function to display the object in an `alert()`. The resultant `alert()` can be seen in Figure 2-35.

Figure 2-35. *ch2_queryToObject.htm result*

dojo.registerModulePath()

You didn't think all this packaging hotness was just for Dojo, did you? Well, guess what? It's not! You can in fact create your own packages and make them available via `dojo.require()` calls just the same as any part of Dojo!

How do you pull this off? Well, it begins with creating a file along the lines seen in Listing 2-1.

Listing 2-1. *myFunc.js*

```
if(!dojo._hasResource["dojo.customPackage.myFunc"]) {
  dojo._hasResource["dojo.customPackage,myFunc"] = true;
  dojo.provide("dojo.customPackage.myFunc");
  dojo.customPackage.myFunc = function() {
    alert("Thank you for calling myFunc!");
  }
}
```

Each JavaScript file that will be loaded via the `dojo.require()` mechanism must contain a `dojo.provide()` call. This registers with Dojo that the resource, the JavaScript file, has been loaded. Wrapped around this call is a check of the `_hasResource` collection that is a member of the `dojo` namespace. This is an object that each resource gets recorded in when it is loaded. So, we check to see whether my custom package has been loaded yet, and if not, we go ahead and register it having been loaded so that Dojo is aware of it.

After that, I add a new `customPackage` namespace to the `dojo` namespace, and within it add a function `myFunc()`.

Now, I can use this as shown in Listing 2-2.

Listing 2-2. *ch2_customPackageTest.htm*

```
<html>
  <head>
    <link rel="StyleSheet" type="text/css"
      href="js/dojo/dojo/resources/dojo.css">
    <script type="text/javascript">
      var djConfig = {
        baseScriptUri : "js/dojo/"
      };
    </script>
    <script type="text/javascript" src="js/dojo/dojo/dojo.js"></script>
    <script language="JavaScript" type="text/javascript">
      dojo.registerModulePath("dojo.customPackage", "../../..");
      dojo.require("dojo.customPackage.myFunc");
      dojo.customPackage.myFunc();
    </script>
  </head>
  <body></body>
</html>
```

Now you can see the call to `dojo.registerModulePath()`. The purpose of this call is to tell Dojo where to find the resource, the JavaScript file, for the `dojo.customPackage` code. The value you pass as the second argument is a path relative to the Dojo root. So here it's simply bringing us back up three levels to get us in the same directory as the HTML file, assuming you run this code from the directory structure provided in the download bundle.

After that I make a test call to `dojo.customPackage.myFunc()`, resulting in an `alert()` pop-up, just to prove everything worked as expected.

I should mention that if you put your source files in the directory structure of Dojo, you shouldn't even need to use `dojo.registerModulePath()`. This example is slightly contrived in that I wanted to demonstrate the function, so I put the JavaScript file alongside the HTML file, which you most likely wouldn't want to do. Keeping it in the same structure as all the Dojo packages that already exist probably makes more sense in "real life," so to speak.

dojo.requireIf()

Remember `dojo.require()`? Well, `dojo.requireIf()` is just an extended version that enables you to do conditional loading of modules. You pass into this function two arguments. The first is some expression that evaluates to a Boolean, and the second is the module name, just like you pass to `dojo.require()`. If the expression evaluates to `true`, the module will be loaded; otherwise, it won't be.

■ Note Of course, Dojo isn't responsible if your downstream code assumes that something is loaded that conditionally was not when using this function! In other words, be careful using `dojo.requireIf()` because you could relatively easily cause code to break if a module doesn't get loaded that your code otherwise expects to be.

---

dojo.setContext()

You should probably have noticed by now that most of the functions that do various lookups in the DOM work in global context by default. In other words, they reference the DOM and the global namespace of the page that contains them, depending on what they're looking up. You should also have noticed that many of those functions, maybe even most of them, allow you to optionally specify another scope, be it a subsection of the DOM, alternate namespace, or the context of an entirely different page (that is, in an IFrame).

With `dojo.setContext()`, you can globally set a new context for these lookups, saving you from having to specify it per call. The `dojo.global` and `dojo.doc` fields are modified as a result of using this function, and `dojo.body()` will get you a different object as well.

dojo.setObject()

With `dojo.setObject()`, you no longer need code like this:

```
if (!o) { o = { }; }
if (!o.names) { o.names = { }; }
o.names.firstName = "Mitch";
```

Instead, you can now do this:

```
dojo.setObject("person.names.firstName", "Mitch");
alert(dojo.toJson(person));
```

What you'll get from that is what you see in Figure 2-36.

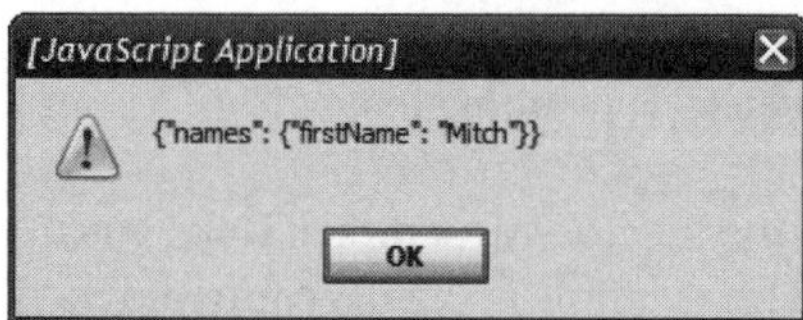

Figure 2-36. *ch2_setObject.htm result*

The `dojo.setObject()` function will add any intermediary objects to an existing object (if `person` was already an instance of some class) or will create the entire thing, as shown in this example. It doesn't get any handier than that!

dojo.setSelectable()

You know, this is an interesting one because, I have to admit, I wasn't even aware you could do this before I saw this function! As it turns out, elements on the page can be made unselectable, meaning you can't highlight them to copy the text. With this function, using

```
dojo.setSelectable('myDiv', false);
```

makes `<myDiv>` unselectable. This function deals with the cross-browser differences, and a quick glance at the source code of this function indicates that each browser pretty much handles things differently than the others, so I'm quite happy to not have to deal with those concerns!

dojo.some()

Let's say you have an array:

```
[ 1, 3, 5, 7, 9, 15 ]
```

Let's further say you want to check whether at least some of the elements in that array are greater than 6:

```
function isGreaterThanSix(val) {
  return val > 6;
}
```

You could then iterate over the array, calling `isGreaterThanSix()` for each element. If you get `true` back for any of them, the condition is met. But, that wouldn't be very Dojo-ish now would it? Well, try `dojo.some()` on for size:

```
alert(dojo.some(a, function(val) { return val > 6; }));
```

This nets you a `true` result, as seen in Figure 2-37.

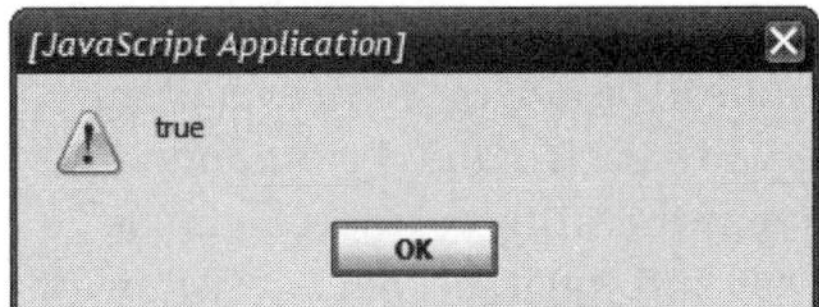

Figure 2-37. *ch2_some.htm result*

Change the value checked for in the function to, say, 22, and you get `false`.

dojo.stopEvent()

Event bubbling is the mechanism in a browser whereby a UI event "bubbles up" from the element that received the event until it is stopped.

Imagine a `<div>` inside another `<div>`. If both register an `onClick` handler, and the inner `<div>` is clicked, the `onClick` handler for that `<div>` will fire, and then the one for the containing `<div>` will fire, and so on through all the containing elements, until the top is reached, or the event is stopped.

So, how do you stop an event? Well, if you're guessing `dojo.stopEvent()` does so, you'd be 100 percent right!

You pass this function either the event object passed to the event handler, or nothing in the case of IE, where it automatically grabs the event object off the window object.

To see it in action, imagine taking this markup:

```
<body onLoad="setup();">
  <div id="outerDiv" style="background-color:#ff0000;width:100px;height:100px;">
     
    <div id="innerDiv" style="background-color:#00ff00;width:50px;height:40px;">
       
    </div>
```

```
  </div>
  <br><br>
  <div id="divOutput" style="width:200px;height:200px;"> </div>
</body>
```

Then imagine this code:

```
function setup() {
  dojo.byId("outerDiv").onclick = doOuterClick;
  dojo.byId("innerDiv").onclick = doInnerClick;
}
function doOuterClick(e) {
  dojo.byId("divOutput").innerHTML += "doOuterClick()<br>";
}
function doInnerClick(e) {
  dojo.byId("divOutput").innerHTML += "doInnerClick()<br>";
  dojo.stopEvent(e);
}
```

The `setup()` function is called `onLoad` to attach the event handlers (needed to be able to pass the event object into the event handler functions in non-IE browsers). Each event handler just writes some content out to the screen to indicate when each of the corresponding events fire. Click the inner green `<div>` and you'll see that only the string `doInnerClick()` is written out. Now, go comment out the `dojo.stopEvent()` call and you'll see that now when the green `<div>` is clicked, `doInnerClick()` is written out, followed immediately by `doOuterClick()`. Note that in the case of IE, no event object is passed in, so passing the argument e is the same as passing null, so the functions work cross-browser with no change.

dojo.style()

This function enables you to both get and set style attributes on a DOM node in a clean, concise way. The first argument is always the DOM node (or ID of the node) to work with. Following that is either one or two arguments. If only one, it is the name of the attribute to retrieve. If two, then the first is the attribute to set, and the second is the value to set.

If you want to see it in action, here you go:

```
alert(dojo.style("myDiv", "color"));
dojo.style("myDiv", "color", "#0000ff");
```

Say you had this markup on the page:

```
<div id="myDiv" style="color:#ff0000;">I am myDiv</div>
```

Executing that code gives you the pop-up in Figure 2-38, and the color of the test in the `<div>` changes to blue after the second line executes.

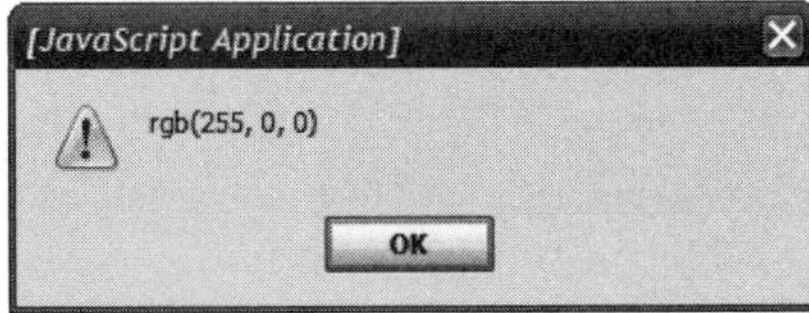

Figure 2-38. *ch2_style.htm result*

dojo.toggleClass()

The `dojo.toggleClass()` function does exactly what it says: it toggles whether a style class is applied to a specified DOM node or not. You pass it a reference to the DOM node, or the ID of the node, and then the name of a style class. If the node already has the style applied, it is removed, and if the node doesn't yet have the style applied, it is applied. Optionally you can pass a third argument that when `true` will apply the style either way, and when `false` will remove it either way.

So, for example:

```
dojo.toggleClass("myDiv", "myClass");
alert("Should now be red");
dojo.toggleClass("myDiv", "myClass");
alert("Should now NOT be red");
dojo.toggleClass("myDiv", "myClass", true);
alert("Should now be red");
dojo.toggleClass("myDiv", "myClass", false);
alert("Should now NOT be red");
```

This yields four `alert()` pop-ups (which I'm going to forego showing here to save a little space). The text on the page changes from red to black, to red again, and then to black again, with the pop-ups in-between each change so you can see it. Because the target `<div>` starts off with no style, the first call to `dojo.toggleClass()` applies it, the second removes it, the third forcibly applies it, and the fourth forcibly removes it.

dojo.toJson()

The `dojo.toJson()` function is a very handy function, especially during debugging. Very simply, it takes a given object and spits out JSON representing the object. It optionally can print the JSON in "pretty" format. (I personally find the non-pretty format to be prettier; your mileage may vary). Check out this code:

```
function MyClass() {
  this.salary = 10000000;
  this.age = 34;
  this.isReality = false;
}
alert(dojo.toJson(new MyClass(), true));
```

The second parameter (true here) tells Dojo to "pretty-print" the JSON, and you can see the results in Figure 2-39.

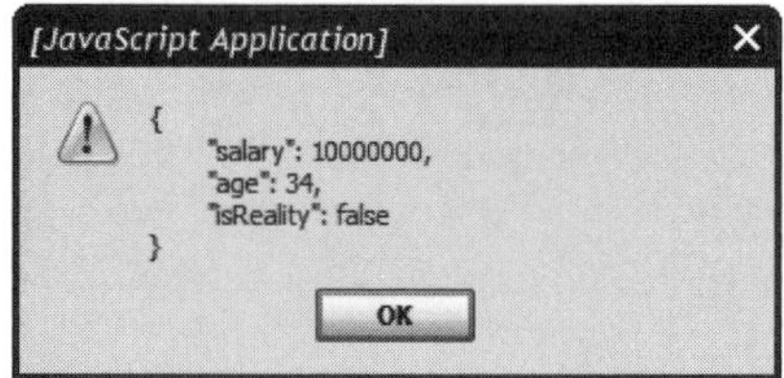

Figure 2-39. *ch2_toJson.htm result*

The only real difference between pretty-printing and, err, ugly-printing, I suppose, is the indenting of objects, arrays, and the placement of brackets.

You will recognize that this is very similar to the `dojo.formToJson()` function you saw earlier, but this works generically for virtually any object.

dojo.trim()

This function trims whitespace from the beginning and end of a string. Later I describe the `dojo.string.trim()` function, which is identical. (I'm frankly not sure why there are two versions of the same thing, but be that as it may.)

dojo.unloaded()

This function is what's called when the environment is being destroyed, usually corresponding to the browser being closed, or the page being navigated away from. This is internally what you're "hooking into," so to speak, when you use `dojo.addOnUnload()` as described previously. There's no need to demonstrate anything here because `dojo.addOnUnload()` is really what you should use (or `dojo.connect()` alternatively, also described previously).

dojo.xhrDelete(), dojo.xhrGet(), dojo.xhrPost(), and dojo.xhrPut()

What we have here is a batch of functions that are the gateway to the world of Ajax in Dojo. All of them do the same basic thing, but they differ in what HTTP method will be used to make the Ajax request.

FOR THOSE WHOSE HOME IS UNDER A ROCK

Ajax is a programming technique that allows for *partial-page refreshes*, meaning portions of the web page that a user is viewing in a browser can be updated without having to ask the server for a whole new page to display. This enables you to have a much richer client-like application because you can begin to make service-oriented requests to your server, which then returns just data, not markup, and your client-side code is then completely responsible for the presentation of that data. You can do all of that without the typical web application paradigm of page ➤ request ➤ next page, which tends to be a lesser user experience in terms of speed, look, feel, and functionality.

Ajax leads to the "single-page" architecture, where a single JSP, PHP, ASP, or plain HTML page provides the full code of your application. (You're of course pulling in a bunch of resources when that page is served, such as JavaScript, images, and style sheets, but it's essentially a single page.) Everything that happens from that point on is controlled (to some extent) by that client-side code, with the server just providing updated data when needed.

Ajax, which stands for *Asynchronous JavaScript and XML*, doesn't have to be asynchronous at all (but nearly always is), doesn't have to use JavaScript (but nearly always does), and doesn't have to use XML (frequently, maybe even mostly nowadays, it doesn't). Ajax has been around for a while now, not even counting how long it's been around before it was even called Ajax (it's nothing new, it's just a new name and a refinement of some techniques that have been around for a while). Ajax is the basis for what we now call rich Internet applications (RIAs). Or, as I like to put it, web applications that don't suck!

Each of these functions accepts a single argument that is an object specifying several optional elements (and one required) that tell Dojo what it needs to make the call for you. A rundown of those elements is presented in Table 2-1.

Table 2-1. *Elements within the Second Argument Object to the dojo.xhr() Function*

Attribute	Description
`content`	This is an object that will be turned into a name/value pair string.
`error`	The callback function to call when an error occurs.
`form`	A reference to a `<form>` element, which will be serialized much as the object for the content element is.
`handleAs`	This specifies what to handle the response as. Valid values are `text` (this the default), `json`, `json-comment-optional`, `json-comment-filtered`, `javascript`, and `xml`.
`headers`	This is an object, just like for the `content` element, that specifies headers to set on the request.
`load`	This is a reference to the callback function to call when the response returns. This function will be passed the response from the server.
`preventCache`	If set to `true`, a `dojo.preventCache` parameter is sent in the request with a value, a timestamp to be more precise, that therefore changes with each request. This attribute is most relevant with `GET` requests because they can be cached by the browser; without setting `preventCache` to `true`, your Ajax requests wouldn't always go to the server and would instead be serviced out of the local cache, which is almost certainly not what you want. (Note that this is never a problem for `POST` requests, which are never cached.)
`sync`	Set to `true` to make the call synchronously, which means all activity in the browser, including JavaScript execution, is blocked until the call returns. This defaults to `false`, making the call asynchronously.
`timeout`	This is the number of milliseconds to wait for the response. If the time elapses with no response, the error callback is called.
`url`	This is the only required element, and it is the URL to contact.

As you can see, only the `url` element is required. Everything else is completely optional. So, how do you use these functions? Well, take a look at Listing 2-3.

Listing 2-3. *ch2_xhr.htm*

```
<html>
  <head>
    <link rel="StyleSheet" type="text/css"
      href="js/dojo/dojo/resources/dojo.css">
    <script type="text/javascript">
      var djConfig = {
        baseScriptUri : "js/dojo/"
      };
    </script>
    <script type="text/javascript" src="js/dojo/dojo/dojo.js"></script>
    <script>
      function doAjax() {
        dojo.xhrGet({ url : "ch2_xhrMockServer.htm",
        content : { var1 : "val1", var2 : "val2" },
          load : function(resp) {
            var o = dojo.fromJson(resp);
            dojo.byId("ajaxResponse").innerHTML = "response1 = " +
              o.response1 + "<br>response2 = " + o.response2;
          }
        });
      }
    </script>
  </head>
  <body onLoad="">
    <input type="button" value="Click for Ajax" onClick="doAjax();">
    <br>
    <div id="ajaxResponse"></div>
  </body>
</html>
```

When you load this code in your browser, you'll have a plain page with nothing but a button on it. After resisting the urge to press the shiny button for a few seconds, click it, and you will see what you see here in Figure 2-40.

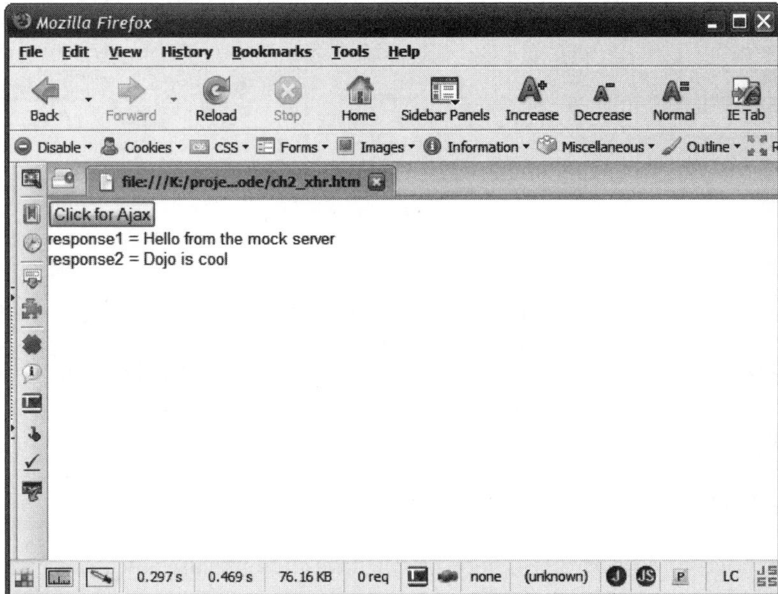

Figure 2-40. *ch2_xhr.htm result*

As you can see, some response text has been inserted into the DOM and is now visible. This was done without refreshing the whole page, so Ajax and Dojo have done their jobs nicely for us.

Now, you may be wondering where the response came from. There doesn't appear to be any server here to have served the response, and that is accurate. What I've done is used a technique known as the *mock server technique*. Basically, this is a fancy way of saying we have an HTML document in the same directory as the HTML document making the Ajax request, playing the part of the server. Assuming you've downloaded the source code for this book, you'll find a file named `ch2_xhrMockServer.htm`, and it's nothing but the following:

```
{ response1 : "Hello from the mock server", response2 : "Dojo is cool" }
```

Yes, that's literally all there is in that file. So, Dojo makes the Ajax request for us, and as you can see from the code, the URL specified is our mock server HTML file. The browser retrieves that file, and it becomes the response to the Ajax request. We then use the `dojo.fromJson()` function to get an object from the response from our "server" and then just pull out the values we're interested in and display them on the page.

The other interesting thing to note here is what the request going across the wire looks like. For that, let's see what Firebug shows us when we click the button, which you can see for yourself in Figure 2-41.

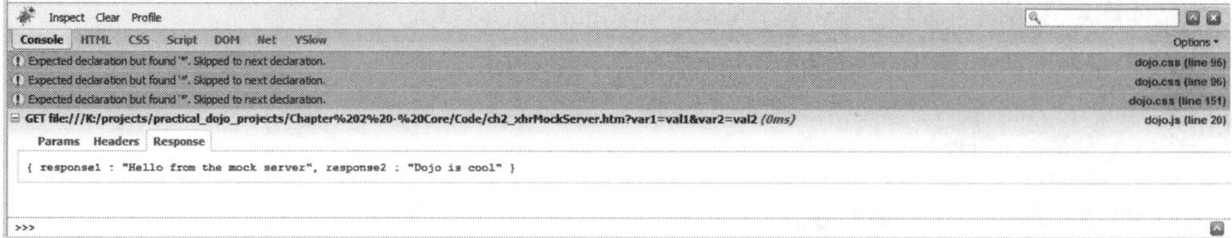

Figure 2-41. *The request, as seen in Firebug*

You can plainly see the two values, var1 and var2, which were added as query string parameters. You can also see the response as it was presented to Dojo.

I could have saved a step here, by the way, if I had passed handleAs:"json" in the call. I then would not have had to make the dojo.fromJson() call myself because the argument passed to my load callback would have been an object equivalent to that returned by dojo.fromJson(). You would also note in that case a message in Firebug saying I should probably use the appropriate Multipurpose Internet Mail Extension (MIME) type to avoid security considerations. My, now, isn't Dojo just *so* helpful?

Now, even though I've used dojo.xhrGet() here, I could have chosen to use any of the other methods; dojo.xhrPost() would have made some sense. This becomes useful especially in RESTful applications where the HTTP method itself has specific meaning to the server process. The point, though, is that the function call is pretty much identical for all of them.

GETTING GOOD REST IS HEALTHY!

REST, which stands for *Representational State Transfer*, is a software architect approach specifically designed for systems that are based around the concept of distributed hypermedia (which is a complicated way of saying the World Wide Web: a collection of documents hyperlinked together).

A RESTful application takes the tact that every single thing that can be retrieved from a server is a resource that is uniquely addressable via a Universal Resource Identifier, or URI. You can do only a few key things with resources: write them, read them, delete them, update them. In other words, you can CRUD them, which means Create, Read, Update, or Delete them. The HTTP methods themselves tells the server what you're doing: PUT means you are creating, GET means you are reading, POST means you are updating, and DELETE literally means you are deleting. (There's some room for using these a little differently in some implementations, and other methods are sometimes employed too, but we're talking high-level concepts here, not implementation-level specific details.)

If this sounds like it's nothing new, that's because it really isn't: the web itself is an example of such an architecture. Some argue that REST as we know it today is an extension of that for various reasons (the use of the HTTP methods specifically is a big one), but it's still an architecture based around URIs, so fundamentally it's really not anything too new.

Properties

Through the `dojo` namespace, you have access to a wealth of information about Dojo, the environment the script is running in, and many other things, all provided by default by Dojo without you having to do any extra work. In this section, I'll go through them so you can get a good feel for what's available. I provide only some limited example code here because these are pretty much "read 'em and go" kinds of things, as all data fields of an object are.

dojo.baseUrl

The `dojo.baseUrl` property tells you the relative path to the root where Dojo is located. This should match the value you set in `djConfig`, if any, or the default otherwise.

dojo.config

The `dojo.config` property is the `djConfig` object that you created before importing `dojo.js` onto the page, or a default version if you've provided no options.

dojo.doc

The `dojo.doc` property is simply an alias for the document object that you already know and love. The API documentation for this states, "Refer to `dojo.doc` rather than referring to `window.document` to ensure that your code runs correctly in managed contexts." I admit I'm not completely sure what that means, but my read on it is that in some situations, perhaps when your code isn't running within the context of a browser, using `dojo.doc` will ensure that your code still works, even if the `document` object isn't defined. I admit that's largely a guess on my part, however. The bottom line is that `dojo.doc` and `window.document` (or just plain `document`) should generally be equivalent, and if using `dojo.doc` provides some sort of additional safety net in some circumstance down the road, that seems like a good idea to me and shouldn't hurt anything in any case.

dojo.global

The `dojo.global` property is an alias for the global namespace, otherwise known as the `window` object when running inside a browser environment. As is the case with many of the aliases Dojo provides for various standard browser objects, this one enables you to stay entirely within the Dojo API when writing your code.

dojo.isBrowser

This property is set to `true` if the application is running within a web browser and the `window` object is defined. You might see this set to `false` if, for instance, you rendered the HTML in memory with the intent of outputting it to a PDF—in which case it wouldn't be rendered in a browser (although it seems a reasonable assumption that JavaScript wouldn't be available in such a case, so this property wouldn't even be set to check—but I assume this serves a purpose in some cases for some people and I further assume there are in fact cases where JavaScript would be available too!).

dojo.isFF

The `dojo.isFF` property is set to a numeric value greater than zero if the application is running Firefox. The value indicates which version of Firefox it's running in. For instance:

```
if (dojo.isFF == 1.5 || dojo.isFF == 2 || dojo.isFF = 3) {
  alert("Running in FF 1.5, 2 or 3");
}
```

dojo.isGears

This property will be set to `true` if the client has Gears installed, `false` if not. This is nice because it keeps you from having to do the check yourself; it's already done for you and the answer is available here.

dojo.isIE

This property is set to a numeric value greater than zero if the application is running in Internet Explorer on a PC. The value indicates which version of IE the application is running in. For instance:

```
if (dojo.isIE == 7) {
  alert("Running in IE 7");
}
```

dojo.isKhtml

This property is set to a numeric value greater than zero if the application is running in a browser using the KHTML render engine. The value returned corresponds to a major version number.

The KHTML engine is an HTML layout engine developed by the KDE Linux desktop project. It is the engine that powers the Konquerer web browser. It is also the basis for the WebKit render engine, which is a fork of KHTML developed by Apple and used in the Safari browser. As such, this property is set to a nonzero value for current versions of Safari (one could imagine this not being the case in the future, but for now it is the case).

As an example, you could do this:

```
if (dojo.isKhtml != 0) {
  alert("Browser uses KHTML layout engine (or derived engine)");
}
```

dojo.isMozilla

This property will tell you whether you're running in a Mozilla-based browser, including Firefox and SeaMonkey. Like all the others, it returns a value greater than zero corresponding to the major version number of the browser, or zero if not running within Mozilla. Note that Firefox will return a nonzero value here, in addition to the value set in `dojo.isFF`.

At this point, I'm going to stop showing examples of these `is*` functions because, frankly, I think you get the idea!

dojo.isOpera

If you aren't seeing a pattern yet, you aren't paying attention! Like all the other browser identification properties, this one returns zero if the browser isn't Opera, or a value greater than zero if it is, with that value indicating the major version number detected.

dojo.isQuirks

This property tells you whether the browser is currently in quirks mode.

■ **Note** *Quirks mode* is a special mode that most browsers support that is for maintaining backward compatibility of older pages. Most modern browsers can render pages adhering to the World Wide Web Consortium (W3C) and Internet Engineering Task Force (IETF) standards, and that's generally what you want to develop to. Older pages, however, frequently aren't standards-compliant. To ensure that these pages render properly, you can tell the browser to render them in quirks mode, which attempts to emulate the behavior of older browsers (in which, presumably, the older page renders fine).

---

dojo.isRhino

This property indicates whether the JavaScript is executing in the Rhino environment. (Rhino is a JavaScript interpreter in Java.)

dojo.isSafari

This is another browser detection property. This one is interesting because it detects Safari, which includes the popular iPhone browser. Once again, zero indicates that the browser is not Safari; nonzero indicates it is and what version is being used.

dojo.isSpidermonkey

SpiderMonkey is Mozilla's implementation of JavaScript in the C language, and the `dojo.isSpidermonkey` property enables you to determine whether your code is running in such an environment. This is useful if you have reason to suspect that your application is running in some sort of embedded environment using SpiderMonkey, in which case you may need to branch to some alternate code in some situations. This property provides a mechanism to determine that.

dojo.jaxer

This property will tell you whether your code is running in Jaxer. Jaxer is a product by Aptana that bills itself as the "world's first true Ajax server." In short, Jaxer takes Firefox and makes it "headless" and runs it on the server, on top of Apache. The idea is to enable you to write your server-side code in JavaScript by using the same techniques, libraries, and so forth as you do on the client. It's not simply a matter of replacing your server-side code with JavaScript, although that's an attractive proposition to many on its own. No, what Jaxer does is takes the next step by providing the mechanism to serialize the DOM created server-side and hand it back to the client.

This enables you to write code that runs on both sides of the network connection, and do so seamlessly. You can do things like manipulate the client DOM from the server side, for example. The key point is that it doesn't stop you from using Dojo, or any other library you like, but now you can use it on the server side too. This `dojo.jaxer` property enables you to know whether that's the case, and possibly branch your code accordingly.

■Note For more information on Jaxer, check out `www.aptana.com/jaxer`. You also might want to have a look at this blog entry from John Resig, famous creator of the jQuery library: `http://ejohn.org/blog/server-side-javascript-with-jaxer`.

---

dojo.keys

The `dojo.keys` property has within it a set of constants that represent key values. For instance, say you have a text field and you want to stop the user from using Backspace. (Why you'd want to do that, I'm not sure, but let's assume you hate your users for just a moment!) You could do this:

```
<html>
  <head>
    <link rel="StyleSheet" type="text/css"
      href="js/dojo/dojo/resources/dojo.css">
    <script type="text/javascript">
      var djConfig = {
        baseScriptUri : "js/dojo/"
      };
    </script>
    <script type="text/javascript" src="js/dojo/dojo/dojo.js"></script>
    <script language="JavaScript" type="text/javascript">
      function noBackspace(e) {
        var keyNum = null;
        if (dojo.isIE != 0) {
          keyNum = window.event.keyCode;
        } else {
          keyNum = e.which;
        }
        if (keyNum == dojo.keys.BACKSPACE) {
          return false;
        } else {
          return true;
        }
      }
    </script>
  </head>
  <body>
```

```
    <input type="text" id="theField" onKeyDown="return noBackspace(event);">
  </body>
</html>
```

When this code is run, your user will not be able to hit Backspace. You can see a couple of things in play here. First, the use of `isIE` can be seen, used to branch the code to get access to the event information, because IE differs from virtually every other browser out there in this regard (the event information is carried in the `window.event` object, whereas most other browsers pass the object into the method, and the actual attribute is different, `keyCode` for IE and `which` for others). Then, the `dojo.keys.BACKSPACE` value is used to determine when that key is pressed.

dojo.locale

This is simply the locale, as defined by Dojo. This is a read-only value and should match the locale as set by the browser, barring any weird goings-on!

dojo.OpenAjax

```
dojo.require("dojo.OpenAjax");
```

Unlike most of the other properties here, this one doesn't tell you something; it provides you something: an instance of the OpenAjax hub.

The OpenAjax hub is a product of the OpenAjax Alliance, which seeks to, among other things, help ensure interoperability of the various client-side libraries out there. The hub is their first concrete product and it is a publish-subscribe bus that libraries (and your own code!) can use to communicate with one another in an event-driven, low-coupling manner. For instance, you can do the following:

```
OpenAjax.hub.subscribe("myMessage", SomeFunction);
```

Then, later on, you can do this:

```
OpenAjax.hub.publish("myMessage", anObject);
```

When that `publish()` function is called, `SomeFunction` will be called and it will be passed the object `anObject`. What's more, *any* function subscribed in such a way will be called. This means, for instance, that if you make an Ajax call, you can publish a message in the Ajax callback function. If there were ten widgets on the screen, all with an `update()` method that was subscribed to the message (which you can name anything you wish by the way; it's an identifier that's meaningful to your code), then those ten `update()` methods would be called, and passed the return from the Ajax call, assuming that was the object you passed to the `publish()` function.

In short, `dojo.OpenAjax` gives you the equivalent of `OpenAjax` seen in those two lines of code. You don't have to worry about instantiating it yourself; it's just there for you to use. Note that you must have a `dojo.require()` statement to make use of this because there is external code Dojo needs to pull in (*external* in this case meaning code outside `dojo.js`, not code from the Internet or anything like that).

dojo.version

As you probably quite reasonably assume, this property gives you the version of Dojo that is running. For instance, in Figure 2-42 you can see the value in the `alert()` pop-up for the version of Dojo that was used for the code throughout this book.

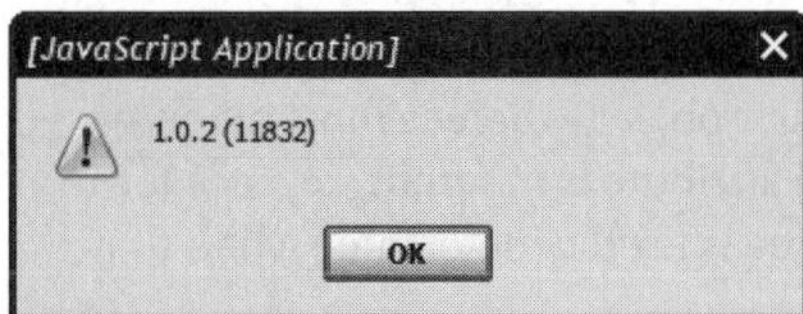

Figure 2-42. *Displaying the dojo.version property via alert()*

dojo.back

One of the biggest problems when writing RIAs that are constructed of a single page and then dynamically load new content via Ajax is that the typical function of the browser's Back and Forward buttons is broken. For example, if you load page A, which happens to be a single HTML page, and you never leave that page but instead reload parts of it (perhaps even the whole content as seen by the user) via Ajax, then when the user clicks back, she will be transported to the last page she visited. The problem is that the user likely expects Back to take her to some previous state of the current application, which is more logical and certainly more user-friendly.

Usually, implementing this functionality isn't the most trivial JavaScript coding one can do, but Dojo provides an elegant mechanism for dealing with this, and all of it is housed within the `dojo.back` namespace.

Functions

Three functions are pretty much all you need to use this powerful feature of Dojo. I'm going to demonstrate them all at once because it's much easier to understand them seen as a single unit in a single example.

dojo.back.addToHistory(), dojo.back.init(), and dojo.back.setInitialState()

```
dojo.require("dojo.back");
```

Okay, so here's the basic premise: to begin with, you call `dojo.back.init()` to get some internal data structures ready. This, interestingly enough, has to be done within the `<body>` of the document to get around some bug in IE. (I couldn't find information on what the bug was, but I'm just as happy to not know!)

Each time your application enters a new state that the user might want to use the Back or Forward buttons to get to again, you make a call to the `dojo.back.addToHistory()` method. This function call takes a single argument, an object with a couple of possible members. One, `back`, is a function that is to be called when the Back button is clicked. Another, `forward`, is the same thing but for the Forward button. Finally is `changeUrl`, which is a Boolean. When `true`, the URL seen in the address box of the browser will have a special code appended to it. More precisely, a unique hash of the URL is created and appended as an internal link location. This is important because it means the user can now bookmark that particular state in your application. When he chooses the bookmark later, assuming your application is smart enough to look for that location value and restore the application to that state, he will be right back where he left off.

Last is the dojo.back.setInitialState() function, which takes the same sort of argument as dojo.back.addToHistory(), but applies specifically to the initial state of the application. My own personal expectation is that this is typically used to deal with that situation where the Back button will cause the user to leave your site, so you may want to alert your users about losing information, or take the opportunity to save it (whatever you need to do).

Now, that explanation is all fine and dandy, but it may not make a ton of sense, so have a look at some code to bring it all into focus, specifically that seen in Listing 2-4.

Listing 2-4. *ch2_back.htm Example*

```
<html>
  <head>
    <link rel="StyleSheet" type="text/css"
      href="js/dojo/dojo/resources/dojo.css">
    <script type="text/javascript">
      var djConfig = {
        baseScriptUri : "js/dojo/"
      };
    </script>
    <script type="text/javascript" src="js/dojo/dojo/dojo.js"></script>
    <script>
      dojo.require("dojo.back");
      dojo.back.setInitialState({
        back : function() { alert("about to leave application") }
      });
      var content = [
        "I am some content (app state 1)",
        "I am some other content (app state 2)",
        "I am yet other content (app state 3)"
      ];
      function gotoContent(inNum) {
        var dc = dojo.byId("divContent");
        dc.innerHTML = content[inNum - 1];
        dojo.back.addToHistory({
          num : inNum, changeUrl : true, back : function() {
            dojo.byId("divContent").innerHTML = content[this.num - 1];
          }
        });
      }
    </script>
  </head>
  <body>
    <script>dojo.back.init();</script>
    <div id="divContent"
```

```
      style="width:300px;height:100px;border:1px solid #000000">
      Hello, welcome to my application!
    </div>
    <br>
    <input type="button" value="Goto Content 1" onClick="gotoContent(1);"> 
    <input type="button" value="Goto Content 2" onClick="gotoContent(2);"> 
    <input type="button" value="Goto Content 3" onClick="gotoContent(3);"> 
  </body>
</html>
```

It will be especially important for you to see this in action, so if you haven't already done so, please download the source code bundle for this book as described previously. Open the directory for Chapter 2 and then locate the `ch2_back.htm` file in the code directory.

When you load this file in your browser, you'll see a simple display with a box and three buttons below it. Clicking any of the buttons will display different content in the box. This changing content corresponds to different states of the application. Now, click the buttons a couple of times and notice that the page isn't reloading. However, notice that after each button click, the URL is different, specifically the value after the hash mark. Now, click back a few times. You should notice that the content changes to the previous content each time, but the page still does not reload. When you get to the point where you hit the initial state again, you should see an `alert()` saying you are about to leave the application.

Now, to explain how this code works: You'll notice the `dojo.back.init()` in the `<body>` as previously mentioned. Up in the `<head>`, in the last `<script>` block specifically, you'll see a call to `dojo.back.setInitialState()`, and you can plainly see the `alert()` assigned to the `back` attribute of the object.

Now, every time one of the three buttons is clicked, `gotoContent()` is called with a number passed into it that is used as an index into the `content` array to retrieve from that array the content to be displayed. The `gotoContent()` function simply updated the `innerHTML` of the `divContent` `<div>`. In addition, it makes a call to `dojo.back.addToHistory()`. The object passed contains a `back` element, which is a function that sets the content of the `<div>` once again, but this time it sets it to the content corresponding to the `num` value stored within it.

In other words, each time the content changes (each time the application state changes), a history record is added to the stack of history records maintained by the `dojo.back` code. This record contains the content that applies to that state. Each time Back is clicked, the last item on the stack is popped off and the function referenced by the `back` element is called, and this function restores the appropriate content.

You can do whatever you like when Back is clicked; that's up to you. Handling Forward would work in much the same way, but I chose to leave the example a little simpler and just handle Back.

As you can see, it's a powerful mechanism that is extremely easy to use.

dojo.behavior

The `dojo.behavior` namespace is concerned with attaching behaviors, which you can for the most part think of as event handlers, to elements. It enables you to do this by creating a collection of behaviors to attach, and then attaching them all in one shot.

Functions

The `dojo.behavior` namespace is quite sparse and contains only two functions, `dojo.behavior.add()` and `dojo.behavior.apply()`.

dojo.behavior.add()

```
dojo.require("dojo.behavior");
```

You begin by creating a behavior object, which describes the behavior you wish to attach. These can come in a variety of forms, based on element ID, class name, and so forth. This object also includes a special found handler, which is called immediately when a matching element in the DOM is found to attach behaviors to.

So, to use this function, you write code along these lines:

```
dojo.behavior.add({
  "#myDiv" : {
    found : function (elem) {
      alert("Found the div: " + elem);
    },
    onmouseover: function (evt) {
      alert("onMouseOver fired");
    },
    onmouseout: function (evt) {
      alert("onMouseOut fired");
    }
  }
});
```

You can call this function as many times as you want. The behaviors are added to the collection each time. When the time is right, `dojo.behavior.apply()` is used.

dojo.behavior.apply()

```
dojo.require("dojo.behavior");
```

After you've used `dojo.behavior.add()` to "collect" one or more behaviors, you use this method to add them to the elements in the DOM, like so:

```
dojo.behavior.apply();
```

After this is done, the events fire and are handled just like any other. For instance, in Figure 2-43 you can see the result of executing a test of this with the preceding code.

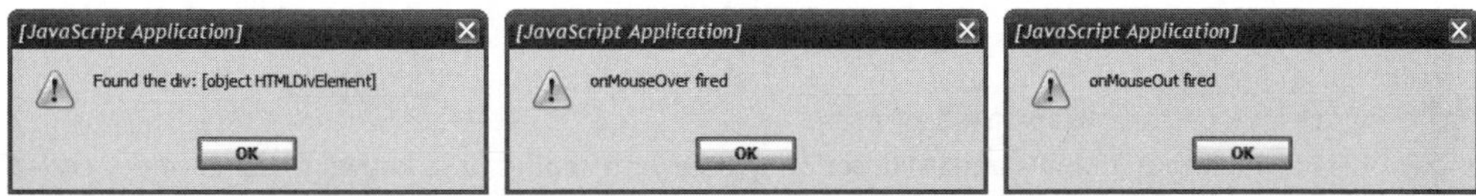

Figure 2-43. *ch2_behavior.htm result*

The first `alert()` you see fires as soon as `dojo.behavior.apply()` is called, or more precisely, when the <div> with the ID of `myDiv` is found. The second `alert()` occurs when you hover over the red <div> that the example shows, and the third occurs when the mouse pointer leaves the <div>.

dojo.cldr

CLDR stands for *Common Locale Data Repository*, and this namespace, so named, is a transformation of some components from the Unicode CLDR project, which describes itself as "... (providing) key building blocks for software to support the world's languages. CLDR is by far the largest and most extensive standard repository of locale data. This data is used by a wide spectrum of companies for their software internationalization and localization: adapting software to the conventions of different languages for such common software tasks as formatting of dates, times, time zones, numbers, and currency values; sorting text; choosing languages or countries by name; and many others."

Functions

Three functions are available to us in this namespace, all tying into the theme of dealing with the world's languages.

dojo.cldr.monetary.getData()

```
dojo.require("dojo.cldr.monetary");
```

The `getData()` method provides a way to get formatting information about a given ISO 4217[3] currency code. This method returns an object with two properties: `places` indicates the number of decimal places present in the currency format, and `round` indicates the number of places the currency should be rounded to.

For example, to get information about the Yen, Japan's currency, call the following:

```
var o = dojo.cldr.monetary.getData("JPY");
var s = "";
for (var f in o) {
  s += f + "=" + o[f] + ",";
}
alert(s);
```

The result of executing this code is seen in Figure 2-44.

---

3. ISO 4217 is the international standard describing three-letter codes (also known as the currency code) to define the names of currencies established by the International Organization for Standardization (ISO).

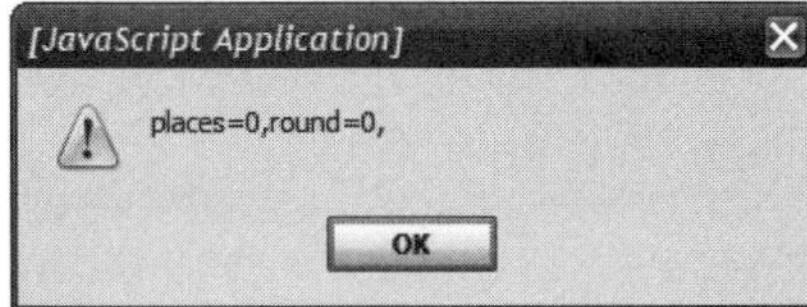

Figure 2-44. *ch2_monetaryGetData.htm result*

dojo.cldr.supplemental.getFirstDayOfWeek()

```
dojo.require("dojo.cldr.supplemental");
```

The `getFirstDayOfWeek()` method can tell you what the first day of the week is, as used by the machine's local Gregorian calendar. The value it gives you is a zero-based index value, 0 for Sunday, 1 for Monday. You can optionally supply this method with a locale to get information for a locale other than that of the machine.

To see it in action you can do this:

```
alert(dojo.cldr.supplemental.getFirstDayOfWeek("us");
```

The pop-up in Figure 2-45 is the result.

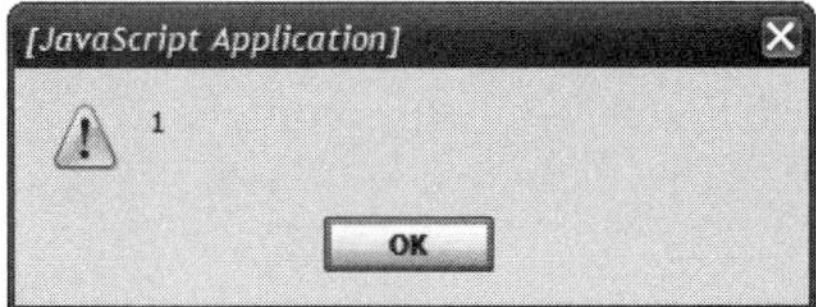

Figure 2-45. *ch2_supplementalGetFirstDayOfWeek.htm result*

dojo.cldr.supplemental.getWeekend()

```
dojo.require("dojo.cldr.supplemental");
```

The `getWeekend()` method returns an object with two properties: `start`, which is the zero-based index of the first day of the weekend, and `end`, which is the zero-based index of the last day of the weekend. Like `getFirstDayOfWeek()`, you can optionally feed this method a locale to get information for.

The following shows how to use `getWeekend()`:

```
var o = dojo.cldr.supplemental.getWeekend("us");
var s = "";
for (var f in o) {
  s += f + "=" + o[f] + ",";
}
alert(s);
```

And of course, Figure 2-46 shows what you see when this code is run.

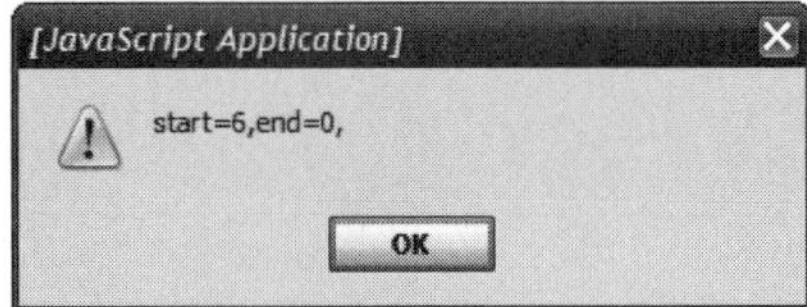

Figure 2-46. *ch2_supplementalGetWeekend.htm result*

dojo.colors

The `dojo.colors` namespace contains a utility functional for working with. . . wait for it. . . *colors*!

Functions

There isn't a whole lot of functionality currently in this namespace. In fact, there is only a single function as of this writing.

dojo.colors.makeGrey()

```
dojo.require("dojo.colors");
```

This function returns a `dojo.Color` object, which is always a grayscale color based on the value you pass in, optionally using an alpha value. This is definitely easier to comprehend in code, so here's an example:

```
alert(dojo.colors.makeGrey(150));
```

The `dojo.Color` object that is returned can be shown via `alert()`, and what you see on the screen is what you see in Figure 2-47.

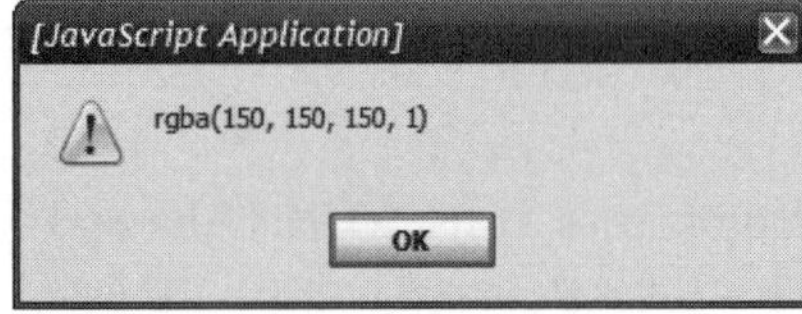

Figure 2-47. *ch2_colorsMakeGrey.htm result*

As you can see, the value passed in simply becomes the red, green, and blue value of the color, which is how it becomes a shade of gray.

dojo.currency

This namespace includes functionality for formatting and parsing currency values with internationalization support built in.

Functions

This namespace consists of nothing but a couple of functions, so it won't take too long to examine.

dojo.currency.format()

```
dojo.require("dojo.currency");
```

When you have a number, and you want to format it with a localized pattern and produce a string from it, this is the function you want to use.

Here's a simple example:

```
alert(dojo.currency.format(123456789.536, null));
```

On my system, which is an English version of Windows, the result is the pop-up shown in Figure 2-48.

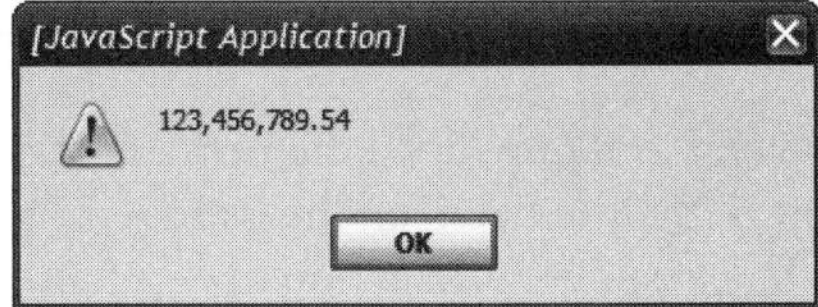

Figure 2-48. *ch2_currencyFormat.htm result*

As you can see, the call to that function has resulted in commas being inserted in the appropriate place. The call has also rounded the fractional portion to two digits as per my system's settings. Running this function on another system with different localization settings might result in a different display.

The null that is passed is an object that sets options for the format. Passing null simply uses the system settings. If you want to do something more explicit, the options that are available to you are the same as those described in the `dojo.number.format()` function a little later, so please refer to that to see what's available here.

dojo.currency.parse()

```
dojo.require("dojo.currency");
```

This function takes in a string, and optionally some currency formatting options, and returns a number. For example:

```
alert("13,873.125 + 1 = " + (dojo.number.parse("13,873.125", null) + 1));
```

The `alert()` you get from this is shown in Figure 2-49.

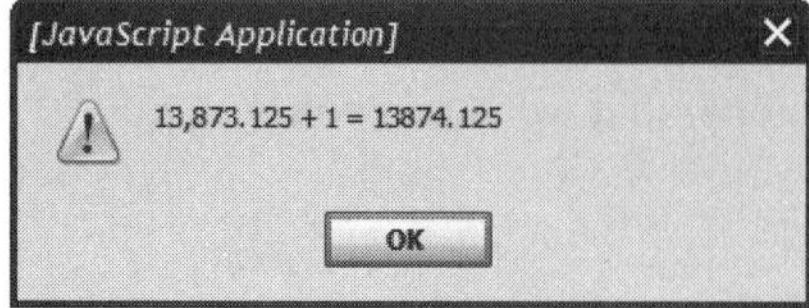

Figure 2-49. *ch2_currencyParse.htm result*

I specifically did a bit of math on the output of the function just to prove it's actually a number.

Just as with `dojo.currency.format()`, you can pass a second argument that specifies options for the parsing. These options are the same as described for `dojo.number.parse()`, with the addition of three new ones here: `symbol`, which overrides the default currency symbol, `places`, which is the number of decimal places to accept, and `fractional`, which enables you to set options with regard to implied decimal places.

dojo.data

The `dojo.data` namespace houses a powerful data access layer that provides a uniform API for working with data in a variety of formats. I'm going to skip going into detail on this namespace, as I've done with a handful of others, because you'll be seeing this in action in depth in at least one of the coming examples and I feel you will be better served being introduced to it there. Rest assured, it's a really cool facility that I think you're going to appreciate. Until then, there's plenty more to feed your hunger for knowledge right here, right now!

dojo.date

The `dojo.date` namespace has quite a few functions for dealing with dates in various ways.

Functions

First we'll take a look at the functions directly below `dojo.date`. I'll combine a few of these examples to save a little time and space on the printed page.

dojo.date.add(), dojo.date.compare(), and dojo.date.difference()

```
dojo.require("dojo.date");
```

If you want to manipulate a given `Date` object in terms of doing date arithmetic on it, `dojo.date.add()` is the way to go. And if you want to be able to compare two `Date` objects, or determine the difference between them, then `dojo.date.compare()` and `dojo.date.difference()` are here for you. Let's go to the code:

```
var d1 = new Date();
var s = "d1 (before) = " + d1 + "\n";
d1 = dojo.date.add(d1, "month", 2);
s += "d1 (after) = " + d1 + "\n";
var d2 = new Date();
s += "d2 = " + d2 + "\n";
```

```
s += "d1 > d2 = " + dojo.date.compare(d1, d2) + "\n";
s += dojo.date.difference(d1, d2, "week");
alert(s);
```

When you run this code, you get the alert() seen in Figure 2-50.

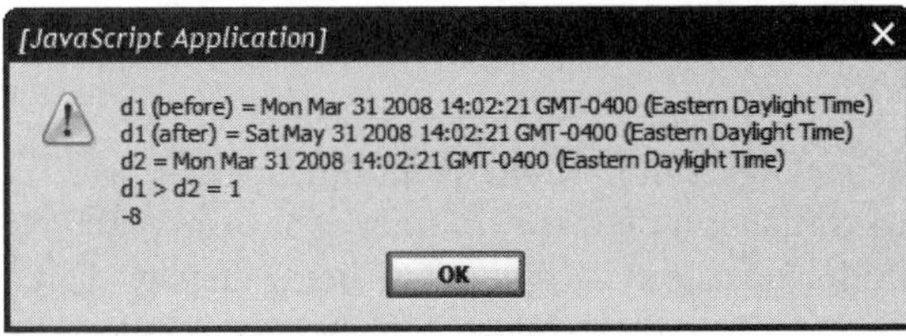

Figure 2-50. *ch2_date1.htm result*

The first line is the Date object before I manipulate it. This Date is created with a simple new Date(); statement, so it's the current date. The second line is that Date object after using the dojo.date.add() function on it. This function accepts three arguments, the first being the Date object to operate on. The second is a string specifying what part of the Date to modify, such as day, week, month, year, and so forth. The third is the amount to change the Date by, and yes, it can be a negative value if you wish. Here, I've added 2 to the month portion, making March become May. The third line is just a new Date object, again set to the current day. The third line is a call to the dojo.date.compare() function. This accepts two Date objects, as well as an optional argument with a value of either date or time, which can be used to compare only the date or time portion of the Date objects (by default it compares both). This function returns zero if the Date objects are equal, a positive number if the first Date is greater than the second, or a negative number if the first Date is less than the second. The final line is the result of a call to dojo.date.difference(), which again accepts two Date objects, plus an optional third string argument that specifies what unit you want the difference in (weeks in this code, for example). Note that for both dojo.date.compare() and dojo.date.difference(), if the second Date object argument is null, the current date will automatically be used.

dojo.date.getDaysInMonth(), dojo.date.getTimezoneName(), and dojo.date.isLeapYear()

```
dojo.require("dojo.date");
```

The next three functions in dojo.date are for getting pieces of information from a given Date object. They all accept a single argument, a Date object, and return some bit of information about it (or by extension, the browser environment). Without further delay, here's some example code:

```
var d = new Date();
alert(dojo.date.getDaysInMonth(d) + "\n" +
  dojo.date.getTimezoneName(d) + "\n" +
  dojo.date.isLeapYear(d));
```

Also without further delay, here's the resultant display on the screen in Figure 2-51.

Figure 2-51. *ch2_date2.htm result*

As you can see, the call to `dojo.date.getDaysInMonth()`, when the month is March, as it was at the time I ran this example, returns 31, which is indeed the number of days in March. The call to `dojo.date.getTimezoneName()` results in Eastern Daylight Time being displayed on my system, but it could be any valid time zone name on your system. Finally, 2008 is indeed a leap year, as indicated by the call to `dojo.date.isLeapYear()`.

dojo.date.stamp.fromISOString() and dojo.date.stamp.toISOString()

```
dojo.require("dojo.date.stamp");
```

These two functions enable you to convert from `Date` objects to string and from string to `Date` objects, where the strings are in a form according to ISO standard 8601 (RFC 3339).[4]

For example, to convert from a string to a date, you might do this:

```
alert(dojo.date.stamp.fromISOString("2005-06-30T08:05:00-07:00"));
```

This code yields Figure 2-52.

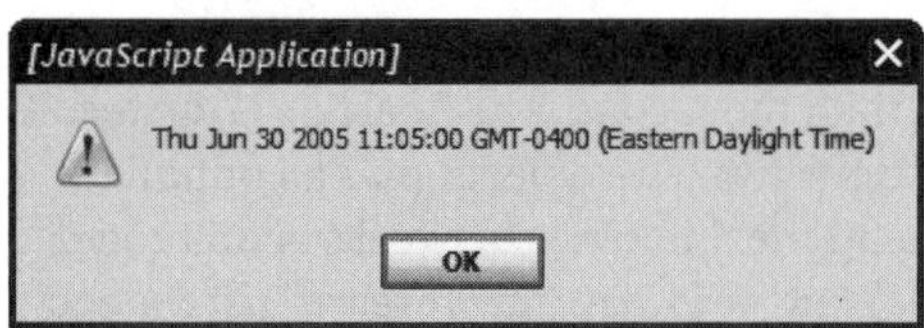

Figure 2-52. *ch2_date3.htm result*

Alternatively, to go the other way, you might do this:

```
alert(dojo.date.stamp.toISOString(new Date()));
```

And that gives you Figure 2-53.

4. For all the gory details on ISO 8601 (RFC 3339), go straight to the source here: `www.ietf.org/rfc/rfc3339.txt`.

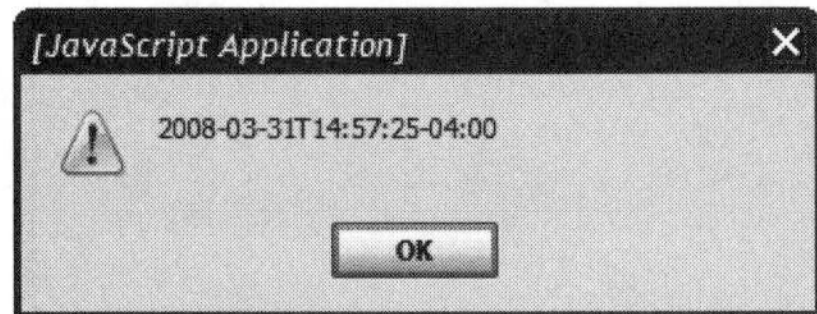

Figure 2-53. *ch2_date4.htm result*

The `dojo.date.stamp.fromISOString()` function accepts two arguments. The first is the string to convert to a `Date` object, and the second, which is optional, is used to supply defaults for values omitted in the first argument. The `dojo.date.stamp.toISOString()` function also accepts two arguments, the first being a `Date` object, and the second being an object that specifies some options. The options available are `milliseconds`, which when `true` outputs milliseconds in the resultant string; `selector`, which can have a value of `date` or `time` and which indicates whether you want just the date or time portion of the `Date` object (both by default); and finally `zulu`, which is a Boolean that when `true` means to use Coordinated Universal Time (UTC, believe it or not!)/Greenwich Mean Time (GMT). UTC and GMT are basically equivalent in most cases for the output time zone.

dojo.fx

The `dojo.fx` namespace houses a few useful animation-related bits of functionality.

Constructors

There is only a single constructor in this namespace, and it's really just a shortcut way of doing something pretty common. We'll have a look at that first.

dojo.fx.Toggler()

Toggling elements on a page between a visible and nonvisible state in some visually pleasing way is a common thing to do, and that's exactly what `dojo.fx.Toggler()` is all about.

Let's check out some code to see how it works. Listing 2-5 is that code.

Listing 2-5. *ch2_fxToggler.htm*

```
<html>
  <head>
    <link rel="StyleSheet" type="text/css"
      href="js/dojo/dojo/resources/dojo.css">
    <script type="text/javascript">
      var djConfig = {
        baseScriptUri : "js/dojo/"
      };
    </script>
    <script type="text/javascript" src="js/dojo/dojo/dojo.js"></script>
    <script>
      dojo.require("dojo.fx");
```

```
      var toggler = null;
      function fxTest() {
        toggler = new dojo.fx.Toggler({
          node : "myDiv",
          showFunc : dojo.fx.wipeIn,
          hideFunc : dojo.fx.wipeOut
        });
        toggler.hide();
      }
    </script>
  </head>
  <body onLoad="fxTest();">
    <div id="myDiv"
      style="background-color:#ff0000;width:40px;top:5px;left:5px;➥
position:absolute;">
     Hello<br>from<br>myDiv</div>
     <br><br><br><br>
     <input type="button" value="Click to show" onClick="toggler.show();">
  </body>
</html>
```

Upon loading, `fxTest()` is called, which instantiates a new `Toggler`. Passed into the constructor is an object with a number of elements. The first is `node`, which is just the ID of the node this Toggler will work on. Next is `showFunc`, which is what animation will be used to show the element, and `hideFunc`, which is what animation will be used to hide the element. This all pretty much just encapsulates two animations and gives you an easy way to execute them, namely calling the `hide()` or `show()` method of the `Toggler`. Here, the element is hidden immediately by calling `toggler.hide()`. Then, when you click the button, `toggler.show()` is called, putting the element back on the screen. All of this is done with the `dojo.fx.wipeIn()` and `dojo.fx.wipeOut()` animations, which we're about to look at!

Functions

As I've done a few times before, I've chosen to come up with a single example that demonstrates all the functions available in this namespace at one time.

dojo.fx.chain(), dojo.fx.combine(), dojo.fx.slideTo(), dojo.fx.wipeIn(), and dojo.fx.wipeOut()

Strictly speaking, there are only three effects here: `dojo.fx.slideTo()`, which simply moves an element from one location to another smoothly; `dojo.fx.wipeIn()`, which takes a given element and makes it appear in a sort of window blind–type effect (it rolls down from no height to the element's natural height); and `dojo.fx.wipeOut()`, which does exactly the opposite as `dojo.fx.wipeIn()`.

The `dojo.fx.chain()` function enables you to create a chain of animations and run them sequentially without having to worry about the details of how to start one when the previous one ends. The `dojo.fx.combine()` function enables you to take a bunch of animations and run them simultaneously in parallel. Once again, Dojo handles the details for you as with `dojo.fx.chain()`; you just feed either one an array of animations and you're off to the races.

Let's see this all in action, shall we? Listing 2-6 is what we're after.

Listing 2-6. *ch2_fx.htm Example*

```
<html>
  <head>
    <link rel="StyleSheet" type="text/css"
      href="js/dojo/dojo/resources/dojo.css">
    <script type="text/javascript">
      var djConfig = {
        baseScriptUri : "js/dojo/"
      };
    </script>
    <script type="text/javascript" src="js/dojo/dojo/dojo.js"></script>
    <script>
      dojo.require("dojo.fx");
      function fxTest() {
        dojo.fx.chain([
          dojo.fx.wipeOut({node:"myDiv"}),
          dojo.fx.combine([
            dojo.fx.slideTo({node:"myDiv",left:"40",top:"40",unit:"px"}),
            dojo.fx.wipeIn({node:"myDiv"})
          ])
        ]).play();
      }
    </script>
  </head>
  <body onLoad="fxTest();">
    <div id="myDiv"
      style="background-color:#ff0000;width:40px;top:5px;left:5px;➥
position:absolute;">
     Hello<br>from<br>myDiv</div>
  </body>
</html>
```

What happens here, when you load this file in your browser, is that a red square appears on the screen with some text in it. Immediately, it will "roll up" by using the `dojo.fx.wipeOut()` function. That is the first animation in a chain constructed by using `dojo.fx.chain()`. The second animation in the chain is created by using `dojo.fx.combine()`. The two animations being combined are a `dojo.fx.slideTo()` and a `dojo.fx.wipeIn()`. So, the net effect on the screen is that the red box disappears when the page loads, and then immediately begins to expand back to full size, while at the same time moving down and to the right. Give it a shot to see it in action, and maybe play with some combinations of animations for yourself to see what's possible.

dojo.i18n

The dojo.i18n namespace (*i18n* being an abbreviated form of *internationalization*, that is, replace the 18 letters between *i* and *n* with *18*) is where you can find functionality for internationalizing an application, that is, making it available in different locales. A *locale*, for the purposes of this discussion, means different languages.

Functions

A stunning two whole functions are available in this namespace, plus one that I'll describe that's actually from the dojo namespace, but they are all you need!

dojo.requireLocalization(), dojo.i18n.getLocalization(), and dojo.i18n.normalizeLocale()

```
dojo.require("dojo.i18n");
```

Strictly speaking, the first function, dojo.requireLocalization(), is part of the dojo namespace, and thus is available without the dojo.require() shown earlier. (I felt it made more sense to describe that function here rather than when you looked at the dojo namespace earlier.)

This is much like the dojo.require() function except that it's for importing internationalized resource bundles. It accepts three parameters, two of which are required. The first is the name of the module (read: namespace) the bundle belongs to. The second is the name of the bundle to load.

You create a resource bundle, which is just a .js file with JSON in it where each from:to pair is a string to translate, in a directory named nls under the module's directory. For instance, taking one that exists already, in the dijit namespace there is a bundle named common in the nls directory.

Optionally, under the nls directory, you can have directories named for language codes—for example, en for English or fr for French. This leads to the optional third parameter, which is the language to load. If you don't specify this, the locale of the requesting user will be used. So for instance, on my American English PC, Dojo would attempt to load the bundle under the dijit/nls/en and dijit/nls/en-us directories. It also attempts to load dijit/nls/<bundle_name>.js.

The next step to using a bundle is to call dojo.i18n.getLocalization(), passing it the name of the module as well as the bundle name, and optionally the language. This returns an object that has all the from:to values as members of it. You can then use simple object access code to get a particular translation. The following code demonstrates all of this:

```
dojo.requireLocalization("dijit", "common",
  dojo.i18n.normalizeLocale("fr"));
alert("buttonCancel = " +
  dojo.i18n.getLocalization("dijit", "common",
    dojo.i18n.normalizeLocale("fr")).buttonCancel);
```

You can see here how the common bundle in the dijit module is first imported. You can also see here usage of the dojo.i18n.localizeLocale() function, which returns the canonical form of a given locale. This ensures that the locale value is one suited for use by the Dojo i18n functions. Next, the dojo.i18n.getLocalization() function is used to retrieve the list of strings from the bundle. The value of the buttonCancel string is then displayed via the alert(), which can be seen in Figure 2-54.

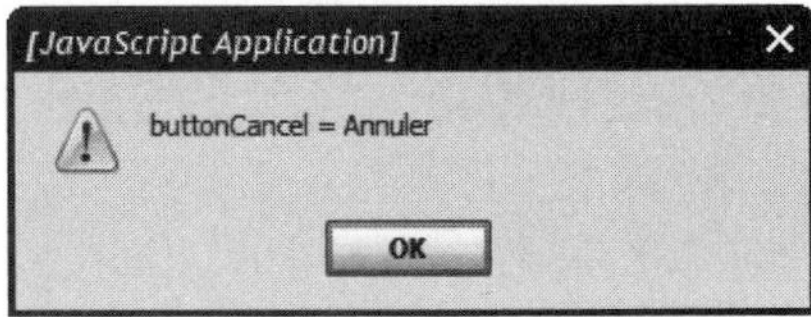

Figure 2-54. *ch2_requireLocalization.htm result*

Not being French-speaking myself, I can only assume Annuler is indeed the correct translation of buttonCancel. Assuming it is, Dojo has done the job for us!

dojo.io

The dojo.io namespace includes a few bits of functionality related to Ajax, but in a tangential sort of way in the sense that it represents alternate transport mechanisms, that is, ways to do Ajax other than the typical XmlHttpRequest object.

Functions

There are five genuinely useful functions to explore here, none of which are terribly complex.

You may be aware that Ajax with XmlHttpRequest must adhere to the *same domain* security policy, that is, you cannot make an Ajax request to a domain that differs from the domain that served the page. Future versions of the object are planned to allow for this, but current implementations do not. In the meantime, people have devised some neat tricks to get around this policy; one deals with IFrames, and another uses something called the dynamic <script> tag trick. The following functions enable you to use these techniques without sweating the details!

dojo.io.iframe.create()

```
dojo.require("dojo.io.script");
```

Sometimes an IFrame is a good mechanism for making remote calls: create an IFrame dynamically, set on it the appropriate URL, insert it into the DOM, and off you go. This is much like the dynamic <script> tag trick, but it's arguably more flexible because now you have a (potentially) full HTML document coming back to work with, including all the life cycle events that come with that. With this function, you don't have to worry about how mechanically to do all that; you just do it!

This function creates a hidden IFrame and provides a way to execute some specified JavaScript when the page loads. Optionally, you can specify a URL to load (if you don't specify it, a blank document provided by Dojo is put into it).

So, for example, you might do this:

```
dojo.io.iframe.create("if1", "alert('loaded');",
  "ch2_iFrameIOResponse1.htm");
```

If the `ch2_iFrameIOResponse1.htm` file contains this:

```
<html><head><title></title></head><body onLoad="alert('hello');"></body></html>
```

. . . then what you'll see are two `alert()` messages, the first saying `hello`, and the second saying `loaded`.

dojo.io.iframe.setSrc()

```
dojo.require("dojo.io.script");
```

As mentioned in `dojo.io.iframe.create()`, you can create an IFrame but not set its source. If you do that and later want to load content into the IFrame, all you need to do is call `dojo.io.iframe.setSrc()` and thy will be done!

dojo.io.script.attach()

```
dojo.require("dojo.io.script");
```

Using the dynamic `<script>` tag trick is not too complex: you construct a new `<script>` tag pointing to a resource that typically is in a different domain, and insert the tag into the DOM. The browser dutifully goes off and retrieves the resource, and because it's a `<script>` tag, the browser treats it like a JavaScript resource and interprets it immediately. If the response is constructed properly, magic happens!

For instance, if the response from the server is nothing but this:

```
myFunction("hello");
```

. . . and if on your page you already had this:

```
function myFunction(inMsg) {
  alert(inMsg);
}
```

. . . then what will happen is that as soon as you insert the `<script>` tag and the browser retrieves that content, you'll get an `alert()` on the screen saying `hello`. This is the basis of what is commonly referred to as JSON-P, or JSON-based web services (or probably a host of other names that all basically refer to this underlying concept).

All of this doesn't help you know how to insert a `<script>` tag dynamically, though. Fortunately, with Dojo, you don't ever have to know! All you need to do is this:

```
dojo.io.script.attach("scriptTag1", "ch2_ scriptIOResponse1.htm");
```

You feed this function an ID for the tag, and the URL to go after. You can optionally, as the third argument, specify the `document` object of an IFrame. When you execute this, you'll see a button on the screen, and after you click it, you'll get Figure 2-55.

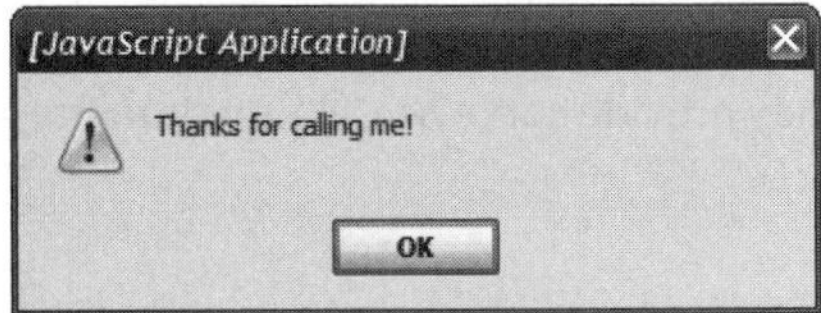

Figure 2-55. *ch2_scriptIO.htm result*

dojo.io.script.get()

```
dojo.require("dojo.io.script");
```

This function is, for all intents and purposes, the same as `dojo.io.script.attach()` except that it provides a few extra options. With this version, you send an object that passes some option attributes. These attributes are the same as those specified in the `dojo.xhr*` functions,[5] with the addition of the following:

- `callbackParamName`: This is the name of the parameter that identifies the JSON-P callback string. In other words, it tells the remote service the name of the callback you wish to be called, and the name of which will be the function call wrapping the JSON response.
- `checkString`: This is a string of JavaScript that is used to verify the response. It performs this check: `if(typeof("+checkString+")!='undefined)`. Note that you should not use this when doing a JSON-P request.
- `frameDoc`: This is the `document` object of an IFrame you want the `<script>` tag attached to.

dojo.io.script.remove()

```
dojo.require("dojo.io.script");
```

It's always nice to clean up after oneself, and that's what this function is for. Recall that when you call `dojo.io.script.attach()`, you pass an ID value to it. Well, if you pass that ID to `dojo.io.script.remove()`, it will remove the dynamically added `<script>` tag (interestingly, it does *not* appear to remove all the code that was retrieved, though).

dojo.number

This namespace provides functions for formatting and parsing numbers with localization capabilities included.

5. The `handleAs` attribute does not apply when using `dojo.io.script.get()`. That attribute is implied by the usage of `callbackParamName`.

Functions

Only four functions are present in this namespace, but they provide some useful functionality for us to explore.

dojo.number.format()

```
dojo.require("dojo.number");
```

As the name implies, this function formats a numeric value. It accepts two arguments. The first is the number to format; the second is an object containing several options. The first option that can be present in that object, `currency`, is an ISO 4217 currency code and can be used to format money. The `locale` option overrides the default locale setting, which determines default formatting rules. The `pattern` option enables you to specify a format mask that will be applied to the number by using the format specification laid out in the Unicode Locale Data Markup Language (LDML) specification.[6] The `places` option specifies how many decimal places to show (the number will be padded out to this many places). The `round` option can be used to round the number (a value of 5 means round to the nearest 0.5; 0 rounds to the nearest whole number, which is the default; and 1 means don't round). The `symbol` option sets the localized currency symbol explicitly. Finally, the `type` option tells the function what type of number this is (`decimal`, `scientific`, `percent`, or `currency`—`decimal` being the default).

Here's a simple example of formatting a dollar amount:

```
alert("1234.56 = " +
  dojo.number.format(new Number(1234.56),
  { pattern : "$#,###.##", places : 4 }));
```

The `alert()` shown in Figure 2-56 is the result.

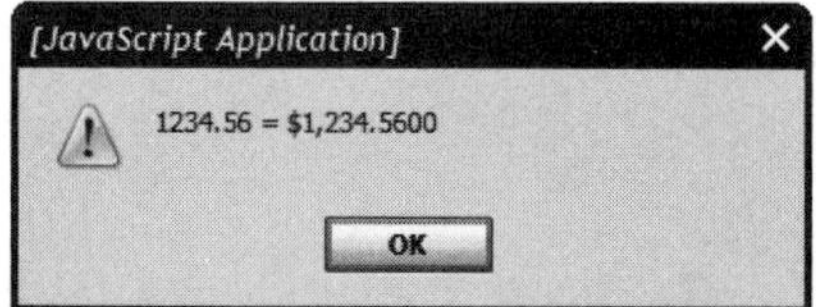

Figure 2-56. *ch2_numberFormat.htm result*

dojo.number.parse()

```
dojo.require("dojo.number");
```

The `dojo.number.parse()` method accepts a string and converts it to a number, using localization information. Like `dojo.number.format()`, it accepts two arguments, and the first is the string to convert. The second is an option object with five possible elements. The first is `currency`, which is itself an object that contains currency information. The `locale` option is next, and it enables you to override the default locale. Next is `pattern`, which indicates the

6. The LDML specification can be seen here: www.unicode.org/reports/tr35/#Number_Format_Patterns.

format specification that will be used to format the user; the default is based on the locale. The `type` option is exactly like that described in `dojo.number.format()`. The final option, `strict`, is not currently documented and I frankly could not determine its function. I can tell you, however, that it defaults to `false`.

Here's a simple example of formatting a dollar amount:

```
alert("3873.12 + 1 = " + (dojo.number.parse("3873.12") + 1));
```

Note that you get back a `Number` object, which you can then use to do some simple math on, as I've demonstrated here and shown in Figure 2-57.

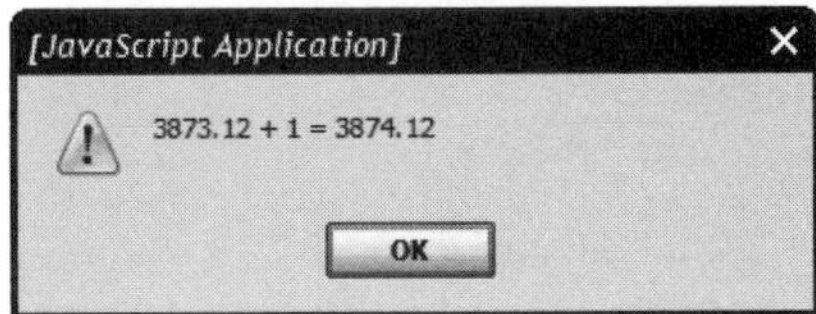

Figure 2-57. *ch2_numberParse.htm result*

dojo.number.regexp()

```
dojo.require("dojo.number");
```

The `dojo.number.regexp()` function returns a regular expression with both a positive and negative match, and group and decimal separators in it. This function accepts an object with options in it, including the now-usual `locale` option to override the default locale, the also previously seen `pattern` option for setting the format mask, `places` and `strict`, as we've also seen before, and `type` as well.

I haven't demonstrated this method here because it isn't terribly exciting or easy to show, so let's just move along, shall we?

dojo.number.round()

The final function in this namespace is `dojo.number.round()`, and as its name implies, it enables us to round numbers. You will need to pass it two parameters, and optionally a third. The first is simply the number to round. The second is the number of decimal places to round to. The third optional parameter specifies that you want to round the next place to the nearest multiple.

As a simple example, have a look at this snippet:

```
alert("1234.56733, 2 = " +
  dojo.number.round(new Number(1234.56733), 2));
```

This results in the display in Figure 2-58. Not exactly the invention of fire, but useful nonetheless!

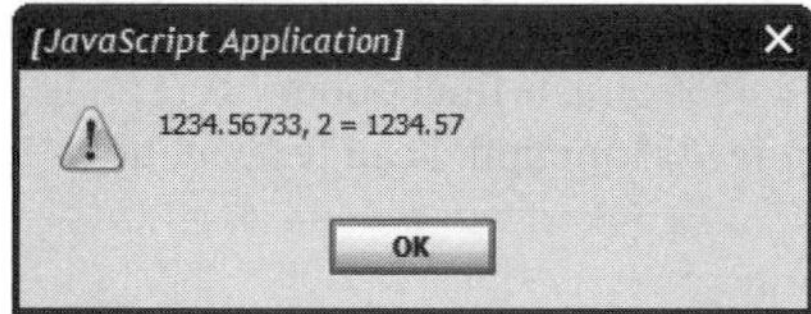

Figure 2-58. *ch2_numberRound.htm result*

dojo.regexp

The `dojo.regexp` namespace provides some functionality for dealing with regular expressions in JavaScript a little easier than you might otherwise be able to.

Functions

There are only three functions coming at you from this namespace: `dojo.regexp.buildGroupRE()`, `dojo.regexp.escapeString()`, and `dojo.regexp.group()`.

dojo.regexp.buildGroupRE()

```
dojo.require("dojo.regexp");
```

This function is used to take an array of values and construct regex subexpressions from each by using a given function. It takes three arguments. The first is the array of values. The second is the function to call for each element to construct the subexpressions. The third, which is optional, uses a noncapturing match when `true`. When it is `false`, matches are retained by regular expression (it defaults to `false`).

Take the following code as an example:

```
alert(dojo.regexp.buildGroupRE([true, false], function (item) {
  return "(http?|gopher?)\\://";
}));
```

(Five points if you know what the gopher protocol is, ten points if you've actually used it—but minus several *million* points if you've used it *recently*!)

This is part of a larger piece of code that constructs a regex for dealing with URLs. The output from running this code can be seen in Figure 2-59.

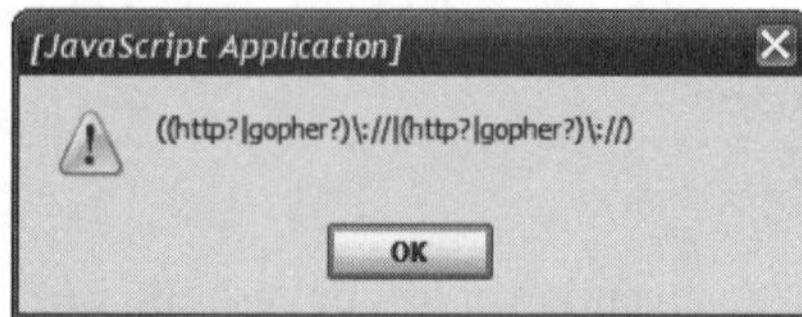

Figure 2-59. *ch2_regex.htm first result*

dojo.regexp.escapeString()

```
dojo.require("dojo.regexp");
```

This function adds escape sequences for special characters in regular expressions. This is simple to demonstrate:

```
alert(dojo.regexp.escapeString("/[]{}"));
```

Run that bit of code and you get the alert() shown in Figure 2-60.

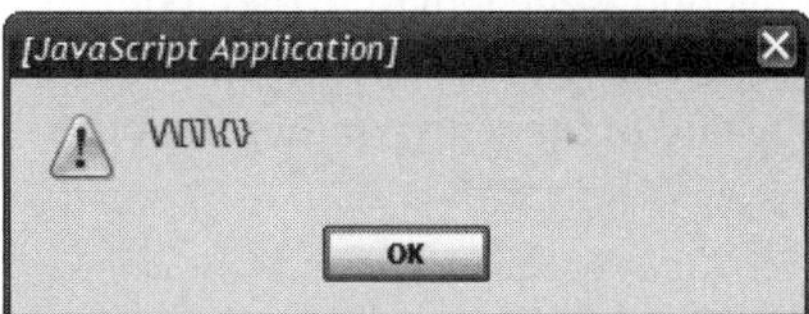

Figure 2-60. *ch2_regex.htm second result*

As you can plainly see, each of the characters in the string has been prefixed with a backslash to escape them for proper use in a regex.

dojo.regexp.group()

```
dojo.require("dojo.regexp");
```

The final function in this namespace is dojo.regexp.group(), and its job is to add group match to an expression. To see it in action, try this code:

```
alert(dojo.regexp.group("test"));
```

It's nothing to write home about, but in Figure 2-61 you can see how it has grouped the string test with parentheses.

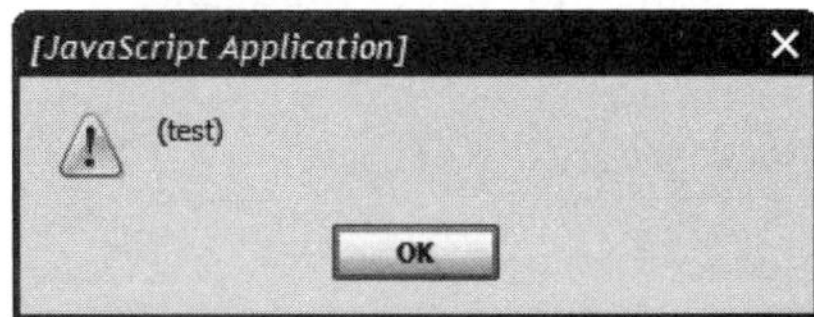

Figure 2-61. *ch2_regex.htm third result*

dojo.string

The dojo.string namespace is, pretty much as you'd expect, where you can find various string utility functions. There's not a whole lot here at present, but I expect that to change pretty rapidly.

Functions

This namespace currently has only three functions underneath it, no constructors or properties to deal with.

dojo.string.pad()

```
dojo.require("dojo.string");
```

The pad() function is your standard "pad my string out to a specified size" function. It accepts four arguments. The first is the string to pad. The second is the length to pad it out to. The third, which is optional, is the character to pad with (this defaults to 0). Finally, the fourth argument, which is optional, is a flag that says to pad at the end of the string, rather than the default of the beginning of the string.

So, to see this in action:

```
alert("dojo.string.pad('frank', 20, '*') = " +
  dojo.string.pad('frank', 20, '*'));
```

This results in the alert() pop-up shown in Figure 2-62.

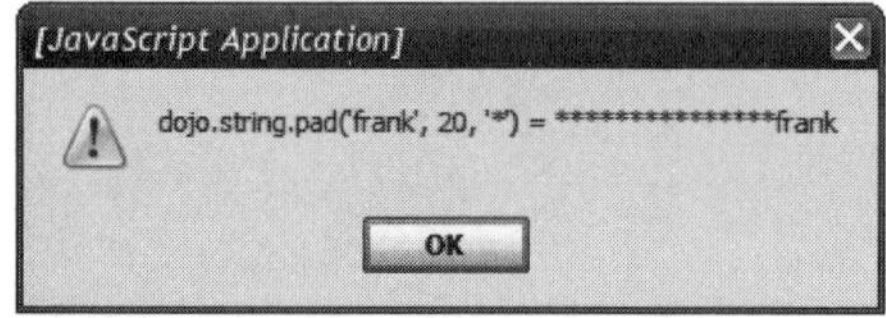

Figure 2-62. *ch2_stringPad.htm result*

dojo.string.substitute()

```
dojo.require("dojo.string");
```

The substitute() function makes replacing tokens in a string with values child's play. With it, you can do things like this:

```
var template = "Hello, ${0}!  I hope you are having a wonderful ${1}!";
var tokenValues = [ "Jason Vorhees", "Friday the 13th" ];
alert(dojo.string.substitute(template, tokenValues));
template = "${name} will see you in your dreams!";
tokenValues = { name : "Freddy Krueger" };
alert(dojo.string.substitute(template, tokenValues));
```

This will result in two alert() pop-ups. The first is shown in Figure 2-63.

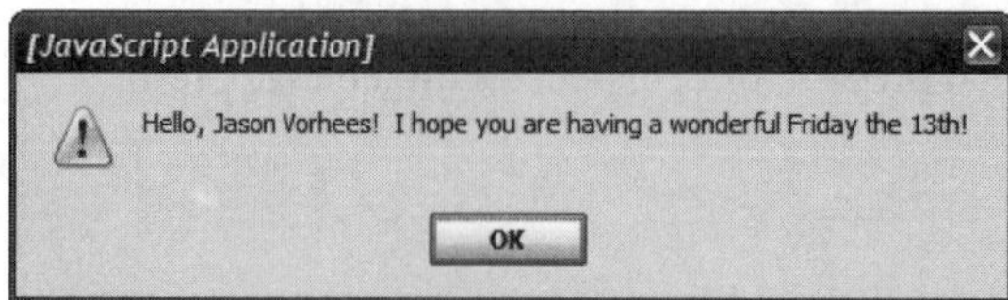

Figure 2-63. *ch2_stringSubstitute.htm first result*

The second `alert()` pop-up is likewise shown in Figure 2-64.

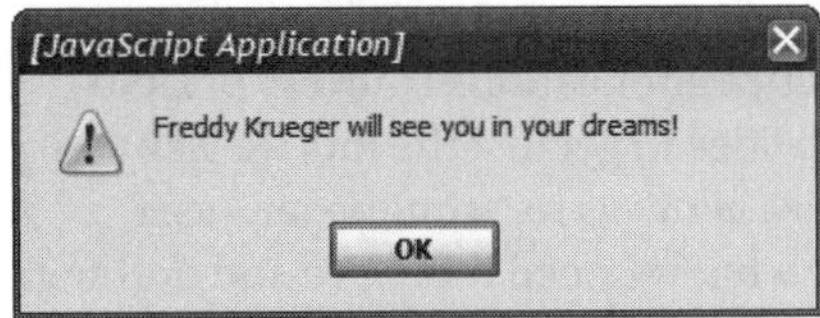

Figure 2-64. *ch2_stringSubstitute.htm second result*

As you can see, you can do the replacements positionally or by name. You can also pass an optional third parameter, which is a function that will be called for each token to do any sort of processing on the values you would like. Finally, there is a fourth parameter, also optional, that tells the `substitute()` function where to look for an optional format function, the default being the global namespace.

dojo.string.trim()

```
dojo.require("dojo.string");
```

The final function in `dojo.string` enables you to trim whitespace from both sides of a string. Amazingly, JavaScript does not by default have this feature! It's a pretty obvious function, frankly, and often needed, so things like this can be done:

```
var s = "   I am an untrimmed string";
if (s == "I am an untrimmed string") {
  alert("Matched without trim");
}
if (dojo.string.trim(s) == "I am an untrimmed string") {
  alert("Matched with trim");
}
```

The only `alert()` pop-up you see is the one shown in Figure 2-65.

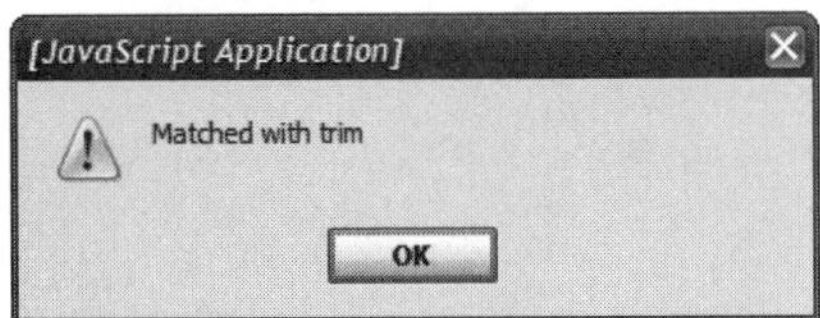

Figure 2-65. *ch2_stringTrim.htm result*

This proves that `trim()` is doing it's job. The first `if` statement doesn't match the string because of the leading spaces. After `trim()` has been called on it, though, it matches the test string that doesn't have spaces on the front. If `trim()` didn't do its job, we wouldn't have seen either `alert()` pop-up.

Summary

In this chapter, we spent a good deal of time looking at the Core component of Dojo. We saw all the nifty-keen functions available to us and our JavaScript applications courtesy of Dojo. We saw how we can use the include mechanism Dojo provides to get just the bits we want on our page. We also saw how Dojo's custom build capabilities allow us to "trim the fat," as it were, and get a version of Dojo on our page that has only what we need it to have and nothing more. At this point, you should have a good feel for what Core offers, and can almost certainly see its value in your own applications. In later chapters, as we explore the projects, you'll see a great deal of what you saw here used in real applications, as opposed to the small example chunks you saw in this chapter.

In the next chapter, we'll delve into Dijit and the Dojo Widgets, and see what UI magic Dojo enables us to perform with little heavy lifting on our parts (just the way we good lazy developers like it!).

CHAPTER 3

Dijit

In the first chapter, we took a fairly high-level look at Dojo, what it is, what it has to offer, and so forth. The second chapter delved into Dojo Base and Core in detail, providing a pretty good idea of what's in there.

In this chapter, we'll examine Dijit in some detail. We'll look at the components that are available, see examples of them, learn about the features they expose to us, and so on. We'll see how to create them declaratively and programmatically, and we'll see how we can interact with them after they are on the page during the course of our application's execution.

This chapter is organized similarly to Chapter 2 in that each component has is own subsection, but I will once again take my cues from the Dojo API documentation and organize the material into higher-level groupings above the components themselves. These groups, if you check out the API documentation, roughly match the namespaces available in the Dijit package, which include `dijit.form` (for form-related dijits—things like check boxes and combos) and `dijit.layout` (for layout-delayed dijits—things like accordions and stack layouts). There are some other namespaces, but they do not typically house dijits, so I will simply discuss them as necessary during the course of the chapter.

You'll also find that there are a number of dijits directly within the `dijit` namespace, so that will become the third general grouping here (it's in fact the *first* group we'll look at).

So, without further ado, let's get right into the thick of things and talk about some Dijit basics before we proceed to look at the individual dijits themselves.

Dijit at a Glance

Dijit, simply stated, is a widget framework that sits on top of Dojo Core and Dojo Base. On top of this framework are built individual dijits. In other words, Dijit is a framework for building widgets, but it's also the general term to describe those widgets.

Dijit as a framework is designed to deal with the problems typically associated with Web 2.0 development—things such as internationalization, currency, number and date formatting in localized ways, keyboard accessibility, and accessibility concerns for people with disabilities. These capabilities are baked into the Dijit framework itself, as well as the individual dijits.

Dijit is fully *skinnable*, or *theme-able*, depending on which term you prefer. This means that you can achieve a consistent look and feel across all dijits by the simple flip of a switch, more specifically, by specifying the theme you wish to use. Dijit comes packaged with a number of themes, Tundra being probably the most popular (and the one I'll be using in this chapter and most of this book). Tundra is a fairly nice-looking theme that enables you to get off the ground quickly and easily and to have a nice-looking UI without any hassle. You can of course tweak this theme to your liking, or obtain or even create one yourself.

To switch themes, all you need to do is import the appropriate style sheet, and set a class on the `<body>` tag, like so:

```
<body class="tundra">
```

Any dijits in the `<body>` of that document will automatically use that theme. You can also set the theme on a per-dijit basis, but this is less convenient and less flexible ironically, in the sense that you'll have a lot more to change when your boss no longer likes your chosen theme! I highly recommend setting the theme on the `<body>` tag and nowhere else—unless you feel the "job security" (ahem) of having all those places to change is somehow valuable to you.

Dijits can be created in one of two ways: declaratively or programmatically. That means you can create your UI with very little, if any, JavaScript coding. All it takes is the appropriate markup, and your UI can spring to life more or less automatically.

Because all dijits are built on top of a common framework, they expose many functions in a consistent manner, enabling you to work with dijits, even those you have no real experience with, quickly and easily. To be sure, you'll need to refer to the documentation often, but you will frequently be able to "guess" what the right answer is without that documentation, which saves a lot of time.

Getting Started with Dijit

To get Dijit onto a page and ready for use requires just a few things. First, you'll need to import some style sheets:

```
<link rel="StyleSheet" type="text/css" href="dojo/resources/dojo.css">
<link rel="StyleSheet" type="text/css" href="dojo/dijit/themes/tundra/tundra.css">
```

In fact, the first one isn't required. However, I've found that it gives you some styles for page margins and such that simply make it all work better and with less thought, so I generally import it unless I have a specific reason not to.

The remaining steps are 100 percent optional. If you want to use the declarative approach to creating dijits, you need to include a new element, `parseOnLoad`, set to `true`, in your `djConfig` object. This instructs Dijit to parse the page when it loads, looking for dijit declarations in markup, and creating dijits from that markup. Finally, and again only if you intend to use the declarative approach, you'll also need to do this:

```
dojo.require("dojo.parser");
```

This is the Dijit code that is responsible for parsing the page upon load. Without this, your dijits will not be created from markup.

Okay, I sort of lied there a bit. There is in fact another step, but it's dependent on which dijits you want to use. You will also need to use `dojo.require()`s for the dijits you want to use. You'll see this as you look at the dijits themselves in just a moment.

Declarative vs. Programmatic Dijits

I've so far mentioned a few times that you can create a dijit declaratively or programmatically, but what does this really mean? The best answer I think is simply to show you! Let's say you want to put a Button dijit on a page, and you want to do so declaratively. All you do is write this in your page:

```
<button dojoType="dijit.form.Button" type="button">I am a button</button>
```

Assuming you've done all the previous steps, including importing the `dijit.form.Button` class via `dojo.require()`, then when this page is loaded, Dijit will go off and create a Button dijit and replace this markup with it. That means it will replace this markup with the markup necessary to display a Button dijit, and will add the applicable JavaScript, if any, to go along with it.

Alternatively, you can do this completely through code. The equivalent button could be created like so:

```
var myDijit = new dijit.form.Button({ label : "I am a button" });
dojo.byId("divButton").appendChild(myDijit.domNode);
```

Now, assuming there is a `<div>` with the ID `divButton` on the page, a new Button dijit will be created and inserted into it.

■Note Parsing the page can be a fairly slow thing to do. The Dojo team has done an amazing job optimizing this process over the past few releases, and the difference between the current versions of Dojo and previous versions is night and day in this regard. Still, if you're finding that the declarative approach is causing a large performance hit, spend a few minutes in the Dojo support forums because you'll find some tweaks you can do to speed it all up, such as telling the parser what DOM nodes to parse, instead of allowing it to parse the entire DOM. Telling it what sub-branch of the DOM tree to inspect can save a lot of processing time.

Now, which you choose is entirely up to you. I think it comes down to a matter of what you're doing. If your UI is known at the time the page loads, declarative is probably the way to go. If, however, you have to build the UI dynamically, perhaps fetching some data from the server before deciding how many buttons to show as an example, that pretty much screams out for doing it programmatically. At the end of the day, Dijit provides for both approaches equally.

■Note If you are told to write 100 percent valid HTML, that is, HTML that will always pass through a validator successfully, Dijit can present a problem for you. Just look at the previous markup: what exactly is `dojoType`? It's not a valid HTML attribute, and therefore a validator (which isn't aware of Dojo anyway) would puke over that. Thankfully, most people seem to be concerned these days with HTML being well formed, which is a completely valid concern, but custom attributes such as `dojoType` seem to be less of a concern. Still, it's something you'll want to be aware of for sure.

Common Dijit Methods and Attributes

Because all dijits extend from a common widget class, they all share some common methods, properties, and behaviors. Table 3-1 lists the common methods. Note that many of them are life-cycle event handlers that you wouldn't typically call as a developer, but you could if you wanted or needed to for some reason.

Table 3-1. *Common Dijit Methods*

Method	Description
`buildRendering`	Called to construct the visual part representation of a dijit.
`connect`	Connects the specified object/event to the specified method of the dijit and registers for `disconnect()` on dijit destroy.
`create`	Begins the life cycle of a dijit.
`destroy`	Destroys the dijit, but leaves its descendants alone.
`destroyDescendants`	Recursively destroys the descendants of the dijit, as well as the descendant's descendants (and so on...hence the term *recursively*!).
`destroyRecursive`	For all intents and purposes, this is synonymous with `destroyDescendants`, but this is the one you should call if needed.
`destroyRendering`	Destroys the DOM nodes associated with this dijit.
`disconnect`	Disconnects a handle created by the `connect()` method. This will also remove the handle from the list of connects maintained by this dijit.
`getDescendants`	Returns all the dijits that are descendants of the dijit.
`isFocusable`	Returns `true` if this dijit can currently be focused, `false` if it can't.
`isLeftToRight`	Checks the DOM for the text direction for bidirectional support.
`onBlur`	Called when the dijit loses focus.
`onClose`	Called when the dijit is being destroyed.
`onFocus`	Called when the dijit gains focus.
`postCreate`	Called after a dijit's DOM has been fully created.
`postMixInProperties`	Called after the parameters to the dijit have been processed, but before the dijit's markup template is processed. This is a handy place to set properties that are referenced in the template itself.
`setAttribute`	Sets a native HTML attribute.
`startup`	Called after a dijit's children, and other dijits on the page, have been created. This provides an opportunity to manipulate any children before they are displayed. This is useful for composite dijits (such as layout dijits) that need to control or lay out subdijits.

In Table 3-2, you can see the common attributes. Of these, the `domNode` attribute is by far the most commonly used attribute in my experience, even more so than `style` and `class`, which you might reasonably expect to be the most commonly used attributes.

Table 3-2. *Common Dijit Attributes*

Attribute	Description
`attributeMap`	A map of attributes, standard HTML attributes usually, to set on the dijit's DOM elements once created.
`class`	HTML class attribute.
`domNode`	This is the visible representation of the dijit. There may be DOM elements that are created for a given dijit, but this is the "top-level" element that all others are nested under.
`id`	This is a unique string identifier that can be assigned by the developer (or by the dijit component manager if not specified).
`lang`	This is not used often, but when it is, its purpose is to override the default Dojo locale used to render the dijit, as typical in the HTML `LANG` attribute.
`srcNodeRef`	This is a pointer to the original DOM node, that is, the element that has the `dojoType` attribute on it. In many cases, this element will be replaced when the dijit is created, so you should take care when using this attribute.
`style`	This is the HTML style attribute value.

You may find other methods and attributes that most dijits share, but these are the most commons ones you'll use, and the ones directly descendant from the base widget class.

GETTING A REFERENCE TO AN EXISTING DIJIT

One other important fact to know is that every dijit created, whether declaratively or programmatically, is controlled by a widget manager. Now, generally you won't care much about that, except for one commonly needed thing: getting a reference to an existing dijit.

Every dijit will have an ID, whether you set it or not. (Of course, if you *don't* set it, getting a reference to it later will be kind of difficult!) There is a simple function to get a reference to a dijit:

```
dijit.byId(<someID>);
```

Feed `dijit.byId()` the ID of a dijit and back will come a reference to the dijit that you can then interact with. You'll see this in action all over the place in this book, but it's important to realize that it's *not* the same as `dojo.byId()`, which gives you back a reference to an arbitrary DOM element. The `dijit.byId()` method is a function of the widget manager and deals with dijits, not DOM elements.

Dijits Directly Under the Dijit Namespace

If you look at the Dojo API documentation, you'll find constructors listed in the `dijit` namespace. Most of them represent dijits that you can create and use. That's where we'll begin our exploration, beginning with ColorPalette.

ColorPalette

```
dojo.require("dijit.ColorPalette");
```

The ColorPalette dijit enables the user to choose a color from a palette of existing colors. This is like virtually any color palette you've ever seen in any program you are familiar with.

The ColorPalette dijit is shown in Figure 3-1.

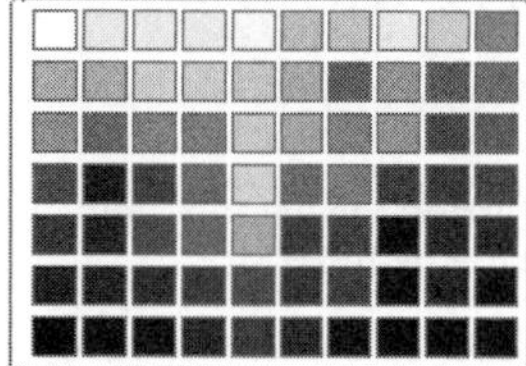

Figure 3-1. *The ColorPalette dijit (using the default 7 × 10 size)*

Naturally, that would be considerably more impressive if it were in color! Such is the problem with the printed page. (I still say type will never die, but this is a good example that says otherwise.)

Anyway, to create this dijit declaratively, you can do this:

```
<div dojoType="dijit.ColorPalette"></div>
```

Yes, it's really that easy!

To create this dijit programmatically, you could do this:

```
var myDijit = new dijit.ColorPalette({
  palette : "3x4", onChange : function(selectedColor) {
    alert(selectedColor);
  }
});
dojo.byId("divProgrammatic").appendChild(myDijit.domNode);
```

This code creates what you see in Figure 3-2.

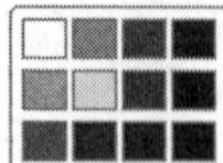

Figure 3-2. *The ColorPalette dijit (specifying the 3 × 4 size)*

You'll of course notice that this ColorPalette dijit is quite a bit smaller. That's thanks to the `palette` attribute. This accepts two values, `3x4` and `7x10`. You can set it declaratively too, of course.

There are two other attributes you can set. The `defaultTimeout` attribute is the number of milliseconds before a held key or button becomes typematic (before it repeats, in other words). The `timeoutChangeRate` attribute is the fraction of time used to change the typematic timer between events. A value of `1` means that each typematic event fires at `defaultTimeout` intervals, while a value less than `1` means that each typematic event fires at an increasingly faster rate.

You'll also see in the programmatic example that I've attached an `onChange` handler to take care of when the user clicks a color. When the user does so, the function is passed a color value in the typical `#rrggbb` form.

Dialog

```
dojo.require("dijit.Dialog");
```

The Dialog dijit enables you to pop up windows, or dialog boxes as they are usually called, anytime you wish. These are not the same types of windows you open with `document.open()` but are instead much prettier and cooler. You can see what I mean by looking at Figure 3-3.

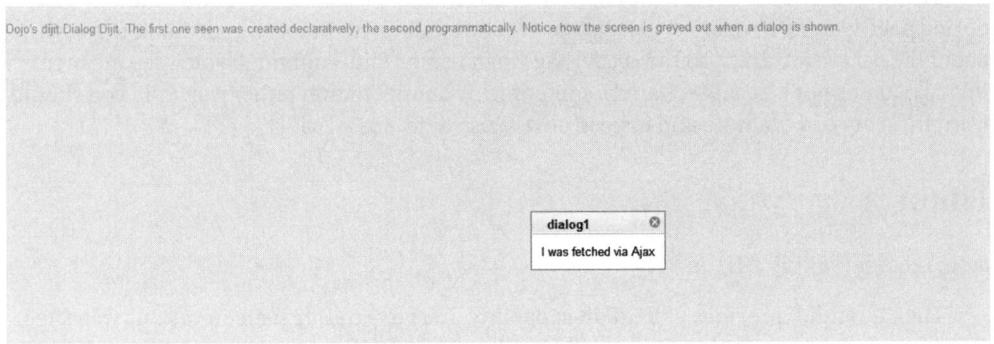

Figure 3-3. *The Dialog dijit*

The Dialog dijit is the part in the middle, but it's interesting to note that the content of the page is grayed out when the Dialog is shown. This is often called the Lightbox effect. What you unfortunately can't see by just looking at this book is that this Dialog fades in and out of existence nice and smooth-like; it doesn't just appear out of nowhere.

So, how do we go about creating a Dialog dijit? Declaratively, it looks like this:

```
<div dojoType="dijit.Dialog" id="dialog1"
  href="ch3_layout_ContentPane_content1.htm"></div>
```

Interestingly, the Dialog dijit is not shown at this point; it is only created and ready for you to use. To show it, you need to make this call:

```
dijit.byId("dialog1").show();
```

Note that until this Dialog is dismissed, nothing other than the Dialog can be interacted with. If there were a button on the page, the user could not click it until after closing the Dialog.

The Dialog can be moved by clicking on its title bar and holding, and then dragging it around.

Now, what about creating a Dialog via code? Easy enough:

```
var myDijit = new dijit.Dialog();
myDijit.setContent("Dialogs are fun!");
dojo.byId("divProgrammatic").appendChild(myDijit.domNode);
myDijit.show();
```

In addition to the `title` attribute, you can also set the `duration` attribute, which is the amount of time in milliseconds that it takes the Dialog to fade in and out. Also, because the Dialog dijit extends from the ContentPane dijit, you can specify things such as `href` to load content from another location, and virtually anything else the ContentPane dijit supports.

Note that in order for this to work in Internet Explorer, you can't use the usual `onLoad` event handler. Instead, use the `dojo.addOnLoad()` function. In this case, the code is as follows:

```
dojo.addOnLoad(showDialogs);
```

The reason you have to use this approach has to do with the timing of when things occur during page loading in relation to Dojo's own code loading. It's in fact a good habit to forget about the `onLoad` attribute on the `<body>` tag when using Dojo—although you'll see me break this rule in this book because, frankly, sometimes it doesn't matter either way. Still, you should learn from my *bad* example and instead always use `dojo.addOnLoad()`.

Editor

```
dojo.require("dijit.Editor");
```

The Editor dijit provides a rich-edit capability. You've certainly seen on various web sites those fancy editors that are trying their best to be Microsoft Word, and frequently not doing too bad a job—you know, the ones where you can make text bold, colored, different sizes, and so forth? Well, with Dojo you can have that very same editor on your site too.

You can see what this editor looks like by taking a look at Figure 3-4.

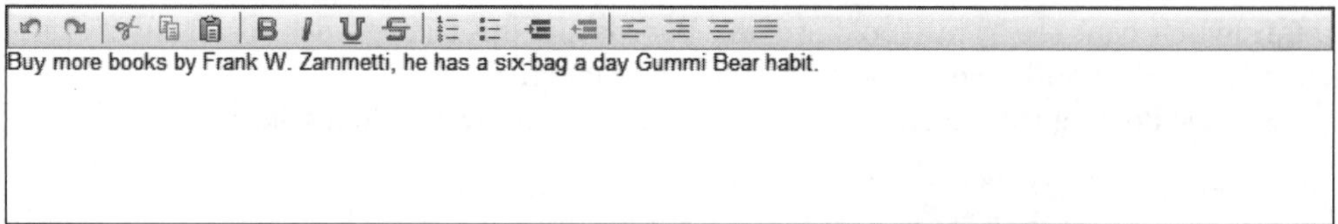

Figure 3-4. *The Editor dijit*

Of course, you can see only some simple text, nothing fancy. So, in Figure 3-5 you can see where I've made some text bold, some italic, and also created an unordered list in the editor.

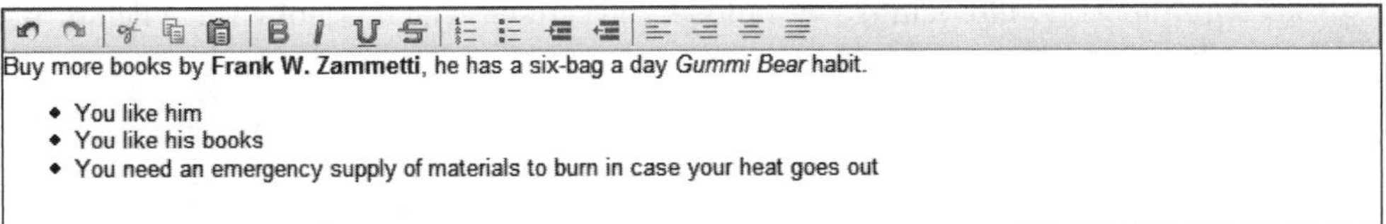

Figure 3-5. *The Editor dijit with some text modified*

So, how do you create this beast? The declarative approach is dirt simple:

```
<textarea name="field" width="200px" height="100px"
  dojoType="dijit.Editor">
  Buy more books by Frank W. Zammetti, he has a six-bag a day
  Gummi Bear habit.
</textarea>
```

The text there is naturally optional. To accomplish the same basic thing from the coding perspective, it looks like this:

```
var descField = document.createElement("textarea");
descField.cols = 42;
dojo.byId("divProgrammatic").appendChild(descField);
var descEditor = new dijit.Editor({id : "description"}, descField);
```

This code is only slightly more complex. As it turns out, you need a `<textarea>` to transform into an Editor dijit, so we have to begin by creating that element. Then we append it to the DOM, and then instantiate our Editor dijit, handing it a reference to the `<textarea>` we created.

InlineEditBox

```
dojo.require("dijit.InlineEditBox");
```

Let's say you have a `<div>` on your page. Let's further say that you want to allow the user to edit the contents of that `<div>` just by clicking it. Interesting thought, no? Well, guess what? That's precisely what the InlineEditBox dijit allows you to do.

It's not too visually impressive, I admit, but Figure 3-6 shows this dijit in action. Here you can see where I've created two versions of the dijit, one declaratively and one programmatically.

Dojo's dijit.InlineEditBox Dijit, created declaratively:

Edit me

Programmatically-created Dijit:

Figure 3-6. *The InlineEditBox dijit*

Clicking either <div> flips it into editor mode. You can see what this looks like in Figure 3-7, where I've clicked the second <div>.

Dojo's dijit.InlineEditBox Dijit, created declaratively:

Edit me

Programmatically-created Dijit:

Hello

Save it | Forget it

Figure 3-7. *The InlineEditBox dijit in editor mode*

So, creating an InlineEditBox declaratively just requires the following:

```
<div style="border:1px solid #000000;width:100px"
  dojoType="dijit.InlineEditBox" title="test">
  Edit me
</div>
```

You can see where I've added the style for the border, which doesn't happen automatically with this dijit. It's not exactly rocket science to create one of these, and doing so programmatically isn't much more difficult, but don't take my word for it:

```
var descEditor = new dijit.InlineEditBox({
  id : "description", autoSave : false, buttonSave : "Save it",
  buttonCancel : "Forget it", width : "100%"},
  dojo.byId("divProgrammatic")
);
```

I have done two things here that I didn't need to do. First, the id attribute is completely optional. Second, there's no requirement that I hold onto a reference to this dijit, but no harm in doing so (and of course, if you know you will need it later—for example, to get the value out of it, better to avoid a call to the dijit manager).

The autoSave attribute ties in with the buttonSave and buttonCancel attributes. As you can see, when the second <div> is being edited, there is a Cancel and a Save button. If autoSave is set to true, which is the default, those buttons are not present, which means the values of buttonSave and buttonCancel will be ignored. This also means the editing is essentially real-time, that is, the value is set in the <div> when the field loses focus (or the user presses Enter).

You'll also notice in the first screenshot that there is a nice little icon in the editor. This is by virtue of the noValueIndicator attribute, which you can set. This is what will appear in the editor if there is no value. What you see in that screenshot is the default, but you can put in anything you like.

You can also set the renderAsHtml attribute to true or false. When true, it means that the editor's value should be interpreted as HTML instead of plain text. You can set the value attribute to set the value of the editor.

You can hook into the onChange event handler by setting the onChange attribute to point to a function that is called whenever the value changes.

Finally, the `width` attribute naturally can be used to set the size of the editor. The default value is actually 100 percent, making my preceding code slightly redundant—but no harm, no foul, I figure.

Menu, MenuItem, and MenuSeparator

```
dojo.require("dijit.Menu");
```

Okay, look, you know what a menu is, right? Of course you do! Well, thanks to Dojo, you can have menus on your web page too! Let's say you want to have a context menu that appears when the user right-clicks a given `<div>`. You can do that. You can also have a menu bar that runs across the top of the page, which is really just a variation on a theme.

Take a gander at Figure 3-8 to see what all the fuss is about.

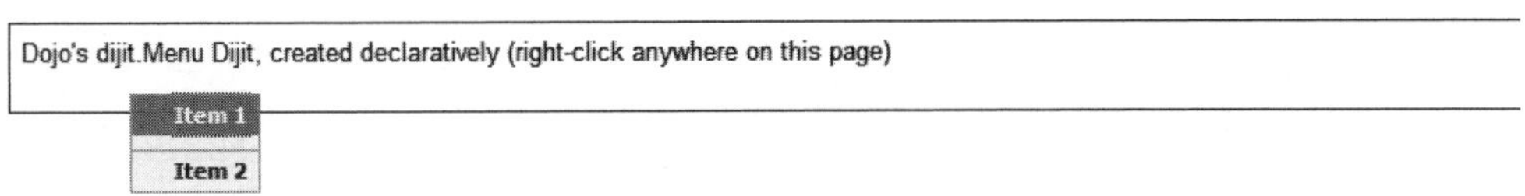

Figure 3-8. *The Menu dijit*

Here, my mouse is hovering over the first item, ready for me to click it. To create such a menu via markup, you have only to do the following:

```
<div dojoType="dijit.Menu" contextMenuForWindow="true"
  style="display:none;">
  <span dojoType="dijit.MenuItem"
    onClick="alert('Item 1')">Item 1</span>
  <span dojoType="dijit.MenuSeparator"></span>
  <span dojoType="dijit.MenuItem"
    onClick="alert('Item 2')">Item 2</span>
</div>
```

In this case, I've told this dijit, via the `contextMenuForWindow` attribute being set to `true`, that it is a context menu for the entire page, so I can right-click anywhere to have it appear. I could limit it to a given DOM node by setting the `targetNodeIds` attribute to the ID or multiple IDs I want to attach it to. As you can see, each item can have an `onClick` handler attached, because there would have to be for this to be worth anything!

Note the style attribute setting of `display:none`, which is required or else the menu will be present all the time, which clearly is not what we want.

There are actually three dijits in play here: the Menu itself, the MenuItem dijit, and the MenuSeparator dijit. The Menu dijit hosts the MenuItem and MenuSeparator dijits, which in markup terms means they are nested under the element with the `dojoType` of `dijit.Menu`. The MenuSeparator dijit just draws a line across the menu to, well, *separate* items!

ProgressBar

```
dojo.require("dijit.ProgressBar");
```

Do you know when you drive on a long trip, and the kids are in the back seat asking "are we there yet?" a million times? Well, imagine that you could put up something in front of them that would give them a constant status report on the progress of the trip. They could at a glance see how close they were to their destination without bugging the heck out of you.

Users of software are much like your children in their desire to know the progress of things, but fortunately Dojo enables you to be a better "parent" to your users with the ProgressBar dijit. You've of course seen a progress bar before, unless this is your first time using a graphical operating system, in which case I'd have to ask what basement you've been stuck in and what VAX[1] you've been using all this time.

Let's take a look first, Figure 3-9 representing said look.

Dojo's dijit.ProgressBar Dijit, created declaratively:

4%

Programmatically-created Dijit:

54%

Figure 3-9. *The ProgressBar dijit*

If I had some sort of paper from Hogwart's,[2] you could see that the percentage is gradually increasing in each, and the bar is gradually filling up with a blue color. (Someday I'll convince Apress to let me publish a book with color pictures so you can see what I'm *really* talking about!)

Creating a ProgressBar dijit is easy:

```
<div dojoType="dijit.ProgressBar" id="pb1"
  places="0" progress="0" maximum="100">
</div>
```

Or:

```
var myDijit = new dijit.ProgressBar({
  id : "pb2", places : 0, progress : "50%", maximum : 100
});
dojo.byId("divProgrammatic").appendChild(myDijit.domNode);
```

---

1. VAX is technically an operating system, but it's more or less become synonymous with mainframe systems that run it and that typically use a text-based interface paradigm.

2. What, you don't read or watch Harry Potter? Hogwart's School of Witchcraft and Wizardry is the school Harry Potter attends in the books (and movies based on the books) by J.K. Rowling. I have to assume you've at least *heard* of Harry Potter because otherwise I'd fear for your sanity! Whether you like them or not is entirely up to you. I happen to like them, and I'm secure in my manhood enough to admit it!

The `places` attribute indicates the number of decimal places to show in the value. Although `0` is the default, I felt the need to set it explicitly because, well, I'm pedantic that way! The `progress` attribute is a string that can be in two forms. If there is a percent sign, the value is a percentage. If there's no percent sign, the value is an absolute numeric value. In either case, this attribute is the current value of the ProgressBar. The `maximum` attribute is the highest value that the ProgressBar can achieve, this being an actual numeric value. There is also an `indeterminate` attribute, which defaults to `false`, but when `true` is used to indicate that the operation the ProgressBar is meant to track has started, but the current progress value is not yet known.

Now, creating a ProgressBar is only half the equation. It won't just move and fill up on its own. No, you have to periodically update it. To do this, you call the `update()` method of the ProgressBar dijit. You pass to it a single argument, an object, which contains a `progress` attribute that is the new `progress` value of the dijit. Typically, you would have an interval set that would periodically call `update()`, using some value that may (or may not) be updated with each iteration of the interval. That way, as you perform some work and reach milestones in the progress of that work, you change the value of the variable that the interval passes to `update()` to reflect the current progress, and the next iteration of the interval will update the ProgressBar automatically.

TitlePane

```
dojo.require("dijit.TitlePane");
```

Before you read this section, I suggest jumping ahead a few pages and reading the section on the ContentPane because, in many ways, you can view the TitlePane as an even more juiced-up ContentPane. (There's a joke in there. Hopefully, it registers after you read about the ContentPane!)

Go ahead, I'll wait.

Okay, all done. Good.

The TitlePane dijit enables you to have a section of a page, as you would typically use a `<div>` for, and allow it to have a title (hence the name TitlePane!), and also be able to "roll it up." Want to see? Absolutely: Figure 3-10 is just the ticket for you.

Dojo's dijit.TitlePane Dijit, created declaratively:

My Title #1

I Am Legend was a vastly overrated movie!

Programmatically-created Dijit:

My Title #2

I was fetched via Ajax

Figure 3-10. *The TitlePane dijit*

We have one created declaratively and one created programmatically, as you've seen before. You can clearly see a title bar and then the actual content. Notice the little icon in the upper-right corner? Figure 3-11 shows what happens when you click one of those bad boys.

Dojo's dijit.TitlePane Dijit, created declaratively:

My Title #1

Programmatically-created Dijit:

My Title #2

I was fetched via Ajax

Figure 3-11. *The TitlePane dijit, rolled up*

The first one has "rolled up" so that only the title bar is still visible. It does this with a very satisfying, smooth animation no less, so it's even better than it appears here.

So, what's the markup look like? It looks like this:

```
<div dojoType="dijit.TitlePane" title="My Title #1">
  I Am Legend was a vastly overrated movie!
</div>
```

Yep, that's all there is! And the code you ask? Here you go:

```
var myDijit = new dijit.TitlePane({
  href : "ch3_layout_ContentPane_content1.htm", title : "My Title #2"
});
dojo.byId("divProgrammatic").appendChild(myDijit.domNode);
myDijit.startup();
```

The call to `startup()` is required only if you're loading content via Ajax. If instead you were to do this:

```
var myDijit = new dijit.TitlePane({
  title : "My Title #2"
});
myDijit.setContent("test");
dojo.byId("divProgrammatic").appendChild(myDijit.domNode);
```

...then that method does not need to be called.

Toolbar

```
dojo.require("dijit.Toolbar");
```

Toolbars are another common user interface metaphor in modern GUI operating systems. Wanting one in web applications is common, and Dojo gives it to you.

A Toolbar dijit looks something like what you see in Figure 3-12.

Dojo's dijit.Toolbar Dijit, created declaratively:

Cut Copy B

Programmatically-created Dijit:

Cut Copy B

Figure 3-12. *The Toolbar dijit*

A toolbar in and of itself is pretty much just a box. To make the box a toolbar requires adding elements to it, typically various types of buttons. Here you can see two toolbars I've created, one declaratively, the other programmatically. They both have the same buttons on them. The button on the far right, which has the typical icon for making text bold, is a toggle button, which means you click it once and it stays "clicked" until you click it again. You can see what I mean in the second toolbar, where I've clicked it once already. You can also see what a button looks like when it's hovered over (the Cut button on the bottom).

Let's see how to create a toolbar without writing a bit of code first:

```
<div dojoType="dijit.Toolbar">
  <div dojoType="dijit.form.Button"
    iconClass="dijitEditorIcon dijitEditorIconCut"
    showLabel="true">Cut</div>
  <div dojoType="dijit.form.Button"
    iconClass="dijitEditorIcon dijitEditorIconCopy"
    showLabel="true">Copy</div>
  <div dojoType="dijit.form.Button"
    iconClass="dijitEditorIcon dijitEditorIconPaste"
    showLabel="false">Paste</div>
  <span dojoType="dijit.ToolbarSeparator"></span>
  <div dojoType="dijit.form.ToggleButton"
    iconClass="dijitEditorIcon dijitEditorIconBold"
    showLabel="false">Bold</div>
</div>
```

As you can see, it's just a `<div>` with the appropriate `dojoType` (`dijit.Toolbar`). Nested underneath that is some other `<div>` elements, and one `<span>` element. Most of the `<div>` elements use a `dojoType` of `dijit.form.Button`, which is basically just a plain old button you can click. Notice the use of the `iconClass` attribute, which is used to set the icon of the button (a button doesn't have to have an icon at all if you don't want it to). I also set the text of the buttons by using the `showLabel` attribute (well, no, that in fact tells the button to show a textual label—the actual text is the content of the `<div>` element). Just like an icon, a button doesn't have to have text; that's up to you.

You can also see the use of the `dijit.ToolbarSeparator` dijit, which is just a line drawn vertically on the Toolbar dijit to separate logically grouped buttons. Finally, the `dijit.form.ToggleButton` is used for that bold button to enable us to have a "sticky" button, so to speak, to set bold on and off.

Now, what about the code-centric approach? Sure, here you go:

```
var myDijit = new dijit.Toolbar({});
dojo.byId("divProgrammatic").appendChild(myDijit.domNode);
myDijit.addChild(new dijit.form.Button({
  iconClass : "dijitEditorIcon dijitEditorIconCut",
  showLabel : "true", label : "Cut"
}));
myDijit.addChild(new dijit.form.Button({
  iconClass : "dijitEditorIcon dijitEditorIconCopy",
  showLabel : "true", label : "Copy"
}));
myDijit.addChild(new dijit.form.Button({
  iconClass : "dijitEditorIcon dijitEditorIconPaste"
}));
myDijit.addChild(new dijit.ToolbarSeparator({}));
myDijit.addChild(new dijit.form.ToggleButton({
  iconClass : "dijitEditorIcon dijitEditorIconBold"
}));
myDijit.startup();
```

I think this is probably self-explanatory, given that it's very much like other dijits we have looked at. The only difference worth mentioning is that the `label` for a button is set via the `label` attribute during construction of a given button.

Tooltip

```
dojo.require("dijit.Tooltip");
```

A tool tip is that little piece of text that appears, usually in some sort of cartoon-like "speech" bubble, when you hover over something in a GUI. The Tooltip dijit provides this functionality for your web pages.

Figure 3-13 shows a visual of a Tooltip dijit.

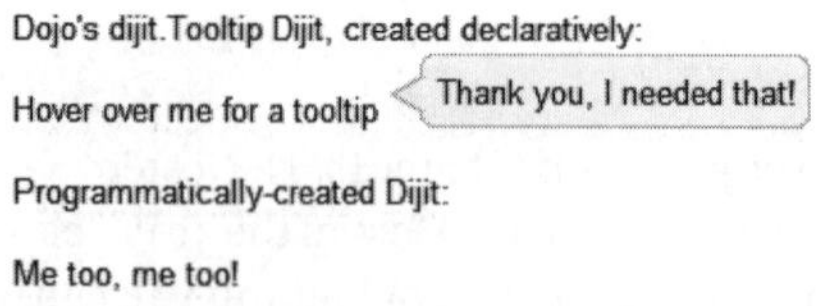

Figure 3-13. *The Tooltip dijit*

As with many dijits, there is nice animation that you get automatically. The Tooltip you see here gently fades in and out of existence when you hover over the text, or stop hovering over it.

What you do is "attach" a Tooltip dijit to a given DOM node. To do this with pure markup requires just this little snippet:

```
<div dojoType="dijit.Tooltip"
  connectId="targetDiv1"
  label="Thank you, I needed that!">
</div>
```

The `connectId` attribute is the ID of the DOM node to attach the Tooltip to. That's all there is to it; all the functionality of the Tooltip is automatic.

What about code you say? Here it is:

```
<span id="divProgrammatic" style="cursor:pointer;"
  onMouseOver="dijit.showTooltip('That too!', dojo.byId('divProgrammatic'));"
  onMouseOut="dijit.hideTooltip(dojo.byId('divProgrammatic'));">
  Me too, me too!
</span>
```

Whoa, that's a little different from what you've seen before. As it turns out, you don't explicitly create a Tooltip programmatically. Instead, a call to `dijit.showTooltip()`, passing it the text for the Tooltip and a reference to the DOM node to attach to, gets it onto the screen. Then you call `dijit.hideTooltip()` later, again passing a reference to the DOM node, to hide it. You still get the nice animation too. I suppose you don't *have* to do this from `onMouseOver` and `onMouseOut` event handlers, but being as those are the events a Tooltip usually appears on, it only makes sense.

Incidentally, you can also set a `duration` attribute, which is the amount of time that the fade-in and fade-out takes. The default value is `200` milliseconds.

Tree

```
dojo.require("dijit.Tree"); and optionally➥
dojo.require("dojo.data.ItemFileReadStore");
```

A Tree dijit is a great way to show hierarchical information. It enables the user to focus attention on a small subset of a larger group of data, to make choices or see relationships. It's another common UI design paradigm that you've no doubt seen plenty before. But just in case, Figure 3-14 is here to offer a first glimpse of a Tree, if it happens to be a new concept for you.

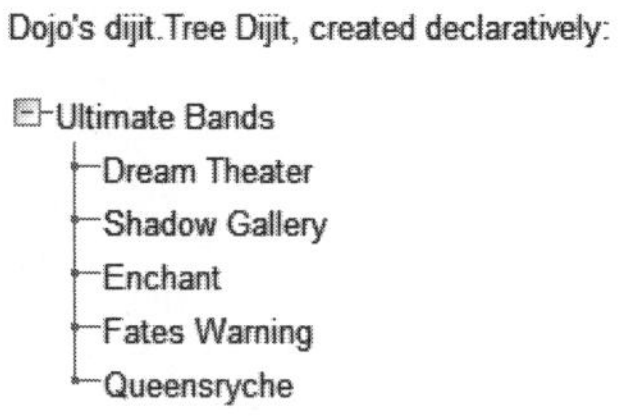

Figure 3-14. *The Tree dijit*

And the magic markup that created this? Here you go:

```
<div dojoType="dojo.data.ItemFileReadStore"
  url="ch3_Tree_data.txt" jsid="bandStore" />
<div dojoType="dijit.Tree" store="bandStore" labelAttr="name"
  label="Ultimate Bands"></div>
```

Okay, wait just a minute—I can see a bunch of band names in that Tree, but I don't see them here in the markup. What gives? Well, what gives is that `<div>` with the `dojoType` of `dojo.data.ItemFileReadStore`.

You see, you can populate a Tree from a file that looks like this:

```
{ label : "name",
  identifier : "name",
  items : [
     { name : "Dream Theater", type :"category" },
     { name : "Shadow Gallery", type : "category" },
     { name : "Enchant", type : "category" },
     { name : "Fates Warning", type : "category" },
     { name : "Queensryche", type : "category" }
  ]
}
```

After you have this file sitting on a server somewhere (or in the same directory as the HTML file, as in this example), you can create a `dojo.data.ItemFileReadStore` thingamajig, and then "bind" a dijit to it. You can think of that `<div>` with the `dojoType` of `dojo.data.ItemFileReadStore` as basically an invisible dijit. Dojo will in fact parse it, because of the `dojoType` attribute, and will create a dijit out of it, but it's one with no visual representation on the screen. You will notice, however, the `jsid` attribute on that same `<div>`. This is an ID for this particular data store, for the data structure created from the file with the data in it.

Now, later you'll see that the second `<div>` with the `dojoType` of `dijit.Tree`, which has of course our actual Tree dijit, references the ID of the data store through the `store` attribute. The only other detail is to tell the Tree which element in the array of data is the test label, `name` in this case as specified by the `labelAttr` attribute, and to give the tree a root label via the `label` attribute, and we're all set. Dojo takes care of doing an Ajax request to get the data file specified by the `url` attribute of the first `<div>` and of populating the Tree for us from the resultant data store.

The dijit.form Package

The `dijit.form` package is where you'll find dijits typically used to build up forms for users performing data entry.

Button

```
dojo.require("dijit.form.Button");
```

The Button dijit creates a button, just like the `<button>` or `<input type="button">` HTML tags, but it does so with a bit more pizzazz! Figure 3-15 shows you what I mean.

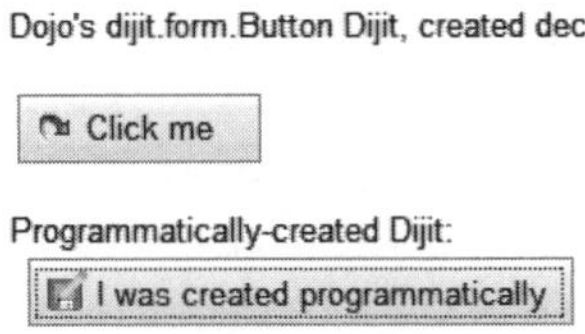

Figure 3-15. *The Button dijit*

Here you can obviously see two buttons, one created declaratively and one created programmatically. The declarative version was created with this markup:

```
<button dojoType="dijit.form.Button"
  iconClass="dijitEditorIcon dijitEditorIconRedo"
  onClick="alert('Stop that!');">
  Click me
</button>
```

You can see a couple of initialize attributes coming into play. The first, `iconClass`, specifies a CSS style element to put an icon on the button. There are two classes specified, both are which are required for the icon to appear because of the way they are declared in the style sheet. Here I've used one of the icons that ships with the Editor dijit, just because they are there! You can also see the `onClick` handler attached for when the user clicks the button.

Creating a button programmatically is similarly easy:

```
var myDijit = new dijit.form.Button({
  label : "I was created programmatically",
  onClick : function() { alert("That tickles!"); },
  iconClass : "dijitEditorIcon dijitEditorIconSave"
});
dojo.byId("divProgrammatic").appendChild(myDijit.domNode);
```

The `label` attribute does the same job as the text does when created declaratively. Otherwise, the attributes map pretty directly. Keep in mind that having an icon is completely optional, and so too is having text on the button. If you just want an icon (or, I suppose, a blank button), you can set the `showLabel` attribute to `false` and you're all set. Note that when creating a button declaratively and setting `showLabel` to `false`, any text present will simply be ignored. There is no harm to text being there in that case.

CheckBox

```
dojo.require("dijit.form.CheckBox");
```

The CheckBox dijit provides a somewhat prettier version of the standard check box form element. In Figure 3-16 you can see this prettiness (relatively speaking at least).

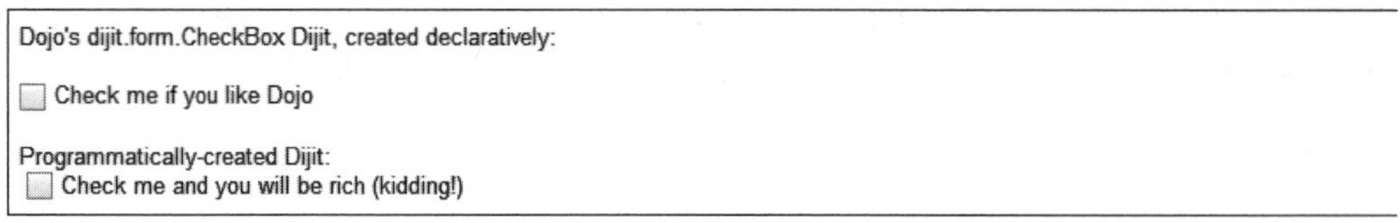

Figure 3-16. *The CheckBox dijit*

Getting one of these bad boys onto the page via straight markup is a trivial exercise, as this code demonstrates:

```
<input type="checkbox" id="cb1"
  dojoType="dijit.form.CheckBox"
/> <label for="cb1">Check me if you like Dojo</label>
```

The `<label>` element is optional, but a check box without text next to it isn't necessary too often, so in all probability you'll want a label. Interestingly, there doesn't seem to be a way to combine the two, that is, there doesn't seem to be something like a label attribute to the dijit itself. No biggie, we can cope. You'll want to be sure to assign an ID to the check box so that later you can retrieve its value, like so:

```
alert(dijit.byId("cb1").checked);
```

This returns `true` or `false`, depending on whether the check box is selected.

To create a check box the hard way, in JavaScript code, you have only to do the following, which isn't much harder:

```
var myDijit = new dijit.form.CheckBox({
  id : "cb2", onClick : function(val) { alert("SUCKER!"); },
  label : "I was created programmatically"
});
dojo.byId("divProgrammatic").appendChild(myDijit.domNode);
dojo.byId("cb2Label").style.display = "";
```

As mentioned before, a label is generally something you'll want, and you could try to build one on the fly, but I found it was easier to simply hide and show it as appropriate. In other words, although the check box is built dynamically, the label is always there; it's just being shown or hidden depending on whether the check box is displayed. Also note that the label is *not* generated by Dojo; it's simply a page element that I put in the markup itself. As you can see here, you can register an `onClick` callback function if you wish. Note that I in fact did put a `label` attribute in, but also notice that it's essentially ignored. That's just to prove the point about the labels that I've been talking about.

Note One more interesting point: you'll find there is a `value` attribute associated with the check box. This, however, is *not* the `true` or `false` value you see by looking at the `checked` property directly. The `value` attribute is instead the value that will be submitted for the check box, if selected, when its parent form is submitted. I found this a little weird at first, frankly because I expected it to be `true` or `false`. Hopefully, being told this saves you a few moments' thought!

ComboBox

```
dojo.require("dijit.form.ComboBox"); and optionally➥
dojo.require("dojo.data.ItemFileWriteStore");
```

A combo box is kind of a chimera, a mixture of two different components. It's a `<select>` element, but it's also a text box. This enables users to choose from a selection of options, as well as giving them the opportunity to enter something else entirely.

The ComboBox dijit goes a step further and combines an autocomplete function. This means that as the user begins typing, the first option in the list of options that matches that entry will be shown so the user can select it quickly. This saves a lot of time for users and makes the interface feel more reactive to their needs.

In Figure 3-17 you can see this dijit in action.

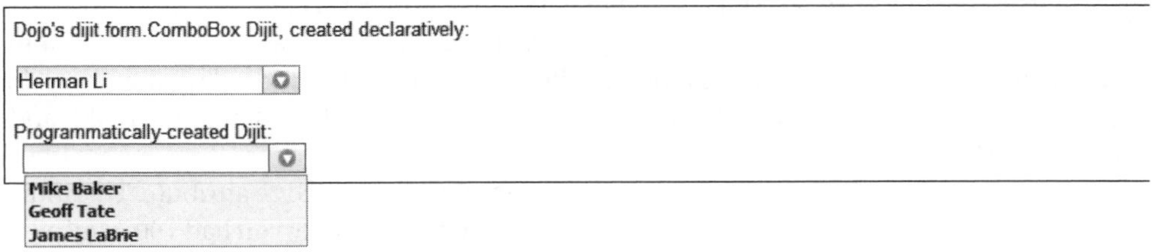

Figure 3-17. *The ComboBox dijit*

Here you can see I've selected one of the options in the first ComboBox. What you can't see, of course, is that all I typed was *H*, at which point the list popped up below the text box (as shown in the select ComboBox), but only those names beginning with *H* were shown. I then used the down-arrow key to highlight *Herman Li* and pressed Enter, at which point the full name was inserted into the text box portion of the ComboBox.

To create the first ComboBox, all I had to do was this:

```
<select dojoType="dijit.form.ComboBox"
  value=""
  autocomplete="true" hasDownArrow="true">
  <option></option>
  <option>Eddie Van Halen</option>
  <option>John Petrucci</option>
  <option>Herman Li</option>
</select>
```

The `hasDownArrow` attribute is set to `true`, which means the arrow the user can click is shown. You can hide this arrow by setting this attribute to `false`. This has the effect of allowing users to start typing and still get the list of matching values below—but they can no longer manually click something to open the drop-down list; the only way to see the list is to actually start typing something.

The second ComboBox you see was created via code, which looks like this:

```
var options = new dojo.data.ItemFileWriteStore({
  data: {
    identifier : "name", items : [
      {name : "Mike Baker"},
      {name : "Geoff Tate"},
      {name : "James LaBrie"}
    ]
  }
});
var myDijit = new dijit.form.ComboBox({
  store : options
});
dojo.byId("divProgrammatic").appendChild(myDijit.domNode);
```

There are a couple of ways you could populate a ComboBox via code, but probably the easiest is to use the Dojo data system. Here, you create a `dojo.data.ItemFileWriteStore`, and in it you create a data structure in a predefined format. After you have that data store, you simply pass it along to a new instance of `dijit.form.ComboBox`, append the dijit to the DOM, and it's ready for use.

There is a neat attribute you can set on the ComboBox: the `pageSize` attribute. This indicates the number of options to display at a time. For example, let's say you had 100 items in the drop-down portion. That's a lot of items for the user to go through. If you set `pageSize` to `10`, the user will see ten at a time, plus an option labeled More Choices. When this option is selected, the user sees another ten, and so on. This is a nice way for the user to easily page through a large number of items, and with no additional work on your part as a developer.

Usually, the ComboBox is case-insensitive when trying to match what the user typed to what is in the drop-down list. If you set `ignoreCase` to `false`, however, case will then matter.

Another nifty configuration option is the `query` attribute, which enables you to specify a query that will be used to filter the options used in the data store. Check the documentation on the data store for how to write such a query.

ComboButton

```
dojo.require("dijit.form.Button");
```

The ComboButton dijit is very much along the lines of the ComboBox dijit, except that there is no free-form data entry available.

Oh yes, and it's a button.

In Figure 3-18, you can see this hybrid for yourself.

Dojo's dijit.form.ComboButton Dijit, created declaratively:

Figure 3-18. *The ComboButton dijit*

As you can see, it doesn't look much different from your average button, except for one thing: the arrow on the right-hand side. If you click the button, you get the normal `onClick` event. If you click the arrow, you get what you see in Figure 3-19.

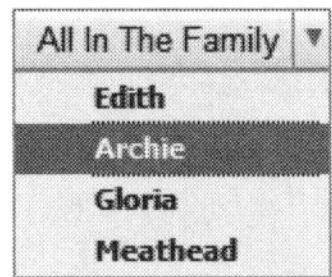

Figure 3-19. *The ComboButton dijit after clicking the arrow*

As you can see, you get a list of options, just as with the ComboBox.

So, how do you create one of these? Here you go:

```
<div dojoType="dijit.form.ComboButton">
  <span>All In The Family</span>
  <div dojoType="dijit.Menu" toggle="fade" style="display:none;">
    <div dojoType="dijit.MenuItem">Edith</div>
    <div dojoType="dijit.MenuItem">Archie</div>
    <div dojoType="dijit.MenuItem">Gloria</div>
    <div dojoType="dijit.MenuItem">Meathead</div>
  </div>
</div>
```

Basically, you create a `dijit.form.ComboButton` object, and then attach a `dijit.Menu` object to it for the selections. The `dijit.Menu` object has some number of `dijit.MenuItem` children, one for each option available.

CurrencyTextBox, DateTextBox, NumberTextBox, and TimeTextBox

```
dojo.require("dijit.form.CurrencyTextBox");➥
dojo.require("dijit.form.DateTextBox");➥
dojo.require("dijit.form.NumberTextBox");➥
dojo.require("dijit.form.TimeTextBox");
```

I grouped four dijits together here because they are all very much along the same lines and so it makes sense to discuss them as one.

It's not at all uncommon to have a text box that you want to *mask*, that is, to allow input of only a certain type and format. Writing the code to do that yourself usually involves looking at each keypress and accepting or rejecting it, or else hooking into the `onChange` event to do much the same thing, or else doing some validation and/or modification to the entered value after the fact. All of that sounds dangerously like a lot of work to me, so a simpler, lazier approach would be nice, and Dojo provides just that!

However, it wouldn't be Dojo if it didn't do a bit more than the basics! So, let's begin by looking at the CurrencyTextBox dijit, as seen in Figure 3-20.

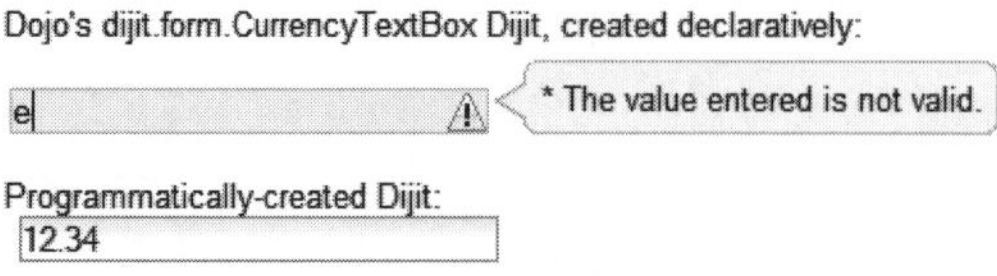

Figure 3-20. *The CurrencyTextBox dijit*

The first thing to be aware of is that if you don't enter the text in an appropriate format, the dijit will be highlighted (in yellow, which you can't see here, of course) and a message will be displayed telling you that you messed up. Here I've entered a letter where only numbers are expected. The message telling me I've borked my entry somehow of course fades in and out of view nicely.

Creating this is a simple matter of using the following code:

```
<input type="textbox" dojoType="dijit.form.CurrencyTextBox">
```

Yes, that's all there is to it! Via code, it's this:

```
var myDijit = new dijit.form.CurrencyTextBox({
  value : 12.34
});
dojo.byId("divProgrammatic").appendChild(myDijit.domNode);
```

The `value` attribute enables you to set an initial default value.

The DateTextBox dijit is even fancier still, as you can plainly see for yourself by looking at Figure 3-21.

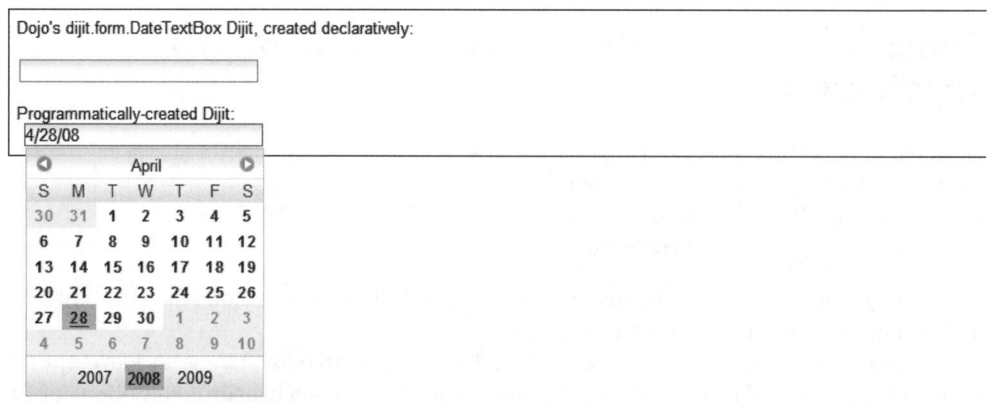

Figure 3-21. *The DateTextBox dijit*

Sure, you can just enter a date in a valid format, but why would you do that? Instead, clicking the text box opens a calendar for you to select from! The same validation and reporting of invalid formats as you saw in the CurrencyTextBox applies here too. The markup to use to create this dijit is this:

```
<input type="textbox" dojoType="dijit.form.DateTextBox">
```

As you can see, I don't need to do anything to get the calendar; it's automatic. The equivalent code is this:

```
var myDijit = new dijit.form.DateTextBox({
  value : new Date()
});
dojo.byId("divProgrammatic").appendChild(myDijit.domNode);
```

Note how the value is an actual JavaScript `Date` object, not some string. This is really nice because dealing with the true data type is more flexible and less error-prone.

The next dijit in this general theme is the NumberTextBox. Although it's in many ways similar to the CurrencyTextBox, it's a little bit different too, as you can see in Figure 3-22.

Dojo's dijit.form.NumberTextBox Dijit, created declaratively:

2,344,354

Programmatically-created Dijit:

42

Figure 3-22. *The NumberTextBox dijit*

One nice thing this dijit does is insert commas as necessary for large numbers. This gives your text box a polished feel. To create this dijit declaratively requires you to do only the following:

```
<input type="textbox" dojoType="dijit.form.NumberTextBox">
```

Via code, it's not much more:

```
var myDijit = new dijit.form.NumberTextBox({
  value : 42
});
dojo.byId("divProgrammatic").appendChild(myDijit.domNode);
```

The final dijit to look at in this section is the TimeTextBox, shown in Figure 3-23, and it's not your momma's text box either!

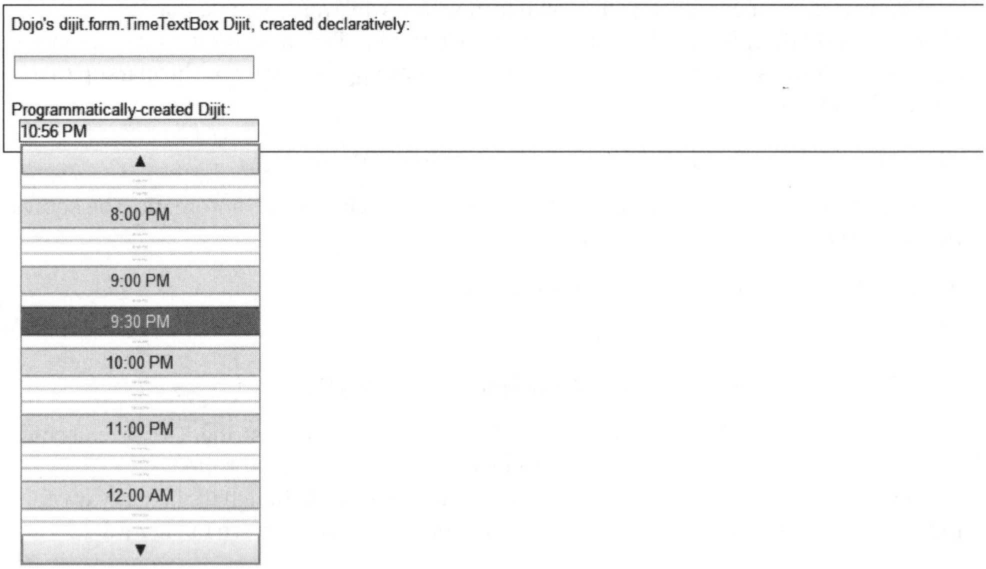

Figure 3-23. *The TimeTextBox dijit*

It's not just a place to enter some numbers, a colon, and an AM/PM indicator! Instead, clicking it gives you a drop-down where you can select the time. You'll notice that the hours show up as large gray bars, but as you scroll over this thing, it expands to reveal times down to 15-minute breakdowns.

Getting this thing onto the screen is a piece of cake, like all the rest:

```
<input type="textbox" dojoType="dijit.form.TimeTextBox">
```

Or, for those who prefer the more pedantic code approach:

```
var myDijit = new dijit.form.TimeTextBox({
  value : new Date()
});
dojo.byId("divProgrammatic").appendChild(myDijit.domNode);
```

These four dijits together enable you to create powerful forms that limit what the user can enter to valid values only. In most cases, these dijits also make it more convenient and easy for the user to enter the data.

DropDownButton

```
dojo.require("dijit.form.Button");
```

A DropDownButton and a ComboButton are nearly identical, except for one key difference: a DropDownButton, when clicked *anywhere*, shows the drop-down portion. There is no `onClick` event with a DropDownButton (well, there *is*, but it's not what you think—it's not typically an event for you to handle).

Figure 3-24 shows a DropDownButton dijit.

Dojo's dijit.form.DropDownButton Dijit, created declaratively:

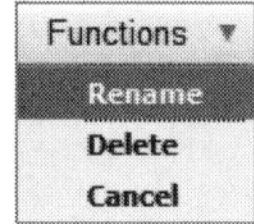

Figure 3-24. *The DropDownButton dijit*

As I mentioned, clicking anywhere on the button gets you the display you see in the figure, not just on the arrow as with the ComboButton.

The markup for creating this dijit is just about identical to that of the ComboButton, however:

```
<div dojoType="dijit.form.DropDownButton">
  <span>Functions</span>
  <div dojoType="dijit.Menu">
    <div dojoType="dijit.MenuItem" label="Rename"
      onclick="alert('Rename');"></div>
    <div dojoType="dijit.MenuItem" label="Delete"
      onclick="alert('Delete');"></div>
    <div dojoType="dijit.MenuItem" label="Cancel"
      onclick="alert('Cancel')"></div>
  </div>
</div>
```

Although you don't typically do anything in response to the `onClick` event of the button itself, you often will want to do something in response to the `onClick` event of a particular option, and you can see I've done that here.

HorizontalSlider and VerticalSlider

```
dojo.require("dijit.form.Slider");
```

Let's say you need the user to choose a number between a maximum and a minimum value. Let's further say that the user will be allowed to choose amounts in discrete "steps." Of course, you want this selection to be done in a graphical, hopefully intuitive way. In such a case, a slider might be the right UI metaphor to use.

A HorizontalSlider dijit allows such a selection in a horizontal orientation (the Vertical-Slider dijit, as I'm sure you realize already, does so in a vertical orientation). Figure 3-25 shows you what the HorizontalSlider looks like.

Dojo's dijit.form.HorizontalSlider Dijit, created declaratively:

10 20 30 40 50 60

Figure 3-25. *The HorizontalSlider dijit*

The VerticalSlider dijit looks the same, but running up and down the page instead of across. As you can see, the user can select a value between (and including) 10 and 60, and can do so in increments of 10. The user simply grabs the little handle that's currently under the number 30 and drags it left or right to make the selection.

The markup for this dijit is as follows:

```
<div dojoType="dijit.form.HorizontalSlider"
  value="30"
  minimum="10"
  maximum="60"
  discreteValues="6"
  showButtons="true">
  <div dojoType="dijit.form.HorizontalRuleLabels"
    container="topDecoration"
    labels="10,20,30,40,50,60"
    style="height:1.2em;font-size:10pt;color:#000000;"></div>
</div>
```

Quite a few attributes are on display here, but they are mostly obvious, I suspect. The `value` attribute is the current value the slider has when it is created. The `minimum` and `maximum` attributes are simply the highest and lowest numbers that appear on the ends of the slider. The `discreteValues` attribute tells the dijit how many "steps" there are between (and including) the minimum and maximum values. This is in turn used to determine the increment that each step has.

You'll also notice there is a HorizontalRuleLabels dijit that goes along with the HorizontalSlider dijit. The HorizontalRuleLabels dijit is used for labeling the HorizontalSlider. The `container` attribute on it determines where the labels will appear, on top here because of the `topDecoration` value assigned to it. The `labels` attribute is just a comma-separated list of the labels for each step on the slider. The `style` attribute is used to "pretty up" the labels a little bit.

By default, you not only can drag the handle to select a value but also can click anywhere on the slider. If you don't want that capability, set the `clickSelect` attribute to `false`. You'll also notice arrows on both ends of the slider. The user can click these to decrement and increment the value, but if you'd prefer that users not be able to do this, set the `showButtons` attribute to `false`.

NumberSpinner

When you want the user to enter a number but you want to do it with a little flair, a NumberSpinner dijit can be just the way to go. You've seen these before, I'm sure: a text box with a down and an up arrow next to it. The user clicks the arrows and increments or decrements the value. Users can still hand-enter a number if they choose to, of course.

Not sure what I'm talking about? Figure 3-26 should clear it right up.

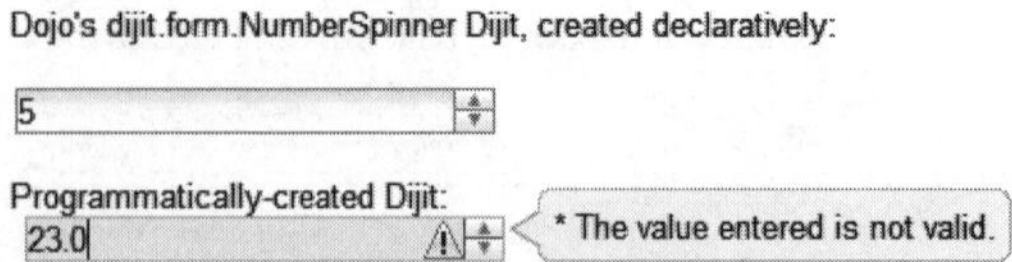

Figure 3-26. *The NumberSpinner dijit*

Here you can see two versions. The difference is that the second forces me to enter two decimal places. In fact, you can see where I've entered only one so far, and I'm getting a validation error at this point. If I enter another number or click the arrow in either direction, that error message goes away.

Interestingly, creating one of these with markup uses the `<input>` tag, as shown here:

```
<input dojoType="dijit.form.NumberSpinner"
  value="1"
  constraints="{min : 0, max : 10, places : 0}">
```

The `value` attribute does what it always does: gives an initial value to the field. The `constraints` attribute is how you tell the NumberSpinner what the maximum and minimum allowed values are, as well as how many decimal places are required (in other words, setting a value of `0` here means that if I enter `12.2`, it's an error).

Creating a NumberSpinner via code is trivial too:

```
var myDijit = new dijit.form.NumberSpinner({
  value : 25, constraints : { min : 20, max : 40, places : 2 }
});
dojo.byId("divProgrammatic").appendChild(myDijit.domNode);
```

This code follows the same basic structure as the markup in terms of the attributes you need to supply. Notice, though, that in both cases, both markup and code, you're passing an object definition as the value. This is a little unusual in Dijit land, but not terribly unusual in Dojo as a whole.

RadioButton

```
dojo.require("dijit.form.CheckBox");
```

Radio buttons enable the user to choose from various options but to choose only one of them at a time (as opposed to check boxes, which allow multiple items to be selected). In Figure 3-27, you can see Dojo's take on the radio button.

Dojo's dijit.form.RadioButton Dijit, created declaratively:

Select me if you like Dojo

Programmatically-created Dijit:

Another

Figure 3-27. *The RadioButton dijit*

To create a RadioButton dijit, you can do this:

```
<input type="radio" id="rb1"
  dojoType="dijit.form.RadioButton"
/> <label for="rb1">Select me if you like Dojo</label>
```

Or you can do this:

```
var myDijit = new dijit.form.RadioButton({
  id : "cb2",
  label : "I was created programmatically"
});
dojo.byId("divProgrammatic").appendChild(myDijit.domNode);
```

Note that the <label> element is optional when creating a RadioButton declaratively, but you'll nearly always want text next to a RadioButton, so you'll usually want a <label> element. Also note that when creating a RadioButton via code, the label attribute is not used; the text still comes from a <label> element (I have text here for the label attribute just to prove that it is in fact not used).

TextBox

```
dojo.require("dijit.form.TextBox");
```

A text box is perhaps the most common UI element out there, save for maybe a button. (I guess windows themselves are more common, but I think you know what I'm sayin' here!) A TextBox dijit gives you a text box as in plain HTML, but with more features.

Figure 3-28 shows an example of this dijit.

Dojo's dijit.form.TextBox Dijit, created declaratively:

Programmatically-created Dijit:
12.34

Figure 3-28. *The TextBox dijit*

This doesn't look much different from a plain ole text box, save for the subtle gradient (which you very likely can't see in the screenshot—but trust me, it's there). It's when you look at some of the available options for this dijit that you start to see it's true worth. Before we get to that, though, let's see what it takes to create one declaratively:

```
<input type="textbox" dojoType="dijit.form.TextBox">
```

Programmatically is nearly as simple:

```
var myDijit = new dijit.form.TextBox({
  value : 12.34
});
dojo.byId("divProgrammatic").appendChild(myDijit.domNode);
```

Here you can see one of the available options, value, which sets the initial value of the TextBox. What are some of the other options? Well, to begin with, you have trim, which defaults to false, but when set to true will trim trailing and leading spaces from the user's entry. The uppercase attribute, which defaults to false, will convert alphabetic characters to uppercase when set to true. In the same vein as uppercase is lowercase, which converts to all lowercase letters, and propercase, which converts the first character of each word to uppercase and all the rest of the letters to lowercase. The maxLength attribute limits how much the user can enter.

Textarea

```
dojo.require("dijit.form.Textarea");
```

A <textarea> is another common UI element, and a Textarea dijit extends its capabilities much like TextBox extends a basic text box. One of the limitations of a plain <textarea> is that it's a static size (assuming you don't resize it via code, I mean). This means that if the user types more than the text area can hold (visually hold, I mean), you get scrollbars to account for the overflow. The Textarea dijit, on the other hand, can expand as the user types, which is often just what you want.

Figure 3-29 shows an example of this dijit.

Dojo's dijit.form.Textarea Dijit, created declaratively:

Programmatically-created Dijit:

Hello, I am a textarea
I have expanded.
And again.

Figure 3-29. *The Textarea dijit*

The second Textarea that you see started off the same size (heightwise at least) as the first one. However, as I typed and pressed Enter a few times, it expanded to accommodate my entry.

What does creating one of these look like? Very much like creating a plain <textarea>, actually:

```
<textarea dojoType="dijit.form.Textarea"
  style="width:200px;"></textarea>
```

Interestingly, you set the size of the Textarea dijit via the style attribute rather than the typical rows and cols attributes on a plain <textarea>. This gives you better control over the size of the text area because rows and cols is dependent on the font size and zoom factor of the page, whereas width and height style attributes are absolute values (browser zoom features still could resize these elements, though).

The code to create a Textarea dijit looks like this:

```
var myDijit = new dijit.form.Textarea({
  value : "Hello, I am a textarea"
});
dojo.byId("divProgrammatic").appendChild(myDijit.domNode);
```

ToggleButton

```
dojo.require("dijit.form.Button"); (and dojo.require("dijit.Toolbar");)
```

A ToggleButton is like a regular button except that when it's clicked, it stays clicked until it's clicked again. This is often used on toolbars for things that "turn on" and persist on, such as turning on bold in your word processor.

A ToggleButton looks a little something like what you see in Figure 3-30.

Dojo's dijit.form.ToggleButton Dijit, created declaratively:

Programmatically-created Dijit:

Figure 3-30. *The ToggleButton dijit*

To create such a dijit, you use markup that looks like this:

```
<div id="toolbar1" dojoType="dijit.Toolbar"
  style="width:26px;">
  <div dojoType="dijit.form.ToggleButton"
    iconClass="dijitEditorIcon dijitEditorIconBold"
    showLabel="false"></div>
  </div>
```

Note that the ToggleButton is nested inside a `dijit.Toolbar` dijit. I found that was necessary for the toggling to work. If it's not inside a Toolbar, the button doesn't stay clicked as it should. You'll note the `iconClass` attribute, which you can optionally use to have an image on the button, as I have here for both of them (I used the images that come with the Editor dijit, just because they're there). The `showLabel` attribute enables you to show text on the button when set to `true` (it would be the content of the `<div>` element in that case).

To create a ToggleButton with code, write something along these lines:

```
var myDijit = new dijit.Toolbar({ style : "width:26px;" });
myDijit.addChild(new dijit.form.ToggleButton({
  iconClass : "dijitEditorIcon dijitEditorIconItalic",
  showLabel : false
}));
dojo.byId("divProgrammatic").appendChild(myDijit.domNode);
```

Once again, I had to create a Toolbar first and then create the ToggleButton and add it as a child of the Toolbar. Otherwise, this is very likely as you'd expect it to look. Note that if you had wanted the button to be depressed by default, you would pass `true` as the value of the `checked` attribute when creating it.

ValidationTextBox

```
dojo.require("dijit.form.ValidationTextBox");
```

The ValidationTextBox is an extended TextBox dijit that enables you to validate user input based on a regular expression. It provides feedback and hints about what format the entry needs to be in. Let's begin with a look at this dijit, shown in Figure 3-31.

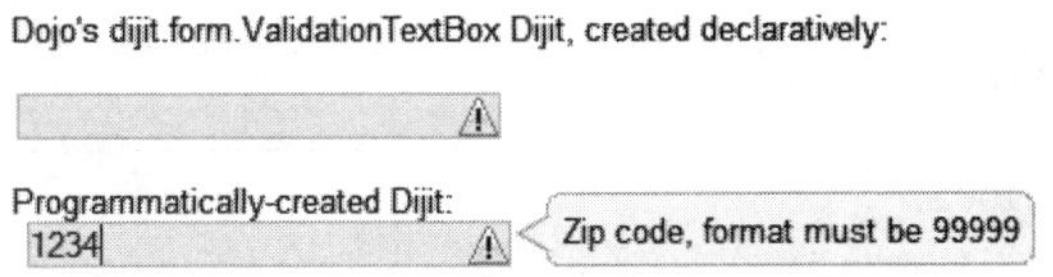

Figure 3-31. *The ValidationTextBox dijit*

Here you can see where I've clicked on the first ValidationTextBox and then clicked away, so it's flagged it as an invalid input (the field requires an entry in the form 99999). The second ValidationTextBox is also flagged as invalid because it's a zip code entry field (at least the first part of a zip code) and the entry also must be in the form 99999. The tool tip has appeared (faded in, actually) to tell me what I need to enter.

To make the magic happen, drop this markup onto your page:

```
<input type="text"
  dojoType="dijit.form.ValidationTextBox"
  regExp="^(\d{5}-\d{4})|(\d{5})$"
  required="true"
  invalidMessage="Format must be 99999">
```

Or, if code is your thing:

```
var myDijit = new dijit.form.ValidationTextBox({
  value : "12345", regExp : "^(\\d{5}-\\d{4})|(\\d{5})$",
  required : false, invalidMessage : "Zip code, format must be 99999"
});
dojo.byId("divProgrammatic").appendChild(myDijit.domNode);
```

In either case, you can see how the `regExp` attribute supplies the regular expression used to validate the field. The `value` attribute supplies the initial value, if any. The `required` attribute, when `true`, is what made the first dijit flag the entry as invalid after I clicked: if there is no entry and the field is required, it gets flagged; otherwise, if the field were blank but not required, it wouldn't be flagged. The `invalidMessage` attribute provides the text to display in the tool tip whenever the field is invalid—if that field has focus (the tool tip isn't present if the field doesn't have focus). You can also set the `prompt` attribute, which will then display a tool tip with that text whenever the field has focus, whether the current value is valid or not.

The dijit.layout Package

The `dijit.layout` package contains a couple of dijits that are used to lay out a page or a section of a page. This enables you to control the structure of the page programmatically, which gives you more flexibility (theoretically at least) and more control (probably). For sure, though, these dijits give you some layout possibilities that would be a lot of work to implement yourself, which makes them well worth using in many situations, theoretical musings aside.

AccordionContainer and AccordionPane

```
dojo.require("dijit.layout.AccordionContainer");
```

Do you use Microsoft Outlook? If you do, then you know exactly what an accordion is: it's a set of bars (usually on the left side) that, when clicked, expand a selection of functions. For instance, clicking the Mail bar "slides" into view all the mail folders. If you don't use Outlook, or aren't otherwise familiar with the accordion, Figure 3-32 shows exactly what it is.

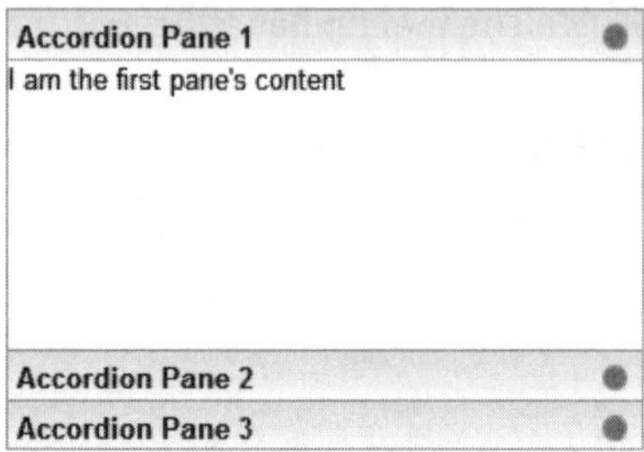

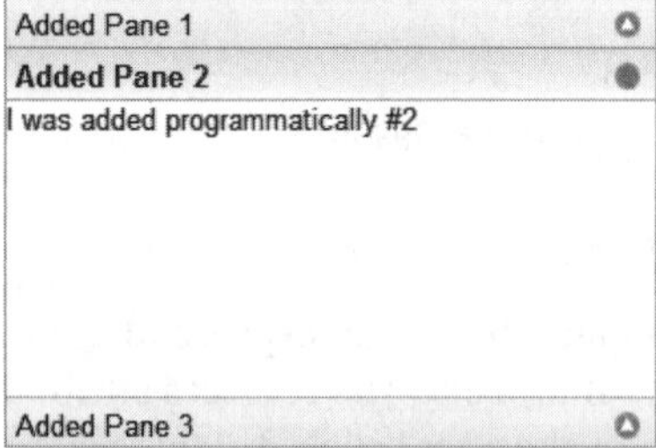

Figure 3-32. *The Accordion (and the AccordionPane) dijits*

Here you can see two accordions, one created with markup and the other created with code. In the first, the first pane is selected. In the second, the second pane is.

The Accordion dijit is the top-level dijit, but underneath it can be any number of AccordionPane dijits. These are the individual *blades*, represented by the gray bars with labels, that contain the actual content for a given category, so to speak. To create an Accordion declaratively, you would write markup like so:

```
<div dojoType="dijit.layout.AccordionContainer" duration="200"
  style=" width:300px;height:200px;">
  <div dojoType="dijit.layout.AccordionPane"
    selected="true" title="Accordion Pane 1">
    I am the first pane's content
  </div>
  <div dojoType="dijit.layout.AccordionPane"
    selected="false" title="Accordion Pane 2">
    I am the second pane's content
  </div>
  <div dojoType="dijit.layout.AccordionPane"
    selected="false" title="Accordion Pane 3">
    I am the third pane's content
  </div>
</div>
```

The `duration` attribute tells the dijit how much time it should take to slide one pane into view. Yes, it's nicely animated! Each AccordionPane can have a `selected` attribute to tell the Accordion which pane is the current one initially. Each pane can have a `title` attribute as well, which is the text displayed on its gray bar. The actual content for the pane is the content of the `<div>`.

You can also load the content for a given pane via Ajax from a remote URL. I'll show how to do this at the same time as I show you how to create an Accordion via code:

```
var myDijit = new dijit.layout.AccordionContainer({
  duration : 300
});
dojo.byId("divProgrammatic").appendChild(myDijit.domNode);
myDijit.domNode.style.width = "300px";
myDijit.domNode.style.height = "200px";
var myPane1 = new dijit.layout.AccordionPane({
  selected : false, title : "Added Pane 1"
});
myPane1.setContent("I was added programmatically #1");
myDijit.addChild(myPane1);
var myPane2 = new dijit.layout.AccordionPane({
  selected : true, title : "Added Pane 2"
});
myPane2.setContent("I was added programmatically #2");
myDijit.addChild(myPane2);
var myPane3 = new dijit.layout.AccordionPane({
  selected : false, title : "Added Pane 3",
  href : "ch3_layout_contentPane_content1.htm"
});
myDijit.addChild(myPane3);
myDijit.startup();
```

After the Accordion itself is instantiated, it is appended to the DOM at the desired location, here as a child of the divProgrammatic <div>. Some style attributes are set to determine its size. Note that the duration of the pane slide animation is slightly longer here (300 milliseconds) than the 200 milliseconds shown in the declarative example.

The next step is to create some number of AccordionPane objects. For each, we pass in whether it is selected (true) or not (false), and its title. Then for each we set its content via a call to setContent(), passing in the text (or HTML) we want to set. The exception is the third pane, which we pass in the href attribute. This is the URL to retrieve the content from. It's just a static HTML file here, but of course it could be anything on your server you wish.

Finally, after an AccordionPane is all set up, we call addChild() on the Accordion object itself to add it. When all AccordionPanes have been added, we have to make a call to the Accordian's startup() method so that it can do the remaining setup work, initialization and what have you, to get the final Accordion, complete with all its children, on the screen and ready to go.

ContentPane

```
dojo.require("dijit.layout.ContentPane");
```

A ContentPane dijit is, for lack of a better description, a <div> tag on steroids! In fact, I'd say it's the Barry Bonds[3] of dijits.

To see it in action is a little anticlimactic, but Figure 3-33 is exactly that.

Dojo's dijit.layout.ContentPane Dijit, created declaratively:

I was fetched via Ajax

Programmatically-created Dijit:

I too was fetched via Ajax

Figure 3-33. *The ContentPane dijit in...err...action*

As I said, it's not too exciting. It looks like two <div> elements with some styling so it has a background color. However, notice the text, which does hint at something interesting. The content you see, the text, was loaded via an Ajax request. This was done without having to write a smidgen of code! Here's the declarative version:

3. Barry Bonds is, depending on who you ask, either the greatest baseball player ever, or a cheat of epic proportions. He is, at the time of this writing (and for a few more years it seems), the all-time leader in home runs. He also holds the single-season home run record, has won multiple MVP awards, Gold Glove awards (earlier in his career), but ironically has no World Series rings to his name. He is also believed by many to have been a steroid user for the last couple of years, perhaps longer, and thus most of his records (the home run records certainly) are invalid because they occurred at a point in his career where his steroid use is believed to have been most prevalent. It should be noted that while there is a ton of circumstantial and anecdotal evidence, there is at this point no hard evidence to prove he ever did steroids.

```
<div dojoType="dijit.layout.ContentPane"
  href="ch3_layout_ContentPane_content1.htm"
  style="background-color:#e0e0e0;">
  I'll  be gone shortly...
</div>
```

See, I wasn't lying! Setting the href attribute is all it takes. The dijit goes off, fetches that document, and sticks it into the <div>.

But wait, there's more!

What if the markup fetched contains dijit declarations? Well, that's not a problem: ensure that the parseOnLoad attribute is set to true and, magically, those dijits will be created as well!

Creating a ContentPane via code is just as easy:

```
var myDijit = new dijit.layout.ContentPane({
  href : "ch3_layout_ContentPane_content2.htm",
  style : "background-color:#e0e0e0;"
});
dojo.byId("divProgrammatic").appendChild(myDijit.domNode);
myDijit.startup();
```

So, it's the usual dijit instantiation, passing some attribute, this time including the href of the content to fetch as well as the style to apply, and then it's just appending it to some DOM node where we want it to appear. We also need to call the startup() method; otherwise, that Ajax request won't occur.

If you are worried about remotely fetched content being stale, you can set the preventCache attribute to true, which will ensure that caching doesn't get in your way. You can also set the loadingMessage and errorMessage attributes if you wish, which tell the dijit what to display while the remote content is being fetched (loadingMessage) and what to display if some sort of error occurs (errorMessage). Also, if you don't wish to fetch content remotely, but do wish to set it dynamically, you can always call setContent() to do just that.

LayoutContainer

```
dojo.require("dijit.layout.LayoutContainer");
```

A LayoutContainer is a dijit that provides for laying out the page by using a *border* paradigm. In other words, it creates a box for content that has a specified size and that contains child dijits in a specified region of the box. In yet other words, it lays out the child dijits along the edges of the box, based on which edge you specify for display, and it then uses another child marked in a specific way to fill up the remaining space in the middle of the box.

This is of course easier to understand by seeing it, so Figure 3-34 should help.

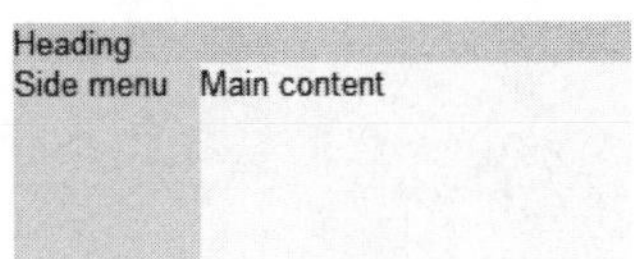

Figure 3-34. *The LayoutContainer dijit*

Here I've created three child dijits (of type `dijit.layout.ContentPane`) and put one on the top edge (the header), one on the left edge (the menu), and one that fills up the rest of the space (the main content). The markup behind this is shown here:

```
<div dojoType="dijit.layout.LayoutContainer"
  style="width:250px;height:100px;">
  <div dojoType="dijit.layout.ContentPane" layoutAlign="top"
    style="background-color:#e0e0e0;">Heading</div>
  <div dojoType="dijit.layout.ContentPane" layoutAlign="left"
    style="width:75px;background-color:#ffe0e0;">Side menu</div>
  <div dojoType="dijit.layout.ContentPane" layoutAlign="client"
    style="background-color:#ffffe0;">Main content</div>
</div>
```

The `layoutAlign` attribute on each `<div>` defines what region of the box that `<div>` will be placed in. The simple style attributes `width` and `height` are used to specify the size of the elements.

Note that there's no reason you have to use a ContentPane for each region. In fact, as a fun little exercise, try using a TitlePane instead and see what happens. In short, it works just fine!

■ **Note** There can be only a single element with a `layoutAlign` value of `client`, but there can be multiple occurrences of each of the others. Try throwing an additional element in to see the effect.

StackContainer and StackController

The StackContainer is a simple dijit. Simply stated, it takes a bunch of elements, `<div>` elements for instance, and stacks them on top of each other so that only one can ever be visible. It then enables you to flip between them programmatically, or more interestingly, use a StackController in a more automated fashion.

Let's begin by having a look at this thing, Figure 3-35 being that look.

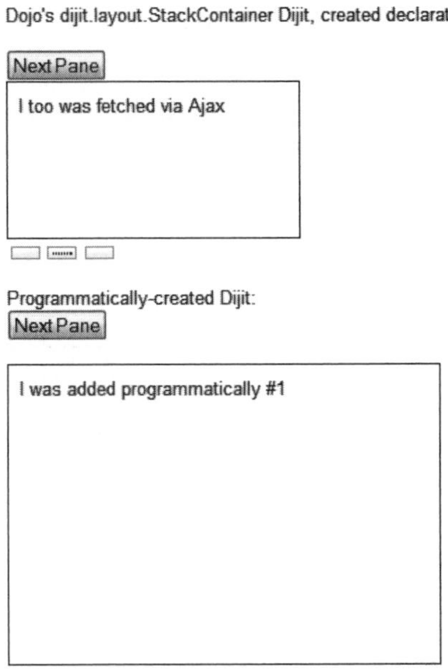

Dojo's dijit.layout.StackContainer Dijit, created declaratively:

Next Pane

I too was fetched via Ajax

Programmatically-created Dijit:

Next Pane

I was added programmatically #1

Figure 3-35. *The StackContainer dijit, along with the StackController dijit*

The first box you see was added declaratively. The button above it enables the user to flip to the next stacked element in sequence. Underneath the box, you'll see three smaller boxes. These represent the visual part of the StackController. What it does is automatically render a small box for each stacked element. Then when those small boxes are clicked, the corresponding stacked element is shown. All of the content for this StackContainer is fetched via Ajax, which is fully supported.

The second box is a StackContainer created programmatically, including its content, which is *not* fetched via Ajax. I also did not attach a StackController to this one just to demonstrate that it's not required to have one.

So, what does the declarative approach take? Not much, as this code shows:

```
<div id="stack" dojoType="dijit.layout.StackContainer"
  style="width:200px;border:1px solid #000000;height:100px;padding:4px;">
  <div id="Page1" dojoType="dijit.layout.ContentPane"
    href="ch3_layout_ContentPane_content1.htm"></div>
  <div id="Page2" dojoType="dijit.layout.ContentPane"
    href="ch3_layout_ContentPane_content2.htm"></div>
  <div id="Page3" dojoType="dijit.layout.ContentPane"
    href="ch3_layout_ContentPane_content3.htm"></div>
</div>
<div dojoType="dijit.layout.StackController" containerId="stack"> </div>
```

As you can see, the href attribute is all it takes to make an Ajax request; the returned content is inserted automatically. You'll notice that the ID attributes are important here because that's how we attach the StackController to the StackContainer.

To create the second StackContainer, the following code was executed:

```
var myDijit = new dijit.layout.StackContainer({
  id : "stack2",
  style : "width:300px;border:1px solid #000000;height:200px;padding:4px;"
});
dojo.byId("divProgrammatic").appendChild(myDijit.domNode);
var myPane1 = new dijit.layout.ContentPane();
myPane1.setContent("I was added programmatically #1");
myDijit.addChild(myPane1);
var myPane2 = new dijit.layout.ContentPane();
myPane2.setContent("I was added programmatically #2");
myDijit.addChild(myPane2);
var myPane3 = new dijit.layout.ContentPane();
myPane3.setContent("I was added programmatically #3");
myDijit.addChild(myPane3);
myDijit.startup();
```

It's slightly more verbose than the markup version, which is typical of most dijits, but not too complex. After we have an instance of a StackContainer, we insert it into the DOM, create some number of `dijit.layout.ContentPane` objects, set some content on it, and add it to the StackContainer. When we're all finished adding children, a call to the `startup()` method of the StackContainer is all it takes to get it all on the screen.

Oh yeah, what about those Next Pane buttons? Well, all it takes to make them work as expected is an `onClick` event handler like this:

```
dijit.byId("stack").forward();
```

■ **Note** Like the LayoutContainer before it, you can add children that aren't just `dijit.layout.ContentPane` instances. A `dijit.TitlePane` will work just as well, for example.

TabContainer

```
dojo.require("dijit.layout.TabContainer");
```

The tabbed interface is one of the most common layout metaphors in user interfaces today, and for good reason: tabs are a great way to present a large amount of information categorized in a way that users can easily understand and easily switch between. Dojo would be less than stellar if it didn't provide tabs, but it does, and does so quite well, as Figure 3-36 demonstrates.

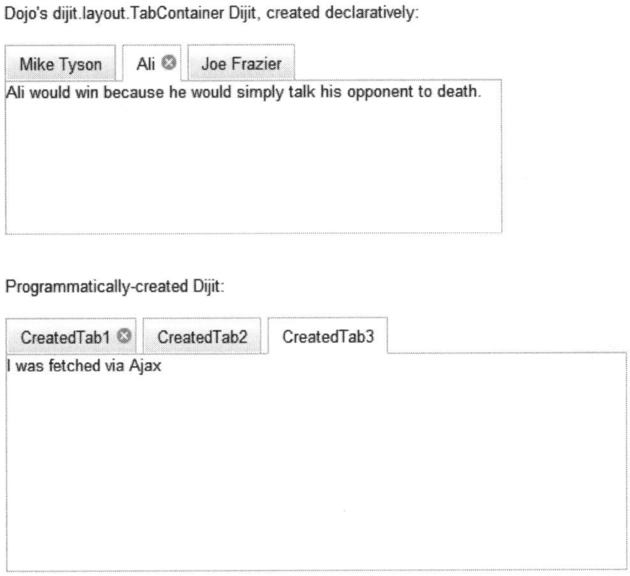

Dojo's dijit.layout.TabContainer Dijit, created declaratively:

Mike Tyson | Ali | Joe Frazier

Ali would win because he would simply talk his opponent to death.

Programmatically-created Dijit:

CreatedTab1 | CreatedTab2 | CreatedTab3

I was fetched via Ajax

Figure 3-36. *The TabContainer dijit*

Of course, Dojo takes things beyond the basics and gives you some really cool capabilities. The capability to load tabs via Ajax? Check. The ability to have closable tabs? Check. (Notice the little X on some of the tabs? Clicking one of those removes that tab.) The capability to have tabs in different positions (top or bottom)? Check.

So, how do you create a set of tabs without writing any code? Simple! Here you go:

```
<div dojoType="dijit.layout.TabContainer"
  style="width:400px;height:150px">
  <div dojoType="dijit.layout.ContentPane" title="Mike Tyson">
    Tyson would win because he'd devour his opponent...LITERALLY.
  </div>
  <div dojoType="dijit.layout.ContentPane" title="Ali" closable="true"
    selected="true">
    Ali would win because he would simply talk his opponent to death.
  </div>
  <div dojoType="dijit.layout.ContentPane" title="Joe Frazier">
    Come on, is there really any doubt Frazier is the best?  Err, ok,
    you're right, Ali is.  Sorry Joe!
  </div>
</div>
```

A TabContainer has some number of ContentPanes underneath it. Each ContentPane has a `title` attribute, which becomes the label on the tab. You can optionally have a `selected` attribute set to `true` to indicate which tab should be selected at startup (by default, it's the first tab on the left). If you wanted to have the tabs on the bottom, you could set the `tabPosition` attribute to `bottom` and you're good to go.

Coding up some tabs isn't rocket science either:

```
var myDijit = new dijit.layout.TabContainer({
  style : "width:500px;height:200px;"
});
dojo.byId("divProgrammatic").appendChild(myDijit.domNode);
var myPane1 = new dijit.layout.ContentPane({
  title : "CreatedTab1", closable : true });
myPane1.setContent("I was added programmatically #1");
myDijit.addChild(myPane1);
var myPane2 = new dijit.layout.ContentPane({
  title : "CreatedTab2" });
myPane2.setContent("I was added programmatically #2");
myDijit.addChild(myPane2);
var myPane3 = new dijit.layout.ContentPane({
  title : "CreatedTab3", selected : true,
  href : "ch3_layout_ContentPane_content1.htm" });
myDijit.addChild(myPane3);
myDijit.startup();
```

This is the same paradigm you've seen a number of times before. Start with an instance of a TabContainer, passing in any attributes desired (just `style` in this case to set the `width` and `height` of the TabContainer). Then append it to the DOM at the desired location. Follow that by creating some number of ContentPanes and adding each one to the TabContainer. Notice that the third pane uses Ajax to get its content via the `href` attribute that you've seen a bunch of times before. At the end of all that, a quick call to the `startup()` method fires it all up and gets it out onto the screen.

Summary

In this chapter, we took the grand tour of Dojo's dijits. We saw them in action, saw how to create them either programmatically or declaratively, saw how to manipulate them and how to use them to an extent. This chapter wasn't really meant to give you every last detail of each dijit because a whole book could be dedicated to that single purpose. Instead, it was meant to give you enough detail that when you see the dijits used in the projects to come, you'll have a good foundation on which to build.

In the next chapter, we'll have a go with DojoX, the "experimental" region of Dojo. We'll see what it has to offer in much the same fashion as this chapter and the previous chapter did.

CHAPTER 4

DojoX

How many times have you watched a movie where a freaky scientist is hacking away at an experiment in his basement, and midway through the movie his creation turns out to embody pure evil, attacks him, and then proceeds to kill his entire family, all his friends, his dog, and his neighbors? Finally, the military shows up, somehow manages to make things worse by blowing up everything in sight, killing a bunch of innocent people, and in the end winds up nuking the town because that's the only thing that can defeat the evil blob/mutant/zombie/alien/robot/cyborg/evil killing thing?

Well, thankfully that happens only in movies (err, unless you visit one of the many tinfoil hat[1]–enthusiast sites on the Internet) and has very little to do with DojoX. In fact, the only thing DojoX has in common with the terribly contrived plots of many B sci-fi movie plots is the idea of experimentation. And thankfully, it has nothing to do with chimpanzees or the decline of Matthew Broderick's career either![2]

DojoX is all about pushing the boundaries. Whenever one of the Dojo development team has the next great idea, DojoX is the natural home for it. After the idea is fully fleshed out (and the risk of it being taken over by a malevolent parasitic alien life form and used for evil is determined to be negligible), it usually will find its way into Dojo proper. Or it will wind up on the cutting room floor perhaps, but either way it won't be the target of a military nuclear strike!

Sometimes, things you find in DojoX are likely to stay there because DojoX isn't strictly about experimentation; it's also about extensions. There may be things that aren't used frequently, in which case the Dojo team may elect to make DojoX their permanent home. Usually you do, however, hear about DojoX being the cutting edge, stuff that's "out there," new, exciting, and basically experimental to a large extent. None of this is meant to imply that what's in DojoX isn't ready for prime-time or that you shouldn't use it. Quite the opposite is true, actually: some of the best stuff is found in DojoX, and you shouldn't be afraid to use it!

---

1. *Wearing a tinfoil hat*, or some variation of that phrase, is generally used to describe overly (or so we think!) paranoid people who believe the government, or aliens, or some combination thereof, are spying on them. In (their) theory, creating headgear from tinfoil stops "the rays" that the nefarious members of society are using against them. I find that wax paper works better, paradoxically, but different strokes for different folks, I guess.

2. *Project X* was one of, if not *the*, lowlight of Matthew Broderick's career. It was about chimpanzees, Air Force science projects, and terrible acting. It's even more depressing to think this was Matthew's follow-up to the iconic *Ferris Bueller's Day Off*!

You should also be aware that because of the nature of DojoX, there's no guarantee that what you see in one version will still be there in the next, or that it won't have changed substantially between versions, or that it even still works from one version to the next. I'm quite sure the Dojo team isn't going to release anything that's outright broken, though; I don't want to imply that they would at all. I'm simply saying that you accept some minimal amount of risk by using things in DojoX because you may sometimes have a porting job to do if you upgrade, or you may even find that what you used is no longer present. Such is life on the bleeding edge!

Some of the most interesting stuff can be found in DojoX, as I hope you'll see in this chapter, and as we use some of this stuff to develop the projects to come (beginning with the next chapter). Before we get to that, let's take a look at what Dr. Frankenstein[3] has sitting on his shelves—that is, what DojoX has to offer! This won't be an exhaustive look, although I'll touch on most of what's in DojoX (at the time this chapter was written at least), and chances are you'll see more of it as we work through the projects too.

Unlike in the previous two chapters, there's not a whole lot in the way of setup, not a whole lot of general-purpose discussion to take place (aside from what you just read, that is). We're pretty much ready at this moment to jump right into DojoX, so . . .

dojox.charting

The `dojox.charting` namespace gives you the ability to generate vector-based charts on the client, without the server rendering images and such. This is quite a big deal because up until now the only good way to generate such things, and have them look good at the same time, was to have images generated on the server, rendered as a GIF or JPG, and then download the image on the client. Sure, you could resort to Flash and Java applets and other browser extensions, but I'm talking native generation here, real-time generation on the client. The `dojox.charting` namespace gives you that.

I'm going to cheat in this section and not write any example code myself because, to put it bluntly, the tests that accompany this package as part of the Dojo download do a far better job of it than I ever could. So, all credit goes to those who wrote these tests because they are excellent and, frankly, allowed me to be really lazy here!

To get started with this namespace, you have to import some resources, beginning with the base Dojo style sheet that you've previously seen. Next is the `Chart2D` class:

```
dojo.require("dojox.charting.Chart2D");
```

Depending on how you'd like your charts to look, you may also need to import some theme classes, like so:

```
dojo.require("dojox.charting.themes.PlotKit.blue");
dojo.require("dojox.charting.themes.PlotKit.cyan");
dojo.require("dojox.charting.themes.PlotKit.green");
dojo.require("dojox.charting.themes.PlotKit.orange");
dojo.require("dojox.charting.themes.PlotKit.purple");
dojo.require("dojox.charting.themes.PlotKit.red");
```

3. Many people mistakenly think the monster was called Frankenstein, but in fact that was the name of the scientist (evil or otherwise—it's debatable) who created the monster. Come to think of it, who am I to call it a monster anyway? Talk about judging a book by its cover!

All of these are imported to make the following examples work, but you of course would need to import only those you wanted to use, if any. After you have all this on your page, you're ready to go.

Line Chart

The first example I want to show you is a simple line chart. Well, you might not even consider it a chart. Certainly it doesn't look much like a typical chart, or at least what you think of when you hear the term *chart*. This is more like a pretty picture based on some data, but whatever the technical term for it, it's important because it quite succinctly demonstrates the basics of `dojox.charting`, so have a look at Figure 4-1 to start with.

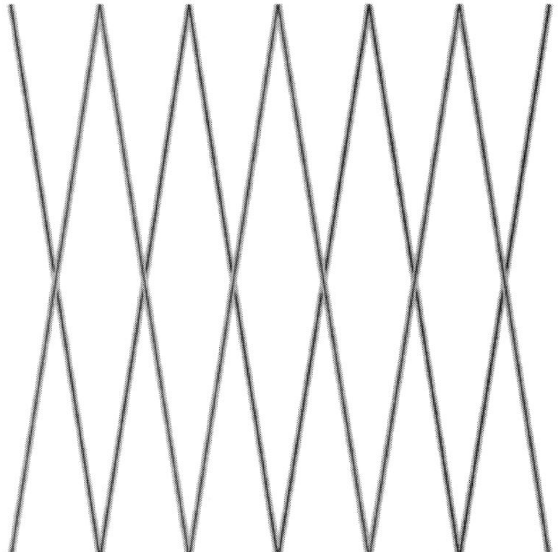
2: Defaults: lines, no axes, and custom strokes.

Figure 4-1. *A very simple line chart . . . err, pretty picture thingy*

Now, let's see what it takes to get this on the screen:

```
var chart1 = new dojox.charting.Chart2D("test1");
chart1.addSeries("Series A", [1, 2, 1, 2, 1, 2, 1]);
chart1.addSeries("Series B", [2, 1, 2, 1, 2, 1, 2]);
chart1.render();
```

So, it's not a whole lot! You just instantiate yourself a `Chart2D` object and pass it the ID of a `<div>`, or other suitable DOM node, to put it in. Then you call the `addSeries()` method one or more times to feed it some data. The first argument is the name of the series, and the second is an array of data points. The chart automatically handles all sizing and spacing concerns for you. For example, trace the line that starts in the lower-left corner, which is actually red on the screen (the other is blue). Starting at the lower-left end, count how many points it has (counting the two ends as points). Note that there are seven of them. Now, look at the data for series A. There are seven elements! As you trace the line, each wave crest represents the number 2, and each trough is the number 1, which you can see matches the data. That's what I mean when I say that the chart automatically sizes and worries about spacing and such for you. You simply supply the points, and the chart itself, based on the size of its containing `<div>`, determines how far apart the points are vertically and horizontally.

Area Chart

An area chart is pretty much just a line chart with the area underneath the lines filled in, as you can see in Figure 4-2.

3: Areas, orange theme, no axes.

Figure 4-2. *An area chart*

The code for creating an area chart doesn't look a whole lot different from what you saw previously:

```
var chart3 = new dojox.charting.Chart2D("test3");
chart3.addPlot("default", {type: "Areas"});
chart3.setTheme(dojox.charting.themes.PlotKit.orange);
chart3.addSeries("Series A", [1, 2, 0.5, 1.5, 1, 2.8, 0.4]);
chart3.addSeries("Series B", [2.6, 1.8, 2, 1, 1.4, 0.7, 2]);
chart3.addSeries("Series C", [6.3, 1.8, 3, 0.5, 4.4, 2.7, 2]);
chart3.render();
```

The `addPlot()` method is used to specify the type of chart being drawn, and options thereof. Using this method isn't necessary for the basic line chart, but it is here. The `setTheme()` method enables you to use one of those themes I mentioned previously, and here we're using the orange theme. Beyond that, our work is just adding the series, like before, and a final call to `render()` to get it on the screen.

Fancy-Pants Line Chart (StackedLines Chart)

Let's say all you need is a simple line chart, but you want it to look a little cooler than usual. How's Figure 4-3 work for ya?

11: Stacked lines, markers, shadows, no axes, custom strokes, fills, and markers.

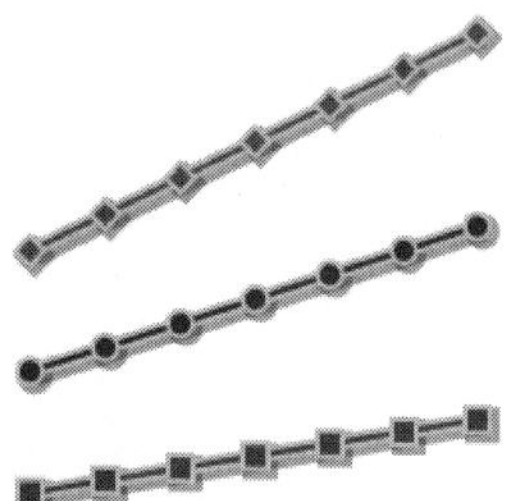

Figure 4-3. *A prettier line chart*

This version has it all: shadows, custom colors on the stroke and fill of the lines, and data markers. Accomplishing this doesn't take much more than you've seen previously:

```
var chart11 = new dojox.charting.Chart2D("test11");
chart11.addPlot("default", {type: "StackedLines",➥
  markers: true, shadows: {dx: 2, dy: 2, dw: 2}});
chart11.addSeries("Series A", [1, 1.1, 1.2, 1.3, 1.4, 1.5, 1.6], {stroke: {➥
  color: "red", width: 2}, fill: "lightpink",➥
  marker: "m-3,-3 l0,6 6,0 0,-6 z"});
chart11.addSeries("Series B", [1, 1.1, 1.2, 1.3, 1.4, 1.5, 1.6], {stroke: {➥
  color: "blue", width: 2}, fill: "lightblue",➥
  marker: "m-3,0 c0,-4 6,-4 6,0 m-6,0 c0,4 6,4 6,0"});
chart11.addSeries("Series C", [1, 1.1, 1.2, 1.3, 1.4, 1.5, 1.6], {stroke: {➥
  color: "green", width: 2}, fill: "lightgreen", ➥
  marker: "m0,-3 l3,3 -3,3 -3,-3 z"});
chart11.render();
```

Here we're calling the `addPlot()` method to add some options, namely telling `dojox.charting` that we want a `StackedLines` chart, a variant on the typical line chart. We're also telling it that we want markers by setting the `markers` attribute to `true`. Finally, we specify some information about shadows, here saying we want a shadow offset 2 pixels down and to the right of the lines. Then, when constructing the series, we pass in attributes defining the stroke, that is, the outline color of each data line, plus the color to fill the line with (because a `StackedLines` chart variety makes thicker lines, not just single-pixel-wide lines). We also specify where to put our markers along each series' line.

Bar Chart

So far we've talked only about line charts, which is nice—but what are bar charts, you ask? Feast your eyes on Figure 4-4!

18: Clustered columns, custom axes, custom strokes, fills, and gap.

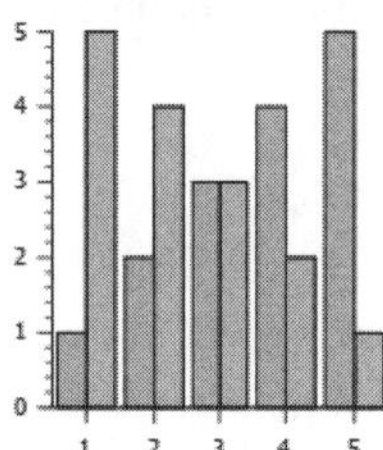

Figure 4-4. *A bar chart example*

The code for this is still very simple:

```
var chart17 = new dojox.charting.Chart2D("test17");
chart17.addPlot("default", {type: "StackedBars"});
chart17.addSeries("Series A", [1, 2, 3, 4, 5], {stroke: {color: "red"},➥
  fill: "lightpink"});
chart17.addSeries("Series B", [2, 1, 2, 1, 2], {stroke: {color: "blue"},➥
  fill: "lightblue"});
chart17.render();
```

In fact, it looks not much different from what you've seen before. That's part of the beauty of `dojox.charting`: a change to the `type` attribute passed into `addPlot()` is most times all you need to transform your data into a different type of chart. Virtually everything else can stay the same all the time. That's a tremendous amount of flexibility right at your fingertips.

dojox.collections

Unless this book is your first foray into programming you almost certainly know what a collection is. But, just in case you just stepped off the Computer Science bus, a *collection* is a group of related data items typically stored in some sort of standard data structure. Examples of such structures include `List`, `Dictionary`, `Stack`, `Queue`, `Map`, `Tree`, `Bag`, `Array`, `Set`, and `Vector`.

In JavaScript there are really only two kinds of built-in collections: arrays and objects (which can be made to function like maps). Generally, if you want the more advanced structures like those listed in the preceding paragraph, you're off coding them yourself.

Or, if you're smart, you're looking at what Dojo has to offer! And thankfully, DojoX is home to a number of useful data structures. The `dojox.collections` namespace is the place to look.

ArrayList

An `ArrayList` is just like an array in that it is a list of values, be it primitives or objects. But unlike an array, an `ArrayList` can grow as elements are added to it. Now, that's the general difference, but the observant reader will note that an array in JavaScript can in fact grow too. So, in the case of JavaScript specifically, you can think of an `ArrayList` as an array on steroids!

An ArrayList provides a host of useful methods that a basic array does not, because an ArrayList is just an object that's been defined. In Listing 4-1, you can see some of those methods on display.

Listing 4-1. *ArrayList Example (ch4_collections_ArrayList.htm)*

```
<html>

  <head>

    <script type="text/javascript">
      var djConfig = {
        baseScriptUri : "js/dojo/",
        parseOnLoad : true
      };
    </script>
    <script type="text/javascript" src="js/dojo/dojo/dojo.js"></script>

    <script>

      dojo.require("dojox.collections.ArrayList");

      function testIt() {
        var al = new dojox.collections.ArrayList();
        al.add("Riggs");
        al.add("Murtaugh");
        al.add("Leo");
        al.add("Mr. Joshua");
        dojo.byId("divOutput").innerHTML +=
          "<br>ArrayList via toString():  " + al;
        dojo.byId("divOutput").innerHTML +=
          "<br>ArrayList via iterator:<br>";
        var it = al.getIterator();
        while (!it.atEnd()) {
          dojo.byId("divOutput").innerHTML += " - " + it.get() + "<br>";
        }
        dojo.byId("divOutput").innerHTML +=
          "ArrayList contains Bill?  " + al.contains("Bill");
        dojo.byId("divOutput").innerHTML +=
          "<br>ArrayList contains Leo? " + al.contains("Leo");
        dojo.byId("divOutput").innerHTML +=
          "<br>Index of Murtaugh: " + al.indexOf("Murtaugh");
        dojo.byId("divOutput").innerHTML +=
          "<br>Item at index 3: " + al.item(3);
        al.reverse();
        dojo.byId("divOutput").innerHTML +=
          "<br>ArrayList after reversing:  " + al;
        al.insert(1, "Lorna");
```

```
        dojo.byId("divOutput").innerHTML +=
          "<br>ArrayList after inserting item at index 1:  " + al;
        al.setByIndex(2, "McCallister");
        dojo.byId("divOutput").innerHTML +=
          "<br>ArrayList after setByIndex(2):  " + al;
        var o = al.item(2);
        al.remove(o);
        dojo.byId("divOutput").innerHTML +=
          "<br>ArrayList after removing McCallister:  " + al;
        al.sort();
        dojo.byId("divOutput").innerHTML +=
          "<br>ArrayList after sorting (default function):  " + al;
        al.clear();
        dojo.byId("divOutput").innerHTML +=
          "<br>ArrayList after clearing:  " + al;
      }

    </script>

  </head>

  <body onLoad="testIt();">
    <br>
    <table border="0" cellpadding="0" cellspacing="0"
      width="800" align="center" style="border:1px solid #000000;padding:6px;">
      <tr><td>
        dojox.collections.ArrayList test:
        <br>
        <div id="divOutput"> </div>
      </td></tr>
    </table>
  </body>

</html>
```

Of course, what this example does isn't all that exciting, but if you're a *Lethal Weapon* fan, you'll certainly appreciate seeing it anyway. Figure 4-5 is your chance!

```
dojox.collections.ArrayList test:

ArrayList via toString(): Riggs,Murtaugh,Leo,Mr. Joshua
ArrayList via iterator:
- Riggs
- Murtaugh
- Leo
- Mr. Joshua
ArrayList contains Bill? false
ArrayList contains Leo? true
Index of Murtaugh: 1
Item at index 3: Mr. Joshua
ArrayList after reversing: Mr. Joshua,Leo,Murtaugh,Riggs
ArrayList after inserting item at index 1: Mr. Joshua,Lorna,Leo,Murtaugh,Riggs
ArrayList after setByIndex(2): Mr. Joshua,Lorna,McCallister,Murtaugh,Riggs
ArrayList after removing McCallister: Mr. Joshua,Lorna,Murtaugh,Riggs
ArrayList after sorting (default function): Lorna,Mr. Joshua,Murtaugh,Riggs
ArrayList after clearing:
```

Figure 4-5. *Output of the ArrayList example*

After an instance of `dojox.collections.ArrayList` has been created, a couple of calls to its `add()` method gets some names into the `ArrayList`. Of course, you aren't limited to strings. You can throw any object or primitive in there you like. The `toString()` method is implemented such that you get a comma-separated list of the values currently in the `ArrayList` as a result. Of course, what you actually get as a value for each element depends on what its `toString()` method gives you (for primitives, you'd get the value itself).

Iterating over the elements in the `ArrayList` is a common thing to want to do, and Dojo gives you the `Iterator` pattern for doing that, which is a common enough approach to this requirement in most languages:

```
var it = al.getIterator();
while (!it.atEnd()) {
  dojo.byId("divOutput").innerHTML += " - " + it.get() + "<br>";
}
```

Here we're getting an `Iterator` from the `ArrayList`, and then doing a `while` loop until it tells us we're at the end of the list. A call to the `Iterator`'s `get()` method gets us the next item in the `ArrayList`.

Finding out what elements are in the `ArrayList` is also common, and although you could always use the `Iterator` to check each element, that's not terribly efficient. Instead, the `contains()` method can be called to see whether the `ArrayList` contains a given object. Likewise, you can use the `indexOf()` method to find the index of a given object.

If you'd like to retrieve a specific item and you know its place in the `ArrayList` (its index in other words), the `item()` method is perfect. Just pass it the index to retrieve, and it will return the corresponding object. Likewise, if you'd like to replace an existing object at a specific location, rather than simply adding on to the end of the list as `add()` does, you can use the `setByIndex()` method. Just pass it the index to set and the object to put there. You can also outright remove a given item from the `ArrayList` with the `remove()` method, which takes the index to remove.

Sorting an ArrayList is also pretty common, and fortunately there's a sort() method just for that. The sort() method by default does your typical binary sort, which often won't give you the results you want (11 gets sorted before 2, for instance). So, you can optionally pass in a reference to a function that will be used to compare each item. This uses the same approach as you've seen in previous chapters for this sort of thing.

Last, clearing an ArrayList can be done with a simple call to the clear() method, not surprisingly!

Dictionary

A Dictionary by any other name is essentially a Map, that is, a list of key values that each map to a specific value. You can retrieve the value by looking up its key. This is probably the second most common data structure in all of programming, right after lists. Here in Listing 4-2 you can see an example of the dojox.collections.Dictionary class in action.

Listing 4-2. *Dictionary Example (ch4_collections_Dictionary.htm)*

```
<html>

  <head>

    <script type="text/javascript">
      var djConfig = {
        baseScriptUri : "js/dojo/",
        parseOnLoad : true
      };
    </script>
    <script type="text/javascript" src="js/dojo/dojo/dojo.js"></script>

    <script>

      dojo.require("dojox.collections.Dictionary");

      function testIt() {
        var dy = new dojox.collections.Dictionary();
        dy.add("Bat Man", "Robin");
        dy.add("Captain America", "Bucky");
        dy.add("Blue Falcon", "Dynomutt");
        dy.add("Scooby", "Scrappy");
        dojo.byId("divOutput").innerHTML +=
          "<br>Dictionary via iterator:<br>";
        var it = dy.getIterator();
        while (!it.atEnd()) {
          dojo.byId("divOutput").innerHTML += " - " + it.get() + "<br>";
        }
        dojo.byId("divOutput").innerHTML +=
          "Dictionary via keyList:<br>";
        var keys = dy.getKeyList();
```

```
      for (var i = 0; i < keys.length; i++) {
        dojo.byId("divOutput").innerHTML += " - " + keys[i] + "<br>";
      }
      dojo.byId("divOutput").innerHTML +=
        "Dictionary via valueList:<br>";
      var vals = dy.getValueList();
      for (var i = 0; i < vals.length; i++) {
        dojo.byId("divOutput").innerHTML += " - " + vals[i] + "<br>";
      }
      dojo.byId("divOutput").innerHTML +=
        "Dictionary contains key Ralph? " + dy.containsKey("Ralph");
      dojo.byId("divOutput").innerHTML +=
        "<br>Dictionary contains key Scooby? " + dy.containsKey("Scooby");
      dojo.byId("divOutput").innerHTML +=
        "<br>Dictionary contains value Roger? " + dy.containsValue("Roger");
      dojo.byId("divOutput").innerHTML +=
        "<br>Dictionary contains value Bucky? " + dy.containsValue("Bucky");
      dojo.byId("divOutput").innerHTML +=
        "<br>Value of key Bat Man: " + dy.entry("Bat Man");
      dy.remove("Blue Falcon");
      dojo.byId("divOutput").innerHTML +=
        "<br>Dictionary size after removing Blue Falcon:  " + dy.count;
      dy.clear();
      dojo.byId("divOutput").innerHTML +=
        "<br>Dictionary size after clearing:  " + dy.count;
    }

  </script>

</head>

<body onLoad="testIt();">
  <br>
  <table border="0" cellpadding="0" cellspacing="0"
    width="800" align="center" style="border:1px solid #000000;padding:6px;">
    <tr><td>
      dojox.collections.Dictionary test:
      <br>
      <div id="divOutput"> </div>
    </td></tr>
  </table>
</body>

</html>
```

As with the ArrayList, the output of the example isn't all that exciting, but hopefully you have an affinity for old Saturday-morning cartoons as I do, in which case Figure 4-6 will be slightly more entertaining than it otherwise might have been.

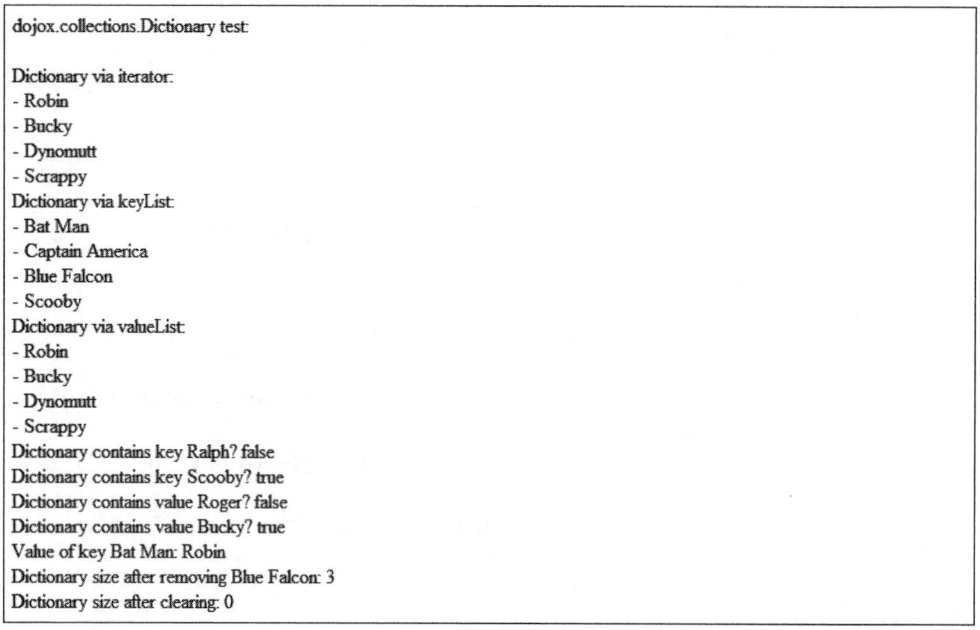

```
dojox.collections.Dictionary test:

Dictionary via iterator:
- Robin
- Bucky
- Dynomutt
- Scrappy
Dictionary via keyList:
- Bat Man
- Captain America
- Blue Falcon
- Scooby
Dictionary via valueList:
- Robin
- Bucky
- Dynomutt
- Scrappy
Dictionary contains key Ralph? false
Dictionary contains key Scooby? true
Dictionary contains value Roger? false
Dictionary contains value Bucky? true
Value of key Bat Man: Robin
Dictionary size after removing Blue Falcon: 3
Dictionary size after clearing: 0
```

Figure 4-6. *Output of the Dictionary example*

The code is pretty similar to the `ArrayList` example. After instantiating `dojox.collections.Dictionary`, as with the `ArrayList`, the `add()` method is used to add elements to the `Dictionary`. In this case, however, the method takes two values: the key and the value to map to the key. We can again iterate over the `Dictionary`, which is actually iterating over the values. If we'd instead prefer to iterate over the keys, we can do so by using the `getKeyList()` method, which returns an array that we can then iterate through:

```
var keys = dy.getKeyList();
for (var i = 0; i < keys.length; i++) {
  dojo.byId("divOutput").innerHTML += " - " + keys[i] + "<br>";
}
```

Similarly, the `getValuesList()` method gives us the same thing as `getIterator()` does, but like `getKeyList()`, it gives us an array rather than an `Iterator`.

We can check whether a given key exists in the `Dictionary` by calling the `containsKey()` method, passing it the key to check for. The `containsValue()` method works the same way but checks the collection of values instead.

We can get the value for a given key by calling `entry()` and passing it the key to look up. The `remove()` method, which is passed a key value, can be used to remove a given key/value pair from the `Dictionary`. The `clear()` method will clear the `Dictionary` entirely, and we can ensure that either worked by checking the `count` attribute, which gives us the number of items currently in the `Dictionary`.

Stack

A Stack is another extremely common data structure. Although there are other kinds, you'll usually deal with what's known as a FILO stack, *FILO* standing for *first in, last out*. So, every time you add an element to a Stack, it's conceptually added to the front (unlike an ArrayList, where the element is added at the end). With a Stack, however, you generally talk about the top of the Stack because the Stack is pictured as being vertical. Each element added pushes down all the other items lower into the Stack. That's called *pushing onto* the Stack. Later you do what's called *popping off* the Stack, which means the item at the top is removed and the next item now moves to the top.

All of that I suspect you already knew just fine, so let's just move on to the code! Listing 4-3 shows an example of using Dojo's Stack implementation.

Listing 4-3. *Stack Example (ch4_collections_Stack.htm)*

```
<html>

  <head>

    <script type="text/javascript">
      var djConfig = {
        baseScriptUri : "js/dojo/",
        parseOnLoad : true
      };
    </script>
    <script type="text/javascript" src="js/dojo/dojo/dojo.js"></script>

    <script>

      dojo.require("dojox.collections.Stack");

      function testIt() {
        var st = new dojox.collections.Stack();
        st.push("Romeo");
        st.push("Juliet");
        st.push("Sam");
        st.push("Diane");
        dojo.byId("divOutput").innerHTML +=
          "<br>Stack via toArray() after 4 push()'s:  " + st.toArray();
        dojo.byId("divOutput").innerHTML +=
          "<br>Stack via iterator:<br>";
        var it = st.getIterator();
        while (!it.atEnd()) {
          dojo.byId("divOutput").innerHTML += " - " + it.get() + "<br>";
        }
        var ret = st.pop();
        dojo.byId("divOutput").innerHTML +=
          "Stack after pop'ing:  " + st.toArray();
```

```
        dojo.byId("divOutput").innerHTML +=
          "<br>Item returned from pop():  " + ret;
        dojo.byId("divOutput").innerHTML +=
          "<br>Item returned from peek():  " + st.peek();
        dojo.byId("divOutput").innerHTML +=
          "<br>Stack after peek'ing:  " + st.toArray();
        dojo.byId("divOutput").innerHTML +=
          "<br>Stack contains Romeo? " + st.contains("Romeo");
        dojo.byId("divOutput").innerHTML +=
          "<br>Stack contains Cleopatra? " + st.contains("Cleopatra");
      }

    </script>

  </head>

  <body onLoad="testIt();">
    <br>
    <table border="0" cellpadding="0" cellspacing="0"
      width="800" align="center" style="border:1px solid #000000;padding:6px;">
      <tr><td>
        dojox.collections.Stack test:
        <br>
        <div id="divOutput"> </div>
      </td></tr>
    </table>
  </body>

</html>
```

Apparently I was in a romantic mood when I wrote this example because I chose to use famous lovers to demonstrate the Stack. Ironically, I didn't choose Sheridan and Delenn,[4] Riker and Troi,[5] or Han and Leia,[6] which are the obvious choices for us sci-fi geeks! Anyway, Figure 4-7 is proof for my wife that I can be romantic at times!

---

4. Captain John Sheridan and Delenn are the two main characters for most of the run of the series *Babylon 5*. They develop a rather strong loving relationship that even crosses species bounds. Talk about a progressive civilization!

5. Will Riker, first officer of the Enterprise-D, and counselor Deanna Troi were of course the long-running relationship on *Star Trek: The Next Generation*. Their relationship was on-again, off-again to say the least, as they each slept with nearly as many people over the course of seven seasons as Captain Kirk did over the entire run of *Star Trek: The Original Series*!

6. If you don't know who Han and Leia are, I suggest you never go to a sci-fi convention because you would very likely be putting your life in real peril!

```
dojox.collections.Stack test:

Stack via toArray() after 4 push()'s: Romeo,Juliet,Sam,Diane
Stack via iterator:
- Romeo
- Juliet
- Sam
- Diane
Stack after pop'ing: Romeo,Juliet,Sam
Item returned from pop(): Diane
Item returned from peek(): Sam
Stack after peek'ing: Romeo,Juliet,Sam
Stack contains Romeo? true
Stack contains Cleopatra? false
```

Figure 4-7. *Output of the Stack example*

After we've gotten ourselves an instance of `dojox.collections.Stack()`, we can begin making calls to `push()` to push objects onto the `Stack` (any kind of object will do, or primitives, whatever floats your boat). We can call `toArray()` to get an array out of the `Stack` if that's something we need. The same `getIterator()` method is available that we've seen before if you need to iterate over the `Stack`.

Calling `pop()` returns the item at the top of the `Stack` and removes that item. What if you just want to see what's at the top of the `Stack` without removing it? You could always `pop()` it, examine it, and then `push()` it back on, but that's just silly. Fortunately, the `peek()` method does precisely all that work for you.

One nice thing about the Dojo `Stack` implementation is the `contains()` method, which enables you to find out whether a given element is in the `Stack`, anywhere, not just at the top. Not all `Stack` implementations can do that, and it's a real handy function to have. Just pass it the item you want to check for, and it will return `true` if the item is in the `Stack` somewhere, `false` if not.

dojox.fx

We previously looked at some FX capabilities that Dojo offers, but as they say in those horrible late-night infomercials: "But wait, there's more!" DojoX is home to additional FX classes and functions, some very interesting.

addClass() and removeClass()

These two functions do precisely what their names indicate: they add or remove a style class from a given node. However, they don't simply add or remove a style class. No, that would be too simple for Dojo! Instead, they *animate* the addition or removal! For instance, say you have a style class that specifies a height of 20 pixels, and another that specifies a height of 100 pixels. If a given `<div>` has that first style applied, and you use the `addClass()` function to add the second class, the `<div>` will indeed be 100 pixels tall at the end, but it will expand to that size over some period of time.

Let's see exactly how you use these things. Listing 4-4 demonstrates.

Listing 4-4. *Add/Remove Class Example (ch4_fx_addClassRemoveClass.htm)*

```
<html>

  <head>

    <script type="text/javascript">
      var djConfig = {
        baseScriptUri : "js/dojo/",
        parseOnLoad : true
      };
    </script>
    <script type="text/javascript" src="js/dojo/dojo/dojo.js"></script>

    <style>
      .oldClass {
        width            : 200px;
        height           : 50px;
        background-color : #eaeaea;
      }
      .newClass {
        width            : 300px;
        height           : 200px;
      }
    </style>

    <script>

      dojo.require("dojox.fx.style");

      function testIt() {
        dojox.fx.addClass({cssClass:"newClass", node:"div1"}).play();
        dojox.fx.removeClass({cssClass:"newClass", node:"div2"}).play();
      }

    </script>

  </head>

  <body onLoad="testIt();">
    <br>
    <table border="0" cellpadding="0" cellspacing="0"
      width="800" align="center" style="border:1px solid #000000;padding:6px;">
      <tr><td>
        dojox.fx.addClass/RemoveClass test:
        <br><br>
        <div id="div1"
          class="oldClass">
```

```
        Class will be added to me
      </div>
      <br>
      <div id="div2"
        class="newClass" style="background-color:#ffff00;">
        Class will be removed from me
      </div>
    </td></tr>
  </table>
</body>

</html>
```

I haven't shown a screenshot here because there just wouldn't be much point. This is definitely an example you need to execute for yourself. But you'll note that the `<div>` with the `id` of `div1` initially has the `oldClass` style class applied, while `div2` has `newClass` applied. Now, `onLoad` we see the `testIt()` function being called, and we see the following code in it:

```
dojox.fx.addClass({cssClass:"newClass", node:"div1"}).play();
dojox.fx.removeClass({cssClass:"newClass", node:"div2"}).play();
```

So, here we're simultaneously adding `newClass` to `div1`, and removing `newClass` from `div2`. Yes, they can be done in parallel; there's nothing that says otherwise. An `Animation` object is returned, which we then call the `play()` method on. Otherwise, the addition or removal won't begin.

■ **Note** This example does not seem to work in Internet Explorer, at least not in IE7. An error occurs down in the bowels of the Dojo code. While I was researching, I noticed some comments in the code that was checked in to the Dojo source tree talking about `addClass()` possibly breaking in IE. It seems here that `removeClass()` is the problem, but I have little trouble believing that an IE issue is at the core of the problem in either case.

---

crossFade()

When you cross-fade two elements, you essentially are morphing one element into another. In other words, you have an element, and you perform some style manipulation on it to get it out of view, while at the same time performing some style manipulation on a second element that happens to be located right on top of the first. The effect is a smooth transition from the first object to the second.

Once again, showing a screenshot here wouldn't do a whole lot of good (a common theme in FX functions), so we'll just jump right to the code again, here in Listing 4-5.

Listing 4-5. *Cross-Fade Example (ch4_fx_crossFade.htm)*

```
<html>

  <head>

    <script type="text/javascript">
      var djConfig = {
        baseScriptUri : "js/dojo/",
        parseOnLoad : true
      };
    </script>
    <script type="text/javascript" src="js/dojo/dojo/dojo.js"></script>

    <script>

      dojo.require("dojox.fx._base");

      function testIt() {
        dojox.fx.crossFade({ nodes : ["node1", "node2"], duration:1000}).play();
      }

    </script>

  </head>

  <body>
    <br>
    <table border="0" cellpadding="0" cellspacing="0"
      width="800" align="center" style="border:1px solid #000000;padding:6px;">
      <tr><td>
        dojox.fx.crossFade test:
        <br><br>
        <input type="button" onclick="testIt()" value="Click to cross-fade">
        <br><br>
        <div style="width:200px;height:100px;position:relative;➥
          border:1px solid #ff0000;">
          <center>
            <div id="node1"
              style="width:100%;height:100%;position:absolute;top:0px;left:0px;➥
               background-color:#e0e0e0;">
              <br>
              I am the first box
              <br>
              I have some content
              <br>
              Click button to cross-fade
            </div>
```

```
          <div id="node2"
            style="width:100%;height:100%;position:absolute;top:0px;left:0px;➥
             opacity:0;background-color:#ffff00;">
            <br>
            I am the second box
            <br>
            I have some different content
            <br>
            Nice cross-fade, huh?!?
          </div>
        </center>
      </div>
    </td></tr>
  </table>
</body>

</html>
```

Here we have two <div> elements, node1 and node2. Note that they are the same size and occupy the same position. Also note that node2's opacity is set to zero, which means it initially is completely transparent. Thus what's behind node2, which is node1, shows through because node1, by virtue of appearing before node2 in the code, automatically has a lower z-index and is thus behind node2. So, when we then call testIt(), the following line executes:

```
dojox.fx.crossFade({ nodes : ["node1", "node2"], duration:1000}).play();
```

That creates an Animation object, and hence we have to call play() on it to start the animation. The arguments it accepts are an array of nodes to cross-fade and the duration attribute, which is the number of milliseconds we want the cross-fade to take—1,000 milliseconds, or 1 second, in this case.

■ Note This cross-fade example also does not seem to work in IE, and again I noticed some comments in Dojo's source tree talking about IE problems. I know IE has historically had issues with opacity in various forms, and opacity is most certainly involved in doing a cross-fade, so it's not too hard to believe that this might not work as expected in IE. We can all hope IE8, which is supposed to be out shortly (it might be out by the time you read this) helps matters a bit.

---

highlight()

The highlight() function is used to implement the yellow fade effect, as described in Chapter 1. However, the highlight doesn't have to be yellow, as the example code in Listing 4-6 shows.

Listing 4-6. *Highlight Example (ch4_fx_highlight.htm)*

```
<html>

  <head>

    <script type="text/javascript">
      var djConfig = {
        baseScriptUri : "js/dojo/",
        parseOnLoad : true
      };
    </script>
    <script type="text/javascript" src="js/dojo/dojo/dojo.js"></script>

    <script>

      dojo.require("dojox.fx._base");

      function testIt() {
        dojox.fx.highlight({ node : "divOutput", color : "#ff0000" }).play();
      }

    </script>

  </head>

  <body>
    <br>
    <table border="0" cellpadding="0" cellspacing="0"
      width="800" align="center" style="border:1px solid #000000;padding:6px;">
      <tr><td>
        dojox.fx.highlight test:
        <br><br>
        <input type="button" onclick="testIt()" value="Click to highlight">
        <br><br>
        <div id="divOutput">I am a highlighted DIV</div>
      </td></tr>
    </table>
  </body>

</html>
```

All it takes to do this effect is a single line of code:

```
dojox.fx.highlight({ node : "divOutput", color : "#ff0000" }).play();
```

This briefly highlights the `<div>` with the `id` `divOutput` in red. As you can see, you can specify the color to use. You're not required to use yellow, contrary to the name of the technique mentioned previously.

sizeTo()

The `sizeTo()` function lets you resize a given element, but it does so in a nice, fancy, animated way. For example, the code in Listing 4-7 when run (and when you click the button) shows a square that gets larger, first vertically, then horizontally, and all gradually.

Listing 4-7. *sizeTo Example (ch4_fx_sizeTo.htm)*

```
<html>

  <head>

    <script type="text/javascript">
      var djConfig = {
        baseScriptUri : "js/dojo/",
        parseOnLoad : true
      };
    </script>
    <script type="text/javascript" src="js/dojo/dojo/dojo.js"></script>

    <script>

      dojo.require("dojox.fx._base");

      function testIt() {
        dojox.fx.sizeTo({
          node:"divOutput", duration: 2000, width: 300, height: 300,
          method: "chain"
        }).play();
      }

    </script>

  </head>

  <body>
    <br>
    <table border="0" cellpadding="0" cellspacing="0"
      width="800" align="center" style="border:1px solid #000000;padding:6px;">
      <tr><td>
        dojox.fx.sizeTo test:
        <br><br>
        <input type="button" onclick="testIt()" value="Click to sizeTo">
        <br><br>
        <div id="divOutput"
          style="background-color:#f0f000;width:100px;height:100px;➥
            position:relative;top:0px;left:0px;">
          I am going to be sized
```

```
      </div>
    </td></tr>
  </table>
</body>

</html>
```

The following code is responsible for performing the effect:

```
dojox.fx.sizeTo({
  node:"divOutput", duration: 2000, width: 300, height: 300,
  method: "chain"
}).play();
```

The `node` attribute tells the function what DOM node to change the size of. The `duration` attribute indicates how long the change should take. The `width` and `height` attributes tell what size the node should wind up being. Finally, the `method` attribute tells the function how to do the resizing. The value `chain` tells it to first do the height and then the width. A value of `combine` can be specified to grow the element both horizontally and vertically at the same time.

slideBy()

The `slideBy()` function is similar in many ways to `sizeTo()`, except that its goal is to move a DOM node, not resize it. Other than that, you use it in a similar way, as you can see in Listing 4-8.

Listing 4-8. *slideBy Example (ch4_fx_slideBy.htm)*

```
<html>

  <head>

    <script type="text/javascript">
      var djConfig = {
        baseScriptUri : "js/dojo/",
        parseOnLoad : true
      };
    </script>
    <script type="text/javascript" src="js/dojo/dojo/dojo.js"></script>

    <script>

      dojo.require("dojox.fx._base");

      function testIt() {
        dojox.fx.slideBy({
          node : "divOutput",
          duration : 1000, top : 100, left: 100
```

```
      }).play();
    }

  </script>

</head>

<body>
  <br>
  <table border="0" cellpadding="0" cellspacing="0"
    width="800" align="center" style="border:1px solid #000000;padding:6px;">
    <tr><td>
      dojox.fx.slideTo test:
      <br><br>
      <input type="button" onclick="testIt()" value="Click to slideBy">
      <br><br>
      <div id="divOutput"
        style="background-color:#f0f000;width:80px;height:60px;">
        I am going to be slid
      </div>
    </td></tr>
  </table>
</body>

</html>
```

The following code is similar, as you can see, and is again the main engine driving this example:

```
dojox.fx.slideBy({
  node : "divOutput",
  duration : 1000, top : 100, left: 100
}).play();
```

Here, instead of specifying `width` and `height` as in `sizeTo()`, we specify `top` and `left` to denote the location we want the node to move to. The `duration` attribute is again used to determine how long it should take the node to get where it's going. There doesn't appear to be a `method` attribute as in `sizeTo()`, though. It seems the element always has to move both vertically and horizontally at the same time.

dojox.gfx

Okay, I'm going to go ahead and say it right up front so there's no confusion: `dojo.gfx` may be the single coolest thing in all of Dojo!

For years now, displaying graphics in a browser has been limited to static images such as JPGs, PNGs, and GIFs, or some browser extension such as Flash or Java applets. (Animated GIFs aren't really static of course—they move after all—but the file itself doesn't change, so in that sense it's static.) One thing you couldn't generally do without some sort of extension was drawing graphic primitives such as lines, circles, and squares. Oh, to be sure, people came up with clever ways of pulling it off anyway, although never with especially good results.

Now, enter `dojo.gfx`, which enables you to do exactly that and much more. For example, check out Figure 4-8.

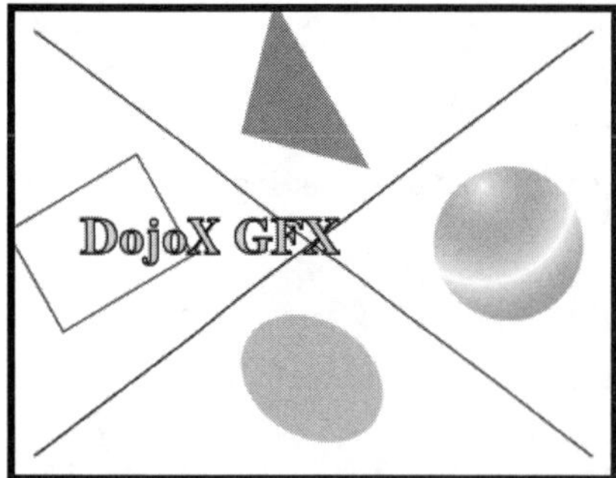

Figure 4-8. *Output of the dojo.gfx example*

What you can't unfortunately see here is that everything except the red and blue lines and the fancy shaded beach ball–looking circle on the right is moving around, rotating, and generally not sitting still. I admit this isn't exactly a graphical tour de force or anything, but it's wickedly cool nonetheless, if you ask me!

So, what's the code behind that look like? Listing 4-9 is your answer.

Listing 4-9. *GFX Example (ch4_gfx.htm)*

```
<html>

  <head>

    <script type="text/javascript">
      var djConfig = {
        baseScriptUri : "js/dojo/",
        parseOnLoad : true
      };
    </script>
    <script type="text/javascript" src="js/dojo/dojo/dojo.js"></script>

    <script>

      dojo.require("dojox.gfx");

      function testIt() {
        var tr1 = 130;
        var tr2 = 80;
        var trd1 = true;
```

```
    var trd2 = true;
    var s = dojox.gfx.createSurface("divSurface", 320, 240);
    s.createLine({x1:10,y1:10, x2:310,y2:230})
      .setStroke({color : "#ff0000"});
    s.createLine({x1:310,y1:10, x2:10,y2:230})
      .setStroke({color : "#0000ff"});
    var t = s.createPolyline([ {x:160,y:15}, {x:110,y:65},
      {x:210,y:65}, {x:160,y:15} ])
      .setFill([0, 255, 0, 1]);
    var r = s.createRect({ x : 15, y : 80, width : 60, height : 80})
      .setStroke({color : "green"});
    var c = s.createCircle({ cx : 265, cy : 120, r : 40})
      .setFill(dojo.mixin(
        { type : "radial", cx : 250, cy : 90},
        { colors: [
          { offset: 0,   color: [255, 0, 0, 0] },
          { offset: 0.5, color: "orange" },
          { offset: 1,   color: [0, 0, 255, 0] }
        ]}
      ));
    var e = s.createEllipse({ cx : 160, cy : 190, rx : 30, ry : 40 })
      .setFill([0, 255, 0, 0.5]);
    var txt = s.createText({x: 90, y: 130, text: "DojoX GFX"});
    txt.setFont({family : "Times", size : "20pt", weight : "bold"});
    txt.setFill("yellow");
    txt.setStroke("black");
    window.setInterval(function() {
      t.applyTransform(dojox.gfx.matrix.rotategAt(5, 155, 50));
      r.applyTransform(dojox.gfx.matrix.rotategAt(-10, 45, 120));
      e.applyTransform(dojox.gfx.matrix.rotategAt(25, 160, 190));
      txt.applyTransform(dojox.gfx.matrix.rotategAt(-15, tr1, tr2));
      if (trd1) {
        tr1 = tr1 + 1;
        if (tr1 > 280) { trd1 = false; }
      } else {
        tr1 = tr1 - 1;
        if (tr1 < 40) { trd1 = true; }
      }
      if (trd2) {
        tr2 = tr2 + 1;
        if (tr2 > 200) { trd2 = false; }
      } else {
        tr2 = tr2 - 1;
        if (tr2 < 40) { trd2 = true; }
      }
    }, 100);
  }
```

```
    </script>

  </head>

  <body onLoad="testIt();">
    <br>
    <table border="0" cellpadding="0" cellspacing="0"
      width="800" align="center" style="border:1px solid #000000;padding:6px;">
      <tr><td>
        dojox.gfx test:
        <br><br>
        <div id="divSurface" style="width:320px;height:240px;➥
          border:4px solid #000000;"></div>
      </td></tr>
    </table>
  </body>

</html>
```

Now, let's look at some of this in more detail to see what `dojo.gfx` has to offer. This won't be an exhaustive look, but more than enough to whet your appetite (and you'll see this, and more, in some projects to come).

Surface

Everything begins with a surface.

A surface gives you something to draw on, simply put. Without it, the rest just wouldn't work. You create a surface like so:

```
var s = dojox.gfx.createSurface("divSurface", 320, 240);
```

You feed it the ID of an element, typically a `<div>`, to create the surface under. You also specify its width and height, and that's all it takes! You can then call the various methods of the `Surface` object to draw things on it, such as a line.

Line

Drawing lines is the basis of just about everything you do with `dojo.gfx`, and the `Surface.createLine()` method gives you that primitive to work with easily. For example, the two lines in the previous screenshot were drawn with this code:

```
s.createLine({x1:10,y1:10, x2:310,y2:230})
  .setStroke({color : "#ff0000"});
s.createLine({x1:310,y1:10, x2:10,y2:230})
  .setStroke({color : "#0000ff"});
```

The first argument to this method is an object containing four attributes: `x`, `y`, `x2`, and `y2`. The `x` and `y` attributes are the coordinates of one end of the line, and `x2` and `y2` are the coordinates of the other end. At this point, it's important to realize that the `Surface` is a grid of pixels with the upper-left corner being pixel 0,0, and the bottom right being 319,239 in the case of a 320 × 240 Surface as we have here.

The setStroke() method is called on the object returned by Surface.createLine(). This method is responsible for setting the color of the line: red for the first line (RGB value 255, 0, 0) and blue for the second (RGB value 0, 0, 255). This is something common to many of these functions, as the code shows.

Polyline

The Surface.createPolyline() method enables you to draw a polygon. It's a collection of points, between which lines will be drawn. You use it by passing it an array of points, like so:

```
var t = s.createPolyline([ {x:160,y:15}, {x:110,y:65},
  {x:210,y:65}, {x:160,y:15} ])
  .setFill([0, 255, 0, 1]);
```

This call to createPolyline() will draw a line between pixel 150,15, another between that and 110,65, another between that and 210,65, and one more from that last pixel to the pixel at location 160,15—which is the first one again; hence it's drawing a closed figure. This is in fact drawing the triangle at the top of the Surface.

You'll also notice the use of the setFill() method. This is something you'll see frequently. This method enables you to fill the shape with a given color, green in this case (RGB value 0, 255, 0). The one on the end enables you to set an opacity level. This is value between 0 and 1, where 1 is completely opaque and 0 is completely transparent.

Rect

Although you could certainly draw a rectangle by using createPolyline(), and although you could draw a polygon by using createLine() too, there are far more convenient ways to do both. In that same vein, Surface.createRect() exists to make drawing rectangles easier, as you can see here:

```
var r = s.createRect({ x : 15, y : 80, width : 60, height : 80})
  .setStroke({color : "green"});
```

All you need to do is specify the upper-left corner's coordinates, tell the method how wide and how tall the rectangle is, and off you go. Notice in the call to setStroke() here that I've specified a color by using a word. You can do this for many common colors, which is nice if you're using the standard ones the method knows about. This applies for most, if not all, of the setStroke() and setFill() calls you can make on any object.

Circle

Drawing circles is another common thing to want to do, and dojo.gfx provides that for you as well:

```
var c = s.createCircle({ cx : 265, cy : 120, r : 40})
  .setFill(dojo.mixin(
    { type : "radial", cx : 250, cy : 90},
    { colors: [
```

```
    { offset: 0,   color: [255, 0, 0, 0] },
    { offset: 0.5, color: "orange" },
    { offset: 1,   color: [0, 0, 255, 0] }
  ]}
));
```

All you need to do is specify the center of the circle, using the cx and cy attributes, and specify the radius with the r attribute, and you'll have yourself a circle! Here as well I show that you can do some more-advanced things with setFill()—for instance, you can create gradients. In this case, I'm creating a radial gradient centered slightly off-center of the circle. I then specify three colors—red (255, 0, 0), orange, and blue (0, 0, 255)—and specify some offset values, which are used to create the gradient.

Ellipse

An ellipse is of course just a squashed circle, so you might think the createCircle() method could do it, but you'd be wrong. There is a createEllipse() method just for drawing ellipses:

```
var e = s.createEllipse({ cx : 160, cy : 190, rx : 30, ry : 40 })
  .setFill([0, 255, 0, 0.5]);
```

All you need to do is specify the center point of the ellipse with the cx and cy attributes, and the horizontal and vertical radiuses with rx and ry, respectively. Then do whatever setFill() and/or setStroke() you want, or none at all if the defaults suit you, and you've got yourself an ellipse.

Text

The dojo.gfx namespace isn't all about simple shapes. You can also create text! Sure, you could always draw the text yourself with primitives, but that's a whole lot of work for what will probably not even wind up being as good of a result. Why not just do this instead:

```
var txt = s.createText({x: 90, y: 130, text: "DojoX GFX"});
txt.setFont({family : "Times", size : "20pt", weight : "bold"});
txt.setFill("yellow");
txt.setStroke("black");
```

You start by creating the text with a call to createText(), feeding it the location to put the text at, and of course the text itself. You can then optionally set the font information, including font family, size, and weight, just like style sheet attributes, and you can also set the outline color of the text with setStroke() and/or the inner color of it with setFill(). At the end of the day, text is just a polyline drawn very finely and automatically for you, but it's still a vector-based drawing.

applyTransform()

The last thing we need to look at is how the objects are animated (you *have* run the example, right?). Doing so is all about transformations. For example, to rotate the triangle, this line of code is used:

```
t.applyTransform(dojox.gfx.matrix.rotategAt(5, 155, 50));
```

Note that when the triangle was created, I kept a reference to it in the variable `t`. That's specifically so I could manipulate it later. It's just a matter of calling `applyTransform()` and giving it a matrix (an instance of `dojox.gfx.Matrix2D`) that describes the transformation. An explanation of transformation matrices is beyond the scope of this book (and I'm probably not the right person to go into it anyway, to be honest, because math and I don't generally get along too well!). Suffice it to say that calling `rotategAt()` is a special case that gives us a matrix suitable for rotating an object. You pass to it the number of degrees to rotate (5 here, a positive number being clockwise, a negative number being counterclockwise) and the x and y location of the point on the screen about which to rotate the object.

For contrast, rotating the rectangle is done with this line:

```
r.applyTransform(dojox.gfx.matrix.rotategAt(-10, 45, 120));
```

As you can see, this rotates counterclockwise and a little faster than the triangle because the degrees value is larger.

Now, for the text rotation, I play some games to basically make it "oscillate" a little. In other words, the point that the rectangle rotates around changes over time so that it moves around a bit, rather than just rotating around a fixed point.

But wait, didn't I gloss over something? I sure did! Each of these transformations will modify the object exactly once. How does the animation happen? Well, that's a simple matter of wrapping all the `applyTransform()` calls in an interval. Ten times a second, the transforms are applied (100 milliseconds = 1/10 of a second). Note that `dojo.gfx` doesn't say anything about how you do animation; that's up to you. It just gives you the facilities to modify vector objects, which is the basics you need to create an animation.

You aren't limited to rotations alone, of course. You can devise any sort of transformation matrix you wish to do mirroring, for example, or making an object bigger, whatever you're mind can dream up (and that it can understand the mathematics for!).

dojox.grid

The `dojox.grid` namespace contains a whole widget, or future dijit, unto itself: the data grid. This is such a common widget that I guess the team felt it deserved its own namespace!

In Figure 4-9 you can see a simple example of the grid in action.

dojox.grid test:

Item	Description	Price	In Stock?
Car Alarm	It's a nice gift idea	99.95	true
Portable DVD Player	Needed with kids in a car	129.99	false
Bagpipes	Does anyone actually like bagpipes?!?	429.89	true
Cabbage Patch Kid	Remember the lines?	39.99	false
Trident Chewing Gum	Is that still made?	0.69	true
1Gb SD Card	Too small, too small!	8.99	false

Figure 4-9. *The dojo.grid example*

The grid supports row highlighting, column sorting, hover effects when mousing around it, multiple rows of columns (that is, a column underneath *Item* in the screenshot), expandable and collapsible rows, subgrids (that is, a grid as the contents of a row in a grid), full styling capability to your liking, editable cells, and much more.

But it all starts with the basics: creating a simple grid. Listing 4-10 shows you how to do that.

Listing 4-10. *GFX Example (ch4_grid.htm)*

```
<html>

  <head>
    <link rel="StyleSheet" type="text/css"
      href="js/dojo/dojo/resources/dojo.css">
    <link rel="StyleSheet" type="text/css"
      href="js/dojo/dojox/grid/_grid/grid.css">

    <script type="text/javascript">
      var djConfig = {
        baseScriptUri : "js/dojo/",
        parseOnLoad : true
      };
    </script>
    <script type="text/javascript" src="js/dojo/dojo/dojo.js"></script>

    <script>

      dojo.require("dojox.grid.Grid");
      dojo.require("dojox.grid._data.model");
      dojo.require("dojo.parser");

      var data = [
        [ "Car Alarm", "It's a nice gift idea", 99.95, true ],
        [ "Portable DVD Player", "Needed with kids in a car", 129.99, false ],
        [ "Bagpipes", "Does anyone actually like bagpipes?!?", 429.89, true ],
        [ "Cabbage Patch Kid", "Remember the lines?", 39.99, false ],
        [ "Trident Chewing Gum", "Is that still made?", .69, true ],
        [ "1Gb SD Card", "Too small, too small!", 8.99, false ],
        [ "Tooth Paste", "5 out of 10 dentists recommend it!", 2.96, true ],
        [ "Ice Cream", "Why can't prices be whole dollars?!?", 4, false ]
    ];

    var model = new dojox.grid.data.Table(null, data);

    var view = {
      cells: [
        [
          { name : "Item", width : "150px"},
```

```
        { name : "Description", width : "175px"},
        { name : "Price", width : "75px"},
        { name : "In Stock?", width : "75px"}
      ]]
    };

    var layout = [ view ];

    </script>

  </head>

  <body>
    <br>
    <table border="0" cellpadding="0" cellspacing="0"
      width="800" align="center" style="border:1px solid #000000;padding:6px;">
      <tr><td>
        dojox.grid test:
        <br><br>
        <div id="myGrid" dojoType="dojox.Grid"
          structure="layout" model="model"
          style="font-size:10pt;font-weight:bold;width:540px;height:200px;" />
      </td></tr>
    </table>
  </body>

</html>
```

After you've imported the necessary style sheets and Dojo components, the next step is to create a data model. This model is just a simple array in which each element is itself an array representing a row in the table, and each element in the inner array is a cell value. After you have populated the array (however it is that you do that in your particular case), you next turn it into an actual data model that the grid understands by calling the following:

```
var model = new dojox.grid.data.Table(null, data);
```

After you have a model, the next step is to create a view for your grid, where a view is a collection of columns. You do this by creating an object that contains a `cells` attribute. The value of this attribute is an array, where each element is itself an array that represents a row of column headers. Remember that a grid can have multiple rows of column headers, hence the needs, potentially anyway, for a multidimensional array. So, in this case we have this:

```
var view = {
  cells: [
    [
      { name : "Item", width : "150px"},
      { name : "Description", width : "175px"},
      { name : "Price", width : "75px"},
      { name : "In Stock?", width : "75px"}
```

```
  ]]
};
```

The last step is to create a layout for the grid. A *layout* is a collection of views. So you create another simple array with each of the view arrays you created as an element. The code for that is this snippet here:

```
var layout = [ view ];
```

Note that in the listing all of this happens in a `<script>` section in the `<head>` of the document. That's because we're going to create the grid declaratively, so we need the model, view, and layout set up before the `<body>` is encountered (remember that the JavaScript in the `<head>` will execute before anything in the `<body>` is processed). The markup for creating the grid is simply this:

```
<div id="myGrid" dojoType="dojox.Grid"
  structure="layout" model="model"
  style="font-size:10pt;font-weight:bold;width:540px;height:200px;></div>
```

See how the data model and layout are referenced here? That's really all the grid code needs to construct itself. I also set some `style` attributes to size the grid itself at least roughly to the data it contains, but it's a little too small vertically so there's scrolling. It'll scroll horizontally as well if you, for instance, increase your browser's font size.

■ **Note** The grid is clearly a very flexible, rich, and powerful component. Check out some of the tests that are packaged with the Dojo download for even more examples. However, the grid is not documented very well (at least not at the time I wrote this), which is to say I could find virtually no documentation. Now, that's not a criticism per se, because after all we're in DojoX land, which we've previously established is largely experimental in nature, and to expect top-notch documentation here isn't exactly fair. Still, the lack of documentation makes it difficult to use the grid to its full potential, and certainly makes it difficult to cover in depth in a book. I suggest that if you need the grid, the examples I mentioned here are most likely your best bet at this moment.

---

dojox.math

The `dojox.math` namespace is home to more-advanced mathematical functions that let you go beyond the basics of adding, subtracting, multiplying, and dividing. I'll say right up front that math was always my worst subject in school, so this namespace holds a little less interest for me than many others. That doesn't matter, though, because even someone as mathematically challenged as I am can see that there's a lot of good stuff here!

We'll begin with an example that demonstrates several things all at the same time. Take a peek at Listing 4-11.

Listing 4-11. *Math Example (ch4_math.htm)*

```
<html>

  <head>

    <script type="text/javascript">
      var djConfig = {
        baseScriptUri : "js/dojo/",
        parseOnLoad : true
      };
    </script>
    <script type="text/javascript" src="js/dojo/dojo/dojo.js"></script>

    <script>

      dojo.require("dojox.math._base");

      function testIt() {
        dojo.byId("divOutput").innerHTML += "<br>90 degrees in radians = " +
          dojox.math.degreesToRadians(90);
        dojo.byId("divOutput").innerHTML += "<br>1.5707963267948966 radians " +
          "in degrees = " + dojox.math.radiansToDegrees(1.5707963267948966);
        dojo.byId("divOutput").innerHTML += "<br>Distance between " +
          "2,2 & 4,2 = " + dojox.math.distance([2,2],[4,2]);
        dojo.byId("divOutput").innerHTML += "<br>Distance between " +
          "18,-23 & -9,4 = " + dojox.math.distance([18,-23],[-9,4]);
        dojo.byId("divOutput").innerHTML += "<br>10 factoral = " +
          dojox.math.factoral(10);
        dojo.byId("divOutput").innerHTML += "<br>A Gaussian random number = " +
          dojox.math.gaussian();
        dojo.byId("divOutput").innerHTML += "<br>Midpoint between " +
          "2,2 & 8,2 = " + dojox.math.midpoint([2,2],[8,2]);
        dojo.byId("divOutput").innerHTML += "<br>A range from 10 to 100 by " +
          "5's = " + dojox.math.range(10, 100, 5);
        dojo.byId("divOutput").innerHTML += "<br>The standard deviation of " +
          "99,45,-17,62 = " + dojox.math.sd([99,45,-17,62]);
      }

    </script>

  </head>

  <body onLoad="testIt();">
    <br>
    <table border="0" cellpadding="0" cellspacing="0"
      width="800" align="center" style="border:1px solid #000000;padding:6px;">
      <tr><td>
```

```
        dojox.math test:
        <br>
        <div id="divOutput"> </div>
      </td></tr>
    </table>
  </body>

</html>
```

The accompanying screen output can be seen in Figure 4-10.

```
dojox.math test:

90 degrees in radians = 1.5707963267948966
1.5707963267948966 radians in degrees = 90
Distance between 2,2 & 4,2 = 2
Distance between 18,-23 & -9,4 = 38.18376618407357
10 factoral = 3628800
A Gaussian random number = 1.296487919119739
Midpoint between 2,2 & 8,2 = 5,2
A range from 10 to 100 by 5's = 10,15,20,25,30,35,40,45,50,55,60,65,70,75,80,85,90,95
The standard deviation of 99,45,-17,62 = 41.91882035553959
```

Figure 4-10. *Output of the math example*

So, what are some of the functions demonstrated in this example? Let's look at them one by one.

degreesToRadians() and radiansToDegrees()

I hear tell that in trigonometry, converting between degrees and radians in either direction is an important thing. Being a horribly bad math student, my exposure to trig was pretty limited and thus I have to take their word for it on the importance of such a thing.

In any case, it's clearly easy to do: a call to `dojox.math.degreesToRadians()`, passing it the degree value to convert, is all it takes to get radians. If you want to go the other way, it's a call to `dojox.math.radiansToDegrees()`. So, if you know what all that gibber-jabber means, it's right there for you!

distance()

Now, I have done a fair bit of game programming in my day, although I'm old-fashioned (math-challenged, as we've already established), which means 3D games and I don't generally get along. I'm a fan of the old 2D world myself, and in that world it's not at all uncommon to need to determine the distance between two points—especially if you're writing a game, say, like Pac-Man, where you need to write a pursuit algorithm of some sort, then that's valuable information.

Dojo is right there to help in such a case. The method `dojox.math.distance()` accepts two arrays with two elements each. The arrays are the coordinates of two points.

So, for instance, in the example you see a call in this form:

```
dojox.math.distance([2,2],[4,2]);
```

The value returned from this call is 2 because that's the distance between the two points. It's a simple method, but a valuable one in many instances.

factoral()

Factoral is a math concept I do know about because I've always had a bit of a fascination with patterns, and that's pretty much all a factoral is. It's simply when you have a series of numbers, say 1, 2, and 3, and you multiply the product of each by the next number. So for instance, 1 × 2 × 3 is 3 factoral (it's notated as 3! technically). Now, that's just 6, which is kind of boring, but what's 10 factoral (10!) instead? Turns out that's a much larger number!

We don't have to do the work ourselves of course because Dojo can do it for us just fine. A quick call to `dojox.math.factoral(10)` gives us the answer, which is 3,628,800 for those keeping score at home.

gaussian()

Generating random numbers via computer is an interesting concept. I remember hearing in my computer science classes that generating truly random numbers is not possible for a computer. I also heard a story about how when US government spy agencies require a random number to encrypt something, they use a telescope that spins around and snaps a picture of the sky. The pixel map that is the resulting image is used as the random number seed, all because that provides a truly random number and therefore better encryption.

I've never been a spook myself, so I don't know if that story is true, and I don't know the current state of the art on computer-based random-number generation. What I do know is that numerous algorithms have been devised over the years to try to get computers to generate better random numbers, and one of those is the Gaussian algorithm.

Without going into detail on how the algorithm works (which I couldn't do anyway because, remember, math weakling here!), I can show you how to generate such a random number: `dojox.math.gaussian()`. Yep, just that simple call does the trick. You'll get back a decimal number between 0 and 1, which you can then use in performing the typical tricks of the trade to get a number in the range you require.

midpoint()

Along with the idea of getting the distance between two points as described previously is the notion of finding the point that is midway between two points. This is another quite common task to have to do in game programming, among other things. And just as with getting the distance between two points, Dojo makes it easy:

```
dojox.math.midpoint([2,2],[8,2]);
```

As you can see, this code uses the same input parameters as `dojox.math.distance()`, which makes sense because we're again dealing with two points. However, `dojox.math.midpoint()` enables you to specify multidimensional arrays as input, so it's even a bit more powerful than `dojox.math.distance()`n.

range()

Quick, how would you write the code to generate a range of numbers between 10 and 100, counting by 5s? Did you envision a for loop of some sort? What if you wanted to be able to change the step value? Thinking of a function with some inputs now? Well, that would all work certainly, but if you're lazy like me, you'd prefer to do this:

```
dojox.math.range(10, 100, 5);
```

What you'll get back is an array of the values as specified. I guess the Dojo folks are a bit lazy, like me, but I'm really thankful for it!

sd(), or Standard Deviation

A *standard deviation* is defined as a measure of the dispersion of outcomes around the mean (or expected value), used to measure total risk. It is the square root of the variance . . .

Err, yeah, I don't get it either.

But if a standard deviation is something you understand and need, then by all means, have at it, and Dojo has you covered. For instance, to calculate the standard deviation of the numbers 99, 45, –17, and 62, you have to do only this:

```
dojox.math.sd([99,45,-17,62]);
```

And of course you get back the obvious answer—41.91882035553959—which obviously anyone would have known without executing the code (ha ha, yeah, right!).

dojox.string

Strings are of course part and parcel of what we as programmers do every day. JavaScript has a String class, and it's fairly powerful, giving you useful methods and attributes to play with. But, it's not always enough, and that's where Dojo and the dojox.string namespace come into play.

The dojox.string namespace provides two useful items: the Builder class and the sprintf() function. Let's see them in action first and then look at each in a little more detail. In truly backward form, Figure 4-11 shows you the output of the code that is in Listing 4-12.

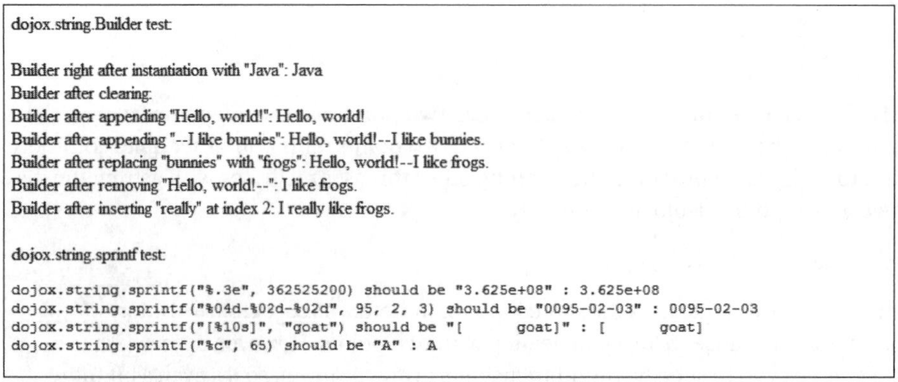

```
dojox.string.Builder test:

Builder right after instantiation with "Java": Java
Builder after clearing:
Builder after appending "Hello, world!": Hello, world!
Builder after appending "--I like bunnies": Hello, world!--I like bunnies.
Builder after replacing "bunnies" with "frogs": Hello, world!--I like frogs.
Builder after removing "Hello, world!--": I like frogs.
Builder after inserting "really" at index 2: I really like frogs.

dojox.string.sprintf test:

dojox.string.sprintf("%.3e", 362525200) should be "3.625e+08" : 3.625e+08
dojox.string.sprintf("%04d-%02d-%02d", 95, 2, 3) should be "0095-02-03" : 0095-02-03
dojox.string.sprintf("[%10s]", "goat") should be "[      goat]" : [      goat]
dojox.string.sprintf("%c", 65) should be "A" : A
```

Figure 4-11. *Output of the string example*

Listing 4-12. *String Example (ch4_String.htm)*

```
<html>

  <head>

    <script type="text/javascript">
      var djConfig = {
        baseScriptUri : "js/dojo/",
        parseOnLoad : true
      };
    </script>
    <script type="text/javascript" src="js/dojo/dojo/dojo.js"></script>

    <script>

      dojo.require("dojox.string.Builder");
      dojo.require("dojox.string.sprintf");

      function testIt() {
        var b = new dojox.string.Builder("Java");
        var s = "Builder right after instantiation with &quot;Java&quot;: " + b;
        b.clear();
        s += "<br>Builder after clearing: " + b;
        b.append("Hello, world!");
        s += "<br>Builder after appending &quot;Hello, world!&quot;: " + b
        b.append("--I like bunnies.");
        s += "<br>Builder after appending &quot;--I like bunnies&quot;: " + b
        b.replace("bunnies", "frogs");
        s += "<br>Builder after replacing &quot;bunnies&quot; with " +
          "&quot;frogs&quot;: " + b;
        b.remove(0, 15);
        s += "<br>Builder after removing &quot;Hello, world!--&quot;: " + b;
        b.insert(2, "really ");
        s += "<br>Builder after inserting &quot;really&quot; at index 2: " + b;
        dojo.byId("divBuilderOutput").innerHTML = s;
        s = "";
        s += "dojox.string.sprintf(&quot;%.3e&quot;, 362525200) " +
          "should be " +
          "&quot;3.625e+08&quot; : " +
          dojox.string.sprintf("%.3e", 362525200);
        s += "<br>dojox.string.sprintf(&quot;%04d-%02d-%02d&quot;, 95, 2, 3) " +
          "should be " +
          "&quot;0095-02-03&quot; : " +
          dojox.string.sprintf("%04d-%02d-%02d", 95, 2, 3);
        s += "<br>dojox.string.sprintf(&quot;[%10s]&quot;, &quot;goat&quot;) " +
          "should be " +
          "&quot;[      goat]&quot; : " +
```

```
        dojox.string.sprintf("[%10s]", "goat");
      s += "<br>dojox.string.sprintf(&quot;%c&quot;, 65) " +
        "should be " +
        "&quot;A&quot; : " +
        dojox.string.sprintf("%c", 65);
      dojo.byId("divSPRINTFOutput").innerHTML = s;
    }

  </script>

</head>

<body onLoad="testIt();">
  <br>
  <table border="0" cellpadding="0" cellspacing="0"
    width="800" align="center" style="border:1px solid #000000;padding:6px;">
    <tr><td>
      dojox.string.Builder test:
      <br><br>
      <div id="divBuilderOutput"> </div>
      <br>
      dojox.string.sprintf test:
      <pre><div id="divSPRINTFOutput"> </div></pre>
    </td></tr>
  </table>
</body>

</html>
```

Let's begin with the Builder class, which is akin to the StringBuilder class in the .NET world, or the StringBuffer class in the Java world.

Builder

The Builder class enables you to construct a large string quicker than you could with the basic JavaScript string functionality. It's essentially a buffer of characters that you can manipulate.

To begin, you have to create an instance of the Builder class like so:

```
var b = new dojox.string.Builder("Java");
```

After that's done, you can call its methods to manipulate it. For example, to display its contents, you can call toString(). However, if you use something like alert(b);, then toString() is called behind the scenes anyway, so you won't typically call it explicitly.

You can call the clear() method on it at any time to clear its contents and start fresh, without having to create a new instance.

Calling the append() method, and passing in some value, appends that value to the end of the Builder. If you instead want to insert a value somewhere other than the end of the string, the insert() method is just the ticket. It accepts two parameters, the first being the index in the Builder to insert at, and the second being the value to insert.

You can also replace strings within the Builder by using the aptly named replace() method. The first parameter it accepts is the value to replace, and the second is the value to replace the first with. All occurrences of the first value will be replaced with the second value.

If you instead want to remove a value, call the remove() method and pass it two values: the start and end index to remove.

sprintf()

If you've ever done any C or C++ programming, sprintf is something you are all too familiar with. Many other languages have taken their cue from C's sprintf() function, and now, thanks to Dojo and DojoX, JavaScript is no exception.

The sprintf() function enables you to format a value in a wide variety of ways by using (relatively) standard formatting strings. For example, if you want to display the value 362525200 in scientific notation, that is, 3.625e+08, you can use this:

```
dojox.string.sprintf("%.3e", 362525200);
```

The string %.3e tells sprintf() how to format the second parameter. Getting into the details of these formatting strings is beyond the scope of this book and could well be a whole chapter all its own, but I will give you a few more examples at least!

Say you have three numbers: 95, 2, and 3. Further, say that they represent year, month, and day values. Even further, say you want to display them as 0095-02-03. (Let's assume that you're writing some sort of historical analysis program and you need to deal with events that occurred not too long after the death of Jesus.) You could accomplish this by doing the following:

```
dojox.string.sprintf("%04d-%02d-%02d", 95, 2, 3);
```

How about one final example? Let's say you want to have an ASCII value, say 65, and you want to see what character that corresponds to. Simple with sprintf():

```
dojox.string.sprintf("%c", 65);
```

That gives us A, which is indeed the character that corresponds to the ASCII value 65.

dojox.timing

The dojox.timing namespace is perhaps one of the more poorly named namespaces out there because when you hear *timing*, you (if you're like me, anyway) think of things to help you tell how long something took. That's not quite what it's all about, although time certainly does play a key role in at least part of it.

The central component in this namespace is the Timer object, which is where we'll begin our exploration.

Timer

The Timer class is in a sense a nice wrapper around the interval capability built into JavaScript. Just like an interval, Timer enables you to fire a given function with each tick of a clock, the interval of those ticks being settable by you, the programmer. The syntax is arguably a little nicer with Timer, which seems to be the main attraction of it.

Listing 4-13 shows an example of its usage.

Listing 4-13. *Timer Example (ch4_timing_Timer.htm)*

```
<html>

  <head>

    <script type="text/javascript">
      var djConfig = {
        baseScriptUri : "js/dojo/",
        parseOnLoad : true
      };
    </script>
    <script type="text/javascript" src="js/dojo/dojo/dojo.js"></script>

    <script>

      dojo.require("dojox.timing._base");

      var t = new dojox.timing.Timer();
      function testIt() {
        t.setInterval(1000);
        t.onTick = function() {
          dojo.byId("divOutput").innerHTML += "Next...";
        }
        t.start();
      }

    </script>

  </head>

  <body onLoad="testIt();">
    <br>
    <table border="0" cellpadding="0" cellspacing="0"
      width="800" align="center" style="border:1px solid #000000;padding:6px;">
      <tr><td>
        dojox.timing.Timer test:
        <br><br>
        <input type="button" onClick="t.stop();" value="Click to stop">
        <br><br>
        <div id="divOutput"> </div>
      </td></tr>
    </table>
  </body>

</html>
```

Figure 4-12 is the result of viewing that file in your browser. In it you can see where four ticks of the clock have already executed. The button there enables you to stop the `Timer`, which is done with a simple call to its `stop()` method.

dojox.timing.Timer test:

Click to stop

Next...Next...Next...Next...

Figure 4-12. *Output of the Timer example*

`Timer` is a class, which means you have to instantiate it. After you do that, calling `setInterval()` on it sets how frequently the clock will tick, measured in milliseconds. The `onTick` attribute should be pointed to a function to be executed with each tick. After that's all done, a call to the `start()` method gets the ball rolling until `stop()` is called.

Sequence

The `Sequence` class is, in my opinion at least, the far more interesting component in the `dojox.timing` namespace. It enables you to queue up a series of function calls and fire them in order. That alone wouldn't be too exciting, but what's more interesting is that you can set all sorts of delays before and after the execution of each!

For example, take a gander at Figure 4-13.

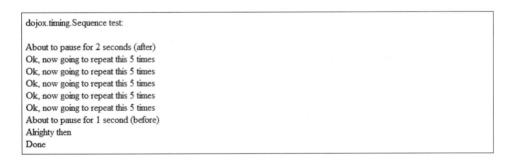

Figure 4-13. *Output of the Sequence example*

Each of the lines after the title line is a function that was called. After the first one, there is a 2-second delay. There is no delay either before or after each of the next five. The sixth line appears, and then there is a 1-second delay, and then the last two appear. All of these delays are specified as part of the list of functions to execute.

Listing 4-14 shows the code behind this example.

Listing 4-14. *Sequence Example (ch4_timing_Sequence.htm)*

```
<html>

  <head>

    <script type="text/javascript">
      var djConfig = {
        baseScriptUri : "js/dojo/",
        parseOnLoad : true
      };
    </script>
    <script type="text/javascript" src="js/dojo/dojo/dojo.js"></script>

    <script>

      dojo.require("dojox.timing.Sequence");

      function writeText(msg) {
        dojo.byId("divOutput").innerHTML += "<br>" + msg;
      }

      function testIt() {
        var s = new dojox.timing.Sequence({});
        var funcs = [
          {func : [writeText, this, "About to pause for 2 seconds (after)"],
            pauseAfter : 2000},
          {func : [writeText, this, "Ok, now going to repeat this 5 times"],
            repeat : 5, pauseAfter : 500},
          {func : [writeText, this, "About to pause for 1 second (before)"]},
          {func : [writeText, this, "Alrighty then"], pauseBefore : 1000}
        ];
        s.go(funcs, function() { writeText("Done"); });
      }

    </script>

  </head>

  <body onLoad="testIt();">
    <br>
    <table border="0" cellpadding="0" cellspacing="0"
      width="800" align="center" style="border:1px solid #000000;padding:6px;">
      <tr><td>
        dojox.timing.Sequence test:
        <br>
```

```
      <div id="divOutput"> </div>
    </td></tr>
  </table>
</body>

</html>
```

As you can see, you instantiate a new `Sequence` object and then call its `go()` method, passing into it an array of objects that each define a function call. Each object in this array has at least one element in it, namely the `func` element, which is itself an array consisting of three elements. The first element is the name of the function to execute, `writeText` in this case. The next is an object that will be the context for the function call (in this case, `this`, which means `writeText` will execute within the context of the `Sequence`). The third (and actually, as many as you like) is a parameter to pass to the function.

Each object that defines a function call can also optionally contain some elements that speak to the delays around its execution. For instance, if you set a value for the `pauseAfter` element, the value (in milliseconds) will specify how long to wait after the function is executed before executing the next. Likewise, `pauseBefore` sets a delay before that particular function is executed. There is also the `repeat` attribute, which enables you to execute a function more than once.

Finally, you have the option of passing in one final function call that is called at the end of processing, separate from the array of objects defining the function calls.

dojox.uuid

A *Universally Unique Identifier*, or *UUID* for short, is a standard method for constructing an ID for a given thing in such a fashion that you can be reasonably sure (although not guaranteed) that the UUID is unique to your thing. UUIDs are seen in computer applications all over the place. Microsoft's GUID is an implementation of the UUID standard as put forth by the Open Software Foundation. A UUID comes in the form df7145b8-2a7c-41cc-82ea-95feba5cb654, which, being as it's a base-16 number (or hexadecimal, for the rest of us!) it clearly allows for some truly huge numbers to be represented, which is one of the ways it ensures, to a large extent at least, uniqueness.

And why shouldn't you have the ability to use UUIDs in JavaScript? Well, now you do, courtesy of Dojo and the `dojox.uuid` namespace! Listing 4-15 shows you an example of using this namespace.

Listing 4-15. *UUID Example (ch4_uuid.htm)*

```
<html>

  <head>

    <script type="text/javascript">
      var djConfig = {
        baseScriptUri : "js/dojo/",
```

```
      parseOnLoad : true
    };
  </script>
  <script type="text/javascript" src="js/dojo/dojo/dojo.js"></script>

  <script>

    dojo.require("dojox.uuid._base");
    dojo.require("dojox.uuid.Uuid");
    dojo.require("dojox.uuid.generateRandomUuid");
    dojo.require("dojox.uuid.generateTimeBasedUuid");

    function testIt() {
      var nuuid = dojox.uuid.generateNilUuid();
      var ruuid = dojox.uuid.generateRandomUuid();
      var tbuuid1 = dojox.uuid.generateTimeBasedUuid();
      var tbuuid2 = dojox.uuid.generateTimeBasedUuid("0a023cffa8ea");
      dojo.byId("divOutput").innerHTML += "<br>A nil UUID: " + nuuid;
      dojo.byId("divOutput").innerHTML += "<br>A random UUID: " + ruuid;
      dojo.byId("divOutput").innerHTML += "<br>A time-based (version 1) " +
        "UUID with no node ID passed in: " + tbuuid1;
      dojo.byId("divOutput").innerHTML += "<br>A time-based (version 1) " +
        "UUID with node ID 0a023cffa8ea passed in: " + tbuuid2;
      dojo.byId("divOutput").innerHTML += "<br>Node read back from 2nd " +
        "time-based UUID: " + dojox.uuid.getNode(tbuuid2);
      dojo.byId("divOutput").innerHTML += "<br>Timestamp read back from " +
        "2nd time-based UUID: " + dojox.uuid.getTimestamp(tbuuid2);
      dojo.byId("divOutput").innerHTML += "<br>Variant of 2nd " +
        "time-based UUID: " + dojox.uuid.getVariant(tbuuid2);
      dojo.byId("divOutput").innerHTML += "<br>Version of 2nd time-based" +
        " UUID: " + dojox.uuid.getVersion(tbuuid2);
      dojo.byId("divOutput").innerHTML += "<br>Is 2nd time-based UUID " +
        "valid? " + dojox.uuid.isValid(tbuuid2);
      dojo.byId("divOutput").innerHTML += "<br>Are 1st and 2nd time-based " +
        "UUIDs equal? " + new dojox.uuid.Uuid(tbuuid1).isEqual(tbuuid2);
      dojo.byId("divOutput").innerHTML += "<br>Is random UUID valid? " +
        new dojox.uuid.Uuid(ruuid).isValid();
    }

  </script>

</head>

<body onLoad="testIt();">
  <br>
```

```
    <table border="0" cellpadding="0" cellspacing="0"
      width="800" align="center" style="border:1px solid #000000;padding:6px;">
      <tr><td>
        dojox.uuid test:
        <br>
        <div id="divOutput"> </div>
      </td></tr>
    </table>
  </body>

</html>
```

The following functions are available in the `dojox.uuid` namespace:

- `dojox.uuid.generateNilUuid()` generates a nil UUID. In other words, it returns the value 00000000-0000-0000-0000-000000000000. This probably has some use somewhere, but I have to admit I'm not sure what it might be!
- `dojox.uuid.generateRandomUuid()` is probably the function you'd use most of the time because it just spits out a random UUID for you. Random UUIDs are, by the way, referred to as *version 4* UUIDs.
- If you'd prefer to generate a UUID based on the current time, `dojox.uuid.generateTimeBasedUuid()` does that for you. This function gives you what's called a *version 2* UUID, for those keeping score at home. You can also optionally pass into this function a 12-character hex string that ostensibly represents an identifier for the hardware node. This theoretically enables you to tie a UUID to a particular hardware node, so given the exact same time of day every time, you should get the same UUID each time you call this with a given node ID.
- If you call `generateTimeBasedUuid()` and pass it a node ID, you can retrieve the node ID from the UUID later by using the `dojox.uuid.getNode()` function (which also proves there is a tie between the UUID and the node ID).
- You can also get the timestamp that was used to generate a version 2 UUID by using the `dojox.uuid.getTimestamp()` function.
- UUIDs are always of a given variant, which is different from its version, and you can always tell what variant was used to generate the UUID by using the `dojox.uuid.getVariant()` function. This returns one of the enumerate values hanging off the `dojox.uuid.variant` object, such as `DCE`.
- If it's the version and not the variant you're after, `dojox.uuid.getVersion()` will give that to you.
- Being able to tell whether a given string, which presumably is a UUID, is a valid UUID, is very common, and thankfully all it takes is a call to `dojox.uuid.isValid()`. Pass it the value to test, and it returns `true` if it's a valid UUID, `false` if not.

dojox.validate

Validating data is an all-too-common requirement in web development, indeed in *any* sort of application development—for example, ensuring that an e-mail address or telephone number is in a valid form or that a number entered by the user is within an acceptable range. Some validations, such as the range check, are fairly easy to write. Others, such as validating that an e-mail address is in a valid form, are not.[7]

Fortunately, Dojo is here to help with many of your validating needs in the form of the dojox.validate namespace in DojoX. In Listing 4-16, you can see an example I threw together that demonstrates some of the more interesting ones, to me at least.

Listing 4-16. *Validation Example (ch4_validate.htm)*

```
<html>

  <head>

    <script type="text/javascript">
      var djConfig = {
        baseScriptUri : "js/dojo/",
        parseOnLoad : true
      };
    </script>
    <script type="text/javascript" src="js/dojo/dojo/dojo.js"></script>

    <script>

      dojo.require("dojox.validate.web");
      dojo.require("dojox.validate._base");
      dojo.require("dojox.validate.creditCard");
      dojo.require("dojox.validate.isbn");

      function testIt() {
        dojo.byId("divOutput").innerHTML += "<br>" +
          "Is john.glenn@nasa.gov a valid eMail address? " +
          dojox.validate.isEmailAddress("john.glenn@nasa.gov");
        dojo.byId("divOutput").innerHTML += "<br>" +
          "Is bert_and_ernie@sesame_street_com a valid eMail address? " +
```

7. RFC 2822 defines what a valid e-mail address should look like. Following the spec, you come up with a regex that looks like this: (?:[a-z0-9!#$%&'*+/=?^_`{|}~-]+(?:\.[a-z0-9!#$%&'*+/=?^_`{|}~-]+)*|"(?:[\x01-\x08\x0b\x0c\x0e-\x1f\x21\x23-\x5b\x5d-\x7f]|\\[\x01-\x09\x0b\x0c\x0e-\x7f])*")@(?:(?:[a-z0-9](?:[a-z0-9-]*[a-z0-9])?\.)+[a-z0-9](?:[a-z0-9-]*[a-z0-9])?|\[(?:(?:25[0-5]|2[0-4][0-9]|[01]?[0-9][0-9]?)\.){3}(?:25[0-5]|2[0-4][0-9]|[01]?[0-9][0-9]?|[a-z0-9-]*[a-z0-9]:(?:[\x01-\x08\x0b\x0c\x0e-\x1f\x21-\x5a\x53-\x7f]|\\[\x01-\x09\x0b\x0c\x0e-\x7f])+)\]). As it happens, that won't even work 100 percent. A truly working one is apparently even longer than this! The point is simply that something that seems relatively trivial isn't necessarily at all!

```
      dojox.validate.isEmailAddress("bert_and_ernie@sesame_street_com");
    dojo.byId("divOutput").innerHTML += "<br>" +
      "Is 6 within the range 3-9? " +
      dojox.validate.isInRange(6, { min : 3, max : 9});
    dojo.byId("divOutput").innerHTML += "<br>" +
      "Is 5 within the range 10-20? " +
      dojox.validate.isInRange(5, { min : 10, max : 20});
    dojo.byId("divOutput").innerHTML += "<br>" +
      "Is 127.0.0.63 a valid IP address? " +
      dojox.validate.isIpAddress("127.0.0.63");
    dojo.byId("divOutput").innerHTML += "<br>" +
      "Is 256.1.1.10 a valid IP address? " +
      dojox.validate.isIpAddress("256.1.1.10");
    dojo.byId("divOutput").innerHTML += "<br>" +
      "Is 901-21-3409 a valid Social Security Number? " +
      dojox.validate.isNumberFormat("901-21-3409",
        { format : "###-##-####" });
    dojo.byId("divOutput").innerHTML += "<br>" +
      "Is (a12)/610-2838 a valid phone number? " +
      dojox.validate.isNumberFormat("(a12)/610-2838",
        { format : "(###)/###-####" });
    dojo.byId("divOutput").innerHTML += "<br>" +
      "Is 4111-1111-1111-1111 a valid credit card number (Visa, should " +
      "return 'vi')? " +
      dojox.validate.isValidCreditCardNumber("4111-1111-1111-1111");
    dojo.byId("divOutput").innerHTML += "<br>" +
      "Is 1111-1111-1111-1114 a valid credit card number? " +
      dojox.validate.isValidCreditCardNumber("1111-1111-1111-1114");
    dojo.byId("divOutput").innerHTML += "<br>" +
      "Is 978-1-4302-1066-5 a valid ISBN number? " +
      dojox.validate.isValidIsbn("978-1-4302-1066-5");
    dojo.byId("divOutput").innerHTML += "<br>" +
      "Is 1-4302-1066-57 a valid ISBN number? " +
      dojox.validate.isValidIsbn("1-4302-1066-57");
    dojo.byId("divOutput").innerHTML += "<br>" +
      "Is 4552 7204 1234 5677 a valid LUHN number? " +
      dojox.validate.isValidLuhn("4552 7204 1234 5677");
    dojo.byId("divOutput").innerHTML += "<br>" +
      "Is 5353535353535353 a valid LUHN number? " +
      dojox.validate.isValidLuhn("5353535353535353");

  }

</script>

</head>
```

```
  <body onLoad="testIt();">
    <br>
    <table border="0" cellpadding="0" cellspacing="0"
      width="800" align="center" style="border:1px solid #000000;padding:6px;">
      <tr><td>
        dojox.validate test:
        <br>
        <div id="divOutput"> </div>
      </td></tr>
    </table>
  </body>

</html>
```

Any of these can be accessed via the `dojox.validate` namespace; each one is just a method call with the appropriate arguments passed in. The result of executing this example is seen in Figure 4-14.

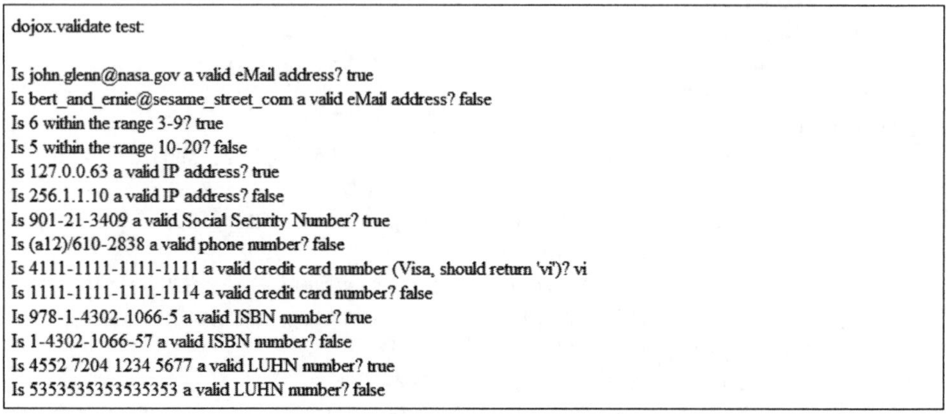

dojox.validate test:

Is john.glenn@nasa.gov a valid eMail address? true
Is bert_and_ernie@sesame_street_com a valid eMail address? false
Is 6 within the range 3-9? true
Is 5 within the range 10-20? false
Is 127.0.0.63 a valid IP address? true
Is 256.1.1.10 a valid IP address? false
Is 901-21-3409 a valid Social Security Number? true
Is (a12)/610-2838 a valid phone number? false
Is 4111-1111-1111-1111 a valid credit card number (Visa, should return 'vi')? vi
Is 1111-1111-1111-1114 a valid credit card number? false
Is 978-1-4302-1066-5 a valid ISBN number? true
Is 1-4302-1066-57 a valid ISBN number? false
Is 4552 7204 1234 5677 a valid LUHN number? true
Is 5353535353535353 a valid LUHN number? false

Figure 4-14. *The dojox.validate example in action*

Now let's take a peek at each of the validations demonstrated here.

isEmailAddress()

Validating an e-mail, as you've seen if you read the previous footnote, can be a tricky venture. But with a simple call to `dojox.validate.isEmailAddress()`, you don't have to bother with the complex regex, or probably more-complex manual code. Just pass the method the e-mail address you want to check, and it'll return `true` if the address is in a valid form, `false` if not. It doesn't get much simpler than that (and that's true of pretty much all these validations).

In the example code, `john.glenn@nasa.gov` is a valid address, while `bert_and_ernie@sesame_street_com` is not because there is no domain specified after the at sign (it would need to be in the form `.com` to be valid).

isInRange()

The `dojox.validate.isInRange()` method enables you to determine whether a number is within a given range. Its call takes this form:

```
dojox.validate.isInRange(5, { min : 10, max : 20})
```

The first argument is the number to check, and the second is an object with two attributes. The `min` attribute defines the lower limit that is valid, and `max` defines the upper limit.

isIpAddress()

The `dojox.validate.isIpAddress()` method helps you validate that a string is a valid IP address. Note that this function is more intelligent than just ensuring that the string is in the form `www.xxx.yyy.zzz`, which would be a valid IP address in terms of form, but it also ensures that the four octets are valid values. For instance:

```
dojox.validate.isIpAddress("256.1.1.10")
```

This returns `false` because the first octet cannot be greater than 255 (none of them can, as a matter of fact). So even though that string is in the correct form for an IP address, it's still not valid because of that first octet's value, and `isIpAddress()` is smart enough to tell you that.

isNumberFormat()

The `dojox.validate.isNumberFormat()` method enables you to validate whether a string matches a given numeric format. This really handy method can be used to validate things like telephone numbers, for example.

This code returns returns `true` because the value matches the format mask specified:

```
dojox.validate.isNumberFormat("901-21-3409",
  { format : "###-##-####" })
```

In contrast, this code returns `false` because of the letter *a* in the second position:

```
dojox.validate.isNumberFormat("(a12)/610-2838",
  { format : "(###)/###-####" });
```

....

The object you pass in as the second argument contains a single `format` attribute, which is the format mask to validate against. The # symbol indicates a number, while the ? symbol can be used to indicate an optional number. Any other character must appear literally in the input string, which is of course the first argument to the method.

isValidCreditCardNumber()

If you've ever written an e-commerce application, especially if you've ever had to write code to validate a credit card number (in fact, most types of account numbers in general), then you know it can be a difficult task to account for every possibility. The `dojox.validate.isValidCreditCardNumber()` method takes care of all of it for you. However, it does so in a slightly more interesting way than a simple `true` or `false` return. For example:

```
dojox.validate.isValidCreditCardNumber("4111-1111-1111-1111")
```

This will return the string `vi` because this is a valid Visa card number. If you pass a MasterCard number, you'll get `mc` back, and so on. You'll get `false` back only if the number is not any sort of valid credit card number. Very handy indeed!

isValidIsbn()

To be honest, validating an International Standard Book Number (ISBN) is a fairly domain-specific thing to do, but because I'm writing a book, I thought I'd mention it nonetheless! If you need to do it, the `dojox.validate.isValidIsbn()` method accepts a single string argument, the ISBN (presumably) to validate, and it returns `true` if it's valid, `false` if not, just as you'd expect it to do!

isValidLuhn()

A *Luhn number* is a number generated by using a specific checksum algorithm (known, not surprisingly, as a Luhn algorithm). Luhn is sometimes called *modules 10* or *mod 10*, because that's the basis of its calculation. It shows up all over the place in all sorts of identification numbers, including credit card numbers and social security numbers (Canadian ones at least). The `dojox.validate.isValidLuhn()` method can tell you whether a given string representing a Luhn number is valid. It returns you a simple `true` or `false` based on the input value.

dojox.widget

The `dojox.widget` namespace contains a couple of new dijits that may someday migrate into Dijit itself, but for now they sit here in DojoX.

Fisheye List

The Fisheye List is my personal favorite widget in all of Dojo. If you've ever seen the Apple Macintosh interface, you know what a Fisheye List is: it's that nifty-keen bar at the bottom where the icons expand and contract in a wickedly cool fashion when you hover over them. Imagine being able to do that in your web apps.

Well, imagine no more! The Fisheye List in Dojo is exactly that! I'm going to skip it here because in the very next chapter we're going to see it in action, and I think it's even cooler when you see it in a more real-world example. So let's exercise a little bit of patience and we'll get to it in just a bit. Believe me, it's worth the wait!

TimeSpinner

A TimeSpinner widget enables a user to easily select a time value. It's not one of the more typical widgets out there, and Figure 4-15 may be your first look at one.

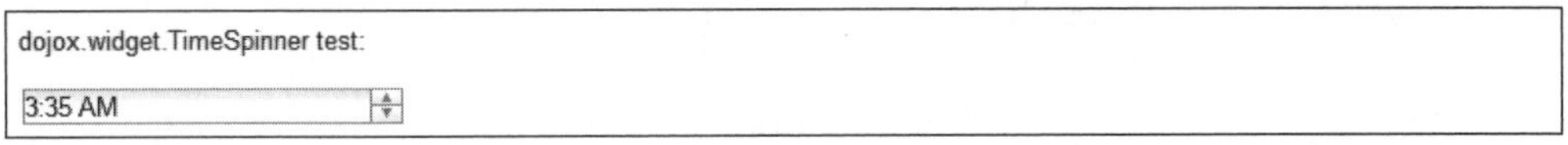

dojox.widget.TimeSpinner test:

3:35 AM

Figure 4-15. *The TimeSpinner widget*

Err, wait a minute, that doesn't look like much. In fact, it just looks like a text box with some arrows on it. But it's exactly those arrows that makes this a TimeSpinner. Clicking the arrows makes the time go up or down in 1-minute intervals, and if you keep one pressed for a while, the speed at which it changes gets faster.

To get one of these onto the page is pretty simple, as is the case with most dijits (of which this is one). Listing 4-17 shows you what it takes.

Listing 4-17. *TimeSpinner Example (ch4_widget_TimeSpinner.htm)*

```
<html>

  <head>

    <link rel="StyleSheet" type="text/css"
      href="js/dojo/dojo/resources/dojo.css">
    <link rel="StyleSheet" type="text/css"
      href="js/dojo/dijit/themes/tundra/tundra.css">

    <script type="text/javascript">
      var djConfig = {
        baseScriptUri : "js/dojo/",
        parseOnLoad : true
      };
    </script>
    <script type="text/javascript" src="js/dojo/dojo/dojo.js"></script>

    <script>
      dojo.require("dojo.parser");
      dojo.require("dojox.widget.TimeSpinner");
    </script>

  </head>

  <body class="tundra">
    <br>
    <table border="0" cellpadding="0" cellspacing="0"
      width="800" align="center" style="border:1px solid #000000;padding:6px;">
      <tr><td>
        dojox.widget.TimeSpinner test:
        <br><br>
        <input id="myTimeSpinner" dojoType="dojox.widget.TimeSpinner"
```

```
            value="3:35 AM" smallDelta="1" />
        </td></tr>
      </table>
    </body>

</html>
```

As with all dijits, you need to import `dojo.parser`, and in this case you also need to grab `dojox.widget.TimeSpinner`. After those are in place, it's a simple matter of adding a `dojoType` with a value of `dojox.widget.TimeSpinner` to an `<input>` element. You can set the initial value of the field by using the `value` attribute, and you can set by how much the arrows change the time by setting the `smallDelta` attribute (a value of `1` here means 1 minute).

Toaster

The Toaster widget enables you to have little pop-up messages appear on the page. It's like a piece of toast popping out of a toaster, hence the name.

In Figure 4-16, you can see an example of a message that has popped up as a result of my having clicked the first button.

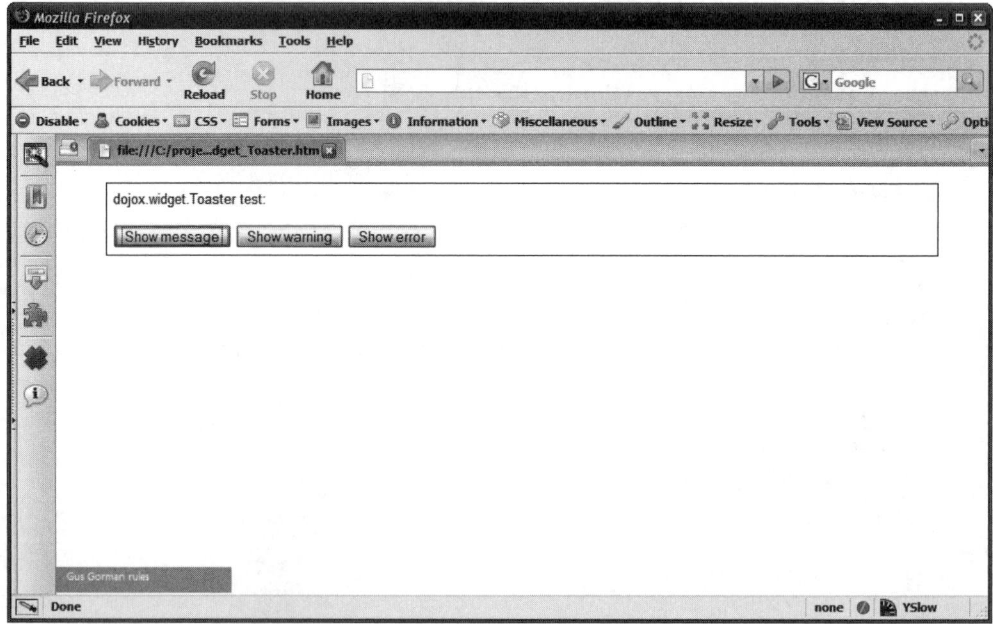

Figure 4-16. *The Toaster widget showing a pop-up message*

The message is highlighted in green on the screen, a fact you can't discern from seeing it here. In any case, the code that produced this is shown in Listing 4-18.

Listing 4-18. *Toaster Widget Example (ch4_widget_Toaster.htm)*

```
<html>

  <head>

    <link rel="StyleSheet" type="text/css"
      href="js/dojo/dojo/resources/dojo.css">
    <link rel="StyleSheet" type="text/css"
      href="js/dojo/dijit/themes/tundra/tundra.css">
    <link rel="StyleSheet" type="text/css"
      href="js/dojo/dojox/widget/Toaster/Toaster.css">

    <script type="text/javascript">
      var djConfig = {
        baseScriptUri : "js/dojo/",
        parseOnLoad : true
      };
    </script>
    <script type="text/javascript" src="js/dojo/dojo/dojo.js"></script>

    <script>

      dojo.require("dojo.parser");
      dojo.require("dojox.widget.Toaster");

      function showMsg(inMsg, inType, inDuration) {
        dojo.publish("toasterTopic", [{
          message : inMsg, type : inType, duration : inDuration
        }]);
      }

    </script>

  </head>

  <body class="tundra">
    <br>
    <table border="0" cellpadding="0" cellspacing="0"
      width="800" align="center" style="border:1px solid #000000;padding:6px;">
      <tr><td>
        dojox.widget.Toaster test:
        <br><br>
        <div dojoType="dojox.widget.Toaster" id="myToaster"
          separator="&lt;hr&gt;" positionDirection="bl-up"
          messageTopic="toasterTopic"></div>
        <button type="submit"
          onClick="showMsg('Gus Gorman rules', 'message', 1000);">
```

```
          Show message
        </button>
        <button type="submit"
          onClick="showMsg('Ash is not a human', 'warning', 2000);">
          Show warning
        </button>
        <button type="submit"
          onClick="showMsg('AVP is a horrendous movie', 'error', 3000);">
          Show error
        </button>
      </td></tr>
    </table>
  </body>

</html>
```

The markup is just some buttons mostly, but there's also creation of the Toaster itself:

```
<div dojoType="dojox.widget.Toaster" id="myToaster"
  separator="&lt;hr&gt;" positionDirection="bl-up"
  messageTopic="toasterTopic"></div>
```

The Toaster uses a publish-subscribe model to do its thing, which is arguably a cleaner approach than calling functions directly on it because it helps isolate the usage of the Toaster from the code using it (that is, you might decide to use another method of showing messages down the road, and so long as it subscribes to the toasterTopic message, it'll work without changing this "client" code). That's why the messageTopic attribute is present: it's the topic ID that the Toaster will subscribe to in order to show messages. The separator attribute is used in the case where more than one message is shown at a time, which the Toaster supports, and which you can see in Figure 4-17. The positionDirection attribute tells the toaster where on the page it should appear and in what direction the messages should pop up from. The value bl-up in this case tells it to show the messages on the bottom left and to have the messages pop upward.

Now, we know that the Toaster is subscribed to the toasterTopic message, but how do we tell the Toaster to show a message? Simple enough, we publish the appropriate message, which you can see here in the showMsg() function:

```
function showMsg(inMsg, inType, inDuration) {
  dojo.publish("toasterTopic", [{
    message : inMsg, type : inType, duration : inDuration
  }]);
}
```

When publishing the message, you send in an object with a couple of attributes, the first being message, which is literally the text of the message to display. The duration attribute tells the Toaster how long to display the message before it fades it off the screen. The type attribute tells the Toaster what type of message it is; some valid values are message, error, and warning. This value affects what color the message is (message is green, warning is yellow, error is red, well, more like orange-ish—try out the example code to see this for yourself).

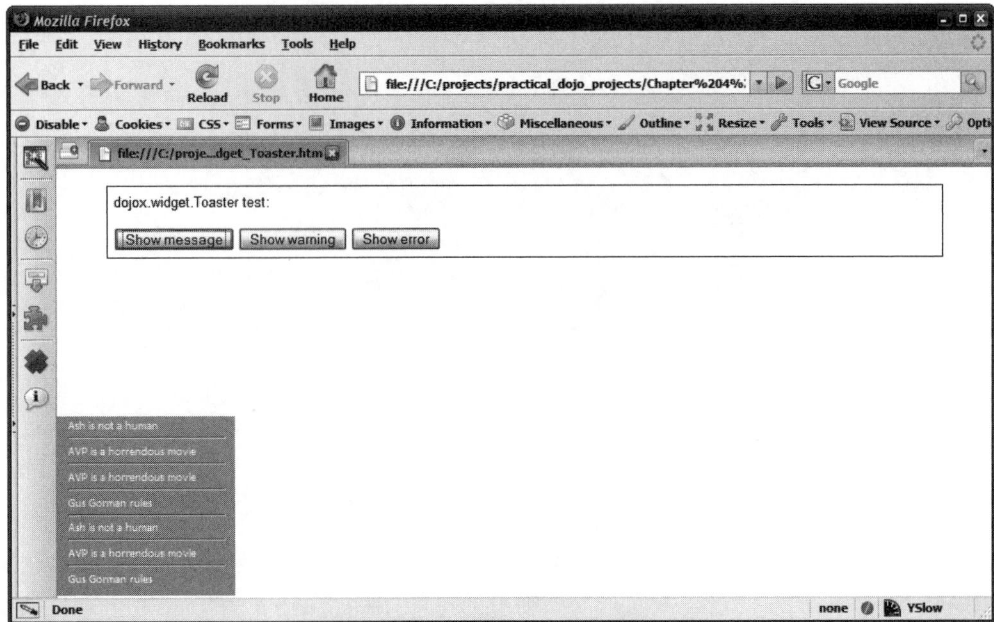

Figure 4-17. *The Toaster widget showing multiple messages*

Summary

If ever there was a convincing argument to be made to Congress to try to fund basic science, DojoX is it because some of the coolest experimenting is going on right here! In this chapter, we got a look at most of what DojoX has to offer. We saw things like some new widgets, effects, basic data structures, collections, some functions for doing more-advanced mathematics, chart creation, some timing-related functionality, and the ability to create vector-based graphics purely on the client. I think there's little doubt that DojoX offers some really wild capabilities, things that just a few short years ago, even just months ago in some cases, you would have swore just weren't possible in JavaScript. We'll be seeing more of DojoX as the projects in the remainder of this book are developed because much of it is just so darned useful!

Speaking of the upcoming projects, the next chapter is our first project-based chapter, and in it we'll see some of DojoX in practice, notably the Fisheye List that I said we should have a little patience for. Well, no longer, it's time to get into it now! Turn the page and off we go!

PART 2

The Projects

The universe is driven by the complex interaction between three ingredients: matter, energy, and enlightened self-interest.

—G'Kar, Narn ambassador to Babylon 5

If you don't push something beyond its boundary of usefulness, how do you find where that boundary is?

—Martin Fowler

Rocket science has been mythologized all out of proportion to its true difficulty.

—John Carmack

I am so clever that sometimes I don't understand a single word of what I am saying.

—Oscar Wilde

Have no fear of perfection—you'll never reach it.

—Salvador Dali

Well, thanks to the Internet, I'm now bored with sex.

—Philip J. Fry, *Futurama*

Technology: the knack of so arranging the world that we don't have to experience it.

—Max Frisch

Technology presumes there's just one right way to do things, and there never is.

—Robert M. Pirsig

I'm sorry. It's just . . . I react to certain doom in a certain way. It's a bad habit.

—Dr. Rodney McKay, *Stargate Atlantis*

CHAPTER 5

That Human Touch: Contact Manager and Client-Side Persistence

We all know that storing information for any length of time in a relatively robust way will usually lead to a database of some sort. In web applications, storing state on the server, whether in a database or in a session, is pretty much expected of most applications. But what happens when you don't have a persistence mechanism on the server or possibly don't want one for some reason? What's the alternative? You almost certainly know that storing nontransient information on the client leads most usually to cookies. We'll be looking at cookies in just a little bit for sure. There is, however, another facility available (after a quick plug-in installation) in modern web browsers that is brought to us by our friends at Google, namely Gears. This storage mechanism is pretty quickly gaining a lot of popularity for very good reason, as we'll soon see.

So, we'll be having a look at that in a fair bit more detail, and we'll put it to use in an application, a simple contact manager to be precise. Perhaps most interesting, though, is that Dojo provides a layer of abstraction above Gears that makes using it even easier than it is natively, and more important, allows us to switch out Gears for an entirely different storage provider with no real impact on our code.

Umm . . . okay, so what was I talking about again? Oh yes, persistence and memory. Okay, on with the show.

Requirements and Goals

In this chapter, we will build ourselves a contact manager application that runs entirely on the client side. This is handy because it means it can be run on virtually any PC without having to have a network connection (although conversely it means that the contact data can't easily be shared between multiple machines). Clearly, persistence will come into play here because the application would be quite useless if we couldn't store contacts.

Let's list some of the key things this project will accomplish and some of the features we'll seek to implement:

- Each contact should include a good amount of data. Not just the basics such as name, phone number, and e-mail address, but a fair amount of extended information, such as birthday, spouse's name, children's names, and so on. However, we want to make these items as free-form as possible so users can use the different data fields however they choose to.
- We'll implement the typical alphabet selector tabs to make finding our contacts easier.
- As you can guess, we'll store our contacts with Gears Database.
- We'll use Dojo to provide some widgets coolness to make the interface fun and nice to look at. We'll also use Dojo to deal with the underlying details of working with the storage provider of our choice, Gears in this case.

Now that we have some goals in mind, let's start figuring out how to make it happen.

How We Will Pull It Off

When one discusses data storage generically, two types of storage are available: persistent and nonpersistent, or transient. *Persistent storage* is any storage mechanism that provides a place for data to be saved between program executions, and often for an indefinite period of time (until explicitly removed from storage). *Transient storage* is any storage mechanism where the data lives only as long as the program is executing (or for some short time thereafter). A database is generally considered a persistent storage mechanism, whereas RAM clearly is not. Writing to a hard drive is usually persistent as well, while session memory generally is not. The term *durable* is also often used to describe persistent storage media.

When discussing persistence in a pure JavaScript-based client-side application, there is a very short list of possible storage mechanisms. The ubiquitous *cookie*, small bits of information stored on the client on a per-domain basis, is one. Another possibility is local shared objects, sometimes called Flash cookies or Flash shared objects, depending on where you read about this technology, provided by the Adobe Flash plug-in. These can be thought of as "cookies on steroids." With local shared objects, you can store a ton more information on the client than you could with plain old cookies, and do so with an API that is a bit more powerful than regular cookies.

■ Note If you'd like more information on Flash shared objects, cruise on over to this address: `http://kb.adobe.com/selfservice/viewContent.do?externalId=tn_16194&sliceId=1`. You could always use a pre-1.0 version of Dojo to mess around with Flash shared objects because with the 1.0 release, the code required to do so was not working (maybe not fully present, I'm really not sure). Hopefully this capability is added back into Dojo soon because with the market penetration of Flash (something around 95+ percent of all computers out there have Flash installed), it's a safe bet most people have this capability available to them already.

Other options include things such as Java applets or ActiveX controls, but they are generally frowned upon these days for various reasons. ActiveX is something many people tend to want to avoid, even more so than applets because of the security risks, whether those risks are legitimate or just perceived. Applets have a bit of a bad reputation in terms of performance, especially when it comes to startup time.

Whatever your feelings on the subject, it's an aside at this point because we'll be using Gears and Dojo to get the job done. But before we get into those two areas, let's see what Dojo offers in the way of plain old cookie functionality, just to get a feel for a possible alternative, and for comparison with what we'll be using in this project.

Dojo and Cookies

We find the cookie functions in the `dojo.cookie` package. This contains a couple of functions that pretty much do exactly as you'd expect. To use these functions, simply include the appropriate package:

```
dojo.require("dojo.cookie");
```

After that's done, you can, as an example, set a cookie by doing the following:

```
dojo.cookie.cookie("myCookie", "someValue");
```

To read the value of a cookie, you use the same function, but passing only the name of the cookie to read:

```
var cookieValue = dojo.cookie("myCookie");
```

You also have the capability to pass a third parameter when setting a cookie that enables you to specify some extended options, which include the following:

- The first is `expires`, which determines the number of days this cookie will live before it expires.
- The next is `path`, which sets the path the cookie is for (that is, for which paths within the domain the cookie is valid and will be returned).
- After that comes `domain`, which sets the domain the cookie is for (that is, for which domain the cookie will be returned).
- Last is `secure`, which determines whether the cookie is secure (that is, when `true`, the cookie will be returned only over a Secure Sockets Layer, or SSL, channel).

If you're wondering how you delete a cookie, it couldn't be simpler:

```
dojo.cookie("myCookie", null, {expires: -1});
```

Yep, that's it, that's one whacked cookie! It's interesting that there's no explicit `dojo.cookie.delete()` method. One function handles setting, getting, and deleting a cookie based on parameters passed or not passed. A little weird perhaps, but effective once you understand it.

Two other functions under `dojo.cookie` are `isSupported()` and `useObject()`. The `isSupported()` function returns `true` if the browser supports cookies, `false` if not. That's always a handy thing to know before storing or reading cookies, no?

The `useObject()` function deserves a look. You use this just as you do `dojo.cookie()` to read and write cookies, but instead of passing strings, you can pass whole objects that Dojo will happily serialize and store for you. For example, you could do the following:

```
dojo.cookie.useObject("myCookie ", { field1 : "value1" } );
```

If you want to read this cookie back and display the value of `field1`, all you need to do is this:

```
var myObj = dojo.cookie.useObject("myCookie");
alert(myObj.field1);
```

Pretty nifty, isn't it? If you're going to do any work with cookies, clearly Dojo has you covered and will make it a much more pleasurable experience. Now, the application in this chapter won't be using cookies, as stated earlier. However, I felt it was important that you see what Dojo has to offer with regard to cookies.

Cookies are of course rather ubiquitous and are used day in and day out in applications all over the place. They are simple, quick, and quite sufficient for a great many tasks. They are, however, not without their limitations:

- First, each domain is limited to a maximum of 20 cookies. You may find some browsers that allow for more, but the HTTP spec states 20 as the required minimum, so it is best to assume that is actually the maximum to ensure your code won't break in browsers that treat 20 as the upper limit.
- Second, each cookie is limited to a 4KB maximum size. So, some quick math tells us we have a maximum of 80KB per domain on the client in cookies. Aside from 80KB not being enough for many tasks, having to break that up between 20 cookies and having to write that code yourself makes cookies less than desirable for many purposes.

Fortunately, the folks at Google have a ready solution for us to get around these limitations, and as you might expect, Dojo is there to take advantage of it and make our lives as developers better.

The Dojo Storage System

Dojo provides a storage package that is billed as a pluggable mechanism for client-side persistence. Its architecture is based on the concept of a storage manager and any number of storage providers. Each provider can store (that is, persist) data via any method it wants to, but the client application writes to a common interface that all providers implement, thereby allowing developers to swap between various storage mechanisms at the drop of a hat without any change to their code. That's very cool, to say the least!

At the time of this writing, the `dojox.storage` package provides only a single storage provider, and that is one that interfaces with Gears. There is another provider that utilizes Adobe Flash Player and its local shared object facility. However, comments in the readme file for that provider indicate it does not currently function. Ironically, this provider was the only one available in pre-1.0 versions of Dojo. I'm certain this provider will eventually be operational if you choose to use it.

Cookies would be a logical fit here too. There was at one time talk of such a provider, but at this time it does not exist. One could also conceive of an ActiveX storage provider that writes directly to a SQL Server database as another possible example, and yet the application that utilized `dojox.storage` wouldn't need to know about the details of that at all, and that's the main point to take away from all this.

The `dojox.storage` package is a wonderful creation that offers a great deal of power to developers. It's essentially a simple architecture (Figure 5-1) that again proves that simplicity is usually the way to go.

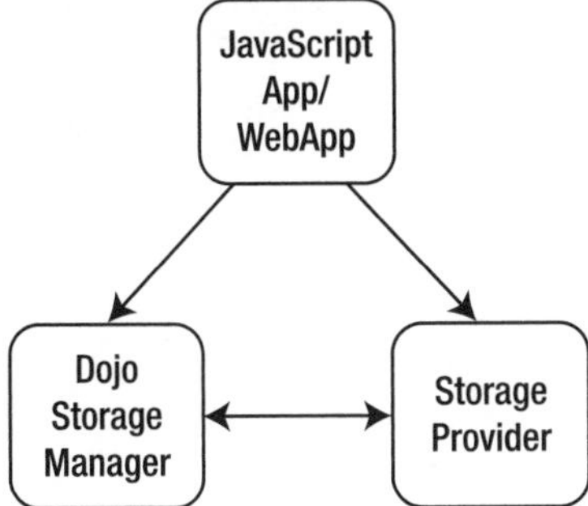

Figure 5-1. *The dojox.storage package architecture*

As you'll see in a bit when you examine the code behind the application in this chapter, the primary interaction your code will have with the Dojo storage system is via `dojox.storage`. The interface to the storage manager is shown in Figure 5-2. Once again, you can see there isn't a whole lot to it, and in fact, for the purposes of the application in this chapter, we won't use more than about half of what it offers.

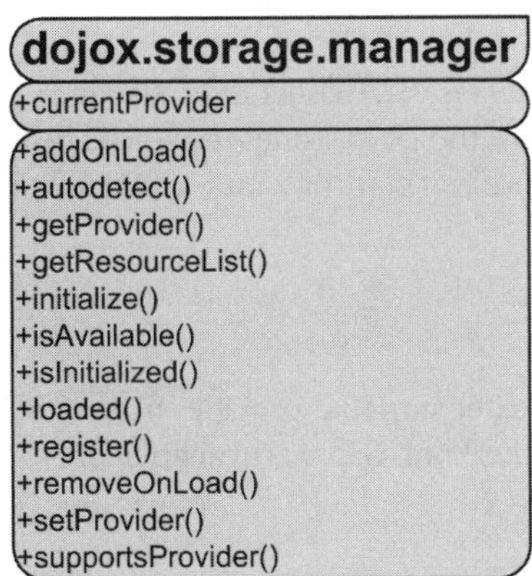

Figure 5-2. *The storage manager interface*

The other important object that you'll interact with is the storage provider. All providers implement a known interface, which you can see in Figure 5-3. Again, this is really just for overview purposes because your code shouldn't typically use a provider directly, but if you had a mind to write your own provider, this is the interface you would be coding to.

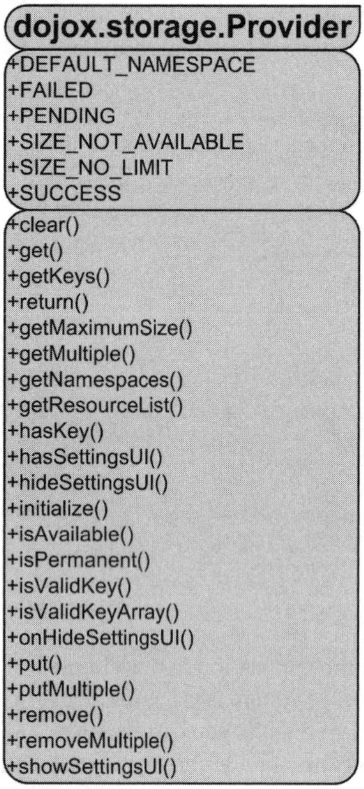

dojox.storage.Provider

+DEFAULT_NAMESPACE
+FAILED
+PENDING
+SIZE_NOT_AVAILABLE
+SIZE_NO_LIMIT
+SUCCESS

+clear()
+get()
+getKeys()
+return()
+getMaximumSize()
+getMultiple()
+getNamespaces()
+getResourceList()
+hasKey()
+hasSettingsUI()
+hideSettingsUI()
+initialize()
+isAvailable()
+isPermanent()
+isValidKey()
+isValidKeyArray()
+onHideSettingsUI()
+put()
+putMultiple()
+remove()
+removeMultiple()
+showSettingsUI()

Figure 5-3. *The storage provider interface*

You'll look at the functions provided in `dojox.storage` itself as you dissect the code, and you'll see that except for one function, all your interaction with the Dojo storage system is in fact via methods hanging directly off `dojox.storage`. But before you start that task, you need to look at one last thing, and that's Gears.

Gears

Gears (`http://gears.google.com`), in a nutshell, is a browser extension that provides functionality in three distinct groups: LocalServer, Database, and WorkerPool. Gears is available for most major browsers and operating systems.

■ **Note** Although Gears is still technically in beta, I think we all recognize Google's MO here: release something solid as beta, call it that for a good, long time, and then finally "flip the switch" on it to make it a final, gold release, even though it's pretty much been that for a while. I suppose this is a lot better than the Microsoft "just release it and we'll fix it up later" approach, but be that as it may . . .

LocalServer

The LocalServer component of Gears enables you to cache and serve the resources that go into rendering a web page from a local cache. This may not sound too exciting at first. In fact, your initial thought may well be, "Browsers already have caches, so what's the big deal?"

The big deal, my friend, is that this cache is under your programmatic control. You can tell it what resources to cache and serve, and when. In other words, you can take an application "offline," assuming all its resources are in the cache, meaning a connection to the server is no longer required.

There is obvious potential in terms of performance too, although interestingly, that's a secondary concern at best. It's that ability to go offline and still have an application work that LocalServer is there to address.

This application won't be using LocalServer, so I won't be going into any more detail on it here. This is, after all, a book on Dojo! The address provided at the start of this section is where you should go to learn more if LocalServer is something that interests you.

WorkerPool

The WorkerPool component is another piece of Gears that isn't used in this application, but it's really cool nonetheless! You are no doubt familiar with how easy it is, owing to the single-threaded nature of JavaScript, to lock up the browser with a `while` loop that never breaks, or similar programming gaffs. You are also no doubt aware that JavaScript doesn't provide threads as a language like Java does. JavaScript has timers and time-outs, which at least approximate threads, but a single thread of execution is still in the interpreter at any given time; timers and time-outs are more an illusion than anything else.

With WorkerPool, Google has given us about as close to real threading as possible in JavaScript. It's especially useful if you have calculation-intensive operations to perform or input/output (I/O) operations in the background to run. There is at least one significant limitation to be aware of, however: threads in a WorkerPool, which are not surprisingly called Workers, can't access the DOM. This limits the Workers' usefulness quite a bit, frankly, but even with that limitation there's still plenty you *can* do with them.

Once again, WorkerPool is not used in this application, but it's definitely worth knowing about, and the aforementioned web site has all the details if you want to explore it further.

Database

Now, we *are* using the Database component of Gears in this application, but indirectly, as Dojo sits between us and it. However, let's look at the Database component in a little detail just so you have a clue about what Dojo must be doing under the covers.

The Database component of Gears provides a client-side relational database system based on the SQLite (`www.sqlite.org`) engine, which is an open source database system. It essentially boils down to two simple classes: `Database` and `ResultSet`.

The architecture that Google talks about is the ability to switch an application from "online" state to "offline" state at the flip of a switch. They way Google recommends doing this is shown in Figure 5-4.

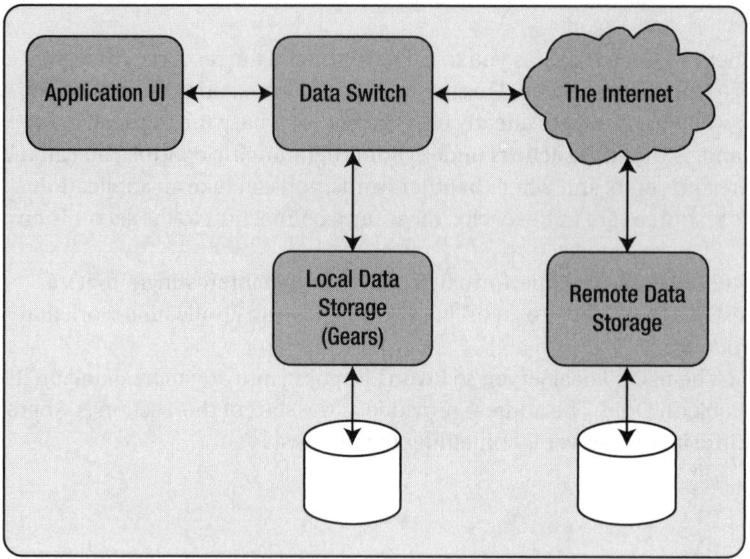

Figure 5-4. *The architecture behind online/offline capabilties made possible by Gears*

In this model, the Data Switch is some code in the client-side of your application that can determine whether the application is online or offline and which is the API your application reads and writes data to. In other words, you wouldn't directly use the Gears Database API. Instead, your application would use some API that you provide that sits between the application code and the Gears Database API. Then, when you detect that your application is online, you write those data reads and writes to your server-side data store, typically via the Internet. When the application is offline, though, you use Gears API instead. When the application goes back online, the Data Switch would be responsible for synchronizing the data in both directions.

Now, all the details about how you detect online vs. offline status, and how data synchronization is done, are left to your discretion. One could imagine this sort of functionality being built into the Dojo storage system. Alas, it looks like the Dojo team is creating a Dojo Offline Project instead, although I wouldn't be surprised if the storage system and the offline project are, or at some point become, tied together.

As an example of using Gears, and the Database component in particular, consider the following HTML:

```
<html>
  <head>
    <script type="text/javascript" src="gears_init.js"></script>

    <script>

      db = google.gears.factory.create("beta.database", "1.0");
      db.open();
      db.execute(
        "CREATE TABLE IF NOT EXISTS test_table (" +
```

```
        "firstName TEXT, " +
        "lastName TEXT, " +
        "age INTEGER" +
        ");"
      );
      db.execute("INSERT INTO test_table " +
        "(firstName, lastName, age) values (" +
        "'Frank','Zammetti','35');");
      db.execute("INSERT INTO test_table " +
        "(firstName, lastName, age) values (" +
        "'Amanda','Tapping','42');");
      var rs = db.execute("select * from test_table");
      while (rs.isValidRow()) {
        alert(rs.field(0) + ", " + rs.field(1) + ", " + rs.field(2));
        rs.next();
      }
      db.close();

    </script>

  </head>
  <body></body>
</html>
```

Yep, that's all it takes! Now, if you have Gears installed and you save that HTML to a file and then load it in your browser, you should see two alert messages displaying the rows of the table. Obviously not rocket science by any stretch! With Dojo on top of Gears, though, working with the Database component becomes even easier because we don't even have to worry about writing SQL statements, or iterating over `ResultSets`, or any of that typical database programming work. Let's get to the application right now so I can stop talking about it and you can see it in action!

■ Note To install Gears, which you'll need to do before you can play with the application in this chapter, or the preceding example, go to `http://gears.google.com` and you should find a big button right there in front of your face to install it. Follow the rather simple instructions and you'll be good to go in no time!

Dissecting the Solution

As we typically do with the projects in this book, let's first get a feel for the lay of the land, so to speak, and see what the contact manager's directory structure looks like. Take a look at Figure 5-5.

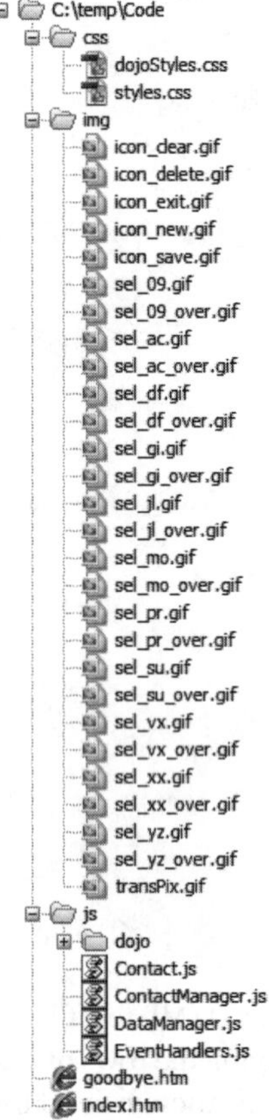

Figure 5-5. *Contact manager's directory structure*

Let's discuss these files and directories:

- In the root directory we find two files, `index.htm` and `goodbye.htm`:
  - `index.htm` is really the heart and soul of the application, as you will soon see.
  - `goodbye.htm` is a simple page that is shown when the user exits the application.
- Under the root we find a couple of directories, starting with the `css` directory. As is typical, the `css` directory is where we find our style sheets. In this case, we have two:
  - The first is `styles.css`, which is the main style sheet for the application.
  - Next is `dojoStyles.css`, which contains styles used specifically for Dojo widgets.
- The next directory we find is `img`, which, obviously enough, contains images used throughout the application. The images are named in a pretty obvious way, so no need to run through them all.
- Last is the `js` directory, which of course is where the JavaScript that composes the application lives. There are four `.js` files present:

- First is `Contact.js`, which defines a class representing a contact.
- Next is `ContactManager.js`, which contains the main application code. It's kind of a traffic cop, more or less, calling the other classes as required.
- Next is `DataManager.js`, which contains the code that actually deals with storing and retrieving our contacts.
- Last is `EventHandlers.js`, which contains the UI event handlers that make our UI work.

Also in the `js` directory we find a subdirectory named `dojo`. This is obviously where the Dojo library lives.

Within the `dojo` directory you will find a number of subdirectories containing other Dojo package source files, as well as HTML and CSS resources, and anything else Dojo needs to function. Although this application uses only a small portion of Dojo, having it all available means that as you want to extend the application and use more of Dojo, it is there, all ready for you. This will in fact be the case in all projects going forward.

And what does the application actually look like you ask? Well, Figure 5-6 gives you the answer to that question.

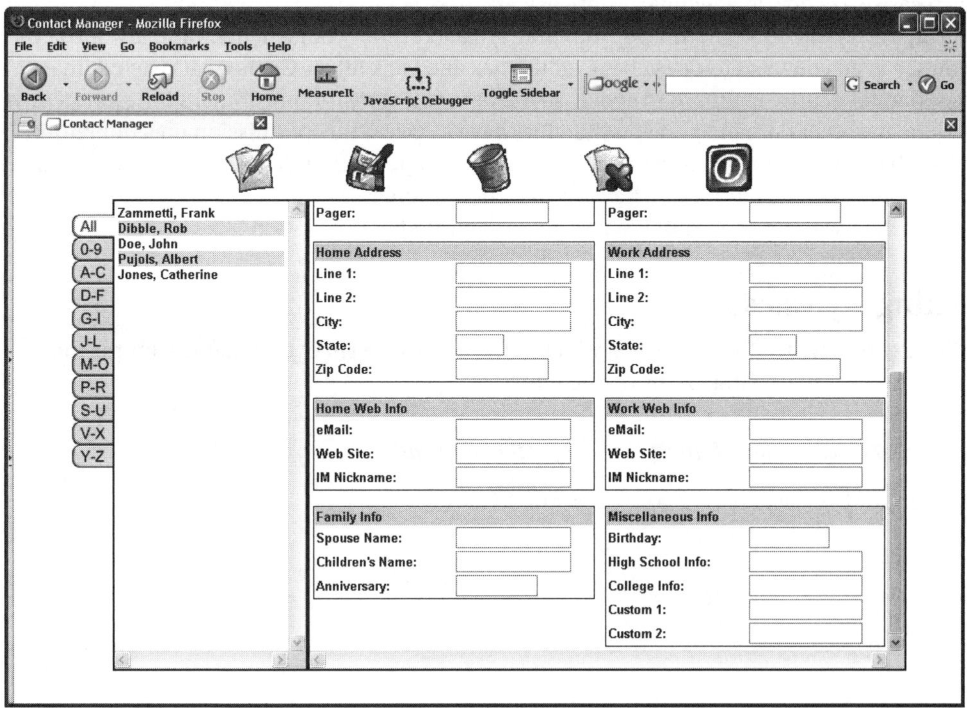

Figure 5-6. *Contact manager—Outlook may not have to worry, but it ain't bad!*

I certainly recommend spending a few minutes playing with the application before proceeding to tear it apart. I think you'll find it to be a fairly clean and useful little contact manager—probably not making anyone on the Microsoft Outlook team lose any sleep, but not bad by any stretch, I think.

There is a good chance when you first run it that you will see a pop-up dialog box generated by Gears that looks like Figure 5-7.

Figure 5-7. *Security warning dialog box seen when you first run the application*

Naturally, the domain listed here won't be `omnytex.com`, unless you've hacked my server, in which case we're now in a technical state of war!

Anyway, if you don't get this pop-up, then great, consider yourself lucky and just move on. If you see it, all you need to do is check off the box and click Allow. Gears treats each domain as a separate security realm, so to speak, so the data you store for one domain is never accessible from any other domain, and you therefore have to give Gears permission on a domain-by-domain basis, which means unless you've ever run an application that used Gears in the same domain as this application, you'll have to give permission now.

And now, without further delay, let's get to some code.

Writing styles.css

Listing 5-1 shows the `styles.css` file, which is the main style sheet that defines, for the most part, all of the visual styling of the application.

Listing 5-1. styles.css, the Main Style Sheet for the Application

```
/* Generic style applied to all elements */
* {
  font-family      : arial;
  font-size        : 10pt;
  font-weight      : bold;
}

/* Style for body of document */
body {
  margin           : 0px;
}
```

```
/* Style for spacer between data boxes */
.cssSpacer {
  height           : 64px;
}

/* Non-hover state of contacts in the contact list */
.cssContactListNormal {
  background-color : #ffffff;
}

/* Non-hover state of contacts in the contact list, alternate row stripping */
.cssContactListAlternate {
  background-color : #eaeaea;
}

/* Hover state of contacts in the contact list */
.cssContactListOver {
  background-color : #ffffa0;
  cursor           : pointer;
}

/* Style for main container box */
.cssMain {
  width            : 100%;
  height           : 580px;
  z-index          : 0;
}

/* Style of the initializing message seen at startup */
.cssInitializing {
  width            : 100%;
  height           : 80px;
  position         : absolute;
  left             : 0px;
  top              : 150px;
}

/* Style for the main content area */
.cssContent {
  display          : none;
}

/* Style of selector tabs */
.cssTab {
  position         : relative;
  left             : 2px;
```

```
  _left            : 4px; /* Style for IE */
}

/* Style of the contact list container */
.cssContactList {
  padding          : 4px;
  height           : 480px;
  border           : 2px solid #000000;
  overflow         : scroll;
}

/* Style of the box surrounding the data boxes */
.cssMainOuter {
  padding          : 4px;
  height           : 480px;
  border           : 2px solid #000000;
  overflow         : scroll;
}

/* Style of a data box */
.cssDataBox {
  width            : 100%;
  border           : 1px solid #000000;
}

/* Style for the header of a data box */
.cssDataBoxHeader {
  background-color : #e0e0f0;
}

/* Style for text boxes */
.cssTextbox {
  border : 1px solid #7f9db9;
}
```

If you're more of a visual person, Figure 5-8 shows a tree view of this style sheet, where you can see the breakdown and classification of the style elements it contains.

The first style class is a neat trick that you may not be aware of. If you define a style by using an asterisk, that style is applied to all elements on the page. The nice thing about this is that it even applies to elements such as tables, which in some browsers often do not inherit styles as you may expect. By using this wildcard, however, you can apply a style even to those elements easily.

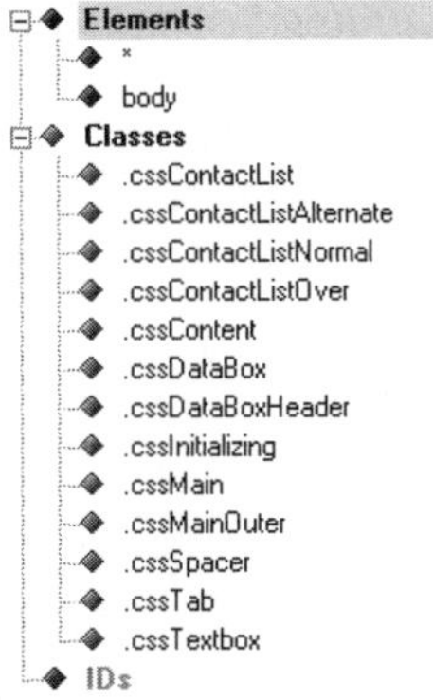

Figure 5-8. *A more visual representation of styles.css*

I suspect most of the rest of the style sheet is pretty self-explanatory and really pretty simple, but one other trick to point out is in the `cssTab` class. This style is used to position the alphabetic selector tabs on the left side. As the visual representation of one of the tabs being the current tab, it has to look different from the other tabs somehow, and that in part requires that the tab overlap the border of the contact list box by a few pixels. Unfortunately, the number of pixels required doesn't seem be consistent between IE and Firefox, so I used a little trick to allow for the difference.

When Firefox encounters an attribute name that begins with an underscore character, it ignores the name. IE, on the other hand, ignores just the underscore, acting as if it wasn't there. So, what essentially happens here is that in both browsers, the first value of `2px` for the `left` attribute is set. Then, when the `_left` attribute is encountered, Firefox ignores it, but IE strips the underscore and treats it as if the `left` attribute was set again, overriding the `2px` value with `4px`. In this way, you can deal with the style sheet differences that sometimes come up between IE and FF without having to write branching code to deal with it, or have alternate style sheets for each browser.

■ **Note** If you find yourself using this trick a lot, you probably want to rethink the way you're styling elements on the page because you may be doing things in a way that is too browser-specific—but here and there, every now and again, this is a good trick to know. Also be aware that in the future, one or both browsers could change this behavior, effectively breaking any page that uses it. It's just something to keep in mind.

Writing dojoStyles.css

`dojoStyles.css` is a style sheet containing just a small number of classes that override default styles in Dojo. Listing 5-2 shows this rather diminutive source.

Listing 5-2. *dojoStyles.css (Whoever Said Size Doesn't Matter Must Have Been Talking About This Style Sheet)*

```
/* Style for the fisheye listbar */
.dojoxFisheyeListBar {
  margin            : 0 auto;
  text-align        : center;
}

/* Style for the fisheye container */
.outerbar {
  text-align        : center;
  position          : absolute;
  left              : 0px;
  top               : 0px;
  width             : 100%;
}
```

And once again, in Figure 5-9, you can see the tree representation of this style sheet file, small though it may be:

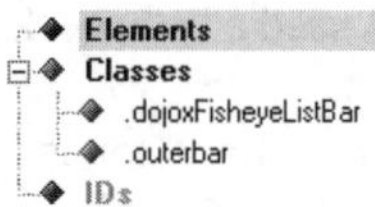

Figure 5-9. *A more visual representation of dojoStyles.css*

Although small, this style sheet provides some important styling, and without it, the way-cool Fisheye icons wouldn't quite look right. The two styles apply to the container that the Fisheye is a child of, and most important, ensure that the Fisheye List is centered on the page.

Writing index.htm

`index.htm` is where we find the bulk of the source that makes up the contact manager application. It is mostly just markup, with just a sprinkle of script in it. Let's begin by taking a look at part of the `<head>` section where the style sheet and JavaScript imports are, as seen in Listing 5-3.

Listing 5-3. *Stylesheet and JavaScript Imports in index.htm*

```
<link rel="StyleSheet" href="css/dojoStyles.css" type="text/css">
<link rel="StyleSheet" href="css/styles.css" type="text/css">
<link rel="StyleSheet"
  href="js/dojo/dojox/widget/FisheyeList/FisheyeList.css"
  type="text/css">
```

```
<script type="text/javascript">
  var djConfig = {
    baseScriptUri : "js/dojo/"
  };
</script>
<script type="text/javascript" src="js/dojo/dojo.js"></script>
<script language="JavaScript" type="text/javascript">
  dojo.require("dojo.parser");
  dojo.require("dojox.widget.FisheyeList");
  dojo.require("dojox.storage");
  dojo.addOnLoad(function(){
    dojo.parser.parse(dojo.byId("divMain"));
  });
</script>

<script type="text/javascript" src="js/Contact.js"></script>
<script type="text/javascript" src="js/EventHandlers.js"></script>
<script type="text/javascript" src="js/DataManager.js"></script>
<script type="text/javascript" src="js/ContactManager.js"></script>
```

First we import our three style sheets, namely the two we've previously seen, as well as one that Dojo supplies for styling the Fisheye List. Next comes a small block of JavaScript that sets up some Dojo properties. The `djConfig` variable is an associative array that Dojo looks for when it starts up (which means this code must come *before* the Dojo imports), and it contains options for various Dojo settings. In this case, only one is important:

- `baseScriptUri` defines the beginning of the path where all Dojo resources can be found, such as source files to be imported, images for widgets, style sheets, and so on. In this case, we have Dojo installed in `js/dojo`, so that is the appropriate value for this attribute.

Other options are available in `djConfig`, and a few minutes looking at the online Dojo docs will turn them up, but for our purposes here, only this one is important.

Following that block is the import of the main part of Dojo itself. Immediately following that is a section with a series of `dojo.require()` function calls. Dojo is of course organized in a package structure, much like in Java and other "grown-up" languages. Dojo also implements the idea of importing small portions of it as required, and even offers wildcard (`.*`) import capabilities, although they aren't being used here.

The import of `dojo.parser` is needed to parse the DOM and create widgets, namely our Fisheye List. The second import is obvious: it's the Fisheye List widget itself. The third import is of course the Dojo storage system. Note that there is no explicit import of the `dojox.storage.manager`, nor any providers. Dojo takes care of those dependencies for us as a result of us importing `dojo.storage`.

This line of code is what tells Dojo to parse the DOM for widgets:

```
dojo.addOnLoad(function(){
  dojo.parser.parse(dojo.byId("divMain"));
});
```

Specifically, it parses the element with the ID `divMain`. Using the `dojo.addOnLoad()` function starts the parsing as soon as the DOM loads, but not necessarily when all resources have loaded. This is different from the typical `onLoad` event handler, which will fire only when all resources have been loaded. Have no fear, though: Dojo ensures that all *its* resources have loaded, so we won't have errors due to widget code that hasn't yet loaded.

Following the Dojo imports and the `addOnLoad()` call are four more plain JavaScript imports bringing in the code that makes up the contact manager application. You will be looking at each in detail shortly.

Before you look at the code further, though, let's get one of those graphical representations I'm apparently so fond of! In Figure 5-10, you can see a high-level tree view of `index.htm`—at least, the elements nested directly under `<body>`. (There's not much sense looking at what's under `<head>` in this way, and there's way more under `<body>` indirectly than I could show in such a diagram.)

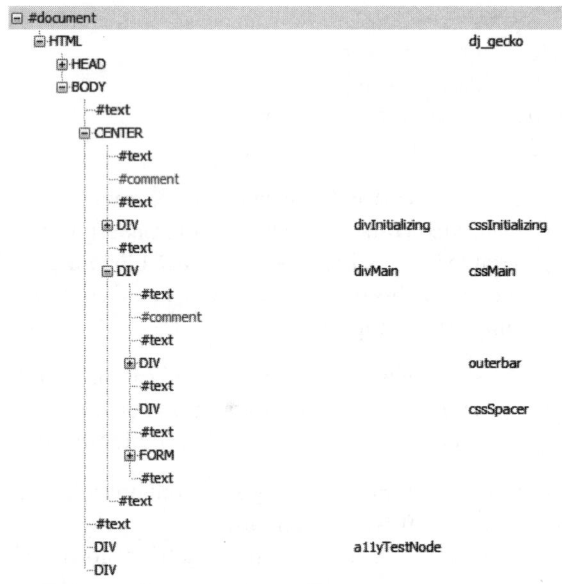

Figure 5-10. *A more visual representation of index.htm*

Adding Bootstrap Code

The last thing we find in `<head>` is a `<script>` block that contains what is essentially bootstrap code to get the application going. This code is seen in Listing 5-4.

Listing 5-4. *The Bootstrap JavaScript in <head> of index.htm*

```
<script>

  // The contactManager instance that is the core of this application.
  var contactManager = new ContactManager();

</script>
```

Here we find the instantiation of the `ContactManager` class, which is basically the core code of the application (you'll see this in just a little bit). The `ContactManager` class has an `init()` method, which will here be called `onLoad` of the page (the call is inlined on the `<body>` tag). This method is what effectively starts the application, as you'll see later.

In keeping with the idea of unobtrusive JavaScript, you'll notice there is precious little on the page so far in terms of executable code. Some would argue that even what I have here should be in external `.js` files, but I personally think you can take that exercise a little too far sometimes. I don't feel it necessary to externalize every last bit of script, but certainly it should be kept to a minimum, and I think you'll agree that is the case here.

Initializing the Application

Now we come to the `<body>` of the page. The first content is this:

```
<div id="divInitializing" class="cssInitializing">
  <center>...Initializing Contact Manager, please wait...</center>
</div>
```

When the page is first loaded, we don't want the user to be able to fire UI events before the UI has fully loaded (that is, clicking the Save button before the persisted contacts have been fully restored might not be such a good thing). So, to start out, the user sees a message saying the application is initializing. After everything is set to go, this `<div>` is hidden, and the main content shown.

Adding the Fisheye List

Now we come to some UI fun. One of the things Dojo does really well, the thing it's probably most famous for, is widgets. One of the singularly most impressive widgets it contains (*the* most impressive for my money) is the Fisheye List. Ever seen the launch bar in Mac OS? Do you like how the icons expand and shrink as you mouse over them? Well, Dojo lets you do it too in your own web apps, as you can see in Figure 5-11. Of course, seeing it statically in print doesn't quite do it justice, so fire up the app and just mouse over the icons a bit. I think you'll have fun doing nothing but that for a few minutes.

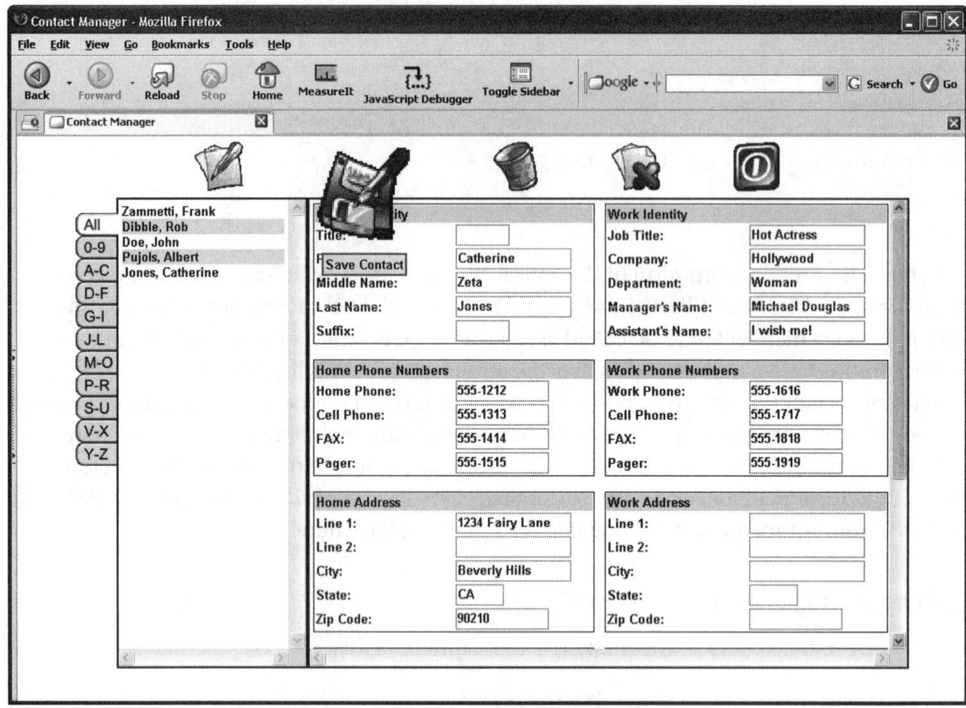

Figure 5-11. *The Dojo Fisheye widget—coolness, 'nough said.*

So, is it difficult to use that widget? Heck no! Dojo allows you to define most, if not all, of its widgets with nothing but HTML. (You can also do it programmatically, and I'll bet in most cases you'll use a mixture of the two approaches.) Listing 5-5 shows the markup responsible for the Fisheye List in this application.

Listing 5-5. *The Fisheye Definition Markup*

```
<div class="outerbar">
  <div dojoType="dojox.widget.FisheyeList"
    itemWidth="64" itemHeight="64"
    itemMaxWidth="128" itemMaxHeight="128"
    orientation="horizontal"
    effectUnits="1"
    itemPadding="10"
    attachEdge="top"
    labelEdge="bottom">
    <div dojoType="dojox.widget.FisheyeListItem"
      onclick="contactManager.doNewContact();"
      label="New Contact"
      iconSrc="img/icon_new.gif">
    </div>
    <div dojoType="dojox.widget.FisheyeListItem"
```

```
      label=""
      iconSrc="img/transPix.gif">
    </div>
    <div dojoType="dojox.widget.FisheyeListItem"
      onclick="contactManager.doSaveContact();"
      label="Save Contact"
      iconSrc="img/icon_save.gif">
    </div>
    <div dojoType="dojox.widget.FisheyeListItem"
      label=""
      iconSrc="img/transPix.gif">
    </div>
    <div dojoType="dojox.widget.FisheyeListItem"
      onclick="contactManager.doDeleteContact();"
      label="Delete Contact"
      iconSrc="img/icon_delete.gif">
    </div>
    <div dojoType="dojox.widget.FisheyeListItem"
      label=""
      iconSrc="img/transPix.gif">
    </div>
    <div dojoType="dojox.widget.FisheyeListItem"
      onclick="contactManager.doClearContacts();"
      label="Clear Contacts"
      iconSrc="img/icon_clear.gif">
    </div>
    <div dojoType="dojox.widget.FisheyeListItem"
      label=""
      iconSrc="img/transPix.gif">
    </div>
    <div dojoType="dojox.widget.FisheyeListItem"
      onclick="contactManager.doExit();"
      label="Exit Contact Manager"
      iconSrc="img/icon_exit.gif">
    </div>
  </div>
</div>
```

When the page loads, Dojo will parse the divMain element as we told it to earlier, looking for tags that it recognizes as defining widgets. It then replaces them with the appropriate markup to form the widget. In this case, adding a dojoType expando attribute to a <div> and giving it the value dojox.widget.FisheyeList gets the job done. You'll notice that this <div> also contains a number of custom expando attributes, starting with dojoType. This is a hallmark of Dojo and is how you configure options for the widgets. Let's look at each of those attributes now, shown in Table 5-1.

Table 5-1. *The Attributes Available for the Fisheye List*

Attribute	Description
`itemWidth`	This is the horizontal size of an icon when it is not hovered over.
`itemHeight`	This is the vertical size of an icon when it is not hovered over.
`itemMaxWidth`	This is the maximum horizontal size of an icon when it is being hovered over and is expanded fully.
`itemMaxHeight`	This is the maximum vertical size of an icon when it is being hovered over and is expanded fully.
`orientation`	This indicates whether the Fisheye List goes horizontally across the page or vertically down it.
`effectUnits`	I couldn't find any definitive documentation of this attribute, but it seems to be a measure of how close the cursor has to come to an icon before it begins to expand.
`itemPadding`	This too I could not find documentation of, but it seems to be, as you might reasonably expect, the amount of space around each icon. The strange thing, to me at least, is that the larger the number, the smaller the icon! So it looks like what happens is that within the bounds of `itemWidth` and `itemHeight`, Dojo will try to force there to be `itemPadding` pixels around the icon. So, if you have `itemWidth` and `itemHeight` of `40`, and `itemPadding` of `30`, the icon will be resized to 10 × 10 regardless of how big it actually is.
`attachEdge`	Geez, are you seeing a pattern? Again, I could find no true documentation, but experimenting seems to indicate this is the edge of the icon that is "attached" to the page, that is, the direction from which growth occurs. A value of `left` or `right` seems to be roughly the same, but `top` and `bottom` give clearly different effects (bottom being rather ugly).
`labelEdge`	This is what edge of the icon the hover label appears on when you hover over the icon. In practice, all but a value of `bottom` made the labels not appear. I don't know if this is a bug or a side effect of the other settings somehow, but in truth I think `bottom` is how you'd generally want it to be anyway.

Each of the icons is simply another `<div>`, this time with a `dojoType` of `dojox.widget.FisheyeListItem`. Note that I have put essentially blank icons between each real icon. There may be another way that I am unaware of, but this is how I was able to space the icons out a bit; otherwise, they looked a little cramped to me.

Feel free to play around with the attributes on the second `<div>`. By manipulating them, you can alter the Fisheye List easily, such as making the expanded icons bigger, changing how far away from an icon you have to be to activate it, and so forth. Experimentation is a great way to learn Dojo. In fact, it's often the *only* way to really figure things out because, to be frank, the documentation isn't always all you'd hope for, as was the case with these attributes. Experimenting and digging through the source code and mailing list/message forum posts is sometimes the best way forward. Dojo is almost always worth the effort, though, so I certainly encourage you to spend some time fiddling with it, and messing with the Fisheye attributes is a good, gentle start.

Continuing on, for each icon we define an `onClick` handler to do whatever it is the icon represents. This is again a situation where completely unobtrusive JavaScript would say the event handlers should not be placed inline. Two points there:

- First, if the event handler is just a call to some JavaScript function that does the actual work, I see no real problem having the handlers inline. In fact, I think it makes more sense for them to be there because they are attributes of the element and therefore should probably be defined with the element. Also, this will aid performance because no script has to process to hook up the event handlers during initial page load and construction.
- Second, because Dojo is generating markup in place of these `<div>` elements, trying to hook up the events after the fact would have been a bit more difficult than usual. The `dojo.event` package may have helped, but it would still have not been straightforward. These points mean I won't lose any sleep tonight because of inline event handlers!

As always, don't blindly follow any guideline, no matter how reasonable it generally seems (and even if it's me putting it forth). Instead, think about each situation and make an appropriate choice.

Okay, putting philosophy aside and getting back to concrete code . . .

Adding the Contact List

Following the Fisheye markup is a chunk of markup that defines the selector tabs on the left. In the interest of brevity, let's just look at the first one and note that the rest are virtually identical:

```
<img src="img/sel_xx_over.gif" id="sel_XX" class="cssTab"
  onClick="contactManager.eventHandlers.stClick(this);"
  onMouseOver="contactManager.eventHandlers.stOver(this);"
  onMouseOut="contactManager.eventHandlers.stOut(this);"><br>
```

This is the All tab, meaning it shows all contacts. The `id` of the tab is used to determine the image it should have, based on its current state (that is, if it's the selected tab, or if it's being hovered over). For instance, in this case, the ID is `sel_XX`, and as you can see, that is the beginning of the name of the image that is the initial source for this tab. When you look at the event handlers (which are again called from inline handlers here), I think you will find that this all makes more sense. As I mentioned, all the tabs that follow are the same, except that the ID is different. For instance, the next tab's ID is `sel_09` because it is the tab for showing contacts beginning with any character from 0 to 9.

Following this section of markup is a very small bit of code:

```
<td width="200" valign="top">
  <div class="cssContactList" id="contactList">
  </div>
</td>
```

The `<div>` `contactList` is, not surprisingly, where our list of contacts will be inserted. The list is filtered by the selector tabs, and this `<div>`'s contents will be rewritten anytime a new tab is selected, or when a contact is added or deleted.

Following this is the remainder of the markup for the data-entry boxes, where we fill in the information for our contacts. This is a big bit of markup that all looks pretty similar, really, so let's just have a look at a representative snippet of it, in particular, the section for entering contact identity (both personal and business) in Listing 5-6.

Listing 5-6. *A Section of the Data-Entry Markup*

```
<tr>
  <!-- Contact Identity -->
  <td width="49%" valign="top">
    <div class="cssDataBox">
      <table border="0" cellpadding="1" cellspacing="1"
        width="100%">
        <tr>
          <td colspan="2" class="cssDataBoxHeader">
            Contact Identity
          </td>
        </tr>
        <tr>
          <td width="50%" valign="middle">Title:</td>
          <td width="50%" valign="middle">
            <input type="text" id="title"
              maxlength="3" size="4" class="cssTextbox">
          </td>
        </tr>
        <tr>
          <td valign="middle">First Name:</td>
          <td valign="middle">
            <input type="text" id="firstName"
              maxlength="15" size="15" class="cssTextbox">
          </td>
        </tr>
        <tr>
          <td valign="middle">Middle Name:</td>
          <td valign="middle">
            <input type="text" id="middleName"
              maxlength="15" size="15" class="cssTextbox">
          </td>
        </tr>
        <tr>
          <td valign="middle">Last Name:</td>
          <td valign="middle">
            <input type="text" id="lastName"
              maxlength="20" size="15" class="cssTextbox">
          </td>
        </tr>
        <tr>
          <td valign="middle">Suffix:</td>
          <td valign="middle">
            <input type="text" id="suffix"
              maxlength="3" size="4" class="cssTextbox">
          </td>
        </tr>
```

```
    </table>
  </div>
</td>
<!-- Divider -->
<td width="2%"> </td>
<!-- Work Identity -->
<td width="49%" valign="top">
  <div class="cssDataBox">
    <table border="0" cellpadding="1" cellspacing="1"
      width="100%">
      <tr>
        <td colspan="2" class="cssDataBoxHeader">
          Work Identity
        </td>
      </tr>
      <tr>
        <td width="50%" valign="middle">Job Title:</td>
        <td width="50%" valign="middle">
          <input type="text" id="jobTitle"
            maxlength="24" size="15" class="cssTextbox">
        </td>
      </tr>
      <tr>
        <td valign="middle">Company:</td>
        <td valign="middle">
          <input type="text" id="company"
            maxlength="25" size="15" class="cssTextbox">
        </td>
      </tr>
      <tr>
        <td valign="middle">Department:</td>
        <td valign="middle">
          <input type="text" id="department"
            maxlength="25" size="15" class="cssTextbox">
        </td>
      </tr>
      <tr>
        <td valign="middle">Manager's Name:</td>
        <td valign="middle">
          <input type="text" id="managerName"
            maxlength="30" size="15" class="cssTextbox">
        </td>
      </tr>
      <tr>
        <td valign="middle">Assistant's Name:</td>
        <td valign="middle">
          <input type="text" id="assistantName"
```

```
            maxlength="30" size="15" class="cssTextbox">
          </td>
        </tr>
      </table>
    </div>
  </td>
</tr>
```

There is certainly nothing unusual here; it is perfectly typical HTML. Note that the sizes of the fields have been limited such that each contact takes up just a hair under 1,024 bytes. This is done so that if you wanted to modify the code to store contacts with plain old cookies instead (hint, hint), you could do so and fit four contacts per cookie (remember, each cookie is limited to 4KB). Also note the `cssTextbox` style class being applied. This is done to avoid a browser quirk I saw that caused the border to not change back when the field loses focus. Setting the border to what's defined in the `cssTextbox` class takes care of it.

And with that, we have only one small bit of markup left to look at, and that's the `goodbye.htm` page.

Writing goodbye.htm

There isn't a whole lot to this file, as Listing 5-7 clearly indicates.

Listing 5-7. *goodbye.htm—Not Much to Look At*

```
<html>
  <head>
    <title>Contact Manager</title>
  </head>
  <body>
    Thanks for using the contact manager... goodbye!
  </body>
</html>
```

This is a simple landing page that the user sees after clicking the Exit icon. It's just always good form to end on a polite, "thanks for stopping by" kind of note.

Writing EventHandlers.js

Let's take a look at the `EventHandlers` class first, because this is something of a stand-alone piece of code. As you looked at `index.htm`, you saw that the selector tabs called event handler functions in this class. Also, as you shall soon see, all of the input fields actually do the same thing (huh? I don't remember seeing any event handlers on the input fields—you are right, but be patient, my young Padawan![1]). The contact list you see on the left uses some functions here

1. A Padawan is the chosen apprentice of a Jedi Knight in Star Wars lore. Probably the most famous Padawan was Anakin Skywalker, who learned under Obi-Wan Kenobi. Obi-Wan was perhaps the second-most famous Padawan, under Qui-Gon Jinn. (It should be noted that Luke Skywalker, perhaps the most famous Jedi in history, was never technically a Padawan.)

as well, but these are all simply UI-related functions. In other words, if you took these functions out, the application would still basically work, although the UI wouldn't be as reactive as it is—the selectors wouldn't turn red when you hovered over them, the input fields wouldn't be highlighted when they gained focus, and the contact list wouldn't have a hover effect at all. These effects are all contained within the EventHandlers class, the class diagram of which is shown in Figure 5-12.

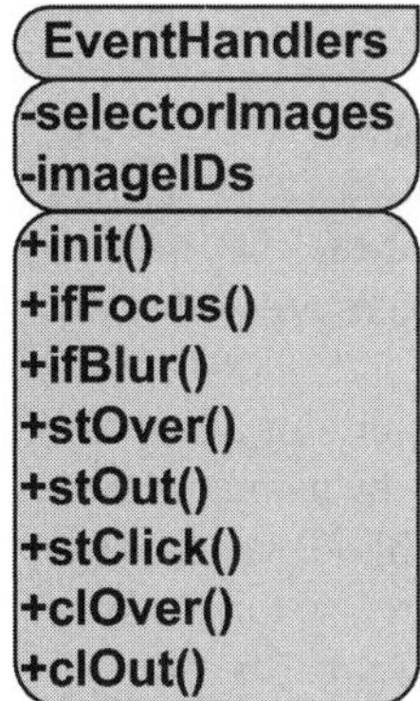

Figure 5-12. *UML class diagram of EventHandlers class*

First, the EventHandlers class is instantiated in the ContactManager class, which we will look at later, and the reference to it is one of the fields on ContactManager (hence the reason all the event handlers in index.htm were in the form contactManager.xxxx()).

The first item we find in the EventHandlers class is the selectorImages field, which is an array that will hold references to the preloaded images for the selector tabs. We next find another array field, imageIDs. This is a list of the selector tab IDs. The filenames of the graphics for each tab can be formed by using these IDs, and so can the ID of the elements on the page, both of which we will need to be able to do.

So, as I mentioned, ContactManager will instantiate EventHandlers, and also initialize it by calling init() on EventHandlers. This init() function is as follows:

```
this.init = function() {

  this.selectorImages = new Array();

  // Load images from the above array and store them in selectorImages.
  for (var i = 0; i < this.imageIDs.length; i++) {
    var sid = this.imageIDs[i];
    this.selectorImages[sid] = new Image();
    this.selectorImages[sid].src = "img/" +
      sid + ".gif";
    this.selectorImages[sid + "_over"] = new Image();
    this.selectorImages[sid + "_over"].src = "img/" +
      sid + "_over.gif";
  }
```

```
  // Get all input fields and attach onFocus and onBlur handlers.
  var inputFields = document.getElementsByTagName("input");
  for (i = 0; i < inputFields.length; i++) {
    inputFields[i].onfocus = this.ifFocus;
    inputFields[i].onblur = this.ifBlur;
  }

} // End init().
```

So, the first task this function performs is preloading the images for the selector tabs. To do so, it iterates over the elements of the `imageIDs` array. For each, it instantiates an `Image` object and sets its `src` attribute to the filename of the image. Two images for each tab are loaded, one in its nonhover state and the other in its hover state. These images are added to the array, keyed by the ID taken from the `imageIDs` array.

What we wind up with is an associative array, `selectorImages`, which contains all the preloaded images for the two states for each tab, and we can get at each image by using the ID as the key (for the hover images, it's the ID plus the string `_over` appended). This all saves us from writing explicit code to load each image. If you wanted to add more tabs later, so long as they follow the same naming scheme, you would have to add only the ID to the `imageIDs` array.

The next task this function performs is hooking up the event handlers to the input fields. Ah yes, there we go, that's how it works. We get the collection of `<input>` fields on the page by using the handy-dandy `document.getElementsByTagName()` function. Then, for each of the fields, we attach `onFocus` and `onBlur` events, pointing to the `ifFocus()` and `ifBlur()` functions of the `EventHandlers` class. Nice to not have to specify these handlers on each input element, huh?

This is another tenet of unobtrusiveness, the idea of attaching event handlers to plain old markup. Although I'm not sure I like the idea of doing so for every event handler on a page, in cases like this where there are a rather large number of elements that need the same event handlers attached, this strikes me as better than having to put the handlers inline with each element in the markup.

I suppose we should look at those `ifFocus()` and `ifBlur()` functions, shouldn't we? Well, here you go:

```
// ********** Input Field focus.
this.ifFocus = function() {

  this.style.backgroundColor = "#ffffa0";

} // End ifFocus();


// ********** Input Field blur.
this.ifBlur = function() {

  this.style.backgroundColor = "#ffffff";

} // End ifBlur().
```

Certainly this is nothing special, just changing the background color of the input field: yellow when it has focus, white when it loses focus. While it's a simple thing to implement, highlighting the current field is something that goes over well with most users, so it's a good (and simple) thing to implement.

One thing to note that *is* of some interest, however, is the use of the keyword `this`, which can be a bit confusing. Recall that the `ifFocus()` and `ifBlur()` functions are attached as event handlers to elements on the page. When they are called, the keyword `this` in the line with `this.style.backgroundColor` refers to the element firing the event because at runtime, the keyword `this` is always evaluated in the context in which it executes. Contrast this to the usage of `this` in the line with `this.ifBlur`. In that case, `this` refers to the `EventHandlers` class because it is defined within that class. You can view this as static vs. dynamic interpretation of the `this` keyword, static being the usage to attach the method to the `EventHandler` class, and dynamic being the usage with the event handler. This is commonly referred to as early vs. late binding. *Late binding* occurs at runtime, while *early binding* occurs at compile time. There is of course no compile time with JavaScript, but it still means before the code actually runs.

After those functions, we find three that deal with the selector tabs:

```
// ********** Selector Tab mouseOver.
this.stOver = function(inTab) {

  inTab.src = this.selectorImages[inTab.id + "_over"].src;

} // End stOver().


// ********** Selector Tab mouseOut.
this.stOut = function(inTab) {

  // Only switch state if not the current tab.
  if (contactManager.currentTab != inTab.id.substr(4, 2)) {
    inTab.src = this.selectorImages[inTab.id].src;
  }

} // End stOut().


// ********** Selector Tab click.
this.stClick = function(inTab) {

  // Reset all tabs before setting the current one.
  for (var i = 0; i < this.imageIDs.length; i++) {
    var sid = this.imageIDs[i];
    dojo.byId(sid).src = this.selectorImages[sid].src;
  }

  inTab.src = this.selectorImages[inTab.id + "_over"].src;
```

```
  // Record the current tab, and redisplay the contact list.
  contactManager.currentTab = inTab.id.substr(4, 2);
  contactManager.displayContactList();

} // End stClick().
```

stOver() and stOut() handle the onMouseOver and onMouseOut events correspondingly. They use the preloaded images stored in the selectorImages array discussed previously. It's a simple matter of changing the src attribute on the tab firing the event to the src of the appropriate image in the array. Of course, if we hover over the current selected tab and then mouse off it, we don't want to reset it to the nonhover state, hence the check in stOut() to be sure the tab that fired the event isn't the currently selected tab.

stClick() is just a little more interesting. When we click a tab, it becomes the current tab, which means it remains in the hover state until another one is clicked. To accomplish this, we first have to reset the currently selected tab to its nonhover state. I decided to do this by resetting all the tabs, and then setting up the new current tab. Note that there wasn't any particular reason I did it this way; I could have just as easily reset only the current tab rather than all of them. You can view it as simply seeing an alternative approach in action. Last, after the tabs are taken care of, we call displayContactList() on the ContactManager object to update the contact list to correspond to only those contacts that should show up on the new current tab.

Last up in this class are the two functions that deal with mouse events on the items in the contact list on the left:

```
// ********** Contact List mouseOver.
this.clOver = function(inContact) {

  inContact.className = "cssContactListOver";

} // End clOver().


// ********** Contact List mouseOut.
this.clOut = function(inContact) {

  if (inContact.getAttribute("altRow") == "true") {
    inContact.className = "cssContactListAlternate";
  } else {
    inContact.className = "cssContactListNormal";
  }

} // End clOut().
```

For the sake of demonstrating a slightly different technique, I decided that unlike the handlers for the input fields, which access style attributes of the target element directly, here instead I would set the style class for the target element as appropriate. I think it is generally better to do it this way, because the styles are abstracted out into style sheets as they probably should be, but now you've seen that you can go the other way too if you feel it is more appropriate.

Here, the only real complexity is in the `clOut()` function. The style to switch the element to when the mouse leaves it can be one of two because the contacts in the contact list are displayed with alternate row stripping, typical of display lists like that. To determine which style should be set, we interrogate the custom `altRow` attribute that each contact in the list carries. When this attribute is set to `true`, we know it is an element with a gray background (meaning the `cssContactListAlternate` style selector); otherwise, it is a white background (using the `cssContactListNormal` selector). Other than that, it's pretty straightforward.

Writing Contact.js

If you are familiar with the concept of a data transfer object (DTO) or value object, this source will be nothing at all special to you because what is defined here is simply a DTO representing a contact. Its class diagram is shown in Figure 5-13.

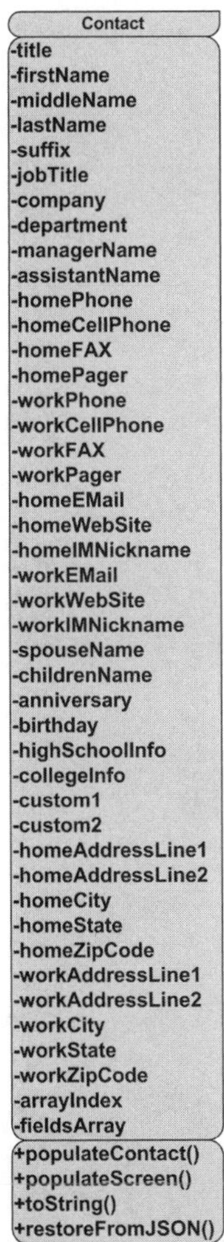

Figure 5-13. *UML class diagram of Contact class*

The first thing we find is a list of properties that represents a contact:

```
this.title = "";
this.firstName = "";
this.middleName = "";
this.lastName = "";
this.suffix = "";
this.jobTitle = "";
this.company = "";
this.department = "";
this.managerName = "";
this.assistantName = "";
this.homePhone = "";
this.homeCellPhone = "";
this.homeFAX = "";
this.homePager = "";
this.workPhone = "";
this.workCellPhone = "";
this.workFAX = "";
this.workPager = "";
this.homeEMail = "";
this.homeWebSite = "";
this.homeIMNickname = "";
this.workEMail = "";
this.workWebSite = "";
this.workIMNickname = "";
this.spouseName = "";
this.childrenName = "";
this.anniversary = "";
this.birthday = "";
this.highSchoolInfo = "";
this.collegeInfo = "";
this.custom1 = "";
this.custom2 = "";
this.homeAddressLine1 = "";
this.homeAddressLine2 = "";
this.homeCity = "";
this.homeState = "";
this.homeZipCode = "";
this.workAddressLine1 = "";
this.workAddressLine2 = "";
this.workCity = "";
this.workState = "";
this.workZipCode = "";

this.arrayIndex = -1;
```

Note that straggler at the end, `arrayIndex`. This is a field that you can think of as transient and is the index into the array of contacts stored in the `DataManager` where this contact is stored. This value will change as contacts are deleted, and will be dynamically calculated when contacts are restored at app initialization. You should note that it *does not* appear in the `fieldsArray` we will discuss next, which is the reason it is transient (the reason it isn't in the list should become apparent as we discuss `fieldsArray` further).

THE DATA TRANSFER OBJECT PATTERN

Say you find yourself making several remote calls in order to satisfy a single client request. Imagine that this comes up rather often, because you have an `Account` object, and you also need a list of `Fund` objects and a list of `Address` objects to display information for the user on a page. It's not far-fetched to think that each of these items is in its own database, and that there are three methods, one to get each type of data.

Instead, you might create a single `AccountDTO` object that has nested within it an array of `Address` objects and an array of `Fund` objects. Then, you have a single method that aggregates the results of the three separate calls (on the server this is), and returns a single `AccountDTO` object. This cuts down network traffic and latency considerably and will nearly always result in better application performance.

That's the idea behind the DTO pattern. It's also a modeling technique because the `Account` object with nested `Address` and `Fund` arrays logically makes a little more sense, although it's not unreasonable either that the data access façade originally provided the three separate methods in order to remain very fine-grained and flexible.

After this we find an interesting bit of code that certainly requires some explanation. It is the `fieldsArray` variable, which is an array containing the names of all the fields of this class, like so:

```
this.fieldsArray = [
  "title", "firstName", "middleName", "lastName", "suffix", "jobTitle",
  "company", "department", "managerName", "assistantName", "homePhone",
  "homeCellPhone", "homeFAX", "homePager", "workPhone", "workCellPhone",
  "workFAX", "workPager", "homeEMail", "homeWebSite", "homeIMNickname",
  "workEMail", "workWebSite", "workIMNickname", "spouseName", "childrenName",
  "anniversary", "birthday", "highSchoolInfo", "collegeInfo", "custom1",
  "custom2", "homeAddressLine1", "homeAddressLine2", "homeCity", "homeState",
  "homeZipCode", "workAddressLine1", "workAddressLine2", "workCity",
  "workState", "workZipCode"
];
```

If you look at the data fields described earlier, and then examine `index.htm` and look at the IDs of the input fields, you'll see that they match. This should be a clue as to what this array is for, but don't worry, we're about to figure it out together!

At various points in the application, we will need to populate an instance of the `Contact` class from the input fields, or populate the screen from the data fields within the `Contact` instance. One could certainly imagine writing code along the lines of this:

```
this.firstName = dojo.byId( "firstName").value;
this.lastName = dojo.byId( "lastName").value;
```

One could also certainly imagine that by jumping off the Brooklyn Bridge on a hot day, a person could possibly survive and get cooled off. But, just like jumping off the bridge, writing code like that isn't the best way to achieve the desired goal. Instead, it would be great if we could write some generic code to populate the object, or the input fields, without that code knowing precisely what fields are available. This is all the better when we want to add elements to a contact. That's exactly the kind of code that is present in the `Contact` class, for instance, in the `populateContact()` function:

```
this.populateContact = function() {

  for (var i = 0; i < this.fieldsArray.length; i++) {
    var fieldValue = dojo.byId(this.fieldsArray[i]).value;
    this[this.fieldsArray[i]] = fieldValue;
  }

} // End populateContact();
```

Now the purpose of that `fieldsArray` member is probably starting to make sense. We iterate over the array, and because the members of the `Contact` class instance to populate are the same as the IDs of the input fields, we can use the values of the array to access both, thereby making this code agnostic about what fields are present in the class and on the screen. If we want to add a field to record a contact's blood type, we could do that by simply adding it to the `fieldsArray` member, and none of the population code would need to change.

Populating the screen, by the way, is even simpler, but is precisely the same concept:

```
this.populateScreen = function() {

  for (var i = 0; i < this.fieldsArray.length; i++) {
    dojo.byId(this.fieldsArray[i]).value = this[this.fieldsArray[i]];
  }

} // End populateScreen().
```

The next function we come to is `toString()`. Recall that as in Java, all JavaScript objects implement a `toString()` function. The basic version inherited from the base `Object` class (which, again like Java, all objects in JavaScript inherit from) may or may not be very useful. However, we can override it simply and provide some output that is more useful. In this case, the output is JSON representing the contact. Here's the `toString()` function:

```
this.toString = function() {

  return dojo.toJson(this);

} // End toString().
```

You may be wondering why I didn't instead have something like a `toJSON()` function. That would have worked perfectly well too, except that overriding `toString()` instead makes the code to get the contact as JSON just a hair cleaner, as you'll see later in the `DataManager` class. Also, it makes debugging a little better because should you want to display a given `Contact` instance, in an `alert()` pop-up for example, what you'll get is something that is a bit more helpful than the default `toString()` provides. Overriding `toString()` is usually better in my opinion precisely because it makes debugging a little easier.

Dojo provides two simple functions: `toJson()` and `fromJson()`. Both hang off the `dojo` instance variable, hence `dojo.toJson()` and `dojo.fromJson()` to use them. With these, the `toString()` method becomes nothing but a one-line piece of code, which is very elegant. You simply pass an object to `toJson()` and you'll get a string of JSON back, or pass a string of JSON to `fromJson()` and you'll get an object back. It couldn't be simpler!

WHAT'S THIS JSON YOU SPEAK OF?

Although I'm willing to bet most people reading this book know what JSON is already, if you aren't familiar with it, *JSON*, which as stated in previous chapters stands for *JavaScript Object Notation*, is a simple data interchange format that is roughly similar to array notation in most C-like languages. JSON is technically a subset of the object literal notation used in JavaScript to define objects.

A quick and simple example of JSON is this:

```
{ firstName:"frank", lastName:"Zammetti" }.
```

If you were to execute `var p = eval(json);` where `json` is the example JSON shown here, what you would have is an object with the fields `firstName` and `lastName` present and pointed to by the variable `p` such that doing `alert(p.firstName);` would result in a pop-up with the text *frank* in it. JSON has quickly become very popular in Ajax development and is at this point perhaps the de facto standard for client-to-server communication in web apps today. Its primary benefits are that it is simple in terms of creation and consuming, lightweight (as compared to the typical alternatives such as XML), and relatively human-readable. It, like XML, is essentially self-describing, assuming the person or system generating it isn't brain-dead.

It allows for common structures needed such as arrays (lists) and maps, as well as arbitrarily complex nesting depths to allow for object hierarchies.

Although it is popular in Ajax development, it is by no means limited to that domain. In fact, because JSON is just a plain-text format, it can readily be used in many circumstances where you have data interchange needs. It's worth noting that many, maybe even most, modern languages have JSON support built in, or as an easily added addition, and this includes parsers, generators, and other general utility functions. As always, Google is your friend! The combination of the language you're working in and the term *JSON* should be all the search terms you need to get what you want quickly. A good place to start is `json.org`.

The last function found in the `Contact` class is `restoreFromJSON()`:

```
this.restoreFromJSON = function(inJSON) {

  var o = dojo.fromJson(inJSON);
  for (var i = 0; i < this.fieldsArray.length; i++) {
    this[this.fieldsArray[i]] = o[this.fieldsArray[i]];
  }

} // End restoreFromJSON().
```

The name says it all: this function populates the `Contact` class instance it is executed on from an incoming string of JSON. I think the beauty of storing the contact as JSON should be pretty apparent here: this code is amazingly simple and compact, especially given `dojo.fromJson()`. We simply iterate over that handy `fieldsArray` again, and for each element, we set the appropriate field in the class from the parsed JSON object. That's a simple approach, and simple is always a good thing!

By the way, remember `arrayIndex` field that I mentioned was transient? Do you see now why that is? By virtue of not being listed in `fieldsArray`, it is neither included in the JSON generated by `toString()` nor is it reconstituted by `restoreFromJSON()`.

Writing ContactManager.js

The `ContactManager` class, defined in the `ContactManager.js` file, is the main code behind this application. Its class diagram is shown in Figure 5-14.

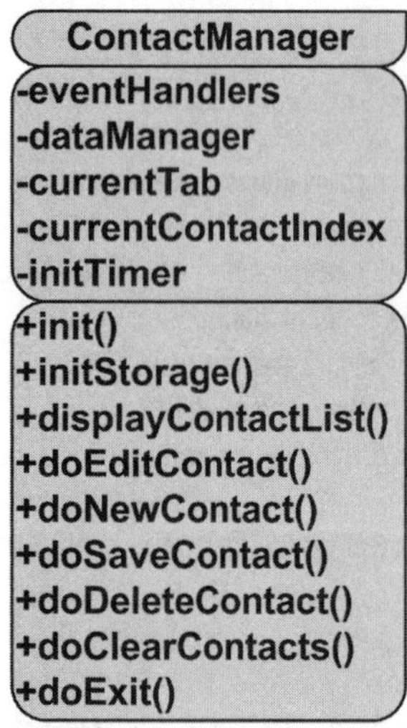

Figure 5-14. *UML class diagram of ContactManager class*

This class starts off with five data fields, described in Table 5-2.

Table 5-2. The Five Data Members of the ContactManager Class

Field Name	Description
`eventHandlers`	This is a reference to an instance of the `EventHandlers` class.
`dataManager`	This is a reference to an instance of the `DataManager` class.
`currentTab`	This is the ID of the currently selected tab.
`currentContactIndex`	This is the index into the array of contacts (stored in the `DataManager` class) of the specific contact currently being edited (or –1 if creating a new contact).
`initTimer`	This is a reference to the timer used during app initialization.

Recall that in index.htm, we hooked up an onLoad event that calls the init() function of the ContactManager class. Well, now it's time to see what's in that function:

```
this.init = function() {

  contactManager.eventHandlers = new EventHandlers();
  contactManager.eventHandlers.init();
  contactManager.dataManager = new DataManager();
  this.initTimer  = setTimeout("contactManager.initStorage()", 500);

} // End init().
```

First, the EventHandlers class is instantiated and the reference to it stored in the eventHandlers field as described in Table 5-1. Then init() is called on that class.

Next, you do the same thing for the DataManager class, but you don't call init() on it right away as you do the EventHandlers instance. Instead you start a timer that every 500 milliseconds calls the initStorage() function of the ContactManager. That function is as follows:

```
this.initStorage = function() {

  if (dojox.storage.manager.isInitialized()) {
    clearTimeout(this.initTimer);
    contactManager.dataManager.init();
    contactManager.displayContactList();
    dojo.byId("divInitializing").style.display = "none";
    dojo.byId("content").style.display = "block";
    this.initTimer = null;
  } else {
    this.initTimer  = setTimeout("contactManager.initStorage()", 500);
  }

} // End initStorage().
```

What's this all about, you ask? Simply, Bad Things™ will happen if we try to use Dojo's storage system before it has properly initialized. When we look at the DataManager class, you'll see that one of the things done in its init() function is to restore saved contacts from persistent storage (read: Gears Database). Therefore, we can't call that function straight away as we did with the EventHandlers instance, and further, we can't call it until the storage system has fully initialized. Hence the reason for the time: every 500 milliseconds, we check with Dojo to see whether the storage system has initialized yet. If not, we just keep firing the timer until it does.

As soon as it initializes, we stop the timer and call init() on the DataManager instance. We also at that point display the contact list so that any restored contacts will be available to the user, and finally we hide the initializing message discussed earlier and show the main content, which is contained within the content <div>. After the DataManager has been initialized, the application is then ready for user interaction.

Recall that the list of contacts restored from persistent storage is displayed during this initialization cycle. The code that generates the list of contacts is this:

```
this.displayContactList = function() {

  // Get a list of contacts for the current tab.
  var contacts = this.dataManager.listContacts(this.currentTab);

  // Generate the markup for the list.
  var html = "";
  var alt = false;
  for (var i = 0; i < contacts.length; i++) {
    html += "<div indexNum=\"" + contacts[i].arrayIndex + "\" ";
    html += "onMouseOver=\"contactManager.eventHandlers.clOver(this);\" ";
    html += "onMouseOut=\"contactManager.eventHandlers.clOut(this);\" ";
    html += "onClick=\"contactManager.doEditContact(" +
      "this.getAttribute('indexNum'));\" ";
    if (alt) {
      html += "class=\"cssContactListAlternate\" altRow=\"true\">";
      alt = false;
    } else {
      html += "class=\"cssContactListNormal\" altRow=\"false\">";
      alt = true;
    }
    html += contacts[i].lastName + ", " + contacts[i].firstName;
    html += "</div>";
  }

  // Display it.
  dojo.byId("contactList").innerHTML = html;

} // End displayContactList().
```

First, the list of contacts is retrieved from the DataManager. We pass the listContacts() function of the DataManager class the currently selected tab so that the list can be filtered accordingly. Next, we cycle through the returned contacts (each element of the returned array is a Contact object) and construct the appropriate markup for the list. Each element in the list has mouse events attached to highlight the contact when the user hovers over it, and it also contains an onClick handler that calls doEditContact() in the ContactManager class, which loads the contact into the input fields on the screen for editing. After the markup is fully constructed, it is inserted into the contactList <div>, which shows it to the user.

Speaking of the doEditContact() function, let's see that now, shall we?

```
this.doEditContact = function(inIndex) {

  // Record contact index, retrieve contact and populate screen.
  this.currentContactIndex = inIndex;
  var contact = this.dataManager.getContact(inIndex);
  contact.populateScreen();

}
```

Wow, really, that's it? Yes indeed. Note in the displayContactList() function that each contact listed has an indexNum custom attribute attached to it. This value corresponds to the value of the arrayIndex member of the Contact class; because we are viewing a subset of the contacts array when a particular tab is set, using this value ensures that a contact's indexNum attribute is the correct index into the array so that when the user clicks on a contact to edit it, we pull the correct data to display.

For instance, if we click the A-C tab, and we see three of ten stored contacts, the array returned by listContacts() in the DataManager class will simply return an array with three elements. But, the index in that array (0, 1, or 2) may not match the index into the contacts array for a given contact. In other words, the first contact returned by listContacts() is index 0 in that returned array, but may actually be the contact at index 9 in the main contacts array. Therefore, if we used the index number of the returned array as the value for indexNum, we wouldn't go after the correct element in the contacts array (that is, 0 instead of 9). We instead need the arrayIndex field of the Contact object.

There are five more functions in the ContactManager class to look at, and each corresponds to one of the five buttons at the top of the page. First up is doNewContact():

```
this.doNewContact = function() {

  if (this.initTimer == null) {

    if (confirm("Create New Contact\n\nYou will lose any unsaved changes.  " +
      "Are you sure?")) {
      document.forms[0].reset();
      this.currentContactIndex = -1;
    }

  }

} // End doNewContact().
```

Not really much going on there, I admit. One thing you will notice in the next five functions is the check of initTimer being null. When the application starts, initTimer has a value of -1. When the initialization cycle is complete, it is set to null. Because we don't want the user to be able to do anything until the application initializes fully, and because Dojo produces the Fisheye icons before initialization completes, we need to ensure that initialization is finished before we process any user events, hence the check that allows the code to execute only after initTimer is null, meaning everything is ready to go.

Once that is the case, we simply make sure the user wants to create a new contact, because if the user had any edits on the page, they would be lost. We then reset the form, which clears all our input fields, and set the currentContactIndex to -1, which indicates to the rest of the code that a new contact is being created.

Next up is the function called when the Save icon is clicked, appropriately named doSaveContact():

```
this.doSaveContact = function() {

  if (this.initTimer == null) {
```

```
    // Make sure required fields are filled in.
    if (dojo.byId("firstName").value == "" ||
      dojo.byId("lastName").value == "") {
      alert("First Name and Last Name are required fields");
      return false;
    }

    // Create a new contact and populate it from the entry fields.
    var contact = new Contact();
    contact.arrayIndex = this.currentContactIndex;
    contact.populateContact();

    // Save the contact.
    this.dataManager.saveContact(contact, this.currentContactIndex);

    // Redisplay the updated contact list.
    this.displayContactList();

    // Reset the entry fields and currentContactIndex.
    document.forms[0].reset();
    this.currentContactIndex = -1;

  }

} // End doSaveContact().
```

This function handles two different save situations: saving a new contact or saving edits to an existing contact. So, after our check of `initTimer` as in `doNewContact()`, we first do a quick edit to ensure that a first name and last name have been entered. These two fields are the only required fields for a contact because they are used to generate the contact list, and this is true whether it is a new contact or an existing one.

After that is done, we instantiate a new `Contact` object and tell it to populate itself from the input fields by calling its `populateContact()` function. We also here set the `arrayIndex` field based on the `currentContactIndex` value, which would be `-1`, as set in `doNewContact()` if this is a new contact, or to the appropriate array index if editing an existing contact.

Next, we call `saveContact()` on the `DataManager`, passing it the contact and the index (we'll be looking at that code shortly). After that, we regenerate the contact list and show it because we may have just added a contact that should be immediately visible (that is, either we're on the tab the contact would appear on naturally, or on the All tab). Last, we reset the input fields and the `currentContactIndex` value (which is a little redundant, but does no harm), and that's how a contact is saved.

The next function to look at is `doDeleteContact()`, and I'll give you just one guess what it does:

```
this.doDeleteContact = function() {

  if (this.initTimer == null) {
```

```
    if (this.currentContactIndex != -1 &&
      confirm("Are you sure you want to delete this contact?")) {

      // Ask the data manager to do the deletion.
      this.dataManager.deleteContact(this.currentContactIndex);

      // Redisplay the updated contact list.
      this.displayContactList();

      // Reset the entry fields and currentContactIndex.
      document.forms[0].reset();
      this.currentContactIndex = -1;

    }

  }

} // End doDeleteContact().
```

After the usual check of `initTimer`, and a confirmation that the user really wants to delete the current contact (which includes a check to be sure there is a contact selected to be deleted), we ask the `DataManager` to do the delete for us, passing it the index of the contact to delete. Once again we regenerate and display the contact list, and reset the input fields and the `currentContactIndex` value. (Yes, it's still a bit redundant here, but it still does no harm, and I prefer variables that aren't based on user input being in known states at any given time—it makes for easier debugging sessions.)

The next function is `doClearContacts()`, which is a giant, shiny "push to destroy the universe" button.[2] Well, maybe not quite, but it *does* delete *all* contacts from persistent storage, so it isn't something that you want the user pressing willy-nilly. For that reason, there is a double verification required, as you can plainly see:

```
this.doClearContacts = function() {

  if (this.initTimer == null) {

    if (confirm("This will PERMANENTLY delete ALL contacts from " +
      "persistent storage\n\nAre you sure??")) {
      if (confirm("Sorry to be a nudge, but are you REALLY, REALLY SURE " +
        "you want to lose ALL your contacts FOREVER??")) {
        this.dataManager.clearContacts();
        // Redisplay now empty contact list.
        this.displayContactList();
```

2. In *The Ren and Stimpy Show* episode "Space Madness," Stimpy is tasked with defending a shiny, red button that the narrator tells us will "eradicate history" and basically ruin everyone's day in the blink of an eye. Needless to say, Stimpy cannot control himself and pushes the button, thereby ending the episode in a hurry!

```
        // Reset form for good measure.
        document.forms[0].reset();
        this.currentContactIndex = -1;
        alert("Ok, it's done.  Don't come cryin' to me later.");
      }
    }

  }

} // End doClearContacts().
```

Only one function remains, and it's a pretty trivial piece of code: `doExit()`:

```
this.doExit = function() {

  if (this.initTimer == null) {

    if (confirm("Exit Contact Manager\n\nAre you sure?")) {
      window.location = "goodbye.htm";
    }

  }

} // End doExit().
```

Nothing fancy here, just a quick confirmation and then the browser is redirected to the `goobye.htm` page we looked at earlier.

Writing DataManager.js

Throughout the `ContactManager` code, we saw a number of calls out to the `DataManager`. Now we come to the point in our show where we need to take a look at that class and see what's going on under the covers. This is the part where we start dealing with Dojo's storage system directly to a large extent. Its class diagram is shown in Figure 5-15.

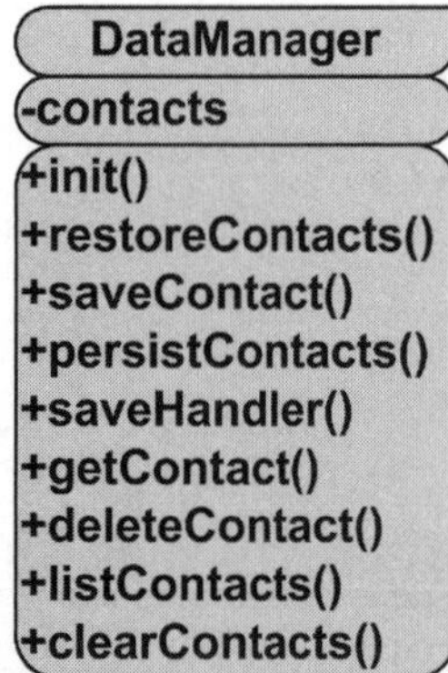

Figure 5-15. *UML class diagram of DataManager class*

It should be noted that I wrote the DataManager with the idea in mind that you could swap it out for another implementation, perhaps one that used an ActiveX control (as evil as those are) to persist the contacts and deal with the underlying storage mechanism. You could in theory not use Dojo at all if you chose not to. As such, its public API is pretty generic and conducive to such a swap. Of course, with Dojo underneath, you'd probably never have to or want to do that anyway because you could just have Dojo use a different persistence mechanism. Still, I'm a Java programmer by day, which means I love abstractions and layers for "flexibility," so that's what I've done here.

The first thing we see in the DataManager class is the contacts array. This is, not surprisingly, the array in which our contacts are stored. This array is loaded from the database when the application initializes, and until the user exits the application, it is essentially kept synchronized with the persistent store. In other words, when we add a contact, it is added to this array, and then the array is persisted to the database. When we delete a contact, it is deleted from the array, and then the array is persisted to the database. When we edit an existing contact, it is updated in the array, and then the array is persisted to the database. Are you seeing a pattern here?

■ **Note** The logical question to ask here is why the entire array is persisted each time. Why not just individual contacts? The answer is that I wrote this application originally to use a different storage mechanism, one that didn't have the necessary capabilities to store individual contacts. Another important reason is that I wanted to allow for an exercise to use cookies instead, which winds up being a little easier if you do the whole array at one time.

When the ContactManager class is instantiated during app initialization, it instantiates the instance of DataManager and keeps a reference to it, as we saw earlier. Also as we saw earlier, it initialized the DataManager by calling its init() function, which we can now look at:

```
this.init = function() {

  // Read in existing contacts from the applicable storage mechanism.
  this.contacts = new Array();
  this.restoreContacts();

} // End init().
```

After the contacts array is initialized, we ask the DataManager to restore any contacts from persistent storage by calling the restoreContacts() function, which is the following:

```
this.restoreContacts = function() {

  // Retrieve stored contacts.
  var storedContacts = dojox.storage.get("js_contact_manager_contacts");

  // Only do work if there actually were any contacts stored.
  if (storedContacts) {
```

```
    // Tokenize the string that was stored.
    var splitContacts = storedContacts.split("~>!<~");
    // Each element in splitContacts is a contact.
    for (var i = 0; i < splitContacts.length; i++) {
      // Instantiate a new Contact instance and populate it.
      var contact = new Contact();
      contact.restoreFromJSON(splitContacts[i]);
      contact.arrayIndex = i;
      // Add it to the array of contacts.
      this.contacts.push(contact);
    }
  }

} // End restoreContacts().
```

Restoring contacts is a pretty simple process. First, we ask Dojo to get our contacts from the underlying storage system. We don't even care what that means! We can imagine that under the covers, there is a SQL query being executed against the SQLite database provided by Gears, but we don't have to worry about those details; we just know that we're asking for something named `js_contact_manager_contacts` to be retrieved form persistent storage, and that just happens to be a string representation of an array of contacts. The code then checks to be sure we got something back: if this is the first time the application is run on this machine, for instance, there would be no object under that name, and hence no contacts to restore.

Assuming there were contacts, what we get back from the `dojox.storage.get()` call is basically a giant string consisting of contacts in JSON form separated by a sequence of characters (`~>!<~` specifically). The reason I chose this sequence of characters is simply that any single character, comma for instance, would not be suitable because it could appear naturally in the data entered by the user, and therefore we would not tokenize the string properly. You could always escape such characters of course, but it's not necessarily as easy as that. So, I wanted a delimiter to separate contacts that wasn't likely to be entered by the user. This seemed like a reasonably safe combination in the sense that it doesn't seem likely that it would naturally occur in real user input. However, it should be pointed out that entering it in any field for a contact will in fact break the code.

■ **Note** To be really bulletproof, the application should check all inputs to be sure that the `~>!<~` sequence doesn't appear. It seems pretty unlikely that it would be entered *except* by someone deliberately trying to break the program, so I can live with the risk.

After the string is tokenized, we start iterating over the tokens, which I remind you are contacts in JSON form. For each, all we need to do is instantiate a new `Contact` object, and then pass the JSON string to the `restoreFromJSON()` function of the `Contact`, which we looked at earlier. It uses the evaluated JSON and populates the `Contact` instance, effectively restoring it. Only two things remain to do: set the `arrayIndex` field of the contact, and add it to the `contacts` array. After all the tokens (read: contacts) have been processed in this way, restoreContacts() has completed its work and we now have a contacts array that is identical to how it was when it was last persisted.

The next function we encounter in our exploration of the DataManager class is the saveContact() function, which is obviously the function called to save a contact, and it looks like this:

```
this.saveContact = function(inContact, inIndex) {

  // Save new contact.
  if (inIndex == -1) {
    inContact.arrayIndex = this.contacts.length;
    this.contacts.push(inContact);
  } else {
    // Update existing contact.
    this.contacts[inIndex] = inContact;
  }
  this.persistContacts();

} // End saveContact().
```

We first do some simple branching based on whether we are saving a new contact (inIndex == -1) or updating an existing one (inIndex != -1). In the case of adding a new index, all we really need to do is set the arrayIndex field of the inContact object, and push it onto the contacts array. When we are updating a contact, we just need to set the appropriate element of the contacts array to the inContact object. After one of those things happens, we call persistContacts() to save the contacts array to the database.

So, what of this persistContacts() function? Let's get to that now. Actually, with persistContacts() goes saveHandler(), which works hand in hand with persistContacts() to do the work of saving to the database:

```
this.persistContacts = function() {

  // First, construct a giant string from our contact list, where each
  // contact is separated by ~>!<~ (that delimiter isn't too likely to
  // naturally appear in our data, I figure!)
  var contactsString = "";
  for (var i = 0; i < this.contacts.length; i++) {
    if (contactsString != "") {
      contactsString += "~>!<~";
    }
    contactsString += this.contacts[i];
  }

  try {
    dojox.storage.put("js_contact_manager_contacts", contactsString,
      this.saveHandler);
  } catch(e) {
    alert(e);
  }
```

```
} // End persistContacts().


// ********** Callback function for storage.
this.saveHandler = function(status, keyName){

  if (status == dojox.storage.FAILED) {
    alert("A failure occurred saving contact to persistent storage");
  }

} // End saveHandler().
```

First we construct that giant string from the contacts array that I talked about earlier when discussing the `restoreContacts()` function. To do so, we simply iterate over the `contacts` array and add each contact to a string, which fires its `toString()` function as described earlier when we looked at the `Contact` class.

We then append our special delimiter character sequence, and continue that until the whole contacts array has been processed into this string. After that's done, we pass this string to the `dojox.storage.put()` function, telling it to store it under the name `js_contact_manager_contacts`. We also pass it a reference to the `saveHandler()` function. This function is a callback that will be called by Dojo when the operation completes. We can examine the outcome of the operation and act accordingly. In this case, all we really care about is a failure, in which case we alert the user. There isn't a whole lot to be done if a failure occurs, so that's the end of things. We could also alert the user if the operation succeeds, but I think the user can surmise that if no error message is shown.

The `getContact()` function comes next, and it's definitely a trivial piece of code—in fact, it's so trivial, I'm not even going to show it. All it does is take in an index number and return that element from the `contacts` array. A single line of code, that's it.

Following `getContact()` is `deleteContact()`, which has a little more meat to it:

```
// ********** Delete a contact.
this.deleteContact = function(inIndex) {

  // Delete from contacts array.
  this.contacts.splice(inIndex, 1);

  // Store the updated contact list.
  this.persistContacts();

  // Finally, renumber all the remaining contacts.
  for (var i = 0; i < this.contacts.length; i++) {
    this.contacts[i].arrayIndex = i;
  }

} // End deleteContact().
```

. . . although I admit, not *a lot* of meat! JavaScript arrays expose a splice() method, which enables us to easily remove elements from an array. We simply specify what index to start removing elements from, and then specify the number of elements to remove.

After the contact has been removed, we ask the DataManager to persist our contacts, effectively updating the shared objects. One last bit of work remains at this point, and that is to renumber the contacts. Recall that the arrayIndex field, which is not persisted with the contact, indicates which element in the contacts array the contact is at. It is important that this be accurate because if and when we click a selector tab and return only a subset of the contacts array, each contact needs to know what position in the array it's at so we can edit and/or delete the appropriate contact if the user requests it.

However, let's say we have three contacts in the contacts array, and we delete the second one. The first contact still has an arrayIndex value of 0, and the second one now has a value of 2, because that's where it was at previously (we're of course assuming they were numbered correctly to begin with). So, if the user clicks that second contact to edit, we'll get an error as we try to access index 2 of the array, which no longer exists. As you can see, the arrayIndex values need to be updated when we delete a contact. Fortunately, this is a simple procedure: we just need to iterate over the array and set the arrayIndex for each contact as we do so. This will remove any gaps in the order left by a deletion, and everything will be set up properly again.

Following deleteContact() is listContacts(), which is called to get some subset of the contacts array (or the entire thing in the case of the All tab). Although it serves an important purpose, there isn't really much to it:

```
this.listContacts = function(inCurrentTab) {

  if (inCurrentTab == "XX") {
    // ALL tab selected, return ALL contact.
    return this.contacts;
  } else {
    // Filter contacts based on current tab.
    var retArray = new Array();
    var start = inCurrentTab.substr(0, 1).toUpperCase();
    var end = inCurrentTab.substr(1, 1).toUpperCase();
    for (var i = 0; i < this.contacts.length; i++) {
      var firstLetter = this.contacts[i].lastName.substr(0, 1).toUpperCase();
      if (firstLetter >= start && firstLetter <= end) {
        retArray.push(this.contacts[i]);
      }
    }
    return retArray;
  }

} // End listContacts().
```

First, we check to see whether the inCurrentTab value is XX, which indicates that the All tab has been selected. In that case, we just return the contacts array, and that's that. For any other tab, we have a little more work to do. First, we create a new array to hold the subset of contacts we'll be returning. Next, we take the first character of inCurrentTab, converted to uppercase, which is the start of the range of characters we want to return contacts for. We do the same for the second character, which is the end of the range.

So, let's say the `inCurrentTab` value is `AC`: in that case, we want to return any contact whose last name begins with *A*, *B*, or *C*. So, we iterate over the contacts and for each we grab the first letter of the last name. After converting it to uppercase, we see whether it falls within the range defined by `start` and `end`, and if so, we add it to the array. After we go through all the contacts, we return the array, which is now some subset of the contacts appropriate for the currently selected tab.

We're just about done with the `DataManager` class now—only one function left to examine:

```
this.clearContacts = function() {

  dojox.storage.clear("");
  this.contacts = new Array();

} // End clearContacts().
```

If the user becomes depressed and wants to cut off all contact with the outside world, that user may decide he no longer wants any contacts, and he may hit the Clear Contacts icon, in which case, this function is called. Two things need to occur to clear contacts. First, we need to clear our persistent storage. Dojo provides the `dojox.storage.clear()` function for this. This function takes as an argument a namespace specification. The `put()` method from before also accepts such an argument, allowing us to have data in multiple namespaces under one domain (which is what the underlying storage provided, Gears, ultimately segregates by). Here, however, because the namespace was not specified in any of the calls to `put()`, an empty string is used by default, and hence that's what we need to pass here to make things work.

After that, we have to clear the `contacts` array in `DataManager`, which is a simple matter of setting it to a new, empty array. After this, the user can go seek professional psychiatric help to deal with his problems.

Suggested Exercises

Although the primary goal of this chapter is to highlight the persistence aspect of the project, that's no reason not to make suggestions that tackle other areas as well. Here are just a few ideas you could explore that would certainly prove to be good learning exercises:

1. Allow for searching on *any* field. For bonus points, use some Dojo transition effects (which you'll see in later projects) to have a search panel slide into view.

2. Allow for sending e-mails by clicking a contact's e-mail address. I purposely left this out because I wanted to leave you one relatively simple suggestion here. This addition shouldn't take much effort.

3. Sort the contacts listed on a given tab.

4. Change the code to not store the entire array each time. Instead, use individual contact objects (well, strings describing a contact, really). This should give you good exposure to the storage system.

5. Implement persistence to cookies. I purposely limited the maximum size that a single contact could take up to just a hair under 1,024 bytes. This should allow you to store four contacts per cookie, so with the limit of 20 cookies per domain you can store 80 contacts. This would give you a chance to play with Dojo's cookie support functions too.

Summary

In this chapter, we explored a couple of mechanisms for storing data in a persistent manner on the client. We took a more in-depth look at Gears and its Database component. We saw how the Dojo library helps make all of this a bit easier by taking care of most of the details for us. Last, we built ourselves a small contact manager application to demonstrate these techniques and in the process saw some Dojo widget magic as well.

CHAPTER 6

A Place for Your Stuff: Dojo Code Cabinet

In this chapter, we'll fulfill the need of our obsessive-compulsive personalities and develop an application to store our code snippets in.

As good developers, we quickly learn that "stealing" is better than creating. That is, the more you can find code that does what you need rather than writing it yourself, the better. This doesn't always mean stealing from others (and *stealing* is just an attempt at humor—it's not actually stealing of course!). Especially after you do this programming thing for a while, you begin to steal from yourself more and more because you remember that you wrote that function to encrypt passwords a couple of projects ago, or you remember that algorithm you put together for processing account numbers, or whatever else.

Being able to find those snippets of code is a challenge, but it's a challenge we're here to meet! With the help of Dojo and Gears, we'll create an application that lets us store our snippets, organize them, and even search for them. That's what this chapter is all about. In the process, we'll get some good experience with some dijits, and we'll get a look at the `dojo.data` namespace.

Let's begin by looking at exactly what we want to accomplish, exactly what we want this application to be able to do.

Requirements and Goals

A *code cabinet*, a virtual filing cabinet for our code snippets, should in many ways model an actual file cabinet. But what does that mean? Here are the bullet points:

- Like a real file cabinet, ours needs drawers. We'll call them *categories* here. We should be able to create categories with any name so we then have a mechanism with which to categorize our snippets. Being a virtual file cabinet, it will be allowed an unlimited number of drawers. In terms of user interface, let's use a Tree dijit to display the categories (although we'll use it essentially like a list in that we won't allow for subcategories—and if you think that sounds like a hint for a suggested enhancement, you're right!).

- Within each category, we can add snippets of code. Each snippet will have pieces of information stored about it including name, description, author, e-mail address (of the author, presumably!), and URL reference (that is, if we found the snippet online and want to remember the site we got it from). We'll also be able to store notes about the snippet and associated keywords with the snippet to make searching possible. We should also let the code and notes be entered in a rich way, not just in plain text.
- Speaking of searching, we want to be able to search for snippets based on several criteria, and in any combination of criteria. We'll include things like being able to search by name, description, author, keywords, and actual code content.
- Clearly the snippets need to be stored in a persistent way, so let's use Gears for this. I'll jump the gun a little and tell you now that we'll use it directly rather than going through Dojo simply because sometimes this is more natural and arguably easier (hopefully, I'll convince you of that as you look at the code!).
- We'll need to be able to delete categories and snippets of course because, hey, we're human and we screw up sometimes!
- The entire user interface should be flexible, that is, we should be able to resize sections of it as we wish. Speaking of sections, let's create a toolbar up top, a list of categories displayed in a Tree dijit on the left, a tabbed section on the upper right (with one tab containing the list of snippets in a given category, and other tabs containing information about the currently selected snippet), and finally a section for scrolling on the lower right.

All right, I think we've got enough here to get going. Now let's look at some of the key technologies that we're going to need to build this.

How We Will Pull It Off

There are two new bits of technology that you'll need to be familiar with to build this application. Well, more precisely, one is new and one is being expanded upon. I'm talking here about the `dojo.data` namespace and the Gears Database component.

The dojo.data Namespace

The goal of `dojo.data` is to provide a data access layer that is independent of the underlying data format. It seeks to allow you to write code against a "database" without having to worry about quaint concepts like drivers and even what format the data is stored in. It's sort of like a Relational Database Management System (RDBMS) in the sense that you deal with SQL, but you don't care how the data is stored underneath, whether as flat files or some sort of binary representation.

The basis of `dojo.data` is the `Item`. An `Item` is, as far as you're concerned when writing code against it, a JavaScript object with fields. The fields are what you would generally think of as columns in a database table, and an `Item` is therefore a record in the table. A data store is, for all intents and purposes, equivalent to a database table.

In `dojo.data` you'll find the `ItemFileReadStore` and `ItemFileWriteStore` classes. These are types of data stores that take in JSON of a specified format and use that as the data. After the

JSON is fed into one of these classes, you can use all the data store methods, without any regard for the fact that the data resides in JSON.

The difference between ItemFileReadStore and ItemFileWriteStore is that the first is read-only, while the latter can be written to. The dojo.data API is broken out into a couple of APIs that a given data store can optionally choose to implement. For example, the ItemFileReadStore implements the dojo.data.api.Read interface, but not the dojo.data.api.Write interface. This is done to allow stores to be as lightweight as they want to be, making it more efficient to download the code.

One of the nice things about dojo.data is that some of the dijits are aware of it, meaning you can essentially bind a dijit to a given data store. Then, changes to the data store are automatically reflected in the dijit's UI (usually—I'll get into some exceptions later on as we dissect the code). This is a really cool capability!

So, what does all of this look like in terms of code? It's pretty simple, really. Let's start with some simple JSON:

```
var d = { "identifier" : "id",
  "label" : "name",
  "items" : [
     { id : 1, "name" : "Bill Gates", "richness" : "Unimaginable" },
     { id : 2, "name" : "Warren Buffet", "richness" : "Mind-boggling" },
     { id : 3, "name" : "Steve Jobs", "richness" : "Are you kidding me?!?" }
  ]
};
```

The identifier attribute will tell the data store that uses this JSON what field represents the unique identifier of an Item. The label attribute tells certain dijits bound to the data store which field is to be used for labels. The items array is the actual data. Each element of the array is an object with whatever fields you wish to have, but it of course has to have the ones named as identifier and name.

When you have that JSON, the next task is to create a data store and "wrap" it around the JSON, like so:

```
var ds = new dojo.data.ItemFileReadStore({data:d});
```

We can now use all the methods provided by the ItemFileReadStore. For instance, to retrieve a specific Item:

```
ds.fetchItemByIdentity({
  identity : 1, onItem : function(item) {
    alert(ds.getValue(item, "richness"));
  }
});
```

Note the asynchronous nature of the call. You specify the function to execute when the retrieval completes by passing it as the value of the onItem attribute; in this case, it's an inline function. Also note the way the richness attribute is retrieved. You shouldn't even directly access the fields of an Item (more on why later); you should instead use the getValue() method of the data store.

Let's say you want to retrieve all the items in the store. You can do that with the fetch() method:

```
ds.fetch({onComplete : function(items) {
  for (var i = 0; i < items.length; i++) {
    alert(ds.getValue(items[i], "name"));
  }
}});
```

There are other methods available, but these are essentially all we're going to need for this application. I suggest reading through the "The Book of Dojo," which can be found in the documentation section of the Dojo web site (http://dojotoolkit.org/book/dojo-book-1-0). The entire API is described pretty well there. You'll see some more capabilities as we go through the application, but this is enough of an introduction to be prepared for it when it comes.

Gears Database Component

If you jumped around and haven't read the previous chapter yet, now is the time to do so. Gears was introduced there, and I'm going to go forward here assuming you've read that already (or are already familiar with Gears). With that assumption in mind . . .

In this project, I thought about how I would likely implement this application if I was dealing with a server component, and it seemed pretty obvious that a database would be the natural storage mechanism. When I further thought about how I would choose to interact with that database, given all the options available in various languages, I decided that straight SQL would likely be my choice (as is, frankly, the case most of the time unless I have a requirement that makes me think otherwise). It's kind of funny to think that nowadays straight SQL is almost considered "bare metal" programming! In Java for instance, there's no shortage of object-relational mapping (ORM) tools available that hide the SQL from you. Those types of abstractions are available in other languages and platforms as well.

In the previous chapter, you saw the Dojo storage system, which hides those details from you in the JavaScript world as well. In fact, the preceding project also used Gears underneath, but I don't have any idea what the final SQL looked like. (I can take some good guesses of course, but I didn't write the SQL myself; that's the important point.)

In this project, however, I wanted more control over how the underlying storage system worked, how it was structured, and how I interacted with it. I therefore decided that going directly against the Gears Database API was the best choice.

What does that API look like, you ask? It couldn't be much simpler! You start by instantiating the database engine:

```
var db = google.gears.factory.create("beta.database");
```

Note that Gears is still technically beta, hence the name of the object being created from the factory.

After you have that engine, you open a database:

```
db.open("myDatabase");
```

If that database doesn't yet exist, Gears goes ahead and creates it for you.

After the database is opened, you can begin executing queries on it. That will, usually, mean creating a new table, which you can do like this:

```
db.execute("CREATE TABLE IF NOT EXISTS people (" +
  "age INT, " +
  "first_name TEXT, " +
  "last_name TEXT" +
")");
```

As you can see, we're dealing in straight SQL here, nothing unusual. The exact dialect is something you'll need to consult the Gears documentation for, but in general it's not too far off standard SQL. (Every RDBMS has its own dialect peculiarities, and the underlying database that Gears sits on top of, SQLite, is no different—but you won't find any shocks here, I dare say.)

After you have some tables, you then use the `execute()` method to execute updates, whether they are deletes, inserts, updates, table drops, or whatever else.

Queries too are done the same way:

```
var rs = db.execute("SELECT age,name,type FROM people ORDER BY name");
while (rs.isValidRow()) {
  alert("age = " + rs.field(0));
  alert("name = " + rs.field(1));
  alert("type = " + rs.field(2));
  rs.next();
}
```

Here we get back a `ResultSet`, which isn't too different from any `ResultSet` (or `RecordSet` as it's sometimes called) in most other languages. We can iterate over it, calling the `isValidRow()` method each time, which will return `false` when we've moved past the last record. We can grab the values of the fields with a simple call to the `field()` method, passing it the index of the field we want back. There's also a `fieldByName()` method we can call, which is useful when doing "select all" statements.

For the `execute()` method, you can also pass an optional second parameter indicating values to be inserted into the SQL. This allows for parametric variables in the SQL. For example:

```
db.execute("INSERT INTO people VALUES (?, ?, ?)", [ 12, "Rick", "Melon" ] );
```

An example like that isn't all that logical because if you were inserting literals like that, you'd probably simply make the values part of the SQL itself. But if you imagine those literals as variable names, the usefulness is a lot more apparent.

On the `Database` object, you can also call `close()`, which is optional but does no harm if the database is already closed. There's also a `lastInsertRowId()` method which, as its name implies, returns the ID of the last inserted row. The Gears documentation states that every row has an ID value, even if you don't explicitly set one up when you create the table, so you'll always get a valid value back from this.

On the `ResultSet` object, you can call `fieldCount()`, which tells you how many fields (columns) were returned. This generally is useful only when you do a "select all" query, because otherwise you'd already know the answer. You can also call `fieldName()`, which takes a field index as `field()` does but gives you the name of the corresponding field.

So, as you can see for yourself, the Gears Database API is quite simple to use. It may not have all the bells and whistles of Oracle, SQL Server, MySQL, or PostgreSQL, but we are talking

JavaScript and the client here! In the end, though, this gives us all we need to write this application and to do a lot of things you otherwise probably couldn't do on the client alone, not without a lot of trouble at least. In fact, we'll use only some of the functions I've described here because we don't need all of them anyway.

With the preliminaries now out of the way, let's dive into the code of this application and see what makes her tick!

Dissecting the Solution

Let's begin our look at the implementation details of this project by having ourselves a peek at the directory structure, as shown in Figure 6-1. There are maybe one or two interesting points to be made about it, but otherwise it's largely like most of the other projects.

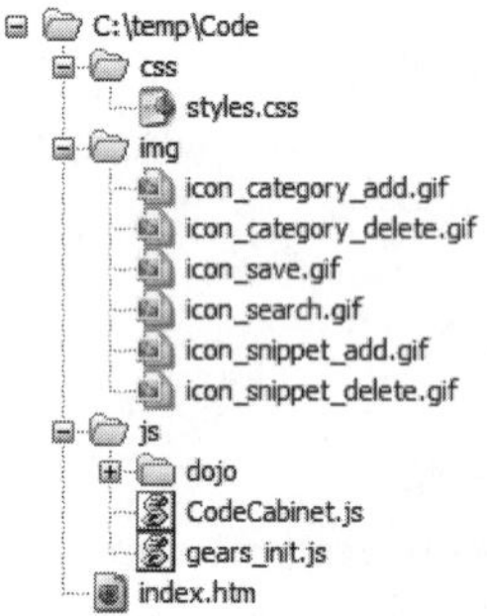

Figure 6-1. *The directory structure of the application*

In the root directory, you'll find `index.htm`, which is the only markup for this project. Naturally, it's the first file loaded, containing all our style sheet and JavaScript imports, some initial "bootstrap" startup code, and of course the HTML making up the application's visual display.

The `styles.css` file lives in the `css` directory, as is my customary approach, and it contains all the style sheet information for this application. You'll find a few style attributes floating around in `index.htm`, but this style sheet is very limited and almost entirely positional/visibility-related, which I feel is generally okay to do in markup.

Within the `img` directory are all the image resources for this application, which are simply the button images for the toolbar and nothing more.

In the `js` directory are two files, `CodeCabinet.js` and `gears_init.js`. The `CodeCabinet.js` file contains all the script for the application itself. The `gears_init.js` file contains some code used to deal with Gears, specifically what happens when it isn't installed. We won't be looking at this code here because it's completely boilerplate and not code I wrote anyway. (This is a file you get from Google, which simply includes it.)

There's also the usual `dojo` directory nested under the `js` directory; it's just Dojo itself in all its glory, unmodified and ready to rock and roll.

And so are we! Let's get into the code without further delay!

Writing index.htm

Essentially, the user interface is defined in one file: `index.htm`. There's a little bit of scripting here as well, but it's pretty limited to largely bootstrap-type code.

Whoa, wait a minute. I think it may help to see the application before seeing the code behind it—you know, put it all in perspective and that sort of thing. So, in Figure 6-2 you can see what the application looks like when you first access it.

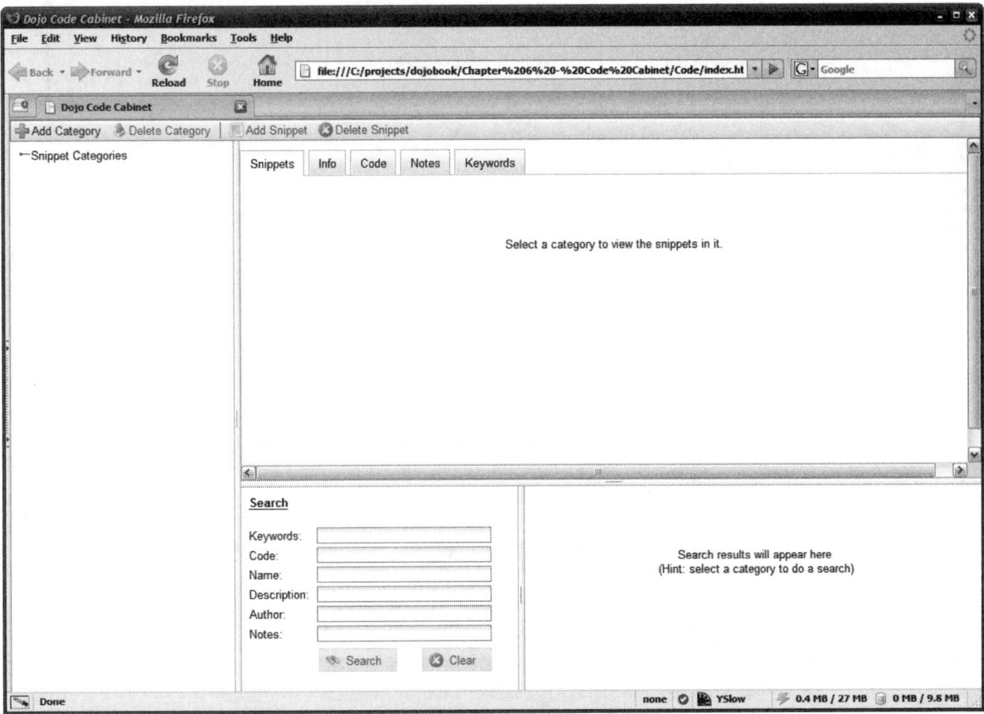

Figure 6-2. *Dojo Code Cabinet, in all its (initial) glory!*

So, we have ourselves a tree of categories on the left, a toolbar up top with some functions we can perform, some tabs on the right, and some search-related stuff on the bottom. It all pretty well matches up with the requirements and goals we laid out before, so we're in good shape so far!

It isn't very exciting, though: we have no categories and no snippets! Take a look at Figure 6-3 and you'll see what the application looks like after we've added a single category and a single snippet.

Yep, that's a little better. Of course, if that's all there was, it wouldn't be a *whole* lot better, but thankfully we have Figure 6-4, which is what you see after you click on that snippet.

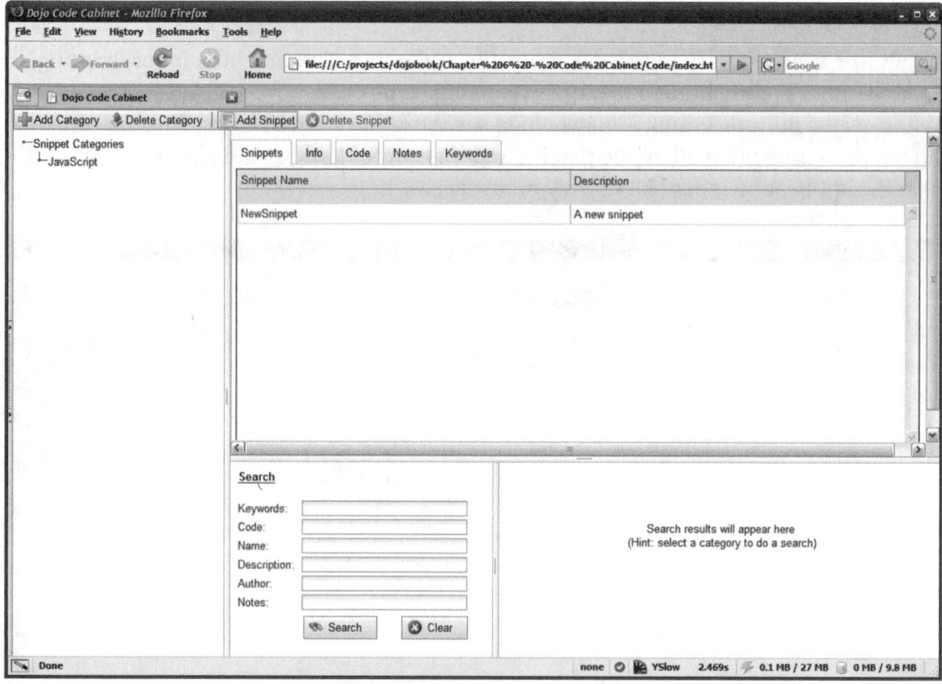

Figure 6-3. *A category selected, snippets in it showing*

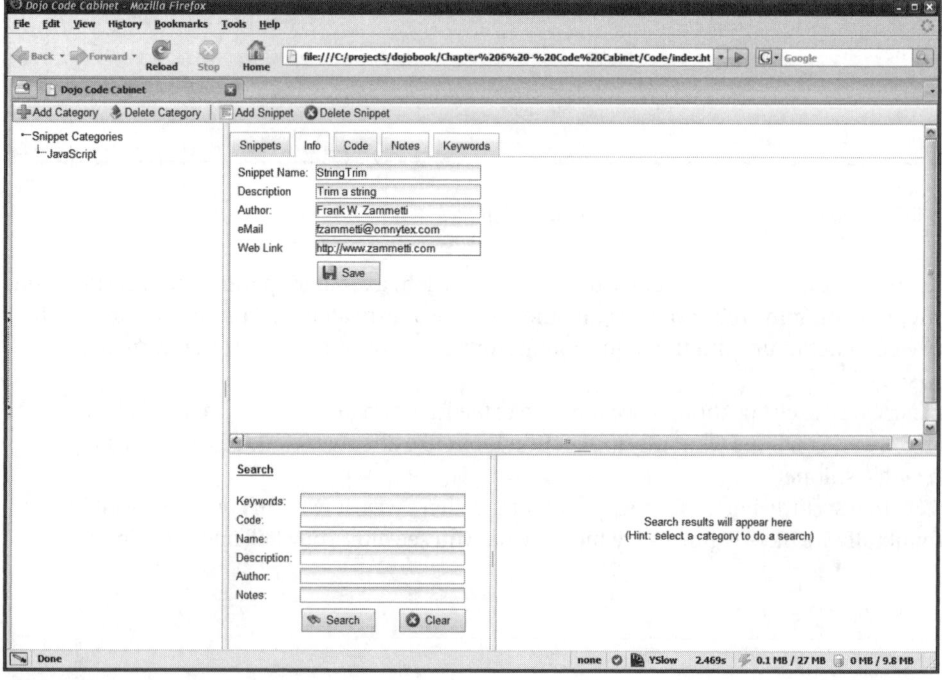

Figure 6-4. *The Info tab*

Yes, now we can see some information about the snippet, which is all well and good of course, but what about, you know, the actual *code* of the *snippet*? In other words, what does that Code tab look like? Figure 6-5 answers that question.

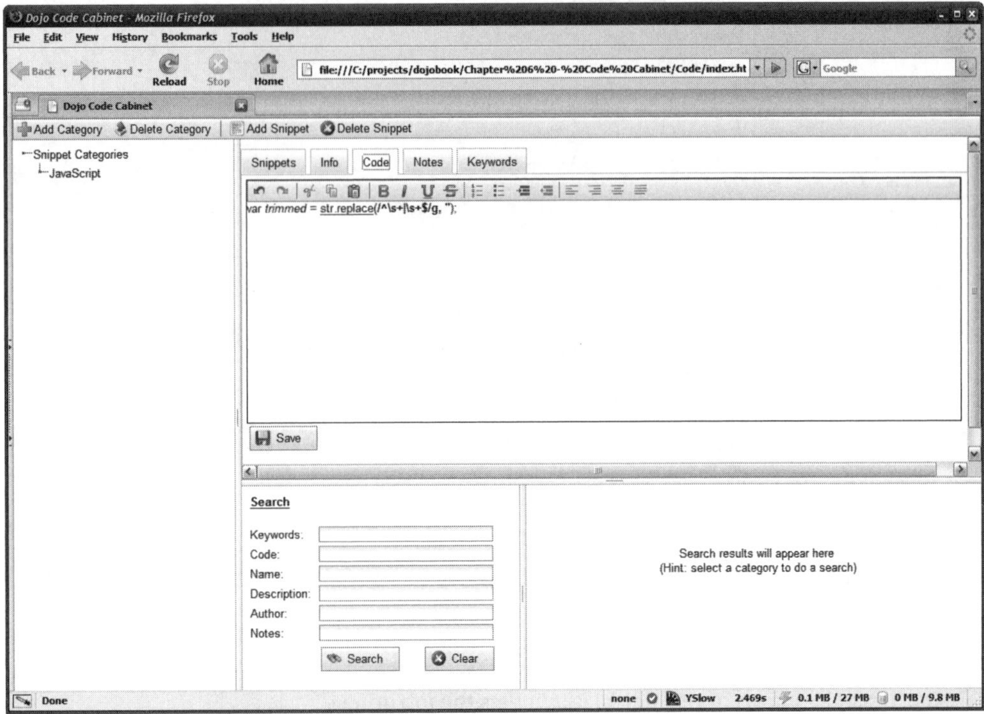

Figure 6-5. *The Code tab*

The interesting thing to note here is how I have some text underlined, some bold, and some italicized. This is a rich text editor, so we can do some basic syntax highlighting and such to give a little more meaning to the code.

The Notes tab looks essentially the same, so I'll skip showing that. It too has a rich text editor, which is nice, especially when you consider that you can create bullet lists and such, the type of thing that can come in handy when writing notes about a snippet.

The last tab is the Keywords tab, and Figure 6-6 shows you that.

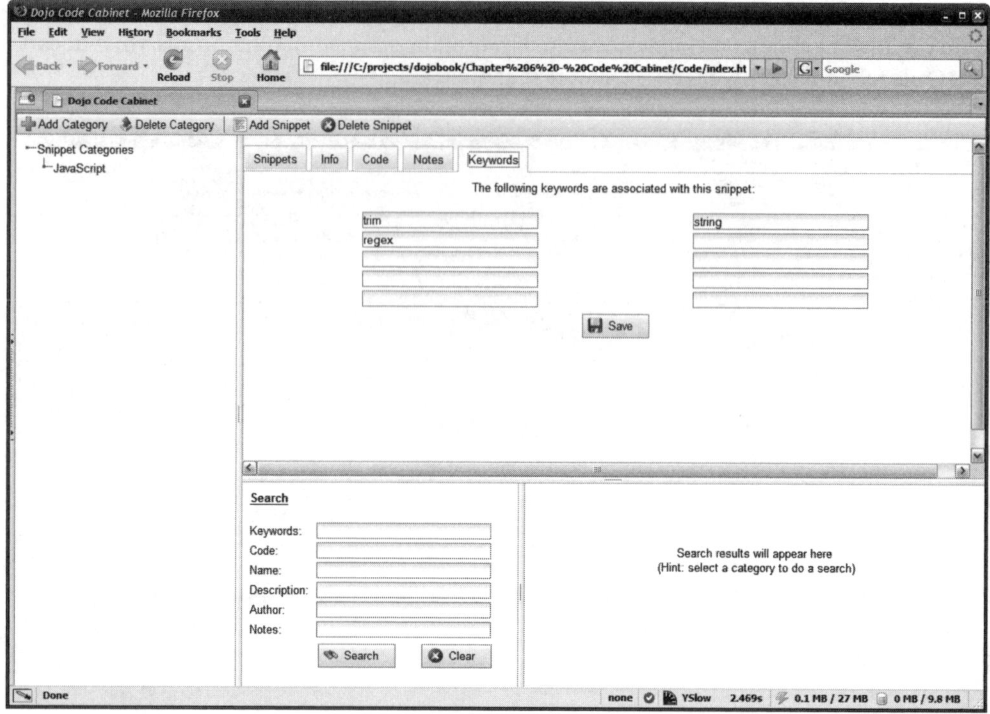

Figure 6-6. *The Keywords tab*

Yep, it's just a bunch of text fields! But, it gets the job done.

Note that the Save button you see on each tab saves everything at once; it doesn't apply just to the tab you're on. This arguably isn't the best UI paradigm, and at first I considered having a single Save button on the toolbar. But even with that little bit of doubt in mind, I still felt it was more natural to have a Save button on each tab. I don't claim it's the best answer, but it's the one I chose! The implication this, err, implies, is that if you make a change on one tab, and then switch to another tab and click Save, the changes on *all* tabs are saved. This might seem unnatural in some ways, but I don't think it's unreasonable.

There are a few more screenshots to be seen but I'll hold off and show them at later points as we discuss the code that they are involved with. Now, *finally*, we're ready for the code!

The Opening Shots

The `index.htm` file begins, as most HTML documents do, with a `<head>` section containing a bunch of resource imports. Take a look at the code and then we'll discuss it a bit:

```
<html>

  <head>

    <title>Dojo Code Cabinet</title>
```

```
<!-- Stylesheet imports. -->
<link rel="StyleSheet" type="text/css"
  href="js/dojo/dojo/resources/dojo.css">
<link rel="StyleSheet" type="text/css"
  href="js/dojo/dijit/themes/tundra/tundra.css">
<link rel="StyleSheet" type="text/css"
  href="js/dojo/dojox/grid/_grid/grid.css">
<link rel="StyleSheet" type="text/css" href="css/styles.css">

<!-- Import Google Gears. -->
<script src="js/gears_init.js"></script>

<!-- Configure and import Dojo. -->
<script type="text/javascript">
  var djConfig = {
    baseScriptUri : "js/dojo/",
    parseOnLoad : true
  };
</script>
<script type="text/javascript" src="js/dojo/dojo/dojo.js"></script>
<script>
  // Import all require Dojo components.
  dojo.require("dojo.parser");
  dojo.require("dijit.layout.ContentPane");
  dojo.require("dijit.layout.LayoutContainer");
  dojo.require("dijit.layout.SplitContainer");
  dojo.require("dijit.layout.TabContainer");
  dojo.require("dijit.Editor");
  dojo.require("dojo.data.ItemFileWriteStore");
  dojo.require("dijit.Tree");
  dojo.require("dijit.form.TextBox");
  dojo.require("dijit.form.Button");
  dojo.require("dojox.grid.Grid");
  dojo.require("dijit.Toolbar");
  dojo.require("dijit.Dialog");
  dojo.require("dojo.string");
</script>

<!-- Import application JavaScript. -->
<script type="text/javascript" src="js/CodeCabinet.js"></script>

<script>
  // Bootstrap initialization.
  dojo.addOnLoad(function() {
    codeCabinet.init();
  });
</script>
```

```
  </head>
  <body class="tundra">
```

First up are a bunch of style sheets, namely the base Dojo style sheet and the style sheet for the Tundra dijit theme. Then is `styles.css`, which is the style sheet specific to the application. We'll look at that shortly, and there are some interesting bits there, although it's not too large a file.

Following that is the first of a couple of `<script>` tags, this one importing `gears_init.js`. This is what enables us to work with Gears; specifically, it allows us to deal with the case where Gears isn't installed in the browser. When we hit the real scripting for this application in `CodeCabinet.js`, we'll come back to that in detail, but for now suffice it to say that this, plus some code on our part, allows the application to gracefully handle Gears not being present.

Next up is the `djConfig` structure, none of which is new at this point, so we won't dwell on it.

Following `djConfig` is a batch of `dojo.require()` statements. Most of them you've seen in previous chapters and are dijits, or Dijit-related. The `dojo.string` namespace is imported so we can use the `dojo.string.trim()` method. There is also one new item that you haven't seen before: `dojo.data.ItemFileWriteStore`. This is primarily what we need to use the `dojo.data` namespace and is the class that represents a data store. We need to use the *write* version because in all cases we need to read *and* write the data in the store.

Following that is the import of `CodeCabinet.js`, which is the main script content of the application. This is where all the interesting coding is, so we'll be tearing that apart in just a bit.

The final bit is the call to `dojo.addOnLoad()`. Recall that using `onLoad` in a Dojo application can often lead to problems and isn't something you should typically do. Especially in IE7 this can lead to an application, specifically using dijits, that just simply doesn't work. So, we use `dojo.addOnLoad()` to avoid those problems here. In this case, the function it executes is nothing but a call to the `init()` method of the `codeCabinet` object, which is an instance of the `CodeCabinet` class defined in `CodeCabinet.js`, which as I said we'll be getting to pretty soon.

A Dialog for Every Occasion

In this application are a number of pop-up dialog boxes, all implemented by using the Dialog dijit. This gives us a nice lightbox effect, and the dialog fading into view, all without lifting a finger. Each of the following dialogs is fairly similar, and requires just simple markup, as you can see here:

```
<!-- Add Category dialog. -->
<div dojoType="dijit.Dialog" id="AddCategoryDialog"
  title="Add Category" style="display:none;">
  Please enter the name of the category to add:
  <br><br>
  <input type="textbox" dojoType="dijit.form.TextBox"
    id="AddCategoryName">
  <button dojoType="dijit.form.Button"
    iconClass="icons iconAddCategory"
    onClick="codeCabinet.addCategory();">
    Add
  </button>
</div>
```

That's the dialog you see when you click the Add Category button. It looks like what you see in Figure 6-7.

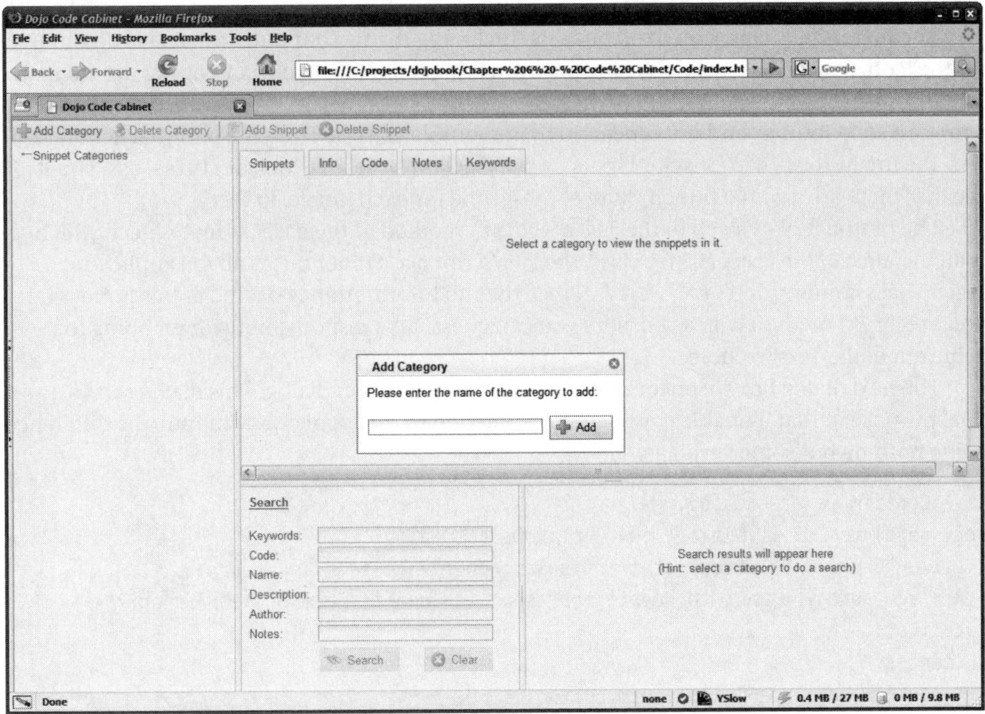

Figure 6-7. *The Add Category dialog box*

This is of course just simple markup, with the additional usage of TextBox and Button dijits rather than the standard HTML form elements. This keeps the UI theme consistent, and they frankly just look better if you ask me! Note that the `style` attribute has a setting of `display:none`, so that the dialog box is initially not visible, not until we tell the Dijit engine to show it.

One interesting bit is the `iconClass` attribute on the button. This is what puts the little green plus sign on the button. The style classes are applied here (two of them are being applied, in case you're unfamiliar with the syntax here):

```
.icons {
  background-repeat   : no-repeat;
  background-position : 0px;
  width               : 20px;
  height              : 18px;
  text-align          : center;
}
```

. . . and . . .

```
.iconAddCategory {
  background-image     : url("../img/icon_category_add.gif");
}
```

The first class is common to all buttons (including the toolbar buttons). It sets up the style for the icon, which is drawn on the button by making it the background image of the element. The second class is the actual icon to use. By splitting these two up, we can abstract out the common style settings and not repeat them in multiple classes. Then the part that actually differs, the image itself, can be set up in its own style class (when we look at `styles.css`, you'll see that there are a whole bunch more of these, one for each image, in fact).

The button makes a call to the `addCategory()` method of the `codeCabinet` object, which is an instance of the `CodeCabinet` class, the JavaScript class that houses all the application logic. That's coming, don't you worry! Notice that no information is passed at this point. The `addCategory()` method will, as I'm sure you can guess, take responsibility for grabbing the value out of the TextBox here.

The next dialog box we encounter is the Confirm Deletion dialog. This dialog serves a dual purpose in that it enables us to confirm deletion of a category or a snippet, the difference being nothing but some verbiage.

```
<!-- Confirm Delete dialog. -->
<div dojoType="dijit.Dialog" id="ConfirmDeleteDialog"
  title="Confirm Deletion" style="display:none;">
  Are you sure you want to delete the <span id="confirmDeleteType"></span>?
  <br><br>
  <center>
    <button dojoType="dijit.form.Button"
      onClick="codeCabinet.confirmDelete(true);">
      Yes
    </button>
        
    <button dojoType="dijit.form.Button"
      onClick="codeCabinet.confirmDelete(false);">
      No
    </button>
  </center>
</div>
```

The `confirmDeleteType` `<div>` is populated with the word *snippet* or *category* as appropriate, and you'll see the code that does that later. When the Yes button is clicked, a call is made to the `confirmDelete()` method of the `codeCabinet` object, passing it a value of `true`. Similarly, when No is clicked, that same method is called but `false` is passed in that case. The code is smart enough to know what's being deleted and act accordingly, as you'll see.

Next is a dialog that appears if, when adding a category, the name you enter is already in use:

```
<!-- Duplicate Category dialog. -->
<div dojoType="dijit.Dialog" id="DuplicateCategoryDialog"
  title="Duplicate Category" style="display:none;">
  A category with that name already exists.
  <br><br>
  <center>
    <button dojoType="dijit.form.Button"
      onClick="dijit.byId('DuplicateCategoryDialog').hide();">
      Ok
    </button>
  </center>
</div>
```

This is purely an informational dialog, so there are no entry fields or decision buttons, just a single OK button. When clicked, it hides the dialog by asking the Dijit engine for a reference to the dialog and then calling the `hide()` method. We get that reference by calling `dijit.byId()`, passing the ID of the dijit we want a reference to. This is just like `dojo.byId()`, which gets a reference to a DOM node, but is specific to dijits.

The next dialog is the one you'll see if Gears isn't available, whether that means it isn't installed or is simply deactivated:

```
<!-- No Gears dialog. -->
<div dojoType="dijit.Dialog" id="NoGearsDialog"
  title="No Gears" style="display:none;">
  Google Gears does not appear to be installed.<br><br>
  Please go <a href="http://gears.google.com/➥
?action=install&message=Google Gears for Dojo Code Cabinet installation">HERE</a>
  to install it, then reload this application.<br><br>
  You can still use this application, but data <b>WILL NOT</b>
  be saved between browser sessions!
  <br><br>
  <center>
    <button dojoType="dijit.form.Button"
      onClick="dijit.byId('NoGearsDialog').hide();">
      Ok
    </button>
  </center>
</div>
```

This dialog appears as shown in Figure 6-8.

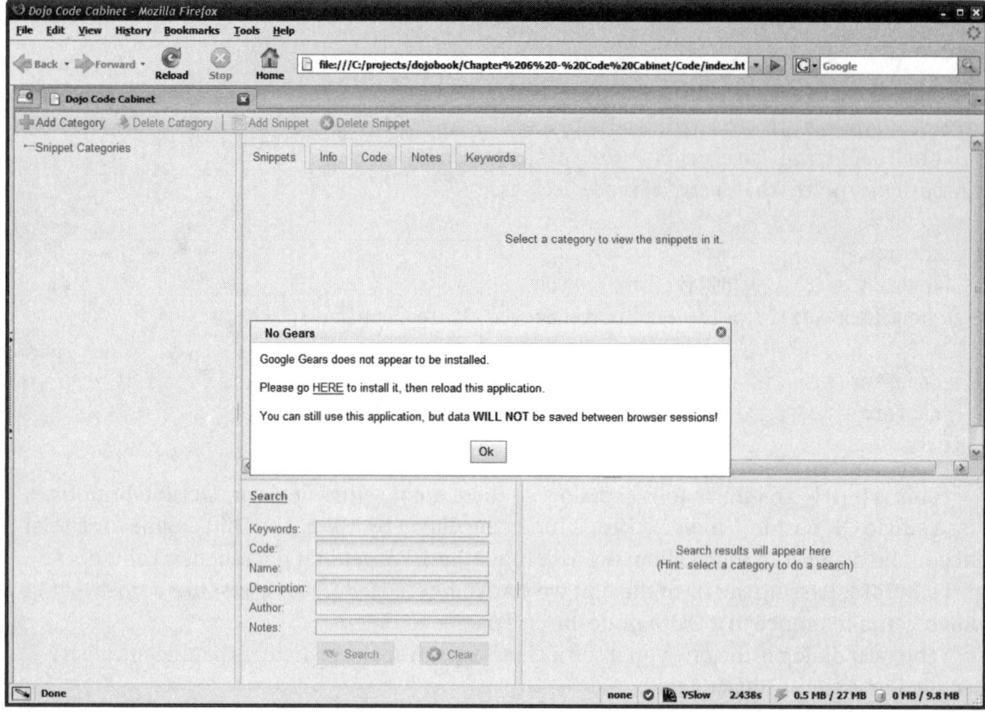

Figure 6-8. *The No Gears dialog box*

This is another information-only dialog, more or less, but it does have a link you can click. When you click it, you are transported to the Gears web page, which guides you through installing Gears. Other than that, it's just like the dialog seen when you try to add a category with a name that already exists, in that it's purely informational in nature.

The final dialog is one you'll see if you enter invalid search criteria, that is, if you forget to enter anything before you click the Search button:

```
<!-- Bad Search Criteria dialog. -->
<div dojoType="dijit.Dialog" id="BadSearchCriteriaDialog"
  title="Bad Search Criteria" style="display:none;">
  To perform a search you must specify at least one search criteria.
  <br><br>
  <center>
    <button dojoType="dijit.form.Button"
      onClick="dijit.byId('BadSearchCriteriaDialog').hide();">
      Ok
    </button>
  </center>
</div>
```

It's another simple informational dialog, much like you've seen a bunch of times already, so I won't go into it here.

We'll just move on to some new material: the beginning of the markup that makes up the application as you see it, not counting the dialogs of course. This includes the beginning of our layout container, and the construction of the toolbar along the top:

```
<!-- Main layout container. -->
<div dojoType="dijit.layout.LayoutContainer" id="mainDiv">

<!-- Toolbar. -->
<div dojoType="dijit.layout.ContentPane" layoutAlign="top"
  class="cssToolbar">
  <div dojoType="dijit.Toolbar">
    <div dojoType="dijit.form.Button"
      iconClass="icons iconAddCategory"
      onClick="codeCabinet.addCategoryClicked();"
      showLabel="true">Add Category</div>
    <div dojoType="dijit.form.Button" id="toolbarDeleteCategory"
      iconClass="icons iconDeleteCategory"
      onClick="codeCabinet.deleteCategoryClicked();"
      showLabel="true" disabled="true">Delete Category</div>
    <span dojoType="dijit.ToolbarSeparator"></span>
    <div dojoType="dijit.form.Button" id="toolbarAddSnippet"
      iconClass="icons iconAddSnippet"
      onClick="codeCabinet.addSnippetClicked();"
      showLabel="true" disabled="true">Add Snippet</div>
    <div dojoType="dijit.form.Button" id="toolbarDeleteSnippet"
      iconClass="icons iconDeleteSnippet"
      onClick="codeCabinet.deleteSnippetClicked();"
      showLabel="true" disabled="true">Delete Snippet</div>
  </div>
</div>
```

First we have the beginning of our layout, the LayoutContainer dijit. This is going to enable us to have a border-type layout, meaning we can define some ContentPane elements as children of it and tell the LayoutContainer to display each on the top, left, right, or bottom. Then, we see this in use on the very next tag: the ContentPane that will contain our Toolbar. The `layoutAlign` attribute declares that this ContentPane should be displayed at the top of the LayoutContainer, running entirely across it horizontally.

The Toolbar itself is easy to define: you nest a series of Button dijits within it and you get a toolbar! Each Button uses the `iconClass` attribute to put images on them, and the styles for these attributes have been discussed already. The content of the tag itself is the text label of the Button. The `showLabel` attribute is set to `true` in order for the text to appear. Each button has an `onClick` event handler defined, which simply calls the appropriate method of the `codeCabinet` object that we'll get to after we're done with `index.htm`.

You can also see usage of the Separator dijit, which gives us a vertical line dividing the buttons dealing with categories from the buttons dealing with snippets.

The Main Content

The main content, simply put, is everything below the toolbar. At the highest level, we have two sides: the left, where the tree of categories lives, and the right, where the snippet information tabs and the search UI parts are. If you played with the application, you may have noticed that you can resize the left and right all you like by dragging the sizer bar around (and likewise between the tabbed area and the search area). This is accomplished by means of the SplitContainer dijit, which is created like this:

```
<!-- Main content. -->
<div dojoType="dijit.layout.SplitContainer" persist="true"
  orientation="horizontal" sizerWidth="8" activeSizing="true"
  layoutAlign="client">
```

The `persist` attribute is a really neat thing. Basically, when set to `true`, it tells Dojo to remember, via a cookie, the split location. In other words, if you resize the tree area, the size you choose will persist between browser sessions, for the life of that cookie at least. That's a really nifty feature to have available just by setting one lousy little attribute!

The `orientation` attribute tells the dijit whether the split runs vertically or horizontally. In the `horizontal` orientation, as this one is, the sections of the container run across the screen. We'll see another SplitContainer later, the one the tabs and the search UI live in, that is split vertically.

The `sizerWidth` attribute tells the SplitContainer how wide, in pixels, the bar you drag around should be. A value of 8 seemed not too small and not too wide, so I think Little Red Riding Hood would approve.

The `activeSizing` attribute tells the container to resize its contents as you drag the sizer bar. When set to `false`, the container won't resize until you release the mouse button. How you set this will depend on the contents. In some cases, your UI may not look right or possibly even work quite right when sized actively, but in this application neither is a concern, so active sizing it is.

Finally, the `layoutAlign` attribute has more to do with the parent LayoutContainer than the SplitContainer in a sense. It is saying here that this SplitContainer should fill all the remaining space of the parent container, the LayoutContainer. This is exactly what we want when you think about it: the Toolbar takes up 24 pixels at the top of the browser window, and this SplitContainer, which is going to contain the tree, the tabs, and everything else, should take up the rest, hence `layoutAlign` set to `client`.

Defining the Tree

Next up is the category Tree. Even before that, though, is the fact that the Tree itself is contained within a ContentPane dijit:

```
<!-- Category tree. -->
<div dojoType="dijit.layout.ContentPane"
  class="cssContentPane" sizeShare="3">
  <div dojoType="dijit.Tree" store="codeCabinet.categoriesStore"
    labelAttr="label" label="Snippet Categories">
    <script type="dojo/method" event="onClick" args="item">
      codeCabinet.categoryClicked(item);
```

```
    </script>
  </div>
</div>
```

This is where you get some exercise in visualization! Imagine the browser window and try to picture the layout we have so far. We have a LayoutContainer. A LayoutContainer has some number of other layout components within it, arranged with a border style. So, to start, we have a Toolbar on the top border. Below that is a SplitContainer, which is a type of layout container dijit, so it fits the bill nicely. A SplitContainer lays out some number of other container dijits either vertical or horizontally. This one lays them out horizontally. So, in the preceding snippet we have another container dijit, a ContentPane specifically. That means that the next container dijit we add will simply sit next to this one, going left to right across the screen.

Do you have that layout hierarchy in your head so far? Good!

So, this ContentPane now is where our Tree dijit will be. But first we should talk about the `sizeShare` attribute on the ContentPane itself. In simplest terms, this is the percentage of the SplitContainer that this ContentPane will take up. But, there is no specific unit for this value, so really what you're dealing with is a ratio. In other words, two ContentPanes, one with a `sizeShare` of `4` and the other with `6`, will wind up occupying the same amount of space, relative to each other, as if you used values of `40` and `60` because the ratio of 4 to 6 is the same as 40 to 60. So, if you're right now guessing there's another ContentPane after this one with a `sizeShare` value of `7`, you'd be right, which means you got it!

The Tree itself is a simple instantiation, except for the new `store` attribute that we talked about briefly earlier. The data store that this Tree uses is an instance variable of the `CodeCabinet` class. The `labelAttr` tells us which attribute of the `Item` from the data store provides the label to be displayed in the Tree.

This is the first time you're seeing the `<script>` tag usage on a dijit, though. It's pretty simple: all dijits have events that you can react to, be they user-triggered, as is the case here, or more lifecycle-type events. In either case, you can have a `<script>` tag nested inside the `<div>` that the dijit is created from to handle these events. The `type` attribute should be set to `dojo/method` in this case, and then the `event` attribute names the event you wish to handle, `onClick` in this case. The `args` attribute tells us the name of the argument(s) that will be passed into the code you write here, and the exact meaning is dependent on the event.

In this case, for example, the `onClick` event results in an `Item` object from the data store being available. By setting `args` to the value `item`, we make a variable named `item` available to the code within the `<script>` tag, which in this case we simply pass along to the `categoryClicked()` method of the `codeCabinet` object. You'll see this event code paradigm a few more times, but this is the basic idea behind it in all cases.

Splitting the Difference: SplitContainer

Now we're inside the ContentPane that houses all the content to the right of the Tree, which means the tabs and the search components. These two sections again use the resizable split paradigm, which means another SplitContainer:

```
<!-- Content/search split container. -->
<div dojoType="dijit.layout.SplitContainer" persist="true"
  orientation="vertical" sizerWidth="8" activeSizing="true"
  sizeShare="7">
```

```
<!-- Content. -->
<div dojoType="dijit.layout.ContentPane" style="padding-top:5px;"
  sizeShare="6">
```

As I hinted at earlier, this one lays out its children vertically, and the `sizeShare` is set to 7, giving us a 30/70 split between the ContentPane the Tree is in and the SplitContainer everything else is in. The actual content, which really means the tabbed section, is in a ContentPane as well.

■ **Note** Interestingly, I could have simply had the tabs themselves in place of the ContentPane because a TabContainer is a type of container dijit too. However, I found that I couldn't quite get the padding to work as I wanted: the tabs themselves bumped up against the toolbar and the sizer bar between them and the tree area, which I just didn't think looked as good. By housing the TabContainer inside this TabContainer, I was able to apply the `cssContentPane` style class to it and get that padding. I thought it was worth pointing out the reason I took the approach I did and letting you know it would have been possible to do it the other way too (aside from the padding issue, that is).

How the Tabs Are Defined

The tabs themselves are nothing but a TabContainer dijit:

```
<!-- Tabs. -->
<div dojoType="dijit.layout.TabContainer" id="tabs">
```

Each tab has a bit of markup to create it. I'm going to go through these relatively quickly because they are for the most part simple HTML, and they all are kind of similar in many ways. But I'll point out the interesting bits for sure as we go.

■ **Note** Not all of the dijits are assigned IDs, but the tabs are. This is because in order to interact with the tabs later, which is something we'll need to do, it has to be possible to get a reference to them. Because we aren't creating these programmatically, in which case we could just hold on to the reference we get when a tab is created, we have to have a way to request a reference to them, and an ID allows that, just as an ID on a DOM node does.

The Snippets tab is up first:

```
<!-- Snippets list tab. -->
<div dojoType="dijit.layout.ContentPane" title="Snippets"
  class="cssContentPane" id="tabSnippets">
  <div id="snippetsGrid" dojoType="dojox.Grid"
    structure="codeCabinet.gridLayout"
```

```
    class="cssSnippetsGrid">
    <script type="dojo/method" event="onRowClick" args="e">
      codeCabinet.snippetClicked(e.rowIndex);
    </script>
  </div>
  <div id="noSnippetsInCategory" style="display:none;">
    <center>
      <br><br><br><br>
      This category currently has no snippets in it.
    </center>
  </div>
  <div id="noCategorySelected">
    <center>
      <br><br><br><br>
      Select a category to view the snippets in it.
    </center>
  </div>
</div>
```

The content for each tab within the TabContainer is contained within a ContentPane. This one is assigned an ID because we'll need to be able to flip to it programmatically, so we'll need to be able to get a reference to it, which means it has to have an ID. (There are probably other ways, such as iterating over the children of the TabContainer looking for the one we want, but that sounds dangerously like effort to me!)

Within the ContentPane is a `<div>` with a `dojoType` of `dojox.Grid`, so this will become our grid where the snippets in the current category are listed. The grid is told what columns it has by assigning a structure to it with the `structure` attribute. Here, it's referencing the `gridLayout` field of the `codeCabinet` object, and you'll see what that's all about shortly.

Note that initially the grid is visible, but it will be immediately hidden when the application starts up. This is important because if you look down, you'll see two other `<div>`s, each with a simple message as its content, and initially only the last one will be visible (because the grid, and the `<div>` with the ID `noSnippetsInCategory`, has its `display` style attribute set to `none`). That's how the two messages are shown instead of the grid, or the grid is shown instead of either of the messages: by manipulating which of the three has a `display` value other than `none`. Unfortunately, in IE7, if the grid is hidden initially via a style setting, the grid itself doesn't work after that point. I'm frankly not sure why that is; in Firefox it works fine that way, so chalk it up to an IE peculiarity (it's not as if it's the first one)!

You can again see how the event handler code is attached to the grid. This is to handle clicking of a snippet in the grid. The `args` value of `e` is an event object specific to the grid, which conveys some information about the state of the grid at the time the event fires. For this case, we care only about the `rowIndex` value, which is the number of the row (0-based) that was clicked. We'll need this in the `snippetClicked()` method to relate it back to the data store for the grid.

Speaking of which, note that the grid is not initially bound to a data store. This binding will be done dynamically when a category is clicked, but that's coming soon to a theater near you!

For Your Information: The Info Tab

The Info tab's markup is pretty straightforward, and here it is:

```
<!-- Info tab. -->
<div dojoType="dijit.layout.ContentPane" title="Info"
  class="cssContentPane" id="tabInfo">
  <form id="infoForm">
    <table border="0" cellpadding="0" cellspacing="4">
      <tr>
        <td nowrap>Snippet Name: </td>
        <td nowrap>
          <input type="textbox" dojoType="dijit.form.TextBox"
            id="infoName">
        </td>
      </td>
      <tr>
        <td nowrap>Description </td>
        <td nowrap>
          <input type="textbox" dojoType="dijit.form.TextBox"
            id="infoDescription">
        </td>
      </tr>
      <tr>
        <td nowrap>Author: </td>
        <td nowrap>
          <input type="textbox" dojoType="dijit.form.TextBox"
            id="infoAuthor">
        </td>
      </tr>
      <tr>
        <td nowrap>eMail </td>
        <td nowrap>
          <input type="textbox" dojoType="dijit.form.TextBox"
            id="infoEMail">
        </td>
      </tr>
      <tr>
        <td nowrap>Web Link </td>
        <td nowrap>
          <input type="textbox" dojoType="dijit.form.TextBox"
            id="infoWebLink">
        </td>
      </tr>
      <tr>
        <td nowrap> </td>
        <td nowrap>
          <button dojoType="dijit.form.Button" id="btnInfoSave"
```

```
            iconClass="icons iconSave" disabled="true"
            onClick="codeCabinet.saveSnippet();">
            Save
          </button>
        </td>
      </tr>
    </table>
  </form>
</div>
```

It's just another ContentPane, with a `<table>` in it. Within the table are a bunch of text labels next to TextBox dijits. Each TextBox has an ID so that we can reference them when the Save button is clicked, which you can see calls the `saveSnippet()` method of the `codeCabinet` object. Nothing needs to be passed. The method takes care of getting all the field values, so that's really all there is to it.

For Code Monkeys: The Code Tab

The Code tab is also very simple (this is a common theme for all of the tabs, frankly, but that's the beauty of Dijit: it saves you from having to write a bunch of complex code or markup):

```
<!-- Code tab. -->
<div dojoType="dijit.layout.ContentPane" title="Code"
  class="cssContentPane">
  <form id="codeForm">
    <div class="cssEditor">
      <textarea dojoType="dijit.Editor"
        width="100%" height="90%" id="codeArea"></textarea>
    </div>
    <button dojoType="dijit.form.Button" id="btnCodeSave"
      iconClass="icons iconSave" disabled="true"
      onClick="codeCabinet.saveSnippet();">
      Save
    </button>
  </form>
</div>
```

Another ContentPane, this time with a `<textarea>` in it that will be turned into an Editor dijit by virtue of its `dojoType` setting of `dijit.Editor`. This gives us a nice rich-text editor for entering code, so we can do some highlighting, listing, aligning, all that good stuff. A simple Button is again present for saving, and it calls the same method as every other Save button does, so I may well not mention it after this!

I Never Took Notes in School: The Notes Tab

For the sake of completeness, I'll show the code for the Notes tab here, but it is essentially identical to the Code tab, aside from some different IDs and such:

```
<!-- Notes tab. -->
<div dojoType="dijit.layout.ContentPane" title="Notes"
  class="cssContentPane">
  <form id="notesForm">
    <div class="cssEditor">
      <textarea dojoType="dijit.Editor"
        width="100%" height="90%" id="notesArea"></textarea>
    </div>
    <button dojoType="dijit.form.Button" id="btnNotesSave"
      iconClass="icons iconSave" disabled="true"
      onClick="codeCabinet.saveSnippet();">
      Save
    </button>
  </form>
</div>
```

One thing worth noting that I haven't mentioned before, though, is that all of these tabs have their fields enclosed in a `<form>` element. That's so I can call `reset()` on that form later to blank out all the fields. The dijits react properly to that method call, so it's a simple way to reset all the fields when entering a new code snippet.

The Keywords Tab

The Keywords tab is a pretty repetitive piece of HTML, as you can see for yourself:

```
<!-- Keywords tab. -->
<div dojoType="dijit.layout.ContentPane" title="Keywords"
  class="cssContentPane">
  <form id="keywordsForm">
    <table border="0" cellpadding="0" cellspacing="4"
      width="90%" align="center">
      <tr><td colspan="2" align="center">
        The following keywords are associated with this snippet:
        <br><br>
      </td></tr>
      <tr>
        <td align="center">
          <input type="textbox" dojoType="dijit.form.TextBox"
            id="keyword0">
        </td>
        <td align="center">
          <input type="textbox" dojoType="dijit.form.TextBox"
            id="keyword1">
        </td>
      </tr>
      <tr>
        <td align="center">
          <input type="textbox" dojoType="dijit.form.TextBox"
```

```
            id="keyword2">
        </td>
        <td align="center">
          <input type="textbox" dojoType="dijit.form.TextBox"
            id="keyword3">
        </td>
      </tr>
      <tr>
        <td align="center">
          <input type="textbox" dojoType="dijit.form.TextBox"
            id="keyword4">
        </td>
        <td align="center">
          <input type="textbox" dojoType="dijit.form.TextBox"
            id="keyword5">
        </td>
      </tr>
      <tr>
        <td align="center">
          <input type="textbox" dojoType="dijit.form.TextBox"
            id="keyword6">
        </td>
        <td align="center">
          <input type="textbox" dojoType="dijit.form.TextBox"
            id="keyword7">
        </td>
      </tr>
      <tr>
        <td align="center">
          <input type="textbox" dojoType="dijit.form.TextBox"
            id="keyword8">
        </td>
        <td align="center">
          <input type="textbox" dojoType="dijit.form.TextBox"
            id="keyword9">
        </td>
      </tr>
      <tr><td colspan="2" align="center">
        <button dojoType="dijit.form.Button" id="btnKeywordsSave"
          iconClass="icons iconSave" disabled="true"
          onClick="codeCabinet.saveSnippet();">
          Save
        </button>
      </td></tr>
    </table>
  </form>
</div>
```

It's also not very interesting from the standpoint of understanding it here. It's just some TextBox dijits, one for each of the ten keywords we allow to be associated with a snippet, plus the ubiquitous Save button at the bottom. There are probably different, and maybe even better, ways of implementing these keywords in terms of UI design, but I felt this got the job done just fine. I figured ten keywords should be sufficient for nearly any situation, but hey, if you think more would be better, please do feel free to expand the UI and make it more dynamic (maybe a button to add a new keywords field, enabling you to therefore have an unlimited number of keywords?).

The Search Markup

We're nearly done with index.htm now. Only one big chunk of markup remains, and that's the search-related markup:

```
<!-- Search. -->
<div dojoType="dijit.layout.ContentPane" sizeShare="6">

  <div dojoType="dijit.layout.SplitContainer" persist="true"
    orientation="horizontal" sizerWidth="8" activeSizing="true"
    layoutAlign="client">

    <!-- Search form. -->
    <div dojoType="dijit.layout.ContentPane"
      class="cssContentPane" sizeShare="6">
      <form id="searchForm">
        <table border="0" cellpadding="0" cellspacing="4">
          <tr><td colspan="2" nowrap>
            <b><u>Search</u><b>
            <br><br>
          </td></tr>
          <tr>
            <td nowrap>Keywords: </td>
            <td nowrap>
              <input type="textbox" dojoType="dijit.form.TextBox"
                id="searchKeywords" disabled="true">
            </td>
          </td>
          <tr>
            <td nowrap>Code: </td>
            <td nowrap>
              <input type="textbox" dojoType="dijit.form.TextBox"
                id="searchCode" disabled="true">
            </td>
          </tr>
          <tr>
            <td nowrap>Name: </td>
            <td nowrap>
              <input type="textbox" dojoType="dijit.form.TextBox"
```

```
          id="searchName" disabled="true">
      </td>
    </tr>
    <tr>
      <td nowrap>Description: </td>
      <td nowrap>
        <input type="textbox" dojoType="dijit.form.TextBox"
          id="searchDescription" disabled="true">
      </td>
    </tr>
    <tr>
      <td nowrap>Author: </td>
      <td nowrap>
        <input type="textbox" dojoType="dijit.form.TextBox"
          id="searchAuthor" disabled="true">
      </td>
    </tr>
    <tr>
      <td nowrap>Notes: </td>
      <td nowrap>
        <input type="textbox" dojoType="dijit.form.TextBox"
          id="searchNotes" disabled="true">
      </td>
    </tr>
    <tr>
      <td nowrap> </td>
      <td nowrap>
        <button dojoType="dijit.form.Button" disabled="true"
          iconClass="icons iconSearch" id="btnSearch"
          onClick="codeCabinet.searchClicked();">
          Search
        </button>
            
        <button dojoType="dijit.form.Button" disabled="true"
          iconClass="icons iconDeleteSnippet" id="btnClear"
          onClick="codeCabinet.searchClearClicked();">
          Clear
        </button>
      </td>
    </tr>
  </table>
</form>
</div>

<!-- Search results. -->
<div dojoType="dijit.layout.ContentPane" class="cssContentPane"
  sizeShare="4">
```

```
        <div id="searchGrid" dojoType="dojox.Grid"
          structure="codeCabinet.gridLayout">
          <script type="dojo/method" event="onRowClick" args="e">
            codeCabinet.searchResultClicked(e.rowIndex);
          </script>
        </div>
        <div id="searchResultsMessage">
          <center>
            <br><br><br><br>
            Search results will appear here
            <br>
            (Hint: select a category to do a search)
          </center>
        </div>
        <div id="searchNoResults" style="display:none;">
          <center>
            <br><br><br><br>
            No snippets were founding matching your search criteria
          </center>
        </div>
      </div>

    </div>

  </div>
```

We start with a ContentPane with a `sizeShare` value of 6. This is the left side of the SplitContainer that contains all the search-related stuff. This way, the user can choose to expand the area containing the search results, but by default it starts with 40 percent of the SplitContainer.

Next is a ContentPane that contains the actual search criteria form. This is pretty straightforward stuff now, especially given our look at the Info tab, so I will leave it to you to look it over. Note that the `disabled` attribute is set to `true` initially for all the fields. This is because they become active only after a category is selected, since searches are constrained to a single category. (And if you think that sounds like an opportunity for a suggested exercise, give yourself a cigar!)

The second ContentPane contains the search results grid. It looks an awful lot like the snippets grid we saw earlier. The same sort of event handler code is also present, but the call this time goes to `codeCabinet.searchResultsClicked()`. There are again two additional `<div>`s that contain simple messages: one seen initially when no search has been performed, and the other shown when a search is done that finds no matching snippets. They are hidden and shown by manipulating the `display` style attribute, just like those we saw on the Snippets tab earlier.

With the markup fully examined at this point, let's have a quick look at the style sheet for this application and then dive right into the real code behind this thing.

Writing styles.css

The `styles.css` file is the style sheet for the application. The meat of it, the styles that deal with the button icons, was already discussed. There's not a whole lot more in it, frankly, but let's have a look just the same, in Listing 6-1.

Listing 6-1. *styles.css, the Main Style Sheet for the Application*

```
/* Size main DIV to take up the whole browser viewport. */
html, body, #mainDiv {
  width                 : 100%;
  height                : 100%;
  border                : 0;
  padding               : 0;
  margin                : 0;
  font-size             : 10pt;
}

/* Styles for toolbar icons. */
.icons {
  background-repeat   : no-repeat;
  background-position : 0px;
  width               : 20px;
  height              : 18px;
  text-align          : center;
}
.iconAddCategory {
  background-image    : url("../img/icon_category_add.gif");
}
.iconRenameCategory {
  background-image    : url("../img/icon_category_rename.gif");
}
.iconDeleteCategory {
  background-image    : url("../img/icon_category_delete.gif");
}
.iconAddSnippet {
  background-image    : url("../img/icon_snippet_add.gif");
}
.iconDeleteSnippet {
  background-image    : url("../img/icon_snippet_delete.gif");
}
.iconSearch {
  background-image    : url("../img/icon_search.gif");
}
.iconSave {
  background-image    : url("../img/icon_save.gif");
}
```

```
/* Styles for the content panes within the layout. */
.cssContentPane {
  padding-top          : 5px;
  padding-left         : 5px;
}

/* Style for the toolbar container. */
.cssToolbar {
  height               : 24px;
}

/* Style for the snippets grid. */
.cssSnippetsGrid {
  width                : 97%;
  height               : 90%;
  border               : 1px solid #000000;
}

/* Style for the code and notes editor. */
.cssEditor {
  border               : 1px solid #000000;
  width                : 97%;
  height               : 80%;
  overflow             : hidden;
}

/* Style for the search results grid. */
.cssSearchGrid {
  width                : 98%;
  height               : 96%;
  border               : 1px solid #000000;
}
```

The first bit of code sets the same style on the `<html>` and `<body>` tags, as well as the `mainDiv` element. This code is responsible for ensuring that the UI takes up the entire area available in the browser, removes all padding and margin space, and sets a default font size across the entire UI.

After that are the styles for the toolbar buttons and buttons throughout the UI. Once again, I think this has been explained well enough already, but note that there are a number of styles, one for each button in fact, with a different icon image for each. That's all there is to it: just apply the correct style class, plus the icon class for all of them, and you get a nice picture on the buttons. Pretty sweet, actually!

After that is the `cssContentPane` class, which is applied to nearly all the ContentPane dijits. This class ensures that there is some padding space at the top and on the left. This is apparent when you look at the UI on all the tabs. If this class wasn't present, text would bump right up against the tabs, and right up on the left of the screen and on the divider between the tree and tabs, which just plain doesn't look very good. This style class takes care of that.

The `cssToolbar` class is used simply to set the proper height on the ContentPane containing the toolbar.

The `cssSnippetsGrid` class is applied to the grid where the snippets in a category are listed. I wanted the grid to take up most of the space available to it and to resize when the window was resized, so percentage-based values just slightly below 100 percent in each direction were the answer. I simply eyed up what seemed to look pretty good to me; there's no fancy theory behind it! Note too that the grid by default doesn't have a border, so I apply one with this style. The `cssSearchGrid` class is almost identical, just with some slightly different percentage values, again pretty much arbitrary, and that class is of course applied to the search results grid on the bottom.

Finally, the `cssEditor` class is applied to both the code and notes editors. As with the grid, I felt these editors looked better with a border around them, so there is one applied there. I also found that I had to set `overflow` to `hidden` to get things to display properly. Otherwise, the editor wound up flowing down *over* the Save button, making it unclickable.

That's the style sheet in its entirety. Nothing too unusual, I dare say. Now we move into the JavaScript of the application, where all the really fun stuff is, in my opinion!

Writing CodeCabinet.js

Note that in some cases I discuss this code in an order different from its actual physical location in the code. This makes it possible to discuss some parts of the code in relation to other parts in a way that will make sense, even though those code segments aren't necessarily adjacent.

The `CodeCabinet.js` file contains, unsurprisingly, the `CodeCabinet` class, which is where all the magic happens. It's where all the client-side coding lives (aside from the event handler script in `index.htm` of course, and the little bit of bootstrap code early on). A single instance of the class, a reference to which is stored in the global `codeCabinet` variable, is created after the class definition. The class diagram for `CodeCabinet` is shown in Figure 6-9.

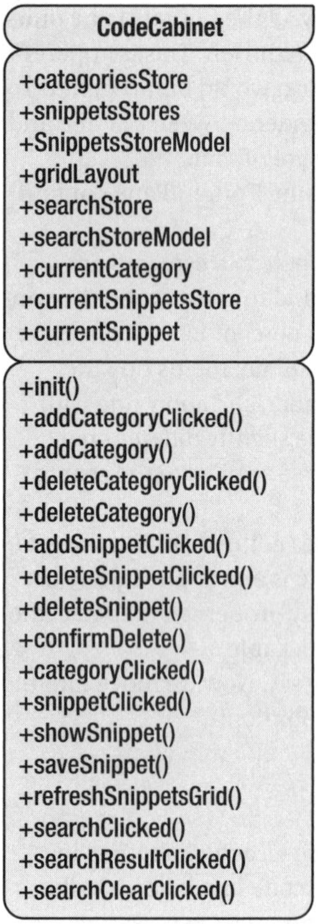

CodeCabinet

+categoriesStore
+snippetsStores
+SnippetsStoreModel
+gridLayout
+searchStore
+searchStoreModel
+currentCategory
+currentSnippetsStore
+currentSnippet

+init()
+addCategoryClicked()
+addCategory()
+deleteCategoryClicked()
+deleteCategory()
+addSnippetClicked()
+deleteSnippetClicked()
+deleteSnippet()
+confirmDelete()
+categoryClicked()
+snippetClicked()
+showSnippet()
+saveSnippet()
+refreshSnippetsGrid()
+searchClicked()
+searchResultClicked()
+searchClearClicked()

Figure 6-9. *UML class diagram of CodeCabinet class*

When we look at the code, we see that there are a bunch of instance fields at the top:

```
/**
 * The main class that is the core code of the application.
 */
function CodeCabinet() {

  /**
   * Declare a custom store for categories so we can implement save.
   */
  dojo.declare("CustomCategoriesItemFileWriteStore",
    dojo.data.ItemFileWriteStore, {
      _saveCustom: function(saveCompleteCallback, saveFailedCallback) {

        // Abort if Gears isn't installed.
        if (!window.google || !google.gears) {
          saveCompleteCallback();
```

```
          return;
        }

        // Gears is available, persist categories.  Do this by iterating over
        // the array of items in this store and inserting each into the
        // Gears database.  Note that this always starts with deleting all
        // categories, so if this store is empty, we're good to go then.
        // While this isn't efficient, it does make it easy: no worries about
        // what got added, modified or deleted, it's just all written fresh.
        var db = google.gears.factory.create("beta.database");
        db.open("DojoCodeCabinet");
        db.execute("DELETE FROM categories");
        var items = this._getItemsArray();
        if (items.length > 0) {
          for (var i = 0; i < items.length; i++) {
            db.execute("INSERT INTO categories VALUES (?, ?, ?)", [
              items[i].id, items[i].name, items[i].type
            ]);
          }
        }

        saveCompleteCallback();

      }
    }
  );
```

The first instance field is a custom data store called `CustomCategoriesItemFileWriteStore`. Recall that `ItemFileWriteStore` is a data store that allows modifications to its data. Also recall that saving data isn't something the existing data stores do for you by default; you have to provide that mechanism. The way you do that is to extend `ItemFileWriteStore`, and the way you extend `ItemFileWriteStore` is to use the `dojo.declare()` function.

As part of that function call, we need to override the `_saveCustom` method, which is what the store will call when we call the `save()` method. This gives us a hook into the store, to be able to implement our save however we wish.

In this case, we're working with Gears. So, the first thing we need to do is ensure that Gears is available. We deal with this in the `init()` method, but recall that the dialog box said the application should still work even without Gears; there just won't be a way to persist data. That's exactly what the first `if` check does. If Gears isn't defined, this method is essentially complete, save for one small task: we need to call `saveCompleteCallback()`, a method of the `ItemFileWriteStore`, in order for the lifecycle of the `save()` call to be completed properly. But most important, we're not doing a thing with Gears at this point. So in other words, the rest of the application works exactly as it always does, but when `save()` is called and Gears is not available, the application simply doesn't save the data. Everything else works as usual, though, so in effect the application works without Gears, just as the dialog promised it would!

Now, assuming Gears is available, we have to persist the categories, being as this is a custom `ItemFileWriteStore` for the categories. I took the simplest possible approach here and decided that anytime a save is done, I will simply delete all the categories and save them all again. This is also done for the snippets. This is in no way, shape, or form the best approach! It's of course inefficient. However, it's also about the easiest way to implement things, and I like simplicity whenever it's possible.

As you can see, we execute a SQL delete query and then call this.`_getItemsArray()` to get the array of `Items` in the data store. We then iterate over that array and execute a SQL insert query for each. When that iteration is complete, we call `saveCompleteCallback()` because again, this completes the save lifecycle properly. And that's it—our categories are now persisted to our local database.

Following that is another custom data store, this time for the snippets. This is, by and large, the same as the custom store for the categories:

```
/**
 * Declare a custom store for snippets so we can implement save.
 */
dojo.declare("CustomSnippetsItemFileWriteStore",
  dojo.data.ItemFileWriteStore, {
    _saveCustom: function(saveCompleteCallback, saveFailedCallback) {

      // Abort if Gears isn't installed.
      if (!window.google || !google.gears) {
        saveCompleteCallback();
        return;
      }

      // Gears is available, persist snippets.  Do this by iterating over
      // the array of items in this store and inserting each into the
      // Gears database.  Note that this always starts with deleting all
      // snippets in the current category, so if this store is empty, we're
      // good to go then.  While this isn't efficient, it does make it easy:
      // no worries about what got added, modified or deleted, it's just all
      // written fresh.
      var db = google.gears.factory.create("beta.database");
      db.open("DojoCodeCabinet");
      db.execute("DELETE FROM snippets WHERE category=" +
        codeCabinet.categoriesStore.getValue(
          codeCabinet.currentCategory, "id")
      );
      var items = this._getItemsArray();
      if (items.length > 0) {
        for (var i = 0; i < items.length; i++) {
          db.execute("INSERT INTO snippets VALUES " +
            "(?, ?, ?, ?, ?, ?, ?, ?, ?, ?)", [
            items[i].id, items[i].category, items[i].name,
            items[i].description, items[i].author, items[i].eMail,
            items[i].webLink, items[i].code, items[i].notes,
            items[i].keywords
          ]);
```

```
        }
      }

      saveCompleteCallback();

    }

  }
);
```

In fact, the only substantive difference is the delete query, which has a where clause in order to delete only the snippets for the current category. (Although I didn't code this as efficiently as I could have, this was one place I didn't take the least efficient route: deleting *all* snippets in *all* categories. I thought that would have just been overkill!). The other difference is the insert query, which has more parameters to it.

One other thing worth mentioning, because this is the first time it's coming up, is the way I get the ID of the current category. Anytime you want to get the value of a field of an Item in a data store, you need to use the getValue() method of the data store rather than access the fields directly. This is because the data store can do anything it wants with the values internally; these values don't have to look anything like the values you'd expect. Maybe they are being compressed, or encoded, or anything else. By using getValue(), you will get back the *actual* value you know is there, not the internal representation of the data as it might appear. In fact, I found a couple of instances where things like simple ID integer values didn't give me an actual integer value back if I accessed the fields directly, and code would break with an error because of it. Using getValue() keeps that from happening.

The getValue() method works in a way that might not be as intuitive as you'd like: you call it on the store that contains the Item, you tell it what attribute of the Item you want, and you actually have to pass it the Item itself! That might seem a little strange at first—it's sort of like saying, "Hey, mister bank teller, can you tell me how much money is in my wallet? And oh yeah, here's my wallet!" You mean to tell me you can't just look in the wallet and see for yourself? As it turns out, no you can't, because maybe there's some sort of foreign currency in there that only the bank teller knows how to convert to a dollar value that you'll understand.

I think it kinda makes sense, but it may seem a little off at first. I suppose it's also kinda irrelevant whether it makes sense to you: that's the way it is! If it's just a little bit of funky syntax, I think we can cope. You'll see this done a bunch of times throughout this code, and now you should understand what it's all about.

The category tree begins empty, so we need to have an empty data store to begin with. Of course we know it's going to be an instance of the CustomCategoriesItemFileWriteStore we created earlier, and here it is:

```
/**
 * The store for the category tree.
 */
this.categoriesStore = new CustomCategoriesItemFileWriteStore({data:{
  label : "name", identifier : "id", items : [
  ]
}});
```

As you can see, the structure of the store is defined such that the name attribute of an Item gives the Tree the label to display, and the unique identifier of an Item is the id field. The items array is empty to begin with, just as you'd expect. You'll see that the init() method will take care of displaying any categories that were persisted to the Gears database.

For each category, there will also be a data store of snippets. These stores will be, err, *stored*, in the snippetsStores array:

```
/**
 * The stores for the snippets grid.  Each category will be its own
 * store within this collection.
 */
this.snippetsStores = new Array();
```

■ **Note** If you're wondering why I didn't choose to have a single data store for all snippets, and just use the data store query capabilities, the simple answer is I couldn't get it to work! I spent quite a few hours on it, asked some questions in various support forums and the Dojo IRC channel, but nothing was helpful. I still don't know whether I was doing something wrong, or there are simply bugs/limitations somewhere in Dojo that made it not work. In the end, having separate stores was the only way I could get the code to work. So, if you're wondering architecturally why I made this choice, I didn't; I had no real choice in the end! Such is the danger of using DojoX components, though: when they work, they're usually really good, but when they don't, it can be frustrating.

A grid also needs a model, essentially an interface between a data store and the data model that the grid will use to be populated. We're going to set this dynamically in code later, but the grid will always reference the snippetsStoreModel, which is a field of the CodeCabinet class as well:

```
/**
 * The model for the snippets grid.  This will wrap one of the stores in the
 * snippetsStores collection.
 */
this.snippetsStoreModel = null;

/**
 * The layout for the snippets and search grids.
 */
this.gridLayout = [{
  cells: [[
    { name : "Snippet Name", field : "name", width : "auto" },
    { name : "Description", field : "description", width : "auto" }
  ]]
}];
```

In addition, the grid needs to know what its layout looks like, that is, what columns it has, how they should be sized, that sort of thing. That's where the gridLayout field comes in. This layout is used by both the snippets grid and the search results grid. We have our array of `cells`, or columns really, despite the attribute name. Each has a `name`, which is again maybe not the best name for the attribute because that's actually the label that will be shown in the column header. The `field` attribute declares what field of an `Item` in the data store that column's data will come from. Finally, the `width` attribute, when set to `auto`, will allow the grid to size the column automatically, according to the size of the data contained within it.

The search results grid has its own data store and model, because those are necessarily different from the ones for the snippets grid:

```
/**
 * The store for the search grid.
 */
this.searchStore = new dojo.data.ItemFileWriteStore({data:{
  label : "name", identifier : "id", items : [ ]
}});

/**
 * The model for the search grid.
 */
this.searchStoreModel = null;
```

We wrap up the instance fields of the `CodeCabinet` class with three fields that give us information about what is currently going on:

```
/**
 * The item of the currently selected category.
 */
this.currentCategory = null;

/**
 * The currently selected catalog's snippets store.
 */
this.currentSnippetsStore = null;

/**
 * The item of the currently selected code snippet.
 */
this.currentSnippet = null;
```

Every time a category is clicked in the Tree, a reference to the appropriate `Item` from the categories data store is stored in `currentCategory`. At the same time, a reference to the appropriate data store for that category's snippets is stored in `currentSnippetsStore`. Finally, when a snippet is selected from the snippets grid, a reference to the `Item` from the `currentSnippetStore` is kept in `currentSnippet`. These fields allow us to write the rest of the code in a fairly generic way: so long as we make sure these fields always have valid and correct values based on what is current, be it a category or snippet, the rest of the code can reference these fields and not have to worry about keeping track of anything else.

Initialization at Startup

The addOnLoad() call in index.htm sets up a call to the init() method of the CodeCabinet class, which we'll now look at, little by little. The first part is this:

```
/**
 * Initialize the application.
 */
this.init = function() {

  // There doesn't appear to be a way to disable tabs, so we have to fake
  // it.  To do so, we connect to the selectChild event and do some work
  // when it fires.
  dojo.connect(dijit.byId("tabs"), "selectChild", null, function(inTab) {
    // If there is no category selected, or if there is a category selected
    // but no snippet selected...
    if (codeCabinet.currentCategory == null ||
      codeCabinet.currentSnippet == null) {
      // And if the tab selected was NOT the snippets tab...
      if (inTab.id != "tabSnippets") {
        // Then we select the snippets tab.  The user will see that when
        // they click one of the other tabs, nothing happens, effectively
        // disabling them.
        dijit.byId("tabs").selectChild(dijit.byId("tabSnippets"));
      }
    }
  });
```

There appears to be a limitation with the Dojo TabContainer dijit: you can't disable a tab. I did some research on this and I don't appear to be the only person looking for this capability, so my guess is we'll see it pretty soon in a new version. For now, it appears to be true that you can't disable a tab. So, we have to essentially fake it. The way we can do that is to use the AOP system in Dojo to connect to the selectChild event, which is fired anytime a tab is selected (whether the user clicks it or we programmatically select it). So, we call dojo.connect(), passing it a reference to the object we want to "observe," which is the TabContainer dijit in this case. We can get a reference to this object by using the diji.byId() function. Then we send the name of the event we want to monitor, selectChild in this case. Finally, we specify the function to call after that event fires, which is an inline function here.

Anytime that event fires, we check whether there's a current category or snippet selected. If there isn't, the user can never access any tab; the UI will be showing the Snippets tab (because it has to show *some* tab, and that one seemed best to me). In this situation, we select the Snippets tab. So what the user sees is that clicking any of the tabs results in nothing happening; effectively, the tabs are disabled. We do this faux-tab disabling only when the clicked tab was not the Snippets tab. (This disabling work would have worked without that inner if check, but why do extra work if we don't have to?)

Of course, if there is both a category and a snippet selected, the user is free to move around, to select any tab desired. So we do nothing in that case, and we in essence have disabled tabs. They don't visually reflect the fact that they are disabled, which probably could have been accomplished with some style sheet manipulation, but this achieves the basic goal, so it's good enough.

The next important step is to deal with the possibility of Gears not being available to us, and to do something about it!

```
// See if Gears is installed.
if (!window.google || !google.gears) {

  // It's not, so show the installation dialog.
  dijit.byId("NoGearsDialog").show();
```

If `window.google` or `google.gears` is not defined, Gears is not available, in which case we display the `NoGearsDialog`. This directs the user where to go to install Gears, and indicates that the application will still work, aside from persistence, if the user chooses not to complete the installation.

Now, assuming Gears *is* available, it's time to get to some real work, which is to read any saved categories and snippets into our data stores so we can let the user get to work:

```
} else {

  // Read categories in and populate the store, creating the table if it
  // doesn't yet exist.
  var db = google.gears.factory.create("beta.database");
  db.open("DojoCodeCabinet");

  // Uncomment the following two lines to clear out the database.  Good
  // for when you're messing around with things and, well, mess up!
  //db.execute("DROP TABLE categories");
  //db.execute("DROP TABLE snippets");
```

We begin by getting a database engine to work with, and opening up the `DojoCodeCabinet` database, which will of course be created for us if it doesn't already exist. You can see where I have two SQL drop statements commented out. This is useful if you want to clear out the database and start from scratch, especially if you're going to be hacking the code; this is a good thing to be able to do to make sure your changes are working.

Whether or not the database was empty to start with, we now need to ensure that we have a categories table to work with. We issue a SQL create table statement, but use the `if not exists` clause so that we'll do this bit only if the table...wait for it...doesn't exist!

```
  db.execute("CREATE TABLE IF NOT EXISTS categories (" +
    "id INT, " +
    "name TEXT, " +
    "type TEXT" +
  ")");
  var rs = db.execute("SELECT id,name,type FROM categories ORDER BY name");
  while (rs.isValidRow()) {
    // Add an item to the tree's store.
    codeCabinet.categoriesStore.newItem({
      id : rs.field(0),
```

```
      name : rs.field(1),
      type : rs.field(2)
    });
    // Also add a store for the snippets in this category.
    codeCabinet.snippetsStores[rs.field(0)] =
      new CustomSnippetsItemFileWriteStore({data:{
        label : "name", identifier : "id", items : [ ]
      }}
    );
    rs.next();
  }
```

The table is a simple one, with a grand total of three fields. The id field is an integer field and will be the unique key of each field. The name field is of type text and stores the actual name of the category, and is also what will be displayed in the Tree. The type field is also of type text, is always the value category, and is needed by the Tree and nothing else. I really didn't need to store this in the database, but I decided to just in case I wanted to extend things later and discovered that variable values come into play. This way, I'm all set for that possibility.

After the table is created (if it had to be in the first place), we query the table for all records so we have a list of all categories (if there are any). We then go through the ResultSet from that query. For each record that we find, we use the newItem() method of the ItemFileWriteStore class to add an item representing the category. For each category, we also add a new CustomSnippetsItemFileWriteStore to the snippetsStores collection so that later, when we read in the snippets, we are assured there is a data store for them to go into.

Speaking of the snippets, they are actually next:

```
// Read snippets in and populate the appropriate store, creating the
// table if it doesn't yet exist.
var db = google.gears.factory.create("beta.database");
db.open("DojoCodeCabinet");
db.execute("CREATE TABLE IF NOT EXISTS snippets (" +
  "id INT, " +
  "category INT, " +
  "name TEXT, " +
  "description TEXT, " +
  "author TEXT, " +
  "eMail TEXT, " +
  "webLink TEXT, " +
  "code TEXT, " +
  "notes TEXT, " +
  "keywords TEXT" +
")");
var rs = db.execute("SELECT id,category,name,description,author," +
  "eMail,webLink,code,notes,keywords FROM snippets");
while (rs.isValidRow()) {
  // Add item to the snippets store for the category associated with the
  // next snippet in the result set.
```

```
      codeCabinet.snippetsStores[rs.field(1)].newItem({
        id : rs.field(0),
        category : rs.field(1),
        name : rs.field(2),
        description : rs.field(3),
        author : rs.field(4),
        eMail : rs.field(5),
        webLink : rs.field(6),
        code : rs.field(7),
        notes : rs.field(8),
        keywords : rs.field(9)
      });
      rs.next();
    }

  } // End if.

  dijit.byId("snippetsGrid").domNode.style.display = "none";
  dijit.byId("searchGrid").domNode.style.display = "none";

  codeCabinet.searchClearClicked();

} // End init().
```

This code is exactly the same sort of thing as for the categories: create the table if it doesn't already exist, and then read in all the records from it, creating an `Item` for each record, and adding it to the appropriate snippets data store. The collection of snippet stores is keyed by the ID of a category, which is stored on each snippet record in the `category` field (so it's a foreign key into the categories table, in other words). Otherwise, it's the same sort of basic code as we saw with the categories, just a few more fields to deal with is all. I think even the table fields are pretty self-evident. Note that the keywords are stored as comma-separated values in a single `keywords` field, rather than any sort of multitable schema where I would have had to use joins to get what I needed. Once again, simplicity, unless there's a good reason to go around it, is usually a good answer, if not the *best* answer.

Note the two lines that hide the `snippetsGrid` and `searchGrid`. This is necessary to get around the IE7 issue that kept the grids from working properly. Again, it would have been nice, as I had originally coded, to hide them in the markup via style settings, but that just didn't work, so I had to go with this approach.

Only one piece remains to the `init()` puzzle, and that's the call to the `searchClearClicked()` method hanging out there by itself. Let's get a quick look at that method now, even though it appears physically a lot later in the `CodeCabinet.js` file:

```
/**
 * Called when the Clear search button is clicked.
 */
this.searchClearClicked = function() {
```

```
    dojo.byId("searchForm").reset();
    dijit.byId("searchGrid").domNode.style.display = "none";
    dojo.byId("searchNoResults").style.display = "none";
    dojo.byId("searchResultsMessage").style.display = "";

} // End searchClearClicked().
```

There's not much to it, but this method is called when the Clear button is clicked, and I didn't want to hang all this code off the inline event handler, and because it's needed in `init()` as well, it's in its own method. All it does is call the `clear()` method on the form encapsulating the search criteria entry fields to clear any entries that may be present in them, and then it hides the `Grid` and message saying no search results were found. Finally, it shows the message saying search results will appear here.

With the initialization code out of the way, we can now move on.

All Things Category

The following batch of methods that we'll look at all deal with categories in some way. For example, the first method, `addCategoryClicked()`, is the method called when the Add Category toolbar button is clicked:

```
/**
 * Called when the toolbar Add Category button is clicked.
 */
this.addCategoryClicked = function() {

  // Show the Add Category dialog.
  dijit.byId("AddCategoryName").setValue("");
  dijit.byId("AddCategoryDialog").show();

} // End addCategoryClicked().
```

This code has a very simple job: clear the TextBox dijit in the Add Category dialog box and show that same dialog.

Now, after the Add button in the dialog is clicked, the `addCategory()` method gets called, and that's next:

```
/**
 * Called when the Add button on the Add Category dialog is clicked.
 */
this.addCategory = function() {

  // Hide dialog and get entered value, if any.
  dijit.byId("AddCategoryDialog").hide();
  var categoryName = dijit.byId("AddCategoryName").getValue();

  // If we got a category name...
  if (categoryName != null) {
    categoryName = dojo.string.trim(categoryName);
```

```
    if (categoryName != "") {
      // And if it's not a duplicate...
      if (codeCabinet.snippetsStores[categoryName]) {
        dijit.byId("DuplicateCategoryDialog").show();
        return;
      }
      // Add it to the store for the categories tree.
      var categoryID = new Date().getTime();
      codeCabinet.categoriesStore.newItem({
        id : categoryID,
        name : categoryName,
        type : "category"
      });
      // Also add a new store for its snippets.
      codeCabinet.snippetsStores[categoryID] =
        new CustomSnippetsItemFileWriteStore({data:{
          label : "name", identifier : "id", items : [ ]
        }}
      );
      // Finally, persist to the underlying persistent store.
      codeCabinet.categoriesStore.save();
    }
  }

} // End addCategory().
```

First, this code hides the dialog. Then, by getting a reference to the `AddCategoryName` TextBox via a call to `dijit.byId()`, it calls `getValue()` to get what the user entered. If the user entered nothing, the `if` block won't be entered and nothing will happen.

If the user entered something, it's time to add a category. Well, after a quick check, that is: Would the category be a duplicate? In other words, is the name entered already in use? To be sure, we trim what the user entered by using the `dojo.string.trim()` function. (The name is always saved after it's been trimmed, so we only have to worry about trimming the user input here, to avoid a mismatch caused by whitespace on the ends of the string.) Then, if something was entered, we try to retrieve the snippets store for that category. Anytime a category is added, so too is a data store for the snippets, so this is a way of checking whether the category is already in use. There are obviously other ways to do it, but this was perhaps the simplest and most straightforward. If we find a data store, we show the `DuplicateCategoryDialog` to inform the user.

Assuming the name is not a duplicate, though, we then get the current time in milliseconds. This is our unique ID for the category. With that in hand, we use the `newItem()` method of the `categoriesStore` to add an `Item` for the category. Here you can see that hard-coded `category` value I talked about earlier.

The next step is to add a data store for the snippets in this category, which is simply a matter of instantiating the `CustomSnippetsItemFileWriteStore` and adding it to the `snippetsStores` collection, under a key that is the ID of the category.

Finally, a call to the save() method of the categoriesStore persists this to the Gears database (assuming Gears is available), which we've already seen, so we're done with adding a category!

Next up is what happens when the user clicks a category in the tree, which results in a call to the categoryClicked() method here:

```
/**
   * Called when a category in the tree is clicked.
   *
   * @param inItem The item from the data store that was clicked.
   */
this.categoryClicked = function(inItem) {

  // Ignore clicks on the top-level element.
  if (!inItem) {
    return;
  }

  // Clear any search results that might be present, and the search form.
  codeCabinet.searchClearClicked();

  // Set up category-related functionality.
  codeCabinet.currentCategory = inItem;
  codeCabinet.currentSnippetsStore =
    codeCabinet.snippetsStores[
      codeCabinet.categoriesStore.getValue(inItem, "id")];
  dijit.byId("toolbarDeleteCategory").setDisabled(false);

  // Set up snippet-related functionality.
  codeCabinet.currentSnippet = null;
  dijit.byId("toolbarAddSnippet").setDisabled(false);
  dijit.byId("toolbarDeleteSnippet").setDisabled(true);
  dijit.byId("btnSearch").setDisabled(false);
  dijit.byId("btnClear").setDisabled(false);
  dijit.byId("searchKeywords").setDisabled(false);
  dijit.byId("searchCode").setDisabled(false);
  dijit.byId("searchName").setDisabled(false);
  dijit.byId("searchDescription").setDisabled(false);
  dijit.byId("searchAuthor").setDisabled(false);
  dijit.byId("searchNotes").setDisabled(false);

  // Clear forms on all entry tabs.
  dojo.byId("infoForm").reset();
  dojo.byId("codeForm").reset();
  dojo.byId("notesForm").reset();
  dojo.byId("keywordsForm").reset();
```

```
  // Update the grid.
  codeCabinet.refreshSnippetsGrid();

} // End categoryClicked().
```

First is a check to see whether inItem is defined. If the user clicks the Snippet Categories root element, inItem won't be defined because it's apparently not considered an item in the tree, so to avoid errors this check is necessary.

After that's done, a call to searchClearClicked() is made. When switching categories we need to ensure that if there were search results displayed, they are hidden. If the user were to click one of the search results at this point, an error would occur because the snippet belongs to a category that is no longer current. The snippet would not exist in the underlying data store, hence an error would occur, and hence the reason for the call to searchClearClicked().

Next, we store a reference to the Item passed to the function in the currentCategory field, and set the currentSnippetStore field to point to the data store where the snippets for the selected category are. The Delete Category toolbar button is then enabled, because that function is now valid to perform.

We then enable all the snippet-related UI elements, such as the Add Snippet button on the toolbar and the search fields. Note that the Delete Snippet button is disabled at this point because no snippet is selected, and that function is therefore not valid. We also set the currentSnippet field to null to indicate that a snippet has not yet been selected.

Next, we call reset() on all the <form> elements, on the various tabs as well as the search form. This ensures that everything else is set up properly from a UI perspective and is nice and clear.

Finally, a call to refreshSnippetsGrid() is performed, which is responsible for displaying the snippets in the selected category. Let's jump ahead and look at that method now:

```
/**
 * This function is called from multiple places to update the snippets grid
 * for the current category whenever a change to a snippet takes place, or
 * when the category is clicked.
 */
this.refreshSnippetsGrid = function() {

  // Switch to the Snippets tab so updates to the grid show up.
  dijit.byId("tabs").selectChild(dijit.byId("tabSnippets"));

  // Retrieve all the items from the store for the current category.
  codeCabinet.currentSnippetsStore.fetch({
    onComplete : function(items, request) {
      // If there are items, we can display them (this avoids an error with
      // the grid... without this check, an empty store causes an error).
      if (items.length > 0) {
        dijit.byId("snippetsGrid").domNode.style.display = "";
        dojo.byId("noSnippetsInCategory").style.display = "none";
        dojo.byId("noCategorySelected").style.display = "none";
        // Wrap the current store in a model and set it on the grid, update
        // occurs automatically after that.
```

```
        codeCabinet.snippetsStoreModel = new dojox.grid.data.DojoData(
          null, codeCabinet.currentSnippetsStore);
        dijit.byId("snippetsGrid").setModel(codeCabinet.snippetsStoreModel);
        dijit.byId("snippetsGrid").update();
      } else {
        dijit.byId("snippetsGrid").domNode.style.display = "none";
        dojo.byId("noCategorySelected").style.display = "none";
        dojo.byId("noSnippetsInCategory").style.display = "";
      }
    }
  });

} // End refreshSnippetsGrid().
```

First, we get a reference to the Snippets tab by calling `diji.byId("tabs")` to get a reference to the TabContainer, and then calling `selectChild("tabSnippets")` to activate that tab. This is necessary because when the grid is populated, I found that if it wasn't visible at that point, it would not get populated on the screen. Flipping to the tab takes care of that, and plus it's the more natural place to be when switching categories because the user will almost certainly be interested in seeing the snippets in that category at that point.

The next step is to fetch all the items in the data store associated with the selected category. This is accomplished by calling the `fetch()` method of the store. This works in a callback way, that is, asynchronously, so we have to set the `onComplete` attribute of the options object passed into `fetch()` to the function we want to execute when the fetch is complete, which is inlined in this case.

After the fetch completes, a check is first done to ensure that there were items returned. This check is necessary because if you try to update the model of the grid with a model that has no items, an error occurs, so this check takes care of it. This is the only reason for doing the fetch at all: it's the only way I could find to tell how many items were in the store. (I suspect this is a case of me just missing something, to be honest, but I looked for a long time and couldn't find anything.) If there are no items, the `else` branch of the `if` statement executes, which simply hides the Grid entirely and puts up the "no snippets in category" message by showing the appropriate `<div>` while hiding the Grid.

Assuming there were items, though, we begin by hiding the message `<div>`s and showing the Grid itself. Then, we need to create a model for the Grid to use based on the data store, so we create a new `dojox.grid.data.DojoData` object, passing into it the `currentSnippetsStore`. Next, we call the `setModel()` method on the Grid, passing in that `DojoData` object, and finally call `update()` on the Grid to make it all show up on the screen.

Deleting a category is next, and that begins with a call to the `deleteCategoryClicked()` method when the Delete Category toolbar button is clicked:

```
/**
 * Called when the toolbar Delete Category button is clicked.
 */
this.deleteCategoryClicked = function() {
```

```
    // Show the delete confirmation dialog.
    dojo.byId("confirmDeleteType").innerHTML = "catalog";
    dijit.byId("ConfirmDeleteDialog").show();

  } // End deleteCategoryClicked().
```

This is a simple matter of showing the `ConfirmDeleteDialog`, which you can see here in Figure 6-10.

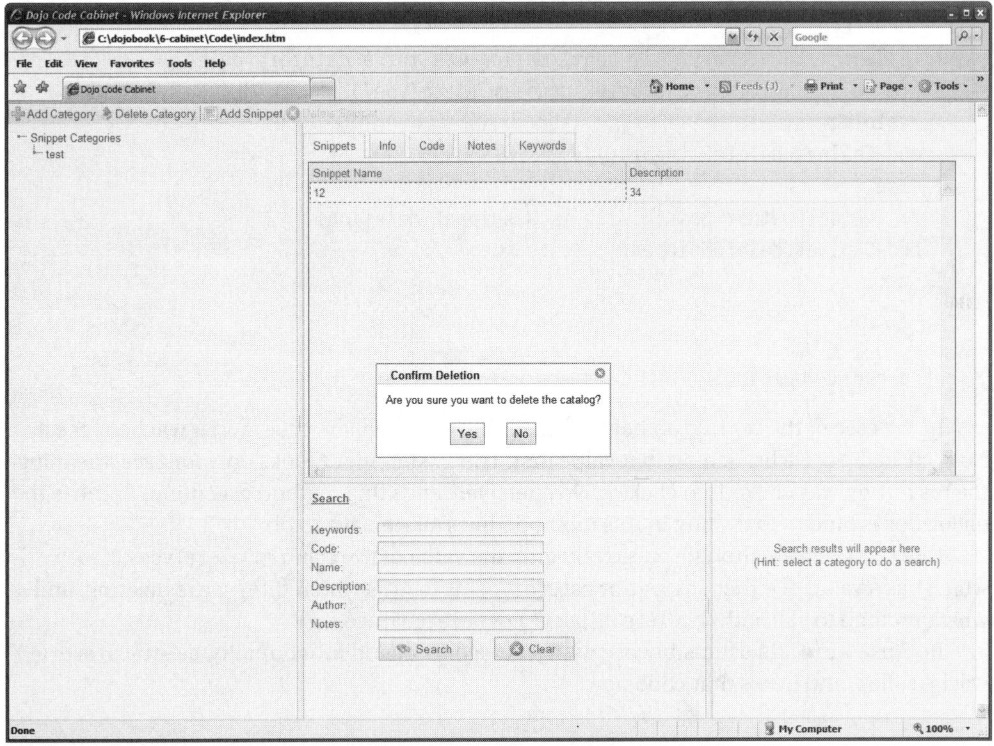

Figure 6-10. *The Confirm Deletion dialog box when deleting a catalog*

This dialog is generic, meaning it works for deleting both categories and snippets, but it will always state the correct one (that is, saying, "Are you sure you want to delete the catalog?" here vs. "Are you sure you want to delete the snippet?" when deleting a snippet). How this happens is answered by this line:

```
dojo.byId("confirmDeleteType").innerHTML = "catalog";
```

The only thing different is the word *snippet* vs. the word *category* in the dialog; everything else about it is the same.

Whichever button the user clicks, the `codeCabinet.confirmDelete()` method is called:

```
/**
 * Called when either of the Yes or No buttons on the delete confirmation
 * dialog is clicked.
```

```
 *
 * @param inProceed True if Yes was clicked, false if No was clicked.
 */
this.confirmDelete = function(inProceed) {

  // Hide the dialog.
  dijit.byId("ConfirmDeleteDialog").hide();

  // See if the deletion was confirmed.
  if (inProceed) {
    // Call deleteCategory() if confirmation was for a category deletion.
    if (dojo.string.trim(dojo.byId("confirmDeleteType").innerHTML) ==
      "catalog") {
      codeCabinet.deleteCategory();
    } else {
      // The only other possibility is a snippet deletion.
      codeCabinet.deleteSnippet();
    }
  }

} // End confirmDelete().
```

In the case of the Yes button being clicked, `inProceed` will be `true`, and it will be `false` if No is clicked. So, we branch on that value first. The `if` statement looks only for `true`, meaning the Yes button was clicked, so clicking No effectively ends this method execution. Because the dialog box is hidden first thing in this method, that's all we have to do.

If Yes was clicked, though, we go and grab the value of the `confirmDeleteType` `<div>`, which has a value of either `snippet` or `category`. This tells us which thing we're deleting, and which method to call, either `deleteSnippet()` or `deleteCategory()`.

Because we're still ostensibly discussing category-related functionality, `deleteCategory()` will be called, and here's that code now:

```
/**
 * Called to delete the currently selected catalog.
 */
this.deleteCategory = function() {

  // Clear any search results that might be present, and the search form.
  codeCabinet.searchClearClicked();

  // Remove the snippets store and clear snippet-related fields.
  delete codeCabinet.snippetsStores[
    codeCabinet.categoriesStore.getValue(
      codeCabinet.currentCategory, "id")];
  codeCabinet.currentSnippetsSore = null;
  codeCabinet.currentSnippet = null;
```

```
// Delete all snippets for this category from the Gears database.  Note that
// this could have been (and some might argue should have been) done by
// iterating over all the items in the snippets store for this category,
// deleting each from the store, then calling save() on the store.  But,
// since we're going to delete the store from the collection of snippet
// stores anyway, this saves a lot of time.
var db = google.gears.factory.create("beta.database");
db.open("DojoCodeCabinet");
db.execute("DELETE FROM snippets WHERE category=" +
  codeCabinet.categoriesStore.getValue(
    codeCabinet.currentCategory, "id")
);

// Update UI with regard to snippets.
codeCabinet.refreshSnippetsGrid();
dojo.byId("noSnippetsInCategory").style.display = "none";
dojo.byId("noCategorySelected").style.display = "";
dijit.byId("snippetsGrid").domNode.style.display = "none";
dijit.byId("toolbarAddSnippet").setDisabled(true);
dijit.byId("toolbarDeleteSnippet").setDisabled(true);
dijit.byId("btnSearch").setDisabled(true);
dijit.byId("btnClear").setDisabled(true);
dijit.byId("searchKeywords").setDisabled(true);
dijit.byId("searchCode").setDisabled(true);
dijit.byId("searchName").setDisabled(true);
dijit.byId("searchDescription").setDisabled(true);
dijit.byId("searchAuthor").setDisabled(true);
dijit.byId("searchNotes").setDisabled(true);

// Remove the Category item from the store.  This automatically updates
// the tree.  Also do other category-related UI setup.
codeCabinet.categoriesStore.deleteItem(codeCabinet.currentCategory);
codeCabinet.currentCategory = null;
dijit.byId("toolbarDeleteCategory").setDisabled(true);

// Finally, persist to the underlying persistent store.
codeCabinet.categoriesStore.save();

} // End deleteCategory().
```

Who would have thought that deleting a category would require so much work? But let's break it down little by little, and I think it'll make a lot of sense.

First, `searchClearClicked()` is called, to clear all the search criteria fields as well as hide the search results grid. This is necessary because at this point no category is selected, and as we previously established, an error would result if the user then went and clicked a row in the search results grid.

Next, we delete the data store from the snippetsStores collection for the category. Yep, deleting a category deletes the snippets too, which pretty much just makes sense! We also ensure that currentSnippetStore and currentSnippet are set to null to avoid any potential errors because of course you can't have a data store for snippets that don't exist, and you can't have a current snippet in a category that is being deleted.

Following that is some Gears code to delete the snippets from the database for this category. Here again is an example of using the getValue() method of the data store to get the ID of the category to delete.

After that is a whole bunch of UI manipulation calls, simply to enable and disable various buttons and fields as appropriate, those fields dealing with snippets. We also at this point call refreshSnippetsGrid(), which we saw earlier and which we now know will result in the grid being hidden because there's no data store for this category anymore.

Next we use the deleteItem() of the data store bound to the Tree to get rid of the category. Unlike the Grid, which we need to manually do some work to refresh, the Tree is truly bound to the data store, and "sees" the changes to it, and thus refreshes itself automatically. At this point, we no longer need the currentCategory either, so we set it to null. We also disable the Delete Category toolbar button, because clicking it is no longer a valid action (not until the user selects a different category).

Finally, a call to the save() method of the categoriesStore persists the categories to the database, effectively updating them for the next browser session.

All Things Snippet

Now that we've seen all the category-related functions, let's get into the snippet-related functions. A lot of these will look pretty familiar as they tend to have a lot in common with the category code we've just looked at, but there are some differences too, beginning with the addSnippetClicked() method:

```
/**
 * Called when the toolbar Add Snippet button is clicked.
 */
this.addSnippetClicked = function() {

  // Add the item to the store.
  codeCabinet.currentSnippetsStore.newItem({
    id : new Date().getTime(),
    category : codeCabinet.categoriesStore.getValue(
      codeCabinet.currentCategory, "id"),
    name : "NewSnippet",
    description : "A new snippet",
    author : "",
    eMail : "",
    webLink : "",
    code : "",
    notes : "",
    keywords : ""
  });
```

```
  // Update the grid.
  codeCabinet.refreshSnippetsGrid();

  // Finally, persist to the underlying persistent store.
  codeCabinet.currentSnippetsStore.save();

} // End addSnippetClicked().
```

As opposed to adding a category, which is a two-step process (show the dialog and then actually add the category), adding a snippet is done in one go. So, all it really takes is adding a (mostly) empty snippet to the `currentSnippetsStore`. The `name` and `description` are populated so you can tell which snippet is the new one in the grid. And speaking of the grid, we have to refresh that as well so that the new snippet shows up, and all it takes is a call to `refreshSnippetsGrid()`. Finally, a call to the `save()` method of the `currentSnippetsStore` is made to get the new snippet saved right away. In retrospect, I think I could convince myself that the new snippet shouldn't be persisted until the user clicks the Save button somewhere, but that's not how I implemented it, for better or worse. (I expect you'll get as much out of what I didn't do as what I did do throughout this book.)

Now that you see how snippets can be added, let's take a look at what happens when we click a snippet in the snippets grid, in effect putting the application into edit mode:

```
/**
 * Called when a snippet in the snippets grid is clicked.
 *
 * @param inRowIndex The index of the row that was clicked.
 */
this.snippetClicked = function(inRowIndex) {

  // Get all items in current snippets collection, then get the clicked
  // item from it.  This has to be done because all we know at this point
  // is the row index from the grid, we can't uniquely identify the item
  // that was clicked, so we have to fetch all the items in order to use
  // that row index.
  codeCabinet.currentSnippetsStore.fetch(
    { onComplete : function(items, request) {
      // Record the clicked snippet as current and show its details.
      codeCabinet.currentSnippet = items[inRowIndex];
      codeCabinet.showSnippet();
    }
  });

} // End snippetClicked().
```

Not much to it, really: first we fetch all the snippets in the `currentSnippetsStore`. Why, you ask? Because all we know at this point is what row in the grid was clicked, but we don't have the necessary information to relate that to an `Item` in the `currentSnippetsStore` directly, that is, we don't have an ID. So, by fetching all the snippets and getting all the `Items` in the array, which just so happens to be populated in the same order as the grid, we can now access the appropriate element from the array to get our snippet Item.

Then a call to showSnippet() is made, which does the work of putting all the details about the snippet on the screen. And oh look, here comes that method now:

```
/**
 * This function is called to show the current snippet's details.
 */
this.showSnippet = function() {

  // Set up UI, start by clearing everything.
  dojo.byId("infoForm").reset();
  dojo.byId("codeForm").reset();
  dojo.byId("notesForm").reset();
  dojo.byId("keywordsForm").reset();
  dijit.byId("toolbarDeleteSnippet").setDisabled(false);

  // Populate Info edit fields.
  dijit.byId("infoName").setValue(
    codeCabinet.currentSnippetsStore.getValue(
      codeCabinet.currentSnippet, "name"));
  dijit.byId("infoDescription").setValue(
    codeCabinet.currentSnippetsStore.getValue(
      codeCabinet.currentSnippet, "description"));
  dijit.byId("infoAuthor").setValue(
    codeCabinet.currentSnippetsStore.getValue(
      codeCabinet.currentSnippet, "author"));
  dijit.byId("infoEMail").setValue(
    codeCabinet.currentSnippetsStore.getValue(
      codeCabinet.currentSnippet, "eMail"));
  dijit.byId("infoWebLink").setValue(
    codeCabinet.currentSnippetsStore.getValue(
      codeCabinet.currentSnippet, "webLink"));

  // Populate code and notes text areas.
  // Have to add a space to the following two because if the value
  // of either if "", an error occurs, it seems there has to be
  // *something* being inserted, even if it's just a single space.
  dijit.byId("codeArea").setValue(
    codeCabinet.currentSnippetsStore.getValue(
      codeCabinet.currentSnippet, "code") + " ");
  dijit.byId("notesArea").setValue(
    codeCabinet.currentSnippetsStore.getValue(
      codeCabinet.currentSnippet, "notes") + " ");

  // Populate keywords.
  var kw = new String(codeCabinet.currentSnippetsStore.getValue(
    codeCabinet.currentSnippet, "keywords")).split(",");
```

```
    for (var i = 0; i < kw.length; i++) {
      dijit.byId("keyword" + i).setValue(kw[i]);
    }

    // Enable all save buttons.
    dijit.byId("btnInfoSave").setDisabled(false);
    dijit.byId("btnCodeSave").setDisabled(false);
    dijit.byId("btnNotesSave").setDisabled(false);
    dijit.byId("btnKeywordsSave").setDisabled(false);

    // Activate Info tab.
    dijit.byId("tabs").selectChild(dijit.byId("tabInfo"));

  } // End showSnippet().
```

I think virtually everything here is just basic UI setup and is pretty self-explanatory, so I'm not going to spend a whole lot of time on it. The keywords, which are stored as a comma-separated list, need to be `split()`, and then each keyword put into its own text box on the Keywords tab. The Info tab is selected at the end because that's probably the first place the user will want to go (arguably the Code tab is, but again, that's a design decision that you could argue either way). Once again, you'll see the use of the `getValue()` method all over the place, but because we have the `Item` going into this method, or more precisely, referenced by the `currentSnippet` field that was set in the `snippetClicked()` method earlier, `getValue()` is easy enough to use.

■ **Note** When the code and notes are inserted into the editors, I append a blank space on the end. I found this was necessary to get the display to work properly. I'm still not sure what the problem was; I suspect it may have been a bug in the editor, but I'm not at all sure. In any case, adding the space on the end takes care of it. Because we trim the code and notes values when we save the snippet, as you'll see shortly, there's no harm in adding the space.

The next thing we will look at is deleting a snippet. A snippet can be deleted only after we've clicked one (because that's when the toolbar button for deleting a snippet is enabled):

```
  /**
   * Called when the toolbar Delete Snippet button is clicked.
   */
  this.deleteSnippetClicked = function() {

    // Show the delete confirmation dialog.
    dojo.byId("confirmDeleteType").innerHTML = "snippet";
    dijit.byId("ConfirmDeleteDialog").show();

  } // End deleteSnippetClicked().
```

The same sort of confirmation that was done with deleting a category is done here, as shown in Figure 6-11. This confirmation is almost entirely the same, except for the text shown in the dialog, which is *snippet* here.

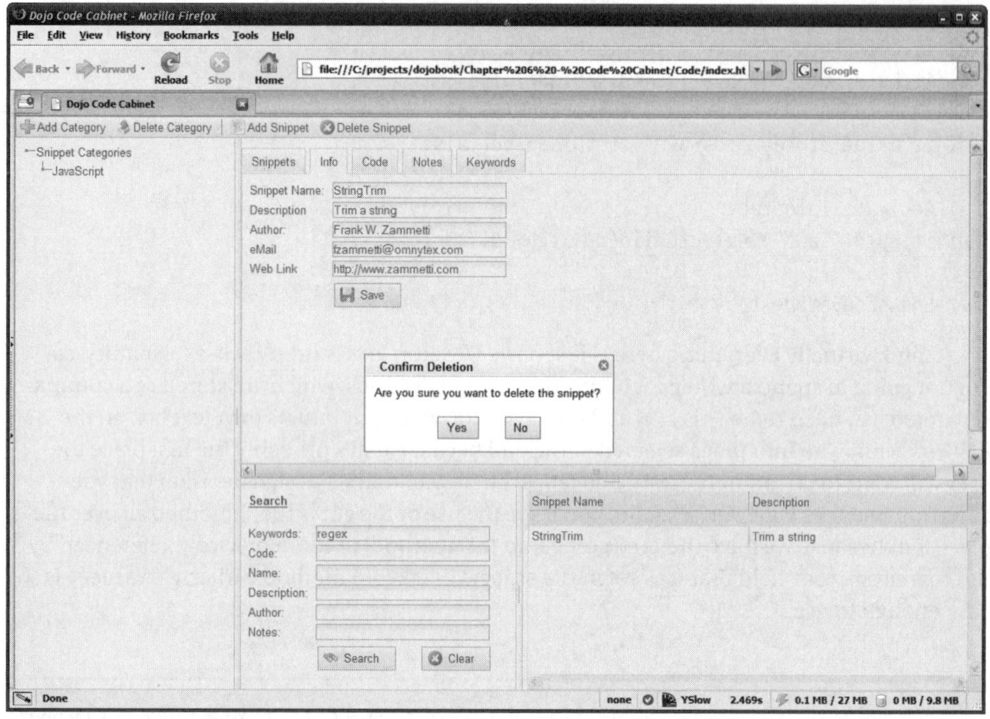

Figure 6-11. *The Confirm Deletion dialog box when deleting a snippet*

So, when the user clicks Yes, `confirmDelete()` will be called, it'll do its thing, and finally the `deleteSnippet()` method will be called:

```
/**
 * Called to delete the currently selected snippet.
 */
this.deleteSnippet = function() {

  // Remove the item from the store.  Note that unlike the tree, this doesn't
  // automatically update the grid, so we'll handle that ourselves next.
  codeCabinet.currentSnippetsStore.deleteItem(codeCabinet.currentSnippet);

  // Set up snippet-related functionality.
  codeCabinet.currentSnippet = null;
  dijit.byId("toolbarDeleteSnippet").setDisabled(true);

  // Update the grid.
  codeCabinet.refreshSnippetsGrid();
```

```
  // Finally, persist to the underlying persistent store.
  codeCabinet.currentSnippetsStore.save();

} // End deleteSnippet().
```

Deleting a snippet is about as easy as deleting a category: call the `deleteItem()` method of the `currentSnippetsStore` to actually delete the `Item` corresponding to the snippet, set `currentSnippet` to `null`, disable the Delete Snippet toolbar button, call `refreshSnippetsGrid()` to show that the snippet has been removed, and finally persist the snippets again by calling `currentSnippetsStore.save()`.

Only one bit of code is left, and that's `saveSnippet()`, the method called anytime one of the Save buttons is clicked:

```
/**
 * Called when any of the Save buttons are clicked.
 */
this.saveSnippet = function() {

  // Construct a CSV of entered keywords, if any.
  var keywords = "";
  for (var i = 0; i < 10; i++) {
    var kw = dijit.byId("keyword" + i).getValue();
    if (kw != null) {
      kw = dojo.string.trim(kw);
      if (kw != "") {
        if (keywords != "") {
          keywords = keywords + ",";
        }
        keywords = keywords + dojo.string.trim(kw);
      }
    }
  }

  // Update the snippets grid to reflect any changes.  To do this, because
  // there seems to be a bug in the grid, we have to delete the item from
  // the store and then add it as a new item.
  codeCabinet.currentSnippetsStore.deleteItem(codeCabinet.currentSnippet);
  codeCabinet.currentSnippetsStore.newItem({
    id : new Date().getTime(),
    category : codeCabinet.categoriesStore.getValue(
      codeCabinet.currentCategory, "id"),
    name : dojo.string.trim((dijit.byId("infoName").getValue() || "")),
    description :
      dojo.string.trim(dijit.byId("infoDescription").getValue() || ""),
    author : dojo.string.trim(dijit.byId("infoAuthor").getValue() || ""),
    eMail : dojo.string.trim(dijit.byId("infoEMail").getValue() || ""),
    webLink : dojo.string.trim(dijit.byId("infoWebLink").getValue() || ""),
    code : dojo.string.trim(dijit.byId("codeArea").getValue() || ""),
```

```
    notes : dojo.string.trim(dijit.byId("notesArea").getValue() || ""),
    keywords : keywords
  });

  // Update the grid.
  codeCabinet.refreshSnippetsGrid();

  // Finally, persist to the underlying persistent store.
  codeCabinet.currentSnippetsStore.save();

} // End saveSnippet().
```

The first task is to take all the keywords that have been entered, if any, and construct a comma-separated string out of them, because that's what is saved to the database. We take care to trim all the strings by using `dojo.string.trim()`, and we also eliminate any empty fields, meaning that if the user enters a keyword in the first field, the third field, and the sixth field, while we can probably rightly ask what they're smoking, the code will handle that just fine; all the keywords will be saved.

Following that, we delete the `Item` for the snippet in the `currentSnippetsStore`, and then use the `newItem()` method to add a new one. You may be wondering why I do this instead of just modifying the existing `Item` from the store, and the simple answer is that this again gave me all sorts of problems. Every time I tried doing that, when I refreshed the grid, the updated data refused to display properly. It always showed a single character in each column. I was unable to get an answer on the support forums about this, and because deadlines are a regular part of writing a book, I simply had to drop back and punt, as it were. This approach works at least, although it has the negative side effect that the "updated" snippet jumps to the bottom of the snippets grid. I think this is acceptable given the alternative of it not working at all!

You'll note that each field's value is obtained by using `getValue()` on the object reference returned by `dijit.byId()`. I handle the possibility of getting `null` back from that call by doing an `|| ""`on the end, so I'm always guaranteed a value.

Finally, a call to `refreshSnippetsGrid()` and a call to `save()` on the `currentSnippetsStore` are done and we're good to go. Our updates are now saved and displayed in the grid.

Searching for Snippets

The final batch of code we have to look at revolves around the search functionality. The first method is the meatiest by far: `searchClicked()`, called when the Search button is, umm, clicked! This is a fairly lengthy method, so I'll break it down into chunks to describe it, starting with this one:

```
/**
 * Called when the Search button is clicked.
 */
this.searchClicked = function() {

  // Get all search parameters.  Trim them, make them lowercase, and make
  // sure we never have nulls here.
```

```
var searchKeywords = dijit.byId("searchKeywords").getValue();
if (searchKeywords == null) { searchKeywords = ""; }
searchKeywords = dojo.string.trim(searchKeywords);
searchKeywords = searchKeywords.toLowerCase();
var searchCode = dijit.byId("searchCode").getValue();
if (searchCode == null) { searchCode = ""; }
searchCode = dojo.string.trim(searchCode);
searchCode = searchCode.toLowerCase();
var searchName = dijit.byId("searchName").getValue();
if (searchName == null) { searchName = ""; }
searchName = dojo.string.trim(searchName);
searchName = searchName.toLowerCase();
var searchAuthor = dijit.byId("searchAuthor").getValue();
if (searchAuthor == null) { searchAuthor = ""; }
searchAuthor = dojo.string.trim(searchAuthor);
searchAuthor = searchAuthor.toLowerCase();
var searchDescription = dijit.byId("searchDescription").getValue();
if (searchDescription == null) { searchDescription = ""; }
searchDescription = dojo.string.trim(searchDescription);
searchDescription = searchDescription.toLowerCase();
var searchNotes = dijit.byId("searchNotes").getValue();
if (searchNotes == null) { searchNotes = ""; }
searchNotes = dojo.string.trim(searchNotes);
searchNotes = searchNotes.toLowerCase();
```

Here we're getting the values of each of the search criteria TextBoxes. The values are trimmed and converted to lowercase, so all our searches will be case-insensitive in effect (assuming of course that when the search is performed, the fields of the snippet `Items` in the `currentSnippetsStore` are likewise trimmed, which they will be). I also ensure that we are never dealing with nulls in any situation by setting the variables to a blank string if `null` is returned by a call to `getValue()`.

After we have all those values, we begin to do some work with them, starting with a validation:

```
// Ensure acceptable criteria are entered.
if (searchKeywords == "" && searchCode == "" & searchName == "" &&
  searchAuthor == "" && searchDescription == "" && searchNotes == "") {
  dijit.byId("BadSearchCriteriaDialog").show();
  return;
}
```

We are simply ensuring that at least one of the search criteria has been entered, and if not, we show the `BadSearchCriteriaDialog`, which just tells the user of the goof and the need to enter something.

The next step is to clear the `searchStore`, which is the data store that will be used to populate the search results grid:

```
// "Clear" the searchStore.
codeCabinet.searchStore = new dojo.data.ItemFileWriteStore({data:{
  label : "name", identifier : "id", items : [ ]
}});
```

Now we need to get the snippets we'll be searching through, which is done via a call to `fetch()`. It's called on the `currentSnippetsStore`, because the search capability works against the current category always:

```
// Fetch all the snippets from the store.
codeCabinet.currentSnippetsStore.fetch(
  { onComplete : function(items, request) {

    // Cycle through them and find the matches.
    var matchesFound = false;
    for (var i = 0; i < items.length; i++) {
```

We then begin to iterate over the array of `Items` returned. We have a variable `matchesFound` set to `false` initially. This will be set to `true` when we find that we have one or more matches.

So, the next step is to get all the data from the next `Item`, and do the same sort of trimming and case conversion that we did with the search criteria to ensure that we'll get matches, if there legitimately are any:

```
// Get the data from the next snippet, trim it nice, and make it
// lowercase so searches are case-insensitive.
var itemKeywords = codeCabinet.currentSnippetsStore.getValue(
  items[i], "keywords");
if (itemKeywords == null) { itemKeywords = ""; }
itemKeywords = dojo.string.trim(itemKeywords);
itemKeywords = itemKeywords.toLowerCase();
var itemCode = codeCabinet.currentSnippetsStore.getValue(
  items[i], "code");
if (itemCode == null) { itemCode = ""; }
itemCode = dojo.string.trim(itemCode);
itemCode = itemCode.toLowerCase();
var itemName = codeCabinet.currentSnippetsStore.getValue(
  items[i], "name");
if (itemName == null) { itemName = ""; }
itemName = dojo.string.trim(itemName);
itemName = itemName.toLowerCase();
var itemAuthor = codeCabinet.currentSnippetsStore.getValue(
  items[i], "author");
if (itemAuthor == null) { itemAuthor = ""; }
itemAuthor = dojo.string.trim(itemAuthor);
itemAuthor = itemAuthor.toLowerCase();
var itemDescription = codeCabinet.currentSnippetsStore.getValue(
  items[i], "description");
if (itemDescription == null) { itemDescription = ""; }
```

```
itemDescription = dojo.string.trim(itemDescription);
itemDescription = itemDescription.toLowerCase();
var itemNotes = codeCabinet.currentSnippetsStore.getValue(
  items[i], "notes");
if (itemNotes == null) { itemNotes = ""; }
itemNotes = dojo.string.trim(itemNotes);
itemNotes = itemNotes.toLowerCase();
```

Because we can enter multiple search criteria, that means we need to look for matches with whatever combination of criteria were entered. If the user enters a value in the Name field and enters a value in the Keywords field, it means we're looking for all snippets that have the name value in its Name field *as well as* the keywords specified. In order to do that, we have a variable named `matched`:

```
// This variable will have a T or F added to it for each search
// criteria that was entered.  If we get to the end and there are any
// Fs in it, then this snippet didn't match one of the entered
// criteria and is therefore not a match.
var matched = "";

// Search includes name.
if (searchName != "") {
  if (itemName.indexOf(searchName) != -1) {
    matched += "T";
  } else {
    matched += "F";
  }
}
```

We'll then check each possible criteria in turn. Anytime a criteria is in play, and anytime a match is found based on those criteria, we'll add a *T* to `matched`. If a given criteria is in play but there is no match, we'll add an *F*. That way, when we get to the end, if we have no *F*s in the matched string, the `Item` is a match on all criteria requested. Not only is this a simple approach, but it also enables us to extend the search facility, by adding new criteria, without having to redesign the underlying matching mechanism.

You can see the first criteria being checked: the name. If `searchName`, which is the value the user entered, is not a blank string, that criteria is in play. (Remember that we're guaranteed to see either the value entered or a blank string, never `null`.) So, we do a simple `indexOf()` search to see whether the entered value appears anywhere in the Name field. If it does, we consider that a match; otherwise, it's not a match.

The code, author, description, and notes search criteria are all essentially identical to the name code, so just have a look at them—I won't bore you by describing them:

```
// Search includes code.
if (searchCode != "") {
  if (itemCode.indexOf(searchCode) != -1) {
    matched += "T";
  } else {
```

```
      matched += "F";
    }
  }

  // Search includes author.
  if (searchAuthor != "") {
    if (itemAuthor.indexOf(searchAuthor) != -1) {
      matched += "T";
    } else {
      matched += "F";
    }
  }

  // Search includes description.
  if (searchDescription != "") {
    if (itemDescription.indexOf(searchDescription) != -1) {
      matched += "T";
    } else {
      matched += "F";
    }
  }

  // Search includes notes.
  if (searchNotes != "") {
    if (itemNotes.indexOf(searchNotes) != -1) {
      matched += "T";
    } else {
      matched += "F";
    }
  }
```

Now, the keywords are just slightly different:

```
  // Search includes keyword(s).
  if (searchKeywords != "") {
    var a = searchKeywords.split(",");
    var foundAny = false;
    for (var j = 0; j < a.length; j++) {
      var nextKeyword = dojo.string.trim(a[j]);
      if (nextKeyword != "") {
        if (itemKeywords.indexOf(nextKeyword) != -1) {
          foundAny = true;
        }
      }
    }
    if (foundAny) {
      matched += "T";
    } else {
```

```
    matched += "F";
  }
}
```

Here we `split()` the keywords the user entered. We then iterate over the resultant array. The next token from the string is trimmed, and as long as it's not blank, we see whether that value appears anywhere in the `keywords` value on the `Item`. If so, we again have a match on this criteria.

Finally, we check whether there are any *F*s in the `matched` string. If there aren't, we have ourselves a match!

```
// If current snippet matches the search criteria, add it to the
// search store.
if (matched.indexOf("F") == -1) {
  matchesFound = true;
  codeCabinet.searchStore.newItem({
    id : codeCabinet.currentSnippetsStore.getValue(items[i], "id"),
    category :
      codeCabinet.currentSnippetsStore.getValue(
        items[i], "category"),
    name :
      codeCabinet.currentSnippetsStore.getValue(items[i], "name"),
    description :
      codeCabinet.currentSnippetsStore.getValue(
        items[i], "description")
  });
}
```

In the case of a match, `matchesFound` is set to `true`, and we add a `newItem()` to the `searchStore`, populating it with the values from the `Item` that was found to be a match:

```
// Update the search results grid, if we found some matches; otherwise
// show the no matches found message.
if (matchesFound) {
  dojo.byId("searchResultsMessage").style.display = "none";
  dojo.byId("searchNoResults").style.display = "none";
  codeCabinet.searchStoreModel = new dojox.grid.data.DojoData(
    null, codeCabinet.searchStore);
  var searchGrid = dijit.byId("searchGrid");
  searchGrid.domNode.style.display = "";
  searchGrid.setModel(codeCabinet.searchStoreModel);
  searchGrid.update();
} else {
  dojo.byId("searchResultsMessage").style.display = "none";
  dojo.byId("searchNoResults").style.display = "";
  dijit.byId("searchGrid").domNode.style.display = "none";
}
```

Then if `matchesFound` is `true`, it's time to update the UI. First, the two message `<div>`s are hidden. Next, we instantiate a new `DojoData` and wrap it around the `searchStore`. This gives us a data model to bind to the search results grid. Following that, we show the grid by updating its `display` style attribute to a blank string. This has to be done, or updating the model won't work, and updating the model is exactly what we do next via a call to `setModel()`, passing it a reference to `searchStoreModel`. Finally, a call to the grid's `update()` method gets the match on the screen.

Now, if no matches were found, we just ensure that the grid isn't showing, and we go ahead and show the "no matches found" message `<div>`.

Assuming there were snippets that matched the search criteria, you'd be greeted with search results, as seen in Figure 6-12.

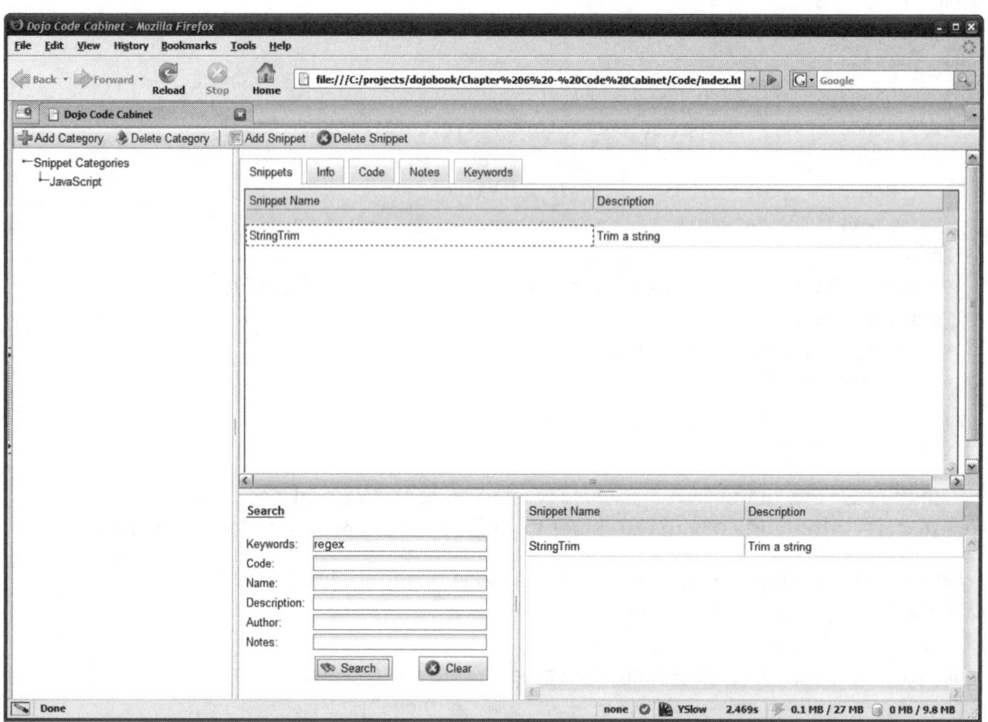

Figure 6-12. *Some search results displayed*

Only one bit of search-related code is left, and that's what is executed when a snippet is clicked from the search results grid:

```
/**
 * Called when a snippet in the search results grid is clicked.
 *
 * @param inRowIndex The index of the row that was clicked.
 */
this.searchResultClicked = function(inRowIndex) {
```

```
  codeCabinet.searchStore.fetch(
    { onComplete : function(items, request) {
      // Get the item from the store corresponding to the clicked row.
      var searchItem = items[inRowIndex];
      // Now find the item in the currentSnippetsStore.
      var snippetID = codeCabinet.searchStore.getValue(searchItem, "id");
      codeCabinet.currentSnippetsStore.fetchItemByIdentity({
        identity : snippetID, onItem : function(item) {
          // Set it as the current snippet.
          codeCabinet.currentSnippet = item;
        }
      });
      // Show all the snippet details.
      codeCabinet.showSnippet();
    }
  });

} // End searchResultClicked().
```

We have to do the same sort of `fetch()` and matchup via `inRowIndex` as we saw in the code that handles clicking on the snippets grid. Again, just having the row index that was clicked isn't sufficient. We need to relate it to the underlying data store, and the only way I could see to do this was to fetch all the records and access the array of `Items` by using `inRowIndex` and the index value. After that's done, we get the `id` field of the `Item`. With that, we can use the `fetchItemByIdentity()` method of the `currentSnippetsStore` to the `Item` of the snippet that was clicked. We set `currentSnippet` to that `Item`, call `showSnippet()`, and we're all done because it will handle everything else, as we saw earlier.

Suggested Exercises

I think the code cabinet as it is presented in this chapter is pretty useful, but as usual I've left some things out. Here are just a few suggestions, all of which would make it a more useful application, not to mention giving you a lot of good experience working with Dojo:

1. Allow for subcategories. Say I want to have a Java category, and below that I want to have a category for string-related snippets, one for math-related snippets, and one for UI-related snippets. As it stands today, I'd have to create three separate Java categories, all at the same level in the tree hierarchy. Allowing for subcategories would make the organizational capabilities of the application that much more robust.

2. Allow for searching across categories. This would make the search capabilities a lot more useful for sure. I originally intended to implement this, but because of time constraints I had to drop it. That's probably fortuitous because now I offer it to you as a suggestion!

3. How about adding a field to the Info tab for the date the snippet was added? For bonus points, use the DateTextBox dijit, and for even more bonus points, add it to the search function.

4. This one's a little bigger but would really make the application nice: history capabilities. In other words, every time you make a change to a snippet, record the state of the snippet before the change. Whether you simply duplicate the entire snippet record or try to do a fancy-pants diff mechanism is up to you. Add a tab that lists all the history records and allow one to be clicked so you can see the state of the snippet at that point. This would almost give this application a source control system type of feel to it.

5. Add a Copy button below the code editor. This is just a minor enhancement but could be a fairly significant convenience for the user. (To be honest, I thought of this only after this chapter was nearly all wrapped up. I feel a little silly for not thinking of it earlier, but hey, it gives me a chance to offer another suggested exercise to you, my dear reader!)

6. Implement some sort of server-side persistence. This book is focused on Dojo and client-side coding, so many of the projects almost scream out for some server interaction, and this one is no exception. Having the ability to save the snippets to a server-side database, and thereby make them available on more than one PC and also give you a backup mechanism, would be really nice but is outside the scope of this book—mostly, at least: the server-side certainly is, but the client-side implementation isn't. Here's a hint: it shouldn't take more than modifying the `_customSave` methods of the snippets and categories stores.

I suspect those suggestions will keep you busy for a while! They will not only make the application more useful but will definitely sharpen your skills in the process, so a definite win-win situation! What are you doing still reading? Get to work!

Summary

In this chapter, we developed an application for coding code snippets. We used a bunch of dijits in the process, got some experience with the `dojo.data` package, and even played with Gears more directly than in the last project. We dealt with a number of issues, including laying out a page in a more programmatic way than usual, how to "save" data, and how to bind dijits to data stores. In the process, we created an application that we can use for a real purpose!

CHAPTER 7

Idiot Blob: The Game!

In the previous chapter, we wrote an application that provides us a place to store our snippets of code, and to organize and find them as quickly as possible. In the chapter before that, we wrote an application to keep track of our contacts and also to organize them in a manner that made it easy to look them up when needed.

Both applications were useful, and both demonstrated some good usages of Dojo. The one thing they clearly were not, though, was fun. When I say that, I mean *fun* in the sense that they weren't created explicitly to be fun to use. I certainly hope they are to some degree, and I certainly hope they were fun to dissect and get into, but their purpose in life was fairly serious. They had real needs they were trying to fulfill.

Well, fun is a need too, and nothing is more fun than a game! Well, nothing we can talk about in mixed company at least (wink, wink). So, in this chapter we'll set about the task of writing a game by using Dojo. I wouldn't expect EGM to be declaring this game of the year, but it'll have some element of enjoyment—at least, that's the plan![1]

Requirements and Goals

Let me tell you about my son Andrew. He's a gamer. No, more specifically, to hear him tell it, he's a gaming god. Now, I'm all for self-confidence, and the fact is, he's usually pretty darned good. He bested me in a Guitar Hero tournament last year, and I'm no slouch at that game to be sure![2]

He also frequently declares his desire to be a video-game designer. Now, some parents might decide that's not a suitable vocation for a child to want to pursue, but those parents haven't looked at the numbers. We all used to say we wanted our kids to grow up to be doctors

1. *EGM* stands for *Electronic Gaming Monthly,* a popular gaming magazine here in the United States.

2. Guitar Hero is a series of games by Activision for various console video-game systems: you play a fake guitar in time to popular songs. If that sounds stupid to you, I'd first ask where you've been lately, and second I'd tell you to give it a try next time you're in a store that has it on display. It's considerably more fun than it sounds! Many video game stores run tournaments, as did the one right up the street from us last year when Guitar Hero III was released. My son and I entered and pretty well demolished everyone else in it. The final match turned out to be me against my son, and he proceeded to whip my butt pretty solidly! Since then he hasn't beaten me nearly as often because I've been practicing my tail off (yes, I'm a sore loser, especially when it's to an obnoxious eight-year-old). But he'll always have those bragging rights from that one tournament win. I think all parents want their children to exceed them; we just don't want it to be so soon and perhaps not as public!

and lawyers, but why? With doctors there's a certain chivalry there, so it's fairly obvious. Why a lawyer, though? Lawyers are generally not very highly regarded—not until you need one at your side at least! I mean, there's a whole web site dedicated to lawyer jokes (`www.lawyer-jokes.us`), and that pretty much says it all right there.

No, the primary reason we tell our kids to be doctors or lawyers (even though we know how the rest of the world will perceive them in the case of becoming a lawyer) is that they tend to make a ton of money, and that ensures that our children will be able to get us into good retirement homes when we reach our golden years!

But what about a video-game designer? Surely that's a foolish goal that won't meet *our* needs of 24/7 bingo and all the Cream of Wheat we can eat, right? Absolutely not! The video game industry is one of the most profitable sectors of the United States economy today,[3] and I suspect that's a trend that is applicable in many other industrialized countries as well. There's clearly good money to be made in this field, so I'd rank it at least up there with lawyers in terms of supporting us parents when we're the ones in need of diapers again!

What does this have to do with the requirements and goals for this project, you ask? Simple: My son provided many of the basics for this game. This is in fact his first foray into video-game design! Now, look, he's only eight years old, so you can't exactly expect Halo or Grand Theft Auto quality here, but it'll suit our needs just fine:

- The game story: You are the proud owner of an idiot blob named Qwamp, not unlike Gloop and Gleep[4] but a lot less intelligent. Qwamp has wandered off into the Cave of the Elements. Each chamber of the cave represents one of the four mythical foundational elements of nature: fire, water, air, and earth. Your job will be to guide him through the cave to safety because you see, being an idiot blob, he's an *idiot*! This means he can't do it himself; you'll have to tell him what to do each step of the way. Now, although idiot blobs are idiots, they listen and obey well. A little *too* well as it happens: If you tell Qwamp to move forward, he will continue to move forward until you tell him to do otherwise, even if that means he walks headlong into a burning fire! This is a problem because the four chambers of the cave are maze-like with narrow bridges going across them. Step off a bridge, and Qwamp plunges into fire, water, or air (which we'll assume is bad for some reason in this game!), or plunges hundreds of feet to the ground below. There are also alien skulls littered across the cave that if touched kill Qwamp dead. Dead ends and rocks can actually be helpful as they stop Qwamp but do not kill him; they're more of an inconvenience (or a help perhaps in some cases).

---

3. The video-game industry in recent years has rivaled the movie industry in overall income. Top game designers can make a pretty penny, to say the least. Like most creative fields, it's pretty hit-or-miss, and there are probably just as many starving game designers as there are starving artists in the world, but the upside is pretty far up there!

4. Gloop and Gleep are the two amoeba-like creatures from the old cartoon *The Herculoids*. If you watched this cartoon on Saturday morning television, you're likely laughing right now. If you've never heard of it, this sounds pretty dumb! Check out Wikipedia for details: `http://en.wikipedia.org/wiki/The_Herculoids`.

- So, based on the preceding story, we know we'll have to draw four levels and enable the user to control Qwamp to move through them. Each level will have a different background of the appropriate element with the bridge maze superimposed over it. There will need to be alien skulls in spots, and control of Qwamp will have to work in the manner described in the story. My son designed the four levels for us (and earned himself $50 in the process—he's well on his way to getting me that nice suite in the Shady Maple Retirement Home!).
- There's no scoring. You either get Qwamp to the end of the fourth level or he dies, so we'll need a win and lose screen to be displayed when applicable.
- To make the game a little more interesting, we'll implement three levels of difficulty. The difference between each is the amount of time you have before Qwamp moves again. Let's say you tell Qwamp to move forward. Remember, he'll keep doing that until you tell him otherwise, or he runs into a dead end, or he dies. So on the hard level, for instance, there will be 1 second between Qwamp moves, which means you'll have just 1 second to decide what Qwamp's next move should be and to click the appropriate button on the screen.
- Speaking of buttons, we'll provide a simple four-way directional group of buttons for controlling Qwamp, plus a button to start a new game.
- We'll want to display the preceding story, plus some simple instructions as well.

So now that you know what my son has planned for you, let's figure out how we as programmers are going to implement the vision of our lead game designer!

How We Will Pull It Off

If you've had occasion to read my previous three books, you'll know that a chapter that revolves around a game project has kind of become my signature. You would also probably realize that I typically advocate a very low-level approach to developing games in the sense that I tend to not want to use libraries for most things and do it all myself. The primary reason is that game programming usually requires you to be in more control over the target environment than many libraries allow you to be. You need to know every instruction that is being executed so you can optimize for performance, more so than you would in a typical business application.

However, this being a book about a specific library, we'll be using Dojo here obviously. Thankfully, it's not a forced usage because Dojo has the `dojox.gfx` namespace that you looked at briefly earlier, and that turns out to be perfect for our needs here.

In Chapter 4, you took a look at `dojox.gfx`. There are only a few new parts of it that we'll be using in this project, and I'm going to introduce them as they are used in the code. With Chapter 4 and this chapter, you should have a decent set of examples for that namespace.

Recall that one of the game's requirements is to show the instructions and the back story to the user. We could do this in any number of ways, but in keeping with the Dojo theme, I decided to use the Dialog dijit for this. Not only does it give us a good solution for displaying this information, but it also looks pretty good, especially if we use the Soria theme, instead of the Tundra theme I've used in the other projects in this book. The Soria theme is a little more "cartoonish" in a way, if for no other reason than it's a bit more colorful, which fits the theme of a game a bit better.

Revenge of the Demented Video Game Designer

One of the interesting problems I faced in this project was how to create the backgrounds. You see, as cool as `dojox.gfx` is, speed isn't one of its strong suits. Now, don't take that to mean that it's slow. In fact, it's surprisingly fast in a great many cases. All I mean is that for some things it's simply not fast enough, and doing complex animations is one of them.

Early on my son decided that the fire, water, and air caverns of the cave should have animated backgrounds. I agreed with him and then said to myself, "How the h**l am I going to pull that off with `dojox.gfx`?" I knew that drawing the background over and over to animate it just wasn't going to work; it wouldn't be nearly fast enough. So I had to figure something else out.

What I discovered is that `dojox.gfx` respects z-indexing. This means that if you draw something on the page, and then overlay a `Surface` on top of it, but don't draw anything on the `Surface`, that `Surface` is essentially transparent and you'll still see what you put underneath it (assuming the `Surface` has a higher z-index). This was a bit of luck because it meant I could use our old friend, the animated GIF, to create a background tile. Then, all I'd really need to draw on the `Surface` would be the bridge, dead ends, start and end markers for a given element cave, and Qwamp himself. The `Surface` would overlay right on top of the animated GIFs (GIFs, plural, because they are going to wind up being a grid of tiles, each tile being an animated GIF that when all put together give the illusion of one giant animated background image). I haven't seen this z-indexing information stated anywhere on the Internet, but I verified that it is the case on both Internet Explorer and Firefox, recent and near-recent versions. It's an extremely handy fact that opens up a lot of possibilities that otherwise wouldn't be possible with just `dojox.gfx` alone.

Finally, we're going to use the overlay "trick" for more than just the background: we'll also use it for Qwamp himself and for rocks. Once again, in the case of Qwamp, this is because of an animation requirement, which `dojox.gfx` isn't too well-suited for—well, setting aside transformations, which it's perfectly good at, but which wouldn't have been much use here. (Tiling the background by using transformations proved to be too slow, and trying to come up with a suitable transformation matrix to get Qwamp to do what I wanted was, to be blunt, mathematics way beyond my pay grade!) The rock is done this way because the shape of the rock required a considerable amount of code to generate with `dojox.gfx`, more so than the alien skulls which *are* done that way. I decided it was easier to use the overlay trick for the rocks as well, even though they are not animated.

PROCEDURAL GRAPHICS: TAKING A CUE FROM THE XBOX 360

One of the things that makes Microsoft's Xbox 360 so powerful is something called *procedural graphics*. This is a fancy term for something pretty mundane: generating graphics via code.

Think of a typical game. Usually, all the graphics you see onscreen are drawn by an artist and then used by a programmer to generate a given scene. There are usually elements created in real time on top of that, such as smoke and sparks and those sorts of things, but elements such as cars, trees, and characters are generally artwork drawn by a person (or previously generated by a computer, as in a Pixar movie, for example).

With procedural graphics, though, some sort of programming algorithm is employed to generate the graphics in real time rather than by an artist beforehand. Now, typically procedural graphics deals with things that can be modeled by using fractal geometry—trees and clouds and such—and not typically for more-complex and specific objects such as cars and spaceships. However, this isn't always the case: if the programmer is skilled enough, she can create just about anything.

Even if the programmer isn't very skilled, or if the requirements aren't that intense, you can generate virtually any graphics procedurally, and that's exactly what we'll do in this game: the alien skulls, level-end markers, and bridges will be drawn procedurally, while the rocks, Qwamp, and backgrounds are typical artwork.

Dissecting the Solution

The directory structure of the application, shown in Figure 7-1, is once again perfectly typical of most, if not all, of the applications throughout this book.

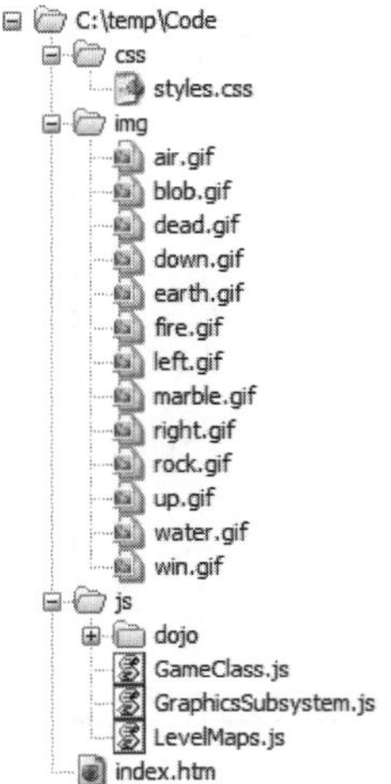

Figure 7-1. *The directory structure of the application*

In the `styles` directory, we find the usual `styles.css` file containing all the style sheet information for the application. In the `img` directory are a bunch of image files. The `air.gif`, `fire.gif`, `earth.gif`, and `water.gif` files are the animated (in the case of air, fire, and water) GIF tiles for the cave chambers' backgrounds. The `blob.gif` file is another animated GIF, this time of Qwamp. The `dead.gif` and `win.gif` files are the images seen when you lose or win the game, respectively. The `left.gif`, `right.gif`, `up.gif`, and `down.gif` files are the icons that will be shown on the four directional control buttons. The `rock.gif` file is an image of a rock that will be overlaid onto the cave. There's also a `marble.gif` file that is a marble texture used for the background of the control area of the screen (and cleverly, to make the bridge that Qwamp must walk on).

Under the `js` directory, we find the `dojo` directory, as you'd expect, as well as three files: `GameClass.js`, which is the main class and logic of the game; `GraphicsSubsystem.js`, which contains generic graphics functionality used in the `GameClass.js` code; and `LevelMaps.js`, which contains the data for the four levels of the game.

In the root directory is the usual `index.htm` that contains the markup for the project and is what you load into your browser.

With that out of the way, let's begin now by taking a quick look at the game itself, starting with Figure 7-2.

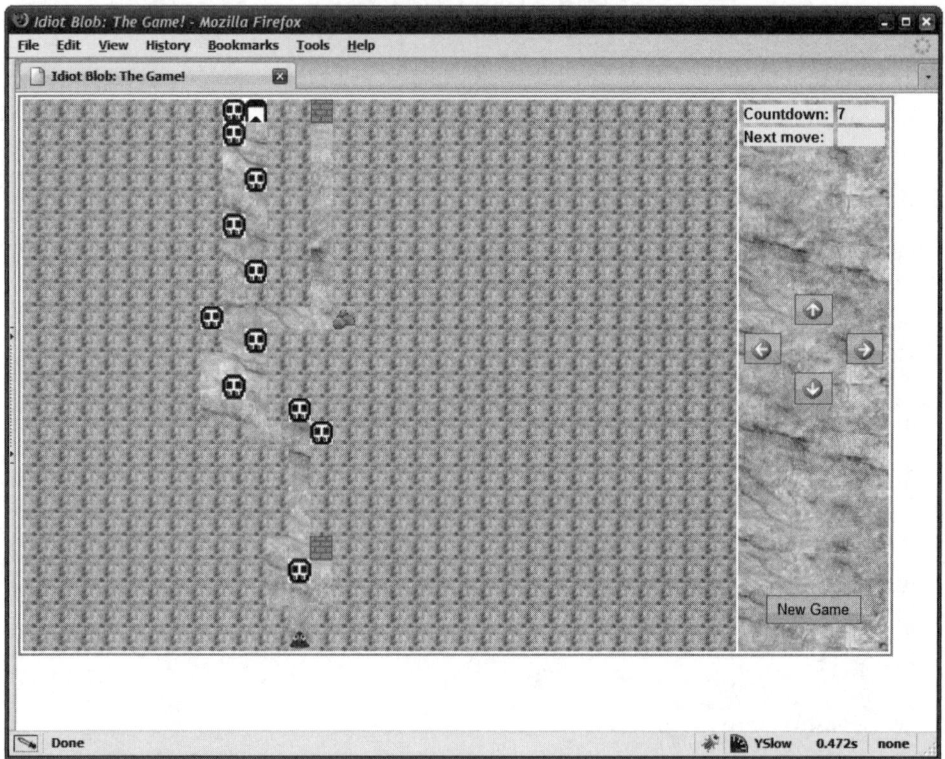

Figure 7-2. *The first level of the game during play*

As you can see, there is the main play area on which you can see Qwamp down there near the bottom, as well as a number of alien skulls, rocks, and dead ends on the bridge. The fire in the background is moving, which obviously you wouldn't know from a picture in a book (not yet, although I hear those digital book readers are set to take off any day now, and you'd presume they could handle something like that!). On the right-hand side is the control area, which houses the four directional control buttons and the New Game button, as well as some information up top showing a countdown before Qwamp's next move and the direction that the move will be in.

In Figure 7-3, you can see the second level of the game, the water chamber of the cave.

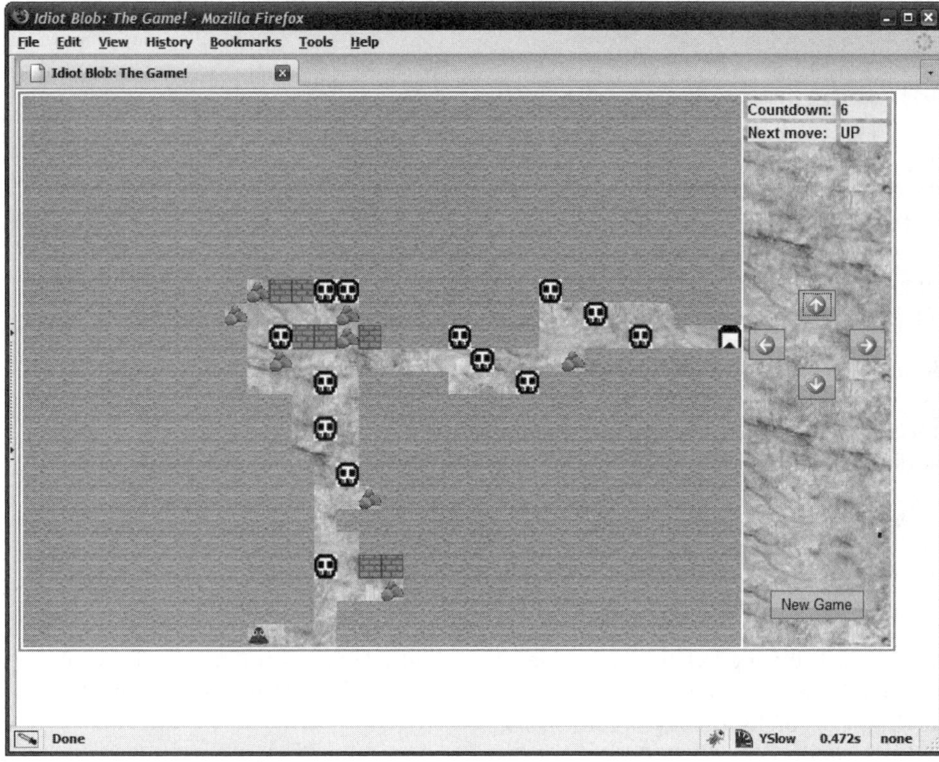

Figure 7-3. *The second level of the game during play*

This isn't much different from the first level, but I thought it would be a good idea to see more than a single level.

Now let's get to the code!

Writing index.htm

The natural place to start is `index.htm`, which can be thought of as the underlying scaffolding that the application is built upon. It's a plain old HTML document, so it begins with a `<head>` section, and within it we find some pretty typical style sheet imports:

```
<!-- Stylesheets. -->
<link rel="StyleSheet" type="text/css"
  href="js/dojo/dojo/resources/dojo.css">
<link rel="StyleSheet" type="text/css"
  href="js/dojo/dijit/themes/soria/soria.css">
<link rel="StyleSheet" type="text/css" href="css/styles.css">
```

The baseline `dojo.css` style sheet is of course imported, as well as the style sheet for the Soria theme. Finally, the application-specific `styles.css` style sheet is imported. We've previously discussed `dojo.css`, and you know about the style sheet for the theme from past experience as well. We'll have a look at `styles.css` right after we're done with `index.htm`.

Following the style sheet imports is our usual starting Dojo configuration and Dojo core import:

```
<!-- Dojo config and load. -->
<script type="text/javascript">
  var djConfig = {
    baseScriptUri : "js/dojo/",
    parseOnLoad : true
  };
</script>
<script type="text/javascript" src="js/dojo/dojo/dojo.js"></script>
```

Because we'll be using the Dialog dijit, and using it in a declarative fashion, we need to make sure widget parsing is turned on, hence the parseOnLoad attribute set to true. Other than that, this is exactly like what you've seen before.

Next are a couple of JavaScript imports to get the actual game code into the page:

```
<!-- Load application code. -->
<script type="text/javascript" src="js/GraphicsSubsystem.js"></script>
<script type="text/javascript" src="js/LevelMaps.js"></script>
<script type="text/javascript" src="js/GameClass.js"></script>
```

As previously mentioned, the core game logic is housed in the GameClass.js file, while general graphics-related code is in GraphicsSubsystem.js, and LevelMaps.js contains the data used to draw each of the four levels of the game.

After that in the code, we find a <script> section that contains what is essentially the bootstrap, or startup code, as well as some Dojo require() statements:

```
<script>
  // Import Dojo components.
  dojo.require("dojox.gfx");
  dojo.require("dojox.timing._base");
  dojo.require("dijit.Dialog");
  dojo.require("dijit.form.Button");
  dojo.require("dijit.form.Slider");
  dojo.require("dojo.parser");

  // The one and only instance of the GameClass.
  var game = new GameClass();

  // Startup tasks.
  dojo.addOnLoad(function() {
    game.init();
  });
</script>
```

We'll of course be using dojox.gfx, so that entire namespace is imported. We'll also be using the dojox.timing.Timer class that we previously looked at, so we need to import dojox.timing._base (that's a little bit of an odd import, the only one I believe we've seen with an underscore in its name, but it's required). We also know we'll need the Dialog dijit imported, as well as the Button dijit. The selection of difficulty level will be done via slider, so we use `require()` `dijit.form.Slider`. Finally, the declarative dijit facility doesn't work without loading in `dojo.parser`, so that's done as well.

Then, an instance of the `GameClass` class is created. This is the JavaScript class contained in the `GameClass.js` file, which we'll look at later.

Finally, we use the `dojo.addOnLoad()` function to hook up some startup code, which is nothing but a call to the `init()` method of the instance of `GameClass` we created.

■ Note As I've mentioned in previous chapters, you can sometimes get away with using the usual page `onLoad` event to do your startup tasks, but it's pretty much just a matter of luck when that works. When you're using Dojo, and dijits specifically, `dojo.addOnLoad()` is the way to go. In this application, you would definitely notice some things that fail to work related to `dojox.gfx` if you tried to use `onLoad`.

This `<script>` block is the last bit of content in the `<head>` section. Next begins the `<body>` section:

```
<body class="soria">
```

The Soria theme will be used here because of its more "playful" nature, that is, it's a bit more colorful and therefore more appropriate for a game in my mind. Please don't take that to mean it can't or shouldn't be used in a serious application; that's not what I'm saying at all! It's just that I felt its visual style better matched the theme of a game than did the Tundra theme I've used in other projects.

Anyway, let's move on to the start of the actual markup:

```
<div class="cssOuterBorder"></div>
```

As you play the game, you'll notice a border around the entire gaming area. That border is a result of this `<div>`. The interesting thing about it is that everything else is *not* a child of this element, as you might expect. That was necessary because of the way everything has to lay out; as children, some elements would have been more difficult to position relative to others that I needed to. Besides that, the only point of this element is to provide for the border. There's no real need for any parent-child relationships in the first place.

After that `<div>`, we find the markup for the first of two dialog boxes that will be seen whenever a new game is begun:

```
<!-- Welcome Dialog One. -->
<div dojoType="dijit.Dialog" id="WelcomeOneDialog" dragable="false"
  title="Welcome - Page One" class="cssDialog1" style="display:none;">
  <div id="divWelcomeOneSurface"></div>
  <center>
    <button dojoType="dijit.form.Button"
      onClick="dijit.byId('WelcomeOneDialog').hide();➥
      dijit.byId('WelcomeTwoDialog').show();">
      Continue
    </button>
```

```
  </center>
</div>
```

The result of this markup can be seen in Figure 7-4.

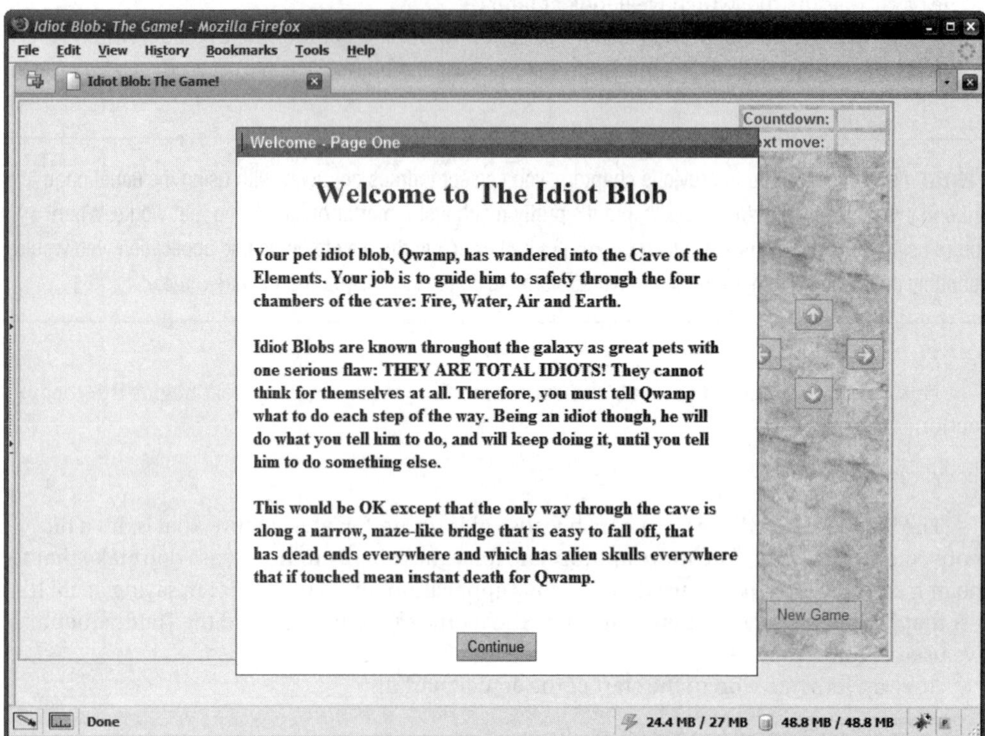

Figure 7-4. *The first "page" of the Welcome dialog*

At this point, unless you're completely asleep (which would mean I haven't done my job well at all!), you will be scratching your head going, "Err, where's the text?" The answer is at least hinted at a little bit by the divWelcomeOneSurface <div> element. The word *surface* in there is a clue that this element will house a dojox.gfx Surface, and if that's the case, it's not much of a stretch to imagine that the text itself is drawn on that Surface. The code that does this drawing will be seen later when we look at the JavaScript files.

The next logical question is, "Why would we do it this way at all?" Why not just put the text in the markup? Certainly that would be easier, but two considerations made me do it this way. First, because this is a book with a goal of teaching you something, I thought this was a good way to demonstrate some of the dojox.gfx text functionality a bit more. Second, and really the more relevant reason (certainly the less contrived reason!) is that in the second dialog box there is a need to display graphics that are drawn with dojox.gfx. In fact, let's look at that markup right now:

```
<!-- Welcome Dialog Two. -->
<div dojoType="dijit.Dialog" id="WelcomeTwoDialog"
  title="Welcome - Page Two" class="cssDialog2" style="display:none;">
```

```
  <div id="divWelcomeTwoSurface"></div>
  <center>
    <div dojoType="dijit.form.HorizontalSlider" class="cssSlider"
      value="2" minimum="1" maximum="3" discreteValues="3"
      showButtons="true" id="sldDifficulty">
      <div dojoType="dijit.form.HorizontalRuleLabels"
        container="topDecoration" labels="Easy,Medium,Hard"
        class="cssSliderLabels">
      </div>
    </div>
    <br><br>
    <button dojoType="dijit.form.Button"
      onClick="dijit.byId('WelcomeTwoDialog').hide();game.startGame();">
      Start Game
    </button>
  </center>
</div>
```

Once again you can see there's no textual content here, just a Button dijit and a Slider dijit, and again a <div> that we can surmise will be where the text is drawn. In Figure 7-5, you can see what this markup, plus the text that is later drawn in the dialog box, looks like.

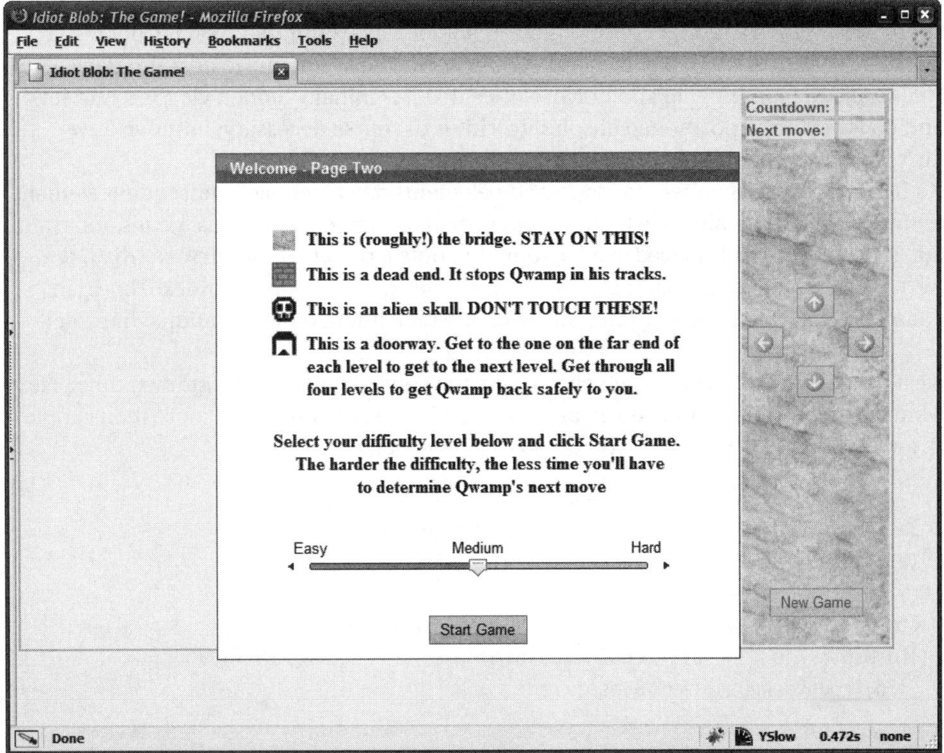

Figure 7-5. *The second "page" of the Welcome dialog box*

Both of these Dialog dijits have a style class applied, cssDialog1 for the first, and cssDialog2 for the second. As you'll see, this is responsible for sizing the dialog box, at least for Internet Explorer. You can also see that the dialog box is initially hidden via the style="display:none;" attribute. The first dialog box has a Button dijit that when clicked hides that dialog box and then shows the second.

The second dialog box also has a Button dijit that when clicked hides that dialog box and then calls the startGame() method of the GameClass instance referred to by the variable game. This dialog box also has a Slider dijit that is used to select difficulty level. This has a HorizontalRuleLabels dijit associated with it for showing the text labels on it. The default difficulty level of Medium, which is a value of 2, is set initially by virtue of the value attribute being set to 2.

Following the markup for the dialogs is the markup for the actual play area of the page:

```
<!-- Play area. -->
<div id="divContainer" class="cssPlayArea">
  <!-- Main surface. -->
  <div id="divSurface" style="display:none;"></div>
  <!-- Blob image. -->
  <img src="img/blob.gif" id="imgBlob"
    style="position:absolute;display:none;">
</div>
```

A single <div> contains the play area, and what that <div> contains is another <div> that will house the dojox.gfx Surface, after it's created in the JavaScript that we'll be looking at shortly. There is also an <img> that is the idiot blob itself. The src points to an animated GIF of our little stupid pet jumping up and down. Notice that it is initially hidden via the style setting and is also set to be positioned absolutely. This is of course necessary; otherwise, we wouldn't be able to move the blob around the screen.

It's important to remember that as you add elements to a page, each subsequent element is effectively (but not literally) at a higher z-index than its predecessors. This means, for example, that if the blob <img> is placed at a location that puts it on top of the Surface <div>, the blob will appear on top of the Surface, even though they have the same z-index. This is an important fact that will work for us not only with the blob but in other situations that you'll see.

Next up we find the side area, which is where the control buttons, Countdown timer, Next Move indicator, and New Game button are housed. This is really not much more than simple HTML and some styling, so I won't spend too much time on it:

```
<!-- In-game data display areas. -->
<div class="cssSideAreaPart" style="top:6px;height:164px;">
  <table cellpadding="4" cellspacing="4" width="100%">
    <tr>
      <td width="1" class="cssInfoBoxes">Countdown: </td>
      <td width="100%" class="cssInfoBoxes"
        id="countdownDisplay"> </td>
    </tr>
    <tr>
      <td width="1" class="cssInfoBoxes">Next move: </td>
      <td width="100%" class="cssInfoBoxes" id="nextMoveDisplay"> </td>
```

```
    </tr>
  </table>
</div>
```

The way these sections lay out is kind of important, though. Basically, the side area has three segments: the area where the game is displayed, the area containing the control buttons, and the area containing the New Game button.

The in-game data display area is the prior snippet. This is where the Countdown timer and Next Move indicator are. Note that the height of this `<div>`, `164px`, is actually more than is needed to display its content. That's by design. When we look at the style sheet, you'll find that each of these segments has a background image attached to it. In order to get the marble background to appear properly in the side area, each segment that makes it up needs to take up the space it needs for its content, and then some, so that the marble background fills up the entire side area.

The second segment is where the directional control buttons are, and the markup for that segment is seen here:

```
<!-- Control buttons. -->
<div class="cssSideAreaPart" style="top:170px;height:230px;">
  <table align="center" border="0" width="100%">
    <tr>
      <td valign="middle" align="center" colspan="2">
        <button dojoType="dijit.form.Button" iconClass="icons iconUp"
          onClick="game.setNextMove('up');" showLabel="false"
          label="up"></button>
      </td>
    </tr>
    <tr>
      <td valign="middle" align="left" width="50%">
        <button dojoType="dijit.form.Button" iconClass="icons iconLeft"
          onClick="game.setNextMove('left');" showLabel="false"
          label="left"></button>
      </td>
      <td valign="middle" align="right" width="50%">
        <button dojoType="dijit.form.Button" iconClass="icons iconRight"
          onClick="game.setNextMove('right');" showLabel="false"
          label="right"></button>
      </td>
    </tr>
    <tr>
      <td valign="middle" align="center" colspan="2">
        <button dojoType="dijit.form.Button" iconClass="icons iconDown"
          onClick="game.setNextMove('down');" showLabel="false"
          label="down"></button>
      </td>
    </tr>
  </table>
</div>
```

Once again, not a whole lot to it, just some relatively simple markup and four Button dijits. Each button, when clicked, calls the `setNextMove()` method of the `GameClass` instance, passing the direction that was clicked.

■Note One problem I discovered is that in Internet Explorer, if you set `showLabel` to `false` and don't include the `label` attribute, you'll encounter an error (you want `showLabel` set to `false` because all you really want to see on the buttons are arrows indicating the direction to move the blob). In Firefox, this is not the case; you can drop the `label` attribute entirely, which logically is what you'd think of doing. That's why there is a `label` attribute on each of these buttons, even though `showLabel` is set to `false`, thereby making the actual `label` value irrelevant.

The final segment is where the New Game button lives:

```
<!-- New Game button. -->
<div class="cssSideAreaPart" style="top:400px;height:86px;">
  <table width="100%" align="center">
    <tr><td align="center">
        <br><br>
        <button dojoType="dijit.form.Button"
          onClick="game.commonGameOverWork();➥
          dijit.byId('WelcomeOneDialog').show();">
          New Game
        </button>
      </a>
    </tr><tr>
  </table>
</div>
```

Once again, just some very simple markup and a Button dijit. A call to `commonGameOverWork()` is required to essentially finish off any current game that might be in progress, including getting the screen ready to display the two Welcome dialog boxes.

Writing styles.css

The style sheet for this game isn't all that large and certainly doesn't contain any especially complicated pieces, but let's have a look just the same, beginning with this snippet:

```
/* Styles for button icons. */
.icons {
  background-repeat   : no-repeat;
  background-position : 0px;
  width               : 20px;
  height              : 18px;
  text-align          : center;
}
```

```
.iconUp {
  background-image    : url("../img/up.gif");
}
.iconDown {
  background-image    : url("../img/down.gif");
}
.iconLeft {
  background-image    : url("../img/left.gif");
}
.iconRight {
  background-image    : url("../img/right.gif");
}
```

This is the exact sort of stuff in previous chapters for putting icons on Button dijits. Here we're putting arrows on the four directional control buttons:

```
/* Style for outer border. */
.cssOuterBorder {
  position            : absolute;
  top                 : 2px;
  left                : 2px;
  border              : 2px solid #a0a0ff;
  width               : 780px;
  _width              : 784px;
  height              : 484px;
  _height             : 488px;
}
```

When we looked at `index.htm`, you'll recall there was a `<div>` whose only purpose in life was to give us a border around the entire play area; it wasn't actually a container of anything. The `cssOuterBorder` class is what's applied to that `<div>`. It's positioned absolutely in the upper-left corner of the page, just 2 pixels from the edge, and it's a slightly bluish solid border that is 2 pixels thick. The `width` and `height` are simply specified as actual pixel values because we know exactly how large to make it based on the fact that we know exactly how big all the parts that will appear to be inside of it are.

However, there is a problem: Internet Explorer and Firefox don't deal with borders in exactly the same way. They always wind up being off by just a little bit (because, I believe, IE doesn't count the border itself in the overall width and height, whereas Firefox does). So, a simple CSS hack is used here. Any attribute name beginning with an underscore is ignored by all browsers other than IE. So, we have a `width` attribute set to `780px`. Firefox will use that value and ignore the `_width` attribute. However, IE will also use the `780px`, but will then *not* ignore the `_width` attribute, thereby overriding the value given by `width` right before it. It's a simple but effective hack. In general, you want to avoid hacks like this, especially given that a future version of IE might not work this way, but for the time being it works well and lets us avoid writing some JavaScript to deal with it.

The next two styles are somewhat interesting:

```
/* Hide close icon on dialog #1. */
#WelcomeOneDialog .dijitDialogCloseIcon {
  display             : none;
}

/* Hide close icon on dialog #2. */
#WelcomeTwoDialog .dijitDialogCloseIcon {
  display             : none;
}
```

I discovered that there is currently no way in Dojo to turn off the Close button that a dialog box usually has. This is annoying because you don't want the user to be able to close the Welcome dialogs; you want them to use the buttons on the bottom to move through them. (The Close button would have provided another path of execution to deal with that I'd prefer not to have to deal with.) The only way to get rid of that button is via CSS, as you can see here.

Two more style classes are present that have to do with the dialog boxes:

```
/* Style for dialog #1.  Note IE hack. */
.cssDialog1 {
  _width              : 565px;
  _height             : 480px;
}

/* Style for dialog #2.  Note IE hack. */
.cssDialog2 {
  _width              : 555px;
  _height             : 380px;
}
```

As it turns out, in Firefox the dialogs size exactly as you'd expect, and everything works right without specifying a width and height. In IE, however, this wasn't the case. Things didn't line up properly, I found, and the solution was to explicitly size the dialogs. However, because I needed to do this only for IE, I used the same sort of CSS hack trick we saw previously, so in Firefox these width and height values are simply ignored.

The next two style classes deal with the difficulty slider on the second Welcome dialog box:

```
/* Style for the difficulty slider. */
.cssSlider {
  width               : 350px;
}

/* Style for the labels on the difficulty slider. */
.cssSliderLabels {
  height              : 1.2em;
  font-size           : 10pt;
  color               : #000000;
}
```

The cssSlider class gives the slider an explicit width so that it fits nicely in the dialog box. The cssSliderLabels class simply sets the style for the text labels above the slider.

Following that is the class applied to the container around the play area:

```
/* Style for the play area container. */
.cssPlayArea {
  position            : absolute;
  left                : 6px;
  top                 : 6px;
}
```

No big deal there; it's nothing but positioning. The cssSideAreaPart that follows is a little more interesting:

```
/* Style for the side area parts (info, control buttons, New Game button. */
.cssSideAreaPart {
  position            : absolute;
  left                : 648px;
  width               : 134px;
  background-image    : url(../img/marble.gif);
}
```

Okay, so we're again positioning it absolutely, 648 pixels to the right to be precise, which puts it just beyond the 32 × 24 grid of tiles that is used to show the current level, and it has a background image of marble. The width is set so that it takes up the space between the right-hand edge of the grid and the right-hand edge of the border around everything. Notice, however, that there is no top attribute specified. The reason is that this same style class will be applied to each of the three segments that make up the info area portion of the screen, but each of those will have a different top setting, as well as a different height setting, which you'll also notice is not specified in the style sheet. In other words, I factored out the style attribute common to all three segments and placed it in cssSideAreaPart and left out the attributes that differ for each segment.

The last class, cssInfoBoxes, is this:

```
/* Style for the info boxes in the side area. */
.cssInfoBoxes {
  font-weight         : bold;
  font-size           : 10pt;
  background-color    : #ffffa0;
}
```

This is used to style the Next Move and Countdown timer text, and also give the yellowish background color to them so they stand out a little bit off the marble background.

With the style sheet and markup now all examined and hopefully making sense in your mind, it's time to get into the JavaScript used in this game. We'll begin with the code that stores the data representing the four levels, or cave chambers, of the game.

Writing LevelMaps.js

The `LevelMaps.js` file contains a single JavaScript class named, not surprisingly I expect, `LevelMaps`. The UML diagram for this class can be seen in Figure 7-6.

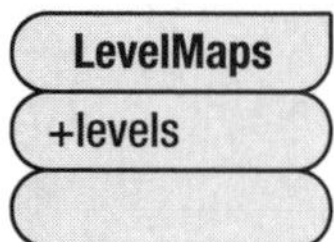

Figure 7-6. *UML class diagram of the LevelMaps class*

It has only a single member (which I think pretty much makes the UML diagram a waste of ink, but for the sake of consistency I included it). As it turns out, that single member, `levels`, is just a multidimensional array. The first dimension consists of four elements, one for each level of the game. The second dimension is a list of "tiles" to display. The data here is quite large, so here are just a few snippets from it, enough to give you a representative idea of what it's all about:

```
function LevelMaps() {

  this.levels = [

    /* LEVEL 1 */
    [
      { background : "fire" },
      { x : 10, y : 0, type : "end" },
      { x : 10, y : 1, type : "bridge" },
      { x : 10, y : 10, type : "skull" },
      { x : 10, y : 11, type : "bridge" },
      { x : 10, y : 12, type : "bridge" },
      { x : 10, y : 13, type : "bridge" },
      { x : 10, y : 14, type : "bridge" },
      { x : 10, y : 2, type : "bridge" },
      { x : 10, y : 3, type : "skull" },
...
      { x : 9, y : 8, type : "bridge" },
      { x : 9, y : 9, type : "bridge" }
    ],

    /* LEVEL 2 */
    [
      { background : "water" },
      { x : 10, y : 23, type : "start" },
      { x : 11, y : 23, type : "bridge" },
      { x : 12, y : 23, type : "bridge" },
      { x : 13, y : 23, type : "bridge" },
...
```

```
      { x : 29, y : 12, type : "bridge" },
      { x : 30, y : 12, type : "bridge" },
      { x : 31, y : 12, type : "end" }
    ]

  ];

} // End LevelMaps().
```

■ **Note** In JavaScript, there are no true multidimensional arrays; there are just arrays of arrays, quite literally. That's pretty much what a multidimensional array is in any language, but in JavaScript there's no syntactic sugar to hide that fact, as there is in some other languages, such as Java.

The way a given level is drawn is like this: The first element of the array for a given level is always an object with a single attribute named `background`. This names the type of background tile to use (it also is used to construct the image filename to use, so fire becomes `img/fires.gif`, for example). When a level is drawn, this element is examined, and a bunch of `<img>` elements, which are created dynamically during application initialization as you'll see, are set to the appropriate image file. These `<img>` elements are drawn at a z-index below the `dojox.gfx` `Surface`. In other words, the `Surface` overlays a grid of `<img>` elements that now have the appropriate image in them, be it fire, water, earth, or air. If nothing is drawn on the `Surface`, it is essentially transparent, so we see the background `<img>` elements and nothing else.

After that, the array for the level is iterated over. Each element of the array is an object with three attributes: `x`, `y`, and `type`. The `x` and `y` attributes tell the code the location of the tile. The playfield is a grid of 32 tiles across by 24 tiles down, and each tile is 20 pixels wide and 20 pixels high. So, an x and y location of 1,0 means it's the second tile from the upper-left corner. The `type` attribute obviously tells the code what type of tile it is. This can be a `bridge` tile, an `end` tile (which triggers going to the next level when the blob reaches it, or winning the game if it's the last level), a `start` tile (where the blob should begin on that level), a `skull`, a `rock`, or a `deadend`.

■ **Note** My son did not only the level designs, but also the coding you see here, which is his first actual programming experience. Sure, I gave him a template, so all he really had to do was copy a line, add a comma to the end, and transcribe the appropriate `x`, `y`, and `type` values from the graph paper he had drawn the map on, but it still counts! He also got to experience the magic of source control when he accidentally messed up a lot of work one time and I was able to get him very close to where he was by reverting changes. (I had him checking code into Subversion frequently; even though he didn't really know what he was doing, at least he could follow my directions well enough!)

This means that we are drawing only the tiles that are needed with `dojox.gfx`, rather than using it to redraw the entire playfield each time. This is a huge performance savings; it in fact cuts the time it takes to draw a level down pretty close to 90 percent. Worst still, the browser is locked up while the drawing occurs, so 1 second is clearly better than 10 (and that's 10 on my fairly beefy PC; it would have been far worse on a more average PC). This is the main reason, aside from the animation requirement, for using the whole "`Surface` superimposed over `<img>` elements" trick.

I figure taking a look at another of the levels couldn't hurt at this point, so here in Figure 7-7 you can see the third level of the game.

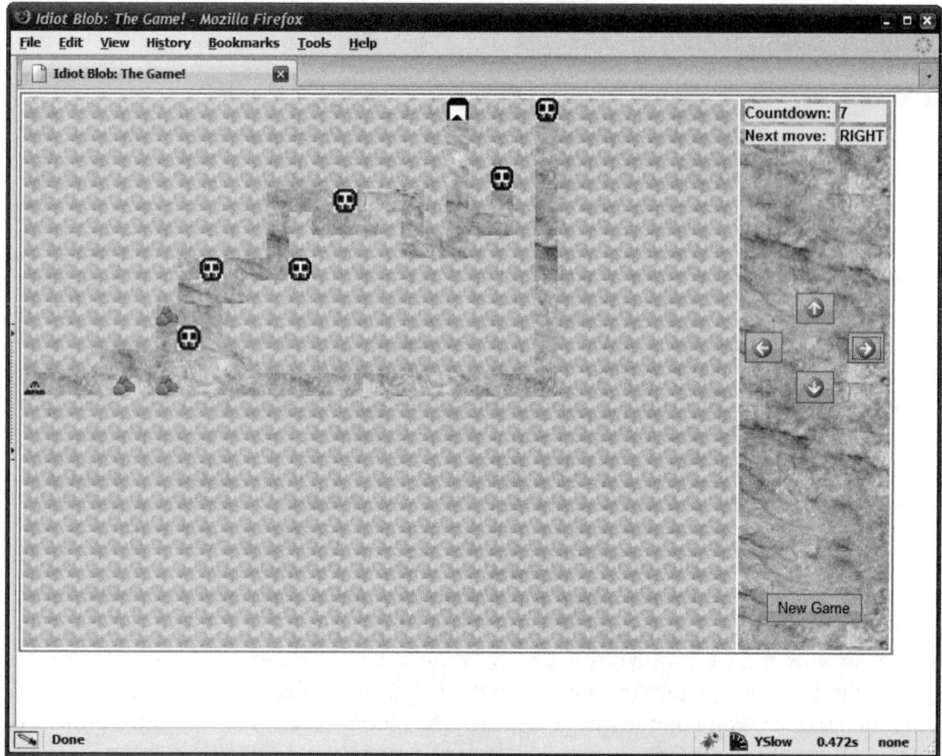

Figure 7-7. *The third level of the game during play*

Now that you have an idea of what the underlying data that describes a level looks like, and are starting to get an idea of how it's all drawn and constructed on the screen, let's delve into that `GraphicsSubsystem.js` file and see the (relatively) low-level graphics functions that are used throughout the main game code to put all this stuff on the screen.

Writing GraphicsSubsystem.js

I've written a fair number of games in my day, but few of them have been cross-platform. A few have been able to run on Windows and Pocket PC, but those platforms are in many ways similar, and the code didn't have to change very much to make that happen. I've often thought about the task of writing a complex game that runs on multiple game consoles plus PCs. This is a pretty tall order! When you think through how to pull that off, you pretty quickly realize that the only way you can do it without having ten different code bases is to break out the more generic "game logic" code from the more platform-specific graphics and audio code. The game logic—things like artificial intelligence (AI), physics, scoring, that sort of stuff—is all pretty platform-agnostic if you write it in a language that itself is platform-agnostic (or at least can be, if used right). C, for example, is such a language. If you stick to basic C, you can pretty well run a game on any platform out there today with minimal changes from platform to platform. C also is powerful enough to write all the core game code in without much trouble.

The graphics code, however, is another story altogether. The Xbox uses one type of graphics chip, while the PlayStation uses another. There are vast differences in programming for the Cell architecture of the PlayStation versus the Power PC–inspired Xenon core of the Xbox. So, you want to abstract out the code that is highly platform-specific from the more generic code.

That's what I've attempted to do with `GraphicsSubsystem.js`. Now, with a JavaScript-based game, you don't really have those platform-specific issues to deal with that you do when programming a multiplatform game. However, what if I later decide I don't want to use `dojox.gfx` for some reason? Maybe a speedier library comes out that does the same thing but with much better performance. In a sense, `dojox.gfx` *is* the platform I'm developing for. So, the less code I have to touch, the better. Ideally, if I've broken things out well, I should have to touch only the code in this file, and none of the code in `GameClass.js`, which is where the more generic "game logic" is.

Let's get the high-level overview of the `GraphicsSubsystem` class, which is what's found in the `GraphicsSubsystem.js` file naturally, by looking at its UML class diagram in Figure 7-8.

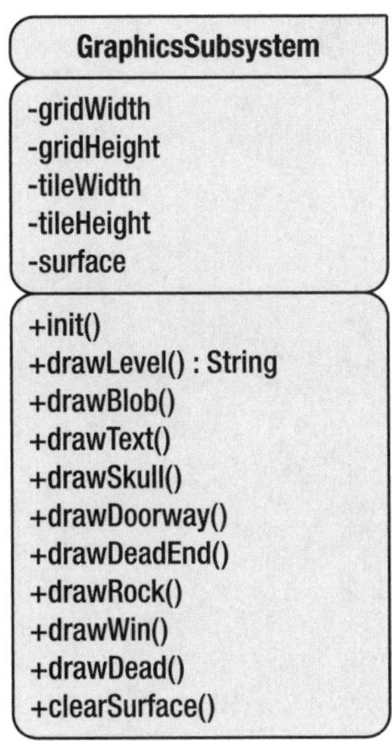

Figure 7-8. *UML class diagram of the GraphicsSubsystem class*

So, we have a couple of private members, and their declaration in the code can be seen here:

```
// Map sizing variables.
var gridWidth = 32;
var gridHeight = 24;
```

```
var tileWidth = 20;
var tileHeight = 20;

// The drawing surface.
var surface = null;
```

The gridWidth and gridHeight members define the number of tiles across and down in the grid that will be used to draw our levels. We'll have a grid of 32 × 24 tiles, and each tile will be 20 pixels wide and 20 pixels tall, as defined by the tileWidth and tileHeight members. Making these variables enables me to resize the play area as I see fit (originally I had this grid sized to 24 × 24 with a tile size of 32 × 32). Note that the border around the play area would need to be resized too, and that would be done through the style sheet. You could have that resized based on these variables too, if you wanted. To be perfectly honest, that didn't occur to me when I wrote the code originally; it was something I realized after the fact based on some comments from my technical reviewer (further proof, as if anyone needed it, that I am not, in fact, perfect!).

The variable surface is a reference to the dojox.gfx Surface object that will be created in the init() method, called when the application loads (indirectly called at least—this will make sense when we look at GameClass), and whose code you can see here:

```
this.init = function() {

  // Calculate actual pixel width and height of grid.
  var gridPixelWidth = gridWidth * tileWidth;
  var gridPixelHeight = gridHeight * tileHeight;

  // Resize container DIV and create Surface.
  var ds = dojo.byId("divSurface");
  ds.style.width = gridPixelWidth + "px";
  ds.style.height = gridPixelHeight + "px";
  ds.style.display = "";
  surface = dojox.gfx.createSurface(
    "divSurface", gridPixelWidth, gridPixelHeight);

  // Create img elements for background tiles.
  var container = dojo.byId("divContainer");
  for (var y = 0; y < gridHeight; y++) {
    for (var x = 0; x < gridWidth; x++) {
      var i = document.createElement("img");
      i.id = "imgBackground_" + x + "_" + y;
      i.style.position = "absolute";
      i.style.display = "none";
      i.style.left = (x * tileWidth) + "px";
      i.style.top = (y * tileHeight) + "px";
      container.appendChild(i);
    }
  }

} // End init().
```

This code begins by calculating the pixel width and height that the surface needs to be, which is simply multiplying the number of tiles across by a tile's width, and doing the same for the height. The divSurface <div> is then sized according to those calculations, and dojox.gfx.createSurface() is called, placing the Surface within divSurface. We now have a canvas on which to draw our game levels.

Now we move on to creating a series of <img> elements. We create an <img> element for each tile in the grid by using a loop within a loop. The outer loop is the height of the grid, and the inner loop is the width of the grid. This is how the background for a given level will be drawn. The src of each <img> element will be, in the drawLevel() method that we'll see next, set to point to the appropriate background tile GIF, as defined in the LevelMaps.js data, as we saw earlier. Each <img> element is created and then positioned absolutely at the appropriate location so that a grid is formed, which is a simple calculation: multiply the x loop value by the width of a tile, and the y loop value by the height of a tile, and that gives you the x and y (left and top style attributes) where the <img> should be located on the page.

The Surface is superimposed over this grid of <img> elements, which just means that it's located at the same location and "covers" the <img> elements. However, because the Surface is essentially transparent, anywhere that nothing is drawn on it, we see the <img> elements "shine through it." I've described all of this more than once now, but it occurs to me a picture is worth a thousand words, so here is Figure 7-9 to save me from typing a thousand more words!

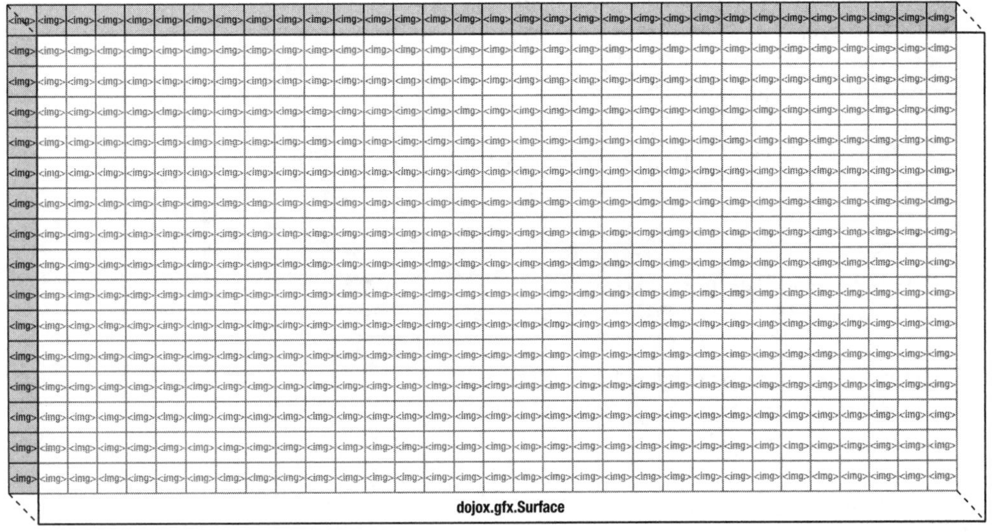

Figure 7-9. *A grid of <img> elements, with a dojox.gfx.Surface located directly over it, is where (and how) our levels will be drawn.*

Note The Surface being "superimposed" over the <img> elements doesn't really mean anything is done in terms of the z-index because again, any part of the Surface where nothing is drawn is transparent, so there's nothing special we have to do to make this work as we want. It's a natural consequence of how the Surface works, and of the fact that the location and size of the Surface is the same as the location and size of the grid of <img> elements.

With init() complete, the next step, at some point anyway (when a game starts to be more specific, or when Qwamp passes along to a new chamber in the cave), is to draw a level. Naturally, we want to have a fairly generic way of doing this, so the drawLevel() method exists, which accepts as an argument the array of data for a given level pulled from LevelMaps:

```
this.drawLevel = function(inLevelMap) {

  var retVal = "";

  // Clear the surface.
  this.clearSurface();

  // Show all background tiles and set the appropriate graphic.
  for (var y = 0; y < gridHeight; y++) {
    for (var x = 0; x < gridWidth; x++) {
      var tile = dojo.byId("imgBackground_" + x + "_" + y);
      tile.style.display = "";
      tile.src = "img/" + inLevelMap[0].background + ".gif";
    }
  }

  // Overlay the actual play tiles.
  for (var i = 0; i < inLevelMap.length; i++) {

    var xBase = inLevelMap[i].x * tileWidth;
    var yBase = inLevelMap[i].y * tileWidth;
    switch (inLevelMap[i].type) {

      // Bridge piece.
      case "bridge":
        // Nothing to draw, background shines through.
        dojo.byId("imgBackground_" + inLevelMap[i].x + "_" +
          inLevelMap[i].y).style.display = "none";
      break;
```

```
      // Dead end.
      case "deadend":
        this.drawDeadEnd(surface, xBase, yBase);
        dojo.byId("imgBackground_" +
          inLevelMap[i].x + "_" + inLevelMap[i].y).style.display = "none";
      break;

      // Rock.
      case "rock":
        this.drawRock(surface, xBase, yBase);
        dojo.byId("imgBackground_" +
          inLevelMap[i].x + "_" + inLevelMap[i].y).style.display = "none";
      break;

      case "skull":
        this.drawSkull(surface, xBase, yBase);
        dojo.byId("imgBackground_" +
          inLevelMap[i].x + "_" + inLevelMap[i].y).style.display = "none";
      break;

      case "start":
        // Nothing to draw, background shines through.
        dojo.byId("imgBackground_" +
          inLevelMap[i].x + "_" + inLevelMap[i].y).style.display = "none";
        // Record the location for the caller.
        retVal = inLevelMap[i].x + "," + inLevelMap[i].y;
      break;

      case "end":
        this.drawDoorway(surface, xBase, yBase);
        dojo.byId("imgBackground_" +
          inLevelMap[i].x + "_" + inLevelMap[i].y).style.display = "none";
      break;

    } // End switch.

  } // End for.

  return retVal;

} // End drawLevel().
```

First, we have a variable `retVal`, which as you'll see returns to the caller the x and y location of the starting tile for the level. You'll see why this is necessary when we look at the core game logic later.

The first task this method performs is to clear the `Surface` via a call to `clearSurface()` on it. We now have a clean slate on which to draw, which is important when moving from level to level. Next, we deal with the background. This is done by ensuring that all the `<img>` elements created in `init()` are showing (they are hidden at various times, as you'll see later). We point all of their `src` attributes to the appropriate GIF, as determined by looking at the first element of the passed-in array. As you'll recall from looking at `LevelMaps.js`, that data contains the name of the tile (fire, water, air, or earth).

If we did nothing else in this method, what you'd see on the screen would be nothing but the background, which wouldn't be a very fun game! So we begin to iterate over the array passed in. With each iteration, we calculate the x and y location of the next tile by using the x and y locations specified in the next element in the array. These values are relative to the grid of tiles, but `xBase` and `yBase` are relative in terms of pixels to the page, so it's a simple calculation, but a necessary one. Because we're going to need these values for just about any tile type, it's smart to calculate it here rather than duplicate the code in multiple places or, worse still, calculate it possibly multiple times, which would be inefficient in a loop like this.

Then, for each element we `switch` on the `type` attribute. For the type `bridge`, there's nothing to draw: we just need to hide the `<img>` element for that tile. This lets the marble background, which was set as the background image of the `<div>` that the `Surface` is in, shine through. This is also the case for the `start` type tile, which is a bridge tile but is slightly special in that the game code knows this tile indicates where Qwamp should be placed to start a level. For the `start` tile, the x and y locations are concatenated with a comma between them, and that value is stored in `retVal` to be returned to the caller. Again, you'll see how this is used in a bit when we look at `GameClass`.

■ **Note** Originally, I had code that drew a `bridge` tile, which maybe looked a little better, but it added seconds to the amount of time it took to draw a level. Using the background marble texture as the bridge shaved a noticeable amount of time off how long it took to draw a level, which I felt was a decent compromise.

For all the other types, there is some drawing to be done, so the appropriate method of `GraphicsSubsystem` is called to do so. Figure 7-10 shows the fourth level of the game.

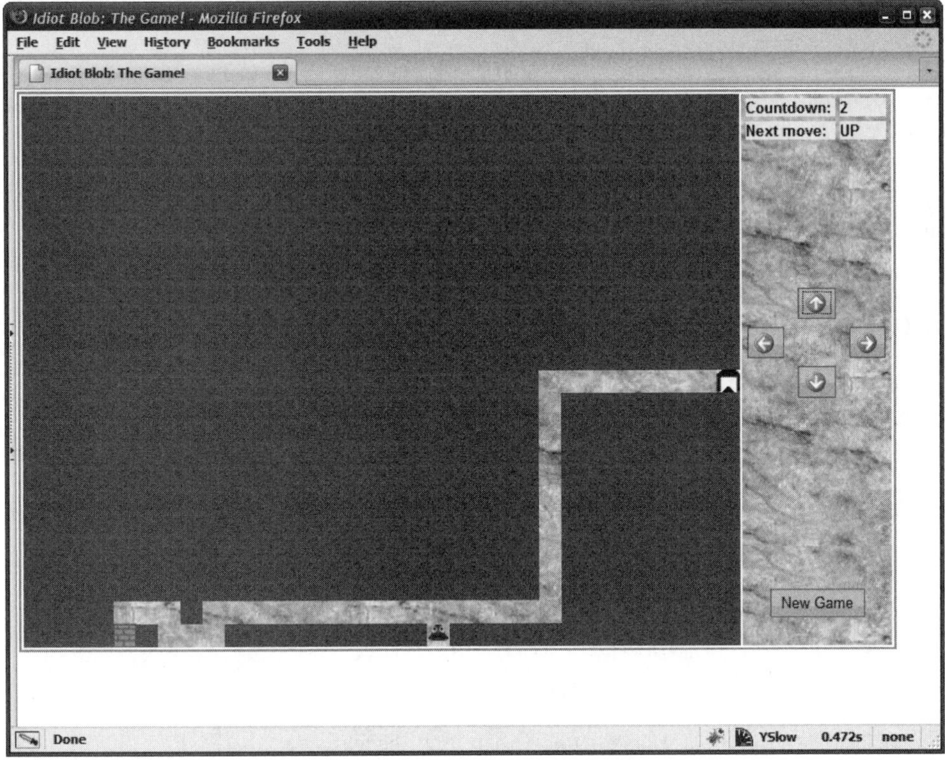

Figure 7-10. *The fourth level of the game during play*

For example, a skull type tile is drawn by calling the drawSkull() method, seen here:

```
this.drawSkull = function(inSurface, inXBase, inYBase) {

  // Fill background to white.
  inSurface.createRect({
    x : inXBase, y : inYBase, width : 20, height : 20
    }).setStroke({ color : "white" }).setFill("white");

  // Draw skull.
  inSurface.createRect({
    x : inXBase + 4, y : inYBase, width : 12, height : 2
    }).setStroke({ color : "black" }).setFill("black");
  inSurface.createRect({
    x : inXBase + 2, y : inYBase + 2, width : 2, height : 2
    }).setStroke({ color : "black" }).setFill("black");
  inSurface.createRect({
    x : inXBase + 16, y : inYBase + 2, width : 2, height : 2
    }).setStroke({ color : "black" }).setFill("black");
  inSurface.createRect({
    x : inXBase, y : inYBase + 4, width : 2, height : 10
```

```
    }).setStroke({ color : "black" }).setFill("black");
  inSurface.createRect({
    x : inXBase + 18, y : inYBase + 4, width : 2, height : 10
    }).setStroke({ color : "black" }).setFill("black");
  inSurface.createRect({
    x : inXBase + 4, y : inYBase + 6, width : 4, height : 5
    }).setStroke({ color : "black" }).setFill("black");
  inSurface.createRect({
    x : inXBase + 12, y : inYBase + 6, width : 4, height : 5
    }).setStroke({ color : "black" }).setFill("black");
  inSurface.createRect({
    x : inXBase + 2, y : inYBase + 14, width : 2, height : 4
    }).setStroke({ color : "black" }).setFill("black");
  inSurface.createLine({ x1 : inXBase + 6, y1 : inYBase + 14,
    x2 : inXBase + 6, y2 : inYBase + 17 }).setStroke({
      color : "black" });
  inSurface.createRect({
    x : inXBase + 9, y : inYBase + 14, width : 2, height : 4
    }).setStroke({ color : "black" }).setFill("black");
  inSurface.createLine({ x1 : inXBase + 13, y1 : inYBase + 14,
    x2 : inXBase + 13, y2 : inYBase + 17 }).setStroke({
      color : "black" });
  inSurface.createRect({
    x : inXBase + 16, y : inYBase + 14, width : 2, height : 4
    }).setStroke({ color : "black" }).setFill("black");
  inSurface.createRect({
    x : inXBase + 4, y : inYBase + 18, width : 12, height : 2
    }).setStroke({ color : "black" }).setFill("black");

} // End drawSkull().
```

Passed into this method is the Surface on which to draw, as well as the base x and y locations, meaning the pixel location of the upper-left corner of the tile to be drawn. All of the dojox.gfx drawing functions called in this method are based on that corner's location.

Here's where we have that procedural-type graphics approach I mentioned before. A skull is put on the screen by executing a bunch of createRect() and createLine() method calls on the Surface, beginning with one meant to give us a 20 × 20 white square on which to draw the black skull. We've seen these functions before, so I don't think there are any real surprises in them, except that the inXBase and inYBase arguments are used to calculate the true x and y location for each drawing operation.

I think perhaps the best way to really grasp what is going on is by looking at Figure 7-11. This shows each of the drawing operations that are performed, numbered in the order they occur. There's no magic to how I did this: it's nothing but a sheet of graph paper, and I draw the image and then figure out the minimum set of operations I could perform to draw it, or at least something close to the minimum. There may have been a more optimal set of operations, but this is fairly close, I think. At the end of the day, the fewer operations that need to be performed, the better, for the sake of performance.

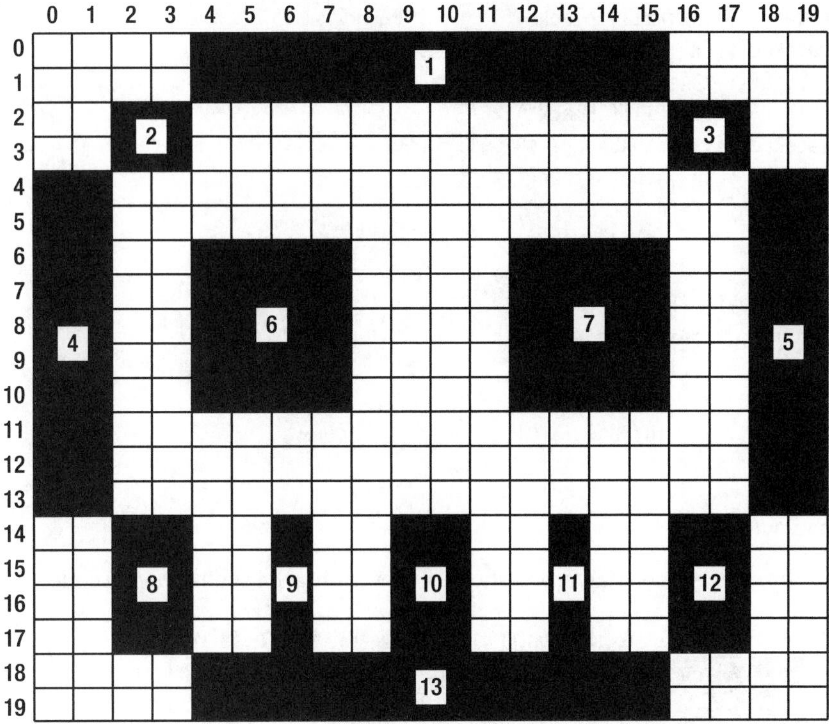

Figure 7-11. *The drawing operations, in sequence, for drawing a skull (not including the very first createRect() call that fills the background with white)*

The next method, `drawDoorway()`, is just like `drawSkull()` but is called to draw a doorway on the last tile of a given level:

```
this.drawDoorway = function(inSurface, inXBase, inYBase) {

  // Fill background to white.
  inSurface.createRect({
    x : inXBase, y : inYBase, width : 20, height : 20
    }).setStroke({ color : "white" }).setFill("white");

  // Draw the archway.
  inSurface.createRect({ x : inXBase + 4, y : inYBase + 0,
    width : 12, height : 2 }).setStroke({
      color : "black" }).setFill("black");
  inSurface.createRect({ x : inXBase + 2, y : inYBase + 2,
    width : 16, height : 2 }).setStroke({
      color : "black" }).setFill("black");
  inSurface.createRect({ x : inXBase, y : inYBase + 4,
    width : 20, height : 2 }).setStroke({
```

```
      color : "black" }).setFill("black");
    inSurface.createRect({ x : inXBase, y : inYBase + 6,
      width : 2, height : 13 }).setStroke({
        color : "black" }).setFill("black");
    inSurface.createRect({ x : inXBase + 18, y : inYBase + 6,
      width : 2, height : 13 }).setStroke({
        color : "black" }).setFill("black");

    // Draw the "perspective" triangle in the middle.
    inSurface.createPolyline([
      { x : inXBase + 4, y : inYBase + 20},
      { x : inXBase + 9, y : inYBase + 15},
      { x : inXBase + 10, y : inYBase + 15},
      { x : inXBase + 15, y : inYBase + 20}
    ]).setFill([0, 0, 0, 1]);

  } // End drawDoorway().
```

Figure 7-12 is the same sort of diagram as shown in describing the skull-drawing code.

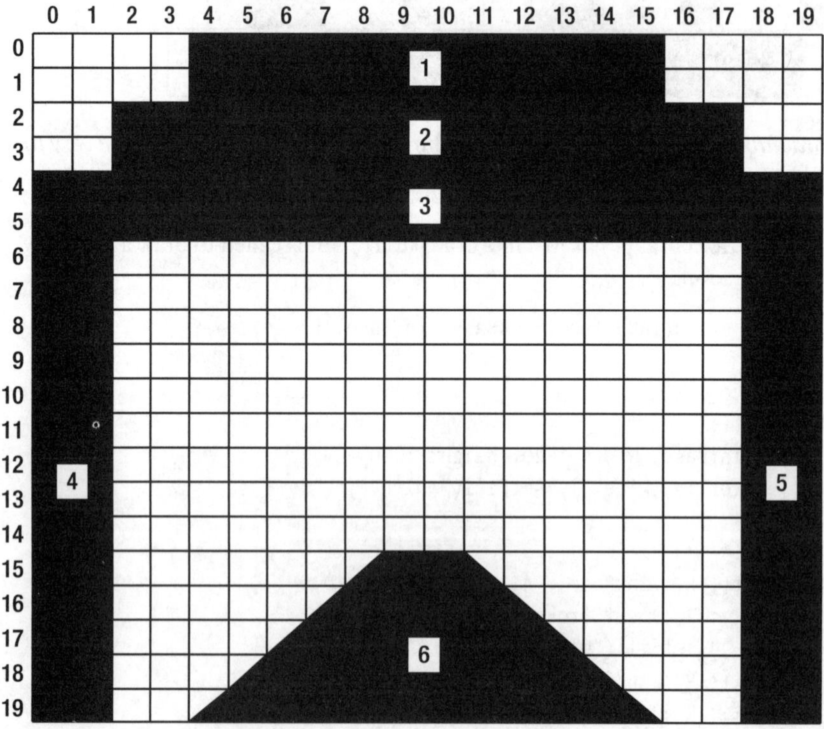

Figure 7-12. *The drawing operations, in sequence, for drawing a doorway (not including the very first createRect() call that fills the background with white)*

Drawing a dead end is next:

```
this.drawDeadEnd = function(inSurface, inXBase, inYBase) {

  inSurface.createRect({
    x : inXBase, y : inYBase, width : 20, height : 20
    }).setStroke({ color : "#4e4e4e" }).setFill("#b0b0b0");
  inSurface.createLine({ x1 : inXBase + 1, y1 : inYBase + 4,
    x2 : inXBase + 20, y2 : inYBase + 4 }).setStroke({ color : "#6e6e6e" });
  inSurface.createLine({ x1 : inXBase + 1, y1 : inYBase + 9,
    x2 : inXBase + 20, y2 : inYBase + 9 }).setStroke({ color : "#6e6e6e" });
  inSurface.createLine({ x1 : inXBase + 1, y1 : inYBase + 14,
    x2 : inXBase + 20, y2 : inYBase + 14 }).setStroke({ color : "#6e6e6e" });
  inSurface.createLine({ x1 : inXBase + 4, y1 : inYBase + 1,
    x2 : inXBase + 4, y2 : inYBase + 4 }).setStroke({ color : "#6e6e6e" });
  inSurface.createLine({ x1 : inXBase + 14, y1 : inYBase + 1,
    x2 : inXBase + 14, y2 : inYBase + 4 }).setStroke({ color : "#6e6e6e" });
  inSurface.createLine({ x1 : inXBase + 9, y1 : inYBase + 5,
    x2 : inXBase + 9, y2 : inYBase + 9 }).setStroke({ color : "#6e6e6e" });
  inSurface.createLine({ x1 : inXBase + 4, y1 : inYBase + 10,
    x2 : inXBase + 4, y2 : inYBase + 14 }).setStroke({ color : "#6e6e6e" });
  inSurface.createLine({ x1 : inXBase + 14, y1 : inYBase + 10,
    x2 : inXBase + 14, y2 : inYBase + 14 }).setStroke({ color : "#6e6e6e" });
  inSurface.createLine({ x1 : inXBase + 9, y1 : inYBase + 15,
    x2 : inXBase + 9, y2 : inYBase + 19 }).setStroke({ color : "#6e6e6e" });

} // End drawDeadEnd().
```

I'm pretty sure you're getting the idea by now without me going into any detail, but for the sake of completeness, Figure 7-13 is another diagram showing the drawing operations performed to draw a dead end.

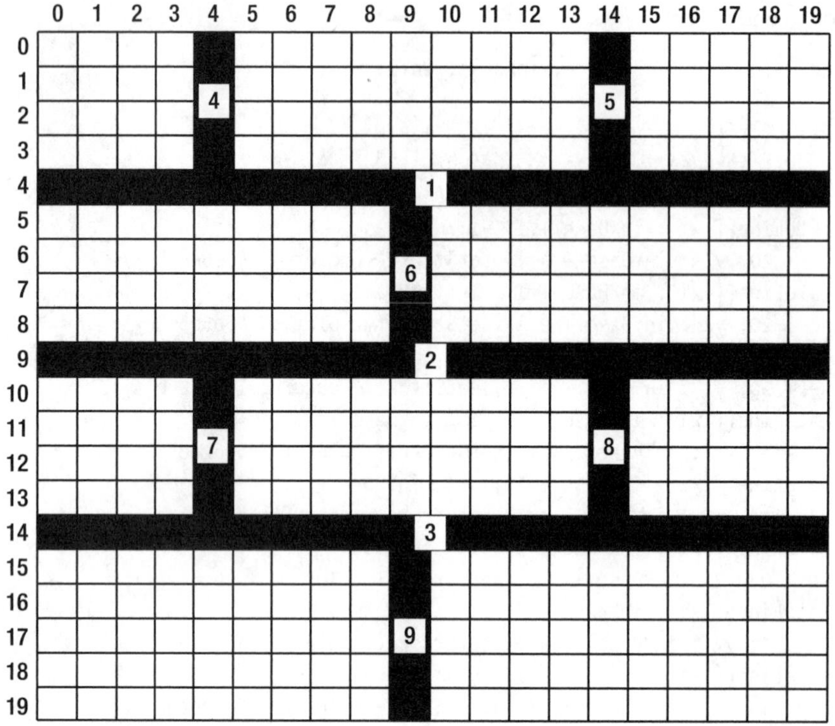

Figure 7-13. *The drawing operations, in sequence, for drawing a dead end (not including the very first createRect() call that fills the background with gray)*

Now we come to `drawRock()`, called to…wait for it…draw a rock! This one is different, however, because the rock isn't drawn as are skulls and dead ends; it is instead an actual GIF image displayed, but in a different fashion than the background tiles. Here, see for yourself:

```
this.drawRock = function(inSurface, inXBase, inYBase) {

  surface.createImage({
    type : "image", width : 20, height : 20, src : "img/rock.gif",
    x : inXBase, y : inYBase
  });

} // End drawRock().
```

The `createImage()` method of the `Surface` class enables you to load an existing image file, `rock.gif` in this case, and display it on the `Surface`. You need to set the type to `"image"`, and you also need to tell the method how wide and tall the image is (and no, the values do *not* need to be real, so you can in fact expand or contract, stretch or shrink the image).

■ **Note** You may at this point be wondering why I didn't use this method for the background tiles. There are a couple of reasons. First and most important, animated GIFs aren't supported by this method, so I wouldn't have been able to create the animated backgrounds called for by my son's level designs. Second, the performance of using this approach, while not poor, wasn't quite as good as the approach I wound up taking. Last, I frankly didn't know about this method to begin with! I discovered it after I had written the code described previously. I did go back and try to use it, which is how I found the first and second reasons were true.

Drawing Qwamp is also a different animal than the previously described methods because the blob is never actually drawn:

```
this.drawBlob = function(inBlobX, inBlobY) {

  var x = inBlobX * tileWidth;
  var y = inBlobY * tileHeight;
  var b = dojo.byId("imgBlob");
  b.style.display = "";
  b.style.left = x;
  b.style.top = y;

} // End drawBlob().
```

You'll recall when we looked at `index.htm` that there is an `<img>` with the ID `imgBlob`. All we need to do to "draw" Qwamp on the screen is ensure that this `<img>` is visible by settings its `display` style attribute to an empty string, and setting the `left` and `top` position values properly based on Qwamp's current location. Once again, using `createImage()` wouldn't have worked here because of the desire to animate Qwamp.

As I mentioned earlier with regard to the Welcome dialogs, the text in them is drawn by using `dojox.gfx` functions. However, as I started writing that code, I discovered that there was a lot of commonality in the text-drawing code for each dialog, so I decided to factor out the common bits and create a `drawText()` method to handle that:

```
this.drawText = function(inSurface, inX, inY, inSize, inColor, inText) {

  var txt = inSurface.createText({ x : inX, y : inY, text : inText });
  txt.setFont({ family : "Times", size : inSize + "pt", weight : "bold" });
  txt.setFill(inColor);

} // End drawText().
```

This method accepts a reference to the `Surface` to draw the text on, the x and y coordinates on that `Surface` to draw the text at, the font size in points, the color of the text, and of course the text itself. The font used will always be a `Times` variant and will always be bold. A call to `createText()`, followed by calls to `setFont()` and `setFill()`, are all that it takes to draw the text on the `Surface`.

When the player gets Qwamp to the last end tile of the fourth level of the game, that player wins the game. When that happens, we show a little graphic declaring the player victorious, and the `drawWin()` method is responsible for doing that:

```
this.drawWin = function() {

  this.clearSurface();
  var w = 361;
  var h = 80;
  surface.createImage({
    type : "image", width : w, height : h, src : "img/win.gif",
    x : ((gridWidth * tileWidth) - w) / 2,
    y : (((gridHeight * tileHeight) - h) / 2) - 10
  });

} // End drawWin().
```

This is a simple matter of using the `createImage()` method to display the `win.gif` image. The only real trick is that we want this graphic to be centered on the `Surface`; thus we need to do a quick little calculation for the x and y coordinates that is based on the width and height of the graphic. Figure 7-14 is the result of this method being executed.

■ **Note** Making the x and y location a calculation is a little more work than necessary because I could have just done the math and had the values statically in the code. I mean, if I wanted to swap in a new graphic, I'd have to go touch the code anyway to update the width and height values. But hey, isn't it a little cooler to have the code do the math? I think so! You also may wonder why I used a graphic at all and not just `drawText()`. There are two reasons. First, I couldn't see a good way to center the text except to precalculate the location and have it statically in the code, but we've already determined that's less cool! Second, and more important, I felt the graphic approach just plain looks better because I could make the text fancier than I could with just the `dojox.gfx` text functions (not without a lot more work, at least work I didn't feel was justified by the results).

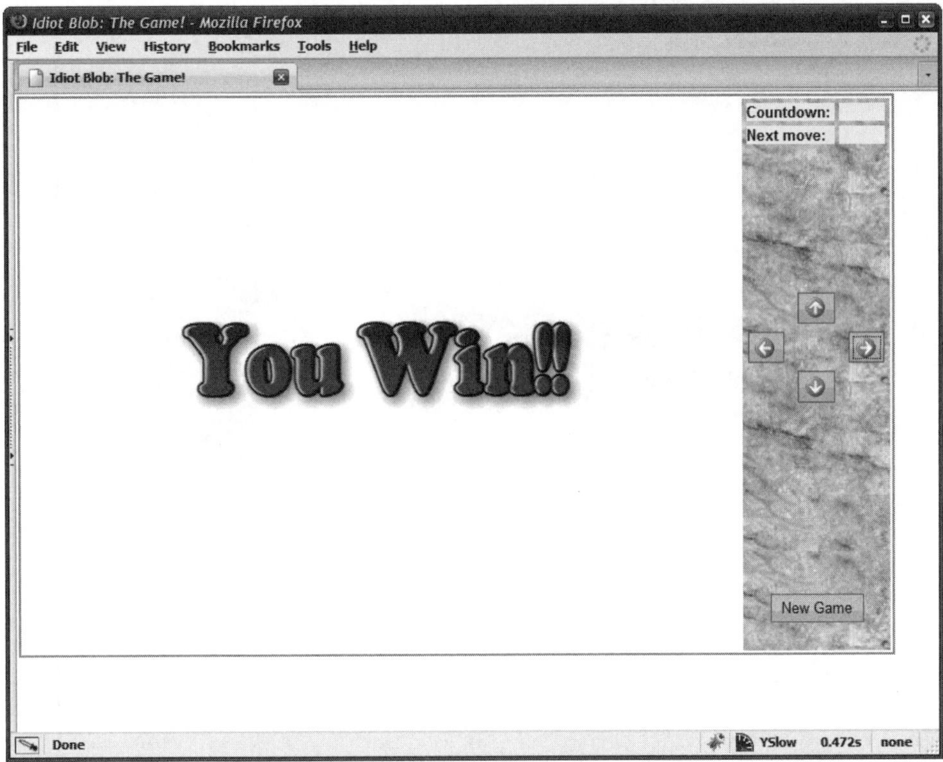

Figure 7-14. *Spoiler alert! This is what you see when you win. Did I ruin it for you?*

Similarly, when Qwamp dies, you get to see a different graphic, generated by the code in the `drawDead()` method:

```
this.drawDead = function() {

  this.clearSurface();
  var w = 422;
  var h = 114;
  surface.createImage({
    type : "image", width : w, height : h, src : "img/dead.gif",
    x : ((gridWidth * tileWidth) - w) / 2,
    y : (((gridHeight * tileHeight) - h) / 2) - 10
  });

} // End drawDead().
```

The result of that method being executed is shown in Figure 7-15. The code is pretty well identical to `drawWin()`, so no sense discussing it again.

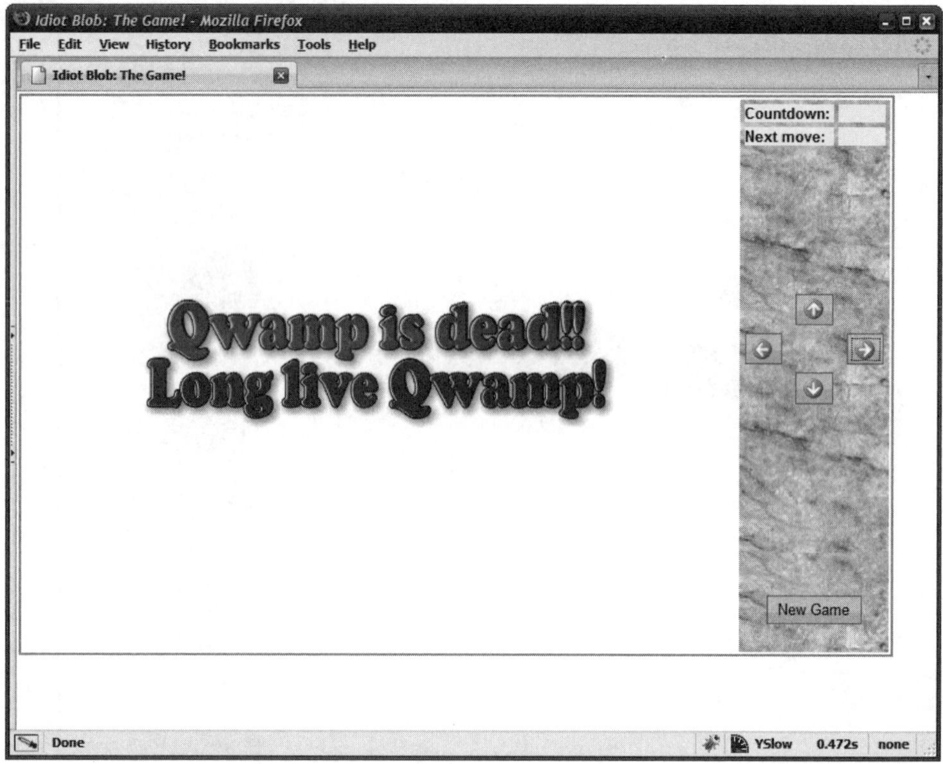

Figure 7-15. *In honor of the British tradition!*

The final method in `GraphicsSubsystem` is `clearSurface()`, which you can see here:

```
this.clearSurface = function() {

  // Clear the surface.
  surface.clear();

  // Hide Qwamp.
  dojo.byId("imgBlob").style.display = "none";

  // Hide all background tiles.
  for (var y = 0; y < gridHeight; y++) {
    for (var x = 0; x < gridWidth; x++) {
      var tile = dojo.byId("imgBackground_" + x + "_" + y);
      tile.style.display = "none";
    }
  }

} // End clearSurface().
```

This method encapsulates some common work that has to be done when clearing the surface at various points in the game's lifecycle. It's not just a simple call to `clear()` on the `Surface` object because of the overlaying of the `Surface` over the `<img>` tiles grid. We also need to hide Qwamp himself, in addition to hiding all those `<img>` elements, and those three tasks are what this method accomplishes.

Now that you've seen how all the graphics functions work, it's time to get into the core game code and see where all those functions are used.

Writing GameClass.js

Now we come to the code in `GameClass.js`, the core game logic code for the Idiot Blob. Have a look at the UML for the `GameClass`, shown in Figure 7-16.

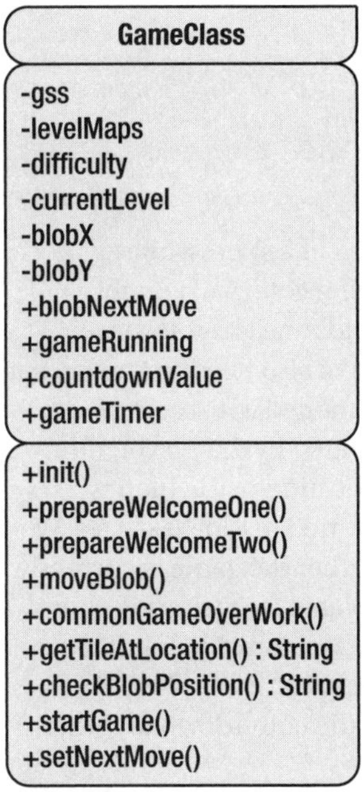

GameClass

-gss
-levelMaps
-difficulty
-currentLevel
-blobX
-blobY
+blobNextMove
+gameRunning
+countdownValue
+gameTimer

+init()
+prepareWelcomeOne()
+prepareWelcomeTwo()
+moveBlob()
+commonGameOverWork()
+getTileAtLocation() : String
+checkBlobPosition() : String
+startGame()
+setNextMove()

Figure 7-16. *UML class diagram of GameClass*

First we have a batch of class members, a few private and a few public:

```
// The GraphicsSubsystem instance.
var gss = new GraphicsSubsystem();

// The LevelMaps instance.
var levelMaps = new LevelMaps();

// Difficulty level being played on (1-3, 3=easy, 2=medium, 1=hard).
var difficulty = null;
```

```
// The current level (0-3) game is on.
var currentLevel = 0;

// Blob location.
var blobX = null;
var blobY = null;

// What direction will the blob move next iteration?
this.blobNextMove = null;

// Is the game currently running?
this.gameRunning = false;

// The current value of the move countdown.
this.countdownValue = null;

// The game Timer.
this.gameTimer = null;
```

So we have an instance of the `GraphicsSubsystem` class we looked at a short while ago, which makes sense because the game wouldn't be much fun if nothing got drawn on the screen! It also makes sense that we'd have an instance of `LevelMaps` floating around so we know what to draw on the screen, and sure enough that's there too. We also need to know what difficulty the game is being played at, and that is stored in the aptly named `difficulty` field. The `currentLevel` field tells us which of the four maps is being navigated by the player, numbered 0–3 so that it lines up with the array index in `LevelMaps`. The location of the blob is stored in `blobX` and `blobY`, and the next move the blob will make is stored in `blobNextMove`. We also have a field, `gameRunning`, that is a simple Boolean to tell us whether the game is currently running. This is necessary to stop things from happening while the game isn't running—for example, the player clicking one of the directional buttons when the Welcome dialogs are showing. The `countdownValue` field is used to do the countdown to the next move. Finally, `gameTimer` is a reference to a `dojox.timing.Timer` object that will do the countdown and then move the blob when the countdown reaches zero.

GAME LOOPS

This is ostensibly a book about Dojo, of course, but that doesn't mean I can't touch on other topics! One of those topics is a basic game theory concept called the *game loop*.

In most games there is a loop that runs, and this is essentially the heartbeat that makes everything work. The loop executes some number of times per second, and with each iteration the screen is updated, characters are moved, the states of onscreen objects are updated, and so on. We have a game loop in the Idiot Blob game, but it doesn't fire multiple times per second. Instead it fires once every tenth of a second. With each iteration, the countdown timer is updated, and we check to see whether it's time to move Qwamp yet, and do so if it is. If Qwamp is moved, we check where he landed to determine whether he is dead, has reached the end of a level, or is bouncing into a dead end or rock that he can't move through, and then we act accordingly.

A game loop is the heartbeat of a game's core logic, and also typically is used to update the screen, so if the game loop fires 30 times a second, for example, the screen may be updated each time, giving you a frame rate of 30 frames per second (fps). This is what you often hear about in game magazines when they say the frame rate is good: the higher the frame rate, and the more consistently it runs, the better, because it will appear smoother to the human eye. (24fps is considered the lowest frame rate where flickering is, for most people, not present. Anything lower shows flickering and doesn't appear smooth.) We of course don't have the need to update the screen every loop iteration in this game, so we don't have those types of concerns, but if you grab my *Practical JavaScript, DOM Scripting, and Ajax Projects* book (Apress, 2007), you'll find an arcade-style game where that consideration definitely does come into play.

We saw in `index.htm` that the `init()` method of `GameClass` is called on startup, which kicks off the game itself, so let's see what goes on in that code now:

```
this.init = function() {

  // Create game timer and define its onTick handler.
  game.gameTimer = new dojox.timing.Timer();
  game.gameTimer.setInterval(100);
  game.gameTimer.onTick = function() {
    dojo.byId("countdownDisplay").innerHTML = game.countdownValue / 100;
    game.countdownValue = game.countdownValue - 100;
    if (game.countdownValue == 0) {
      game.gameTimer.stop();
      game.moveBlob();
      if (game.gameRunning) {
        game.countdownValue = difficulty * 1000;
        game.gameTimer.start();
      }
    }
  };

  // Initialize graphics subsystem.
  gss.init();

  // Prepare the welcome dialog's two surfaces, one for each page.
  this.prepareWelcomeOne();
  this.prepareWelcomeTwo();

  // Show the first Welcome dialog.
  dijit.byId("WelcomeOneDialog").show();

} // End init().
```

First is the instantiation of our `Timer` that will run our main game loop. We set its interval to 1/10 of a second, or 100 milliseconds, and create an `onTick` event handler function for it. In that function, we're updating the countdown timer, which requires that we divide the countdownValue by 100 so that we're displaying tenths of seconds and not milliseconds. We then check whether we've reached zero, and if so we stop the timer and call the moveBlob() method, which naturally moves Qwamp based on the current direction he's set to move in. As you'll see, it's that method that contains the real logic of the game—for example, determining if the player has won or if Qwamp has died. After the call to moveBlob(), we check whether gameRunning is still true. It would have been set to false if Qwamp died or if the player won, but if neither of those things occurred, we need to start the timer again. At this point, we also reset the countdownValue to its initial value, which is based on the difficulty level. If the difficulty is Easy, the player has three seconds to determine Qwamp's next move. Because the Timer will fire 30 times within three seconds, that means that we need to reduce the value of countdownValue by 100 each time, which means it needs to start at 3000, hence the multiplication in setting its value. A difficulty of Medium gives 2 seconds, and Hard gives 1 second, so I'm sure you can see how the values work in those cases as well.

The next task is to initialize the GraphicsSubsystem, which you saw previously, so a quick call to gss.init() does that for us. After that we need to prepare the two Welcome dialogs and begin things by showing the first dialog.

Speaking of the first dialog, here is what "preparing" it actually means:

```
this.prepareWelcomeOne = function() {

  // Create the surface for page one.  Note different widths for IE vs. FF.
  var surface = dojox.gfx.createSurface(
    "divWelcomeOneSurface", (dojo.isIE?540:445), 400);

  // Title.
  gss.drawText(surface, (dojo.isIE?90:60), 30, 20, "red",
    "Welcome to The Idiot Blob");

  // First paragraph.
  gss.drawText(surface, 5, 80, 12, "black",
    "Your pet idiot blob, Qwamp, has wandered into the Cave of the");
  gss.drawText(surface, 5, 100, 12, "black",
    "Elements.  Your job is to guide him to safety through the four");
  gss.drawText(surface, 5, 120, 12, "black",
    "chambers of the cave: Fire, Water, Air and Earth.");

  // Second paragraph.
  gss.drawText(surface, 5, 160, 12, "black",
    "Idiot Blobs are known throughout the galaxy as great pets with");
  gss.drawText(surface, 5, 180, 12, "black",
    "one serious flaw: THEY ARE TOTAL IDIOTS!  They cannot");
  gss.drawText(surface, 5, 200, 12, "black",
    "think for themselves at all.  Therefore, you must tell Qwamp");
  gss.drawText(surface, 5, 220, 12, "black",
    "what to do each step of the way.  Being an idiot though, he will");
  gss.drawText(surface, 5, 240, 12, "black",
    "do what you tell him to do, and will keep doing it, until you tell");
```

```
  gss.drawText(surface, 5, 260, 12, "black",
    "him to do something else.");

  // Third paragraph.
  gss.drawText(surface, 5, 300, 12, "black",
    "This would be OK except that the only way through the cave is");
  gss.drawText(surface, 5, 320, 12, "black",
    "along a narrow, maze-like bridge that is easy to fall off, that");
  gss.drawText(surface, 5, 340, 12, "black",
    "has dead ends everywhere and which has alien skulls everywhere");
  gss.drawText(surface, 5, 360, 12, "black",
    "that if touched mean instant death for Qwamp.");

} // End prepareWelcomeOne().
```

You'll recall when we looked at the markup for this dialog that the text wasn't present on it and I said it was drawn on with `dojox.gfx` functions. See, I wasn't lying, here is that code! A `Surface` is created in the `<div>` reserved for it in the `Dialog` markup. Note the difference for IE and Firefox, which results in slightly different values for the width, as well as the x location of the first text drawn, and the title. (I don't typically like *magic numbers*, which is what these are, but I couldn't find a good way to do all this positioning in a more automatic way.) The `drawText()` method of the `GraphicsSubsystem` class that we looked at earlier is used throughout to draw the text, and I've simply precalculated the locations for each string of text so that it is positioned nicely in the dialog.

■ **Note** *Magic numbers* are a code smell, that is, something that most programmers consider bad form. A magic number is a "naked" number statically present in code whose meaning and derivation isn't immediately obvious from the code. Generally, constants and/or variables are a better choice because they give the numbers some semantic meaning. For instance, I could have had a variable named `surfaceWidth` and then had an `if…else` block that set it to the appropriate value based on whether `dojo.isIE` was `true` or `false`. This arguably would have made the code more readable, but also would have meant there was more code to parse, and sometimes a more concise form is preferable, even if it means using a magic number. It's a stylistic choice here, but magic numbers really do make code harder to read most of the time, and you should therefore take this as a counterexample of what you should, typically anyway, do in your own code!

The second dialog is similar, but is also a bit different, as you can see by examining the code here:

```
this.prepareWelcomeTwo = function() {

  // Create the surface for page two.
  var surface = dojox.gfx.createSurface(
    "divWelcomeTwoSurface", (dojo.isIE?530:445), 300);
```

```
  // Bridge tile and description.
  surface.createImage({
    type : "image", width : 20, height : 20, src : "img/marble.gif",
    x : 40, y : 30
  });
  gss.drawText(surface, 70, 44, 12, "black",
    "This is (roughly!) the bridge.  STAY ON THIS!");

  // Dead end and description.
  gss.drawDeadEnd(surface, 40, 60);
  gss.drawText(surface, 70, 75, 12, "black",
    "This is a dead end.  It stops Qwamp in his tracks.");

  // Skull and description.
  gss.drawSkull(surface, 40, 90);
  gss.drawText(surface, 70, 105, 12, "black",
    "This is an alien skull.  DON'T TOUCH THESE!");

  // Doorway and description.
  gss.drawDoorway(surface, 40, 120);
  gss.drawText(surface, 70, 135, 12, "black",
    "This is a doorway.  Get to the one on the far end of");
  gss.drawText(surface, 70, 155, 12, "black",
    "each level to get to the next level.  Get through all");
  gss.drawText(surface, 70, 175, 12, "black",
    "four levels to get Qwamp back safely to you.");

  // Difficulty level information.
  gss.drawText(surface, 40, 220, 12, "black",
    "Select your difficulty level below and click Start Game.");
  gss.drawText(surface, 60, 240, 12, "black",
    "The harder the difficulty, the less time you'll have");
  gss.drawText(surface, 115, 260, 12, "black",
    "to determine Qwamp's next move");

} // End prepareWelcomeTwo().
```

In this case, the Dialog shows the various obstacles for Qwamp to avoid, as well as what the bridge and end of a level look like, so there is a need to draw them (which is, incidentally, why I've used a Surface in these Dialogs rather than just static text). So, you can see the drawing functions that we examined previously in GraphicsSubsystem being used. You also now should understand why those methods accept a reference to a Surface, rather just assuming it would be the Surface on which the level is drawn: they are needed not just on the main game Surface, but on this Dialog-based Surface as well.

After the user clicks the Button dijit in the second Welcome dialog, a new game is begun, which results in a call to startGame():

```
this.startGame = function() {

  // Set background image so we get a bridge.
  dojo.byId("divContainer").style.backgroundImage = "url(img/marble.gif)";

  // Set up initial conditions.  Reverse the values 1 and 3 on the slider
  // because it's essentially backwards right now.
  difficulty = dijit.byId("sldDifficulty").getValue();
  if (difficulty == 1) {
    difficulty = 3;
  } else if (difficulty == 3) {
    difficulty = 1;
  }
  currentLevel = 0;
  game.gameRunning = true;
  game.blobNextMove = null;
  game.countdownValue = difficulty * 1000;

  // Draw the level map and blob.
  var blobLocation = gss.drawLevel(levelMaps.levels[currentLevel]);
  blobX = parseInt(blobLocation.split(",")[0]);
  blobY = parseInt(blobLocation.split(",")[1]);
  gss.drawBlob(blobX, blobY);

  // Start the main game "loop".
  game.gameTimer.start();

} // End startGame().
```

The first task is to set the `backgroundImage` of the `<div>` that the play grid is in to the `marble.gif` texture image. Recall from looking at `GraphicsSubsystem` that when a level is drawn and a tile that is a bridge tile is hit, the tile is not drawn and the corresponding background `<img>` is hidden. This enables the background of the `divContainer <div>` to shine through, giving us a bridge tile (a bridge made out of marble—but hey, this is the Cave of the Elements, so you'd imagine it'd be a bit fancier than just a wooden bridge!).

Next, the difficulty level is determined by getting the value of the Slider dijit. However, the values in a slider go up, from left to right, but remember that the higher the difficulty, the *lower* the amount of time the player has to move. That means that laying the difficulty levels out on the slider from left to right doesn't match the values because it's logical for the difficulty to increase as you read left to right across the slider, but the values are going to increase going in the same direction, which is the opposite of what we want. So, we have a little `if…else` block here that reverses the `1` and `3` values (`2`, Medium, is of course `2` no matter what).

After that, a bunch of variables are set to the correct initial values to start a game, including `currentLevel` set to `0` so that the game begins on the first level, setting `gameRunning` to `true` to indicate to the rest of the code that the game is in progress, setting `blobNextMove` to `null` so that to begin with Qwamp isn't moving, and setting `countdownValue` to the initial value based on the difficulty.

Following that setup is a call to `gss.drawLevelMap()`, which you'll recall accepts an array of tiles to draw taken from `LevelMaps`, which is just an array, so we use the value of `currentLevel` as an index into that array to get the appropriate-level data.

The call to `drawLevelMap()` returns a string in the form x,y where x and y are the coordinates Qwamp starts at. This is determined by looking for the special start tile in the level data, as you'll recall, so here finally is how that information is used. The values are parsed so we have numbers and not string values, and a call to `gss.drawBlob()` is made, passing those values into it.

At this point, we have the first level on the screen, and Qwamp at his starting location, so the only step left is to start the game loop `Timer` and we're off to the races!

The game loop looks at the value of `blobNextMove` during each iteration to determine how, if at all, to move Qwamp. How does that value get set, you ask? It's set when the player clicks one of the directional buttons, and the method that gets called is `setNextMove()`:

```
this.setNextMove = function(inDirection) {

  if (game.gameRunning) {
    game.blobNextMove = inDirection;
    dojo.byId("nextMoveDisplay").innerHTML = inDirection.toUpperCase();
  }

} // End setNextMove().
```

As you can see, there's not much to it. We first check to ensure that the game is currently running; otherwise, clicking the buttons shouldn't do anything (this is really to deal with the user clicking the buttons after Qwamp has died, that and when the player wins is the only time this can happen because otherwise the game is running, or one of the Welcome dialogs is showing, which makes the buttons unclickable). The argument passed in is the string value `up`, `down`, `left`, or `right`, which we store in `blobNextMove`, and we display it in the info area on the right. Note that Qwamp isn't actually moved at this time. That won't happen until the next iteration of the game loop, which means the player has the chance to change his mind before the countdown timer expires. Actually moving the blob is accomplished by calling `moveBlob()`, seen here:

```
this.moveBlob = function(inDirection) {

  // Skip if blob isn't moving this iteration.
  if (!game.blobNextMove) {
    return;
  }

  // Update blob location.
  var oldX = blobX;
  var oldY = blobY;
  switch (game.blobNextMove) {
    case "up": blobY = blobY - 1; break;
    case "down": blobY = blobY + 1; break;
    case "left": blobX = blobX - 1; break;
```

```
    case "right": blobX = blobX + 1; break;
  }

  // Check the tile the blob is now on.  If it's a dead end, revert the
  // location changes.
  var result = this.checkBlobPosition();
  if (result == "deadend" || result == "rock") {
    blobX = oldX;
    blobY = oldY;
  }

  // Draw the blob at its (potentially) new location.
  gss.drawBlob(blobX, blobY);

  // Check for win or loss and react accordingly.
  if (result == "dead") {
    this.commonGameOverWork();
    gss.drawDead();
  } else if (result == "win") {
    this.commonGameOverWork();
    gss.drawWin();
  }

} // End moveBlob().
```

First, a trivial rejection: Is there a move queued up? If not, the method ends with a return and that's that. If there's a move to make, though, we first update Qwamp's coordinates. In some cases, we'll need to basically revert the changes, so we begin by storing the current `blobX` and `blobY` values. Next it's just a simple `switch` block to determine how to modify Qwamp's coordinates.

After the coordinates have been updated, we have what is really the only game "logic," and that's to see if Qwamp is still alive, or if he's hit a dead end or a rock. A call to `checkBlobPosition()` is made, which returns a string that tells us the current state of Qwamp. There are a couple of possible return values. One is `deadend`, and another is `rock`. These are more or less the same thing because both mean Qwamp can't move in the direction requested, and in this case we need to revert the changes to his location, which is just a matter of setting `blobX` to `oldX`, and `blobY` to `oldY`.

At this point, we call `drawBlob()` so that Qwamp is shown at his new location (which may in fact be where he started, if he hit a rock or a dead end).

The last step is to see whether Qwamp is alive. If he's dead, the game is over and the player has lost, in which case we need to perform some common cleanup tasks by calling `commonGameOverWork()`. Then we call `gss.drawDead()` to show the "You're a loser" graphic. If Qwamp has landed on the end tile on the fourth level, the player has won and we need to show the "You're worth something" win graphic. This is achieved by the same `commonGameOverWork()` call, and then a call to `gss.drawWin()`.

The other possible return value from `checkBlobPosition()` is `ok`, which means Qwamp is alive and well and should move. In that case, there's nothing else to do because everything necessary has already occurred, so the method just ends.

We'll look at the checkBlobPosition() method next, because we just discussed how it's used:

```
this.checkBlobPosition = function() {

  var retVal = null;

  var tileType = this.getTileAtLocation(blobX, blobY);
  switch (tileType) {

    // Blob is still on a bridge tile or start tile, game continues.
    case "bridge": case "start":
      retVal = "ok";
    break;

    // Blob is on end tile, jump to next map or end win game.
    case "end":
      if (currentLevel == 3) {
        retVal = "win";
      } else {
        game.blobNextMove = null;
        dojo.byId("nextMoveDisplay").innerHTML = "";
        currentLevel = currentLevel + 1;
        var blobLocation = gss.drawLevel(levelMaps.levels[currentLevel]);
        blobX = parseInt(blobLocation.split(",")[0]);
        blobY = parseInt(blobLocation.split(",")[1]);
        gss.drawBlob(blobX, blobY);
        retVal = "ok";
      }
    break;

    // Blob ran into skull and is now dead.
    case "skull":
      retVal = "dead";
    break;

    // They hit a dead end or a rock, so revert the last move so it looks
    // like they didn't go anywhere, but the game continues.
    case "deadend": case "rock":
      retVal = "deadend";
    break;

    // Blob must be on a background tile, meaning they fell off
    // the bridge.
    default:
      retVal = "dead";
    break;
```

```
  } // End switch.

  return retVal;

} // End checkBlobPosition().
```

First a call to getTileAtLocation() is made, passing it the current location of Qwamp. That method is this:

```
this.getTileAtLocation = function(inX, inY) {

  // Cycle through tiles for this map and find the appropriate one and
  // return its type, or null if not found.
  retVal = null;
  for (var i = 0; i < levelMaps.levels[currentLevel].length; i++) {
    if (levelMaps.levels[currentLevel][i].x == inX &&
      levelMaps.levels[currentLevel][i].y == inY) {
      retVal = levelMaps.levels[currentLevel][i].type;
      break;
    }
  }
  return retVal;

} // End getTileAtLocation().
```

Recall that the data for a level does not include every single tile on the grid, nor does it have to be in any particular order. Therefore, there's no direct, straightforward way to retrieve the tile at location x,y without systematically scanning through the level data looking for the element with x and y attribute values that match the inX and inY values passed in, hence the need to do this loop. After the appropriate element is found, its type is returned.

Getting back to checkBlobPosition() now . . . after getTileAtLocation() gives us the type of tile Qwamp is standing on, it checks that type and acts accordingly. If the tile is a bridge or start type, checkBlobPosition() will need to return ok so that the caller, the moveBlob() method specifically, knows that Qwamp is alive and well. If the type is skull, Qwamp is dead, and that's the return value. Likewise, if the call to getTileAtLocation() returns null, that indicates that Qwamp has fallen off the bridge and is similarly toast. If the tile type is rock or deadend, the return value is deadend, which tells moveBlob() that the move needs to be reverted because Qwamp can't move on that tile.

I skipped over the case where the tile is the end tile until now because in this case there is more work to do than the other possibilities. When Qwamp steps on an end tile, it's either time to go to the next level or the game has been won. The check is simple: if the currentLevel value is 3, which is the last level, the game has been won, and the return value is win. If, however currentLevel is not 3, it's time to move on to the next level. In this case, all the game status variables are reset to their values when the game started, currentLevel is incremented by one (there's no way to go backward through the levels), and the new level is displayed. Qwamp is put on the starting tile, just like when the game first began, and the player is ready to start that level.

■ **Note** You can make the argument that the `getTileAtLocation()` belongs in the `LevelMaps` class, and I wouldn't argue too strenuously against that. Architecturally speaking, I think there's some logic to that position. Still, I chose to put `getTileAtLocation()` here simply because this is the only place it is used, and sometimes I find it makes more sense to keep code elements that call one another as close to each other as possible.

The final method to examine is really just a fairly simple utility method that saves us from having some duplicate code in a couple of places:

```
this.commonGameOverWork = function() {

  game.gameTimer.stop();
  game.gameRunning = false;
  gss.clearSurface();
  dojo.byId("divContainer").style.backgroundImage = "";
  dojo.byId("nextMoveDisplay").innerHTML = "";
  dojo.byId("countdownDisplay").innerHTML = "";

} // End commonGameOverWork().
```

The `commonGameOverWork()` method does some things that always have to occur when a game ends, regardless of how the game ended. The game timer is first stopped, and then `gameRunning` is set to `false`. The `Surface` is cleared, and the `backgroundImage` of the `divContainer` <div> is cleared. The result of these last two tasks is that the play area is completely blank. Finally, the information display fields on the right are cleared, and that's a wrap.

Suggested Exercises

For this project, I'm going to go fairly light on the suggestions because creating a game is pretty much all up to your imagination, more so than most other projects. After all, we *are* talking about a game called the Idiot Blob, so clearly imagination factors into it right from the word *go*! However, here are a few that might be good experience, and fun, which is the name of the…wait for it…*game*!

1. Add more levels. This won't give you much in the way of experience with Dojo, but seeing another level in there will give you a good sense of accomplishment. Of course, you'll have to modify the underlying story because there would no longer be the four basic "elements" at play, but that's up to you! Actually, come to think of it, I take back what I said. Doing this in fact *would* give you some play time with Dojo because you'll have to modify at least the second Welcome dialog, so go for it!
2. Add some other obstacles and draw them with `dojox.gfx`. This could be anything you want. Maybe a lava pit, or a snake, or whatever you can dream up.

3. Make the win and lose screens a little fancier and do it all with `dojo.gfx`. I like the way the graphics look on both these screens, but maybe some spinning text or something would be a good option too, and `dojo.gfx` can do that!

4. Add a scoring system. Maybe there are some "power crystals" that Qwamp needs to pick up in order to be able to get through a given level.

Summary

In this chapter, we took a break from the ordinary for a little while and developed a game by using Dojo. We got to play around with `dojo.gfx` a bit, and we also saw some tricks for blending what it can do with more-traditional types of graphics. We got a little more experience with Dijit too. Hopefully, in the process of all that we developed a game that is at least a *little bit* fun.

In the next chapter, we'll get back to some "serious" work and develop an application that uses Dojo to access some remote services in order to watch our stock portfolio grow and grow and grow. (Sorry, I don't know what happened, I slipped into optimistic mode there—that's not like me at all! I don't know what *your* stock portfolio has been doing lately, but I know mine has most certainly not been growing and growing and growing, that's for sure!)

CHAPTER 8

When the Yellow Pages Just Isn't Cool Enough: Local Business Search

Sit right back and you'll hear a tale, a tale of a big yellow book . . . I know, it doesn't quite fit the melody of the *Gilligan's Island* theme, but work with me here!

You kids today with your Internets[1] and your iPhones and your Tellmes,[2] you don't know what it was like! Back in the day, if you wanted to find a business in your home town, you either asked a neighbor or pulled out this huge yellow book called, very creatively, the *Yellow Pages*. Within this book, you could flip through an alphabetically sorted listing of all sorts of businesses in your vicinity. It was a manual process: you actually had to turn pages! You couldn't just type something into a computer and have it spit out a list of businesses; you had to burn some calories and expand some mental effort.

Ah, but I like progress as much as the next guy, so now I get to play the part of old curmudgeon and tell these stories about how we used to walk to school in the snow, uphill, both ways, and use the yellow pages. I also get to write books and show how the world is much better now that we can write an application to save us all that work.

That's precisely what this chapter is all about! We'll be writing an application that enables us to search for local businesses. We'll be able to see a map of where the business is located, and we'll be able to jump directly to the business's web site, if there is one. We'll also have the ability to store a business as one of our favorites so that, if you can believe it, we'll be able to expend even *less* energy next time to find it again! Dojo will make all of this a piece of cake, of course, and we'll have a pretty useful little application by the time we're finished.

1. During the 2000 presidential campaign, George W. Bush uttered the term *Internets*. Clearly, the Internet should never be pluralized like that—it's a pretty dumb thing to say—which is why people now use this phrase in a humorous context (and sometimes in an insulting way, depending on how it's used).
2. Tellme (`www.tellme.com`) is a voice-activated service that enables you to call a 1-800 number and get information such as weather, sports scores, business listings, and more, all just by speaking into the phone. It's a very handy service to have handy in your cell phone's contact list.

Application Requirements and Goals

Let's get the silly terminology out of the way first, shall we? What we're actually creating here is a mashup. A *mashup*, as it has come to be known, is basically a web site or application that takes content from multiple sources (usually via some sort of public programmatic interface, a remote API in other words), and integrates it all into a new experience, that is, a new application.

The term mashup might sound a bit silly (it does to me!) but it's the term that's been applied to what is at its core an extremely powerful vision: people provide various services and data over the Internet, and anyone can come along and combine them to create applications. In other words, we're talking about a relatively simple, open, platform-agnostic service-oriented architecture (SOA).

MORE ON SOA

The idea of SOA has been gaining steam over the past few years. Most notably, the concept of web services has been evolving rapidly over that time. However, the meaning of that term has been evolving as well. People now often consider things such as the Yahoo services that will be used in this application to be web services, even though they don't use the full web services stack (that is, SOAP, WS-Security, and all the other specifications that can go along with it).

Whatever line of demarcation you choose to use, the bottom line is that you're developing using a SOA, which means you have loosely coupled components that expose a remote service interface that, usually, is platform- and language-agnostic and can therefore be married together in nearly limitless ways.

The benefits of this approach are numerous. The simple fact that you aren't generally tied to any particular technology or language is a big one. The ease with which updates can be done, assuming the interface doesn't change, is another big one (this is the same reason people love web apps in general). The ability to use all sorts of automated tools to both create and consume services is another (although this isn't always a good thing, of course, if those tools become a crutch that allow you to not actually understand what you're doing). Realizing the goal of building your application on top of established standards is another. Reusing existing assets and therefore increasing the speed with which solutions can be delivered is another (some would argue this is the biggest benefit). There are plenty more; these are just some that come to mind immediately.

You've almost certainly heard the term *web services* before. Web services are sometimes involved in mashups. However, web services, as most people mean when they use the term, can be pretty complicated beasts! SOAP, Universal Description, Discovery, and Integration (UDDI) directories, Web Services Description Language (WSDL) documents, not to mention a whole host of other specifications, are the types of things you deal with in working with web services. Although there's nothing that says that stuff can't be involved when writing a mashup, typically they aren't.

Today, the term *mashup* most usually refers to a web app that, by and large, runs within your browser. In fact, for many people, mashup implies a JavaScript-based application that can run locally with no server interaction (aside from loading it in the first place, which is actually optional too, and calling on remote servers). Mashup has generally come to mean browser-based JavaScript clients aggregating content through public APIs from various companies and vendors to form new applications. These APIs are often referred to as web services, and even though they may not truly be web services in the sense of using the full technology stack, they fulfill the same basic goal as those types of web services. They provide services and function over a network (specifically, the Web), so calling them web services isn't really too far-fetched!

Many companies are getting into the API business, including companies you've certainly heard of: Google, Yahoo, Amazon, and eBay, just to name a few. Google and Yahoo have really led the charge, and Yahoo, in particular, originated a neat trick that will be central to the application we'll build in this chapter, namely the dynamic `<script>` tag trick, or `<script>` injection trick (it's sometimes referred to both ways—just depends on who you're talking to). Now with the preliminaries out of the way, let's go ahead and spell out what this application is going to do:

- We will be able to perform a search for businesses given an address or some components of a location, by using a remote service. We'll be able to see a list of search results, page through large result sets, and select one to view in more detail.
- Those "more details" will be things like the address of the business, phone number, web site, and average user ratings.
- We'll also be able to view a map of the location around the business and be able to zoom in and out of that map.
- We can save a selected business as a favorite so that we can quickly call up its details later. These favorites will be stored in a local database via Gears.
- The address used for a search can be saved as the default location to save time later.
- A lot of Dijit will be used for the user interface, so we'll have a good-looking application automatically.

Now let's have a look at the web services we're going to be using to pull this off, and look at exactly how we're going to be calling on them.

The Yahoo APIs and the Dynamic <script> Tag Trick

Yahoo did something very cool a little while ago, and it is this one cool thing that makes the application in this chapter possible. Before we can discuss that, though, we have to discuss what was going on before the coolness occurred.

For a while now, many companies have been exposing public APIs for people to use, Yahoo among them. For instance, you could perform a Yahoo search remotely, or you could get a Yahoo map from your own application, and so on. These APIs, these "web services," if you will, usually used XML as their data-transport mechanism. You would post some XML to a given URL, and you would get an XML response back. It was (and still is) as simple as that. These types of services don't require all the web services such as SOAP, UDDI, WSDL, and the like.

If you wanted to use these APIs from a JavaScript-based client running in a browser, you quickly ran into a major stumbling block, though. Ajax, using the `XMLHttpRequest` object, has what's known as the *same-domain security restriction* in place. This means that the `XMLHttpRequest` object will not allow a request to a domain other than the domain from which the document it is in was served. For instance, if you have a page named `page1.htm` located at `http://www.omnytex.com`, you can make requests to any URL at `www.omnytex.com`. However, if you try to make a request to something at `www.yahoo.com`, the `XMLHttpRequest` object won't allow it. This means that the APIs Yahoo exposes aren't of much use to you if you try to access them directly from a browser. Because Ajax is the only way (apparently!) to make an asynchronous call from a browser that doesn't result in the full page being reloaded, it seems we're up a stream of feces without a means of locomotion! Even if you use a library such as Dojo, it can't work around the limitations imposed by the underlying browser technology, so there's no relief to be had there.

There are of course ways around this same-domain restriction. Probably the most common is to write a server-side component on your own server that acts as a proxy. This enables your code to make requests via `XMLHttpRequest` to something like `www.omnytex.com/proxy`, which makes a request to something at `www.yahoo.com` on behalf of the calling code and returns the results. This is very cool, but it requires your own server in the mix, which is limiting.

Wouldn't it be so much more useful if the JavaScript running in the browser could make the request directly to Yahoo and not need a server-side component? Yes, indeed it would be! And as you probably have guessed, there is a clever way to do it. Take a look at the following bit of JavaScript:

```
var scriptTag = document.createElement("script");
scriptTag.setAttribute("src", "www.yahoo.com/someAPI");
scriptTag.setAttribute("type", "text/javascript");
var headTag = document.getElementsByTagName("head").item(0);
headTag.appendChild(scriptTag);
```

So, what we have here is a new `<script>` tag being created. We set the `src` attribute to point to some API at Yahoo (which at the end of the day is just a specific URL), and finally we append that new tag to the `<head>` of the document. The browser will go off and retrieve the resource at the specified URL, and then evaluate it, just as it does for any imported JavaScript file. To understand this fully, keep in mind that anytime the browser encounters a `<script>` tag in the HTML document that it is parsing, it stops, retrieves the code at the URL specified by the `src` attribute of the `<script>` tag, and evaluates it, right then and there. Fortunately, if you create a `<script>` tag and insert it into the `<head>` as this code does, the browser does the exact same thing: it goes off and retrieves the JavaScript resource and evaluates it.

Now, in and of itself, that isn't very useful. As I said, the Yahoo APIs return XML, and XML being evaluated by the browser won't do much. (Some browsers may generate a DOM object from the XML, but even still, that on its own isn't of much use.) Unlike with the `XMLHttpRequest` object, you don't get any events to work with, callback functions that can act upon what was returned, and so on.

Now we come to the bit of coolness that Yahoo came up with that I mentioned before!

Let's say we have some XML being returned by a Yahoo service, like so:

```
<name>Frank</name>
```

It may not be very interesting, but it's perfectly valid XML. Now let's ask the probing question: what is the JSON equivalent to that XML? It's nothing more than this:

```
{ "name" : "Frank" }
```

Okay, now suppose that we pass that JSON to a JavaScript function, like so:

```
someFunction( { "name" : "Frank" } );
```

What is the parameter passed to someFunction()? As it turns out, it's an object constructed from the JSON. (Remember that *JSON* stands for *JavaScript Object Notation*: it is literally a notation format that defines an object.) This means that if someFunction() is this . . .

```
function someFunction(obj) {
  alert(obj.name);
}
```

. . . the result is an alert() pop-up that reads, *Frank*.

Are you maybe starting to see what Yahoo might have done? If you are thinking that what the service returns is something like this . . .

```
someFunction( { "name" : "Frank" } );
```

. . . then give yourself a big round of applause; you just came to the same wonderful discovery that Yahoo did a while ago!

What Yahoo came up with is the idea of returning JSON in place of XML from an API service call, and wrapping the JSON in a function call. When you call the API function, you tell it what the callback function is. In other words, you tell the remote service what JavaScript function on your page you want passed the JSON that is returned. So let's say you wanted to interact with some Yahoo API that returns a person's name, as we've been discussing as our example. Your page might look something like this:

```
<html>
  <head>
    <title>Dummy Yahoo API Test</title>
    <script>
      function makeRequest() {
      var scriptTag = document.createElement("script");
      scriptTag.setAttribute("src", "www.yahoo.com/someAPI/callback= ➥
        myCallback&output=json");
      scriptTag.setAttribute("type", "text/javascript");
      var headTag = document.getElementsByTagName("head").item(0);
      headTag.appendChild(scriptTag);
    }
    function myCallback(inJSON) {
      alert(inJSON.name);
    }
    </script>
  </head>
  <body>
  <input type="button" value="Test" onClick="makeRequest();">
  </body>
</html>
```

When you click the button, makeRequest() is called, and it uses that dynamic <script> tag trick to call the Yahoo API function. Notice the URL, which specifies the name of the callback function and also specifies that we want to get back JSON instead of the usual XML. Now, when the response comes back, the browser evaluates what was inserted into the document via the `<script>` tag, which would be this:

```
myCallback( { "name" : "Frank" } );
```

`myCallback()` is called at that point, with the object resulting from evaluation of the JSON being passed to it. You can load this page from any domain, and it will work. Hence, we've done what the `XMLHttpRequest` object does (in a basic sense, anyway), and we've gotten around the same-domain limitation. Sweet!

Yahoo was the first to use this hack (that I am aware of), but many others such as Google have begun to follow suit because what this allows is purely client-side mashups and API utilization. No longer do you need a server-side proxy. You can now make the requests across domains directly. This is an extremely powerful capability that leads to some really cool possibilities, such as the type of application in this chapter.

■ **Note** While this technique is very useful because it allows you to make direct requests to any server you want, it also has the potential for malicious code to be introduced. Remember that what is being returned is script that winds up executing with the same privileges as any other script on the page. This provides a potential for scams including stealing cookies, spoofing, phishing, and so on. You therefore want to take care in your choice of services and organizations. Accessing APIs from Yahoo or Google, for instance, isn't likely to present any security issues, but less-well-known companies may not be quite as safe.

JSON-P and Dojo

The approach to web services where JSON is returned wrapped in a JavaScript function call has come to be known as *JSON with Padding*, or *JSON-P*. It is also sometimes referred to as *JSON-based web services*. Whatever the term, it all means the same thing.

The example we just looked at is nice, not too complicated codewise, but as I'm sure you can guess, Dojo makes it even easier. Dojo provides the `dojo.io.script.get()` function, which looks something like this:

```
dojo.io.script.get({
  callbackParamName : "callback",
  url : "http://local.yahooapis.com/MapsService/V1/mapImage",
  content : {
    "appid" : "xxx", "output" : "json",
    "longitude" : "xxx",
    "latitude" : "xxx",
    image_width : 480, image_height : 460
  }
}).addCallback(function(response) {
  // Do something
});
```

We'll get into the details of this later, but as you can see, it's just a single function call to which we pass some information. The `callbackParamName` attribute is the name of the parameter that the remote service looks for to determine the name of the JavaScript function to call. In other words, the value of the callback HTTP parameter will name the JavaScript function on the page that we want called back. In this case, Dojo takes care of the callback function itself, but it still has to be told the name of the parameter that the remote service will look at to get the function name to wrap the JSON in. The `url` attribute is obviously the URL of the remote service. The `content` attribute contains all the parameters to be passed to the service. This is of course all determined by the service being called and can and will vary from service to service; it isn't dictated by Dojo in any way. Finally, we use the `addCallback()` method to add the function to execute when our response comes back. With all that in place, Dojo takes care of all the details of implementing the dynamic `<script>` tag trick. Very clean, very simple, typical Dojo!

JSON-P AND ERROR HANDLING—THAT IS, THE LACK THEREOF!

JSON-P is, I think without question, a really handy technique. However, to call it anything other than a trick, even a hack, would mean we aren't being quite intellectually honest! It's most definitely thinking outside the box, that's for sure!

As neat a trick as it is, it has one significant flaw: error handling. That is to say, there really is none. There is no error callback as with a typical Ajax request, no interrogating HTTP status codes, or any of that. Your script simply doesn't do something you expected it to do. Oh, you may well see a failed outbound request in a debug tool such as Firebug, but that's about it, and that won't generally help your end users any.

There is one way you can get at least *some* degree of error handling: use a time-out. In other words, you fire off a request, and you start a JavaScript time-out, say to fire some function in 5 seconds. In the callback to the JSON-P request, you cancel the time-out. So, if the request takes longer than 5 seconds to execute, you take that to mean that the call failed, and the function the time-out fires is essentially your error handler. (If the response comes back in less than 5 seconds, that function will never fire because the time-out is cancelled first.) This clearly isn't ideal: who's to say the request didn't just go long and really is taking a little more than 5 seconds to complete? In fact, you could arguably make matters worse because you might flash an error message and then a short time later process a completed request that you just told the user had failed! You could code for this possibility too and avoid it with a system of status flags, but hopefully you see that in any case, this simply isn't a robust error-handling mechanism.

As an FYI, note that in this application I took the tact that because the error-handling scheme is pretty poor anyway, and could potentially even be worse than none at all, I simply went with none at all. If a service call hangs, the application hangs with the Please Wait dialog box showing. Not great by any stretch of the imagination, but such is the difficulty with the `<script>` injection technique underlying this all.

Yahoo Web Services Registration

Before you go looking at the web services we're going to be using to build this application, you need to get some paperwork out of the way first.

Most API services require you to register to use their APIs, and Yahoo is no exception. Every time you make a Yahoo service call, you need to pass an `appid` parameter. The value of this parameter is a unique identifier assigned to your application. Not passing this value, or passing an invalid value, will result in the call failing. Before you can play with the application in this chapter, you will have to register and get your own appid. It's a painless process that you can go through by accessing the following page:

```
http://api.search.yahoo.com/webservices/register_application
```

You should plug your own appid into the App class (in the App.js source file, aptly named appID field) before you spend time with the application, just so you are playing nice with Yahoo. I'll use XXX in the following sections when referencing appid to indicate that you should plug your ID in there.

There are some limitations associated with using the APIs in terms of request volume, but the upper limit is so high as to not be a realistic concern for your adventures with this application! If you are intent on building a production-level application by using these services, you will need to consult with Yahoo for other registration options that allow for high volumes. Again, for our purposes, the number of requests allowed is more than sufficient.

Yahoo Local Search Service

Yahoo offers some very nice search services that you can play with, and one of them is the Yahoo Local search service. Simply stated, it enables you to search for businesses around a given geographic location. For each search result, the service provides a plethora of information, including the business location, contact information (phone number, web site, and so forth), and user rating information.

Using this service requires you to access a given URL, for example:

```
http://local.yahooapis.com/LocalSearchService/V3/➥
localSearch?appid=XXX&query=pizza&zip=94306&results=2
```

The query parameter enables you to specify a keyword to search for, zip is just a US zip code to center the search around, and results is the maximum number of results you want to return. The appid is an ID you get when you register for the services, as discussed in the previous section. If you go ahead and paste that into the address bar of your web browser, assuming you replace the XXX appid with a valid ID as described in the previous section, you'll see the following response:

```
<?xml version="1.0"?>
<ResultSet xmlns:xsi=http://www.w3.org/2001/XMLSchema-instance➥
xmlns="urn:yahoo:lcl" xsi:schemaLocation="urn:yahoo:lcl➥
http://api.local.yahoo.com/LocalSearchService/V3/➥
LocalSearchResponse.xsd" totalResultsAvailable="459"➥
totalResultsReturned="1" firstResultPosition="1"><ResultSetMapUrl>➥
http://maps.yahoo.com/broadband/?q1=Palo+Alto➥
%2C+CA+94306&amp;tt=pizza&amp;tp=1</ResultSetMapUrl➥
><Result id="28734629"><Title>➥
Patxi's Chicago Pizza</Title><Address>➥
441 Emerson St</Address><City>Palo Alto</City>➥
<State>CA</State><Phone>(650) 473-9999</Phone><Latitude>➥
37.445242</Latitude><Longitude>-122.163427</Longitude><Rating>➥
```

```
<AverageRating>4.5</AverageRating><TotalRatings>➥
30</TotalRatings><TotalReviews>21</TotalReviews>➥
<LastReviewDate>1203959693</LastReviewDate>➥
<LastReviewIntro>I'd give this place 4.5 Stars, but➥
since I can't tie goes to the Restaurant. This is➥
a good alternative to the legendary Zachary's with➥
the benefit that there isn't usually a wait.  In➥
many ways I like this place better than Zachary's➥
since it seems to have figured out a way to do➥
Chicago deep dish without the heaviness of the➥
oils, It could be the sauce being more of a puree➥
instead of chopped tomatoes balances the oils out.➥
While I am mostly a NY Thin Crust kind of guy, this➥
is top notch pizza.</LastReviewIntro></Rating>➥
<Distance>2.67</Distance><Url>➥
http://local.yahoo.com/details?id=28734629&amp;➥
stx=pizza&amp;csz=Palo+Alto+CA&amp;➥
ed=5Ft25a160SwgYwogEsXfvFF62jUOrNK1trfxXbRawD4AClLt➥
Hub4_iH_GpomidnTfCwCqJBK</Url><ClickUrl>➥
http://local.yahoo.com/details?id=28734629&amp;➥
stx=pizza&amp;csz=Palo+Alto+CA&amp;ed=5Ft25a160➥
SwgYwogEsXfvFF62jUOrNK1trfxXbRawD4AClLtHub4_iH_➥
GpomidnTfCwCqJBK</ClickUrl><MapUrl>➥
http://maps.yahoo.com/maps_result?➥
name=Patxi%27s+Chicago+Pizza&amp;desc=6504739999➥
&amp;csz=Palo+Alto+CA&amp;qty=9&amp;cs=9&amp;➥
gid1=28734629</MapUrl><BusinessUrl>➥
http://www.patxispizza.com/</BusinessUrl>➥
<BusinessClickUrl>http://www.patxispizza.com/➥
</BusinessClickUrl><Categories><Category id="96926243">➥
Pizza</Category><Category id="96926236">Restaurants➥
</Category><Category id="96926237">➥
American Restaurants</Category>➥
<Category id="96926190">Italian Restaurants</Category>➥
</Categories></Result></ResultSet>

<!-- ws02.search.re2.yahoo.com compressed/➥
chunked Fri Jul 25 22:45:33 PDT 2008 -->
```


To turn this into a JSON-P request, we have only to add two parameters to the request: `output`, with a value of `json`, and `callback`, with a value of the name of the function to call. So, if we do this . . .

```
http://local.yahooapis.com/LocalSearchService/V3/localSearch?appid=XXX➥
&query=pizza&zip=94306&results=1&output=json&callback=myCallback
```

. . . the response we get back is this:


```
myCallback({"ResultSet":{"totalResultsAvailable":"459",➥
"totalResultsReturned":"1","firstResultPosition":"1",➥
"ResultSetMapUrl":"http:\/\/maps.yahoo.com\/broadband\/➥
?q1=Palo+Alto%2C+CA+94306&tt=pizza&tp=1","Result":➥
{"id":"28734629","Title":"Patxi's Chicago Pizza",➥
"Address":"441 Emerson St","City":"Palo Alto","State":"CA","Phone":➥
"(650) 473-9999","Latitude":"37.445242",➥
"Longitude":"-122.163427","Rating":{"AverageRating":"4.5",➥
"TotalRatings":"30","TotalReviews":"21",➥
"LastReviewDate":"1203959693","LastReviewIntro":➥
"I'd give this place 4.5 Stars, but since I can't➥
tie goes to the Restaurant. This is a good alternative➥
to the legendary Zachary's with the benefit that there➥
isn't usually a wait.  In many ways I like this place➥
better than Zachary's since it seems to have figured out➥
a way to do Chicago deep dish without the heaviness of➥
the oils, It could be the sauce being more of a puree➥
instead of chopped tomatoes balances the oils out.  While➥
I am mostly a NY Thin Crust kind of guy, this is top notch➥
pizza."},"Distance":"2.67","Url":"http:\/\/➥
local.yahoo.com\/details?id=28734629&stx=pizza&➥
csz=Palo+Alto+CA&ed=5Ft25a160SwgYwogEsXfvFF62jUOr➥
NK1trfxXbRawD4AClLtHub4_iH_GpomidnTfCwCqJBK",➥
"ClickUrl":"http:\/\/local.yahoo.com\/details?➥
id=28734629&stx=pizza&csz=Palo+Alto+CA&ed=5Ft25➥
a160SwgYwogEsXfvFF62jUOrNK1trfxXbRawD4AClLtHub4➥
_iH_GpomidnTfCwCqJBK","MapUrl":"http:\/\/➥
maps.yahoo.com\/maps_result?name=Patxi%27s+➥
Chicago+Pizza&desc=6504739999&csz=Palo+Alto+➥
CA&qty=9&cs=9&gid1=28734629","BusinessUrl":➥
"http:\/\/www.patxispizza.com\/","BusinessClickUrl":➥
"http:\/\/www.patxispizza.com\/","Categories":➥
{"Category":[{"id":"96926243","content":"Pizza"},➥
{"id":"96926236","content":"Restaurants"},➥
{"id":"96926237","content":"American Restaurants"},{"id":"96926190",➥
"content":"Italian Restaurants"}]}}}}});
```


It's not much to look at on the page, I admit, but it's golden in the code: if we called this by using the `<script>` injection trick, what would happen is that `myCallback()` would get called and passed into it would be an object with a bunch of data fields we can reference. For instance, the Latitude and Longitude fields tell us where this business is located, Rating tells us the average user rating, and Distance tells us how far away the business is. The set of data returned by the service is pretty large, and a lot of it won't be used in this application, but if you cruise on over to `http://developer.yahoo.com/search/local/V3/localSearch.html`, you can get all those details, plus a lot more, about this particular service.

Yahoo Maps Map Image Service

Yahoo is also going to be providing the maps that you can see on the Map tab of the application. (Yes, take a break and go play with the application a bit now!) Yahoo Maps is a service that has been around for a while, even before a public JSON-P interface was provided for it. It enables you to get maps for a given address, as well as access other features, such as traffic and local places of interest. The API Yahoo provides has a number of different services, but for our purposes, we'll be focusing on the Map Image service.

The Yahoo Maps Map Image API enables you to get a reference to a graphic of a map generated according to the parameters you specify in your request. You may specify latitude and longitude or address in your request (we'll be specifying longitude and latitude in the application itself, but in this discussion it'll just be an address, more precisely, a component of an address).

This service is referenced via a simple HTTP request, such as the following:

```
http://local.yahooapis.com/MapsService/V1/mapImage?appid=XXX&location=11719
```

The location parameter specified is just a US zip code, and the appid is once again your registered application ID. If you go ahead and paste that into the address bar of your web browser, you'll see the following response:


```
<?xml version="1.0"?>
<Result xmlns:xsi="http://www.w3.org/2001/XMLSchema-instance">➥
http://gws.maps.yahoo.com/mapimage?MAPDATA=n6Oehud6wXUJUYM_tJcfOwsQpG9JUAzuPg➥
gQRTTce9N8zspONMdiDVuUVXTcOkJcBUZXUolGqZulnHzcPOkjcpYTF82_DXtJgf4ISRYS8gqVHa➥
BiWhmY3OqSK9C9PR4.k.HNxwaJJO2UQqOOexH6&amp;mvt=m?cltype=onnetwork&amp;.➥
intl=us</Result>
<!-- ws01.search.re2.yahoo.com compressed/chunked➥
Fri Jul 25 10:32:36 PDT 2008 -->
```


What you've gotten back includes a reference to an image now sitting on Yahoo's servers. If you pluck out the following URL . . .

```
http://gws.maps.yahoo.com/mapimage?MAPDATA=n6Oehud6wXUJUYM_tJcfOw➥
sQpG9JUAzuPggQRTTce9N8zspONMdiDVuUVXTcOkJcBUZXUolGqZulnHzcPOkjcpYT➥
F82_DXtJgf4ISRYS8gqVHaBiWhmY3OqSK9C9PR4.k.HNxwaJJO2UQqOOexH6&amp;➥
mvt=m?cltype=onnetwork&amp;.intl=us
```

. . . and put that in the address bar of a web browser, you'll see an image that is a map of the Bellport/Mastic Beach area of Long Island, New York, as shown in Figure 8-1.

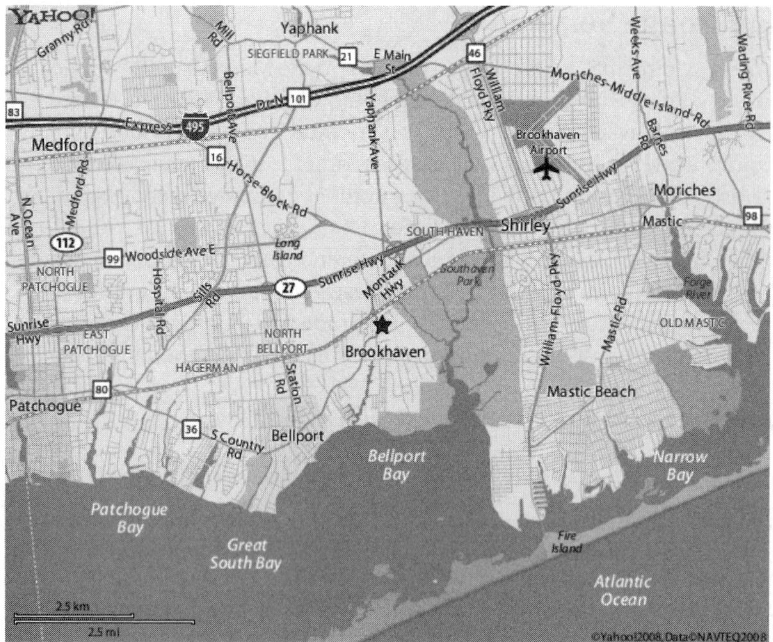

Figure 8-1. *The map resulting from accessing the URL in the example*

You can also add some parameters to the original request. For instance, you can specify that you want a GIF back (by default, you get a PNG file), and you can specify that instead of XML, you want JSON back. The URL would then look like this:

```
http://local.yahooapis.com/MapsService/V1/mapImage?appid=XXX&➥
location=11719&image_type=gif&output=json&callback=myCallback
```

Now the response you get is this:

```
myCallback({"ResultSet":{"Result":"http:\/\/gws.maps.yahoo.com\/mapimage?➥
MAPDATA=cxsuGud6wXXyiBJ69MPrKK..1HUkskJsw7lifuUcFkwxzQ4OjwJp.wHqkuSE➥
pCr9RhHUtwrTtNO.b4WNfkBNid1D6TAblazXIF8anq5PqbaLIF5iAmHGbbh8LZtPjnvs➥
LP8Ndkoiu1qWNWduAGHC&mvt=m?cltype=onnetwork&.intl=us"}});
```

A few other parameters are used in the application, and these are summarized in Table 8-1.

Table 8-1. *Some Yahoo Map Image Service Parameters Used in This Application*

Parameter	Meaning
`latitude`	The latitude that is the center of the map.
`longitude`	The longitude that is the center of the map.
`image_width`	The width of the map image.

Parameter	Meaning
`image_height`	The height of the map image.
`zoom`	The zoom factor to apply to the map. This is a value in the range 1–12, where 1 represents street level and 12 represents regional level (a little wider than state level).

As with the local search service, I encourage you to examine the Yahoo Maps APIs more (`http://developer.yahoo.com/maps/rest/V1`) because they can definitely do more than this application demonstrates. This is about all we need for the purposes of this chapter, though, so you're now armed with all the knowledge you need to go forth and dissect this application!

Dissecting the Solution

Let's begin by taking a quick look at the application itself, beginning with Figure 8-2.

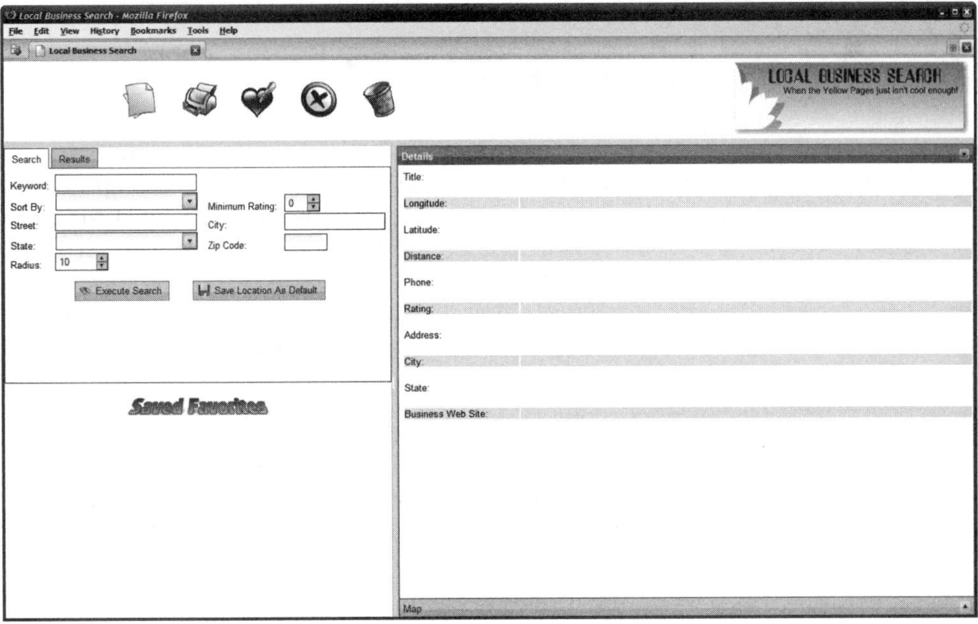

Figure 8-2. *The local business search in all its glory*

The basic structure and layout of the application is simple: at the top we have a Fisheye dijit that gives us access to common functions such as adding and deleting favorites and printing the currently selected item. There is also a logo in the upper-right corner of the screen. Below that the screen is split vertically in two. On the left side we have a tabbed section: one tab for entering search criteria, another for displaying the results of a search. Below that is a list of favorites you have saved. On the right we have an Accordion dijit with two panes, one for details about the currently selected business, the other for displaying a map. Note that the vertical split can be resized to the user's liking.

Moving right along . . . the directory structure for this application should by now be absolutely nothing new, because it's in no way a departure from the previous applications. We'll look at it just the same, beginning with Figure 8-3.

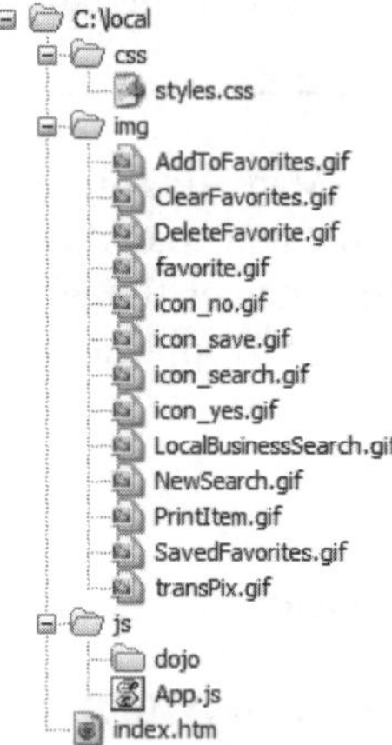

Figure 8-3. *The directory structure of the application*

The `css` directory has the typical `styles.css`, the style sheet for the application. The `img` directory has all our images. This includes the icons for the Fisheye dijit at the top (`AddToFavorite.gif`, `ClearFavorites.gif`, `DeleteFavorite.gif`, `NewSearch.gif`, and `PrintItem.gif`). We also have the application's logo that you see in the upper-right corner, which is the file `LocalBusinessSearch.gif`. The file `SavedFavorites.gif` is the little header you see above your list of saved favorites. The `favorite.gif` file is the little heart shown next to each saved favorite. The files `icon_no.gif`, `icon_yes.gif`, `icon_save.gif`, and `icon_search.gif` are the images seen on various buttons throughout the application, such as confirmation pop-ups and the search form. Finally, `transPix.gif` is a transparent single-pixel image for spacing out the Fisheye dijit, as seen in the Chapter 5 project. The `js` directory contains a single file, `App.js`, which houses all the JavaScript for this application. Finally, in the root directory we find `index.htm`, the starting point and markup for the application, which is where we're headed next.

Writing index.htm

Every web app needs to start with at least one HTML page, and this one is no exception. The `index.htm` file begins as any well-formed HTML document does, with a `<head>` section. (Well, it technically begins with an `<html>` tag, as my technical reviewer pointed out, but a well-formed HTML document begins with a `<head>` *section*, which is different from an `<html>` *tag*, so nyah-nyah to Herman van Rosmalen!)

<head> Contents

The first thing we need to do is get all the style sheets imported into the page that we're going to need:

```
<link rel="StyleSheet" type="text/css"
  href="js/dojo/dojo/resources/dojo.css">
<link rel="StyleSheet" type="text/css"
  href="js/dojo/dijit/themes/soria/soria.css">
<link rel="StyleSheet" type="text/css"
  href="js/dojo/dojox/widget/FisheyeList/FisheyeList.css">
<link rel="StyleSheet" type="text/css" href="css/styles.css">
<link rel="StyleSheet" type="text/css"
  href="js/dojo/dojox/grid/_grid/grid.css">
```

We have the `dojo.css` style sheet as always, plus the one for the Soria theme, namely `soria.css`, because that's what we're going to use for all our dijits this time around. Then we have the `FisheyeList.css` files, needed for our Fisheye dijit to work right. Next we import `styles.css`, the application-specific style sheet. Finally, because we'll be using a Grid dijit in this application, we also need to import `grid.css`.

The next step is to configure Dojo:

```
<script type="text/javascript">
  var djConfig = {
    baseScriptUri : "js/dojo/",
    parseOnLoad : true
  };
</script>
<script type="text/javascript" src="js/dojo/dojo/dojo.js"></script>
```

This is of course just like code you've seen a bunch of times before, so no need to go over it again.

Next we have to get the JavaScript that represents the core of this particular application, so we need to bring in `App.js`:

```
<script type="text/javascript" src="js/App.js"></script>
```

Now it's time to go ahead and import all the Dojo components we're going to be using. You've previously seen each of these in other applications or in examples in previous chapters, so there shouldn't be any surprises here:

```
  dojo.require("dijit.Dialog");
  dojo.require("dijit.Toolbar");
  dojo.require("dijit.form.Button");
  dojo.require("dijit.form.ComboBox");
  dojo.require("dijit.form.Form");
  dojo.require("dijit.form.NumberSpinner");
  dojo.require("dijit.form.ValidationTextBox");
  dojo.require("dijit.form.Slider");
  dojo.require("dijit.form.TextBox");
  dojo.require("dijit.layout.AccordionContainer");
  dojo.require("dijit.layout.ContentPane");
  dojo.require("dijit.layout.LayoutContainer");
  dojo.require("dijit.layout.SplitContainer");
  dojo.require("dijit.layout.TabContainer");
```

```
  dojo.require("dojo.data.ItemFileWriteStore");
  dojo.require("dojo.io.script");
  dojo.require("dojo.parser");
  dojo.require("dojo.string");
  dojo.require("dojox.collections.Dictionary");
  dojo.require("dojox.fx._base");
  dojo.require("dojox.grid.Grid");
  dojo.require("dojox.storage");
  dojo.require("dojox.widget.FisheyeList");
```

The next step is to kick off the application, so to speak:

```
  var app = new App();

  dojo.addOnLoad(function() {
    app.init();
  });
```

We create a single instance of the App class, which again is the real code behind the application. Then we hook up an event to fire when the page and all Dojo initialization is complete, using the `dojo.addOnLoad()` function. All we need to do is call the `init()` method of the App instance—all the real work is done there, as you'll see a little later.

Now we can move on to the markup content in the <body> of `index.htm`, starting with the definitions of the dialog boxes that the user can see in this application.

The Four Dialogs of the Apocalypse

There are four types of dialog boxes that can be displayed in this application. The first one is the Print dialog (these don't appear here, or in the code, in any sort of important order):

```
<div dojoType="dijit.Dialog" id="printDialog"
  title="Local Business Search"
  style="display:none;width:100%;height:100%">
  Title: <span id="print_title"></span>
  <br><br>
  <img id="print_map">
  <br><br>
  Longitude: <span id="print_longitude"></span><br>
  Latitude: <span id="print_latitude"></span><br>
  Distance: <span id="print_distance"></span><br>
  Phone: <span id="print_phone"></span><br>
  Rating: <span id="print_rating"></span><br>
  Address: <span id="print_address"></span><br>
  City: <span id="print_city"></span><br>
  State: <span id="print_state"></span><br>
  Business Web Site: <span id="print_businessUrl"></span><br>
</div>
```

Dialog boxes are nothing new at this point; you've seen a bunch of them in other applications. This one has some content that will be populated dynamically: the map and the details for the selected business. These are the same details shown in the Accordion section of the main UI. A dialog is used for printing so that all the information can be presented in one consolidated view. This isn't the case on the main UI because you are either viewing business details *or* the map, never both at the same time, so there had to be some sort of new display mechanism to present both simultaneously. A dialog, maximized so that it covers everything else, meaning the main UI, does the job perfectly. Later in the JavaScript you'll see that each of the `<div>`s with `id`s beginning with `print_` are populated with the information, and the `<img>` `print_map` is pointed at the appropriate map image, all as you'd expect.

The next dialog is the Please Wait dialog, and it's a very simplistic beast:

```
<div dojoType="dijit.Dialog" id="pleaseWaitDialog"
  title="Please Wait" style="display:none;width:200px;">
    <p align="center" id="pleaseWaitText"></p>
</div>
```

An example of the Please Wait dialog can be seen in Figure 8-4. This is in fact what you'll see when the application is first loaded and initialization of the Dojo storage system is in process.

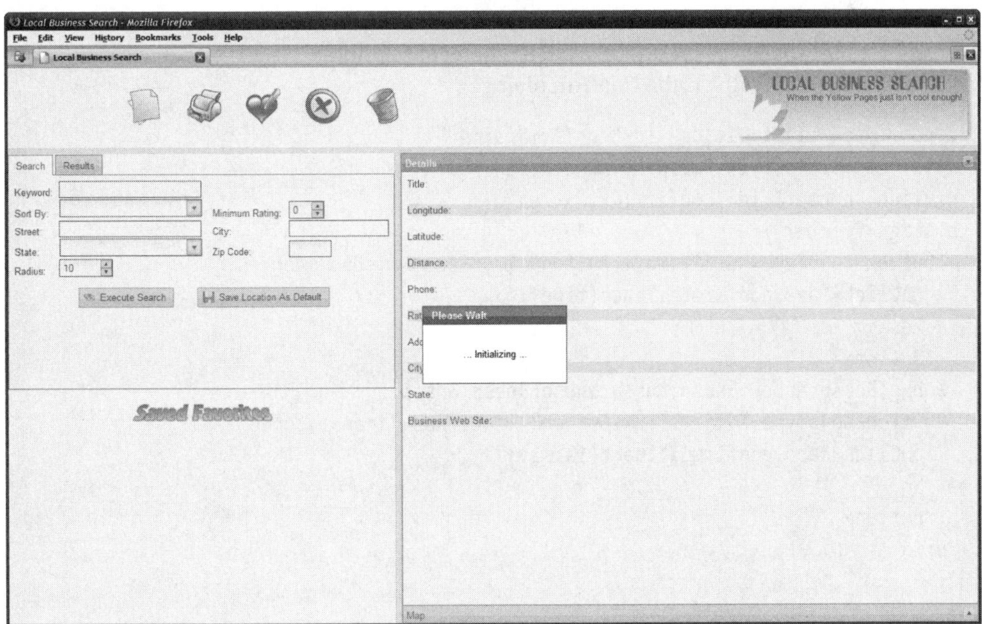

Figure 8-4. *An example of the Please Wait dialog box, the "initializing" dialog*

The text to be displayed, *Initializing* in this case, is inserted into the `pleaseWaitText` `<p>` element (you will see the code for doing this later). This type of dialog is meant to block the user from interacting with the UI in any way; hence the typical Close button that usually appears on a dialog is hidden, and there is no button to dismiss the dialog as you'll see that other types have. This type of dialog is used, in addition to during initialization, when searches are being performed.

The info type of dialog is next. This is similar to the Please Wait dialog in that it blocks the user from interacting with the UI, except in one way: the user can dismiss the dialog by clicking an OK button. The idea behind this type of dialog is that the user needs to be presented with some information and can continue only after acknowledging the dialog, by clicking the OK button:

```
<div dojoType="dijit.Dialog" id="infoDialog"
  title="Attention Human!" style="display:none;width:300px;">
  <p align="center" id="infoText"></p>
  <p align="center">
    <button dojoType="dijit.form.Button"
      onClick="dijit.byId('infoDialog').hide();">
      Ok
    </button>
  </p>
</div>
```

As you can see, the OK button hides the dialog. In fact, each of the four types of dialogs are always hidden or shown; they are never destroyed and re-created after the initial creation. This is just more efficient because it means less work for Dojo to have to do (that is, creating a dijit can be a bit expensive—better to avoid it wherever possible).

The final type of dialog is the Confirm dialog:

```
<div dojoType="dijit.Dialog" id="confirmDialog"
  title="Confirm" style="display:none;width:300px;">
  <p align="center" id="confirmText"></p>
  <p align="center">
    <button dojoType="dijit.form.Button" iconClass="icons iconYes"
      onClick="app.confirmCallback(true);">
      Yes
    </button>
            
    <button dojoType="dijit.form.Button" iconClass="icons iconNo"
      onClick="app.confirmCallback(false);">
      No
    </button>
  </p>
</div>
```

A confirmation dialog requires that the user make a decision via a yes or no response. Hence, as you can see, there are two buttons that can be clicked. The Close button is hidden on this dialog as well, so the user will have to answer whatever question is being asked—the user can't just skip it (well, he could just close the application entirely). The text is dynamically inserted into `confirmText <p>`, similar to the other three dialog types. The buttons call the `confirmCallback()` method of the `App` class, passing either `true` if Yes is clicked or `false` if No is clicked. You'll see how this mechanism works later, but these two buttons are the triggers, one way or another, for that mechanism.

The Menu

The next bit of markup we encounter as we explore `index.htm` is the markup responsible for rendering our menu, the Fisheye List dijit. Figure 8-5 shows what this menu looks like in action, specifically when the Add to Favorites icon is hovered over.

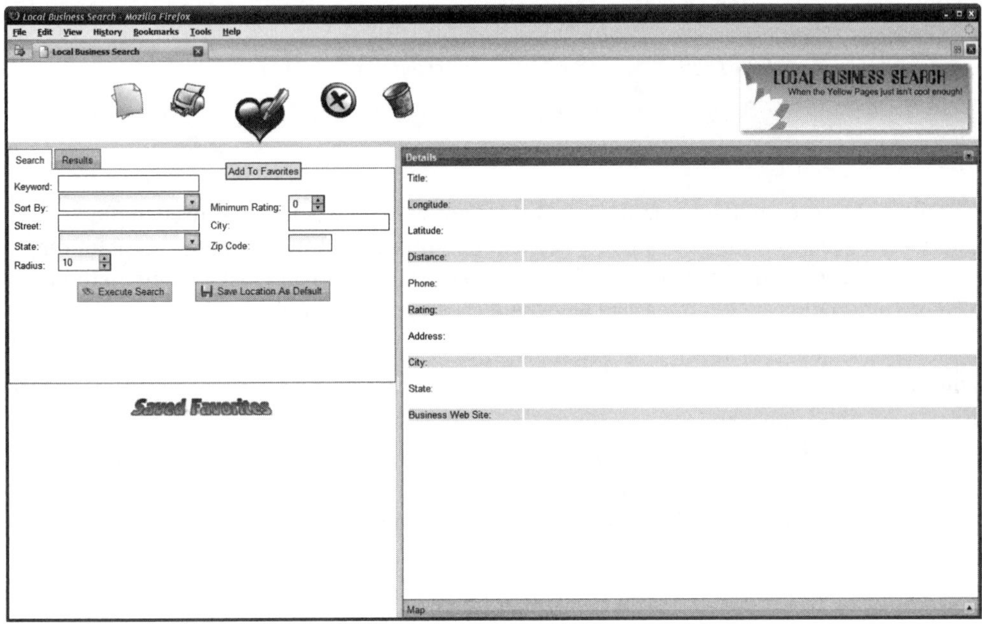

Figure 8-5. *The Fisheye dijit in action, with the Add to Favorites item being hovered over*

You've seen the Fisheye List dijit in action before in the Chapter 5 project, but darn, it's so pretty I just *had* to show it again! Anyway, the markup for generating the menu is this:

```
<div class="outerbar" id="fisheyeList">
  <div dojoType="dojox.widget.FisheyeList"
    itemWidth="84" itemHeight="84"
    itemMaxWidth="128" itemMaxHeight="128"
    orientation="horizontal" effectUnits="1" itemPadding="20"
    attachEdge="top" labelEdge="bottom">
    <div dojoType="dojox.widget.FisheyeListItem"
      onclick="app.newSearch();"
      label="New Search" iconSrc="img/NewSearch.gif">
    </div>
    <div dojoType="dojox.widget.FisheyeListItem"
      onclick="app.printCurrentItem();"
      label="Print Item" iconSrc="img/PrintItem.gif">
    </div>
    <div dojoType="dojox.widget.FisheyeListItem"
      onclick="app.addToFavorites();"
      label="Add To Favorites" iconSrc="img/AddToFavorites.gif">
```

```
    </div>
    <div dojoType="dojox.widget.FisheyeListItem"
      onclick="app.deleteFavorite();"
      label="Delete Favorite" iconSrc="img/DeleteFavorite.gif">
    </div>
    <div dojoType="dojox.widget.FisheyeListItem"
      onclick="app.clearFavorites();"
      label="Clear Favorites" iconSrc="img/ClearFavorites.gif">
    </div>
  </div>
</div>
```

This is almost completely identical to the definition of the Fisheye List used in the Chapter 5 project, so I won't go into any detail here. None of it should be new, except for the methods that each of the icons executes when clicked. All of them are just straight method calls—no arguments are being passed anywhere—so it's pretty simple stuff.

Main Contents

The main content of the UI is next, and it begins with the definition of the mainContainer, which is a LayoutContainer that houses all the UI components except the Fisheye List. (The Fisheye List is positioned relative to the upper-left corner of the browser window, as the style sheet definition that we'll look at after index.htm shows.) Here is the markup for the mainContainer:

```
<div dojoType="dijit.layout.LayoutContainer" id="mainContainer">

  <div dojoType="dijit.layout.ContentPane" layoutAlign="top"
    class="cssTitle">
    <table border="0" cellpadding="0" cellspacing="0" width="100%"><tr>
      <td align="right">
        <img src="img/LocalBusinessSearch.gif" hspace="8" vspace="4">
      </td>
    </tr></table>
  </div>
```

The mainContainer ContentPane enables us to maximize usage of the browser window—take up the entire usable area, in other words. The first ContentPane beneath it is where the application's logo lives.

Below that ContentPane comes the first of three SplitContainer dijits:

```
<div dojoType="dijit.layout.SplitContainer" persist="true"
  orientation="horizontal" sizerWidth="8" activeSizing="true"
  layoutAlign="client">
```

This SplitContainer lays out its children horizontally, so it gives us the split between the search section/favorites section and the business details/map section. Note that persist is set to true so that the sizes of the two sections are stored via a cookie and are used the next time the application is loaded (the user can choose the sizes). This is the only SplitContainer that will persist its sizing (in fact, the others are not even resizable).

We next find another SplitContainer:

```
<div dojoType="dijit.layout.SplitContainer" persist="false"
  orientation="vertical" sizerWidth="0" activeSizing="false"
  sizeShare="4">
```

This time we are laying out the children of this SplitContainer vertically. This SplitContainer divides the left side of the display between the search and favorites sections. Note that the `sizerWidth` value of `0`, plus the `activeSizing` value of `false`, results in this SplitContainer not being resizable by the user. This becomes strictly a means to lay out the two sections (search and favorites) and assign them sizes based on a percentage of the total window height. This SplitContainer is not something the user can interact with, as is the preceding one.

The first child of this SplitContainer (the one dividing the left side of the page) is a TabContainer where the Search and Results tabs will live:

```
<div dojoType="dijit.layout.TabContainer" id="searchTabs"
  sizeShare="5">
```

There's not much to see there, but moving down into the children of this TabContainer there's definitely more to see.

The Search Criteria Pane

Next up we find a ContentPane that houses the search criteria form. This is where the user enters the values used to perform a search—things like a keyword, address, and minimum rating. This is also the first of two tabs within the TabContainer named `searchTabs`. The markup for the Search tab looks like this:

```
<div dojoType="dijit.layout.ContentPane" title="Search"
  id="tabSearch">
  <form id="searchForm">
    <table width="100%" style="padding-left:6px;padding-top:6px;">
      <tr>
        <td valign="bottom">Keyword: </td>
        <td colspan="3" valign="bottom">
          <input type="textbox" dojoType="dijit.form.TextBox"
            id="queryKeyword"> 
        </td>
      </tr>
      <tr>
        <td valign="bottom">Sort By: </td>
        <td valign="bottom">
          <select dojoType="dijit.form.ComboBox" id="sortBy"
            autocomplete="false" hasDownArrow="true">
            <option></option>
            <option>Distance</option>
            <option>Relevance</option>
            <option>Title</option>
            <option>Rating</option>
          </select> 
```

```
          </td>
          <td valign="bottom">Minimum Rating: </td>
          <td valign="bottom">
            <input dojoType="dijit.form.NumberSpinner" value="0"
              constraints="{min:0,max:5,places:0}"
              style="width:50px;" id="minimumRating">
          </td>
        </tr>
        <tr>
          <td valign="bottom">Street: </td>
          <td valign="bottom">
            <input type="textbox" dojoType="dijit.form.TextBox"
              id="street"> 
          </td>
          <td valign="bottom">City: </td>
          <td valign="bottom">
            <input type="textbox" dojoType="dijit.form.TextBox"
              id="city" style="width:140px;">
          </td>
        </tr>
        <tr>
          <td valign="bottom">State: </td>
          <td valign="bottom">
            <select dojoType="dijit.form.ComboBox" id="state"
              autocomplete="true" hasDownArrow="true">
              <option></option>
              <option>Alabama</option><option>Alaska</option>
              <option>Arizona</option><option>Arkansas</option>
              <option>California</option><option>Colorado</option>
              <option>Connecticut</option><option>Delaware</option>
              <option>Florida</option><option>Georgia</option>
              <option>Hawaii</option><option>Idaho</option>
              <option>Illinois</option><option>Indiana</option>
              <option>Iowa</option><option>Kansas</option>
              <option>Kentucky</option><option>Louisiana</option>
              <option>Maine</option><option>Maryland</option>
              <option>Massachusetts</option><option>Michigan</option>
              <option>Minnesota</option><option>Mississippi</option>
              <option>Missouri</option><option>Montana</option>
              <option>Nebraska</option><option>Nevada</option>
              <option>New Hampshire</option>
              <option>New Jersey</option>
              <option>New Mexico</option><option>New York</option>
              <option>North Carolina</option>
              <option>North Dakota</option>
              <option>Ohio</option><option>Oklahoma</option>
```

```
            <option>Oregon</option><option>Pennsylvania</option>
            <option>Rhode Island</option>
            <option>South Carolina</option>
            <option>South Dakota</option><option>Tennessee</option>
            <option>Texas</option><option>Utah</option>
            <option>Vermont</option><option>Virginia</option>
            <option>Washington</option>
            <option>West Virginia</option>
            <option>Wisconsin</option><option>Wyoming</option>
          </select> 
        </td>
        <td valign="bottom">Zip Code: </td>
        <td valign="bottom">
          <input type="textbox"
            dojoType="dijit.form.ValidationTextBox"
            id="zipCode" style="width:60px;" regExp="\d{5}"
            invalidMessage="Invalid zip code">
        </td>
      </tr>
      <tr>
        <td valign="bottom">Radius: </td>
        <td valign="bottom" colspan="3">
          <input dojoType="dijit.form.NumberSpinner" value="10"
            constraints="{min:5,max:1000,places:0}" smallDelta="5"
            largeDelta="25" style="width:75px;" id="radius"> 
        </td>
      </tr>
      <tr>
        <td colspan="4" align="center" style="padding-top:10px;">
          <button dojoType="dijit.form.Button"
            iconClass="icons iconSearch" onClick="app.search();">
            Execute Search
          </button>
          <img src="img/transPix.gif" width="20">
          <button dojoType="dijit.form.Button"
            iconClass="icons iconSaveLocation"
            onClick="app.saveLocation();">
            Save Location As Default
          </button>
        </td>
      </tr>
    </table>
  </form>
</div>
```

By this point in this book, there probably isn't anything new in there, but I'll just point out a few interesting tidbits. First, notice that the `sortBy` ComboBox has its `autocomplete` attribute set to `false`. Because there are only a limited set of options to choose from here, I didn't see much sense in having `autocomplete` enabled. The `state` ComboBox, on the other hand, has `autocomplete` set to `true` because I think that makes sense, seeing as it has 50 options.

The `minimumRating` field is implemented by using a NumberSpinner, which is a dijit you haven't seen used in a project yet. This is perfect for situations when there is a finite set of numeric options to choose from and they are contiguous, as is the case here (0–5). You could certainly argue that other controls would have been just as appropriate, perhaps even more so—maybe radio buttons, maybe a combo box, and I wouldn't argue too strenuously against you—but a NumberSpinner is a good choice too, and because we haven't used it yet, I thought it was a good choice.

The `zipCode` field is interesting in that we have a `regExp` defined, namely five numbers. So if you try to enter a letter there, for instance, you'll see an error pop up, as shown in Figure 8-6.

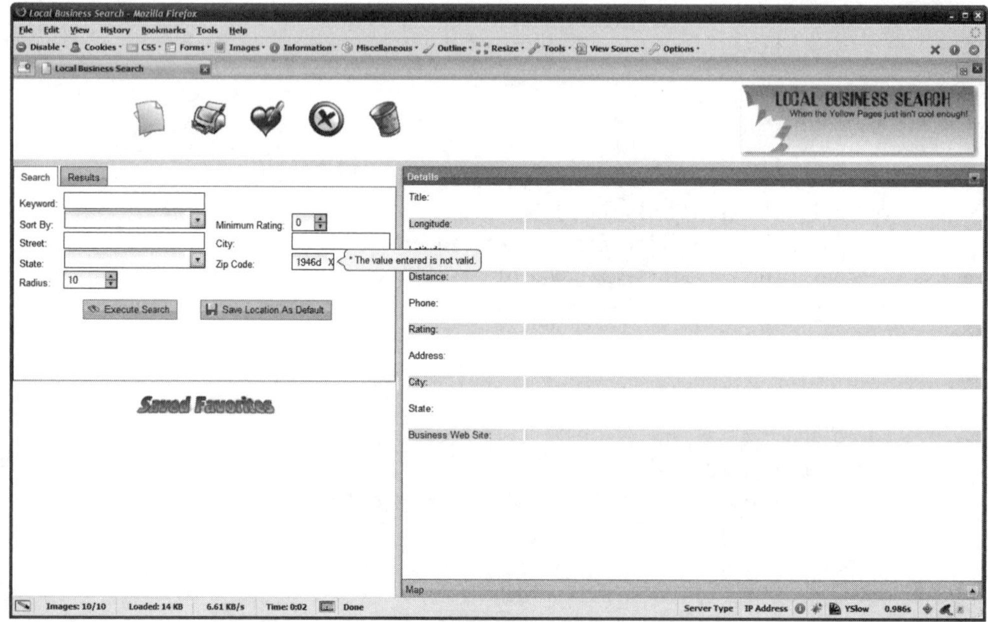

Figure 8-6. *An error resulting from entering a letter in the Zip Code field*

To perform a search, the user enters some search criteria, as seen in Figure 8-7. The criteria always requires a keyword to be entered, as you see in the figure, and at least some portion of the location fields (zip code at minimum). The Sort By and Minimum Rating fields are completely optional, but give users a way to limit the results further to get only matches that will be suitable to them.

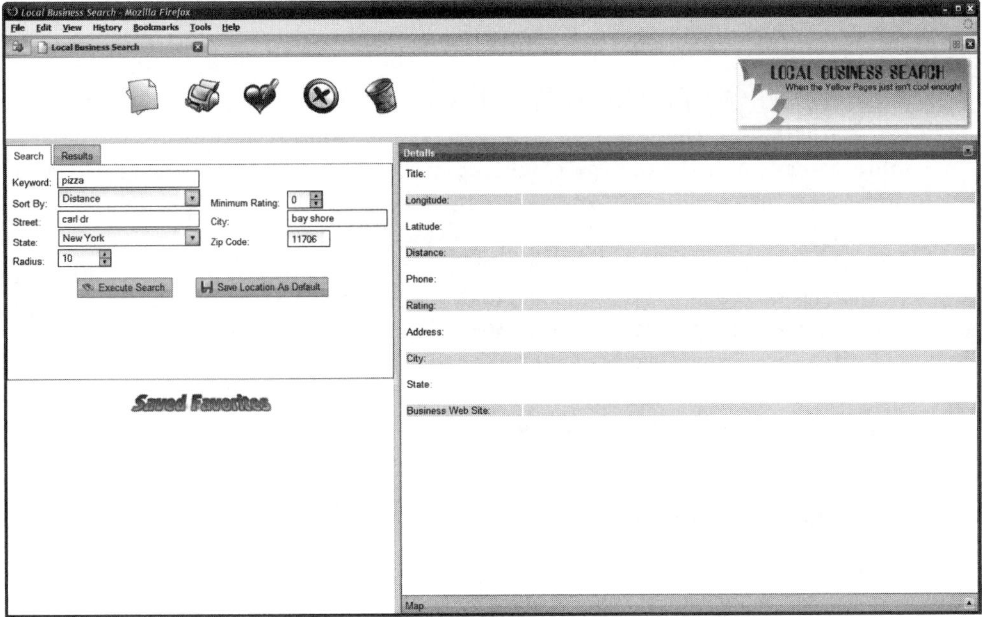

Figure 8-7. *The search form, populated with some entries*

When the user clicks the Execute Search button, the search is performed via a call to Yahoo's web service, and results are returned (assuming there were matches—otherwise, the user would have seen a dialog indicating there were no matches). How those results are displayed, markup-wise at least, is where we're headed next.

The Search Results Pane

The second ContentPane also contains the contents for the second tab, where search results are displayed. The markup is straightforward, as you can see for yourself:

```
<div dojoType="dijit.layout.ContentPane" id="tabResults"
  sizeShare="8" title="Results">
  <div dojoType="dijit.layout.SplitContainer" persist="false"
    orientation="vertical" sizerWidth="0" activeSizing="true"
    layoutAlign="client">
    <div dojoType="dijit.layout.ContentPane"
      sizeShare="8">
      <div id="searchResultsGrid" dojoType="dojox.Grid"
        structure="app.searchResultsGridLayout"
        class="cssSearchResultsGrid"
        style="width:100%;height:100%;">
        <script type="dojo/method" event="onRowClick" args="e">
          app.itemClicked(e.rowIndex);
```

```
        </script>
      </div>
    </div>
    <div dojoType="dijit.layout.ContentPane" sizeShare="2"
      style="padding-top:6px;">
      <table border="0" cellpadding="0" cellspacing="0"
        align="center" width="98%"><tr>
        <td width="28%" colspan="2" id="totalCount"> </td>
        <td align="center" width="18%" nowrap>
          <button dojoType="dijit.form.Button" id="vcrFirst"
            onClick="app.pageResults(app.PAGERESULTS_FIRST);"
            disabled="true">First</button>
        </td>
        <td align="center" width="18%" nowrap>
          <button dojoType="dijit.form.Button" id="vcrPrevious"
            onClick="app.pageResults(app.PAGERESULTS_PREVIOUS);"
            disabled="true">Previous</button>
        </td>
        <td align="center" width="18%" nowrap>
          <button dojoType="dijit.form.Button" id="vcrNext"
            onClick="app.pageResults(app.PAGERESULTS_NEXT);"
            disabled="true">Next</button>
        </td>
        <td align="center" width="18%" nowrap>
          <button dojoType="dijit.form.Button" id="vcrLast"
            onClick="app.pageResults(app.PAGERESULTS_LAST);"
            disabled="true">Last</button>
        </td>
      </tr></table>
    </div>
  </div>
</div>
```

Inside this ContentPane is a SplitContainer. The reason for this is that we have to show the Grid with the actual search results, and below it are buttons for paging through large result sets, and for displaying the current position within that larger list. Although this is a SplitContainer, note that `sizerWidth` is set to `0`, which as we've previously seen, effectively makes it not resizable, precisely what we want here.

Within the SplitContainer is a ContentPane. This is the top half where the Grid goes, and sure enough that's exactly what you see in it. The Grid gets its structure by pointing to the `searchResultsGridLayout` member of the `App` class instance. A simple `onClick` handler is attached, which is the only function this Grid really has.

Below this ContentPane is another, and this is where our VCR buttons are, as you can see in Figure 8-8.

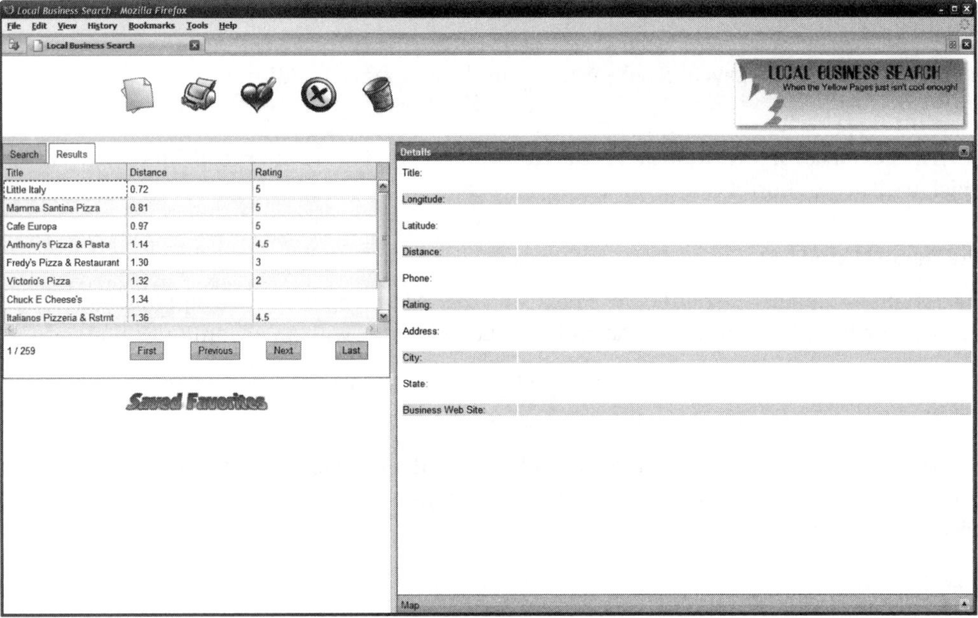

Figure 8-8. *The search results after executing a search*

VCR buttons are a common interface metaphor and are so named because they typically are organized and work like the control buttons on an old-fashioned (by today's standards!) videocassette recorder, or VCR. That means there is a rewind button (labeled First here), a fast-forward button (Last), and, stretching the analogy just a bit, slow-motion forward (Next), and back (Previous) buttons. In today's age of TiVo and digital video recorders (DVRs), maybe *next scene* and *previous scene* are closer.

Be that as it may, these buttons are simply Button dijits, each calling the `App` class's `pageResults()` method and passing to it the appropriate constants to tell that method what function to perform. You'll see how that works later, but that's how it works from a UI perspective.

Note The term *constant* is of course a misnomer in JavaScript as there is no such animal. However, you can have an object that has fields with values that you can reference and *pretend* they are constants. If you follow the semistandard convention of making them all uppercase with underscores separating words, they at least *look* like constants, to a reasonable approximation. That's as reasonable an approximation as is currently possible in JavaScript.

The Favorites Pane

Below the tabbed section where the Search and Results tabs are is the section where favorites are listed. This content is dynamically generated, save for the header image, but I'll show the markup for this nonetheless:

```
<div dojoType="dijit.layout.ContentPane" sizeShare="5">
<p align="center"><img src="img/SavedFavorites.gif"></p>
<div dojoType="dijit.layout.ContentPane" id="cpFavorites"></div>
</div>
```

The actual list of favorites will be inserted into cpFavorites later via code in the App class, which we'll get to shortly.

The Details Pane

The Details section on the right comes next, and this is implemented via a dijit that you haven't seen in real action yet, the Accordion dijit. This starts with an AccordionContainer:

```
<div dojoType="dijit.layout.AccordionContainer" sizeShare="6"
  duration="200" id="detailsTabs">
```

This is a container dijit, which means it hosts child dijits. More specifically, it hosts some number of AccordionPane dijits. The first we have is the Details section, where the details for a selected business are displayed:

```
<div dojoType="dijit.layout.AccordionPane" title="Details"
  id="tabDetails">
  <table style="padding-left:6px;padding-top:6px;" width="100%">
    <tr>
      <td width="20%">Title: </td><td id="details_title"></td>
    </tr>
    <tr><td colspan="2"> </td></td>
    <tr class="cssAltRow">
      <td>Longitude: </td>
    <td id="details_longitude"></td></tr>
    <tr><td colspan="2"> </td></td>
    <tr>
      <td>Latitude: </td><td id="details_latitude"></td>
    </tr>
    <tr><td colspan="2"> </td></td>
    <tr class="cssAltRow">
      <td>Distance: </td><td id="details_distance"></td></tr>
    <tr><td colspan="2"> </td></td>
    <tr><td>Phone: </td><td id="details_phone"></td></tr>
    <tr><td colspan="2"> </td></td>
    <tr class="cssAltRow">
      <td>Rating: </td><td id="details_rating"></td>
    </tr>
    <tr><td colspan="2"> </td></td>
    <tr><td>Address: </td><td id="details_address"></td></tr>
    <tr><td colspan="2"> </td></td>
    <tr class="cssAltRow">
      <td>City: </td><td id="details_city"></td>
    </tr>
```

```
    <tr><td colspan="2"> </td></td>
    <tr><td>State: </td><td id="details_state"></td></tr>
    <tr><td colspan="2"> </td></td>
    <tr class="cssAltRow">
      <td>Business Web Site: </td>
      <td id="details_businessUrl"></td>
    </tr>
  </table>
</div>
```

As you can see, there's nothing special there; it's just a table-based layout, straight-up HTML, nothing more. Note, however, that the AccordionPane has an `id` assigned, which is important because that's necessary to be able to flip back to this pane at various times, such as when starting a new search.

The Map Pane

The other section in the details area is where the map is displayed, and that's simply another AccordionPane, as you can see here:

```
<div dojoType="dijit.layout.AccordionPane" title="Map"
  id="tabMap">
  <br>
  <div style="text-align:center;width:100%;">
    <div dojoType="dijit.form.HorizontalSlider"
      value="6" minimum="1" maximum="12" discreteValues="12"
      showButtons="true" id="sldZoom" style="width:95%;"
      onChange="app.showMap(arguments[0]);">
      <div dojoType="dijit.form.HorizontalRuleLabels"
        container="topDecoration"
        labels="Street,2,3,4,5,6,7,8,9,10,11,Country"
        class="cssSliderLabels">
      </div>
    </div>
    <img id="imgMap" src="img/transPix.gif" vspace="6"
      style="border:1px solid #000000;display:none;">
  </div>
</div>
```

We have ourselves a HorizontalSlider, just as we saw in the previous chapter's project. This time, however, we have 12 discrete values, which is the number of levels of zoom Yahoo's map service supports, and this is exactly what this slider is for. For the labels, I decided to use words for the two end conditions, Street and Country, so that there is some sort of contextual meaning to the numbers. This way, it's obvious that as the numbers go up, you're actually zooming *out*. Otherwise, you might reasonably think that the higher the number, the higher the magnification, which is in fact the opposite of how it works.

The `<img>` element will have its `src` updated to point to the appropriate map when the time comes, but it's initially hidden via `display:none` so as to avoid there being just a small square in the middle of the pane. (Because the `<img>` tag is defined with a border and a `vspace` attribute on it, you'd have a small box in the middle, which would just look a bit ugly.)

In Figure 8-9, you can see an example of what this pane looks like with a map displayed.

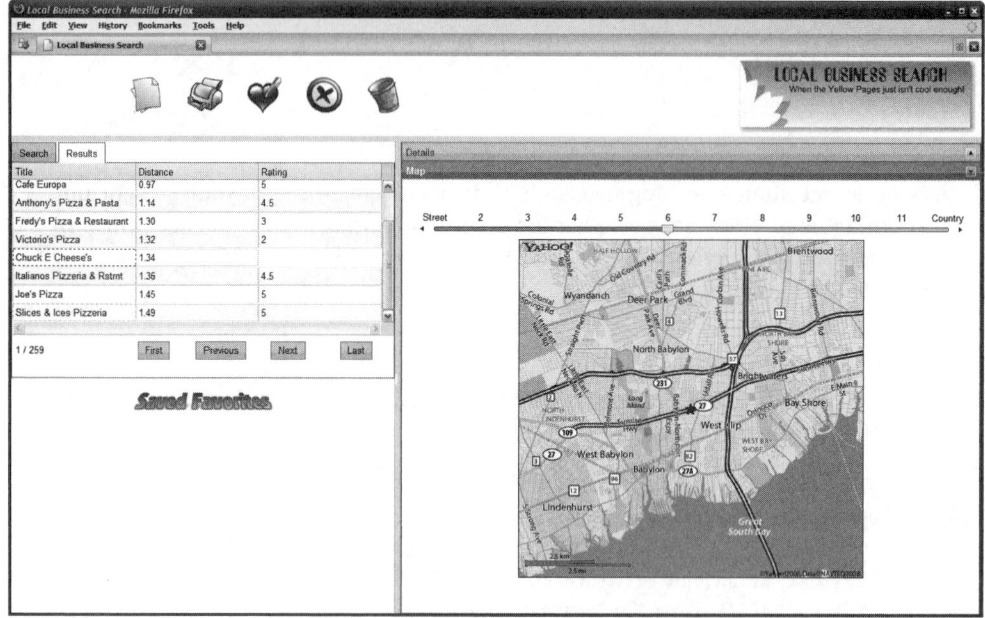

Figure 8-9. *Viewing the map for a selected search result*

And with that, we're finished with the markup for this application. Let's now look at the style sheet that contains the styles that you saw applied to the elements in `index.htm`.

Writing styles.css

The style sheet for this application is really pretty sparse, and a large portion of it is all but identical to things you've seen in other applications. We'll go through it, at least briefly, nonetheless, starting with a "god" style, so to speak:

```
html, body, #mainContainer {
  width                : 100%;
  height               : 100%;
  border               : 0px;
  padding              : 0px;
  margin               : 0px;
  font-family          : arial;
  font-size            : 10pt;
  overflow             : hidden;
}
```

These style settings result in there being no padding or margin around all the content in the browser window, and also ensure that we have a consistent font setting for everything. We also indicate that no scrolling should occur.

Next we have some styles associated with the icons on the buttons throughout the application:

```
.icons {
  background-repeat   : no-repeat;
  background-position : 0px;
  width               : 20px;
  height              : 18px;
  text-align          : center;
}
.iconSearch {
  background-image    : url("../img/icon_search.gif");
}
.iconSaveLocation {
  background-image    : url("../img/icon_save.gif");
}
.iconYes {
  background-image    : url("../img/icon_yes.gif");
}
.iconNo {
  background-image    : url("../img/icon_no.gif");
}
```

This works just as you saw in previous projects, so if you can't make heads or tails of what you see here, taking a look at previous chapters once more would be very helpful indeed.

Next is a simple style applied to the ContentPane that is housing the application's logo:

```
.cssTitle {
  height              : 110px;
  border-bottom       : 8px solid #dee8f7;
}
```

The point to this is twofold: first, to ensure that the ContentPane is tall enough for the image; and second, to give it a border on the bottom that *looks* like the divider seen in a SplitContainer, but isn't. I thought it looked a little odd without this border because there didn't seem to be a clear delineation between the logo and menu and the rest of the UI. To be consistent, it had to look like a splitter, but there was no point in actually making it a splitter (meaning to use a SplitContainer), so just using a border did the trick nicely.

The next handful of styles have to do with the four dialogs we saw earlier:

```
#InitializingDialog .dijitDialogCloseIcon {
  display             : none;
}
#pleaseWaitDialog .dijitDialogCloseIcon {
  display             : none;
}
```

```
#infoDialog .dijitDialogCloseIcon {
  display              : none;
}
#confirmDialog .dijitDialogCloseIcon {
  display              : none;
}
```

This is just the same trick seen in previous chapters to hide the Close icon typically seen in a dialog.

The next style is applied to the <div> that houses the Fisheye List dijit:

```
.outerbar {
  position             : absolute;
  left                 : 150px;
  top                  : 12px;
  z-index                : 9999;
}
```

This style's only purpose in life is to position the menu relative to the upper-left corner of the browser viewport, which is another way of saying to position it absolutely. Remember that positioning something absolutely is always done based on a coordinate of 0,0 representing the upper-left corner of the viewport where the page is drawn. So saying something is positioned absolutely is equivalent to saying it's positioned relative to the upper-left corner. I know, it sounds like I'm running for office with the double-speak, but it's an accurate bit of double-speak at least!

I lied there a little: positioning isn't the style's *only* purpose in life. In fact, in IE7, the Fisheye List didn't work right; the items could not be clicked. The solution was setting the z-index attribute as you see here. This project turned up several IE7 problems with various dijits, and this was just one of them. Thankfully, they weren't too hard to address.

The next style is applied to the labels on the map zoom slider:

```
.cssSliderLabels {
  height               : 1.2em;
  font-size            : 10pt;
  color                : #000000;
}
```

This just sets the size and font size of the text of the labels, nothing more.

The final style is this one:

```
.cssAltRow {
  background-color     : #eaeaea;
}
```

This is applied to every other row of the <table> where the business's details are shown, thus giving the display a striped appearance to help the user's eyes keep track of the information a little better.

Now it's time to move on to the JavaScript that makes up the core of the application, housed in the file App.js.

Writing App.js

Now, at last, we come to what is, in my opinion anyway, the most interesting part of the application, namely the JavaScript behind it. All of the code for this application is enclosed in a single class called, not very creatively I admit, `App`. And, as if I wasn't being lazy enough, it's in the file `App.js`!

In Figure 8-10, you can see the UML class diagram for `App`, which gives you an overview of what we'll be looking at next.

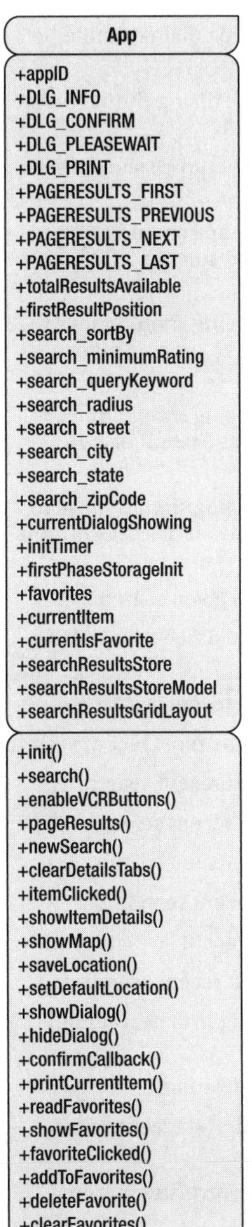

Figure 8-10. *UML class diagram of App class*

To get started, let's have a look at the data fields in the class, as listed in Table 8-2.

Table 8-2. *The Data Fields of the App Class*

Field Name	Description
appID	The application ID you get when you registered to use Yahoo's services.
DLG_INFO	Pseudo-constant to indicate an info-type dialog should be shown. Will be passed to showDialog() method.
DLG_CONFIRM	Pseudo-constant to indicate a confirmation-type dialog should be shown. Will be passed to showDialog() method.
DLG_PLEASEWAIT	Pseudo-constant to indicate a Please Wait–type dialog should be shown. Will be passed to showDialog() method.
DLG_PRINT	Pseudo-constant to indicate the Print dialog should be shown. Will be passed to showDialog() method.
PAGERESULTS_FIRST	Pseudo-constant used to indicate result set paging should move to the first item. Passed into pageResults() as a result of a VCR button being clicked.
PAGERESULTS_PREVIOUS	Pseudo-constant used to indicate result set paging should move to the previous 10 items. Passed into pageResults() as a result of a VCR button being clicked.
PAGERESULTS_NEXT	Pseudo-constant used to indicate result set paging should move to the next 10 items. Passed into pageResults() as a result of a VCR button being clicked.
PAGERESULTS_LAST	Pseudo-constant used to indicate result set paging should move to the last item. Passed into pageResults() as a result of a VCR button being clicked.
totalResultsAvailable	Stores the total number of matches found for a given search.
firstResultPosition	Stores the first result showing in the results grid. Used for result set paging.
search_sortBy	Value of the sortBy field used during the most recent search.
search_minimumRating	Value of the minimumRating field used during the most recent search.
search_queryKeyword	Value of the keyword field used during the most recent search.
search_radius	Value of the radius field used during the most recent search.
search_street	Value of the street field used during the most recent search.
search_city	Value of the city field used during the most recent search.
search_state	Value of the state field used during the most recent search.
search_zipCode	Value of the zipCode field used during the most recent search.
currentDialogShowing	Records what dialog, if any, is currently showing. Will be a value matching one of the DLG_* fields.
initTimer	Handle to timer used during application initialization.
firstPhaseStorageInit	Flag to indicate whether application is in the first stage (true) of initialization or the second stage (false).
Favorites	A Dictionary object where the list of the user's favorites is stored during application run.

Field Name	Description
`currentItem`	A reference to the current search result whose details are being shown.
`currentIsFavorite`	Flag that is set to `true` if the item whose details are being displayed is a favorite, `false` if it's not.
`searchResultsStore`	The data store for the search results grid.
`searchResultsStoreModel`	The data model for the search results grid.
`searchResultsGridLayout`	The layout specification for the search results grid.

Many of those are obvious based on their names. Still others you should have a pretty good idea about based just on the brief descriptions in the table. The rest will become clear as you see them used in the code, which we're now ready to begin looking at, starting with the application initialization procedure.

Initialization

As we saw in `index.htm`, the `init()` method of the `App` class is called `onLoad` (via the Dojo `onLoad` mechanism) to perform application initialization. It's about time we look at that code, wouldn't you say? Here it is:

```
this.init = function() {

  if (dojo.exists("firstPhaseStorageInit", app)) {
    // Perform these tasks the first timer iteration only.
    app.showDialog(app.DLG_PLEASEWAIT, "... Initializing ...");
    // Make sure Gears is available, abort if not.
    if (!dojox.storage.manager.supportsProvider(
      "dojox.storage.GearsStorageProvider")) {
      app.hideDialog();
      app.showDialog(app.DLG_PLEASEWAIT,
        "Gears is not installed or is disabled, cannot continue.");
      return;
    }
    // Make sure we use Gears, then move on to second phase of initialization.
    dojox.storage.manager.setProvider(dojox.storage.GearsStorageProvider);
    app.firstPhaseStorageInit = false;
    app.initTimer = setTimeout("app.init()", 500);
  } else {
    // Do this as many times as necessary (phase 2 initialization).
    if (dojox.storage.manager.isInitialized()) {
      clearTimeout(app.initTimer);
      app.initTimer = null;
      app.readFavorites();
      app.showFavorites();
      app.setDefaultLocation();
      app.hideDialog();
       // Deal with an IE issue that caused Sort By and Minimum rating
```

```
        // fields to not be visible initially.
        dijit.byId("searchTabs").selectChild(dijit.byId("tabResults"));
        dijit.byId("searchTabs").selectChild(dijit.byId("tabSearch"));
      } else {
        app.initTimer  = setTimeout("app.init()", 500);
      }
    }

  } // End init().
```

As I alluded to earlier, initialization is performed in two phases. Each time this method is called, it checks whether the firstPhaseStorageInit field is present on the App instance. This check is performed by using the dojo.exists() function. If that field is present, dojo.exists() returns true. In this case, the "initializing" dialog is shown. This is done via a call to the showDialog() method of the App class. As a preview of that method, which we'll look at in detail later, you pass to it a code that tells it what type of dialog to show (using one of the constants we saw earlier) and the text to display on the dialog (*Initializing*, in this case).

The next step of this first phase of initialization is to see whether the dojox.storage. GearsStorageProvider is a supported storage provider for the Dojo storage system. This is done via a call to dojox.storage.manager.supportsProvider(), passing it the name of the provider we want to check for (dojox.storage.GearsStorageProvider, in this case). This function will return false if the provider isn't available, meaning Gears isn't available. In that case, the "initializing" dialog is hidden via a call to hideDialog(), and then a new dialog is shown stating that Gears isn't available and the application can't continue.

Assuming Gears is available, firstPhaseStorageInit is set to false, indicating that the second phase of initialization is now in progress. Next, a time-out is set to fire in 500 milliseconds, and the function to execute at that time is init() again. A reference to the time-out is stored in the initTimer field of the App instance.

Now, when init() fires again, we're still in the second phase, so the else branch of the initial if check executes. At this point, a call to dojox.storage.manager.isInitialized() is made. If this returns true, the Dojo storage system is all set and we can continue. The time-out is first cleared, and then favorites are read in via a call to readFavorites(). This gets the favorites from the local Gears database, if there are any favorites to get. Then a call to showFavorites() is made, which displays the favorites on the screen. The method setDefaultLocation() is then called, which will set the search criteria to the saved default location, if there is one. Finally, the "initializing" dialog is hidden, and initialization is complete.

■ **Note** A problem was observed running in IE7 that caused the Sort By and Minimum Rating fields to not appear when the application started up. So a bit of hackery was employed: by flipping to the Results tab and then back to the Search tab, the fields appear. I don't know the root cause of the issue—it appears to be something IE7-specific that Dojo doesn't like—but at least this solution works without too much fuss.

Now, if that check to see whether the Dojo storage system is initialized returns false, a time-out is set again, and init() will execute as many times as necessary, waiting for the storage system to initialize.

To make certain the entire flow through initialization is clear, have a look at Figure 8-11. Hopefully, that clears up any nagging doubt you may have.

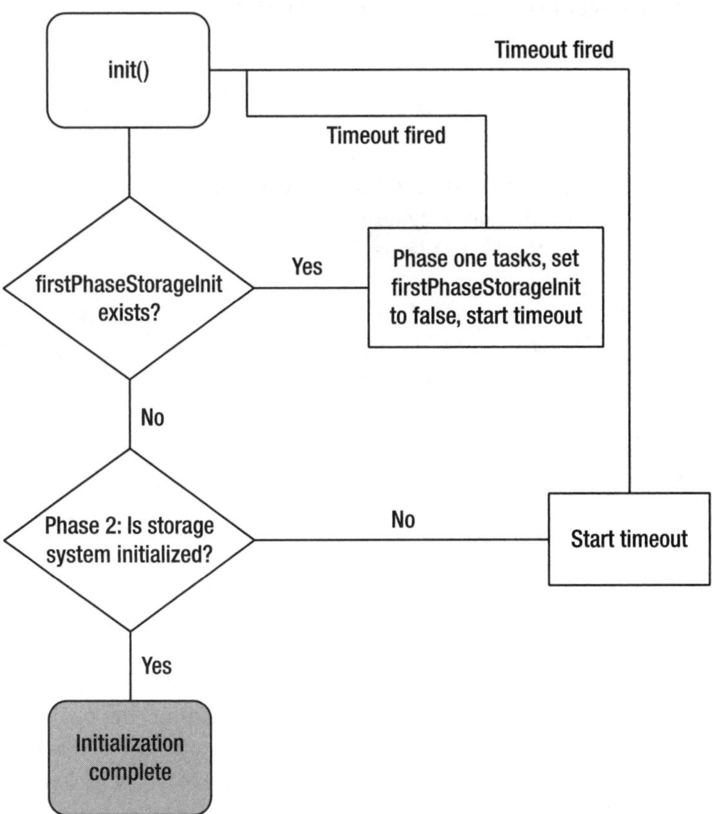

Figure 8-11. *Initialization process flow*

Performing a Search

Now it's time to perform a search! Because this method is fairly long, we're going to look at it in chunks, just to make things a little easier to digest. The first chunk is this:

```
this.search = function(inUseCurrent) {

  if (!inUseCurrent) {
    app.search_sortBy = dijit.byId("sortBy").getValue();
    app.search_minimumRating = dijit.byId("minimumRating").getValue();
    app.search_queryKeyword = dijit.byId("queryKeyword").getValue();
    app.search_radius = dijit.byId("radius").getValue();
    app.search_street = dijit.byId("street").getValue();
    app.search_city = dijit.byId("city").getValue();
    app.search_state = dijit.byId("state").getValue();
    app.search_zipCode = dijit.byId("zipCode").getValue();
    app.totalResultsAvailable = 0;
    app.firstResultPosition = 1;
    dojo.byId("totalCount").innerHTML = "";
    app.enableVCRButtons(true);
  }
```

This method can be called in two situations. The first is obviously when the Execute Search button is clicked. The second is when one of the VCR buttons is clicked to page through results.

In the first case, `inUseCurrent` will be `true`. In this case, we retrieve the values of each of the search criteria fields and store them in fields of the `App` instance. For example, the `radius` UI field is stored in the `search_radius` `App` instance field. At this point, the code also resets the `totalResultsAvailable` and `firstResultPosition` fields to their default values. These fields will be populated when a search is performed (or when paging is performed, in the case of `firstResultPosition`). The code also clears the <div> where the total number of search results, and the current position within the result set, are displayed. Finally, a call to the method `enableVCRButtons()` is made, passing it a value of `true`. This enables all the VCR buttons (passing `false` would disable them all).

When `inUseCurrent` is `false`, this entire branch is skipped because in that case the user is paging through results, not initiating a new search, so none of these tasks is necessary.

The next chunk we encounter is this:

```
  if (app.search_queryKeyword == "") {
    app.showDialog(app.DLG_INFO, "You must enter a keyword to search for");
    return;
  }
  if (app.search_street == "" && app.search_city == "" &&
    app.search_state == "" && app.search_zipCode == "") {
    app.showDialog(app.DLG_INFO,
      "You must enter a location to search around " +
      "(just zip code at a minimum)");
    return;
  }
```

```
if (app.search_street != "" &&
  (app.search_city == "" || app.search_state == "")) {
  app.showDialog(app.DLG_INFO,
    "When street is entered you must also enter city and state");
  return;
}
```

This is just some simple checking to ensure that we have required fields. A keyword is always required, and at least one of the location fields (street, city, state, zip code) is required. If a street is entered, the city and state are then required.

Next we have a single line:

```
app.showDialog(app.DLG_PLEASEWAIT, "... Performing Search ...");
```

This shows a dialog to indicate that a search is in progress. That line is followed by another single line:

```
if (app.search_sortBy == "") { app.search_sortBy = "distance"; }
```

This sets a default for the sort condition if none was selected by the user.

The next chunk is a bit longer:

```
var contentObj = {
  "appid" : app.appID, "output" : "json", "sort" :
  app.search_sortBy.toLowerCase(), start : app.firstResultPosition,
  results : 10
};

if (dojo.exists("search_queryKeyword", app)) {
  contentObj.query = dojo.string.trim(app.search_queryKeyword);
}
if (dojo.exists("search_minimumRating", app)) {
  contentObj.minimum_rating = app.search_minimumRating;
}
if (dojo.exists("search_radius", app)) {
  contentObj.radius = app.search_radius;
}
if (dojo.exists("search_street", app)) {
  contentObj.street = dojo.string.trim(app.search_street);
}
if (dojo.exists("search_city", app)) {
  contentObj.city = dojo.string.trim(app.search_city);
}
if (dojo.exists("search_state", app)) {
  contentObj.state = app.search_state;
}
if (dojo.exists("search_zipCode", app)) {
  contentObj.zip = app.search_zipCode;
}
```

The contentObj object will be passed to the dojo.io.script.get() function that will be called next. These are the parameters to be passed to the web service. The dojo.exists() function is used on each of the possible search criteria. As opposed to the previous instance when we saw this function used, this time there are two arguments being passed. The first is of course the field to look for, and the second is a scope to look in. In other words, it tells the function what object to examine. This defaults to the current object. That's why the first time we saw this function in action, it had only one argument: it was checking for the existence of the given field on the object pointed to by the standard this reference. Any field that is found to exist is added to contentObj.

There are also a few parameters in contentObj that don't come from search criteria. The appid parameter is the application ID you registered to access the Yahoo web services. The output parameter tells the web service what kind of output you want, json in this case. Because the sort parameter will always have a value, one way or another, it too is added. Next, the start parameter, based on the web service documentation, tells the service what the first result you want returned is. For a new search, this will be zero, as you saw in the first chunk of code here. If search() is called as a result of a VCR button being clicked, that value will be something else. Finally, the results parameter tells the service the maximum number of results we want returned, ten in this case.

Now it's time to actually make the call to the web service, and Dojo of course makes that simple for us:

```
dojo.io.script.get({
  callbackParamName : "callback", content : contentObj,
  url : "http://local.yahooapis.com/LocalSearchService/V3/localSearch"
}).addCallback(function(response) {
```

I've broken down what is actually a single JavaScript statement into discrete pieces because, again, it'll be a bit easier to follow this way. The first part is the call to dojo.io.script.get(). As you can see, it accepts an object as an argument. This object has a couple of attributes, beginning with callbackParamName. Recall that the way JSON-P works is that you tell the remote service the name of the JavaScript function you want to use as the callback. The service generates its response in JSON, and then wraps that JSON in a function call using the function name you specified. When you use dojo.io.script.get(), however, Dojo is taking care of that callback for you. In other words, you have no clue regarding the name of the function that the remote service should wrap the JSON response in; Dojo determines the name behind the scenes. However, Dojo needs to know the name of the parameter that the remote service will look at to determine the name of the callback function, and the Yahoo service uses the parameter callback for that, so that's where the value of callbackParamName comes from.

Next, the contentObj object that we previously built up is handed to the function via the content attribute. Dojo takes care of making sure those parameters get sent to the remote service for us. Finally, the URL of the remote service is specified via the url attribute.

Now, also notice that at the end of this portion of code a call to addCallback() is made. So, dojo.io.script.get() is returning some object, on which addCallback() is called. We pass to addCallback() a reference to a function, which in this case is an inlined function, shown here:

```
if (!dojo.exists("ResultSet.Result", response)) {
  app.hideDialog();
  app.showDialog(app.DLG_INFO,
    "No businesses were found matching your search criteria");
  return;
}
```

At least, that's the first portion of the function! Here, we are again using the `dojo.exists()` function to look for an attribute `ResultSet.Result` on the `response` object returned by the web service (which is the object resulting from the returned JSON). If the object doesn't exist, the dialog saying a search is in progress is hidden, and then another is shown saying there were no matches. That's it; the callback is done at that point and is exited.

Assuming there were some matches, the remainder of the callback code executes. Before we look at that code, although it's not all that relevant to understanding the application, let's have a look at the request to and response from the Yahoo Local Search web service. In Figure 8-12, you can see the request parameters, courtesy of your friendly neighborhood Firebug.

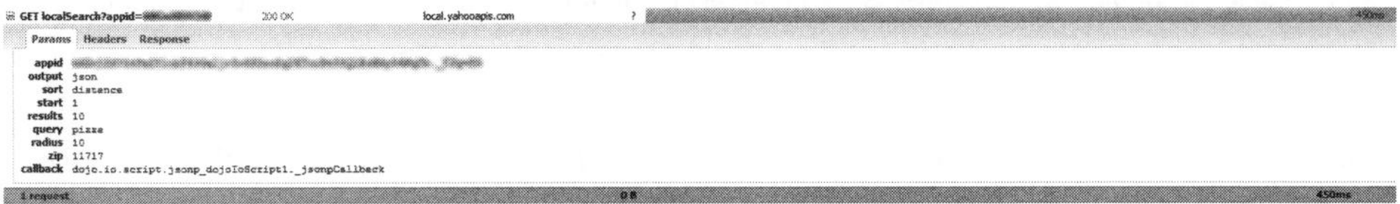

Figure 8-12. *Request parameters of the local search API call*

The `appID` has been blurred in all of these to protect the innocent. (I wouldn't want Yahoo to come knocking on my door because someone deployed this app on Facebook and everyone on the planet is running it against my registered ID!)

Figure 8-13 shows the headers for the same request.

GET localSearch?appid= 200 OK local.yahooapis.com
Params Headers Response
Response Headers
Date Thu, 31 Jul 2008 20:42:31 GMT
P3P policyref="http://p3p.yahoo.com/w3c/p3p.xml", CP="CAO DSP COR CUR ADM DEV TAI PSA PSD IVAi IVDi CONi TELo OTPi OUR DELi SAMi OTRi UNRi PUBi IND PHY ONL UNI PUR FIN COM NAV INT DEM CNT STA POL HEA PRE GOV"
Connection close
Transfer-Encoding chunked
Content-Type text/javascript; charset=utf-8
Request Headers
Host local.yahooapis.com
User-Agent Mozilla/5.0 (Windows; U; Windows NT 5.1; en-US; rv:1.9) Gecko/2008052906 Firefox/3.0
Accept */*
Accept-Language en-us,en;q=0.5
Accept-Encoding gzip,deflate
Accept-Charset ISO-8859-1,utf-8;q=0.7,*;q=0.7
Keep-Alive 300
Connection keep-alive
1 request

Figure 8-13. *Request headers of the local search API call*

Finally, Figure 8-14 shows the actual response. Note that I showed only the first result in the result set because the whole set is quite a bit larger than I could reasonably display in a screenshot in this book.

⊟ json	Object ResultSet=Object
⊟ ResultSet	Object totalResultsAvailable=308 totalResultsReturned=10
⊟ Result	[Object id=11458825 Title=Drago Pizza, Object id=11461914 Title=Pizza Hut Address=717 Suffolk Ave, Object id=11462173 Title=Guarino's Pizza Pasta Rstrnt, 7 more...]
⊟ 0	Object id=11458825 Title=Drago Pizza
Address	"743 Suffolk Ave"
BusinessClickUrl	""
BusinessUrl	""
⊞ Categories	Object Category=[3]
City	"Brentwood"
⊞ ClickUrl	"http://local.yahoo.com/details?id=11458825&stx=pizza&csz=Brentwood+NY&ed=TKNKFK160SzPrrZhfY.t7HaRugwk_aiXSmX0e2tXFw7znesszcsq0XrKIqIKHxO1bNnj2k9e"
Distance	"0.30"
Latitude	"40.780825"
Longitude	"-73.248287"
⊞ MapUrl	"http://maps.yahoo.com/maps_result?name=Drago+Pizza&desc=6312314492&csz=Brentwood+NY&qty=9&cs=9&gid1=11458825"
Phone	"(631) 231-4492"
⊞ Rating	Object AverageRating=4 TotalRatings=5 TotalReviews=5
State	"NY"
Title	"Drago Pizza"
⊞ Url	"http://local.yahoo.com/details?id=11458825&stx=pizza&csz=Brentwood+NY&ed=TKNKFK160SzPrrZhfY.t7HaRugwk_aiXSmX0e2tXFw7znesszcsq0XrKIqIKHxO1bNnj2k9e"
id	"11458825"
⊞ 1	Object id=11461914 Title=Pizza Hut Address=717 Suffolk Ave

Figure 8-14. *Response of the local search API call*

Note It's really cool just how powerful Firebug is. To generate Figure 8-14, all I had to do was drill down through the DOM hierarchy starting with the `dojo` object, then into `io`, then into `script`. I was able to find the actual JSON response from the call in there. That's a really powerful capability to have at your fingertips. If you aren't using Firebug on a regular basis, all I can say is, Shame on you! What are you waiting for?

Getting back to the code of the callback function, we are now ready to take the response and process it, which is done by the following chunk of code:

```
app.searchResultsStore = new dojo.data.ItemFileWriteStore({data:{
  label : "title", identifier : "id", items : [ ]
}});
for (var i = 0; i < response.ResultSet.Result.length; i++) {
  var ratingVal = response.ResultSet.Result[i].Rating.AverageRating;
  app.searchResultsStore.newItem({
    id : parseInt(response.ResultSet.Result[i].id),
    title : response.ResultSet.Result[i].Title,
    distance : response.ResultSet.Result[i].Distance,
    phone : response.ResultSet.Result[i].Phone,
    rating : (isNaN(ratingVal) ? 0 : ratingVal),
    address : response.ResultSet.Result[i].Address,
    city : response.ResultSet.Result[i].City,
    state : response.ResultSet.Result[i].State,
    latitude : response.ResultSet.Result[i].Latitude,
    longitude : response.ResultSet.Result[i].Longitude,
    businessUrl : response.ResultSet.Result[i].BusinessUrl
  });
}
```

Here we're creating a new DataStore for the results Grid to bind to. The structure of the JSON returned by the web service is fairly simple. There is a `ResultSet` attribute that is the overall set of matching businesses. Within that is a `Result` attribute that is an array of the matches. So, we iterate over this array and call `newItem()` on the DataStore for each match. The data from the next match in the array is transferred into the new item.

After that's done, it's time to do some UI setup, beginning with this:

```
dijit.byId("searchTabs").selectChild(dijit.byId("tabResults"));
app.searchResultsStoreModel = new dojox.grid.data.DojoData(null, null, {
  store: app.searchResultsStore, query: {id:"*"}
});
dijit.byId("searchResultsGrid").setModel(app.searchResultsStoreModel);
dijit.byId("searchResultsGrid").update();
```

This code gets a reference to the tab container with the Search and Results tabs, and selects the Results tab. Then it creates a new data model from the DataStore we just populated. Here, the query parameter is used to get all the items in the DataStore. This query attribute allows you to retrieve only matching elements from the store, but here we need them all, so a simple wildcard query does the trick. Then, the model of the results Grid is pointed to the model we just created and update() is called on the Grid. At this point, we have search results in the Grid!

The next task is to deal with the display of total results:

```
app.totalResultsAvailable =
  parseInt(response.ResultSet.totalResultsAvailable);
app.firstResultPosition =
  parseInt(response.ResultSet.firstResultPosition);
dojo.byId("totalCount").innerHTML = app.firstResultPosition + " / " +
  app.totalResultsAvailable;
```

This code displays the current position within the overall result set, and the total number of matches in the form X / Y, where X is the current position and Y is the total number of matches.

Finally, the following is executed to get rid of the dialog box indicating that a search is in progress:

```
    app.hideDialog();
  });

} // End search().
```

Dealing with Result Paging

Now, seeing how a search is done pretty well prepares you for seeing how paging works, because paging is built directly on top of the search capability. Let's begin with that enableVCRButtons() method we saw referenced earlier:

```
this.enableVCRButtons = function(inEnabled) {

  if (inEnabled) {
    dijit.byId("vcrFirst").setDisabled(false);
    dijit.byId("vcrPrevious").setDisabled(false);
    dijit.byId("vcrNext").setDisabled(false);
    dijit.byId("vcrLast").setDisabled(false);
  } else {
```

```
    dijit.byId("vcrFirst").setDisabled(true);
    dijit.byId("vcrPrevious").setDisabled(true);
    dijit.byId("vcrNext").setDisabled(true);
    dijit.byId("vcrLast").setDisabled(true);
  }


} // End enableVCRButtons().
```

Yes, that's all there is to it!

■ **Note** You might argue that the name of the method isn't exactly accurate, but then you'd have to make the same argument about `setDisabled()` on the buttons themselves. I mean, how can a method called `setDisabled()` actually *enable* something, right? But I digress . . .

Now we come to the `pageResults()` method, which is called whenever one of the VCR buttons is clicked:

```
this.pageResults = function(inCommand) {

  switch (inCommand) {
    case app.PAGERESULTS_FIRST:
      if (app.firstResultPosition > 1) {
        app.firstResultPosition = 1;
        app.search(true);
      }
    break;
    case app.PAGERESULTS_PREVIOUS:
      if (app.totalResultsAvailable > 10) {
        app.firstResultPosition = app.firstResultPosition - 10;
        if (app.firstResultPosition < 1) {
          app.firstResultPosition = 1;
        }
        app.search(true);
      }
    break;
    case app.PAGERESULTS_NEXT:
      if (app.totalResultsAvailable > 10) {
        app.firstResultPosition = app.firstResultPosition + 10;
        if (app.firstResultPosition >= app.totalResultsAvailable) {
          app.firstResultPosition = app.totalResultsAvailable - 10;
        }
        app.search(true);
      }
    break;
```

```
    case app.PAGERESULTS_LAST:
      if (app.totalResultsAvailable > 10 && app.firstResultPosition <
        (app.totalResultsAvailable - 10)) {
        app.firstResultPosition = app.totalResultsAvailable - 10;
        app.search(true);
      }
    break;
  }

} // End pageResults().
```

The inCommand argument tells this method what paging operation is being performed, whether it's jumping to the first result, last result, or moving forward or back ten items. The value passed in is taken from one of the PAGERESULTS_* constants seen previously. The code switch is based on inCommand. In the case of PAGERESULTS_FIRST, the process is simple: assuming some paging has occurred already, we set the firstResultPosition to 1, which is where it starts out when a new search is performed, and call search(), passing true. Recall that when search() gets true as its argument, it *does not* grab the entries from the search criteria fields; it instead uses the values stored when the last search was performed, which is precisely what we want to happen here. Now, if no paging has occurred yet, that means firstResultPosition is already 1, so there's no sense in calling the web service again, so in that case nothing happens here.

When inCommand is PAGERESULTS_PREVIOUS, a check is performed to see whether there are more than ten total search results. If there are not, obviously paging can't occur, so nothing would happen here. If there are more than ten, the next step is to subtract ten from firstResultPosition. This assumes that some paging has already occurred, which may not be the case. That's where the if check to see if firstResultPosition is now less than one. If it is, firstResultPosition is set to 1 and a search is performed. This just makes paging a little simpler: rather than keeping track of what has happened and acting accordingly, assumptions are made about what *could* have happened, and bounds checking is instead done to ensure that paging doesn't break around the edge conditions. It's a design choice, but I find that this approach results in less code and is easier to understand, paradoxically.

When inCommand is PAGERESULTS_NEXT, the task to perform is similar to PAGERESULTS_PREVIOUS. First we see whether there are more than ten results. If there are, we add ten to firstResultPosition. Now we have to check the boundary condition: if firstResultPosition is greater than or equal to the total number of results, we need to back it off ten so that we don't wind up with a starting position beyond the end of the result set.

Finally, when inCommand is PAGERESULTS_LAST, there are two checks to perform. Again, we make sure that there are more than ten total results, and then we need to see whether the current firstResultPosition is less than the total number of results, less ten. The second condition comes into play when there are fewer than an even ten results in the last "group" of results—for example, if we have 43 results. That gives us ten groups of four results, plus one group on the end of three. If both conditions pass, we subtract ten from the total number of results and use that value as the new value of firstResultPosition and we're good to go.

Initiating a New Search and Clearing Details

When the New Search icon is clicked on the Fisheye menu, the current search needs to be cleared and things prepared for a new search to be initiated. It's just a lot of cleanup work really and nothing too complex. The newSearch() method does it all:

```
this.newSearch = function() {

  // Clear current data.
  app.currentItem = null;
  app.currentIsFavorite = false;
  app.totalResultsAvailable = 0;
  app.firstResultPosition = 1;
  app.search_sortBy = null;
  app.search_minimumRating = null;
  app.search_queryKeyword = null;
  app.search_radius = null;
  app.search_street = null;
  app.search_city = null;
  app.search_state = null;
  app.search_zipCode = null;

  // Clear search results grid by connecting an empty store to it.
  app.searchResultsStore = new dojo.data.ItemFileWriteStore({data:{
    label : "title", identifier : "id", items : [ ]
  }});
  dijit.byId("searchTabs").selectChild(dijit.byId("tabResults"));
  app.searchResultsStoreModel = new dojox.grid.data.DojoData(null, null, {
    store: app.searchResultsStore
  });
  dijit.byId("searchResultsGrid").setModel(app.searchResultsStoreModel);
  dijit.byId("searchResultsGrid").update();

  // Clear search criteria form.
  dijit.byId("searchTabs").selectChild(dijit.byId("tabSearch"));
  dojo.byId("searchForm").reset();

  // Clear details tabs and other UI reset work.
  app.clearDetailsTabs();
  app.enableVCRButtons(false);
  dojo.byId("totalCount").innerHTML = "";

  // Reset to stored default values for convenience, and reset a few others
  // to sensible defaults.
  app.setDefaultLocation();
  dijit.byId("minimumRating").setValue(0);
  dijit.byId("radius").setValue(10);

} // End newSearch().
```

The currentItem field is set to null because obviously there is no currently selected item now. Likewise, currentIsFavorite is set to false because that could be true only if the user selects one of her favorites. The totalResultsAvailable and firstResultPosition are also reset to their correct initial values. Any previously stored search criteria are cleared next. Then, an empty DataStore is created, as well as a new model based on it. The results Grid is pointed to that model and update() is called, all of which clears any previous search results. Then, the search criteria fields are cleared, which is done via a call to reset() (they are all nested inside a <form>, so that's all it takes). The Search tab is made current at this point as well.

The method clearDetailsTab() is called next:

```
this.clearDetailsTabs = function() {

  dijit.byId("detailsTabs").selectChild(dijit.byId("tabDetails"));
  dojo.byId("details_title").innerHTML = "";
  dojo.byId("details_latitude").innerHTML = "";
  dojo.byId("details_longitude").innerHTML = "";
  dojo.byId("details_distance").innerHTML = "";
  dojo.byId("details_phone").innerHTML = "";
  dojo.byId("details_rating").innerHTML = "";
  dojo.byId("details_address").innerHTML = "";
  dojo.byId("details_city").innerHTML = "";
  dojo.byId("details_state").innerHTML = "";
  dojo.byId("details_businessUrl").innerHTML = "";
  dojo.byId("imgMap").src = "img/transPix.gif";
  dojo.style("imgMap", "display", "none");
  dijit.byId("sldZoom").setValue(6);

} // End clearDetailsTabs().
```

This code flips over to the Details AccordionPane and clears all the <div>s containing the details of the currently selected business, if any. It also points the imgMap <img> element to the transparent pixel image and hides the map. It also resets the zoom slider to its initial value of 6.

Back in newSearch(), the enableVCRButtons() method is called, passing false, so all those buttons are disabled. Then, a call to setDefaultLocation() resets all the location-related search criteria to the stored default location, if any, just like during application initialization. The Minimum Rating and Radius fields are also set to their default values.

At this point, everything is reset to how it was at application initialization, and the user can perform a new search with a clear slate.

Showing a Selected Item's Details and Map

After a search has been performed, the user will look at the list of results and select one. The details for that business then need to be displayed, and the appropriate map retrieved from the Yahoo Map service. The same occurs when one of the user's saved favorites is clicked. In both these cases, the itemClicked() method is called (indirectly in the case of favorites, but ultimately it is called):

```
this.itemClicked = function(inIndex) {

  // Get all items in current snippets collection, then get the clicked
  // item from it.  This has to be done because all we know at this point
  // is the row index from the grid, we can't uniquely identify the item
  // that was clicked, so we have to fetch all the items in order to use
  // that row index.
  dijit.byId("detailsTabs").selectChild(dijit.byId("tabDetails"));
  app.searchResultsStore.fetch(
    { onComplete : function(items, request) {
      // Get the Item from the data store, and create a simple object out of
      // it with all the attributes on it.
      app.currentIsFavorite = false;
      var attrs = app.searchResultsStore.getAttributes(items[inIndex]);
      var item = new Object();
      for (var i = 0; i < attrs.length; i++) {
        item[attrs[i]] = app.searchResultsStore.getValue(items[inIndex],
          attrs[i]);
      }
      app.currentItem = item;
      app.showItemDetails();
    }
  });

} // End itemClicked().
```

First, we need to retrieve the appropriate `Item` from the results Grid's DataStore. You've seen how this works in previous projects, so it shouldn't be any surprise. All items in the DataStore are fetched, and then the index of the item clicked in the Grid is used to get the corresponding `Item`. Because this is an actual `Item` object, an object specific to the DataStore, I decided it was better, and would make other code that needed this object later simpler, so I created a more simplistic object. So, a new `Object` is created, and then the attributes of the DataStore `Item` are iterated over. For each, a field is added to the `Object` and the value of it set. This means that this is the only place that the `getValue()` technique is needed. From here on out, we can reference `currentItem.longitude`, for instance, without having to worry about asking Dojo to get the value and possibly translate it from its internal representation to the real value. We simply have the real value all the time.

After the `Item` is transferred to the more basic `Object`, and the `currentItem` field is set to reference that `Object`, `showItemDetails()` is called to display the details on the screen:

```
this.showItemDetails = function() {

  // Iterate over attributes in the item.
  for (var attr in app.currentItem) {
    // If the current attribute has a corresponding field on the screen,
    // go ahead and populate it.
    var fieldOnScreen = dojo.byId("details_" + attr);
    if (fieldOnScreen) {
```

```
        if (attr == "businessUrl") {
          fieldOnScreen.innerHTML = "<a href=\"" + app.currentItem[attr] +
            "\" target=\"new\">" + app.currentItem[attr] + "</a>";
        } else {
          fieldOnScreen.innerHTML = app.currentItem[attr];
        }
      }
    }

    // Show map.
    app.showMap();

} // End showItemDetails().
```

This is a simple enough matter: iterate over the attribute of currentItem, and for each construct an ID for a <div> by concatenating details_ with the attribute name. Then, try to get a reference to that <div>. If it's found (remember that there may be some fields in the object that don't have a corresponding display <div> on the screen), then populate the <div>'s innerHTML attribute. In the special case of the field being businessUrl, the markup to be inserted into innerHTML is a little more complex—not just the value of the attribute as it is for all the others, but instead a hyperlink so the user can jump to the business's web site.

The results of all this effort can be seen in Figure 8-15.

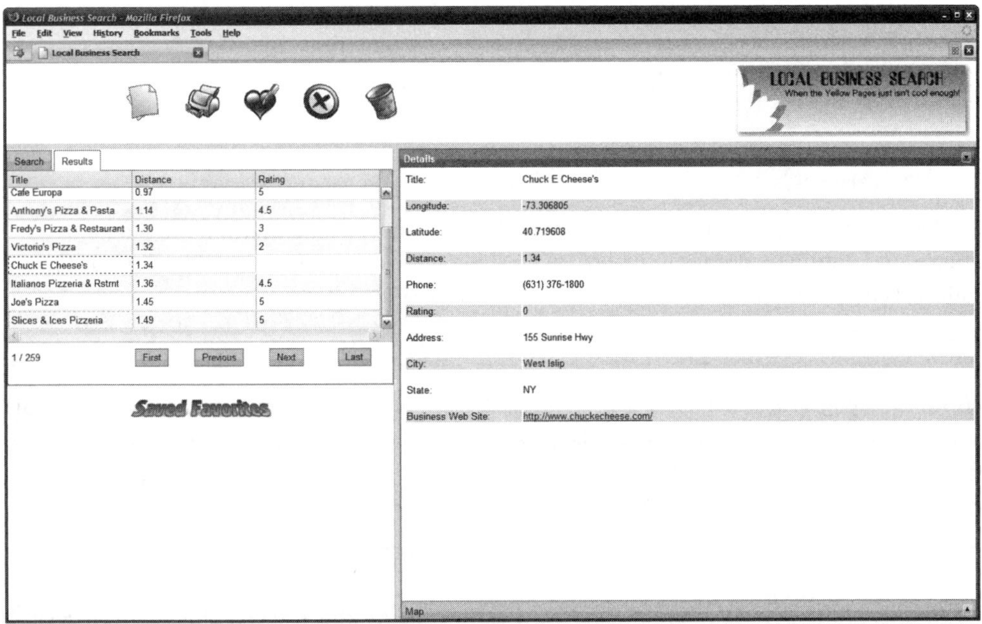

Figure 8-15. *Viewing the details for a given item*

Now, you'll notice that at the end of showItemDetails(), a call is made to showMap(). This is responsible for displaying the map for the business, which means we have to make another web service call. The showMap() method is this:

```
this.showMap = function(inZoomLevel) {

  // Make call to Yahoo! Map service.
  if (dojo.exists("currentItem", app)) {
    if (!inZoomLevel) {
      inZoomLevel = 6;
    }
    dijit.byId("sldZoom").setValue(inZoomLevel);
    dojo.io.script.get({
      callbackParamName : "callback",
      url : "http://local.yahooapis.com/MapsService/V1/mapImage",
      content : {
        "appid" : app.appID, "output" : "json",
        "longitude" : app.currentItem.longitude,
        "latitude" : app.currentItem.latitude,
        image_width : 480, image_height : 460, zoom : inZoomLevel
      }
    }).addCallback(function(response) {
      // Show map.
      dojo.style("imgMap", "display", "");
      dojo.byId("imgMap").src = response.ResultSet.Result;
    });
  }

} // End showMap().
```

This method is also called when the zoom slider is moved, and that's where the inZoomLevel argument comes into play. When showMap() is called from showItemDetails(), nothing is passed in, in which case the default value 6 is set.

■ **Note** Modifying an input parameter like this is usually something I frown upon, but it *does* often make the code somewhat less verbose, as is the case here, because there's no local variable whose value is taken from inZoomLevel. Still, you should probably take this as a good example of what *not* to do, generally speaking!

Then, another dojo.io.script.get() invocation occurs, this time passing the longitude and latitude field values from the currentItem. We also specify the size of the map image we want back, 480 × 460, as well as the zoom level. The callback here is very simple: just update the src attribute of the imgMap <img> element to point to the response.ResultSet.Result element, which is the URL of the map image generated by the service invocation.

Figure 8-16 shows you the net result of all this work.

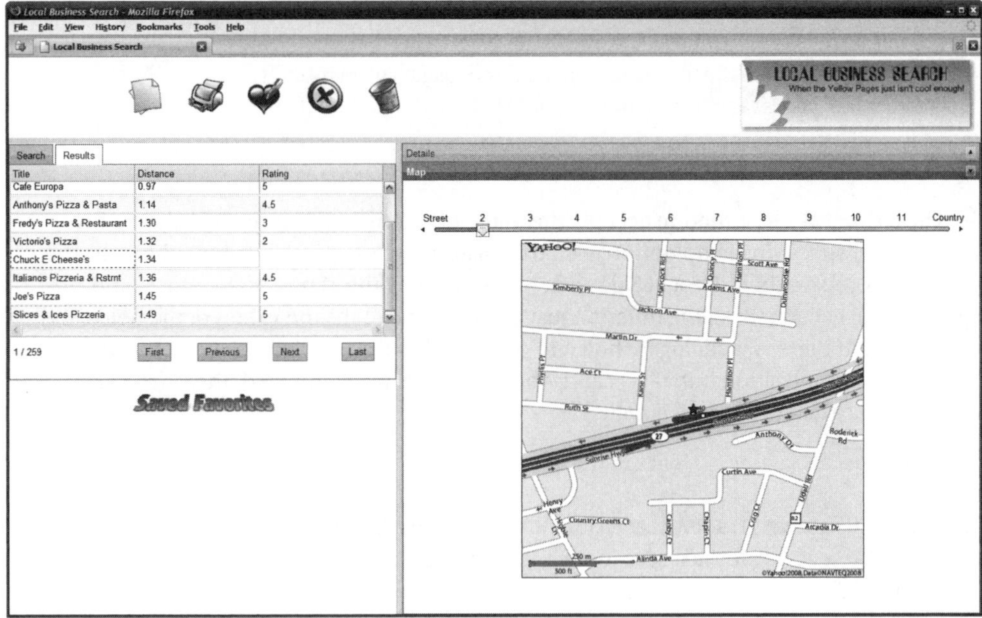

Figure 8-16. *A map that has been zoomed*

The slider has the following attribute on it in `index.htm`:

```
onChange="app.showMap(arguments[0]);"
```

The `arguments[0]` part is a fancy way of getting the current value of the slider, so as you can see, another web service call will be made, and the `imgMap` `<img>` will again be updated, every time the value of the slider changes. That's all it takes to implement that zoom feature!

Dealing with Default Location

In this application, the user has the ability to save whatever location search criteria he currently has entered and use that as his default location. This information is stored in a cookie. When the Save Location as Default Button is clicked, the `saveLocation()` method is called:

```
this.saveLocation = function() {

  // Save location values for one year.
  dojo.cookie("defaultLocation_street",
    dijit.byId("street").getValue(), { expires : 365 });
  dojo.cookie("defaultLocation_city",
    dijit.byId("city").getValue(), { expires : 365 });
  dojo.cookie("defaultLocation_state",
    dijit.byId("state").getValue(), { expires : 365 });
  dojo.cookie("defaultLocation_zipCode",
    dijit.byId("zipCode").getValue(), { expires : 365 });
```

```
  // Tell the user we're done.
  app.showDialog(app.DLG_INFO,
    "This location has been saved and will be used automatically " +
    "next time you start the application");

} // End saveLocation().
```

The dojo.cookie() function accepts the name of the cookie to save, the value to save, and an object specifying extra options—in this case, just the expires attribute that tells the browser this cookie should last 365 days, or one year. Only the street, city, state, and zipCode fields get stored, so the function just goes out and grabs the values of the fields and stores them. At the end, a dialog is shown to confirm that the location has been saved.

When the application initializes, and when a new search is initiated, the setDefaultLocation() method is called:

```
this.setDefaultLocation = function() {

  dijit.byId("street").setValue(dojo.cookie("defaultLocation_street"));
  dijit.byId("city").setValue(dojo.cookie("defaultLocation_city"));
  dijit.byId("state").setValue(dojo.cookie("defaultLocation_state"));
  dijit.byId("zipCode").setValue(dojo.cookie("defaultLocation_zipCode"));

} // End setDefaultLocation().
```

The multifaceted dojo.cookie() function is again used, but this time only the name of the cookie to retrieve is specified. The value of the entry fields are set to whatever the value of the cookie is. If the cookie isn't set, meaning no default location has been saved yet, the field's value winds up being blank anyway, which is perfect.

■ **Note** You might be wondering why this default location information is stored in a cookie rather than in the Gears database. The answer is simply this: I wanted to demonstrate using the Dojo cookie functions to you! You already have seen plenty of Gears interaction in this application and others, so I took this opportunity to go in a different direction and show off more of Dojo. Feel free to rewrite the code to store it in the database if you wish; that wouldn't be a bad exercise.

Dialog Functionality

A number of times now you've seen the showDialog() and hideDialog() methods used, and now it's time to see what they're all about. I hope you aren't disappointed, but they frankly aren't very complex at all!

```
this.showDialog = function(inWhich, inMessage) {

  var textField = dojo.byId(inWhich + "Text");
  if (textField) {
    textField.innerHTML = inMessage;
  }
```

```
  dijit.byId(inWhich + "Dialog").show();
  app.currentDialogShowing = inWhich;

} // End showDialog().
```

The showDialog() method accepts two arguments. The first is a code telling it which type of dialog to display. These codes are the values of the DLG_* fields. So, passing in DLG_INFO shows an info-type dialog, for example. This method also accepts a string of text to display in the dialog. Recall from when we looked at index.htm that each dialog has a <div> where the text is inserted. Further recall that the ID of those <div>s are things like infoText, pleaseWaitText, and confirmText. As you can see, the inWhich argument, more precisely, the values of the DLG_* fields, are values such as info, pleaseWait and confirm. Because of that, the ID of the appropriate <div> to insert the text into can be constructed easily. Then, a reference to that <div> is retrieved via dojo.byId(). Assuming the reference is found, the text is inserted. (This won't occur for the Print dialog because no such <div> is present; there's no dynamic text insertion for that dialog.) Then the dialog is shown, and again the correct ID is constructed dynamically based on the inWhich value passed in. Finally, the currentDialogShowing field is updated to store the value of inWhich. That's primarily done so that this next method can do its thing:

```
this.hideDialog = function() {

  dijit.byId(app.currentDialogShowing + "Dialog").hide();
  app.currentDialogShowing = null;

} // End hideDialog().
```

The hideDialog() method uses the value of currentDialogShowing to hide whatever the currently showing dialog is. This method doesn't have to perform any conditional logic, though; the value of currentDialogShowing is all that's needed to construct the proper ID. Then of course currentDialogShowing has to be set to null because no dialog would be showing at that point.

The final dialog-related method to look at is confirmCallback(), and this is the method called when either the Yes or No button on a confirm-type dialog is clicked:

```
this.confirmCallback = function(inYesOrNo) {

  app.hideDialog();
  var confirmText = dojo.byId("confirmText").innerHTML;
  if (inYesOrNo) {
    if (confirmText.indexOf(
        "Are you sure you want to delete the favorite") != -1) {
      app.deleteFavorite(true);
    } else {
      app.clearFavorites(true);
    }
  }

} // End confirmCallback().
```

First, the dialog is hidden. Then, the content of the `confirmText` `<div>` is retrieved. Next, `inYesOrNo` is branched on. If it's `true`, we then look at the value retrieved from `confirmText`. If it contains the string "Are you sure you want to delete the favorite," we know the dialog was the result of the user wanting to delete the currently selected favorite, so we can then call `deleteFavorite()` if `inYesOrNo` was `true` (meaning Yes was clicked). If that string is not present, then we're clearing favorites, because those are the only two operations that are performed in this application that require confirmation by the user. In that case, `clearFavorites()` is called.

■ Note The calls to `deleteFavorite()` and `clearFavorites()` are both passed `true`. The reason for this will be apparent when we look at those methods, but here's a hint: it's similar conceptually to how `init()` works.

A confirmation-type dialog, by the way, is what you see in Figure 8-17.

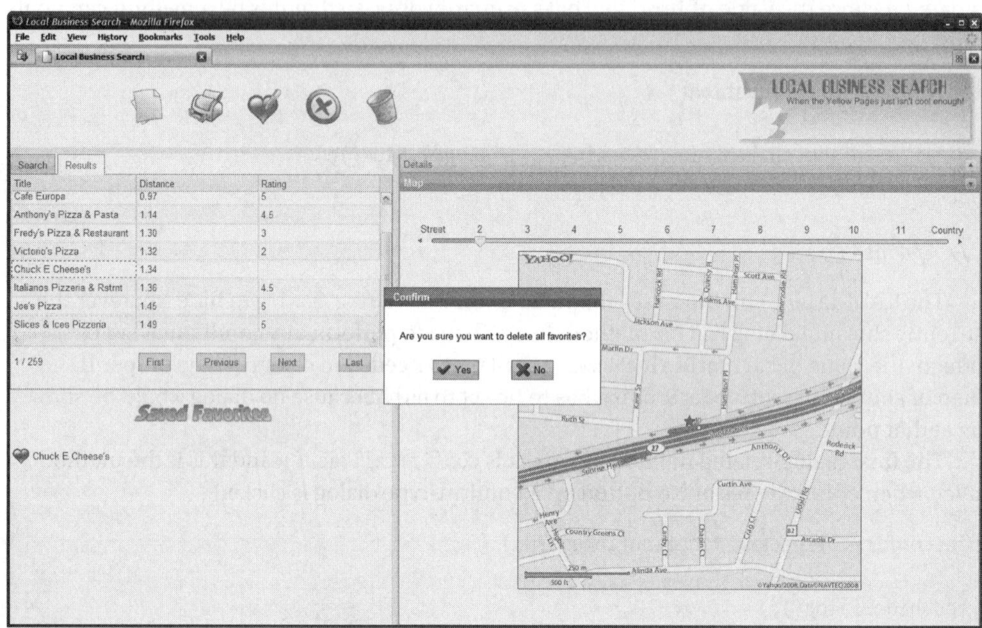

Figure 8-17. *A confirmation dialog box*

As you can see, the user has a choice to make. The user can't just close the dialog because the Close icon is hidden, so we are guaranteed that `confirmCallback()` will be called, one way or another.

Printing an Item

Printing an item is also a pretty simple function:

```
this.printCurrentItem = function() {

  // Make sure we have a current item to print.
  if (!dojo.exists("currentItem", app)) {
    app.showDialog(app.DLG_INFO,
      "Please select an item (either a favorite or a search result) " +
      "to print it");
    return;
  }

  // Show print dialog, then reset the currentDialogShowing field, since it
  // won't be done via the usual call to hideDialog().
  app.showDialog(app.DLG_PRINT);
  app.currentDialogShowing = null;

  // Populate details of current item, including map.
  for (var attr in app.currentItem) {
    var field = dojo.byId("print_" + attr);
    if (field) {
      field.innerHTML = app.currentItem[attr];
    }
  }
  dojo.byId("print_map").src = dojo.byId("imgMap").src;

  // Pop info dialog.
  app.showDialog(app.DLG_INFO,
    "You can now print, and remember to close this maximized dialog " +
    "when you are done to return to the application");

} // End printCurrentItem().
```

The display that the user sees when printing an item is seen in Figure 8-18. As you can see, it's implemented as a maximized dialog that contains the map and business details. There is also a dialog that appears on top of that, informing the user that he has to close the dialog when he is finished. This is necessary because calling the `print()` method automatically, as you'd expect you want to do, runs into timing issues and what winds up printing is the underlying UI and not the Print dialog. This little bit of user interaction avoids that problem and is therefore an acceptable alternative.

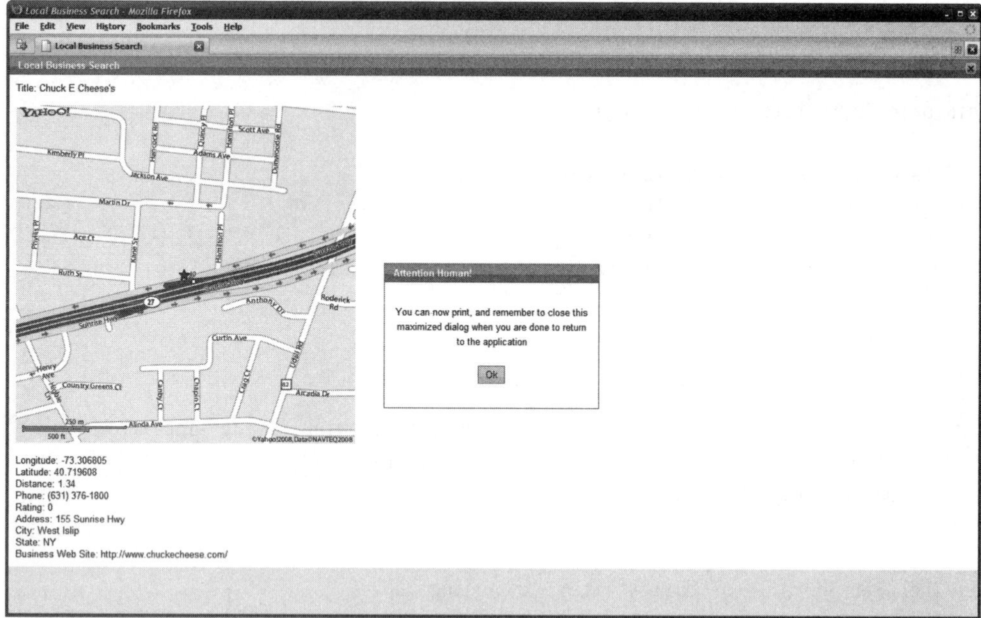

Figure 8-18. *Printing a selected item*

The code itself begins with a simple check to ensure that there is an item currently selected. If there isn't, a quick info dialog is displayed, indicating that the user needs to select an item (or favorite) first.

If an item is selected, the next step is to show the Print dialog itself. Because the user will manually close the dialog, and we don't have a triggering event to hook into, the `currentDialogShowing` field is set to `null` right then and there. This is just like what occurs when `hideDialog()` is called, but because `hideDialog()` won't actually be called here, the code has to do the job of `hideDialog()` itself.

Then, the `currentItem` object (the currently selected search item or favorite, in other words) is iterated over. For each member, we construct an ID based on its name prefixed with `print_`. So, if the next member during the iteration process is `zipCode`, for instance, we construct an ID string value of `print_zipCode`, and we then use this value to try to get a reference to a DOM node with that ID. If one is found, `innerHTML` is set to the value of that member of the `currentItem` object. Because some of the members of `currentItem` may not have a corresponding field in the Print dialog, we need to see whether a reference to the field was retrieved before trying to set its `innerHTML` property, or else Bad Things™ would happen (read: a JavaScript error).

Implementing Favorites Functionality

The next bit of functionality to explore is everything having to do with favorites, beginning with `readFavorites()`, which is responsible for retrieving any stored favorites the user might have from the Gears database:

```
this.readFavorites = function() {

  app.favorites = new dojox.collections.Dictionary();
  // Get all keys in Gears database and iterate over them, retrieving each
  // favorite and adding it to the collection.
  var favKeys = dojox.storage.getKeys("DojoLocalBusinessSearch");
  dojo.forEach(favKeys, function(inVal) {
    var favorite = dojox.storage.get(inVal, "DojoLocalBusinessSearch");
    app.favorites.add(favorite.id, favorite);
  });

} // End readFavorites().
```

I decided to use a `dojox.collections.Dictionary` object to store these in the `App` instance because doing so makes it easy to retrieve a given favorite when it's clicked from the list. A `Dictionary` is a `Map` after all, so keying the favorites by the `id` field is a pretty natural thing to do.

So, we ask the Dojo storage system to give us all the keys stored in the `DojoLocalBusinessSearch` namespace. Then, using the `dojo.forEach()` function, we iterate over that collection of keys. For each, we execute a function (inlined in the `dojo.forEach()` call) that gets the value associated with the given key. This value is in fact a serialized version of the simple object that was created previously when a given DataStore `Item` is clicked. So, when this value is added to the favorites `Dictionary`, what we're actually adding is in fact an object, one that has attributes where all the data on that business is stored! All the details of how this works are neatly tucked behind the Dojo storage system, making it really drop-dead simple.

After favorites have been read in during application initialization, or after any add or delete from the collection of favorites is performed, the UI's favorites display is updated via a call to `showFavorites()`:

```
this.showFavorites = function() {

  var htmlOut = "<br>";
  var it = app.favorites.getIterator();
  while (!it.atEnd()) {
    var fav = it.get().value;
    htmlOut = htmlOut + "<div onClick=\"app.favoriteClicked('" + fav.id +
      "');\" style=\"width:100%;margin-bottom:10px;cursor:pointer;\" " +
      "onmouseover=\"dojo.style(this, 'backgroundColor', '#ffff00');\" " +
      "onmouseout=\"dojo.style(this, 'backgroundColor', '');\" " +
      "id=\"fav_" + fav.id + "\">" +
      "<img src=\"img/favorite.gif\" hspace=\"4\" align=\"absmiddle\">" +
      fav.title + "</div>";
  }
  dijit.byId("cpFavorites").setContent(htmlOut);

} // End showFavorites().
```

The getIterator() method of the Dictionary class gives us an Iterator that we can then use to . . . wait for it . . . iterate over the elements in the Dictionary. Each element has a key attribute and a value attribute, but it's only the value attribute we're interested in here. Using the value (which, remember, is an object), we can generate some markup that becomes the list of favorites. Each favorite is in its own <div> with onMouseOver and onMouseOut event handlers attached to give us a nice little hover effect. Each also has an onClick handler that calls the favoriteClicked() method of the App class, passing it in the id of the clicked favorite. After the HTML is fully constructed, it is inserted into the cpFavorites <div>, and we have a list of favorites on the screen for the user to interact with.

When a favorite is clicked, the favoriteClicked() method is called:

```
this.favoriteClicked = function(inID) {

  dijit.byId("detailsTabs").selectChild(dijit.byId("tabDetails"));
  app.currentItem = app.favorites.entry(inID).value;
  app.currentIsFavorite = true;
  app.showItemDetails();

} // End favoriteClicked().
```

See? It's just a simple matter of getting the corresponding element from the Dictionary via the entry() method, getting the value of that entry, setting currentItem to the retrieved object, and calling showItemDetails(). We also set the currentIsFavorite flag to true so that the other code in the App class knows this is a favorite rather than a clicked search result, which is important in some cases, as you've seen.

Adding a favorite is the next piece of the puzzle:

```
this.addToFavorites = function() {

  if (dojo.exists("currentItem", app)) {
    dojox.storage.put(app.currentItem.id,
      app.currentItem, function(status, keyName) {
        if (status == dojox.storage.FAILED) {
          app.showDialog(app.DLG_INFO,
            "A failure occurred saving favorite to persistent storage");
        } else if (status == dojox.storage.SUCCESS) {
          app.favorites.add(app.currentItem.id, app.currentItem);
          app.showFavorites();
          dojox.fx.highlight(
            { node : "fav_" + app.currentItem.id, color : "#ffff00" }
          ).play();
        }
      }, "DojoLocalBusinessSearch"
    );
  } else {
    app.showDialog(app.DLG_INFO,
```

```
            "You must perform a search and select an item before " +
            "you can add a favorite");
    }

} // End addToFavorites().
```

First, a check is performed to ensure that there is an item currently selected. If there's not, the else branch executes and a dialog is displayed, telling the user to select an item first. Assuming an item is selected, though, all it takes is a call to `dojox.storage.put()` to save it. To this function we pass the id of the `currentItem`, plus the `currentItem` itself. That is the value being saved, and you should note that there's no work here on our part to serialize the object; `dojox.storage.put()` takes care of that for us entirely. All we're dealing with are JavaScript objects, nothing more.

We also pass a callback function that will be called when the operation completes. If the outcome was `dojox.storage.FAILED`, a dialog is popped saying the favorite couldn't be saved. If the outcome was `dojox.storage.SUCCESS`, the favorite is also added to the favorites `Dictionary` on the `App` instance, and a call to `showFavorites()` is made to update the UI. Then, the `dojo.fx.highlight()` function is used to create a yellow fade effect on the newly added favorite. Figure 8-19 attempts to show this, although obviously you can't see the animation, nor will the color be apparent, but you can see a slight coloration at least. (Run the app and try it, that's of course the best answer here!)

The final argument passed to `dojox.storage.put()` is the namespace to save the data under, `DojoLocalBusinessSearch` in this case.

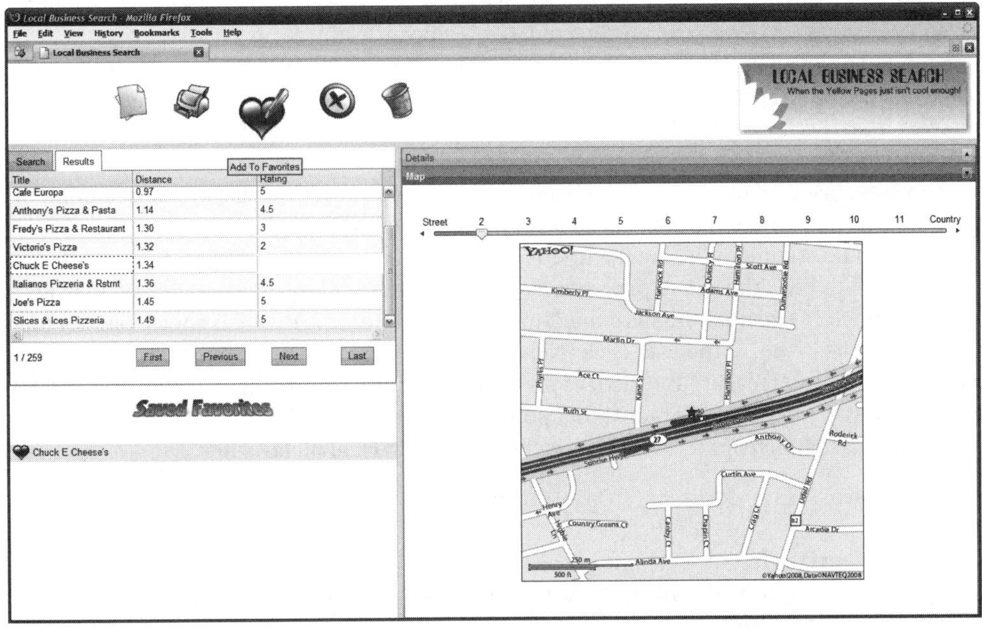

Figure 8-19. *Adding a favorite, which is displayed with the yellow fade effect*

Deleting a favorite is the next function required of the favorites facility, and here it is:

```
this.deleteFavorite = function(inDoDeleteNow) {

  if (dojo.exists("currentIsFavorite", app)) {
    if (inDoDeleteNow) {
      dojox.storage.remove(app.currentItem.id, "DojoLocalBusinessSearch");
      app.favorites.remove(app.currentItem.id);
      app.showFavorites();
      app.currentItem = null;
      app.currentIsFavorite = false;
      app.clearDetailsTabs();
    } else {
      app.showDialog(app.DLG_CONFIRM,
        "Are you sure you want to delete the favorite '" +
        app.currentItem.title + "'?");
    }
  } else {
    app.showDialog(app.DLG_INFO,
      "Please select a favorite first to delete it");
  }

} // End deleteFavorite().
```

First, we ensure that the currently showing item is actually a favorite; otherwise, a dialog is displayed saying this item can't be deleted. If it is a favorite, the `dojox.storage.remove()` function is employed to delete the favorite from the database. This simply requires the `id` to delete and the namespace it's under. After being deleted from the database, the item is also removed from the `favorites` Dictionary. Then `showFavorites()` is called to reshow the updated list of favorites on the screen, and details and such are reset.

However, I glossed over something here. Did you take note of the `inDoDeleteNow` argument? Here's how it works: when the Delete Favorite Fisheye menu icon is clicked, `deleteFavorite()` is called with no argument. Inside the first `if` branch, the value of the `inDoDeleteNow` argument is checked. If it's `true`, the delete proceeds as described. If it's `false`, or wasn't passed in at all, the `else` branch is executed. In this situation, a confirmation-type dialog is shown, asking the user whether he is sure. If the user clicks No, nothing happens and we're finished. If the user clicks Yes, `confirmCallback()` is called, as previously discussed, and that will ultimately call `deleteFavorite()`, passing in `true`. At that point, the delete proceeds.

The last function related to favorites is the function to clear all favorites:

```
this.clearFavorites = function(inDoDeleteNow) {

  if (app.favorites.count == 0) {
    app.showDialog(app.DLG_INFO, "You currently have no favorites saved");
  } else {
    if (inDoDeleteNow) {
```

```
      dojox.storage.clear("DojoLocalBusinessSearch");
      app.favorites.clear();
      app.showFavorites();
      app.currentItem = null;
      app.currentIsFavorite = false;
      app.clearDetailsTabs();
    } else {
      app.showDialog(app.DLG_CONFIRM,
        "Are you sure you want to delete all favorites?");
    }
  }

} // End clearFavorites().
```

This does the same sort of two-phase process as `deleteFavorite()` did because a confirmation-type dialog is involved here as well. First, however, we check to be sure there are elements in the `favorites` Dictionary. If there aren't, an information-type dialog is displayed.

If there are favorites to be cleared and the user confirms the operation, the `dojox.storage.clear()` method is called, passing it the namespace we want cleared, and the Dojo storage system takes care of that. The `clear()` method on the `favorites` Dictionary is called to clear that out. Then, `showFavorites()` is called, which effectively clears the list of favorites from the UI because there are no favorites to display now. The Details tab is cleared as well, other variables are reset, and that's it for favorites.

And that's it for this application as well!

Suggested Exercises

This is now my fourth book, and each one was an Apress "practical' book, which means I've written a whole lot of mini-applications over the past few years! I myself refer back to them when I have questions or need to remember how to do something. This application, however, is the first that I've found myself actually *using* on a pretty regular basis! I find it to be genuinely useful in my day-to-day life.

That being said, I think there are some things that could be added to make it even more useful, and I think they would be good learning exercises for you to undertake as well, so here are a few ideas:

1. Add a link to the Yahoo page with the details for the selected business. Look through the documentation for the local search service and you'll find that such a link is part of the data returned. This would enable you to see things like user ratings and reviews.

2. Add a Google search pane to the Accordion. This would enable you to see a list of search hits for a given business as provided by Google. I say *Google* for two reasons: first, as for most of the planet, it is my search engine of choice because I find the results are generally better than other engines, and second, just to prove that there's no inherent limitation on mashing up services from two sources.

3. Store the last, say, three searches in the Gears database and provide a way to quickly pull them up. I mean store the search *results*, not just the search criteria. No sense pinging Yahoo's servers if you can avoid it!

4. Add the ability to get directions to a selected business. You may have to look around for a service that gives you this capability; I'd check into what else Yahoo offers first, and then Google's map APIs.

Summary

In this chapter, we looked at the concept of a mashup and saw how Dojo provides some very nice functions for being able to call on remote web services, allowing for a completely client-side mashup to be developed. We of course developed such an application and saw some of the services Yahoo provides. We also learned about JSON-P, the technique underlying the functions Dojo provides. We got to play with some more of Dijit and saw some more Core functions in action. We saw more of Dojo's storage subsystem and how it lets us interact with Gears in a simple way. Plus, we wound up with what I think is a pretty useful application, which is definitely a win in my book!

Index

Special Characters

* (asterisk) to define styles, 228
37signals Basecamp product
  web site address, 9
  yellow fade effect usage in, 9

A

Academic Free License (AFL), 13
Accordion dijit, 148–150, 406
AccordionContainer dijit, 148–150
AccordionPane dijit, 148–150
AccordionPane objects, 150
ActiveX, 216
AdapterRegistry object, 46–47
Add Category dialog box (Code Cabinet application), 277
addCategory() method, 278
addCategoryClicked() method, 306
addClass()/removeClass() functions, 171, 173
addOnLoad() function, 232, 276
addPlot() method, 160–161
addSeries() method, 159
addSnippetClicked() method, 314
Ajax (Asynchronous JavaScript and XML), 80–81
Anderson, Mark, 13
Animation objects, 175
API (Application Programming Interface)
  App class data fields, 412–413
  dojo.data, 267
  Gears Database, 268, 270
  Yahoo APIs, 381, 384
app() method, 194
App.js (Local Business Search application)
  App class data fields, 412–413
  default locations, 429–430
  dialog functionality, 430–432
  favorites functionality, 434–439
  initialization, 413–415
  initiating new searches, 424–425
  performing searches, 416–421
  printing items, 433–434
  result paging, 421–423
  showing selected item details, 425–429
applications, initializing, 233
applyTransform() function, 184–185
Aptana (Jaxer), 87
area charts, 160
ArrayLists, 162–166
aspect-oriented programming (AOP), 53–54
attributes, Fisheye List, 235–236
autocomplete function (ComboBox dijit), 135
autoSave attribute (InlineEditBox dijit), 124

B

Babylon 5, 69
Ballmer, Steve, 7
bar charts, 161–162
Base
  baseScriptUri, 34, 231
  vs. Dojo Core, 41–42
body section (Idiot Blob application), 337
<body> tags, 116
Boodman, Aaron, 13
The Book of Dojo, 268
bootstrap JavaScript code (Contact Manager application), 232–233
borders, 343
BSD license, 13
Builder class, 194–195
build.txt file, 43–45

Button dijit, 133, 336
buttonCancel attribute (InlineEditBox dijit), 124
buttonSave attribute (InlineEditBox dijit), 124

C

callbackParamName attribute (dojo.io.script.remove function), 107
Cartman, Eric, 34
categories (Code Cabinet application)
  category-related functions, 306–314
  category Tree, 282–283
  overview, 265
ch2_back.htm example, 91–92
ch2_xhr.htm, 82
Chart2D class, 158
charting
  charting namespace (DojoX). *See* dojox.charting namespace
  in DojoX, 26–27
check boxes
  assigning IDs to, 134
  CheckBox dijit, 133–134
  creating in JavaScript code, 134
checked attribute (ToggleButton dijit), 146
checkString attribute (dojo.io.script.remove function), 107
circles, drawing, 183, 184
clear() method, 166
Clearleft, 9
clearSurface() method, 364–365
clickSelect attribute (HorizontalRuleLabels dijit), 142
client-side application, building. *See* contact manager application (client-side)
clOut() function, 245
code cabinet application
  category-related functions, 306–314
  category Tree, 282–283
  Code tab, 273–287
  CodeCabinet.js, writing, 295–301
  dialog boxes, 276, 281
  directory structure, 270
  dojo.data namespace, 266–268
  features and goals, 265–266
  Gears Database component, 268–270
  head section, 274–276
  index.htm overview, 271–274
  Info tab, 273–287
  initialization at startup, 302–306
  Keywords tab, 274–288, 290
  learning exercises, 327–328
  main content, 282
  Notes tab, 287–288
  overview, 265
  search functions, 320–327
  search-related markup, 290–292
  snippet-related functions, 314–320
  SplitContainer, 283–284
  styles.css, writing, 293–295
  tab definitions, 284–285
code monkey, 14–15
Code tab (code cabinet application), 273–287
CodeCabinet.js (code cabinet application), 295–301
Cold Stone Creamery, 70
collections
  classes, in DojoX, 30
  collections namespace, DojoX. *See* dojox.collections namespace
  defined, 162
ColorPalette dijit, 120–121
ComboBox, creating, 135–136
ComboBox dijit, 135–136
ComboButton dijit, 136–137
Common Locale Data Repository (CLDR). *See* Dojo, dojo.cldr namespace
com.omnytex.AnotherClass, 58–59
configuring Dojo, 34
Confirm Deletion dialog, 278
Confirm dialog (Local Business Search application), 396
confirmCallback() method, 396, 431

connectId attribute (Tooltip dijit), 131
constants in JavaScript, 405
constraints attribute (NumberSpinner dijit), 143
contact manager application (client-side)
  bootstrap JavaScript code, adding, 232–233
  contact list, adding, 237–240
  Contact.js, 245–250
  Contact.js, writing, 245–250
  ContactManager.js file, 250–256
  ContactManager.js file, writing, 250–256
  cookies and Dojo, 217–218
  data storage, 216–217
  DataManager.js, writing, 256–262
  directory structure, 223–226
  Dojo storage system, 218–220
  dojoStyles.css, writing, 229–230
  EventHandlers.js, writing, 240
  features and goals, 215–216
  Fisheye List, adding, 233–237
  Gears Database overview, 220–223
  goodbye.htm, writing, 240
  index.htm, writing, 230–232
  initializing application, 233
  learning exercises, 262–263
  styles.css file, writing, 226–229
container attribute (HorizontalRuleLabels dijit), 142
contains() method, 171
containsKey() method, 168
containsValue() method, 168
ContentPane dijit, 150–151
contextMenuForWindow attribute (Menu dijit), 125
cookies
  Dojo and, 217–218
  dojo.cookie() function, 430
  Flash, 216
Core
  automatic functionality, 17–20
  component, 41. *See also* Dojo Core
  manually added functionality, 19–20
Coulton, Jonathan, 15
Crawford, Christina, 6
Crawford, Joan, 6
createImage() method, 360, 362
createText() function, 184
credit cards, validating, 205
crossFade() function, 173–175
cryptographic algorithms, 30
css classes (Code Cabinet application), 295
CSS3 selectors, 72–73
cssOuterBorder class, 343
cssSlider class, 345
cssTab class, 229
cssTextbox style class, 240
currency code. *See* ISO 4217 currency code
CurrencyTextBox dijit, 137–138
customDOJO.js, 45
customPackage namespace, 74
cylindrical bar chart, 26

D

data-entry markup (Contact Manager application), 237–240
data storage (Contact Manager application), 216–217
Data Switch code, 222
data transfer object (DTO) pattern, 247
Database component (Gears), 221–223
DataManager.js (Contact Manager application), 256–262
DateTextBox dijit, 138–139
defaultTimeout attribute (ColorPalette dijit), 120
degressToRadians()/radiansToDegrees() functions, 190
deleting
  categories (Code Cabinet application), 310–314
  cookies, 217
  favorites, 438
  snippets, 319
Details AccordionPane, 425
Details pane (Local Business Search application), 406–408

dialog boxes
  Code Cabinet application, 276–281
  Idiot Blob application, 344
  Local Business Search application, 394–396, 430–432
Dialog dijit, 121–122, 331, 336
Dictionary class, 166–168, 436
digit.layout, 115
Dijits
  attraction of, 20–21
  attributes, 118–119
  common methods and attributes, 118–119
  creating, 116
  creation of, 35
  declarative vs. programmatic, 116–117
  dijit.form, 115
  dijit.form package, 132–147
  dijit.form.ComboBox, 136
  dijit.form.ComboButton object, 137
  dijit.form.ToggleButton digit, 129
  dijit.hideTooltip(), 131
  dijit.layout package, 148–156
  dijit.showTooltip(), 131
  dijit.ToolbarSeparator dijit, 129
  Dojo widget, 20–25
  example of i18n support, 22
  form elements, 21
  getting references to existing, 119
  getting started with, 116
  at a glance, 115–117
  mail reader application, 21
  methods, 118
  namespace, 115, 119–132
  themes packaged with, 115–116
  toolbars provided by, 23
Direct Web Remoting (DWR) library, 12
directory structure
  Contact Manager application, 223–226
  Idiot Blob application, 333–335
Display for Menu dijit, 125
distance() method, 190–191
djConfig object, 34, 85
djConfig variable, 231
Document Object Model (DOM), 4
document.getElementsByTagName() function, 242
Dog Heaven silent film, 3
Dojo. *See also* Dojo Toolkit
  applied, 30–36
  automatic Core functionality, 17–19
  Base. *See* Base
  components of, 16–30
  configuring, 34
  creating custom build, 43–45
  data system, 136
  directory structure of, 32
  dojo-developer list, 13
  dojo.AdapterRegistry() object, 46–47
  dojo.addClass() function, 48–49
  dojo.addOnLoad() function, 49–50, 122, 337
  dojo.addOnUnload() function, 50
  dojo.back namespace, 90–92
  dojo.back.addToHistory() function, 90–92
  dojo.back.init() function, 90–92
  dojo.back.setInitialState() function, 91–92
  dojo.baseUrl property, 85
  dojo.behavior namespace, 92–94
  dojo.behavior.add() function, 93
  dojo.behavior.apply() function, 93–94
  dojo.blColors() function, 50
  dojo.body() function, 50
  dojo.byId() function, 50–51
  dojo.cldr namespace, 94, 94–95
  dojo.cldr.monetary.getData() function, 94
  dojo.cldr.supplemental.getFirstDayOfWeek() function, 95
  dojo.cldr.supplemental.getWeek() function, 95
  dojo.clone() function, 51
  dojo.Color(), 47–48
  dojo.colorFromArray() function, 52
  dojo.colorFromHex() function, 52
  dojo.colorFromRgb() function, 53

dojo.colorFromString() function, 53
dojo.colors namespace, 96
dojo.colors.makeGrey() function, 96
dojo.config property, 85
dojo.connect() function, 53–55
dojo.connectPublisher() function, 55–56
dojo.cookie() function, 57, 430
dojo.cookie package, 217–218
dojo.coords() function, 57
dojo.currency, 96–98
dojo.currency.format() function, 97
dojo.currency.parse() function, 97–98
dojo.data namespace, 98, 266–268
dojo.data.ItemFileReadStore type, 132
dojo.data.ItemFileWriteStore, 136, 276
dojo.date namespace, 98–101
dojo.date.add() function, 98
dojo.date.compare() function, 98–99
dojo.date.difference() function, 98–99
dojo.date.getDaysInMonth() function, 99–100
dojo.date.getTimezoneName() function, 99–100
dojo.date.isLeapYear() function, 99–100
dojo.date.stamp.fromISOString() function, 100–101
dojo.date.stamp.toISOString() function, 100–101
dojo.declare() function, 58–59, 297
dojo.disconnect() function, 55
dojo.doc property, 85
dojo.eval() function, 59
dojo.every() function, 59
dojo.exists() function, 59–60, 414, 418–419
dojo.ext() function, 60–61
dojo.fadeIn() function, 61
dojo.fadeOut() function, 61
dojo.filter() function, 61–62
dojo.forEach() function, 62, 435
dojo.formToJson() function, 62–63
dojo.formToObject() function, 62–63
dojo.formToQuery() function, 62–63
dojo.fx namespace, 101–103, 171–179
dojo.fx.chain() function, 102–103
dojo.fx.combine() function, 102–103
dojo.fx.slideTo() function, 102–103
dojo.fx.Toggler() constructor, 101–102
dojo.fx.wipeIn() function, 102–103
dojo.fx.wipeOut() function, 102–103
dojo.getComputedStyle() function, 63–64
dojo.getObject() function, 64
dojo.gfx packages, 27
dojo.global property, 85
dojo.hasClass() function, 64
dojo.i18n namespace functions, 104–105
dojo.i18n.getLocalization() function, 104–105
dojo.i18n.normalizeLocale() function, 104–105
dojo.indexOf() function, 65
dojo.io namespace functions, 105–107
dojo.io.iframe.create() function, 105–106
dojo.io.iframe.setSrc() function, 106–107
dojo.io.script.attach() function, 106
dojo.io.script.get() function, 107, 384
dojo.io.script.remove() function, 107
dojo.isArray() function, 47, 65–66
dojo.isArrayLike() function, 66
dojo.isBrowser property, 85
dojo.isDescant() function, 66–67
dojo.isFF property, 86
dojo.isFunction() function, 67
dojo.isGears, 86
dojo.isIE property, 86
dojo.isKhtml property, 86
dojo.isMozilla property, 86
dojo.isObject() function, 67–68
dojo.isOpera property, 87
dojo.isQuirks property, 87
dojo.isRhino property, 87
dojo.isSafari property, 87
dojo.isSpidermonkey property, 87
dojo.isString() function, 47, 68
dojo.jaxer property, 87–88

dojo.keys property, 88–89
dojo.lastIndexOf() function, 68–69
dojo.loaded() function, 48
dojo.locale property, 89
dojo.map() function, 69
dojo.mixin() function, 70
dojo.number namespace, 107–109
dojo.number.format() function, 97, 108
dojo.number.parse() function, 108–109
dojo.number.regexp() function, 109
dojo.number.round() function, 109
dojo.objectToQuery() function, 70–71
dojo.OpenAjax property, 89
dojo.parser, 231
dojo.place() function, 71
dojo.platformRequire() function, 72
dojo.provide() call, 74
dojo.publish() function, 55–56
dojo.query() function, 72–73
dojo.queryToObject() function, 73–74
dojo.regexp namespace, 110–111
dojo.regexp.buildGroupRE() function, 110
dojo.regexp.escapeString() function, 111
dojo.regexp.group() function, 111
dojo.registerModulePath() function, 74–75
dojo.removeClass() function, 48–49
dojo.require() function, 231
dojo.required() function, 42–43
dojo.required() statement, 35
dojo.requireIf() function, 75
dojo.requireLocalization() function, 104
dojo.setContext() function, 76
dojo.setObject() function, 76
dojo.setSelectable() function, 76
dojo.some() function, 77
dojo.stopEvent() function, 77–78
dojo.string namespace, 111–113
dojo.string.pad() function, 112
dojo.string.pad() namespace, 112–113
dojo.string.substitute() function, 112–113
dojo.string.trim() function, 113, 307, 320
dojo.style() function, 78
dojoStyles.css (Contact Manager application), 229–230
dojo.subscribe() function, 55–56
dojo.toggleClass() function, 79
dojo.toJson() function, 79–80
dojo.trim() function, 80
dojo.unloaded() function, 80
dojo.unsubscribe() function, 55–56
dojo.version property, 90
Foundation, 14
functions, 48
help and information, 36–38
history of, 13–14
importing dojo.js, 17
importing other parts of, 35
importing style sheets, 33–34
include() mechanism, 17
including optional components in, 35
manually added functionality, 19–20
My First Dojo app, 31–32
object constructors, 46–48
object properties, 85–90
online API documentation, 37–38
overall architecture of, 42
overview, 3
page access, 32–33
philosophy of, 15–16
pros and cons of, 38–39
storage system, 218–220
TabContainer dijit, 302
Tundra theme, 33
version 1.0.2 releases, 44
Dojo Core
vs. Base, 41–42
in detail, 45
Dojo Toolkit
Core component of, 41
open-source JavaScript library, 13–14
Dojo widgets. *See also* Dijits
accessibility of, 21
attraction of, 20–21
dojox.widget namespace, 206–210
ease of creating, 21

internationalization and localization supported by, 21
programming interface provided by, 20
skinnability of, 20
DojoX
charting in, 26–27
collection classes in, 30
ColorPicker widget, 29
dojo.fx. *See* Dojo, dojo.fx namespace
dojox.charting namespace. *See* dojox.charting namespace
dojox.collections. *See* dojox.collections namespace
dojox.gfx. *See* dojox.gfx namespace
dojox.grid namespace, 185–188, 285
dojo.xhr() function, 81–82
dojo.xhrDelete() function, 80–84
dojo.xhrGet() function, 80–84
dojo.xhrPost() function, 80
dojo.xhrPut() function, 80–84
dojox.math namespace. *See* dojox.math namespace
dojox.storage package, 218–220
dojox.storage.put() function, 437
dojox.storage.remove() function, 438
dojox.string namespace. *See* dojox.string namespace
dojox.timing namespace. *See* dojox.timing namespace
dojox.uuid namespace, 199–201
dojox.validate namespace, 202–206
dojox.widget namespace, 206, 210
drawing in, 27–30
Fisheye List widget, 30
Grid widget, 28
ImageGallery widget, 29
implementations of cryptographic algorithms in, 30
Lightbox widget, 29
math functions in, 30
Offline, capabilities provided by, 27–28
other things included in, 30
overview, 157–158
validation functions in, 30
widgets, 28–30
XML functionality package in, 30
dojox.charting namespace
area charts, 160
bar charts, 161–162
line charts, 159–160
overview, 158–159
StackedLines charts, 161
dojox.collections namespace
ArrayLists, 162–166
Dictionary class, 166–168
overview, 162
Stacks, 169, 171
dojox.collections.Dictionary objects, 435
dojox.gfx namespace
applyTransform() function, 184–185
circles, drawing, 183–184
ellipses, drawing, 184
Idiot Blob application and, 331–332
lines, drawing, 182–183
overview and example, 179–182
Polylines, 183
Rect() function (rectangles), 183
surfaces, creating, 182
text, creating, 184
dojox.math namespace
degreesToRadians()/radiansToDegrees() functions, 190
distance() method, 190–191
factoral() function, 191
gaussian() function, 191
midpoint() function, 191
overview and example, 188–190
range() function, 192
sd() (standard deviation) function, 192
dojox.string namespace
Builder class, 194–195
overview and example, 192–195
sprintf() function, 195
dojox.timing namespace
Sequence class, 197–199
Timer class, 195–197
drawing shapes. *See* DojoX, dojox.gfx
drawText() method, 369

DropDownButton dijit, 140–141
DTO (data transfer object) pattern, 247
duration attribute
  in Accordion dijit, 149
  setting for Tooltip dijit, 131
Dynamic HTML, 7

E

early binding, 243
Eckel, Bruce, 1
ECMAScript, 9
Editor dijit, 122–123, 287
Eich, Brendan, 4
ellipses, drawing, 184
emails, validating, 204
error handling, JSON-P and, 385
errorMessage attribute (ContentPane dijit), 151
European Computer Manufacturers Association (ECMA), 9–10
EventHandlers.js (Contact Manager application), 240
execute() method, 269
expando attribute (dojo type), 36
extraLocale for configuring Dojo, 34

F

factoral() function, 191
favorites
  Favorites pane, 405
  Local Business Search application, 434–439
fetch() method, 310
field() method, 269
fieldCount() method, 269
FILO (first in, last out) stacks, 169
Firebug, 420
Fisheye List
  dijit, 397–398
  widget, 206, 233–237
Flash shared objects, 216
form element, 288
frameDoc attribute (dojo.io.script.remove function), 107
frames in Netscape Navigator 2.0, 4
fromJson() function, 249

G

game application. *See* Idiot Blob application
game loops, 366
GameClass.js, writing (Idiot Blob application), 365–376
gaussian() function, 191
Gears Database
  API, 222
  Code Cabinet application, 268–270
  installing, 223
  overview, 220–223
getIterator() method, 436
getValue() method, 299
getValuesList() method, 168
Gibbs, Mark, 1
GNU General Public License (GPL), 13
goodbye.htm (Contact Manager application), 240
Google, origins of, 3
GraphicsSubsystem.js, writing (Idiot Blob application), 348–365
grid namespace (DojoX). *See* DojoX, dojox.grid namespace
gridWidth/gridHeight, 350

H

head section
  Code Cabinet application, 274–276
  Idiot Blob application, 335
  Local Business Search application, 392–394
hideDialog() method, 430
highlight() function, 175–176
HorizontalRuleLabels dijit, 142
HorizontalSlider dijit, 141
HorizontalSliders, 407

I

i18n (internationalization), 104
iconClass attribute (ToggleButton dijit), 146
Idiot Blob application
  body section, 337
  dialog boxes, 344
  directory structure, 333–335
  dojox.gfx namespace, 331–332
  exercises for further learning, 376–377
  game loops, 366
  GameClass.js, writing, 365–376
  GraphicsSubsystem.js, writing, 348–365
  head section, 335–336
  index.htm, writing, 335–342
  LevelMaps.js, writing, 346–348
  procedural graphics, 332
  requirements and goals, 330–331
  script section, 336
  styles.css, writing, 342–345
ifBlur() function, 242–343
ifFocus() function, 242–243
ignoreCase attribute, 136
img elements, 351–352
include() mechanism (Dojo), 35, 42
indeterminate attribute (ProgressBar dijit), 127
index.htm
  Code Cabinet application, 271–274
  Contact Manager application, 230–232
  Idiot Blob application, 335–342
index.htm (Local Business Search application)
  Details pane, 406–408
  dialog boxes, 394–396
  Favorites pane, 405
  head contents, 392–394
  main contents, 398–399
  menu markup, 397–398
  search criteria pane, 399–403
  search results pane, 403–405
indexOf() method, 165
Info dialog box (Local Business Search application), 395
Info tab (Code Cabinet application), 273, 286–287
init() function (DataManager class), 251
initializing
  Code Cabinet application, 302–306
  Contact Manager application, 233
  Local Business Search application, 413–415
initTimer, 253
InlineEditBox dijit, 123–125
interceptor() function, 54
Internet Explorer problems, 173, 175
Internet Movie Database (IMDb), 69
invalidMessage attribute (ValidationTextBox dijit), 147
ISBN numbers, validating, 206
isEmailAddress() function, 204
isInRange() function, 205
isIpAddress() function, 205
isNumberFormat() function, 205
ISO 4217 currency code, 94
ISO standard 8601 (RFC 3339), 100
isSupported() function (dojo.cookie), 217
isValidCreditCardNumber() function, 205
isValidIsbn() function, 206
isValidLuhn() function, 206
isValidRow() method, 269
item() method, 165
itemClicked() method, 425
ItemFileReadStore/ItemFileWriteStore classes, 266, 276
Items, defined (dojo.data), 266
Iterator pattern, 165

J

Java applets, 216
Java import statement vs. dojo.required() statement, 43
JavaScript
  acceptance of, 10–11
  birth of, 3
  current version, 11–12

developer reluctance toward, 7–9
early perceptions of, 8–9
effects in, 8
evolution of, 3–13
LiveScript renamed as, 4
memory usage in early versions, 7
object-oriented design in, 11–12
performance issues in early versions, 7
problems with, 6–7
problems with early releases of, 5–6
reasons for rise of, 5
standardization by ECMA, 9–10
JavaScript libraries, 12–13
Jaxer web site, 88
jQuery library, 12, 88
JSON (JavaScript Object Notation), 249, 383–385
JSON-P (JSON with Padding), 384–385

K

Kay, Alan, 1
Keywords tab (Code Cabinet application), 274, 288–290
Konquerer web browser, 86

L

label attribute (Button dijit), 133
label element
for CheckBox dijit, 134
for RadioButton dijit, 144
labels attribute (HorizontalRuleLabels dijit), 142
lastInsertRowId() method, 269
late binding, 243
layout, defined, 188
LayoutContainer dijit, 151–152
LayoutContainers, 281, 283
Lesser General Public License (LGPL), 13
LevelMaps.js, writing (Idiot Blob application), 346–348
Lightbox effect in Dialog dijit, 121
Lin, Leonard, 13
Linderman, Matthew, 9
line charts, 159–160
lines, drawing, 182–183
listContacts() function, 261
LiveScript, 4
LiveWire, development of, 4
loadingMessage attribute (ContentPane dijit), 151
Local Business Search application
exercises for further development, 439–440
features and goals, 381
JSON-P, 384–385
mashups, 380–381
overview, 379
script tag trick, 382
structure and layout, 391–392
styles.css, writing, 408–410
Yahoo APIs, 381–384
Yahoo Local search service, 386–388
Yahoo Maps Image service, 389–391
Yahoo web services registration, 385–386
Local search service, Yahoo, 386–388
local shared objects, 216
LocalServer component (Gears), 221
loops, game, 366
lowercase attribute (TextBox dijit), 144
Luhn numbers, defined, 206

M

Macintosh windows effect, 7
magic numbers, 369
main contents
Code Cabinet application, 282
Local Business Search application, 398–399
mainContainer ContentPane, 398
Maps Image service, Yahoo, 389–391
mashups, 380–381
match() method, 47
math functions in DojoX, 30
math namespace. *See* dojox.math namespace
maximum attribute (ProgressBar dijit), 127
maxLength attribute (TextBox dijit), 145

menus
- markup (Local Business Search application), 397–398
- Menu dijit, 125
- MenuItem dijit, 125
- MenuSeparator dijit, 125

Microsoft Windows, performance test for, 7
midpoint() function, 191
mock server technique, 83
modules 10, 206
Mollari, Londo, 1
MooTools, 13
My First Dojo app, 31–32
myFunc() function, 74
myMessage event, subscribing to, 56

N

Netscape Navigator browser, 4
netWindows library, 13
newSearch() method, 424
Notes tab (Code Cabinet application), 287–288
noValueIndicator attribute (InlineEditBox dijit), 124
numbers
- determining range of, 205
- generating random, 191
- Luhn numbers, 206
- NumberSpinner dijit, 142, 143
- NumberTextBox dijit, 139
- validating, 205

O

object-oriented design in JavaScript, 11–12
O'Brien, Larry, 1
onChange attribute (InlineEditBox dijit), 124
onChange handler (ColorPalette dijit), 121
open-source software, 15–16

P

pageResults() method, 405, 422
pageSize attribute (ComboBox), 136
palette attribute (ColorPalette dijit), 120
Park, Joyce, 13
parseOnLoad option (Dojo config), 34
parser component in Dojo, 35
pauseAfter/pauseBefore elements, 199
peek() method, 171
performance test for Microsoft Windows, 7
Perlis, Alan J., 1
persistContacts() function, 259
persistent storage, defined, 216
places attribute (ProgressBar dijit), 127
Please Wait dialog box (Local Business Search application), 395
Polylines (polygons), 183
pop-up dialog boxes (Code Cabinet application), 276
popping off stacks, 169
populateContact() function, 248
Practical JavaScript, DOM Scripting, and Ajax Projects (Apress), 364–365
prefixes section, listing of modules in, 45
preventCache attribute (ContentPane dijit), 151
Print dialog box (Local Business Search application), 394
print() method, 433
printing items (Local Business Search application), 433–434
procedural graphics, 332, 356
progress attribute (ProgressBar dijit), 127
ProgressBar dijit, 126
- creating, 126–127
- updating, 127

prompt attribute (ValidationTextBox dijit), 147
propercase attribute (TextBox dijit), 145
Prototype library (JavaScript), 13
provider, storage, 219
publish() function, 89
publish-subscribe model, 210
pushing onto stacks, 169

Q

query attribute (ComboBox), 136
quirks mode, 87

R

RadioButton dijit, 143–144
range() function, 192
ranges of numbers, determining, 205
Rect() function (rectangles), 183
regExp attribute (ValidationTextBox dijit), 147
remove() method, 168, 195
removeClass()/addClass() functions, 171–173
replace() method, 195
Resig, John, 88
REST (Representational State Transfer), 84
restoreContacts() function, 257
result paging, 421–423
ResultSet object, 269
Russell, Alex, 13

S

same-domain security restriction (Ajax), 381
saveContact() function, 259
saveHandler() function, 260
saveLocation() method, 429
saveSnippet() method, 319
Schiemann, Dylan, 13
Schontzler, David, 13
script injection trick, 385, 388
script-kiddie language, 6
script tag trick (Local Business Search application), 382
script.aculo.us (JavaScript library), 13
sd() (standard deviation) function, 192
search criteria pane (Local Business Search application), 399–403
searches
  initiating new (Local Business Search application), 424–425
  Local Business Search application, 416–421
searching
  search functions (Code Cabinet application), 320–327
  search-related markup (Code Cabinet application), 290–292
  search results pane (Local Business Search application), 403–405
  searchClicked() method, 320
  Yahoo Local search service, 386–388
selected attribute (AccordionPane dijit), 149
Separator dijit, 281
Sequence class, 197–199
setByIndex() method, 165
setDefaultLocation() method, 430
setFill() method, 183
setInterval() function, 197
setStroke() method, 183
setTheme() method, 160
shared objects, local, 216
showButtons attribute (HorizontalRuleLabels dijit), 142
showDialog() method, 430
showFavorites() method, 435, 439
showLabel attribute
  setting for Button dijit, 133
  for ToggleButton dijit, 146
showMap() method, 428
showMsg() function, 210
ShrinkSafe JavaScript compressor, 45
sizeTo() function, 177–178
slideBy() function, 178–179
sliders, horizontal and vertical dijits for, 141
snippets (Code Cabinet application)
  searching for, 320–327
  snippet-related functions, 314–320
  Snippets tab, 284
  snippetsStores array, 300
SOA (service-oriented architecture), 380
sort() method, 166
splice() method (JavaScript), 261
SplitContainer (Code Cabinet application), 283–284

SplitContainer dijits, 398
SplitContainers, 282, 283
sprintf() function, 195
SQLite engine, 221
StackContainer dijit, 152–154
StackedLines chart, 161
stacks, 169, 171
standard deviation (sd) function, 192
stClick() function, 244
storage
provider object, 219
storage.clear() function, 262
system, Dojo, 218–220
transient storage, defined, 216
strings
string namespace. *See* dojox.string namespace
string.trim() function (Dojo), 307, 320
string.trim() method, 276
style attribute
on HorizontalRuleLabels dijit, 142
for Textarea dijit, 145
styles.css file (Contact Manager application), 226–229
styles.css, writing
Code Cabinet application, 293–295
Idiot Blob application, 342–345
Local Business Search application, 408–410
surface objects, 182, 332

T

tabs
coding in TabCotainer dijit, 156
creating without writing code, 155
tab definitions (Code Cabinet application), 284–285
TabContainer dijit, 154, 156, 284, 302
targetNodeIds attribute (Menu dijit), 125
text, creating, 184
Textarea dijit, 145
TextBox dijit, 144–145
themes
packaged with Digit, 115–116
setting on a per-digit basis, 116
switching, 116
Theme Tester application, 23–25
timeoutChangeRate attribute (ColorPalette dijit), 120
Timer class, 195, 197
TimeSpinner widget, 206–208
TimeTextBox dijit, 139–140
timing namespace. *See* dojox.timing namespace
title attribute (AccordionPane dijit), 149
TitlePane dijit, 127–128
Toaster widget, 208–210
ToggleButton dijit, 146
toJson() function, 249
Toolbar dijit, 128–130
Tooltip dijit, 130–131
toString() function, 248–249
transient storage, defined, 216
Tree, category, 282–283
Tree dijit, 131–132
Trenka, Tom, 13
Tundra theme
packaged with Digit, 115
using in Dojo, 33

U

Unicode Locale Data Markup Language (LDML) specification, 108
unregister() method (AdapterRegistry object), 47
update() method (ProgressBar dijit), 127
uppercase attribute (TextBox dijit), 144
useObject() function (dojo.cookie), 218
uuid namespace (DojoX), 199–201

V

validation
functions (DojoX), 30
namespace. *See* dojox.validate namespace

validate namespace (DojoX), 202–206
ValidationTextBox dijit, 147
value attribute
check box, 134
NumberSpinner dijit, 143
VCR buttons, 405
VerticalSlider dijit, 142

W

web services
fundamentals, 380
Yahoo web services registration, 385–386
web sites, for downloading
Gears Database installation, 223
SQLite engine, 221
web sites, for further information
37signals Basecamp product, 9
The Book of Dojo, 268
Clearleft contact form, 9
Cold Stone Creamery, 70
Dojo 1.0.2, 44
Dojo help and information, 37
ECMA, 9
Flash shared objects, 216
Google information, 3
Internet Movie Database (IMDb), 69
ISO standard 8601 (RFC 3339), 100
Jaxer, 88
Jonathan Coulton, 15
Matthew Linderman blog, 9
Unicode Locale Data Markup Language (LDML) specification, 108
Yahoo Maps APIs, 391
widgets. *See* Dojo widgets; DojoX
width attribute (InlineEditBox dijit), 125
Willison, Simon, 13

X

XML functionality package (DojoX), 30

Y

Yahoo! UI Library (YUI), 12
yellow fade effect, 9